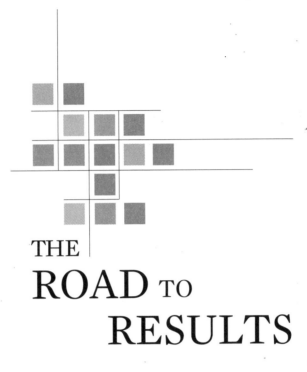

# THE
# ROAD TO
# RESULTS

# THE
# ROAD TO
# RESULTS

Designing and Conducting
Effective Development
Evaluations

Linda G. Morra Imas
Ray C. Rist

THE WORLD BANK

© 2009 The International Bank for Reconstruction and Development / The World Bank
1818 H Street NW
Washington DC 20433
Telephone: 202-473-1000
Internet: www.worldbank.org
E-mail: feedback@worldbank.org

1 2 3 4 12 11 10 09

ISBN: 978-0-8213-7891-5
eISBN: 978-0-8213-7911-0
DOI: 10.1596/978-0-8213-7891-5

*Library of Congress Cataloging-in-Publication Data*

Morra-Imas, Linda G.
   The road to results : designing and conducting effective development evaluations / Linda G. Morra-Imas, Ray C. Rist.
      p. cm.
   ISBN 978-0-8213-7891-5 -- ISBN 978-0-8213-7911-0 (electronic)
   1. Economic development--Evaluation. I. Rist, Ray C. II. Title.
   HD75.M666 2009
   338.91068'4--dc22

                              2009013401

Cover design: Naylor Design, Washington, DC

# DEDICATION

*For my husband, Silvio, who so supports and encourages me in my professional endeavors, and with special gratitude to two strong women who have been my evaluation role models and mentors: Eleanor Chelimsky and Lois-ellin Datta*

LINDA G. MORRA IMAS

*For Molly, Ethan, Madeleine, Lukas, Nina, and Anna: my six grandchildren who bring joy into my life every day*

RAY C. RIST

*The Road to Results* is available as an interactive textbook at **http://www.worldbank.org/r2r.**

This tool enables students and teachers to share notes and related materials for an enhanced, multimedia learning experience.

# CONTENTS

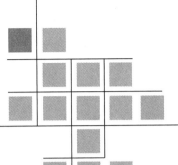

**Boxes**

**Figures**

**Illustration**

**Tables**

# PREFACE

Development evaluation is an exciting component of the larger evaluation mosaic. It addresses the profound, the complex, and the emergent areas of development. Evaluating poverty alleviation, globalization and its impacts on the poor, the consequences of global warming on weak countries, the structural inequalities of the global financial systems, and strategies to help postconflict countries are but a few of the areas in which development evaluation is making contributions to our understanding of, indeed, our response to these pressing issues.

As pressures grow across the globe for accountability by governments and organizations for the consequences of their actions for greater responsiveness to internal and external stakeholders for their performance, and most profoundly for greater development effectiveness, evaluation is emerging as a key way in which to systematically address and answer the question, "So what?" It is not enough to document that one is busy, it is now a requirement to document that one is (or is not) effective.

Development evaluation is also an emergent area of inquiry. Finding ways of evaluating is tenuous when governmental data systems are weak or nonexistent, corruption of information for political ends is frequent, information gaps are large and real, and there is no assurance that information provided is reliable. In the face of these challenges, development evaluation is resilient, innovative, and creative in finding ways to help provide information to citizens, government officials, donors, civil society, and the media on whether government programs are making a difference.

This textbook seeks to contribute to the strengthening of development evaluation as a tool to inform the creation and implementation of policies and programs in particular and governance systems in general. Evaluation can be a powerful public management tool to improve the way governments and organizations perform and achieve results. Its contribution does not end at the doorstep of the public sector. Evaluation can be a powerful tool for civil society, nongovernmental organizations, and donor organizations that seek to support development among the poor.

The material in this book was adapted from the International Program for Development Evaluation Training (IPDET), a development evaluation training program offered by the World Bank and Carleton University every summer (see www.IPDET.org). IPDET brings participants from across the globe together to spend a month studying development evaluation. The material in this volume is an elaboration of the core course provided by IPDET. It is provided with the aim of expanding and sharing the content of the IPDET course with others interested in development evaluation.

We, the authors, are indebted to a number of individuals who gave counsel, read parts of the manuscript and provided critiques, and encouraged us to continue to make this book a reality. The full list of people we wish to thank is provided at the back of the book (Appendix 1). A select group of people must be thanked here: Michael Patton, Patrick Grasso, Martin Abrams, Niels Dabelstein, Gregg Jackson, Gene Swimmer, and Nancy Porteous, each of whom read and critiqued sections of the book. For their efforts, we are thankful. Santiago Pombo Bejarano of the Office of the Publisher, World Bank, has been a strong wind at our backs. His encouragement to continue to work on this manuscript has not faltered.

We are also thankful for the two people who have been our partners in making IPDET a reality at Carleton University: Karen Ginsberg and Barbara Levine. There would be no book if there were no IPDET. They are wonderful partners and wonderful friends.

Finally, we have to acknowledge the outstanding contribution of Diane Schulz Novak, who worked with us throughout the entire process of writing and rewriting the manuscript. Her dedication, care, and craft in working with us have been so essential that in her absence we would not be writing this preface, as there would be no book to follow.

The two of us have been friends and colleagues for nearly 30 years. We first met and began working together at the U.S. Government Accountability Office in 1981. We have been together at the World Bank now for more than a decade. The collaboration and friendship have grown stronger and stronger. It is right that as we come toward the apex of our careers, we are able to give to the evaluation community this fruit of our joint labors.

# ABOUT THE AUTHORS

Linda G. Morra Imas is an advisor in the Independent Evaluation Group of the World Bank Group. She is widely known as "the mother of IPDET," the International Program in Development Evaluation Training, and is its Co-Director. She advises and trains on monitoring and evaluation in countries worldwide. She has been an Adjunct Professor at George Washington University and at Carlton University. Dr. Morra Imas joined the Bank Group in 1996 and has led numerous evaluations. She was a Senior Director at the United States Government Accountability Office and has been a frequent testifier for Congressional Committees on education and employment programs.

Ray C. Rist is an advisor in the Independent Evaluation Group of the World Bank. He joined the Bank in 1997. His career includes 15 years in the United States government, with appointments in both the executive and legislative branches. Dr. Rist has held academic appointments at Cornell University, The Johns Hopkins University, and The George Washington University. Dr. Rist was the Senior Fulbright Fellow at the Max Planck Institute in Berlin, Germany, in 1976–77. He has authored, edited, or coedited 25 books, written 135 articles, and has lectured in more than 75 countries.

# ABBREVIATIONS

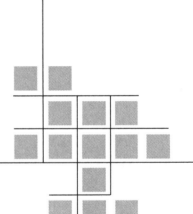

ADBA        Asian Development Bank
AEA         American Evaluation Association
AfDB        African Development Bank
ANOVA       analysis of variance
ANSI        American National Standards Institute
ASEAN       Association of Southeast Asian Nations

BE          Business Environment

CAHMI       Child and Adolescent Health Measurement Initiative
CAQDAS      computer-assisted qualitative data analysis software
CATI        computer-assisted telephone interviewing
CES         Canadian Evaluation Society
CESE        Central, Eastern, and Southern Europe
CGD         Center for Global Development
CIDA        Canadian International Development Agency
CIS         Commonwealth of Independent States
CODE        Committee on Development Effectiveness
CSF         Community Support Framework
CSR         corporate social responsibility

DAC         Development Assistance Committee
DANIDA      Danish International Development Agency
DfID        Department for International Development
DEC         Disasters Emergency Committee

EBRD        European Bank for Reconstruction and Development
ECI         Early Communication Indicator

| | |
|---|---|
| EDUCO | El Salvador's Community-Managed Schools Program |
| EET | exempt-exempt-taxed |
| ESEA | Elementary and Secondary Education Act |
| ESRC | Economic and Social Research Council |
| EU | European Union |
| | |
| FAO | Food and Agriculture Organization of the United Nations |
| FATF | Financial Action Task Force on Money Laundering |
| FDI | foreign direct investment |
| FIT-ED | Foundation for Information Technology and Education Development |
| | |
| GAD | gender and development |
| GAO | Government Accountability Office |
| GDP | gross domestic product |
| GICHD | Geneva International Centre for Humanitarian Demining |
| GMI | guaranteed minimum income |
| GPRA | Government Performance Results Act |
| GRPPs | Global and Regional Partnership Programs |
| | |
| HIPC | Heavily Indebted Poor Countries |
| HSSP2 | Health Sector Strategic Plan 2 |
| HZZO | Croatian Institute for Health Insurance |
| | |
| IBSTPI | International Board of Standards for Training, Performance, and Instruction |
| IDEAS | International Development Evaluation Association |
| IDRC | International Development Research Centre |
| IFAD | International Fund for Agricultural Development |
| IFC | International Finance Corporation |
| IISD | International Institute for Sustainable Development |
| ILO | International Labour Organization |
| IMF | International Monetary Fund |
| IOB | Policy and Operations Evaluation Department (the Netherlands) |
| IOM | International Organization for Migration |
| IPDET | International Program for Development Evaluation Training |
| IRBM | integrated results-based management system |
| INTOSAI | International Organization of Supreme Audit Institutions |
| IOCE | International Organisation for Cooperation and Evaluation |

| | |
|---|---|
| JEEAR | Joint Evaluation of Emergency Assistance to Rwanda |
| JICA | Japan International Cooperation Agency |
| | |
| LGAB | look good—avoid blame |
| LOA | level of adoption |
| LSMS | Living Standards Measurement Survey Study |
| | |
| M&E | monitoring and evaluation |
| MATR | Management Action Tracking Record |
| MBS | Modified Budgeting System |
| MDBs | Multilateral Development Banks |
| MDGs | Millennium Development Goals |
| MFPED | Ministry of Finance, Planning, and Economic Development |
| MIS | management information system |
| MMV | Medicines for Malaria Venture |
| MSH | Management Sciences for Health |
| | |
| NAD | National Audit Department |
| NCSTE | Chinese National Centre for Science and Technology Evaluation |
| NDC | notional defined-contribution |
| NEIR TEC | Northeast and the Islands Regional Technology in Education Consortium |
| NGO | nongovernmental organization |
| NHIFA | National Health Insurance Fund Administration (Hungary) |
| NORAD | Norwegian Agency for Development Cooperation |
| NSGPR | National Strategy for Growth and Reduction of Poverty |
| NSSI | National Social Security Institute (Bulgaria) |
| | |
| ODA | official development assistance |
| OECD | Organisation for Economic Co-operation and Development |
| | |
| PEAP | Poverty Eradication Action Plan |
| POW | Health Sector Program of Work |
| PPBS | Planning, Programming, and Budgeting System |
| PPBS | Program Performance Budgeting System |
| PRSP | Poverty Reduction Strategies Paper |
| | |
| RFP | request for proposals |

| SDC | Swiss Agency for Development and Cooperation |
| SHIPDET | Shanghai International Program for Development Evaluation Training |
| SIDA | Swedish International Development Cooperation Agency |
| SIEF | Spanish–World Bank Trust Fund for Impact Evaluation |
| SIR | subjective interpretation of reality |
| SWAps | sectorwide approaches |
| | |
| TI | Transparency International |
| TOR | terms of reference |
| | |
| UNDP | United Nations Development Programme |
| UNEG | United Nations Evaluation Group |
| UNEP | United Nations Environment Programme |
| UNESCO | United Nations Educational, Scientific and Cultural Organization |
| UNFPA | United Nations Population Fund |
| UNHCR | United Nations High Commissioner for Refugees |
| UNICEF | United Nations Children's Fund |
| UNSD | United Nations Statistics Division |
| USAID | U.S. Agency for International Development |
| | |
| WHO | World Health Organization |
| WID | women in development |
| WTO | World Trade Organization |
| | |
| ZUS | Social Insurance Fund (Poland) |

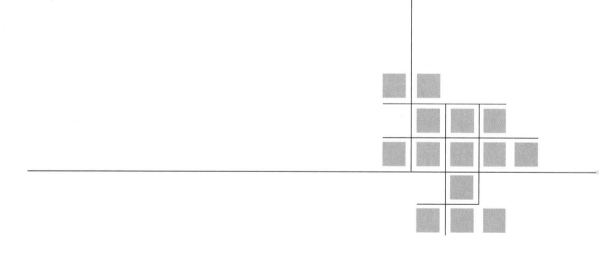

# Introduction

The analytical, conceptual, and political framework of development is changing dramatically. The new development agenda calls for broader understandings of sectors, countries, development strategies, and policies. It emphasizes learning and continuous feedback at all phases of the development cycle.

Indeed, development evaluation can be considered a kind of public good:

> Evaluation extends beyond the boundaries of any single organization. A good evaluation study can have positive spillover effects throughout the development community. Development evaluation has the characteristics of an international public good. (Picciotto and Rist, 1995, p. 23)

As the development agenda grows in scope and complexity, development evaluation follows suit. Development evaluators are moving away from traditional implementation and output-focused evaluation models toward results-based evaluation models, as the development community calls for results and embraces the Millennium Development Goals. As the development community shifts its focus away from projects in order to comprehensively address country challenges, development evaluators are seeking methods with which to assess results at the country, sector, theme, policy, and even global levels. As the development community recognizes the importance of not only a comprehensive but also a coordinated approach to developing country challenges and emphasizes partnerships, development evaluators are increasingly engaged in joint evaluations. These joint evaluations, while advantageous in many respects, add to the complexity of development evaluation (OECD 2006). Additionally, development evaluators increasingly face the measurement challenge of determining the performance of an individual development organization in this broader context and of identifying its contribution.

With the advent of this more complex and demanding approach to development, evaluation has become more difficult to design. It encompasses more intricate methodological demands and sets high standards for establishing impacts.

Demand for new evaluation approaches and a new mix of skills goes beyond economics. Urgent issues, such as climate change, call for new approaches to evaluating sustainability. The scope of environmental problems, multinational consequences, difficulties in obtaining comparable measures, and persistent evidence of unanticipated consequences all necessitate a complex, multimethod approach to evaluation.

> It may well be that no single discipline can be expected to dominate in an endeavor that deals with the multiple challenges, hopes, and exertions of the majority of humankind. In the absence of a single intellectual rallying point, trespassing across disciplinary boundaries is common, and evaluators are increasingly eclectic and venturesome in their use of social science instruments. (Picciotto and Rist, 1995, p. 169)

The building of evaluation capacity—creating evaluation units trained in development evaluation practices and methods—is a challenge facing most developing countries. The rise of developing country national evaluation associations as well as regional evaluation groups are important first steps in increasing the professionalism of the development evaluation community. In the young International Development Evaluation Association (IDEAS), development evaluators now find an international professional organization dedicated to their needs. Also helping to build development evaluation capacity is the growth of graduate-level university courses and regional training centers.

This text is intended as a tool for use in building development evaluation capacity. It aims to help development evaluators think about and explore the new evaluation architecture and especially to design and conduct evaluations that focus on results in meeting the challenges of development.

The International Program for Development Evaluation Training (IPDET) was created by the Operations Evaluation Department (now the Independent Evaluation Group [IEG]) of the World Bank in 2001. IEG partnered with Carleton University, with support from the World Bank Institute, to hold the first program, in Ottawa, Canada. Since 2003, the program has offered one- and two-week customized versions of IPDET, which have been delivered in a dozen countries. In 2007, the Shanghai International Program for Development Evaluation Training (SHIPDET) was established.

While IPDET has continually evolved to reflect the changing nature of development, it remains broadly aimed at all those working, or about to work, in development evaluation. It seeks to provide the generic tools to evaluate development interventions (policies, programs, and projects) at the local, national, regional, and global levels. It is targeted to evaluation staffs of bilateral and multilateral development agencies, developing country governments, nongovernmental organizations, as well as to parliamentarians and private consultants.

IPDET's overall goal is to enhance participants' knowledge, skills, and abilities to design and conduct effective development evaluations for evidence-based decision making. It is based on 14 instructional modules that together overview the road to effective evaluation of development interventions.

This volume builds on and expands these modules, presenting a comprehensive discussion of issues facing development evaluators as well as a guide to undertaking development evaluation. Through this text, many more of those working in development will have the generic tools to produce strong evaluations of development results.

## References

OECD (Organisation for Economic Co-operation and Development). 2006. DAC *Guidance for Managing Joint Evaluations.* Paris: OECD. http://www.oecd.org/dataoecd/28/14/37484787.pdf.

Picciotta, Robert, and Ray C. Rist. 1995. *Evaluating Country Development Policies and Programs: New Approaches for a New Agenda.* San Francisco: Jossey-Bass.

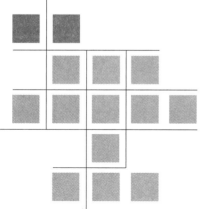

# FOUNDATIONS

*"True genius resides in the capacity for evaluation of uncertain, hazardous, and conflicting information."*

—WINSTON CHURCHILL

**Chapter 1: Introducing Development Evaluation**
- Evaluation: What Is It?
- The Origins and History of the Evaluation Discipline
- The Development Evaluation Context
- Principles and Standards for Development Evaluation
- Examples of Development Evaluations

**Chapter 2: Understanding the Issues Driving Development Evaluation**
- Overview of Evaluation in Developed and Developing Countries
- Implications of Emerging Development Trends

**CHAPTER 1**

# Introducing Development Evaluation

This chapter introduces the definition of and general concepts behind the evaluation of projects, programs, and policies. It then turns to the evaluation of development interventions, often called *development evaluation*.

**This chapter has five main parts:**

- Evaluation: What Is It?
- The Origins and History of the Evaluation Discipline
- The Development Evaluation Context
- Principles and Standards for Development Evaluation
- Examples of Development Evaluations

## Evaluation: What Is It?

To begin understanding development evaluation, it is important to understand what is meant by evaluation, its purposes, and how it can be used. This part of the chapter

* defines evaluation
* identifies the purpose of evaluation
* lists the benefits of evaluation
* indicates what evaluators evaluate
* describes the uses of evaluation
* examines the relation between monitoring and evaluation
* identifies the roles and activities of professional evaluators.

### Definition of Evaluation

■ **Evaluation:**
Determination of the value of a project, program, or policy

*Evaluation* has been defined in many ways. The Oxford English Dictionary defines it as:

> 1. the action of appraising or valuing (goods, etc.); a calculation or statement of value; 2. the action of evaluating or determining the value of (a mathematical expression, a physical quantity, etc.) or of estimating the force of probabilities, evidence, etc.

Within the evaluation discipline, the term has come to have a variety of meanings. Differences in definitions reflect differing emphases on the purpose of evaluation—accountability versus learning—or the timing of evaluation in relation to the maturity of the program, project, or policy. Indeed, there is no universal agreement on the definition itself.

> In fact, in considering the role of language in evaluation, Michael Scriven, one of the founders of modern evaluation, recently noted that there are nearly sixty different terms for evaluation that apply to one context or another. These include: *adjudge, appraise, analyze, assess, critique, examine, grade, inspect, judge, rate, rank, review, score, study, test....* (Fitzpatrick, Sanders, and Worthen 2004, p. 5)

Most evaluation definitions include the concept of making a judgment of the value or worth of the subject of the evaluation. Indeed, this "valuing" is used to differentiate evaluation from research and monitoring activities.

The definition used in this volume is from the Organisation for Economic Co-operation and Development (OECD)/Development Assistance Committee (DAC) Glossary (OECD 2000, p. 21):

Evaluation refers to the process of determining the worth or significance of an activity, policy, or program. [It is] as systematic and objective as possible, of a planned, on-going, or completed intervention.

Evaluations can be formative, summative, or prospective:

Formative evaluations are evaluations intended to improve performance, [and] are most often conducted during the implementation phase of projects or programs. Formative evaluations may also be conducted for other reasons, such as compliance, legal requirements or as part of a larger evaluation initiative. Summative evaluations, by contrast, are studies conducted at the end of an intervention (or a phase of that intervention) to determine the extent to which anticipated outcomes were produced. Summative evaluation is intended to provide information about the worth of a program. (OECD 2002, pp. 21–22)

A *formative evaluation* looks into the ways in which a program, policy, or project is implemented. It examines whether or not the assumed "operational logic" corresponds with actual operations and identifies the (immediate) consequences the implementation (stages) produces. This type of evaluation is conducted during the implementation phase of a project or program. Formative evaluations are sometimes called *process evaluations,* because they focus on operations.

■ **Formative evaluation:** Evaluation of ways in which a program, policy, or project is implemented

An example of a formative evaluation is the evaluation conducted for the International Development Research Centre (IDRC) of its initiative for managing natural resources in Latin America and the Caribbean (known as Minga) (Adamo 2003). The general objective of the Minga initiative was to contribute to the formation of natural resource management professionals, women and men, in Bolivia, Ecuador, and Peru.

One component of the program initiative that interested IDRC was gender mainstreaming. To learn more about how gender was being mainstreamed into the program, IDRC contracted for a formative evaluation. The methodology for the formative evaluation began with a review of program documents related to gender mainstreaming and activities. The evaluators also reviewed trip reports to assess the extent to which gender was being addressed during visits. Interviews were conducted with program staff members to examine their individual efforts and experiences and to mainstream gender into their work and the lessons they learned along the way.

One type of formative evaluation is a midterm or midpoint evaluation. As its name implies, a midterm evaluation is conducted about halfway through a project, program, or change in policy. The purpose of a midterm evaluation is to help identify which features are working well and which features are not. Midterm evaluations can begin to focus on lessons learned, as well as relevance, effectiveness, and efficiency. Lessons learned are important in guiding future interventions and improving current ones.

■ **Summative evaluation:** Evaluation conducted at the end of an intervention to determine the extent to which it achieved desired results

A ***summative evaluation***, often called an *outcome or impact evaluation*, is conducted at the end of an intervention or on a mature intervention to determine the extent to which anticipated results were realized. Summative evaluation is intended to provide information about the worth and impact of the program. Summative evaluations include impact evaluations, cost-effectiveness investigations, quasi-experiments, randomized experiments, and case studies.

An example of a summative evaluation is one completed by the Asian Development Bank (ADB) to evaluate the Second Financial Sector Program in Mongolia (ADB 2007). The program involved financial sector reforms that included restructuring and transforming the financial sector from a mono-banking system into a two-tier system supported by the ADB. A summative evaluation was completed at the end of the second phase of this program. Summative evaluations are used to answer questions of relevance, performance, impacts, sustainability, external utility, and lessons learned.

The difference between a formative and a summative evaluation can be stated as follows:

- Formative evaluations focus on project, program, and policy implementation and improvement.
- Summative evaluations focus on results. They enable people to make decisions regarding continuing, replicating, scaling up, or ending a given project, program, or policy.

Typically, both kinds of evaluation are needed and used by organizations at different times in the cycle of a project, program, or policy.

■ **Prospective evaluation:** Evaluation of the likely outcomes of a proposed project, program, or policy

A ***prospective evaluation*** assesses the likely outcomes of proposed projects, programs, or policies. It is somewhat similar to an evaluability assessment. An evaluability assessment answers the questions "Is this program or project worth evaluating?" and "Will the gains be worth the effort/resources expended?" A prospective evaluation synthesizes evaluation findings from earlier studies to assess the likely outcomes of proposed new projects, programs, or policies. For example, congressional committees in the United States frequently ask the Government Accountability Office (GAO) for advice in forecasting the likely outcomes of proposed legislation.[1]

A dated, but nevertheless interesting, example of a prospective evaluation is the 1986 GAO study *Teenage Pregnancy: 500,000 Births a Year but*

*Few Tested Programs* (U.S. GAO 1986). This evaluation used four procedures. It analyzed the main features of two congressional bills, reviewed statistics on the extent of teenage pregnancy, examined the characteristics of federal and nonfederal programs, and reviewed evaluation studies on the effectiveness of previous programs for assisting pregnant and parenting teenagers as well as teenagers at risk of becoming pregnant. The evaluators reconstructed the underlying program theory and the operational logic of both congressional bills to find out why it was believed that these initiatives would work as proposed in the legislation. They then compared the evidence found with the features of the proposed legislation.

This type of prospective evaluation is sometimes called an *ex ante (before the fact) evaluation* (Rossi and Freeman 1993). Ex ante or prospective evaluations often include program theory reconstruction or assessment and scenario studies as well as summaries of existing research and evaluation to ascertain the empirical support for proposed initiatives.

### Purpose of Evaluation

Evaluation can be used for a variety of purposes. Within the discipline, there are different views about what the purpose or goal of evaluation should be in a given context.

A prevalent view is that evaluation has four distinct purposes:

- *ethical purpose:* to report to political leaders and citizens on how a policy or program has been implemented and what results have been achieved. This purpose combines the objectives of using better accountability, processing information, and serving of democracy.
- *managerial purpose:* to achieve a more rational distribution of financial and human resources among "competing" programs, improve program management, and increase program benefits.
- *decisional purpose:* to pave the way for decisions on the continuation, termination, or reshaping of a policy or program.
- *educational and motivational purpose:* to help educate and motivate public agencies and their partners by enabling them to understand the processes in which they are engaged and to identify themselves with their objectives (Scientific and National Councils of Evaluation 1999).

Prominent evaluators in the field describe the following purposes of evaluation:

- Obtain social betterment.
- Promote the fostering of deliberative democracy.

- Provide oversight and compliance.
- Ensure accountability and transparency.
- Build, share, and manage knowledge.
- Contribute to organizational improvement.
- Promote dialogue and cooperation among key stakeholders.
- Determine project, program, or policy relevance, implementation, efficiency, effectiveness, impact, and sustainability.
- Generate lessons learned.

Chelimsky and Shadish (1997) take a global perspective by extending the context of evaluation to worldwide challenges. The challenges they cite include the impact of new technologies, demographic imbalances across nations, environmental protection, sustainable development, terrorism, human rights, and other issues that extend beyond one program or even one country.

Ultimately, the purpose of any evaluation is to provide information to decision makers to enable them to make better decisions about projects, programs, or policies. Evaluation should help decision makers understand what is likely to happen, is happening, or has happened because of an intervention and identify ways to obtain more of the desired benefits.

## Benefits of Evaluation

Evaluation helps answer questions about interventions such as the following:

- What are the impacts of the intervention?
- Is the intervention working as planned?
- Are there differences across sites in how the intervention is performing?
- Who is benefiting from this intervention?

People benefit from evaluations in different ways. Some benefit directly. Others are indirect beneficiaries—people who are not involved in the intervention but nonetheless reap benefits from it. Some interventions yield short-term benefits; others provide benefits over the long term.

To illustrate how people benefit in different ways, consider the following example. The U.S. Department of Housing and Urban Development (1997) evaluated a midnight basketball program for boys and girls age 16–20 residing in public housing. Surveys were administered to participants both before and after the program was implemented. The survey findings showed that before the program, 92 percent of respondents reported that they expected to get into some kind of trouble and two-thirds thought that they would be victims of violent acts over the next three months. Following implementation of the basketball program, 20 percent of respondents stated that they expected to get into some kind of trouble, and only 5 percent expected to be crime victims.

The evaluation of the midnight basketball program showed a 78 percent reduction in the juvenile offender crime rate among 16- to 20-year-olds in the precinct in which the public housing development was located. The primary reason for the decline, according to survey respondents, was that having a midnight basketball program gave them something positive to do. In this example program participants are the direct beneficiaries of the program, which they believe will help them stay out of trouble and avoid being victims of violent crime.

Community residents were also surveyed. Respondents reported feeling that both their community and their children were safer because of the midnight basketball program. In this case, community residents are indirect and at least short-term beneficiaries (depending on how long the gains last). Although they are not involved in the program, they feel safer as a result of it.

The summary findings above could be used to demonstrate to residents and the community at large that this program was successful in preventing and reducing violence. Program administrators could also present the findings to the city council to justify a request for continued funding. Program administrators are indirect beneficiaries if continued funding allows them to keep their jobs longer.

In the long term, society at large also benefits if young people stay out of jail, because it does not bear the costs of incarceration and lost productivity. Rather than sit in jail, these young people can perhaps become employable, productive, tax-paying citizens.

An evaluation can also provide information on the process of implementing a program. Other public housing agencies (unintended beneficiaries) will be able to benefit from lessons learned during the program implementation phase and subsequent evaluation.

In a second example, an intervention to build and maintain a water treatment plant brings safe drinking water to residents. The direct immediate benefit is clean drinking water to residents. A longer-term direct benefit to individuals in the community and the community at large would be decreased incidence of waterborne diseases. Indirect medium-term benefits may include attracting industries to the community because it has safe drinking water.

## What to Evaluate

Evaluations can look at many different facets of development (table 1.1). The following are some facets that can be evaluated:

- **projects:** a single intervention in one location or a single project implemented in several locations
- **programs:** an intervention that includes various activities or projects that are intended to contribute to a common goal
- **policies:** standards, guidelines, or rules established by an organization to regulate development decisions
- **organizations:** multiple intervention programs delivered by an organization
- **sectors:** interventions across a specific policy area, such as education, forestry, agriculture, or health
- **themes:** particular issues, often cross-cutting, such as gender equity or global public goods
- **country assistance:** country progress relative to a plan, the overall effect of aid, and lessons learned.

## Uses of Evaluation

The results of evaluation can be used in many ways. Evaluations provide clients, government agencies, nongovernmental organizations (NGOs), the public, and many others with feedback on policies, programs, and projects. The results provide information on how public funds are being used. They can give managers and policy makers information on what is working well and what is not in terms of meeting original or revised objectives.

**Table 1.1  Examples of Policy, Program, and Project Evaluations**

| Type of evaluation | Application | |
| --- | --- | --- |
| | Privatizing water systems | Resettlement |
| Policy evaluation | Comparing model approaches to privatizing public water supplies | Comparing strategies used to resettle villagers to new areas |
| Program evaluation | Assessing fiscal management of government systems | Assessing the degree to which resettled village farmers maintain their previous livelihood |
| Project evaluation | Comparing the improvement in water fee collection rates in two provinces | Assessing the farming practices of resettled farmers in one province |

*Source:* Authors.

Evaluations can help make projects, programs, and policies accountable for how they use public funds. They can identify projects, programs, and policies for replication, scaling up, improvements, or possible termination.

Weiss (2004) stresses the importance of identifying the intended uses for an evaluation from the initial planning stage. "If you cannot identify and articulate the primary intended users and uses of the evaluation you should not conduct the evaluation," she notes. "Unused evaluation is a waste of precious human and financial resources" (p. 1).

From beginning to end, the evaluation process should be designed and carried out according to the needs of the primary intended user. These primary users will bear responsibility for implementing change based on their involvement in the process or the evaluation findings.

Evaluations can serve many purposes and uses (box 1.1). They can

- help analyze why intended results were or were not achieved
- explore why there may have been unintended results or consequences
- assess how and why results were affected by specific activities
- shed light on implementation processes, failures, or successes that occur at any level
- help provide lessons, highlight areas of accomplishment and potential, and offer specific recommendations for improvement and reform.

In summary, evaluations can be useful in focusing on

- the broad political strategy and design issues ("Are we doing the right things?")
- operational and implementation issues ("Are we doing things right?")
- whether there are better ways of approaching the problem ("What are we learning?").

---

**Box 1.1   Uses of Evaluation**

Evaluation can be used in a variety of ways:

- to help make resource allocation decisions
- to help rethink the causes of a problem
- to identify emerging problems
- to support decision making on competing or best alternatives
- to support public sector reform and innovation
- to build consensus on the causes of a problem and how to respond.

*Source:* Kusek and Rist 2004.

---

### Relation between Monitoring and Evaluation

To be consistent, we use the OECD/DAC *Glossary of Key Terms in Evaluation* definition of **monitoring**:

**■ Monitoring:** Collection of data with which managers can assess extent to which objectives are being achieved

> Monitoring is a continuing function that uses systematic collection of data on specified indicators to provide management and the main stakeholders of an ongoing development intervention with indications of the extent of progress and achievement of objectives and progress in the use of allocated funds. (OECD 2002, pp. 27–28)

Monitoring is a routine, ongoing, internal activity. It is used to collect information on a program's activities, outputs, and outcomes to track its performance.

An example of a monitoring system is the use by Malawi's Ministry of Health of 26 indicators to monitor the quality of health provided at Central Hospital. Indicators include the number of patients seen by specialists within four weeks of referral, the number of in-patient deaths, the number of direct obstetric deaths in the facility, and the number of in-patient days (Government of Malawi 2007).

Regular provision of data on the indicators provides the minister of health with a trend line. Any dramatic swings can be investigated. A marked increase in the number of in-patient deaths, for example, may reflect a high hospital infection rate that needs to be reduced immediately. A marked decrease in infection rates may suggest that the use of a new disinfectant is effective, suggesting that its use should be promoted.

Evaluations are generally conducted to answer the "why" question behind the monitoring of data—questions such as why caesarean sections are up in 5 hospitals or why 3 of 50 sites have particularly high survival rates for premature babies. Evaluations are also needed to attribute results to a specific intervention rather than to other possible causes.

Both monitoring and evaluation measure and assess performance, but they do so in different ways and at different times (table 1.2).

- Monitoring takes place throughout program or project implementation.
- Evaluation is the periodic assessment of the performance of the program or project. It seeks to answer the question "why?"

Monitoring is an internal activity carried out by project staff. It is generally the project management's responsibility to see that monitoring is conducted and the results used. In contrast, evaluation can be carried out internally or externally. It is the responsibility of the evaluator together with program staff members (Insideout 2005).

**Table 1.2 Comparison of Monitoring and Evaluation**

| Monitoring | Evaluation |
|---|---|
| Ongoing, continuous | Period and time bound |
| Internal activity | Internal, external, or participatory |
| Responsibility of management | Responsibility of evaluator together with staff and management |
| Continuous feedback to improve program performance | Periodic feedback |

*Source:* Insideout 2005.

## Roles and Activities of Evaluators

As the concept and purposes of evaluation have evolved over time, so have the roles and activities of evaluators. Evaluators play a multitude of roles and engage in numerous activities. Their role depends on the nature and purpose of the evaluation. As Fitzpatrick, Sanders, and Worthen (2004, p. 28) note, "Evaluators play many roles, including scientific expert, facilitator, planner, collaborator, aid to decision makers, and critical friend." They also act as judges, trusted people, teachers, and social change agents.

### Who conducts the evaluation?

Evaluators may be part of internal, external, or participatory evaluations. The OECD/DAC glossary defines *internal evaluation* as

> evaluation of a development intervention conducted by a unit or individuals reporting to the management of the donor, partner, or implementing organization. (2002, p. 26)

It defines *external evaluation* as

> evaluation of a development intervention conducted by entities and/or individuals outside the donor, partner, and implementing organization. (2002, p. 23)

There are advantages and disadvantages to using internal and external evaluators. Internal evaluators usually know more about a program, project, or policy than do outsiders. The person who develops and manages the intervention may also be charged with its evaluation. These people usually know more about the history, organization, culture, people involved, and problems and successes. Because of this knowledge, internal evaluators may be able to ask the most relevant and pertinent questions; they know where to go backstage in the organization to find out what is really going on.

■ **Internal evaluation:** Evaluation conducted by people within the organization

■ **External evaluation:** Evaluation conducted by people from outside the organization

This advantage can also be a disadvantage, however. Internal evaluators may be so close to the program, project, or policy that they do not see it clearly and may not be able to recognize solutions or changes that others may see. Internal evaluators may also have the disadvantage of being more subject to pressure or influence from program decision makers who also make personnel decisions. They may see the whole organization only from their own position within it. Moreover, external stakeholders may perceive their findings as less credible than those of external evaluators.

External evaluators usually have more credibility and lend the perception of objectivity to an evaluation. In addition, most external evaluators have more specialized skills, which may be needed to perform effective evaluations. They are also independent from the administration and financial decisions about the program (Fitzpatrick, Sanders, and Worthen 2004).

An external evaluation is not a guarantee of independent and credible results, however, particularly if the consultants have prior program ties. External consultants also may be overly accommodating to management in the hopes of obtaining future work.

Participatory evaluation is increasingly considered as a third evaluation method. Participatory evaluators work together with representatives of agencies and stakeholders to design, carry out, and interpret an evaluation (OECD 2002). Participatory evaluation differs from internal and external evaluation in some fundamental ways.

> Participatory evaluation represents a further and more radical step away from the model of independent evaluation. . . . [It] is a form of evaluation where the distinction between experts and layperson, researcher and researched is deemphasized and redefined. . . . Evaluators . . . [act] mainly [as] facilitators and instructors helping others to make the assessment. (Molund and Schill 2004, p. 19)

Note the distinction between participatory evaluation and participatory methods. Participatory methods may be used in both internal and external evaluations.

### Evaluator activities

Evaluators carry out activities that correspond to their various roles. Internal evaluators may work on project or program design, implementation, and outreach strategies. External evaluators typically limit their involvement in program management. All evaluators generally

- consult with all major stakeholders
- manage evaluation budgets

- plan the evaluation
- perform or conduct the evaluation or hire contract staff to do so
- identify standards for effectiveness (based on authorizing documents or other sources)
- collect, analyze, interpret, and report on data and findings.

To accomplish their goals, evaluators need diverse skills. As part of the evaluation process, they can help build knowledge and disseminate lessons learned.

## The Origins and History of the Evaluation Discipline

The modern discipline of evaluation emerged from social science research, which is based on the scientific method. But evaluation has ancient traditions. Indeed, archaeological evidence shows that the ancient Egyptians regularly monitored their country's output of grain and livestock production more than 5,000 years ago. The ancient Chinese and Greeks also conducted evaluation:

> In the public sector, formal evaluation was evident as early as 2000 BC, when Chinese officials conducted civil service examinations to measure the proficiency of applicants for government positions. And, in education, Socrates used verbally mediated evaluations as part of the learning process. (Fitzpatrick, Sanders, and Worthen, p. 31)

Some experts trace the emergence of modern evaluation methods to the advent of the natural sciences and the emphasis on observed phenomena (the empirical method) in the 17th century. In Sweden, ad hoc policy commissions that performed some kind of evaluations came into being at that time. Indeed, the commission system is still used in Sweden today, with several hundred commissions currently in existence.

In the 1800s, evaluation of education and social programs began to take root in several Anglo-Saxon countries. Program evaluation was conducted in Britain by government-appointed commissions that were called upon to investigate and evaluate dissatisfaction with educational and social programs. The current-day external inspectorates for schools grew out of these earlier commissions.

In the United States, pioneering efforts were made during the 1800s to examine the quality of the school system using achievement tests. These efforts continue to the present day, when student achievement scores remain a key measure for determining the quality of education in schools.

The beginnings of accreditation for secondary schools and universities in the United States also began during this period.

## History of Evaluation in the 20th Century

Formal evaluation and accreditation of U.S. and Canadian medical schools was first instituted in the early 1900s. Other areas of investigation/ measurement and evaluation during this period included health, housing, work productivity, democratic and authoritarian leadership, and standardized educational testing. Most were small-scale efforts conducted by government agencies and social services.

Rossi and Freeman (1993) trace commitment to the systematic evaluation of programs in the United States to turn-of-the-century efforts to improve literacy, provide occupational training, and reduce deaths from infectious diseases. In the development arena, the "attempt to introduce water boiling as a public health practice in villages in the Middle East is one of the landmark studies in the pre–World War II empirical sociological literature" (Rossi and Freeman 1993, p. 10).

Applied social research grew rapidly in the United States after President Franklin D. Roosevelt instituted the New Deal. The federal government grew rapidly, as new agencies were created to manage and implement national programs. These programs included agricultural subsidies to farmers, public works and job creation schemes, rural electrification, and social security. Because these large-scale programs were new and experimental in nature, the need for evaluating their effectiveness in jump-starting the economy, creating jobs, and instituting social safety nets grew.

The need for evaluation increased during and after World War II, as more large-scale programs were designed and undertaken for the military, urban housing, job and occupational training, and health. It was also during this time that major commitments were made to international programs that included family planning, health and nutrition, and rural community development. Expenditures were large and consequently accompanied by demands for knowledge of results.

In the 1950s and 1960s, evaluation became used more routinely in the United States and Europe to assess programs related to education, health and mental health, human services, prevention of delinquency, and rehabilitation of criminals. President Lyndon B. Johnson's "War on Poverty" program during the 1960s stimulated increased interest in evaluation. Work in developing countries around the world also expanded, with some evaluation conducted of programs in agriculture, community development, family planning, health care, and nutrition. For the most part, these assessments relied on traditional social science tools, such as surveys and statistical analysis.

In 1949, the first Hoover Commission recommended that budget information for the national government in the United States be structured in terms of activities rather than line items. It also recommended that performance measurements be provided along with performance reports (Burkhead 1956; Mikesell 1995). This type of budget reform became known as *performance budgeting* (Tyler and Willand 1997).

In 1962, the U.S. Department of Defense, under Secretary of Defense Robert McNamara, developed the Planning, Programming, and Budgeting System (PPBS). The purpose of the PPBS was to increase efficiency and improve government operations. It involved

- establishing long-range planning objectives
- analyzing the costs and benefits of alternative programs that would meet those objectives
- translating programs into budget and legislative proposals and long-term projections.

The PPBS changed the traditional budgeting process by emphasizing objectives and linking planning and budgeting (Office of the Secretary of Defense 2007). The early efforts of the PPBS would eventually lead to the "monitoring for results" movement.

In the late 1960s, many Western European countries began to undertake program evaluation. In the Federal Republic of Germany, for example, the Bundestag started to require the federal government to report on the implementation and impact of various socioeconomic and tax programs. Reports included those on the Labor Market and Employment Act (1969), the General Educational Grants Law (1969), the joint federal-state program to improve the regional economic structure (1970), the hospital investment program (1971), and various reports on subsidies and taxes (Derlien 1999). During this period, the Canadian government also began to move toward evaluating government programs and performance. Canadian government departments were encouraged to establish planning and evaluation units.

Early efforts did not yield significant results. In Canada, the Federal Republic of Germany, and Sweden, "despite institutionalization of program evaluation in various policy areas, their systems remained rather fragmented and the number of studies carried out seems to be relatively low" (Derlien 1999, p. 146).

The Elementary and Secondary Education Act (ESEA) of 1965 was a landmark for evaluation in the United States. This legislation mandated the government to assess student performance and teacher quality standards. It also provided resources (the first U.S. government budgetary set-aside for evaluation) to undertake these activities, thereby institutionalizing evaluation. With federal money going into evaluation in the late 1960s and early 1970s, numerous articles and books on evaluation began to appear in the United States and some OECD countries. Graduate school university programs focusing on evaluation were developed to train a new cadre of evaluators to meet the increasing demands for accountability and effectiveness in government-financed socioeconomic programs, such as elementary and secondary education grants, and "Great Society" programs, which included poverty reduction programs, Head Start preschools, civil rights activities, and the creation of a job corps.

Canada, the Federal Republic of Germany, and Sweden undertook program evaluation in the 1960s to assess new government-financed education, health, and social welfare programs.

> In this context formal planning systems emerged, which either were limited to medium-term financing planning (in the Federal Republic of Germany) or even attempted to integrate budgeting with programming (in Sweden and Canada). In any case, evaluation was either regarded logically as part of these planning systems or as necessitated by the information needs of the intervention programs. . . . Evaluations, then, were primarily used by program managers to effectuate existing and new programs. (Derlien 1999, pp. 153–54)

From the mid-1970s to the mid-1980s, evaluation became a full-fledged profession in many OECD countries. Professional evaluation associations were created, more programs to train evaluators were introduced, evaluation journals were started, and evaluation began to expand beyond the purview of government-financed programs to corporations, foundations, and religious institutions. In France, for example, public policy evaluation was systematically developed, with many universities—including the **Grandes Écoles**—offering courses and information about evaluation as part of their curricula.

Many OECD countries have established evaluation training programs for civil servants either within the government or through outside contractors. New methodologies and models have been explored, with greater emphasis on the information needs of consumers, the examination of unintended outcomes, and the development of values and standards. The evaluation literature has also grown in quantity and quality (Fontaine and Monnier 2002).

Since 1985 computers and technology have vastly increased the ability of evaluators to collect, analyze, and report on evaluation findings and to share them with others.

## Development Evaluation and Auditing

Development evaluation evolved out of the audit and social science traditions. There are important similarities, differences, and linkages between the two traditions.

### The auditing tradition

Auditing traces its roots to 19th-century Britain, when growing commercial and industrial development gave rise to the

> need for verifiably accurate and dependable financial records. . . . Auditors' work lent credibility to the growing capitalist infrastructure of the West. Auditors' opinions carried weight because of their technical craftsmanship and because auditors were outsiders. (Brooks 1996, p. 16)

The auditing tradition has an investigative, financial management, and accounting orientation. It seeks to determine whether a program did what it was supposed to do and whether the money spent was done so within the rules, regulations, and requirements of the program. It uses concepts such as internal controls, good management and governance, and verification. Its emphasis is on accountability and compliance. The OECD/DAC glossary (OECD 2002) defines several types of audits:

- *standard audit:* an independent, objective assurance activity designed to add value to and improve an organization's operations (It helps an organization accomplish its objectives by bringing a systematic, disciplined approach to assess and improve the effectiveness of risk management, control, and governance processes.)
- *financial audit:* an audit that focuses on compliance with applicable statutes and regulations
- *performance audit:* an audit that is concerned with relevance, economy, efficiency, and effectiveness.

Auditing can be an internal or an external function (box 1.2). The internal audit function helps an organization accomplish its objectives by bringing a systematic, disciplined approach to evaluating and improving the effectiveness of risk management, control, and governance processes. Governments use external auditors when independence from a program's management is needed.

■ **Standard audit:** Objective assurance activity designed to improve an organization's operations

■ **Financial audit:** Audit that focuses on compliance with applicable statutes and regulations

■ **Performance audit:** Audit that assesses relevance, economy, efficiency, and effectiveness

The fact that the auditing tradition is strong in developing countries led to a strong tradition of compliance auditing in evaluation. Malaysia's National Audit Department (NAD), for example, has played a role in ensuring public accountability for 100 years. NAD conducts audits to

- ensure compliance with laws and regulations
- expose unwarranted factors that lead to inefficiency, ineffectiveness, or uneconomical procedures
- determine whether the financial statements prepared are true and fair and the records were properly prepared according to generally accepted accounting and auditing standards.

■ **Internal auditing:**
Audit done within an organization to assess financial activities and operations

**Internal auditing** encompasses a wide array of "financial activities and operations including systems, production, engineering, marketing, and human resources" (http://www.theiia.org). It gains strength from the fact that professional accreditation is offered, which is not yet the case with evaluation (chapter 15 discusses the pros and cons of accrediting evaluators).

Development evaluation drew from the auditing profession a strong focus on compliance with legal and procedural requirements. This can be observed in the objectives-based project evaluation frameworks of bilateral donors and development banks. For example, the "Good Practice Standards for Evaluation of MDB–Supported Public Sector Operations," developed by the Evaluation Cooperation Group of the Multilateral Development Banks (MDB), include the achievement of objectives, on the grounds that "evaluation against objectives enhances accountability" (Evaluation Cooperation Group of the Multilateral Development Banks n.d., p. 9.)

### The continuum between auditing and evaluation

Auditing and evaluation can be viewed as part of a continuum, providing related but different kinds of information about compliance, accountability, impact, and results. There is some "overlap in areas such as efficiency of operations and cost effectiveness . . . with evaluation concerned with analysis of policy and outputs, and auditing with internal financial controls and management systems" (Treasury Board of Canada Secretariat 1993, para. 3). Both auditing and evaluation aim to help decision makers "by providing them with systematic and credible information that can be useful in the creation, management, oversight, change, and occasionally abolishment of programs" (Wisler 1996, p. 1).

Much has been written on the differences between and the overlap of auditing and evaluation. Differences stem from their origins, with auditing deriving largely from financial accounting and evaluation deriving largely from the social sciences. Auditing tends to focus on compliance with requirements, while evaluation tends to focus on attributing observed changes to a policy, program, or project. Auditors tend to seek answers to normative questions (what is versus what should be), while evaluators tend to seek answers to descriptive and cause-and-effect questions (Wisler 1996).

### The social science tradition

As governments and organizations moved from an emphasis on verification and compliance to an emphasis on impact, social science techniques were incorporated into evaluation. Development evaluation drew on scientific and social research methods.

The scientific method is a systematic approach to acquiring information that objectively attempts to separate truth from belief. Under this approach, data are collected through observation and experiment and are based on the formulation and testing of hypotheses. Researchers using the scientific method

- identify a problem, research it, and consider previous explanations
- develop a hypothesis about a cause-and-effect relationship, and state it in measurable terms

- test the hypothesis by conducting an experiment and collecting data
- analyze the data and draw a conclusion
- document and disseminate their findings
- use the results to refine the hypothesis.

Evaluation drew other methods from the social sciences, including sociology, anthropology, political science, and economics.

> The application of social research methods to evaluation coincides with the growth and refinement of the methods themselves, as well as with ideological, political, and demographic changes that have occurred this century. Of key importance were the emergence and increased standing of the social sciences in universities and increased support for social research. Social science departments in universities became centers of early work in program evaluation and have continued to occupy an influential place in the field. (Rossi and Freeman 1993, p. 9)

Evaluation also draws heavily from social science research in areas such as theory construction, design, approach, data collection methodology, analysis and interpretation, statistics, surveys, and sampling.

## The Development Evaluation Context

Development evaluation has emerged as a subdiscipline of evaluation. It began mainly with the post–World War II reconstruction and development efforts. The World Bank was created in 1944 and established the first independent evaluation group in 1972. The European Bank for Reconstruction and Development (EBRD) was founded in 1991. Other multilateral development banks were also founded in the 1990s. Bilateral organizations, such as the United Kingdom's Department for International Development (DfID) and the Canadian International Development Agency (CIDA), were also established. The origins of development evaluation begin with the establishment of these organizations, as donors were accountable for project funds and results. In turn, developing countries' ministries needed to meet requirements for reporting project findings using project evaluation systems developed by donors for learning and accountability.

As the notion of development has changed over the past decades, so has development evaluation. Since its inception, for example, the World Bank has shifted its emphasis, with implications for the complexity of development evaluation (table 1.3).

The OECD has played an important role in advancing development evaluation. Established in 1961, the mission of the OECD has been to "help

**Table 1.3 The World Bank's Changing Approach to Development, 1950–2000**

| Decade | Focus | Approach | Discipline |
|---|---|---|---|
| 1950s | Rebuilding, reconstruction, technical assistance, and engineering | Technical assistance | Engineering |
| 1960s | Economic growth, financing, and the creation of projects, in the hope that stronger economic growth would lift more people out of poverty | Projects | Finance |
| 1970s | Social sectors or basic needs (education, health, and social welfare); longer-term planning and social sector investments | Sector investment | Planning |
| 1980s | Structural adjustment policies and lending; adjustment lending linked to specific conditionalities used to support major policy reforms and to help countries cope with financial and debt crises | Adjustment lending | Neoclassical economics |
| 1990s | More comprehensive country based as opposed to individual projects; more emphasis given to building capacity and institutions within developing countries | Country assistance | Multidisciplinary |
| 2000s | Poverty reduction, partnerships, participation, sectorwide approaches, and a results orientation | Partnerships | Results-based management |

*Source:* Based on Picciotto 2002.

governments achieve sustainable economic growth and employment and rising standards of living in member countries while maintaining financial stability, so contributing to the development of the world economy" (http://www.oecd.org). The members of the OECD meet in specialized committees, including the Development Assistance Committee (DAC), which has long had a working group on development evaluation (currently the DAC Network on Evaluation). The purpose of the DAC Network on Evaluation is to increase the effectiveness of international development programs by supporting robust, informed, and independent evaluation. It brings together 30 bilateral and multilateral development agencies.

The DAC's definition of development evaluation has been widely adopted. It differs somewhat from the generic definition of evaluation given at the beginning of this chapter. According to the DAC, a development evaluation is

> the systematic and objective assessment of an on-going or completed project, program or policy, its design, implementation and results. The aim is to determine the relevance and fulfillment of objectives, development efficiency, effectiveness, impact, and sustainability. An evaluation should provide information

that is credible and useful, enabling the incorporation of lessons learned into the decision making process of both recipients and donors. [OECD 1991b, p. 4]

A wide variety of methodologies and practices has been used in the development evaluation community. It has become generally accepted that a mix of theories, analysis strategies, and methodologies often works best in development evaluation, especially given the growing scale and complexity of development projects, programs, or policies. Mixing approaches can help strengthen the evaluation.

This mix of methods, called ***methodological triangulation***, refers to

the use of several theories, sources or types of information, and/or types of analysis to verify and substantiate an assessment. By combining multiple data sources, methods, analyses, or theories, evaluators seek to overcome the bias that comes from single informants, single methods, single observers, or single theory studies. (OECD 2002, p. 37)

As Chelimsky and Shadish (1997, p. 11) note:

Evaluation continues to become ever more methodologically diverse. It is by now well established that the full array of social science methods belongs in the evaluator's methodological toolkit—tools from psychology, statistics, education, sociology, political science, anthropology, and economics.

The choice of evaluation design and methodology (or combination of designs and methodologies) will be determined by the questions being asked and the information being sought.


## Growth of Professional Evaluation Associations

Professional evaluation associations create a support system and allow for professionalism within the evaluation community. This support contributes to capacity development in development evaluation.

In the 1980s, there were only three regional or national evaluation societies. Since then there has been explosive growth in new national, regional, and international evaluation associations, which have sprung up around the world; currently, there are more than 75 evaluation associations in developing and developed countries (http://www.ioce.net/members/eval_associations.shtml). Much of the growth comes from the establishment of evaluation associations in developing countries. At the national level, for example, associations have been in place in Malaysia and Sri Lanka since 1999 and in Uganda since 2002. At the regional level, the Australasian Evaluation Society was established in 1991, the European Evaluation Society in 1994, and the African Evaluation Association in 1999.

An important international organization for evaluation is the International Organisation for Cooperation in Evaluation (IOCE), a loose alliance of regional and national evaluation organizations (associations, societies, and networks) from around the world. The IOCE aims to build evaluation leadership and capacity in developing countries and to foster the cross-fertilization of evaluation theory and practice around the world. To do so, evaluation professionals must take a more global approach to contributing to the identification and solution of world problems (http://ioce.net/overview/general.shtml).

Another important international organization for evaluation is the International Development Evaluation Association (IDEAS). IDEAS was created in 2001 to help build evaluation capacity in developing countries. Its mission is "to advance and extend the practice of development evaluation by refining methods, strengthening capacity, and expanding ownership" (http://www.ideas-int.org). IDEAS is the only association for professionals who practice development evaluation.

IDEAS' strategy is to

- promote development evaluation for results, transparency, and accountability in public policy and expenditure
- give priority to evaluation capacity development
- foster the highest intellectual and professional standards in development evaluation.

## Principles and Standards for Development Evaluation

The evaluation community needs principles and standards, which promote accountability, facilitate comparability, and enhance the reliability and quality of services provided (Picciotto 2005). Most development-related organizations use the OECD/DAC principles, standards, and criteria. A key document (OECD 1991a) identifies five criteria for evaluating development assistance:

- *relevance:* the extent to which the objectives of a development intervention are consistent with beneficiaries' requirements, country needs, global priorities, and the policies of partners' and development agencies
- *effectiveness:* a measure of the extent to which an aid activity attains its objectives
- *efficiency:* a measure of outputs—qualitative and quantitative—in relation to inputs (This economic term signifies that aid uses the least costly

resources possible to achieve the desired results. Measuring efficiency generally requires comparing alternative approaches to achieving the same outputs to determine whether the most efficient process was adopted.)

- ***impact:*** the positive and negative changes produced by a development intervention, directly or indirectly, intended or unintended (Measuring impact involves determining the main impacts and effects of an activity on local social, economic, environmental, and other development indicators. The examination should be concerned with both intended and unintended results and must include the positive and negative impact of external factors, such as changes in terms of trade and financial conditions.)

- ***sustainability:*** the resilience to risk of the net benefit flows over time (The notion of sustainability is particularly relevant to assess [not measure] whether the benefits of an activity or program are likely to continue after donor funding is withdrawn. Projects and programs need to be environmentally as well as financially sustainable [OECD 1991b].)

DAC developed principles for the evaluation of development assistance (OECD 1991b). These principles address the following issues:

- the purpose of evaluation
- impartiality and independence
- credibility
- usefulness
- participation of donors and recipients
- donor cooperation
- evaluation programming
- design and implementation of evaluations
- reporting, dissemination, and feedback
- application of these principles.

A review of the DAC "Principles for Evaluation of Development Assistance" was conducted in 1998. It compared the DAC principles with those of other organizations and looked for consistency and possible areas to expand. Members' recommendations for possible revisions to the principles included the following:

- Modify the statement of purpose.
- Directly address the question of decentralized evaluations and participatory evaluations.
- Elaborate more on the principles and practices for recipient participation and donor cooperation.

- Introduce recent developments in evaluation activity, such as performance measurement, status, and success rating systems, and developing a typology of evaluation activity (OECD 1998).

This review laid the groundwork for further DAC publications.

In 1994, the American Evaluation Association (AEA) published its "Program Evaluation Standards in the United States." These standards were approved by the American National Standards Institute (ANSI) as the American National Standards for Program Evaluation. They were updated in 1998 and have been adapted by other evaluation associations, including those of developing countries.

In March 2006, the DAC Evaluation Network established the "DAC Evaluation Quality Standards" (OECD 2006) (box 1.3). The standards, currently being used on a trial basis, for test phase application, identify the key pillars needed for a quality evaluation process and product:

- Provide standards for the process (conduct) and products (outputs) of evaluations.
- Facilitate the comparison of evaluations across countries (meta-evaluation).
- Facilitate partnerships and collaboration on joint evaluations.
- Better enable member countries to make use of one another's evaluation findings and reports (including good practice and lessons learned).
- Streamline evaluation efforts.

---

**Box 1.3  The 10 Parts of the DAC Evaluation Quality Standards**

The OECD has set 10 criteria for assessing evaluation quality:

- rationale, purpose, and objectives of an evaluation
- evaluation scope
- context
- evaluation methodology
- information sources
- independence
- evaluation ethics
- quality assurance
- relevance of the evaluation results
- completeness.

*Source:* OECD 2006.

---

At the request of the OECD/DAC Evaluation Network and other evaluation networks, the World Bank's Independent Evaluation Group developed indicative consensus principles and standards for evaluating the Global and Regional Partnership Program (GRPP), which have some unique features that make evaluation complex. These indicative principles and standards are being tested through use and will be revised and endorsed within a few years. (The link to the Web site for these principles and standards appears at the end of this chapter. Principles and standards are discussed further in chapter 14.)

**■ Independent evaluation:**
Evaluation conducted by people who are not beholden to those who designed and implemented the intervention

An important component of credibility of development evaluation is independence. The OECD/DAC glossary defines an **independent evaluation** as "an evaluation carried out by entities and persons free of the control of those responsible for the design and implementation of the development intervention" (OECD 2002, p. 25). It notes:

> The credibility of an evaluation depends in part on how independently it has been carried out. Independence implies freedom from political influence and organizational pressure. It is characterized by full access to information and by full autonomy in carrying out investigations and reporting findings.

Independence does not mean isolation: The interaction between evaluators, program managers, staff, and beneficiaries can enhance the evaluation and its use. An evaluation can be conducted internally or externally, by evaluators organizationally under those responsible for making decisions about the design and implementation of the program interventions (that is, management). Such evaluations are not independent evaluations. They serve a learning purpose rather than an accountability purpose.

The heads of evaluation of the multilateral development banks, who meet regularly as members of the Evaluation Cooperation Group, have identified four dimensions or criteria of evaluation independence:

- organizational independence
- behavioral independence
- protection from external influence
- avoidance of conflicts of interest.

Table 1.4 presents criteria and indicators for assessing the independence of an evaluation organization. Both come from a variety of sources.

**Table 1.4    Criteria and Indicators for Determining the Independence of Evaluation Organizations**

| Criterion | Aspect | Indicators |
|---|---|---|
| Organizational independence | Structure and role of the evaluation unit is appropriate. | Whether evaluation unit has a mandate statement that clarifies that its scope of responsibility extends to all operations of the organization and that its reporting line, staff, budget, and functions are organizationally independent from the organization's operational, policy, and strategy departments and related decision making |
| | Unit is accountable to, and reports evaluation results to, the head or deputy head of the organization or its governing board. | Whether there is direct reporting relationship between the unit and the management or board of the institution |
| | Unit is located organizationally outside the staff or line management function of the program, activity, or entity being evaluated. | Unit's position in organization relative to the program, activity, or entity being evaluated |
| | Unit reports regularly to the larger organization's audit committee or other oversight body. | Reporting relationship and frequency of reporting to the oversight body |
| | Unit is sufficiently removed from political pressures to be able to report findings without fear of repercussions. | Extent to which evaluation unit and its staff are not accountable to political authorities and are insulated from participation in political activities |
| | Unit staffers are protected by a personnel system in which compensation, training, tenure, and advancement are based on merit. | Extent to which merit system covering compensation, training, tenure, and advancement is in place and enforced |
| | Unit has access to all needed information and information sources. | Extent to which evaluation unit has unrestricted access to the organization's staff, records, co-financiers and other partners, clients, and those of programs, activities, or entities it funds or sponsors |
| Behavioral independence | Unit has ability and willingness to issue strong, uncompromising reports. | Extent to which evaluation unit has issued reports that invite public scrutiny (within appropriate safeguards to protect confidential or proprietary information and to mitigate institutional risk) of the lessons from the organization's programs and activities; propose standards for performance that are in advance of those in current use by the organization; and critique the outcomes of the organization's programs, activities, and entities |

*(continued)*

Table 1.4 (continued)

| Criterion | Aspect | Indicators |
|-----------|--------|------------|
| | Unit has ability to report candidly. | Extent to which organization's mandate provides that evaluation unit transmits its reports to management/the board after review and comment by relevant corporate units but without management-imposed restrictions on their scope and comments |
| | Reporting of evaluation findings is transparent. | Extent to which organization's disclosure rules permit evaluation unit to report significant findings to concerned stakeholders, both internal and external (within appropriate safeguards to protect confidential or proprietary information and to mitigate institutional risk) |
| Protection from outside interference | Evaluation is properly designed and executed. | Extent to which evaluation unit is able to determine the design, scope, timing, and conduct of evaluations without management interference |
| | Evaluation study is adequately funded. | Extent to which evaluation unit is unimpeded by restrictions on funds or other resources that would adversely affect its ability to carry out its responsibilities |
| | Evaluator judgments on report content are not overruled. | Extent to which evaluator's judgment as to appropriate content of a report is not subject to overruling or influence by external authority |
| | Independent human resource procedures are documented for evaluation unit head. | Extent to which mandate or equivalent document specifies procedures for the hiring, firing, term of office, performance review, and compensation of evaluation unit head that ensure independence from operational management |
| | Unit has control over staff hiring, promotion, and/or dismissal. | Extent to which evaluation unit has control over staff hiring, promotion, pay increases, and firing, within a merit system |
| | Evaluator's continued employment is not based on results of evaluation. | Extent to which evaluator's continued employment is based only on job performance, competency, and the need for evaluator services |
| Avoidance of conflicts of interest | Official, professional, personal, or financial relationships do not exist that might cause an evaluator to limit the extent of an inquiry, limit disclosure, or weaken or slant findings. | Extent to which policies and procedures are in place to identify evaluator relationships that may interfere with independence of the evaluation, policies and procedures are communicated to staff through training and other means, and they are enforced |

| Criterion | Aspect | Indicators |
|---|---|---|
| | Evaluator does not hold preconceived ideas, prejudices, or social/political biases that could affect evaluation findings. | Extent to which policies and procedures are in place and enforced that require evaluators to assess and report personal prejudices or biases that could imperil their ability to bring objectivity to the evaluation and on which stakeholders are consulted as part of evaluation process to ensure against evaluator bias |
| | Evaluator is not currently and was not previously involved with a program, activity, or entity being evaluated at a decision-making level or in a financial management or accounting role and is not seeking employment with such a program, activity, or entity while conducting the evaluation. | Extent to which rules or staffing procedures are present and enforced that prevent staff members from evaluating programs, activities, or entities for which they have or had decision-making or financial management roles or with which they are seeking employment |
| | Evaluator has no financial interest in the program, activity, or entity being evaluated. | Extent to which rules or staffing procedures are in place and enforced to prevent staff members from evaluating programs, activities, or entities in which they have a financial interest |
| | Immediate or close family members are not involved in or in a position to exert direct and significant influence over the program, activity, or entity being evaluated. | Extent to which rules or staffing procedures are in place and enforced to prevent staff members from evaluating programs, activities, or entities in which family members have influence |

*Source:* Danish Ministry of Foreign Affairs 1999; OECD 1991b; CIDA 2000; Institute of Internal Auditors 2000; European Federation of Accountants 2001; INTOSAI 2001; U.S. GAO 2002.

# Examples of Development Evaluations

Boxes 1.4–1.8 are from evaluation reports (ALNAP 2006). Each exemplifies one of the criteria described above: relevance, effectiveness, efficiency, impact, and sustainability.

---

**Box 1.4    Relevance: The World Food Programme's Evaluation of Food Aid for Relief and Recovery in Somalia**

This evaluation was carried out by two expatriates who visited Somalia for three weeks in mid-July 2001. The evaluation assessed three years of support that distributed 63,000 million tonnes of food commodities to 1.3 million people, at a cost of US$55 million. Of this support, 51 percent was supposed to have gone toward rehabilitation and recovery, 30 percent to emergency relief, and 19 percent to social institutions. The primary aim of the protracted relief and recovery operation was to "contribute to a broader framework for integrated rehabilitation programs in Somalia, while maintaining flexibility to both grasp development opportunities and respond to emergency situations" (WFP 2002, p. 4). The evaluation therefore needed to examine the relevance of this mix of allocations as well as the appropriateness of each type of intervention.

The overall relevance of the intervention was considered in the context of the political economy of aid in Somalia. The evaluation considered the rationale for providing food aid in Somalia. Arguments against food aid included the facts that Somalia is usually in food deficit, that people in many locations are isolated from customary markets, and that many Somalis lost both their primary occupations and their assets. Arguments against food aid suggested that it might make more sense to give beneficiaries funds with which to purchase local food where available, either in the form of a cash-for-work or food-for-work award. Such commitments tend to be long-term projects, however, with no clear exit strategy. This evaluation's examination of both wider and specific issues means that its analysis of relevance is comprehensive.

---

**Box 1.5  Effectiveness: DfID's Evaluation of Support for the World Food Programme's Efforts in Bangladesh**

In September 2000, floods in six southwestern districts of Bangladesh seriously affected about 2.7 million people. DfID supported the World Food Programme in providing three distributions of food, including a full ration of rice, pulses, and oil. In the first distribution, 260,000 beneficiaries received food support; in the second and third distributions, 420,000 beneficiaries received food support. The DfID evaluation (DfID 2001) provided a comprehensive analysis of whether the project objectives were met, with respect to ration sizes, commodity mixes, and distribution schedules.

The evaluation included both quantitative and qualitative methods. Quantitative data were collected in 2,644 randomly selected households in villages throughout the project zone. Qualitative data were collected during livelihood assessments in six representative villages on the livelihoods' systems, status, and prospects in flood-affected communities. A second, smaller evaluation team was deployed about five weeks after the end of the first qualitative assessment to explore community perceptions and behaviors related to the food ration, including issues such as the timeliness of distribution, the desirability of the commodities provided, and usage patterns. The quantitative and qualitative data sets were used in combination in the analysis.

The report includes most key elements for the evaluation of effectiveness, including

- examination of the development of the intervention objectives, including an analysis of the logical framework
- assessment of criteria used for selection of beneficiaries, including primary stakeholders' views of these criteria
- analysis of implementation mechanisms, including levels of community participation
- estimation of targeting accuracy, disaggregated by gender and socioeconomic grouping
- assessment of resources provided (both the size of the ration and the commodity mix), including the reasons why they were provided (this area can also be assessed under the relevance criterion)
- examination of the adequacy of distribution schedules
- analysis of beneficiaries' views of the intervention.

**Box 1.6    Efficiency: Evaluation of the Disasters Emergency Committee's Mozambique Flood Appeal Funds**

After the 2000 floods in Mozambique, the Disasters Emergency Committee (DEC) evaluation took a close look at the humanitarian response undertaken by DEC agencies (DEC 2001). The purpose of the evaluation was to report to the British public on how and where its funds were used and to identify good practice for future emergency operations. The method for the evaluation included extensive interviews, background research, field visits, and a detailed beneficiary survey.

The chapter dedicated to efficiency contains many of the key elements necessary for evaluation, including analysis of

- the use of military assets by DEC agencies, assessed in terms of lack of collaborative use of helicopters to carry out the needs assessment; the high costs of using Western military forces rather than commercial facilities for humanitarian relief; and the comparative costs of the Royal Air Force, the U.S. military, and the South African National Defence Forces (the report notes that expensive military operations consumed large amounts of funding, which limited later donor funding of NGO projects)
- the effects on efficiency of an underdeveloped market for contracted services (for example, although use of national contractors enabled agencies to implement equipment-heavy works, such as road repairs, without having to make large capital investments, the contractors used by the DEC agencies often failed to meet their obligations in a timely manner)
- the efficiency of choice of response (intervening directly with operational programs, working through local partners, or working through international network members); the evaluation found that staff composition was a more important factor determining efficiency than choice of response (this area could also have been considered under the relevance criterion)
- whether it was more efficient for agencies to build their response on existing capacity in-country or international staff
- whether agencies with existing partners were more efficient than those without such partners
- how investment in preparedness led to a more efficient response
- the efficiency of accounting systems.

An attempt was made to compare input costs across agencies, but doing so proved impossible given the different items provided and delivery channels used. Instead, the evaluation relied on the general cost implications of practices followed, such as warehousing and transportation costs. The evaluation also included a breakdown of expenditure of funds by sectors and for each of the DEC agencies by supplies and material, nonpersonnel and personnel, and agency management costs.

### Box 1.7 Impact: Joint Evaluation of Emergency Assistance to Rwanda

The Joint Evaluation of Emergency Assistance to Rwanda (JEEAR 1996) is the largest and most comprehensive evaluation of humanitarian action ever conducted. It involved 52 consultants and researchers. The report set standards for the joint assessment of the impact of political action (and the lack thereof) in complex emergencies.

JEEAR assessed impact mainly in terms of a lack of intervention in Rwanda by the international community despite significant signs that forces in Rwanda were preparing the climate and structures for genocide and political assassination. It employed a definition of humanitarian action that included both political and socioeconomic functions. This definition led to an analysis of political structures that largely determine humanitarian response and impact.

Lack of intervention was considered in two parts: an analysis of historical factors that explained the genocide and a detailed description of the immediate events leading up to the genocide. The value of the joint evaluation is that it went beyond the confines of examination of single-sector interventions to an analysis of political economy. The political economy approach was then linked to the evaluation of the effectiveness of the humanitarian response.

This approach can be contrasted with that used in evaluations of other crises, such as the conflict and its aftermath in Kosovo, the effects of Hurricane Mitch, and interventions in Afghanistan. In each of these cases, decisions were made to carry out single-agency, single-sector evaluations, which largely failed to capture the political nature of the event and the response to it. In the Kosovo and Afghanistan cases, this led to a lack of attention by evaluators to issues of protection and human rights (ALNAP 2001, 2004. In the case of Hurricane Mitch, it led to lack of attention to how far humanitarian action supported the transformative agenda proposed in the Stockholm Declaration (ALNAP 2002).

JEEAR is unusual in its assessment of impact because it places strong emphasis on why there was little interest in intervening in Rwanda (principally because of its lack of geopolitical significance) rather than listing events and their consequences. One of the lessons for evaluators is that evaluations of impact need to look not only at what interventions took place but also at what may have happened given other circumstances and different kinds of intervention.

**Box 1.8  Sustainability: JICA's Evaluation of the Third Country Training Program on Information and Communication Technology**

The Japan International Cooperation Agency (JICA) conducted an evaluation of a project in the Philippines. This project aimed to provide an opportunity for participants from Cambodia, Lao PDR, Myanmar, and Vietnam to improve their knowledge and techniques in the field of information and communication technology for entrepreneurship.

The evaluation (JICA 2005b) concluded that sustainability was high, given the commitment by the Foundation for Information Technology and Education Development (FIT-ED) to take on future training programs to achieve project objectives. FIT-ED has established an e-group to allow networking among participants and enable FIT-ED to share knowledge and enhance its capacities. As an institution committed to help increase information technology awareness in government and business sectors in the Association of Southeast Asian Nations (ASEAN) countries, FIT-ED will continue to be at the forefront of ASEAN activities related to information and communication technology.

FIT-ED's adequate and timely allocation of resources for the three training courses proved its commitment to sustain the training program. Participants also expressed commitment to support the initiative. They recognized the importance of information and communication technology in their businesses, with 84 percent of those interviewed already having applied knowledge and skills acquired during the training program (in Web site development, communications, textiles and apparel, import and export of handicrafts, construction, coffee production, and government undertakings, among other areas) in their work. Respondents reporting having benefited greatly from the course, which they viewed as the beginning of the training program. In addition to using the strategic e-business plan drafted during the training program as a reference, participants also made use of the Internet to apply the knowledge gained from the course to promote the sectors cited above.

## Summary

Evaluation has taken place for centuries. Only recently, however, has it looked at the effects of interventions on development.

Evaluation takes three forms (formative, summative, and prospective) and serves four purposes (ethical, managerial, decisional, and educational and motivational). It can provide information on strategy (are the right things being done?), operations (are thing being done right?), and learning (are there better ways?). Evaluation can be conducted internally, externally, or in a participatory manner.

Development evaluation evolved from social science research, the scientific method, and auditing. The role of the evaluator has changed over time, from an emphasis on evaluator as auditor, accountant, and certifier to an emphasis on evaluator as researcher and facilitator of participatory evaluations.

Development evaluation is based on the OECD/DAC criteria of relevance, effectiveness, efficiency, impact, and sustainability. The OECD/DAC has also developed specific principles for evaluation of development assistance and evaluation quality standards.

An important part of credibility is independence. The heads of the multinational development banks have identified four dimensions or criteria of evaluation independence: organizational independence, behavioral independence, avoidance of conflicts of interest, and protection from outside interference.

## Chapter 1 Activity

### Application Exercises 1.1

1. You have been asked to justify why development evaluation should be a budgeted expense for a new national program. The program was designed to improve the education of families about effective health practices. What would you say in defense of development education?

2. Interview an evaluator in your field to determine the extent to which standards and guiding principles are addressed in the evaluations he or she has seen. (If you do not have access to an evaluator, review recent evaluation reports conducted in your field.) Where do the strengths seem to be? Where are the weaknesses? Share your findings with evaluation colleagues and listen to their comments and experiences. Do you see any patterns?

## Notes

1. The U.S. General Accounting Office changed its name to the Government Accountability Office in July 2004. It still uses the abbreviation GAO.

## References and Further Reading

Adamo, Abra. 2003. *Mainstreaming Gender in IDRC's MINGA Program Initiative: A Formative Evaluation.*
https://idl-bnc.idrc.ca/dspace/bitstream/123456789/30972/1/121759.pdf.

ADB (Asian Development Bank). 2007. *Mongolia: Second Financial Sector Program.*
http://www.oecd.org/dataoecd/59/35/39926954.pdf.

ALNAP (Active Learning Network for Accountability and Performance in Humanitarian Action). 2001. *Humanitarian Action: Learning from Evaluation. ALNAP Annual Review 2001.* ALNAP/Overseas Development Institute, London.

———. 2002. *Humanitarian Action: Improved Performance through Improved Learning. ALNAP Annual Review 2002.* ALNAP/Overseas Development Institute, London.

———. 2006. *Evaluating Humanitarian Action Using the OECD/DAC Criteria.* Overseas Development Institute, London.
http://www.odi.org.uk/alnap/publications/eha_dac/pdfs/eha_2006.pdf.

Bhy, Y. Tan Sri Data' Setia Ambrin bin Huang. 2006. *The Role of the National Audit Department of Malaysia in Promoting Government Accountability.* Paper presented at the Third Symposium of the Asian Organisation of Supreme Audit Institutions (ASOSAI), Shanghai, September 13.
http://apps.emoe.gov.my/bad/NADRole.htm.

Brooks, R. A. 1996. "Blending Two Cultures: State Legislative Auditing and Evaluation." In *Evaluation and Auditing: Prospects for Convergence,* ed. Carl Wisler, 15–28. *New Directions for Evaluation* 71 (Fall). San Francisco: Jossey-Bass.

Burkhead, J. 1956. *Government Budgeting.* New York: John Wiley & Sons.

Callow-Heusser, Catherine. 2002. *Digital Resources for Evaluators.*
http://www.resources4evaluators.info/CommunitiesOfEvaluators.html.

Chelimsky, Eleanor. 1995. "Preamble: New Dimensions in Evaluation." In *Evaluating Country Development Policies and Programs,* ed. Robert Picciotto and Ray C. Rist, 3-8. *New Approaches for a New Agenda* 67 (Fall). Publication of the American Evaluation Association. San Francisco: Jossey-Bass Publishers.

———. 1997. "The Coming Transformations in Evaluation." In *Evaluation for the 21st Century: A Handbook*, eds. E. Chelimsky and W. R. Shadish, pp. 1–26. Thousand Oaks, CA: Sage Publications.

Chelimsky, Eleanor, and William R. Shadish. 1997. *Evaluation for the 21st Century: A Handbook.* Thousand Oaks, CA: Sage Publications

CIDA (Canadian International Development Agency). 2000. *CIDA Evaluation Guide.* Ottawa.

Danida, Ministry of Foreign Affairs. 1998, 1999. Guidelines for an Output and Outcome Indicator System. Copenhagen: Danida.

DEC (Disasters Emergency Committee). 2001. *Independent Evaluation of DEC Mozambique Floods Appeal Funds: March 2000–December 2000*. London.

Derlien, Hans-Ulrich. 1999. "Program Evaluation in the Federal Republic of Germany." In *Program Evaluation and the Management of Government: Patterns and Prospects across Eight Nations*, ed. Ray C. Rist, 37–52. New Brunswick, NJ: Transaction Publishers.

DfID (Department for International Development). *Sector Wide Approaches (SWAps)*. London. http://www.dfid.gov.uk/mdg/aid-effectiveness/swaps.asp.

———. 2001. *Emergency Food Aid to Flood-Affected People in South-Western Bangladesh: Evaluation report*. London.

European Federation of Accountants. 2001. *The Conceptual Approach to Protecting Auditor Independence*. Bruxelles.

Evaluation Cooperation Group of the Multilateral Development Banks. n.d. *Good Practice Standards for Evaluation of MDB–Supported Public Sector Operations*. Working Group on Evaluation Criteria and Ratings for Public Sector Evaluation. https://wpqp1.adb.org/QuickPlace/ecg/Main.nsf/h_B084A3976FF5F808482571D90027AD16/1E8F8A367033183248257463002F0726/

Feuerstein, M. T. 1986. *Partners in Evaluation: Evaluating Development and Community Programs with Participants*. London: MacMillan, in association with Teaching Aids at Low Cost.

Fitzpatrick, Jody L., James, R. Sanders, and Blaine R. Worthen. 2004. *Program Evaluation: Alternative Approaches and Practical Guidelines*. 3rd ed. New York: Pearson Education, Inc.

Fontaine, C., and E. Monnier. 2002. "Evaluation in France." In *International Atlas of Evaluation*, eds. Jan-Eric Furubo, Ray C. Rist, and Rolf Sandahl, 63–76. New Brunswick, NJ: Transaction Publishers.

Furubo, Jan-Eric, Ray C. Rist, and Rolf Sandahl, eds. 2002. *International Atlas of Evaluation*. New Brunswick, NJ: Transaction Publishers.

Furubo, Jan-Eric, and R. Sandahl. 2002. "Coordinated Pluralism." In *International Atlas of Evaluation*, eds. Jan-Eric Furubo, Ray C. Rist, and Rolf Sandahl, 115–28. New Brunswick, NJ: Transaction Publishers.

Government of Malawi. 2007. "National Indicators for Routine Monitoring of Quality of Health Services at Central Hospital." http://www.malawi.gov.mw/MoHP/Information/Central%20Hospital%20Indicators.htm.

Human Rights Education Associated. 1997. *Evaluation in the Human Rights Education Field: Getting Started*. Netherlands Helsinki Committee. http://www.hrea.org/pubs/EvaluationGuide/.

Insideout. 2005. "M&E In's and Out's." *Insideout* 3 (October/November) p. 1. http://www.insideoutresearch.co.za/news_1/Newsletter_issue%203.pdf.

Institute of Internal Auditors. 2000. *Professional Practices Framework*. Altamonte Springs, Florida.

Inter-American Development Bank. 2004. *Proposal for Sector-wide Approaches*. http://idbdocs.iadb.org/wsdocs/getdocument.aspx?docnum=509733.

INTOSAI (International Organization of Supreme Audit Institutions). n.d. *Draft Strategic Plan 2004 to 2009*. Vienna, Austria. http://www.gao.gov/cghome/parwi/img4.html.

———. 2001. *Code of Ethics and Auditing Standards*. Stockholm.

JEEAR (Joint Evaluation of Emergency Assistance to Rwanda). 1996. *The International Response to Conflict and Genocide: Lessons from the Rwanda Experience, 5 volumes*. JEEAR Steering Committee, Copenhagen.

JICA (Japan International Cooperation Agency). 2005a. *JICA Evaluation: Information and Communication*. Tokyo.
http://www.jica.go.jp/english/operations/evaluation/.

———. 2005b. *Results of Evaluation, Achievement of the Project Joint Evaluation of Emergency Assistance to Rwanda*. Tokyo.

KRA Corporation. 1997. *A Guide to Evaluating Crime Control of Programs in Public Housing*. Report prepared for the U.S. Department of Housing and Urban Development.
http://www.ojp.usdoj.gov/BJA/evaluation/guide/documents/guide_to_evaluating_crime.html.

Kusek, Jody Zall, and Ray C. Rist. 2004. *Ten Steps to a Results-Based Monitoring and Evaluation System*. World Bank, Washington, DC.
http://www.oecd.org/dataoecd/23/27/35281194.pdf.

Lawrence, J. 1989. "Engaging Recipients in Development Evaluation: The 'Stakeholder' Approach." *Evaluation Review* 13 (3): 243–56.

MEASURE Evaluation. n.d. *Monitoring and Evaluation of Population and Health Programs*. University of North Carolina, Chapel Hill.
http://www.cpc.unc.edu/measure.

Mikesell, J. L. 1995. *Fiscal Administration: Analysis and Applications for the Public Sector*, 4th ed. Belmont, CA: Wadsworth Publishing Company.

Molund, Stefan, and Göran Schill 2004. *Looking Back, Moving Forward: SIDA Evaluation Manual*. Swedish International Development Agency, Stockholm.

OECD (Organisation for Economic Co-operation and Development). 1991a. *DAC Criteria for Evaluating Development Assistance*. Development Assistance Committee.
http://www.oecd.org/document/22/0,2340,en_2649_34435_2086550_1_1_1_1,00.html.

———. 1991b. *Principles for Evaluation of Development Assistance*. Development Assistance Committee.
http://siteresources.worldbank.org/EXTGLOREGPARPRO/Resources/DACPrinciples1991.pdf.

———. 1998. *Review of the DAC Principles for Evaluation of Development Assistance*. Development Assistance Committee.
http://www.oecd.org/dataoecd/31/12/2755284.pdf.

———. 2002. *OECD Glossary of Key Terms in Evaluation and Results-Based Management*. Development Assistance Committee, Paris.

———. 2006. *Evaluation Quality Standards for Test Phase Application*. Development Assistance Committee.
http://www.oecd.org/dataoecd/30/62/36596604.pdf.

———. 2007a. General information.
http://www.oecd.org/document/48/0,3343,en_2649_201185_1876912_1_1_1_1,00.html.

———. 2007b. Development Co-operation Directorate DCD-DAC. http://www.oecd.org/department/0,2688,en_2649_33721_1_1_1_1_1,00.html.

Office of the Secretary of Defense Comptroller Center. 2007. *The Historical Context.* http://www.defenselink.mil/comptroller/icenter/budget/histcontext.htm.

Picciotto, Robert. 2002. "Development Evaluation as a Discipline." International Program for Development Evaluation Training (IPDET) presentation, Ottawa, July.

———. 2005. "The Value of Evaluation Standards: A Comparative Assessment." *Journal of Multidisciplinary Evaluation* 3: 30–59. http://evaluation.wmich.edu/jmde/content/JMDE003content/PDFspercent 20JMDE percent20003/4_percent20The_Value_of_Evaluation_Standards_A_ Comparative_Assessment.pdf.

Quesnel, Jean Serge. 2006. "The Importance of Evaluation Associations and Networks." In *New Trends in Development Evaluation* 5, UNICEF Regional Office for Central and Eastern Europe, Commonwealth of Independent States, and International Program Evaluation Network. http://www.unicef.org/ceecis/New_trends_Dev_EValuation.pdf.

Quinn, Michael 1997. *Utilization-Focused Evaluation.* 3rd ed. Thousand Oaks, CA: Sage Publications.

Rossi, Peter, and Howard Freeman. 1993. *Evaluation: A Systematic Approach.* Thousand Oaks, CA: Sage Publications.

Scientific and National Councils for Evaluation. 1999. *A Practical Guide to Program and Policy Evaluation.* Paris: National Council of Evaluation.

Sonnichsen, R. C. 2000. *High-Impact Internal Evaluation.* Thousand Oaks, CA: Sage Publications.

Treasury Board of Canada Secretariat. 1993. "Linkages between Audit and Evaluation in Canadian Federal Developments." http://www.tbs-sct.gc.ca/pubs_pol/dcgpubs/TB_h4/evaluation03_e.asp.

Tyler, C., and J. Willand. 1997. "Public Budgeting in America: A Twentieth Century Retrospective." *Journal of Public Budgeting, Accounting and Financial Management* 9 (2): 189–219. http://www.ipspr.sc.edu/publication/Budgeting_in_America.htm.

U.S. Department of Housing and Urban Development. 1997. "A Guide to Evaluating Crime Control of Programs in Public Housing." Paper prepared by the KRA Corporation, Washington, DC. http://www.ojp.usdoj.gov/BJA/evaluation/guide/documents/benefits_of_ evaluation.htm.

U.S. GAO (General Accounting Office). 1986. *Teenage Pregnancy: 500,000 Births a Year but Few Tested Programs.* Washington, DC: U.S. GAO.

———. 2002. "Government Auditing Standards, Amendment 3," GAO, Washington, DC.

Weiss, Carol. 2004. "Identifying the Intended Use(s) of an Evaluation." *Evaluation Guideline* 6. http://www.idrc.ca/ev_en.php?ID=58213_201&ID2=DO_TOPIC p 1.

WFP (World Food Programme). 2002. *Full Report of the Evaluation of PRRO Somalia 6073.00, Food Aid for Relief and Recovery in Somalia.* Rome.

Wisler, Carl, ed. 1996. "Evaluation and Auditing: Prospects for Convergences." In *New Directions for Evaluation* 71 (Fall), 1–71. San Francisco: Jossey-Bass.

World Bank. 1996. *World Bank Participation Sourcebook.* http://www.worldbank.org/wbi/sourcebook/sbhome.htm.

## Web Sites

### Evaluation Organizations

African Evaluation Association. http://www.afrea.org/.

American Evaluation Association. http://www.eval.org.

Australasian Evaluation Society. http://www.aes.asn.au.

Brazilian Evaluation Association. http://www.avaliabrasil.org.br.

Canadian Evaluation Society. http://www.evaluationcanada.ca.

Danish Evaluation Society. http://www.danskevalueringsselskab.dk.

Dutch Evaluation Society. http://www.videnet.nl/.

European Evaluation Society. http://www.europeanevaluation.org.

Finnish Evaluation Society. http://www.finnishevaluationsociety.net/.

French Evaluation Society. http://www.sfe.asso.fr/.

German Society for Evaluation Standards. http://www.degeval.de/.

Institute of Internal Auditors. http://www.theiia.org.

International Development Evaluation Association (IDEAS). http://www.ideas-int .org/. (IDEAS Web page with links to many organizations: http://www.ideas-int .org/Links.aspx.)

International Organisation for Cooperation in Evaluation. http://ioce.net/ overview/general.shtml.

International Organization of Supreme Audit Institutions (INTOSAI). http://www .intosai.org/.

International Program Evaluation Network (Russia and Newly Independent States). http://www.eval-net.org/.

Israeli Association for Program Evaluation. http://www.iape.org.il.

Italian Evaluation Association. http://www.valutazioneitaliana.it/

Japan Evaluation Society. http://ioce.net/members/eval_associations.shtml

Latin American and Caribbean Programme for Strengthening the Regional Capac-ity for Evaluation of Rural Poverty Alleviation Projects (PREVAL). http://www .preval.org/.

Malaysian Evaluation Society. http://www.mes.org.my.

Nigerian Network of Monitoring and Evaluation. http://www.pnud.ne/rense/.

Polish Evaluation Society. http://www.pte.org.pl/x.php/1,71/Strona-glowna.html.

Quebecois Society for Program Evaluation. http://www.sqep.ca.

Red de Evaluacion de America Latina y el Caribe. http://www.relacweb.org.

South African Evaluation Network. http://www.afrea.org/webs/southafrica/.

South African Monitoring and Evaluation Association. http://www.samea.org.za.

Spanish Evaluation Society. http://www.sociedadevaluacion.org.

Sri Lankan Evaluation Association. http://www.nsf.ac.lk/sleva/.

Swedish Evaluation Society. http://www.svuf.nu.

Swiss Evaluation Society. http://www.seval.ch/de/index.cfm.

Ugandan Evaluation Association. http://www.ueas.org.

United Kingdom Evaluation Society. http://www.evaluation.org.uk.

Wallonian Society for Evaluation. http://www.prospeval.org.


## Evaluation Standards

African Evaluation Association. *Evaluation Standards and Guidelines*. http://www
.afrea.org/.

American Evaluation Association. *Guiding Principles*. http://www.eval.org/
Publications/GuidingPrinciples.asp.

Australasian Evaluation Society. *Ethical Guidelines for Evaluators*. http://www.aes
.asn.au/content/ethics_guidelines.pdf.

ECGnet [The Evaluation Cooperation Group] https://wpqp1.adb.org/QuickPlace/
ecg/Main.nsf/h_B084A3976FF5F808482571D90027AD16/1E8F8A36703318324
8257463002F0726/.

German Society for Evaluation. *Standards*. http://www.degeval.de/standards/
standards.htm.

Italian Evaluation Association. *Guidelines*. http://www.valutazioneitaliana.it/
statuto.htm#Linee.

OECD (Organisation for Economic Co-operation and Development). *Evaluation
Quality Standards* (for test phase application). Development Assistance Committee. http://www.oecd.org/dataoecd/30/62/36596604.pdf.

———. *Evaluating Development Co-Operation: Summary of Key Norms and Standards*. Development Assistance Committee, Network on Development Evaluation. http://www.oecd.org/dac/evaluationnetwork.

Program Evaluation Standards (updated 1998). http://www.eval.org/Evaluation
Documents/progeval.html.

Swiss Evaluation Society. *Standards*. seval.ch/.

UNEG (United Nations Evaluation Group). *Norms for Evaluation in the UN System*.
http://www.uneval.org/docs/ACFFC9F.pdf.

———. *Standards for Evaluation in the UN System*. http://www.uneval.org/docs/
ACFFCA1.pdf.

UNFPA (United Nations Population Fund). n.d. *List of Evaluation Reports and Findings*. http://www.unfpa.org/publications/index.cfm.

UNICEF Regional Office for Central and Eastern Europe, Commonwealth of Independent States, and International Program Evaluation Network. 2006.
*New Trends in Development Evaluation* 5. http://www.unicef.org/ceecis/New_
trends_Dev_EValuation.pdf.

United Nations Development Project Evaluation Office. http://www.undp.org/eo/.

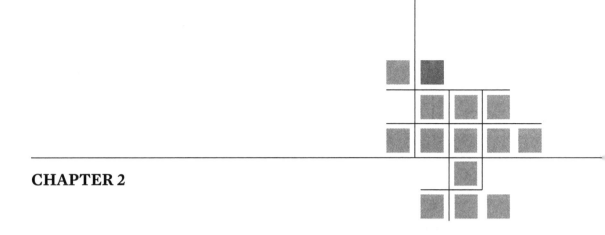

**CHAPTER 2**

# Understanding the Issues Driving Development Evaluation

The field of development evaluation is a relatively new one that changes in response to emerging issues in developed and developing countries. This chapter looks at some of the current issues that affect both developed and developing countries.

**This chapter has two main parts:**

- Overview of Evaluation in Developed and Developing Countries
- Implications of Emerging Development Issues

# Overview of Evaluation in Developed and Developing Countries

Evaluation can assist countries in learning about how well, and to what extent, they are achieving their development goals, including the Millennium Development Goals (MDGs). Policy makers and others can use key insights and recommendations drawn from evaluation findings to initiate change. Evaluation enables countries to use experience to improve the design and delivery of current projects, programs, and policies; change future directions; or both.

Many developed and developing countries have put monitoring and evaluation (M&E) systems in place to assist with development. These systems can be set up in different ways, depending upon needs and available resources.

## Evaluation in Developed Countries

Most of the 30 countries of the Organisation for Economic Co-operation and Development (OECD) now have mature M&E systems. Putting them in place was neither an easy nor a linear process. These countries differ, often substantially, in their paths, approach, style, and level of development.

Furubo, Rist, and Sandahl (2002) mapped evaluation cultures in OECD countries in order to explain the observed patterns. They examined 9 variables in 23 countries, giving each country a score between 0 (low) and 2 (high) for each of the following variables:

1. Evaluation takes place in many policy domains.
2. There is a supply of evaluators specializing in different disciplines who have mastered different evaluation methods and who conduct evaluations.
3. There is a national discourse concerning evaluation in which more general discussions are adjusted to the specific national environment.
4. There is a profession with its own societies or frequent attendance at meetings of international societies and at least some discussion concerning the norms and ethics of the profession.
5. There are institutional arrangements in the government for conducting evaluations and disseminating their results to decision makers.
6. Institutional arrangements are present in parliament or other legislative bodies for conducting evaluations and disseminating them to decision makers.

7. An element of pluralism exists—that is, within each policy domain there are different people or agencies commissioning and performing evaluations.
8. Evaluation activities also take place within the supreme audit institution.
9. Evaluations should not focus only on technical production or the relation between inputs and outputs. Some public sector evaluations must have program or policy outcomes as their object (Furubo, Rist, and Sandahl 2002).

According to these criteria, Australia, Canada, the Netherlands, Sweden, and the United States had the highest "evaluation culture rankings" among OECD countries in 2002.

OECD countries have developed evaluation cultures and M&E systems in response to varying degrees of internal and external pressures. France, Germany, and the Netherlands, for example, developed an evaluation culture in response to both strong internal and external (mostly European Union–related) pressures. In contrast, countries such as Australia, Canada, the Republic of Korea, and the United States were motivated largely by strong internal pressures (Furubo, Rist, and Sandahl 2002).

The first wave of OECD countries was motivated to adopt evaluation cultures largely because of strong internal pressures, such as domestic planning, programming, and budgeting imperatives for new socioeconomic spending programs, as well as legislative oversight. Several factors contributed to the adoption of an evaluation culture in the pioneering countries. Many of the earliest adopters were predisposed to do so because they had democratic political systems, strong empirical traditions, civil servants trained in the social sciences (as opposed to strict legal training), and efficient administrative systems and institutions.

Countries with high levels of expenditure on education, health, and social welfare adopted evaluation mechanisms in these areas, which then spilled over into other areas of public policy. The OECD countries that were early adaptors of an evaluation culture were also instrumental in spreading evaluation culture to other countries, by disseminating evaluation ideas and information and by launching evaluation organizations, training institutes, networks, and consulting firms.

In contrast, many of the latecomer OECD countries (including Ireland, Italy, and Spain) tended to respond to evaluation issues mainly because of strong external pressures, primarily European Union (EU) membership requirements, including access to EU structural development funds. These latecomers were heavily influenced by the evaluation culture of the first-wave countries, as well as by the evaluation culture rooted in the international organizations with which they interact.

The Tavistock Institute (2003) describes a model, or map, for a journey toward developing evaluation capacity that has four stages and intermediate destinations:

- Stage 1: Mandating evaluation
- Stage 2: Coordinating evaluation
- Stage 3: Institutionalizing evaluation
- Stage 4: Building an evaluation system.

Stage 1 usually begins with external pressure that requires evaluation through norms, regulations, or policy objectives. Even when the driving force comes from within, a certain degree of external scrutiny is likely.

Stage 2 includes two kinds of actions in response to the formal and rule-based first-stage evaluation policy. The first provides guidelines and basic tools; the second emphasizes professionalizing the staff as a way of improving quality.

Stage 3 usually begins after a central unit is up and running. It includes two steps, usually adopted simultaneously: creating decentralized units and improving supply of evaluation expertise.

Stage 4 involves building a fully operative evaluation system in which evaluation is incorporated into policy making, program management, and governance. It includes establishing stronger internal links within the system and opening up the network to external stakeholders.

The pioneering and latecomer OECD countries differed in their approach to creating monitoring and evaluation systems. They adopted one of three approaches:

- whole-of-government approach
- enclave approach
- mixed approach.

### The whole-of-government approach

■ **Whole-of-government approach:** Broad-based, comprehensive establishment of monitoring and evaluation across the government

The **whole-of-government approach** was adopted in some of the early M&E countries, such as Australia. This approach involves a broad-based, comprehensive establishment of M&E across the government. A whole-of-government approach framework cannot be developed overnight; it can take at least a decade to embed such a framework in a sustainable manner (World Bank 1999).

For such an approach to succeed, the support of the government must be won and sustained, necessary skills must be developed, and civil service structures and systems must be set up to make full use of M&E findings. Developing countries must also ensure steady support from development assistance agencies.

With adoption of the MDGs, many developing countries are looking to design and implement comprehensive whole-of-government evaluation systems. With the growing emphasis on results in international aid lending, more donors, governments, and other institutions are providing support to developing countries to help them build evaluation capacity and systems.

*Australia's approach to evaluation.* Australia was a pioneer in developing monitoring and evaluation systems, starting in 1987. Intrinsic advantages that were conducive to building a sound evaluative culture and structure included the following:

• strong human, institutional, and management capacity in the public sector
• a public service known for integrity, honesty, and professionalism
• well-developed financial, budgetary, and accounting systems
• a tradition of accountability and transparency
• credible, legitimate political leaders.

Two main factors contributed to success in building strong evaluation systems in Australia. First, budgetary constraints prompted the government to look at ways of achieving greater value for money. Second, Australia also had two important institutional champions for evaluation—the Department of Finance and the Australian National Audit Office. It also had the support of cabinet members and key ministers, who placed importance on using evaluation findings to better inform decision making (Mackay 2002).

The first generation of evaluation (1987–97) began during a time of severe budget pressures. Many public sector reforms involved giving line departments and agencies autonomy, but they failed to conduct monitoring and evaluation. For this reason, governments forced departments and agencies into evaluation. The objectives of this first generation of M&E systems were to aid budget decision making, strengthen accountability within the government, and assist managers in ministries and agencies.

The first-generation M&E system was designed and managed by the Department of Finance. Evaluations were mandatory, to be conducted every three to five years for every program. Sector ministries were required to prepare rolling, three-year plans for major evaluations.

A broad range of evaluation types were used. By the mid-1990s, some 160 evaluations were underway at any given time. Little formal requirements were given for collecting or reporting on performance indicators.

All evaluation findings were shared with the cabinet, which took the findings very seriously. In fact, nearly 80 percent of new policy proposals and two-thirds of savings options influenced cabinet budget decision making. Other strengths of this system were the heavy use of evaluation findings by sector departments and agencies and the fact that evaluation became a collaborative endeavor.

The first-generation system also had weaknesses. The quality of the evaluations was uneven. There was insufficient central support for advanced evaluation training and insufficient formal requirements for collecting and reporting on performance indicators. Ministries claimed that the system placed a burden on the administration.

The second generation of evaluation in Australia began with the election of the new conservative government. Changes included a significant reduction in the size of the civil service, the dismantlement of the policy-advising system for the budget process, a reduction in central oversight and "bureaucratic" rules, and substantial downsizing of the Department of Finance, which reduced its role in providing advice during the budget process.

In response to these changes in government, the M&E system needed to change. The old evaluation strategy was dismantled, and evaluation was "deregulated"—encouraged but not required. An emphasis was placed on performance monitoring of outputs and outcomes, which were reported to Parliament both ex ante and ex post.

The Australian National Audit Office reported that performance on this second-generation system was highly inadequate. Data collection was poor because of weak standards. Little use was made of targets or benchmarking. Much information was collected on government outputs but little on outcomes. Real analysis of performance information was lacking. These shortcomings made the parliamentary committees very unhappy with the information they received. Despite this, a few ministries (family and community services, education, and health) still learned from good-practice evaluations.

The third generation (from 2006) was motivated by ongoing concerns about difficulties in implementing complex government programs and with "connectivity" (that is, coordination across ministries and agencies, both federal and state). There was also a desire on the part of the Department of Defense to rebuild its role in budget and policy advising (Mackay 2007).

Two types of review were set up to ensure that spending was efficient, effective, and aligned with government priorities. Strategic reviews (seven per year) focused on the purpose, design, management, results, and future improvements needed to major policy and spending areas. Program reviews (also seven per year) focused on individual programs and their alignment with government objectives, effectiveness, duplication, overlap, and savings.

The Department of Defense was set to manage the reviews, and the decision was made to mainstream the system. The government committed US$17 million for reviews over four years. Retired civil servants were hired to head two pilot programs. They also maintained the requirements from generation two for the performance-monitoring framework.

What lessons were learned from the evolution of Australia's evaluation program?

- The issues of program coordination, implementation, and performance (results) are permanent challenges for all governments.
- The nature of government decision making determines the level of demand for M&E (and review) information.
- It takes time to build an M&E review system.
- It is difficult to balance top-down/centralized and bottom-up/decentralized needs for information.
- Most departments are not naturally inclined to conduct evaluations, which they consider costly and dangerous.

*The U.S. Government Performance Results Act of 1993.* A key development in government evaluation in the United States in the past 20 years was passage of the Government Performance Results Act (GPRA) of 1993, which instituted results-based evaluation in all U.S. government agencies. The law directly affects how evaluation is conducted across the U.S. government. GPRA is a whole-of-government approach that began with pilots before phasing in the changes.

Performance measurement in the United States began with local governments in the 1970s. It then spread to state governments and eventually to the federal level, with enactment of the GPRA in 1993. The federal government in the United States adopted performance measurement later than other levels of government in the United States.

The goals of the GPRA are to

1. improve the confidence of the American people in the capability of the federal government, by systematically holding federal agencies accountable for achieving program results
2. initiate program performance reform with a series of pilot projects in setting program goals, measuring program performance against those goals, and reporting publicly on their progress

3. improve federal program effectiveness and public accountability by promoting a new focus on results, service quality, and customer satisfaction
4. help federal managers improve service delivery, by requiring that they plan for meeting program objectives and by providing them with information about program results and service quality
5. improve congressional decision making by providing more objective information on achieving statutory objectives, and on the relative effectiveness and efficacy of federal programs and spending
6. improve internal management of the federal government. The GPRA mandated federal agencies to focus on their missions and goals, how to achieve them, and how to improve the structural organizations and business processes. Under the law, agencies are required to submit five-year strategic plans for their programs and to update them every three years. They must also identify any "key external factors" that may have a significant effect on the ability of the agency to achieve its goals and objectives. Agencies must publish annual program performance reports. (U.S. Department of Labor, 1993, para. 1)

Agencies must also measure their performance to ensure that they are meeting goals and making informed decisions. Performance measures need to be based on program-related characteristics and must be complete, accurate, and consistent. The data collected must be used to improve organizational processes, identify gaps, and set performance goals (U.S. GAO 2003).

A 2003 survey of 16 programs across 12 United States government agencies found that many federal programs had already made use of regularly collected outcome data to help them improve their programs. Outcome data, for example, were used to trigger corrective action, to identify and encourage "best practices," to motivate and recognize staff, and to plan and budget.

At the same time, the survey found some continuing obstacles to the use of outcome data, including

- lack of authority or interest to make changes
- limited understanding and use of outcome data
- problems with outcome data (old data, nondisaggregated data, lack of specificity, need for intermediate data, and so forth)
- fear of "rocking the boat" (Hatry and others 2003).

The GPRA was extended in 2003 to integrate performance and budgeting. Efforts were also made across the government to time more closely

GPRA strategic and annual planning and reporting. ChannahSorah summarizes GPRA as

> just good business. Its requirements have provided government departments with tools for very basic ways of conducting business in sensible ways: set performance goals and measure both long and short-term outcomes. Any organization seeking to provide improved quality of life, greater quantity of services, and enhanced overall quality of customer services must have a vision and a mission, set goals and objectives, and must measure results. (2003, pp. 5–6)

In a 2003 study, the GAO found that many U.S. agencies faced significant challenges in establishing an agencywide results orientation. Federal managers surveyed reported that agency leaders did not consistently demonstrate a strong commitment to achieving results. Furthermore, according to these managers, agencies did not always positively recognize employees for helping the agency accomplish its strategic goals. The GAO also reported that high-performing organizations seek to shift the focus of management and accountability from activities and processes to contributions and achievement of results. However, although many federal managers surveyed reported that they were held accountable for the results of their programs, only a few reported that they had the decision-making authority they needed to help the agencies accomplish their strategic goals. Finally, the GAO found that although managers increasingly reported having results-oriented performance measures for their programs, the extent to which these managers reported using performance information for key management activities had declined since earlier surveys. The GAO study noted the need to transform organizational cultures so that they are more results oriented, customer focused, and collaborative.

Leading public organizations in the United States and other countries have found that strategic human capital management must be the centerpiece of any serious change management initiative and efforts to transform the cultures of government agencies. Performance management systems are integral to strategic human capital management. Such systems can be key tools for maximizing performance by aligning institutional performance measures with individual performance and creating a "line of sight" between individual and organizational goals. Leading organizations use their performance management systems as a key tool for aligning institutional, unit, and employee performance; achieving results; accelerating change; managing the organization day to day; and facilitating communication throughout the year so that discussions about individual and organizational performance are integrated and ongoing.

### The enclave approach

The ability to set up an evaluation system often varies across ministries. For this reason, the whole-of-government strategy may not be able to move all ministries simultaneously; there may be a need for sequencing ministries in developing these systems. Innovations at one level often filter both horizontally and vertically to other levels of government.

The **enclave approach** focuses on one part or sector of the government, such as a single ministry. Mexico, for example, has focused on social development, Jordan on planning, and the Kyrgyz Republic on health. Working with one ministry that has a strong champion may be the best course of action in countries that lack the capacity for a whole-of-government approach.

### The mixed approach

Countries such as Ireland have adopted a **mixed approach** to evaluation. While some areas (such as projects financed by EU structural funds) are comprehensively evaluated, other areas receive less attention. The government of Ireland began creating its evaluation system with an enclave approach, but it moved in the direction of a more comprehensive approach with respect to government expenditure programs (Lee 1999). The mixed approach may also be a valid alternative for some developing countries.

*Increasing evaluation capacity development in Ireland.* Like many other countries in the late 1960s, Ireland had an interest in rational analysis and its application to planning and budgeting. Government policy makers identified the need for objective studies of social programs and the development of and need for those involved to acquire the skills to implement these studies (Friis 1965; Public Services Organisation Review Group 1969). Several initiatives were undertaken to develop evaluation skills.

Despite these initiatives, the scope of these evaluations was limited, and they had little influence on decision making until the late 1980s. This lack of influence was caused partly by the absence of a strong tradition of evaluation of policies and programs in Ireland and partly by the fact that the evaluations were conducted during a time of economic crisis, when evaluation as a tool of good governance was not considered as important as the drive to control public expenditure.

An exception to the lack of influence was the EU expenditure in Ireland. EU funds are applied through a number of operational programs, which are run under a joint Irish–EU Community Support Framework

**■ Enclave approach:** Establishment of monitoring and evaluation systems in one part or sector of the government at a time, such as a single ministry.

**■ Mixed approach:** Comprehensive establishment of monitoring and evaluation systems in some parts of government, while other parts of government receive less attention.

(CSF) plan. The EU—a major source of funding support—demanded consistent and systematic evaluation. The EU–funded program evaluations significantly affected two main policy areas: (a) industrial training and employment-creating schemes and (b) antipoverty and other community development programs. The labor market area tended to focus on quantitative measurement of outcomes, while the community development initiatives focused on qualitative methods concerned with description rather than outcome measurement (Boyle 2005).

Between 1989 and 1993, two independent evaluations units were established, one by the European Social Fund, the other by an industry evaluation unit. Since 1989, evaluation of the EU Structural Funds was a formal requirement of those receiving assistance that led to further developments in evaluation. During 1994–99, a central evaluation unit was established under the Department of Finance. A third evaluation unit was established to cover evaluations in agriculture and rural development, and external evaluators were appointed for operational program expenditures and the CSF plan. Between 1999 and 2006, there was renewed interest in national evaluation of public expenditure in Ireland. The capacity of the central evaluation unit was increased to allow it to take on extra responsibilities, and the independent evaluation units were abolished. External evaluators were contracted to conduct the midterm evaluation of the operational programs and the national development plan (Boyle 2005).

*Adopting a new approach to evaluation in France.* Until 2001, France was among the group of OECD countries that was slowest to move toward a mature evaluation system. Indeed, France lagged behind many transition economies and developing countries in this regard. Various incremental reform efforts were attempted during the late 1980s and throughout the 1990s.

Then in 2001, the government passed sweeping legislation, replacing the 1959 financial constitutional, eliminating line item budgeting, and instituting a new program approach. The new constitutional by-law, phased in over a five-year period (2001–06), had two primary aims: (a) to reform the public management framework, in order to make it results and performance oriented and (b) to strengthen legislative supervision. As then-prime minister Lionel Jospin noted, "The budget's presentation in the form of programs grouping together expenditure by major public policy should give both members of Parliament and citizens a clear picture of the government's priorities and the cost and results of its action" (Republic of France 2001). About 100 programs were identified, and financial resources were budgeted against them. Every program budget submitted to the legislature was required to have a statement of precise objectives and performance indicators. Public managers had greater freedom and autonomy with respect to the allocation of resources, but in return they were held more accountable for results. Thus the new budget process was results driven.

Budget requests for additional funds had to include annual performance plans detailing the expected versus actual results for each program. Annual performance reports also were included in budgetary reviews. These steps were intended to improve legislators' ability to evaluate the performance of governmental programs.

This reform initiative altered some of the political and institutional relationships within the French government, giving the legislature increased budgetary powers. "Article 40 of the Constitution previously prohibited members of [the legislature] from tabling amendments that would increase spending and reduce revenue. They are able to change the distribution of appropriations among programs in a given mission." The legislature is able to vote on revenue estimates, appropriations for individual missions, limits on the number of state jobs created, and special accounts and specific budgets. In addition, the legislative finance committees have monitoring and supervisory responsibilities concerning the budget.

Public servants reacted to the changes immediately. There was a new bureaucracy of control, new accountants, more audits, more questionnaires about the audit offices and inspectors, more requests for reporting, and so forth. Managers had difficulty adapting to the constraints of achieving output (quantity) results while ignoring the quality of services, which did not appear in the objectives.

As for the quality of service, "no mechanism of competition or of strong consumerist pressures make it possible to guarantee it" (Trosa 2008, p. 8). Societies are very complex. Some people need financial assistance, others need trust and the assumption of responsibility; yet others are living happily. The question is how to summarize these tensions in one formula (Trosa 2008).

Combining the previous model of evaluation with the new one did not allow freedom of management, creativity, and innovation. Trosa indicates that an alternative model is needed. Another lesson learned from the French experience is that "enhancing internal management cannot be done without linking it to the internal governance of public sectors" (Trosa 2008, p. 2). According to Trosa, the new system does not need to be demolished but rather widened by clearly discussing required purposes while encouraging the logics of action, not merely the use of tools.

## Evaluation in Developing Countries

Developing countries face challenges similar to and different from those faced by developed countries in moving toward and building their own evaluation systems. For an evaluation system to be established and take hold in any country, interested stakeholders and commitments to transparency and good governance are necessary. Demand for and ownership of an evaluation system may be more difficult to establish in developing countries.

Weak political will and institutional capacity may slow progress. Difficulties in interministerial cooperation and coordination can impede progress toward strategic planning. Indeed, a lack of sufficient governmental cooperation and coordination can be a factor in both developed and developing countries.

To emerge and mature, evaluation systems need political will in the government and champions who are highly placed and willing to assume the political risks of advocating on behalf of evaluation. The presence of a national champion or champions can go a long way in helping a country develop and sustain an evaluation system. Conversely, we know of no instance in which an M&E system has emerged in the public sector of a developing country without a champion.

Many developing countries are still struggling to put together strong, effective institutions. Some may require civil service reform or reform of legal and regulatory frameworks. Toward this end, the international development community is trying to improve basic building blocks to support them. The challenge is to build institutions, undertake administrative and civil service reforms, and/or revamp legal and regulatory codes while at the same time establishing evaluation systems. Instituting evaluation systems could help inform and guide the government to undertake needed reforms in all of these areas.

Developing countries must first have or establish a foundation for evaluation. Many are moving in this direction. Establishing a foundation means having basic statistical systems and data as well as key budgetary systems. Data and information must be of appropriate quality and quantity. Like developed countries, developing countries need to know their baseline conditions—where they currently stand in relation to a given program or policy. Capacity in the workforce is needed to develop, support, and sustain these systems. Officials need to be trained in modern data collection, monitoring methods, and analysis—challenges that can be difficult in many developing countries (Schacter 2002).

In response to these challenges, many aid organizations have ramped up their efforts to build institutional capacity. The methods include technical and financial assistance to build statistical systems, training in monitoring and evaluation, diagnostic readiness assessments and results, and performance-based budget systems. The trend toward results-based Country Assistance Strategies may help model practices. Assistance to developing countries in producing country-led poverty reduction strategies may also help build such capacity.

As part of the efforts to support local capacity in developing countries, development organizations are also moving to create development networks, such as on-line computer networks and participatory communities that share expertise and information. Examples are the Development Gateway and Asian Community of Practice. It can be argued that circumstances in a particular country are unique and that the experience of one country will not necessarily translate to another. But once it is accepted that there is very little generic development knowledge—that all knowledge has to be gathered and then analyzed, modified, disassembled, and recombined to fit local needs—the source is immaterial. The new motto is "Scan globally; reinvent locally" (Fukuda-Parr, Lopes, and Malik, 2002, p. 18).

### International Program for Development Evaluation Training

In 1999, the Independent Evaluation Group of the World Bank conducted a survey to identify training in development evaluation. It found little except for a few one-off programs for development organizations. These findings led to the creation of the International Program for Development Evaluation Training (IPDET) in 2001, as part of a major effort to build evaluation capacity in developing countries and in organizations focused on development issues.

IPDET trains professionals working, or about to begin working, in designing and conducting evaluations in the development context. Held annually, in Ottawa, Canada, on the Carleton University campus and supported by other organizations, the four-week training program is a collaboration between the Independent Evaluation Group of the World Bank, the Faculty of Public Affairs at Carleton University, and other organizations, including the Canadian International Development Agency (CIDA), the United Kingdom's Department for International Development (DfID), the Swiss Agency for Development and Cooperation (SDC), the Norwegian Agency for Development Cooperation (NORAD), the International Development Research Centre (IDRC), the Geneva International Centre for Humanitarian Demining (GICHD), the Swedish International Development Cooperation Agency (SIDA), the Commonwealth Secretariat, the Dutch Ministry of Foreign Affairs, the African Development Bank (AfDB), and the Danish International Development Agency (DANIDA).

The IPDET course begins with a two-week core program that devotes special attention to monitoring and evaluating the implementation of poverty reduction strategies and emphasizes results-based M&E and stakeholder participation. The core program offers more than eighty instructional hours, complete with tools, case studies, discussion groups, and readings. Almost one-third of instructional time is devoted to structured work group sessions, which give participants with similar interests the opportunity to work together on real-world development evaluation issues and produce a preliminary evaluation design for a program that one of the group participants must evaluate on his or her return to the work place.

Following the two-week core program are two weeks of customizable training provided through 30 workshops offered by an array of highly respected and well-known instructors. Examples of workshops include the following:

- designing impact evaluations under constraints
- designing and building results-based M&E systems
- understanding World Bank country, sector, and project evaluation approaches
- using mixed methods for development evaluations
- using participatory M&E
- evaluating postconflict situations and conducting international joint evaluations
- evaluating HIV/AIDS programs
- evaluating hidden and marginal populations.

IPDET is one of the few programs in development evaluation that is offered annually. It has trained more than 2,000 professionals from government ministries, bilateral and multilateral aid organizations, nongovernment organizations (NGOs), and other development entities.

The IPDET core program is now offered regionally and nationally. Customized versions of IPDET have been delivered, for example, in Australia (for the Australasian NGO community), Botswana, Canada, China, India, South Africa, Tunisia, Thailand, Trinidad and Tobago, and Uganda. These shorter regional programs—known as "mini–IPDETs"—are highly interactive, employing a mix of presentations, discussion groups, group exercises, and case studies. The programs are designed to maximize opportunities for peer learning, with a focus on discussing real-world issues and learning practical solutions to them.

On the basis of the demonstrated success of IPDET through annual and impact evaluations, the Independent Evaluation Group is now partnering with the Chinese Ministry of Finance (International Department), the Asia-Pacific Finance Department Center, and the Asian Development Bank on the first institutionalized regional offering. The program, called Shanghai IPDET (SHIPDET), is offered twice a year, once nationally and once regionally. Its creation illustrates efforts to help develop capacity in evaluation within developing countries and regions.

### New evaluation systems

Attempts to develop an evaluation system and to shed light on resource allocation and actual results may meet with political resistance, hostility, and opposition. Given the nature of many developing country governments, building an evaluation system can also lead to a reshaping of political relationships. Creating a mature evaluation system requires interdependency, alignment, and coordination across multiple governmental levels. Achieving such conditions can be a challenge. In many developing countries, governments are only loosely interconnected and are still working toward building strong administrative cultures and transparent financial systems. As a result, some governments may have only vague information about the amount and allocation of available resources. They may need more information about whether these resources are being used for their intended purposes. Measuring government performance in such an environment is an exercise in approximation.

Many developed and developing countries are still working toward linking performance to public expenditures framework or strategy. If these linkages are not made, there is no way to determine if the budgetary allocations that the support programs are ultimately supporting are successful.

Some developing countries are beginning to make progress in this area. For example, in the 1990s Indonesia started to link evaluation to its annual budgetary allocation process. "Evaluation is seen as a tool to correct policy and public expenditure programs through more direct linkages to the National Development Plan and the resource allocation process" (Guerrero 1999, p. 5). Some middle-income countries—including Brazil, Chile, and Turkey—have made progress toward linking expenditures to output and outcome targets. The government of Brazil issues separate government reports on outcome targets (OECD and PUMA 2002).

Many developing countries still operate with two budget systems, one for recurrent expenditures and another for capital/investment expenditures. Until recently, Egypt's Ministry of Finance oversaw the recurrent budget and its Ministry of Planning oversaw the capital budget. Consolidating these budgets within a single ministry has made it easier for the government to consider a broad-based evaluation system in order to ensure that the country's goals and objectives are met.

Given the particular difficulties of establishing evaluation systems in developing countries, adopting an enclave, or partial, approach (in which a few ministries or departments pilot and adopt evaluation systems) may be preferable to a whole-of-government approach. Attempting to institute a whole-of-government approach to evaluation may be too ambitious. A 2002 World Bank readiness assessment for the Kyrgyz Republic, for example, recommended that the Ministry of Health (where some evaluation capacity already existed) be supported as a potential model for eventual governmentwide implementation of an evaluation system.

China, Malaysia, and Uganda have pursued an enclave approach. Their efforts are described below.

*Growth-motivated evaluation in China.*    Evaluation is a relatively new phenomenon in China. Indeed, before the early 1980s, it was almost unknown. This unfamiliarity with evaluation reflected the orientation of the social sciences at that time, the virtual absence of evaluation literature published in Chinese, and the lack of systematic contacts by Chinese nationals with those practicing evaluation in other parts of the world.

The Chinese did conduct some activities that are related to evaluation, including policy analysis, economic and management studies, survey research, project completion reviews, and summarizing of experience. Social science institutional and technical/analytical capacity existed at some economic policy and research institutes.

It was not until 1992, however, that key central agencies, including the State Audit Administration, the Ministry of Finance, and the State Planning Commission, began to develop and put forth specific proposals for building performance M&E capacity in the State Council. The Center for Evaluation of Science & Technology and the Netherland's Policy and Operations Evaluation Department conducted a first joint evaluation of science and technology programs (NCSTE and IOB 2004).

With capital and development assistance going into China over the past 20 years, the country has seen an increase in capability in, and understanding of, technological and engineering analysis, financial analysis, economic analysis and modeling, social impact analysis, environmental impact analysis, sustainability analysis, and implementation studies. It is rather dramatic how quickly the capacity in China has emerged.

The driving force for evaluation in China is the massive and sustained surge in national development and economic growth. Annual gross domestic product (GDP) increased by more than 7.8 percent a year for the nine years ending in 2007. Interest in addressing evaluation questions comes from China's concern with development. Some central agencies, including the China International Engineering Consulting Company, a government-owned consulting firm; the Ministry of Construction; and the State Development

Bank have now established evaluation capacities at the highest levels of their organizations.

Although most evaluation is ex post project assessment, there is increasing recognition that evaluation issues should also be embedded in all stages of the development project cycle. There is growing awareness within China that the evaluation function is applicable to all stages of the project cycle. There is now interest in linking evaluation to project and program formulation and implementation. Some ongoing evaluation has already been undertaken, though comprehensively doing so remains infrequent.

One example of such an evaluation occurred in 2006, when China built a systematic M&E component into its five-year plan for the first time. This system included in the 11th Five-Year Plan is based on the 10 steps identified by Kusek, Rist, and White (2004).

In April 2006 China launched the twice-yearly SHIPDET to train national and regional evaluators. Partners in the training program are the Ministry of Finance, the World Bank, the Asian Development Bank, and the Asia-Pacific Finance and Development Center. China is also building a foundation for evaluation, although no grand edifice is in place.

In the Chinese governmental structure and administrative hierarchy, several key tasks must be accomplished if evaluation is to continue to develop. These include the following:

- establishment of a strong central organization for overall evaluation management and coordination
- establishment of formal evaluation units, policies, and guidelines in all relevant ministries and banks
- recognition that the time is right for provincial and local governments to start their own evaluations
- establishment in the State Audit Administration of an auditing process of the evaluation function, so that ongoing oversight and auditing of the evaluations undertaken within line ministries and the evaluation policies and guidelines issued by the central evaluation organizations, the relevant ministries, provinces, and the banks can be conducted
- development of advanced evaluation methods across units and organizational entities
- strengthening of the monitoring and supervision function in investment agencies
- development of a supply of well-trained evaluators for the many national ministries, provinces, and banks moving into the evaluation arena (Houqi and Rist 2002).

China has identified the important issue of raising demand for evaluation results. This key issue is a challenge in many countries without a tradition of transparent government.

*Outcome-based budgeting, nation building, and global competitiveness in Malaysia.* Among developing countries, Malaysia has been at the forefront of public administration reforms, especially in the areas of budget and finance. These reforms were initiated in the 1960s as part of an effort by the government to strategically develop the country. Because the public sector was seen as the main vehicle of development, the need to strengthen the civil service through administrative reform was emphasized.

In 1969, Malaysia adopted the Program Performance Budgeting System (PPBS), which it continued to use until the 1990s. The system replaced line-item budgeting with an outcome-based budgeting system. While agencies used the program-activity structure, in practice implementation still resembled the line-item budgeting and an incremental approach.

Budgetary reform focused on increasing accountability and financial discipline among the various government agencies entrusted to carry out Malaysia's socioeconomic development plans. The government also undertook a number of additional reforms, including efforts to improve financial compliance, quality management, productivity, efficiency in governmental operations, and management of national development efforts.

Malaysia's budget reform efforts have been closely linked with the efforts at nation building and global competitiveness. One of the driving forces for these reform efforts has been to link reform to the program Vision 2020, which aims to make Malaysia a fully developed country by the year 2020.

In 1990, the government replaced the PPBS with the Modified Budgeting System (MBS). Under the PPBS system, there were minimal links between outputs and inputs; policies continued to be funded even when no results were being systematically measured. Under the MBS greater emphasis was placed on outputs and impact of programs and activities in government.

In the late 1990s, Malaysia developed its integrated results-based management system (IRBM). The components of the system were a results-based budgeting system and a results-based personnel performance system. Malaysia also developed two other results-based systems—a results-based management information system (MIS) and a results-based M&E framework—to complement its management system (Thomas 2007).

The IRBM system provides a framework for planning, implementing, monitoring, and reporting on organizational performance. It is also able to link organizational performance to personnel performance. A number of countries (including Afghanistan, Botswana, India, Mauritius, and Namibia) are integrating IRBM systems in stages, with results-based budgeting and results-based M&E at the forefront. In Malaysia the budget system is the main driver of the IRBM system (Thomas 2007).

The MIS and M&E systems, which provide the performance measurement dimension to the strategic planning framework, make the IRB more dynamic. MIS and M&E are closely linked to ensure that the system produces the right information for the right people at the right time. Indicators must be both operational and results based. An electronic version of the integrated performance management framework has been developed and used in Malaysia (Thomas 2007).

The Malaysian government identified several lessons learned from its experience:

- A capacity-building program for key levels of government needs to be sustained.
- Monitoring and reporting are time consuming.
- The performance planning process needs to be strengthened to be more comprehensive rather than incremental.
- Rewards and sanctions are not commensurate at all levels.
- There is limited integration with other initiatives (Rasappan 2007).

It also proposed several recommendations:

- Work toward full vertical and horizontal linkages.
- Avoid disillusionment at both policy and operational levels.
- Review and strengthen all support policies and systems.
- Work toward an integrated results-based management system that focuses on whole-of-government performance (Rasappan 2007).

Although Malaysia has been at the forefront of public administration and budget reforms, its reforms have not been smooth or consistent over the years. Nonetheless, the MBS was an important initiative on the part of the government, demonstrating foresight, innovativeness, dynamism, and commitment to ensure value for money in the projects and policies being implemented (World Bank 2001).

*Poverty reduction as an impetus for evaluation in Uganda.* The government of Uganda has committed itself to effective public service delivery in support of its poverty-reduction priorities. The recognition of service delivery effectiveness as an imperative of national development management is strong evidence of its commitment to results. This commitment is also evident in several ongoing public management priorities and activities.

Over the past decade, Uganda has undergone comprehensive economic reform and achieved macroeconomic stabilization. In response to the Comprehensive Development Framework, it developed a Poverty Eradication Action Plan (PEAP), which is incorporated into its Poverty Reduction Strategy Paper. The PEAP calls for a reduction in the absolute poverty rate from 44 percent as of the late 1990s to 10 percent by 2017. The PEAP and the MDGs are broadly similar in focus and share the overall objective of holding government and development partners responsible for development progress.

Uganda became the first country to be declared eligible and to benefit from the Heavily Indebted Poor Countries Initiative (HIPC). In 2000 it qualified for enhanced HIPC relief, in recognition of the effectiveness of its poverty reduction strategy, its consultative process involving civil society, and its continuing commitment to macroeconomic stability.

Uganda has introduced new measures to make the budget process more open and transparent to internal and external stakeholders. The government is modernizing its fiscal systems and embarking on a decentralization program of planning, resource management, and service delivery to localities. The Ministry of Finance, Planning, and Economic Development (MFPED) is also introducing output-oriented budgeting. In addition, government institutions will be strengthened and made more accountable to the public.

The country is still experiencing coordination and harmonization difficulties with respect to evaluation and the PEAP. "The most obvious characteristic of the PEAP M&E regime is the separation of poverty monitoring and resource monitoring, albeit both coordinated by the MFPED. The two strands of M&E have separate actors, reports, and use different criteria of assessment. Financial resource monitoring is associated with inputs, activities and, increasingly, outputs, whereas poverty monitoring is based on analyzing overall poverty outcomes" (Hauge 2001). Other evaluation coordination issues concern the creation of a new National Planning Authority and the sector working groups.

At the end of 2007, the Office of the Prime Minister (OPM) presented a working note for discussion of the M&E of the national development plan. Two goals of this paper were to review the strengths and weaknesses of the PEAP and to propose a way forward for the M&E of the new national plan (Uganda OPM 2007a).

The working note reported several problems with the system:

- "Sector ministry outcomes and outputs, measurable indicators with associated baselines and targets, efficient monitoring systems, and the strategic use of evaluation to determine performance and causality" (Uganda OPM 2007b, p. 4) are not clear.

- Accountability is based on spending rather than substantive performance measures.
- The amount of data being collected has not been balanced by the demand for data and the capacity to use data.
- As a result of duplicative and uncoordinated monitoring, a complex and formidable burden of inspection activity, indicator data collection, and reporting formats has been created. The result is a large volume of data on compliance with rules and regulation that do not provide a clear basis for assessing value for money and cost-effectiveness in public sector delivery. A study conducted by the Uganda OPM (2007a, p. 6) reports that "the reasons for poor coordination and duplication of effort may relate more to the incentive structure of the civil service, where monitoring activities are driven in part by the desire for per diems as important salary supplements."
- Lack of incentives and issues of overlapping mandates on planning and related M&E issues have made it difficult to convene a national &E working group that addresses M&E challenges.
- Although numerous evaluations are conducted, they are typically conducted within sectors and ministries without use of common standards.
- At the local level, people still do not feel involved in decision making.

The working note also proposed several recommendations:

- Link budget allocations to the achievement of results.
- Consider establishing public service agreements or performance contracts.
- Provide information on results in a timely and usable manner to policy makers.
- Ensure that information and data demands are reflected in the data supply.
- Establish mechanisms for quality control and assurance.
- Ensure that analysis will be useful for policy makers.
- Separate the monitory and evaluation functions.
- Clarify roles and responsibilities across government for planning, monitoring, evaluation, and other related quality assurance functions.

Regarding future evaluation, Uganda faces the challenge of keeping track of and learning from its progress toward poverty reduction via the PEAP and the National Poverty Reduction Strategy. Evaluation cannot be isolated from the decision-making practices and incentives that underpin national development systems and processes (Hauge 2001).

## Implications of Emerging Development Issues

Emerging development issues are making evaluation more complex. This section provides a brief overview of these issues, highlighting the implications for evaluation.

Patton (2006) begins a discussion of recent trends in evaluation by identifying evaluation as a global public good. He describes the growth of professional organizations, associations, and societies for evaluation around the world and the standards and guidelines being established by these organizations. He also points to the development of more than 100 new models for evaluation as an emerging trend.

Patton uses an analogy to help illustrate the emerging complexity of evaluation. In the past, evaluators could often follow a kind of recipe in conducting evaluations. Patton describes the merits of a recipe as follows:

- Recipes are tested, ensuring replicability.
- While no particular expertise is needed, knowing how to cook increases success.
- Recipes produce standard products.

Recipes work well in cooking; they do not yield standard results in development, however, where a model is needed in which the evaluator must react to complex questions. Patton's analogy for the emerging trend in development evaluation is that of raising a child. A recipe is a step-by-step process. In contrast, raising a child is a highly complex process, in which caregivers use knowledge to help them make decisions and react to new situations.

Patton describes another trend in development evaluation: moving to more formative situations. The kinds of formative situations he discusses are evaluations in which

- the intended and hoped-for outcomes are specified, but the measurement techniques are being piloted
- a model for attaining outcomes is hypothesized, tested, and refined
- implementation of the intervention is not standardized but studied and improved as problems in the intervention are worked out (a kind of iterative approach)
- the attribution is formulated with the possibility of testing causality as part of the challenge.

Another recent trend is that of going beyond individual evaluation studies to streams (Rist and Stame 2006). Rist and Stame describe how the evaluation community is now relying on systems of evaluative knowledge, not individual evaluators or individual evaluations, to produce evaluative knowledge. Basic to their thesis is that simply accumulating more and more evaluation reports has little to no impact on the resultant knowledge that could be gained from synthesizing across these same studies.

What happens in development affects evaluation. The development agenda will continue to evolve in response to current and emerging issues, including globalization, the growing incidence of conflict around the world, terrorism and money laundering, the widening gap between the world's rich and poor, the increasing number of players on the development scene, the drive toward debt reduction, and the new focus on improved governance. Addressing these issues places new demands on the evaluator.

The global drive toward comprehensive, coordinated, participatory development and the demonstration of tangible results also presents new challenges to the development evaluation community. There have been significant shifts from partial to comprehensive development, from an individual to a coordinated approach (partnerships), from growth promotion to poverty reduction, and from a focus on implementation to a focus on results. With respect to comprehensive development, for example, bilateral and multilateral donors "must now position each project within a larger context and examine its sustainability and potential effects on society, politics and the broad economy" (Takamasa and Masanori 2003, p. 6). As they note:

> Development theorists have also come to believe that the most important factor for economic development is not capital but appropriate policies and institutions. This shift was caused by the tremendous impact that economists such as North . . . , Stiglitz . . . and Sen . . . had on the discipline of economics, including development economics. These developments resulted in the current situation where the central theme of international development assistance is poverty reduction in a broad sense, which includes the expansion of human dignity and political and economic freedom for people in developing countries.

The MDGs are one concrete manifestation of this new thinking in development. The *World Development Report* 2005 (World Bank 2005b) focuses on what governments can do to create better investment climates in their societies, measuring progress through sets of indicators designed to tap elements of business climates. The report recommends institutional and behavior improvements: designing better regulation and taxation, reducing barriers to competition, improving business incentives, tackling corruption, fostering public trust and legitimacy, and ensuring proper implementation of regulations and laws.

Many of the new issues in development assistance involve bilateral and multilateral development partners and the potential burden of their multiple evaluations on developing countries. Their involvement underlies the rationale for conducting joint international evaluations. Such evaluations can be conducted at the project, country, sector, or thematic level. They may yield efficiencies of cost and scale for the development organizations, as well as harmonization of evaluation methods that facilitate comparison of results.

What follows is a brief discussion of some of the major drivers of the international development agenda and their implications for evaluation. These drivers include the following:

- the MDGs
- the Monterrey Consensus
- the Paris Declaration on Aid Effectiveness
- the Heavily Indebted Poor Countries (HIPC) Initiative
- the role of foundations
- conflict prevention and postconflict reconstruction
- governance
- anti–money laundering and terrorist financing
- workers' remittances
- gender
- private sector development and the investment climate
- environmental and social sustainability
- global public goods.

The authors note that the list of drivers is always under movement. As this book goes to press, a key driver that might lead the list is now the effects of the global financial crisis on the developing world.

## The Millennium Development Goals

In September 2000, 189 UN member countries and numerous international organizations adopted the United Nations Millennium Declaration, from which the MDGs were, in part, derived. The **MDGs** consist of a set of development goals for the international community to meet by 2015, as a result of the active participation of developed and developing countries alike (box 2.1). These ambitious goals are aimed at poverty reduction, human development, and the creation of global partnerships to achieve both. They represent a shift away from the earlier emphasis in the development community on economic growth, which decision makers had hoped would lift people out of poverty. The MDGs specifically target a series of measures aimed at reducing poverty and improving living conditions for the world's poor.

**MDGs:** Set of development goals for the international community to meet by 2015

The eight MDGs include a set of 18 targets and 48 indicators by which to measure progress. (Developing countries have different mixes of the 18 targets and different dates for achieving them, depending on their situations.) The MDGs are results-based goals that must be measured, monitored, and evaluated accordingly. They pose major challenges to evaluation systems in all countries.

Many developing countries lack the capacity to perform M&E. To fill this gap, development organizations have provided statistical and M&E capacity building, technical assistance, and support.

The MDGs are driving developing countries to build M&E capacity and systems. Development organizations are being called upon to provide technical assistance and financing for these efforts. Many developing countries are in the early stages of building M&E systems and are slowly working their way toward the construction of results-based systems that will help determine the extent to which the MDGs are being achieved. Assessing success toward meeting the MDGs will require the development and effective use of evaluation systems. The evaluation system will, in turn, need to be integrated into the policy arena of the MDGs so that it is "clear to all why it is important to collect the data and how the information will be used to inform the efforts of the government and civil society to achieve the MDGs" (Kusek, Rist, and White 2004, pp. 17–18).

Every year the World Bank and the International Monetary Fund (IMF) publish an annual *Global Monitoring Report* on the MDGs. The report provides a framework for accountability in global development policy.

The *Global Monitoring Report 2004* focused on how the world is doing in implementing the policies and actions needed to achieve the MDGs and related development outcomes. It highlights several priorities for strengthening the monitoring exercise. These include

- strengthening the underlying development statistics, including through timely implementation of the action plan agreed upon by international statistical agencies
- conducting research on the determinants of the MDGs, on critical issues such as effectiveness of aid, and on the development of more robust metrics for key policy areas, such as governance and the impact on developing countries of rich country policies
- deepening collaboration with partner agencies in this work, building on comparative advantage, and ensuring that the approach to monitoring and evaluation is coherent across agencies (World Bank 2004b).

The *Global Monitoring Report 2005* pointed to opportunities created by recently improved economic performance in many developing countries. It outlined a five-point agenda designed to accelerate progress:

- *Ensure that development efforts are country owned.* Scale up development impact through country-owned and -led poverty reduction strategies.
- *Improve the environment for private sector–led economic growth.* Strengthen fiscal management and governance, ease the business environment, and invest in infrastructure.
- *Scale up delivery of basic human services.* Rapidly increase the supply of health care workers and teachers, provide greater and more flexible and predictable financing for these recurrent cost-intensive services, and strengthen institutional capacity.
- *Dismantle barriers to trade.* Use an ambitious Doha Round that includes major reform of agricultural trade policies to dismantle trade barriers, and increase "aid for trade."
- *Double development aid in the next five years.* In addition, improve the quality of aid, with faster progress on aid coordination and harmonization (World Bank 2005a).

The *Global Monitoring Report 2006* highlighted economic growth, better-quality aid, trade reform, and governance as essential elements to achieve the MDGs (World Bank 2006a). The 2007 report highlighted two key thematic areas: gender equality and empowerment of women (the third MDG) and the special problems of fragile states, where extreme poverty is increasingly concentrated (World Bank 2007f).

## The Monterrey Consensus

In March 2002 government representatives from more than 170 countries, including more than 50 heads of state, met to discuss a draft of the Monterrey Consensus on Financing for Development. The draft reflected an attempt to distribute more money to the world's poorest people, those living on less than US$1 a day.

Most significantly for development evaluation, the Monterrey Consensus stressed mutual responsibilities in the quest to achieve the MDGs. It called on developing countries to improve their policies and governance and on developed countries to step up their support, especially by opening up access to their markets and providing more and better aid. The document recognized the need for greater financial assistance to raise the living standards of the poorest countries, but it did not set firm goals for increasing aid, relieving most debt burdens, or removing trade barriers (Qureshi 2004).

At the midway point between the year in which the MDGs were adopted and their 2015 target date, the Economic Commission for Africa published a report assessing Africa's progress toward meeting the commitments to Africa for the Monterrey Consensus. The report concluded that substantial progress had been made in the area of external debt relief but that very limited progress had been made in the other core areas of the Consensus. Of interest to evaluators, the report notes:

> There is the understanding that monitoring of the commitments made by both African countries and their development partners is essential if the objectives of the Monterrey Consensus are to be realized. African leaders have recognized this and put in place a mechanism to monitor progress in the implementation of their commitments as well as those of their development partners. The recent institutionalization of an African Ministerial Conference on Financing for Development is a bold step by African leaders in this area. The international community has also put in place a mechanism to monitor donor performance. For example, they have established an African Partnership Forum and an African Progress Panel, both of which will monitor progress in the implementation of key commitments on development finance. Ultimately, the effectiveness of these monitoring mechanisms shall be assessed in terms of how they are able to turn promises made by development partners into deeds. For it is only through the implementation of these commitments that African countries and the international community can reduce poverty in the region and lay the foundation for a brighter future for its people. (Katjomulse and others 2007, p. vi)

## The Paris Declaration on Aid Effectiveness

The Paris Declaration on Aid Effectiveness was an international agreement to continue to increase efforts for managing aid to developing countries. More than 100 ministers, heads of agencies, and other senior officials endorsed the agreement on March 2, 2005.

One feature of this declaration that is important to evaluation was the agreement to use monitorable actions and indicators as a part of the implementation of the agreement. Twelve indicators were developed to help track and encourage progress toward attaining more effective aid. Targets were set for 11 of the 12 indicators for 2010 (OECD 2005b).

The indicators and targets that were endorsed are organized around five key principles:

- *Ownership*. Partner countries exercise effective leadership over their development policies and strategies and coordinate development actions.
- *Alignment.* Development organizations base their overall support on partner countries' national development strategies, institutions, and procedures.
- *Harmonization*. Development organizations' actions are more harmonized, transparent, and collectively effective.
- *Managing for results*. Governments are moving toward an emphasis on managing resources and improving decision making for results.
- *Mutual accountability*. Development organizations and partners are accountable for development results (Joint Progress toward Enhanced Aid Effectiveness 2005).

In 2007, the OECD published a landmark report summarizing the results of a baseline survey of the state of affairs in 2005. The report (OECD 2007b) assesses the effectiveness of aid both globally and for development organizations.

The OECD conducted a survey to monitor progress in improving aid effectiveness as emphasized in the Monterrey Consensus and made more concrete in the Paris Declaration. It drew the following conclusions:

- The Paris Declaration has increased awareness and promoted dialogue at the country level on the need to improve the delivery and management of aid.
- The pace of progress in changing donor attitudes and practices on aid management has been slow, and the transactions costs of delivering and managing aid remain very high.
- There is a need to strengthen national development strategies, improve the alignment of donor support to domestic priorities, increase the

credibility of the budget as a tool for governing and allocating resources, and increase the degree of accuracy in budget estimates of aid flows.

- Changing the way in which aid is delivered and managed involves new costs, which donors and partners need to take into account.
- Countries and donors should use performance assessment frameworks and more cost-effective results-oriented reporting. Donors need to contribute to capacity building and make greater use of country reporting systems.
- More credible monitoring systems need to be developed to ensure mutual accountability (Katjomulse and others 2007).

### The Heavily Indebted Poor Countries Initiative

In 1996 the World Bank and the IMF proposed the HIPC Initiative, the first comprehensive approach to reduce the external debt of the world's poorest and most heavily indebted countries. One hundred and eighty countries endorsed the initiative.

HIPC is designed to reduce debts to sustainable levels for poor countries that pursue economic and social policy reforms. It is used in cases where traditional debt relief mechanisms would not be enough to help countries exit the rescheduling process. HIPC reduces debt stock, lowers debt service payments, and boosts social spending.

The initiative includes both bilateral and multilateral debt relief. External debt servicing for HIPC countries is expected to be cut by about US$50 billion. As of January 2009, debt reduction packages had been approved for 34 countries, 28 of which were in Africa; 7 additional countries were found eligible for assistance (IMF 2009).

HIPC is linked to comprehensive national poverty reduction strategies. In 1999 the international development community agreed that national Poverty Reduction Strategies Papers (PRSPs) should be the basis for concessional lending and debt relief. These strategies include agreed-upon development goals over a three-year period. They include a policy matrix, an attendant set of measurable indicators, and an M&E system through which to measure progress. If a country meets its goals, its debt is reduced, providing incentives to speed up reforms and increase country ownership. As a condition for debt relief, recipient governments must be able to monitor, evaluate, and report on reform efforts and progress toward poverty reduction. This condition created demand for M&E capacity building and assistance.

Some developing countries, such as Uganda, have made progress in evaluation and have qualified for enhanced HIPC relief. Lack of capacity for evaluation has been a problem for other participating HIPC countries, including Albania, Madagascar, and Tanzania. These countries require additional assistance to develop their evaluation capacity.

In providing countries that have very high levels of debt with concessional loans or grants to mitigate the risk of future debt crises, HIPC raised a new evaluation issue: How would grant, as opposed to loan, effectiveness be evaluated and according to what criteria? This question creates new challenges for development evaluators.

September 2006 marked 10 years of the HIPC Initiative. Since 1999, the poverty-reducing expenditures of HIPCs have increased while debt-service payments have declined (World Bank 2007e). This finding suggests that HIPC is resulting in progress.

## The Role of Foundations

An OECD study estimated the amount of funds given to developing countries by philanthropic foundations. The study

> attempted a serious estimate of the amount of funds distributed by 15 of the largest philanthropic foundations with some international giving, for 2002. The total was almost US$4 billion dollars and the total international giving was about US$2 billion dollars. This represents about 4 percent of all development aid and is about one-half of the contributions attributed by the official Development Assistance Committee to . . . NGOs as a whole (a group that includes the foundations. (Oxford Analytica 2004a)

The U.S. Council on Foundations counts 56,000 private and community foundations in the United States, distributing US$27.5 billion annually. The European Foundation Centre found some 25,000 foundations in nine EU countries with annual spending of more than US$50 billion.

Several large foundations dominate the global scene. They include the Bill & Melinda Gates Foundation, the Ford Foundation, the Susan Thompson Buffet Foundation, and the Soros Foundation/Open Society.

The Soros Foundation/Open Society Institute network is an influential player on the international development scene, with programs in more than 50 countries. Programs provide support for education, media, public health, women, human rights, arts and culture, and social, economic, and legal reforms (SOROS Foundations Network 2007).

## Conflict Prevention and Postconflict Reconstruction

In the post–Cold War years of 1989–2001, there were 56 major armed conflicts in 44 different locations. In 2003, conflicts were estimated to affect more than 1 billion people. The majority of conflicts during this period lasted seven years or more. The global costs of civil wars in particular are enormous. "By creating territory outside the control of any recognized government, armed conflicts foster drug trafficking, terrorism and the spread of disease" (Collier and others 2003).

Poverty is both a cause and a consequence of conflict. Sixteen of the world's 20 poorest countries experienced a major civil war. On average, countries emerging from war face a 44 percent chance of relapsing in the first five years of peace.

Dealing with postconflict reconstruction involves coordinating large numbers of bilateral and multilateral development organizations. For example, 60 development organizations were active in Bosnia-Herzegovina, 50 were active in the West Bank and Gaza, and 82 were active in Afghanistan. Rebuilding after a conflict has placed strains on aid coordination mechanisms to ensure that needs are met and duplication and gaps in aid avoided.

Postconflict reconstruction involves more than simply rebuilding infrastructure. Reconstruction often involves providing support for institution building, democracy and elections, NGOs and civil society, civilian police forces, budgetary start-up and recurrent costs, debt relief, balance-of-payments support, gender issues, demining, resettlement of refugees and internally displaced people, and demobilization and reintegration of excombatants.

Because of concerns about corruption and the need to leverage official development assistance, postconflict reconstruction has often entailed the creation of new lending instruments and mechanisms. In the West Bank and Gaza, for example, a multilateral development organization trust fund has been created to support start-up and recurrent budgetary expenditures for the new Palestinian administration. Such instruments and mechanisms are now common in postconflict regions in other parts of the world.

Postconflict reconstruction programs—multisector programs that cost billions of dollars—bring a new level of difficulty and scale to evaluation (Kreimer and others 1998). Evaluators must examine the impact that such heavily front-loaded development approaches have on postconflict reconstruction and reconciliation. Evaluating a coordination process that brings together a large and diverse group of bilateral, multilateral, and other supporters presents new challenges.

Evaluators must examine new projects and programs in untraditional areas of development assistance, such as demobilizing and reintegrating excombatants and demining land. They must also evaluate new types of development organization mechanisms and lending instruments, such as multilateral development organization trust funds.

Increasingly, bilateral and multilateral development organizations are looking at the economic causes and consequences of conflict and seeking ways to prevent conflict. There is a greater emphasis on social, ethnic, and religious communities and relations; governance and political institutions; human rights; security; economic structures and performance; the environment and natural resources; and external factors. This means that evaluators must also look at what is being done and what could be done in the development context to prevent conflicts from erupting.

## Governance

While often acknowledged behind closed doors, the issue of governance and corruption came to the forefront of development only in the mid-1990s. Since then international conventions have been signed to address the problem of corruption around the world. The United Nations and the OECD have adopted conventions on corruption that include provisions on prevention and criminalization of corruption, international cooperation on asset recovery, and antibribery measures.

Multilateral development banks have also instituted anticorruption programs. Lending is directed toward helping countries build efficient and accountable public sector institutions. Governance and anticorruption measures are addressed in country assistance strategies. Governance programs seek to promote

- anticorruption
- public expenditure management
- civil service reform
- judicial reform
- administration, decentralization, e-government, and public services delivery.

Transparency International (TI), an NGO whose aim is to put "corruption on the global agenda," was created and launched in the early 1990s. It currently has chapters in 88 countries. It works with local, national, regional and international partners (governmental and nongovernmental) to combat corruption (http://www.transparency.org/).

TI's annual Corruption Perception Index ranks about 140 countries based on public officials' perceptions of corruption. Its annual Bribe Payers Index ranks exporting countries based on the incidence of bribery.

Some estimates report that more than US$1 trillion is lost to corruption annually. Measuring corruption and the costs of corruption has been a challenge for the international community, but the

increasing availability of surveys and polls by many institutions, containing data on different dimensions of governance, has permitted the construction of a worldwide governance databank. Utilizing scores of different sources and variables, as well as a novel aggregation technique, the databank now covers 200 countries worldwide and contains key aggregate indicators in areas such as rule of law, corruption, regulatory quality, government effectiveness, voice and accountability, and political instability (World Bank 2007c, p. 1).

Development organizations and evaluators can use these data as a measure of aid effectiveness. Findings suggest that where corruption is higher, the possibility that aid is being wasted is commensurately higher.

Results-based management is being used to identify and monitor the most vulnerable determinants and institutions in a country's governance structure. The data help demystify and treat more objectively issues of governance that were previously obscured. The data generated will also aid evaluators in compiling more quantitative evaluation findings related to lessons learned. At the same time, evaluating investment climates and business environments will involve difficult and thorny concepts (see the section below on private sector development and the investment climate).

This new area is evolving quickly. It will require that evaluators address new developments and data in a timely fashion.

### Anti–Money Laundering and Terrorist Financing

Money laundering and terrorist financing are part of the broader anticorruption landscape.

■ **Money laundering:** Practice of engaging in financial transactions in order to conceal the identities, sources, and destinations of the money in question

**Money laundering** is the practice of engaging in financial transactions in order to conceal the identities, sources and destinations of the money in question. In the past, the term "money laundering" was applied only to financial transactions related to otherwise criminal activity. Today its definition is often expanded by government regulators, such as the Securities and Exchange Commission (SEC), to encompass any financial transaction which is not transparent based on law. As a result, the illegal activity of money laundering is now commonly practised by average individuals, small and large business, corrupt officials, and members of organized crime, such as drug dealers or Mafia members. (Investor Dictionary.com 2006)

With an estimated US$1 trillion (2–5 percent of world gross domestic product) laundered annually, according to the IMF, money laundering is a serious and growing international problem, affecting developing and developed countries alike (Camdessus 1998, p. 1). Globalization and the opening or easing of borders have facilitated transnational criminal activities and the attendant illegal financial flows. Global anti–money laundering initiatives have taken on new importance with the spread of terrorism.

Money laundering can take an especially heavy toll on developing countries.

> Emerging financial markets and developing countries are . . . important targets and easy victims for money launderers, who continually seek out new places and ways to avoid the watchful eye of the law. The consequences of money laundering operations can be particularly devastating to developing economies. Left unchecked, money launderers can manipulate the host's financial systems to operate and expand their illicit activities . . . and can quickly undermine the stability and development of established institutions. (IFAC 2004, p. 5)

The OECD's Financial Action Task Force on Money Laundering (FATF) was created in 1989 by the G-7. It now includes 31 member countries and territories and 2 regional organizations. This intergovernmental policy-making body aims to develop and promote national and international policies to combat money laundering and terrorist financing.

Monitoring and evaluation of implementation is a part of the FATF's mandate. It is carried out multilaterally, by peer review, and by mutual evaluation. The M&E process entails the following:

> Each member country is examined in turn by the FATF on the basis of an on-site visit conducted by a team of three or four selected experts in the legal, financial and law enforcement fields from other member governments. The purpose of the visit is to draw up a report assessing the extent to which the evaluated country has moved forward in implementing an effective system to counter money laundering and to highlight areas in which further progress may still be required. (FATF 2007, p. 1)

The FATF has established a series of measures to be taken in the event of noncompliance.

### Workers' Remittances

Annual global remittances sent by migrant workers to their countries of origin outpaced annual official development assistance. Annual remittances rose from US$60 billion in 1998 to US$80 billion in 2002 and an estimated US$100 billion in 2003. These figures compare with about US$50–$60 billion a year in official development assistance and US$143 billion dollars in private capital flows in 2002. Remittances tend to be more stable than private capital flows (World Bank 2003; Oxford Analytica 2004b).

Global remittances have a strong impact on poverty reduction. "On average, a 10 percent increase in the share of international migrants in a country's population will lead to a 1.9 percent decline in the share of people living in poverty (US$1.00/person/day)" (Adams and Page 2003, p. 1). Global remittances help fund local consumption in housing, agriculture, industry, and the creation of new small and medium-size enterprises in the recipient country.

Developed and developing countries and organizations are cognizant of these trends and are seeking ways to capitalize on these flows for investment purposes. A recent G-8 Summit Plan called on members and developing country governments to

> facilitate remittance flows from communities overseas to help families and small entrepreneurs [businesses], including by encouraging the reduction of the cost of remittance transfers, and the creation of local development funds for productive investments; improving access by remittance recipients to financial services; and enhancing coordination. (G-8 2004a, p. 7)

Remittances through the banking system are likely to rise, as restrictions on informal transfers increase because of more careful monitoring regulations to stem financing to terrorist organizations through informal mechanisms (see below) and a decrease in banking fees as a result of increased competition in the sector to capture the global remittance market.

The impact of remittances on developing countries has yet to be fully articulated and tested. Tracking global remittances and funneling them to new types of investments and funds will pose new challenges for evaluators. As development practitioners have not yet devised ways to capture remittances and leverage them for poverty reduction, evaluators will watch this area with great interest.

### Gender: From Women in Development to Gender and Development to Gender Mainstreaming

■ **Gender analysis:** Examination of access to and control over resources by men and women

Gender refers to the socially constructed roles ascribed to females and males. **Gender analysis** examines access to and control over resources by men and women. It also refers to a systematic way of determining men's and women's often differing development needs and preferences and the different impacts of development on women and men. Gender analysis takes into account how class, race, ethnicity, and other factors interact with gender to produce discriminatory results. Gender analysis has traditionally been directed toward women because of the gap between men and women in terms of how they benefit from education, employment, services, and so forth.

Women make up a little more than half the world's population and play a key role in economic development. Yet their full potential to participate in socioeconomic development has yet to be realized. Indeed, women and children still represent the majority of the world's poor.

> Women produce half the food in some parts of the developing world, bear most of the responsibility for household food security, and make up a quarter of the workforce in industry and a third in services.... Yet because of more limited access to education and other opportunities, women's productivity relative to that of men remains low. Improving women's productivity can contribute to growth, efficiency and poverty reduction—key development goals everywhere. (World Bank 1994, p. 9)

Recent trends regarding the role of women in development have evolved away from the traditional "women in development" (WID) approach to "gender and development" (GAD) to a more comprehensive "gender mainstreaming" approach. The WID strategy focused on women as a special target or interest group of beneficiaries in projects, programs, and policies. "WID recognizes that women are active, if often unacknowledged, participants in the development process, providing a critical contribution to economic growth . . . as an untapped resource; women must be brought into the development process" (Moser 1995, p. 107).

The GAD approach focuses on the social, economic, political, and cultural forces that determine how men and women participate in, benefit from, and control project resources and activities. It highlights the often different needs and preferences of women and men. This approach shifts the focus of women as a group to the socially determined relations between men and women.

Progress in gender equality and the empowerment of women is embodied in the MDGs, which include targets and indicators for measuring and evaluating progress. The OECD's Development Assistance Committee (DAC) has also produced guiding questions to assist managers in evaluating development activities. Questions include the following:

- Has the project succeeded in promoting equal opportunities and benefits for men and women?
- Have women and men been disadvantaged or advantaged by the project?
- Has the project been effective in integrating gender into the development activity? (Woroniuk and Schalkwyk 1998)

Gender budgeting is one way of implementing and assessing how much of the national budget benefits men and women. Another way to measure and evaluate assistance is by examining the extent to which development assistance benefits sectors "that involve women, help women, empower women, and generate results for women" (Jalan 2000, p. 75). Given the current emphasis on comprehensive approaches and partnerships, evaluation of gender mainstreaming policies must also be conducted and integrated and coordinated within and between development partner countries, organizations, and agencies. In every evaluation, it is important to look at how the project, program, or policy differentially affects men and women.

### Private Sector Development and the Investment Climate

A host of issues falls under the rubric of private sector development and the investment climate. These issues include the role of the private sector and foreign direct investment in poverty reduction; privatization; private participation in infrastructure services and public-private partnerships; and creation and support of micro, small-, and medium-sized enterprises through fiscal intermediaries.

#### Private sector investment

Private sector investment has become increasingly recognized as critical to reducing poverty in the developing world. In 1990, private sector investment in developing countries was about US$30 billion a year, while development assistance amounted to about US$60 billion. By 1997, private sector investment in developing countries had reached US$300 billion, while development assistance had fallen to US$50 billion. Private sector development thus grew from half of the size of development assistance to six times its size in the space of less than 10 years.

#### Official development assistance

■ **Official development assistance:**
Flows of official financing administered at concessional rates to promote economic development and welfare of developing countries

One measure of the investment climate is **official development assistance** (ODA), which the *OECD Glossary of Statistical Terms* (2002a) defines as follows:

> Flows of official financing administered with the promotion of the economic development and welfare of developing countries as the main objective, and which are concessional in character with a grant element of at least 25 percent (using a fixed 10 percent rate of discount). By convention, ODA flows comprise contributions of donor government agencies, at all levels, to developing countries ("bilateral ODA") and to multilateral institutions. ODA receipts comprise disbursements by bilateral donors and multilateral institutions. [From a Web page identified as Official Development Assistance.]

In 1997 aid levels rose before hitting a plateau that continued until 2001. Total ODA from DAC members rose 7 percent in 2001 and 5 percent in 2003. In 2005 official development assistance from DAC members rose 32 percent, largely as a result of the increase in aid following the 2004 tsunami and debt relief for Iraq and Nigeria (OECD 2005a). In 2006, ODA fell 4.6 percent, as a result of the exceptionally high debt and humanitarian relief in 2004 (OECD 2006).

ODA has grown steadily over the past decade, and it is expected to continue to rise, as donors have committed to scale up aid significantly to achieve the MDGs. To make effective use of such scaled-up aid at the country level, donors and recipients need to address a number of implementation challenges, particularly

- achieving complementarity across national, regional, and global development priorities and programs
- strengthening recipient countries' ability to make effective use of potentially scaled-up, fast-disbursing ODA, such as budget support (World Bank 2007a).

### Foreign direct investment

Another measure of the investment climate is **foreign direct investment** (FDI), which plays an extraordinary and growing role in global business. FDI is a cross-border investment of at least 10 percent of an enterprise's equity capital that is made by an investor in order to establish a lasting financial interest in the enterprise and exert a degree of influence over its operations. It is often cited as a leading driver of economic growth and thought to bring certain benefits to national economies (InvestorDictionary.com 2006).

The largest increase in FDI between the 1970s and 1999 occurred in developing countries, where annual flows increased from an average of less than US$10 billion in the 1970s and less than US$20 billion in the 1980s to US$179 billion in 1998 and US$208 billion in 1999. These flows accounted for a large portion of global FDI (Graham and Spaulding 2005).

The United Nations Conference on Trade and Development (UNCTAD) (2008) reported global growth of FDI in 2007. The report documents a rise in FDI in all three groups of economies: developed countries, developing economies, and South-East Europe and the Commonwealth of Independent States (CIS). The results reflect the high growth propensities of transnational corporations and strong economic performance in many parts of the world, as well as increased corporate profits and an abundance of cash, which boosted the value of cross-border mergers and acquisitions. Such transactions constituted a large portion of FDI flows

■ **Foreign direct investment:** Cross-border investment of at least 10 percent of an enterprise's equity capital made in order to establish a lasting financial interest in the enterprise and exert a degree of influence over its operations

in 2007, although the value of mergers and acquisitions declined in the second half of the year.

FDI flows to developed countries rose for the fourth consecutive year in 2007, reaching US$1 trillion. FDI inflows to developing countries and transition economies in South-East Europe and the CIS rose 16 percent and 41 percent, respectively, reaching record levels.

### Privatization

Privatization of state-owned enterprises was a particularly strong trend in the 1990s, as many countries sought to move from socialist to market-oriented economies. It is still a major force in many countries, where the state continues to own and operate many economic assets.

"More than 100 countries, on every continent, have privatized some or most of their state-owned companies, in every conceivable sector of infrastructure, manufacturing, and services. . . . [A]n estimated 75,000 medium and large-sized firms have been divested around the world, along with hundreds of thousands of small business units. . . ." Total generated proceeds are estimated at more than US$735 billion (Nellis 1999). Privatization is controversial; the debate over if, when, and how best to go about privatization continues. It is not a panacea for economic ills, but it has proved to be a useful tool in promoting net welfare gains and improved services for the economy and society.

### Implications for evaluation

How has the development evaluation community responded to these initiatives? The International Finance Corporation (IFC) evaluates the effects on interventions at the project level. It uses Business Environment (BE) Snapshots to "present measurable indicators across a wide range of business environment issues and over time" (IFC 2007). This new tool compiles disparate data, indicators, and project information on the business environment for a country and makes it easily accessible in a consistent format. Development practitioners and policy makers can use BE Snapshots to obtain a comprehensive picture of the business environment in particular countries. BE Snapshots can also be used as a monitoring tool or a planning tool.

How does one go about evaluating these kinds of activities? On a general level, one may look at four possible indicators:

- business performance
- economic sustainability
- environmental effects
- private sector development.

The *World Development Report 2005* highlights investment climate surveys and business environment and firm performance, which can help identify how governments can improve the investment climate for firms of all types. The surveys covered 26,000 firms in 53 developing countries and 3,000 micro and informal enterprises in 11 countries.

These surveys allow for comparison of existing conditions and the benchmarking of conditions to monitor changes over time. The survey instrument is a core set of questions and several modules that can be used to explore in greater depth specific aspects of the investment climate and its links to firm-level productivity.

Questions can be categorized into three groups:

- those generating information for the profiling of businesses
- those used for the profiling of the investment climate in which businesses operate
- those generating indicators of firm performance.

The indicators used were

- policy uncertainty (major constraint: unpredictable interpretation of regulations)
- corruption (major constraint: bribes)
- courts (major constraint: lack confidence that courts uphold property rights)
- crime (major constraint: losses from crime). Other sources of investment climate indicators included a business risk service, country credit ratings (Euromoney Institutional Investor), country risk indicators (World Markets Research Center), a country risk service (Economist Intelligence Unit), and the *Global Competitiveness Report* (World Economic Forum).

Multilateral development banks, international financial institutions, development organizations, and the private sector are all involved in such surveys, providing valuable information and advice. Ongoing and periodic assessments and evaluations of investment climates are also conducted in countries around the world. One notable example is the Doing Business database, which provides objective measures of business regulations and their enforcement. Comparable indicators across 145 economies indicate the regulatory costs of business. These indicators can be used to analyze specific regulations that enhance or constrain investment, productivity, and growth (World Bank 2007d). However, a World Bank Independent Evaluator's Group 2008 report pointed out needed improvements in the Doing Business indicators (IEG 2008).

**Corporate social responsibility:** Acceptance by private companies of need to take into account the economic, environmental, and social impacts and consequences of their activities

**Corporate social responsibility** (CSR) involves actively taking into account the economic, environmental, and social impacts and consequences of business activities. Private sector companies, organizations, and governments are looking at new ways of ensuring that business activities and services do not harm the economy, society, or the environment in the countries and sectors in which they operate. The British government, for example, has adopted various policies and legislation to encourage CSR in general and environmental and social sustainability in particular.

> The Government sees CSR as the business contribution to our sustainable development goals. Essentially it is about how business takes account of its economic, social and environmental impacts in the way it operates—maximizing the benefits and minimizing the downsides. . . . The Government's approach is to encourage and incentivize the adoption and reporting of CSR through best practice guidance, and, where appropriate, intelligent regulation and fiscal incentives. (BEER 2004, para. 1)

**Equator Principles:** Industry approach for determining, assessing, and managing environmental and social risk in private sector project financing

An example of an international environmental and social sustainability effort is the **Equator Principles**, signed by 10 Western financial institutions in 2003. The Equator Principles were developed by private sector banks. They are an industry approach for determining, assessing, and managing environmental and social risk in private sector project financing. In 2006, a revised version of the Equator Principles was adopted. The new version reflects the revisions to IFC's own *Performance Standards on Social and Environmental Sustainability*. The 2006 version of the Equator Principles apply to all countries and sectors and to all project financings with capital costs exceeding US$10 million.

The IFC and 61 leading commercial banks (in North America, Europe, Japan, and Australia) have voluntarily adopted the Equator Principles in their financing of projects around the world. The institutions are seeking to ensure that the projects they finance are developed in a socially responsible manner and reflect sound environmental management practices. The Equator Principles are intended to serve as a common baseline and framework for the implementation of individual internal environmental and social procedures and standards for project financing activities across all industry sectors globally. In adopting these principles, the institutions undertake to carefully review all proposals for which their customers request project financing. They pledge not to provide loans directly to projects if the borrower will not or cannot comply with their environmental and social policies and processes. Standards cover environmental, health and safety, indigenous peoples, natural habitats, and resettlement (Equator Principles 2007).

Making a public commitment to the principles is one thing but applying them in good faith is quite another. BankTrack, a network of 18 international NGOs specializing in the financial sector, has played an important role in helping monitor the way the Equator Principles are implemented. It is critical of the Equator Principles' reporting requirements and the way in which it monitors financial institutions (BankTrack 2008).

## Global Public Goods

Economists define **private goods** as those for which consumption by one person reduces the amount available for others, at least until more is produced (Linux Information Project 2006). Private goods tend to be tangible items. Most products are private goods.

Economists define **public goods** as products that individuals can consume as much as they want of without reducing the amount available for others (Linux Information Project 2006). Clean air, for example, is a public good, because breathing clean air does not reduce the amount of clean air available to others. Public goods tend to be intangible items; many fall into the category of information or knowledge.

**Global public goods** are public goods that affect the entire world. Examples of global public goods are property rights, safety, financial stability, and a clean environment. Indeed, development evaluation can be considered a kind of public good because it extends beyond the boundaries of any single organization. A good evaluation study can have positive spillover effects throughout the development community (Picciotto and Rist 1995, p. 23).

Global public goods are important because with increased openness of national borders, the public domains of countries have become interlocked. A public good in one country often depends on domestic policy and events and policy choices made by other countries or internationally (gpgNet 2008). Everyone depends on public goods; neither markets nor the wealthiest individual can do without them.

Evaluation is largely absent at the global level:

> Collaborative programs designed to deliver global public goods are not subjected to independent appraisal and, as a result, often lack clear objectives and verifiable performance indicators. In addition, the impact of developed country policies on poor countries is not assessed systematically even though aid, debt, foreign investment, pollution, migration patterns, and intellectual property regimes are shaped by the decisions of developed country governments. (Picciotto 2002b, p. 520)

■ **Private goods:** Goods whose consumption by one person reduces the amount available for others

■ **Public goods:** Goods whose consumption by one person does not reduce amount available for others

■ **Global public goods:** Public goods that are nonrival and nonexcludable throughout the whole world rather than only within a country's borders

Controlling the spread of and ultimately eliminating HIV/AIDS is another example of a global public good that is at the top of many international agendas. The impact of globalization on the poor has yet to be assessed. Development evaluation needs to become more indigenous, more global, and more transnational (Chelimsky and Shadish 1997).

In 2004 the Independent Evaluation Group of the World Bank released an evaluation of the Bank's involvement in global programs. The report, *Evaluating the World Bank's Approach to Global Programs: Addressing the Challenges of Globalization*, investigated 26 Bank-supported global programs, drawing lessons about the design, implementation, and evaluation of global programs (World Bank 2004a). The report emphasizes 5 of its 18 findings:

- The Bank's strategy for global programs is poorly defined.
- Global programs have increased overall aid very little.
- Voices of developing countries are inadequately represented.
- Global programs reveal gaps in investment and global public policy.
- Oversight of independent global programs is needed.

The report makes the following recommendations:

- Establish a strategic framework for the Bank's involvement in global programs.
- Link financing to priorities.
- Improve the selectivity and oversight of the global program portfolio.
- Improve the governance and management of individual programs.
- Conduct additional evaluation.

## Summary

Countries have adopted various approaches in establishing evaluation systems. The whole-of-government approach involves the broad-based, comprehensive establishment of the system across the government. The enclave approach focuses on one part or sector of the government. In the mixed approach, some parts or sectors of the government are comprehensively evaluated while others receive more sporadic treatment.

Creating an evaluation system is more difficult in developing countries, which often lack democratic political systems, strong empirical traditions, civil servants trained in the social sciences, and efficient administrative systems and institutions. Development organizations are focusing on assisting developing countries in acquiring the capacity to create and maintain evaluations systems.

Many complex issues in development are influencing evaluation. Some of the major drivers for the development agenda include the following:

- the MDGs
- the Monterrey Consensus
- the Paris Declaration on Aid Effectiveness
- the HIPC Initiative
- the role of foundations
- conflict prevention and postconflict reconstruction
- governance
- anti–money laundering and terrorist financing
- workers' remittances
- gender
- private sector development and the investment climate
- environmental and social sustainability
- global public goods.

The list is not static but changes in response to global events.

# References and Further Reading

Adams, Richard H. Jr., and John Page. 2003. "International Migration, Remittances and Poverty in Developing Countries." World Bank Policy Research Working Paper 3179, Washington, DC.

BankTrack. 2008. *The Equator Principles.*
http://www.banktrack.org/.

Barslund, Mikkel, and Finn Tarp. 2007. "Formal and Informal Rural Credit in Four Provinces of Vietnam." Discussion Paper 07-07, Department of Economics, University of Copenhagen.

BEER (U.K. Department for Business Enterprise & Regulatory Reform). 2004. "What Is CSR?" London.
http://www.csr.gov.uk/whatiscsr.shtml.

Boyle, Richard. 2002. "A Two-Tiered Approach: Evaluation Practice in the Republic of Ireland." In *International Atlas of Evaluation*, eds. Jan-Eric Furubo, Ray Rist, and Rolf Sandahl, 261–72. New Brunswick, NJ: Transaction Publishers.

——. 2005. *Evaluation Capacity Development in the Republic of Ireland.* ECD Working Paper Series 14, World Bank, Evaluation Capacity Development, Washington, DC.

Camdessus, Michael. 1998. "Money Laundering: The Importance of International Countermeasures." Address by Managing Director of the International Monetary Fund, Washington, DC.

CGAP (Consultative Group to Assist the Poor). 2003. *CGAP Publications on Assessment and Evaluation.*
http://www.cgap.org/portal/site/CGAP/menuitem.9fab704d4469eb016780801 0591010a0/.

ChannahSorah, Vijaya Vinita. 2003. "Moving from Measuring Processes to Outcomes: Lessons Learned from GPRA in the United States." Paper presented at the joint World Bank and Korea Development Institute conference on "Performance Evaluation System and Guidelines with Application to Large-Scale Construction, R&D, and Job Training Investments," Seoul, July 24–25.

Chelimsky, Eleanor, and William R. Shadish, eds. 1997. *Evaluation for the 21st Century: A Handbook.* Thousand Oaks, CA: Sage Publications.

Chemin, Matthieu. 2008. "Special Section on Microfinance. The Benefits and Costs of Microfinance: Evidence from Bangladesh." *Journal of Development Studies* 44 (4): 463–84.

Collier, Paul, V., L. Elliott, Håvard Hegre, Anke Hoeffler, Marta Reynal-Querol, and Nicholas Sambanis. 2003. *Breaking the Conflict Trap: Civil War and Development Policy.* Washington, DC: Oxford University Press for the World Bank.

Economic Commission for Europe. 1998. *Public–Private Partnerships: A New Concept for Infrastructure Development.* BOT Expert Group, United Nations, New York.
http://rru.worldbank.org/Documents/Toolkits/Highways/pdf/42.pdf.

Equator Principles. 2004. http://www.fatf-gafi.org/dataoecd/14/53/38336949.pdf.

——. 2007. "A Milestone or Just Good PR?"
http://www.equator-principles.com/principles.shtml.

FATF (Financial Action Task Force on Money Laundering). 2007. *Monitoring the Implementation of the Forty Recommendations.* http://www.fatf-gafi.org/document/60/0,3343,en_32250379_32236920_340392 28_1_1_1_1,00.html.

Feuerstein, M. T. 1986. *Partners in Evaluation: Evaluating Development and Community Programs with Participants.* London: MacMillan, in association with Teaching Aids at Low Cost.

Fitzpatrick, Jody L., James R. Sanders, and Blaine R. Worthen. 2004. *Program Evaluation: Alternative Approaches and Practical Guidelines.* New York: Pearson Education, Inc.

Friis, H. 1965. *Development of Social Research in Ireland.* Institute of Public Administration, Dublin.

Fukuda-Parr, Sakiko, Carlos Lopes, and Khalid Malik, eds. 2002. *Capacity for Development: New Solutions to Old Problems.* London: Earthscan Publications.

Furubo, Jan-Eric, and Rolf Sandahl. 2002. "Coordinated Pluralism." In *International Atlas of Evaluation*, eds. Jan-Eric Furubo, Ray Rist, and Rolf Sandahl, 115–28. New Brunswick, NJ: Transaction Publishers.

Furubo, Jan-Eric, Ray Rist, and Rolf Sandahl, eds. 2002. *International Atlas of Evaluation.* New Brunswick, NJ: Transaction Publishers.

G-8. 2004a. *G-8 Action Plan: Applying the Power of Entrepreneurship to the Eradication of Poverty.* Sea Island Summit, June.

———. 2004b. *G-8 Plan of Support for Reform.* Sea Island Summit, June.

Gerrard, Christopher. 2006. "Global Partnership Programs: Addressing the Challenge of Evaluation." PowerPoint presentation. http://www.oecd.org/secure/pptDocument/0,2835,en_21571361_34047972_ 36368404_1_1_1_1,00.ppt.

gpgNet. 2008. *The Global Network on Global Public Goods.* http://www.sdnp.undp.org/gpgn/#.

Graham, Jeffrey P., and R. Barry Spaulding. 2005. *Going Global: Understanding Foreign Direct Investment.* JPG Consulting. http://www.going-global.com/articles/understanding_foreign_direct_ investment.htm.

Guerrero, R. Pablo 1999. "Evaluation Capacity Development: Comparative Insights from Colombia, China, and Indonesia." In *Building Effective Evaluation Capacity: Lessons from Practice*, eds. Richard Boyle and Donald Lemaire, 177–94. New Brunswick, NJ: Transaction Publishers.

Hatry, Harry P., Elaine Morely, Shelli B. Rossman, and Joseph P. Wholey. 2003. *How Federal Programs Use Outcome Information: Opportunities for Federal Managers.* IBM Endowment for the Business of Government, Washington, DC.

Hauge, Arild. 2001. "Strengthening Capacity for Monitoring and Evaluation in Uganda: A Results-Based Perspective." ECD Working Paper 8, World Bank, Operations Evaluation Department, Evaluation Capacity Development, Washington, DC.

Hougi, Hong, and Ray C. Rist. 2002. "Evaluation Capacity Building in the People's Republic of China." In *International Atlas of Evaluation*, eds. Jan-Eric Furubo, Ray Rist, and Rolf Sandahl, 249–60. New Brunswick, NJ: Transaction Publishers.

IDA (International Development Association), and IMF (International Monetary Fund). 2007. *Heavily Indebted Poor Countries HIPC Initiative and Multilateral Debt Relief Initiative MDRI: Status of Implementation.* http://siteresources.worldbank.org/DEVCOMMINT/Documentation/21510683/DC2007-0021 E HIPC.pdf.

IDS (Institute of Development Studies). 2008. "Impact Evaluation: The Experience of Official Agencies." *IDS Bulletin* 39 (1). http://www.ntd.co.uk/idsbookshop/details.asp?id=1030.

IEG (Independent Evaluation Group). 2008. "Doing Business: An Independent Evaluation. Taking the Measure of the World Bank–IFC Doing Business Indicators."

IFAC (International Federation of Accountants). 2004. *Anti–Money Laundering,* 2nd ed. New York.

IFC (International Finance Corporation). 2004. *Strengthening the Foundations for Growth and Private Sector Development: Investment Climate and Infrastructure Development.* Development Committee, Washington, DC. http://siteresources.worldbank.org/IDA/Resources/PSDWBGEXT.pdf.

———. 2007. *Business Environment Snapshots.* Washington, DC. http://rru.worldbank.org/documents/BES_Methodology_Note_External.pdf.

IMF (International Monetary Fund). 2009. "A Fact Sheet: Debt Relief under the Heavily Indebted Poor Countries (HIPC) Initiative." http://www.info.org/external/np/exr/facts/hipc.htm.

Investor Dictionary.com. 2006. "Money Laundering." http://www.investordictionary.com/definition/money+laundering.aspx.

Jalan, Bimal. 2000. "Reflections on Gender Policy." In *Evaluating Gender Impact of Bank Assistance*, 75–76. World Bank, Operations Evaluation Department, Washington, DC.

Joint Progress toward Enhanced Aid Effectiveness, High-Level Forum. 2005. *Paris Declaration on Aid Effectiveness: Ownership, Harmonization, Alignment, Results, and Mutual Accountability.* http://www1.worldbank.org/harmonization/Paris/FINALPARIS DECLARATION.pdf/.

Katjomulse, Kavazeua, Patrick N. Osakwe, Abebe Shimeles, and Sher Verick. 2007. *The Monterrey Consensus and Development in Africa: Progress, Challenges, and Way Forward.* United Nations Economic Commission for Africa (UNECA), Addis Ababa.

Kreimer, Alcira, John Eriksson, Robert Muscat, Margaret Arnold, and Colin Scott. 1998. *The World Bank's Experience with Post-Conflict Reconstruction.* World Bank, Operations Evaluation Department, Washington, DC. http://lnweb90.worldbank.org/oed/oeddoclib.nsf/b57456d58aba40e585256ad400736404/f753e43e728a27b38525681700503796/$FILE/PostCon.pdf.

Kusek, Jody Zall, Ray C. Rist, and Elizabeth M. White. 2004. "How Will We Know Millennium Development Results When We See Them? Building a Results-Based Monitoring and Evaluation System to Give Us the Answer." World Bank Africa Region Working Paper 66, Washington, DC.

Lawrence, J. 1989. "Engaging Recipients in Development Evaluation: The 'Stakeholder' Approach." *Evaluation Review* 13 (3): 243–56.

Lee, Yoon-Shik. 1999. "Evaluation Coverage." In *Building Effective Evaluation Capacity: Lessons from Practice*, eds. Richard Boyle and Donald Lemaire, 75–91. New Brunswick, NJ: Transaction Publications.

Linux Information Project. 2006. "Public Goods: A Brief Introduction." http://www.linfo.org/public_good.html.

Mackay, Keith. 2002. "The Australian Government: Success with a Central, Directive Approach." In *International Atlas of Evaluation*, eds. Jan-Eric Furubo, Ray C. Rist, and Rolf Sandahl, 157–74. New Brunswick, NJ: Transaction Publishers.

———. 2007. "Three Generations of National M&E Systems in Australia." PowerPoint presentation to the Third Latin America and Caribbean Regional Conference on Monitoring and Evaluation, Lima, July 23–24.

———. 2008. *M&E Systems to Improve Government Performance: Lessons from Australia, Chile and Columbia*. PowerPoint presentation to the High-Level Delegation from the People's Republic of China, Washington, DC, March 6.

Moser, Caroline O. N. 1995. "Evaluating Gender Impacts." *New Directions for Evaluation* 67 (Fall): 105–17.

NCSTE (China National Center for Evaluation of Science & Technology), and IOB (Netherland's Policy and Operations Evaluation Department). 2004. *A Country-Led Joint Evaluation of the ORET/MILIEV Programme in China*. http://www.euforic.org/iob/docs/200610201336433964.pdf.

Nellis, John. 1999. "Time to Rethink Privatization in Transition Economies?" IFC Discussion Paper 38, International Finance Corporation, Washington, DC.

OECD (Organisation for Economic Co-operation and Development). 2002a. *OECD Glossary of Statistical Terms*. http://stats.oecd.org/glossary/index.htm.

———. 2002b. "Public Management and Governance: Overview of Results-Focused Management and Budgeting in OECD Member Countries." Paper presented at the 23rd annual meeting of OECD senior budget officials, Washington, DC, June 3–4.

———. 2003. *Joint OECD DAC/Development Centre Experts' Seminar on Aid Effectiveness and Selectivity: Integrating Multiple Objectives into Aid Allocations*. Development Assistance Committee. http://www.oecd.org/document/51/0,2340,en_2649_34435_2501555_119808_1_1_1,00.html.

———. 2004a. *Final ODA Data for 2003*. http://www.oecd.org/dataoecd/19/52/34352584.pdf.

———. 2004b. *The Istanbul Ministerial Declaration on Fostering Growth of Innovative and Internationally Competitive SMEs*. http://www.oecd.org/document/16/0,3343,en_2649_201185_32020176_1_1_1_1,00.html.

———. 2005a. "Aid Rising Sharply, According to Latest OECD Figures." http://www.oecd.org/dataoecd/0/41/35842562.pdf.

———. 2005b. *The Paris Declaration*. Development Co-operation Directorate. http://www.oecd.org/document/18/0,2340,en_2649_3236398_35401554_1_1_1_1,00.html.

———. 2006. *Final ODA Data for 2005*. http://www.oecd.org/dataoecd/52/18/37790990.pdf.

———. 2007a. "Development Aid from OECD Countries Fell 5.1 Percent in 2006." http://www.oecd.org/document/17/0,3343,en_2649_33721_38341265_1_1_1_1,00.html.

———. 2007b. *Final ODA Flows in 2006*. http://www.oecd.org/dataoecd/7/20/39768315.pdf.

———. 2007c. "Monitoring the Paris Declaration." http://www.oecd.org/department/0,3355,en_2649_15577209_1_1_1_1_1,00.html.

OECD, and PUMA (Public Management Committee). 2002. "Overview of Results-Focused Management and Budgeting in OECD Member Countries." Twenty-third annual meeting of OECD Senior Budget Officials, Washington, DC, June 3–4.

Oxford Analytica. 2004a. "Foundations Muscle into Aid Arena." August 10, Oxford.

———. 2004b. "Remittances Fund Investment Growth." September 7, Oxford.

Patton, M. Q. 1997. *Utilization-Focused Evaluation*. 3rd ed. Thousand Oaks, CA: Sage Publications.

———. 2006. "Recent Trends in Evaluation." Paper presented to the International Finance Corporation, Washington, DC, May 8.

Picciotto, Robert. 2002a. "Development Cooperation and Performance Evaluation: The Monterrey Challenge." World Bank, Operations Development Department, Washington, DC.

———. 2002b. "Development Evaluation as a Discipline." International Program for Development Evaluation Training (IPDET) presentation, Ottawa, June.

———. 2003. "International Trends and Development Evaluation: The Need for Ideas." *American Journal of Evaluation* 24: 227–34.

Picciotto, Robert, and Ray C. Rist. 1995. *Evaluating Country Development Policies and Programs: New Approaches and a New Agenda*. San-Francisco: Jossey-Bass Publishers.

Pollin, Robert. 2007. *Microcredit: False Hopes and Real Possibilities*. Foreign Policy in Focus. http://www.fpif.org/fpiftxt/4323.

Public Services Organisation Review Group. 1969. *Report of the Public Services Organization Review Group*. Dublin: Stationary Office.

Qureshi, Zia. 2004. *Millennium Development Goals and Monterrey Consensus: From Vision to Action*. World Bank, Washington, DC. http://wbln0018.worldbank.org/eurvp/web.nsf/Pages/Paper+by+Qureshi/US$File/MOHAMMED+QURESHI.PDF.

Rasappan, Arunaselam. 2007. "Implementation Strategies and Lessons Learnt with Results-Based Budgeting Malaysia." Training course on program and performance budgeting, ITP Pune, India, October 1–5. http:// blog-pfm.imf.org/pfmblog/files/rasappan_implementation_strategies_lessons_malaysia.pdf.

Republic of France. 2001. Ministry of the Economy, Finance, and Industry. "Towards New Public Management." *Newsletter on the Public Finance Reform* 1 (September), Paris.

Rist, Ray C., and Nicoletta Stame, eds. 2006. *From Studies to Streams: Managing Evaluative Systems.* New Brunswick, NJ: Transaction Books.

Schacter, Mark. 2000. "Sub-Saharan Africa: Lessons from Experience in Supporting Sound Governance." ECD Working Paper 7, World Bank, Evaluation Capacity Department, Washington, DC.

Soros Foundations Network. 2007. "About OSI and the Soros Foundation Network." http://www.soros.org/about/overview.

Takamasa, Akiyama, and Kondo Masanori, eds. 2003. "Global ODA since the Monterrey Conference." Foundation for Advanced Studies on International Development (FASID), International Development Research Institute, Tokyo. http://www.fasid.or.jp/english/publication/research/pdf/global.pdf.

Tavistock Institute, in association with GHK and IRS. 2003. *The Evaluation of Socio-Economic Development: The GUIDE.* http://coursenligne.sciences-po.fr/2004_2005/g_martin/guide2.pdf.

Thomas, Koshy. 2007. "Integrated Results-Based Management in Malaysia." In *Results Matter: Ideas and Experiences on Managing for Development Results.* Asian Development Bank. http://www.adb.org/Documents/Periodicals/MfDR/dec-2007.pdf.

Trosa, Sylvie. 2008. "Towards a Postbureaucratic Management in France." *Politique et management public* (2).

Uganda Office of the Prime Minister (OPM). 2007a. *National Integrated Monitoring and Evaluation Strategy (NIMES) : 2006–2007 Bi-Annual Implementation Progress Report.* Kampala.

———. 2007b. "Working Note: Monitoring and Evaluation of the National Development Plan." October, Kampala.

UNCTAD (United Nations Conference on Trade and Development). 2008. "Foreign Direct Investment Reached New Record in 2007." Press Release. http://www.unctad.org/Templates/Webflyer.asp?docID=9439&intItemID=2068&lang=1.

UNECA (United Nations Economic Commission for Africa). 2007. "Financing Development Section, Trade, Finance, and Economic Commission for Africa, Addis Ababa." http://www.uneca.org/eca_programmes/trade_and_regional_integration/documents/MonterreyConsensusMainReport.pdf.

United Nations Office on Drugs and Crime. 2006. *The United Nations Convention against Transnational Organized Crime and Its Protocols.* http://www.unodc.org/unodc/en/treaties/CTOC/index.html.

U.S. Department of Labor. 1993. Government Performance and Results Act. Employment & Training Administration, Washington, DC. http://www.doleta.gov/performance/goals/gpra.cfm.

U.S. GAO (Government Accountability Office). 2003. *Executive Guide: Effectively Implementing the Government Performance and Results Act.* http://www.gao.gov/special.pubs/gpra.htm.

World Bank. n.d. "About Private Participation in Infrastructure."
http://www.worldbank.org/infrastructure/ppi/.

———. 1994. *Enhancing Women's Participation in Economic Development.* Washington, DC: World Bank.
http://books.google.ca/books?id=CJBmEClPci8C&dq=World+Bank.+1994.+
Enhancing+Women%E2%80%99s+Participation+in+Economic+Development.+
Washington,+DC:+World+Bank.&printsec=frontcover&source=bn&hl=en&ei=
IPy2SdntFYueMoTU_NcK&sa=X&oi=book_result&resnum=4&ct=result#
PPA5,M1.

———. 1996b. *World Bank Participation Sourcebook.*
http://www.worldbank.org/wbi/sourcebook/sbhome.htm.

———. 1999. "Monitoring and Evaluation Capacity Development in Africa." *Précis*
Spring (183).
http://wbln0018.worldbank.org/oed/oeddoclib.nsf/7f2a291f9f1204c6852568080
06a0025/34b9bade34aca617852567fc00576017/US$FILE/183precis.pdf.

———. 2001. *Strategic Directions for FY02–FY04.* Washington, DC.
http://lnweb18.worldbank.org/oed/oeddoclib.nsf/24cc3bb1f94ae11c852568080
06a0046/762997a38851fa0685256f8200777e15/US$FILE/gppp_main_report_
phase_2.pdf#page=21.

———. 2003. *Global Development Finance 2003.* Washington, DC: World Bank.
http://siteresources.worldbank.org/INTRGDF/Resources/GDF0slide0-
show103010DC0press0launch.pdf.

———. 2004a. "Evaluating the World Bank's Approach to Global Programs: Addressing the Challenges of Globalization." Independent Evaluation Group, Washington, DC.
http://www.worldbank.org/oed/gppp/.

———. 2004b. *Global Monitoring Report 2004: Policies and Actions for Achieving the Millennium Development Goals.* Washington, DC: World Bank.

———. 2005a. *Global Monitoring Report 2005: Education for All.* Washington, DC: World Bank.

———. 2005b. *World Development Report 2005: A Better Investment Climate for Everyone.* Washington, DC: World Bank.

———. 2006a. *Global Monitoring Report 2006: Equity and Development.* Washington, DC: World Bank.

———. 2007a. *Aid Architecture: An Overview of the Main Trends in Official Development Assistance Flows, Executive Summary.*
http://siteresources.worldbank.org/IDA/Resources/Aidarchitecture-exec
summary.pdf.

———. 2007b. *Conflict Prevention and Reconstruction.*
http://lnweb18.worldbank.org/ESSD/sdvext.nsf/67ByDocName/Conflict
PreventionandReconstruction.

———. 2007c. *The Data Revolution: Measuring Governance and Corruption.*
http://web.worldbank.org/WBSITE/EXTERNAL/NEWS/0,,contentMDK:
20190210~menuPK:34457~pagePK:34370~piPK:34424~theSitePK:4607,00.html.

———. 2007d. *Doing Business: Economy Profile Reports.* Washington, DC: World Bank. http://rru.worldbank.org/DoingBusiness/.

———. 2007e. *The Enhanced HIPC Initiative: Overview.* http://web.worldbank.org/WBSITE/EXTERNAL/TOPICS/EXTDEBTDEPT/ 0,,contentMDK:21254881~menuPK:64166739~pagePK:64166689~piPK:64166646 ~theSitePK:469043,00.html.

———. 2007f. *Global Monitoring Report 2007: Development and the Next Generation.* Washington, DC: World Bank.

———. 2008. *Online Atlas of the Millennium Development Goals: Building a Better World.* http://devdata.worldbank.org/atlas-mdg/.

Woroniuk, B., and J. Schalwyk. 1998. "Donor Practices: Evaluation and Preparation Tipsheet." OECD, Paris.

## Web Sites

### Finance

CGAP (Consultative Group to Assist the Poor). http://www.cgap.org/.

———. *Assessment and Evaluation.* http://www.cgap.org/publications/assessment_ evaluation.html.

The Equator Principles. http://www.equator-principles.com/index.shtml.

Tedeschi, Gwendolyn Alexander. 2008. *Overcoming Selection Bias in Microcredit Impact Assessments: A Case Study in Peru.* http://www.informaworld.com/ smpp/content~content=a792696580~db=all~order=page.

World Bank. *Doing Business: Economy Profile Reports.* http://rru.worldbank.org/ DoingBusiness/.

### Gender

OECD (Organisation for Economic Co-operation and Development). "Gender Tip-sheet, Evaluation." Development Assistance Committee. http://www.oecd.org/ dataoecd/2/13/1896352.pdf.

### Governance

Transparency International. http://www.transparency.org/.

World Bank. 2007a. *Governance Matters.* http://info.worldbank.org/governance/ wgi2007/ and http://info.worldbank.org/governance/wgi2007/pdf/booklet_ decade_of_measuring_governance.pdf.

———. 2007b. Untitled Video. http://web.worldbank.org/WBSITE/EXTERNAL/ NEWS/0,,contentMDK:21400275~menuPK:51416191~pagePK:64257043~piPK: 437376~theSitePK:4607,00.html.

## Millennium Development Goals

United Nations. *Millennium Development Goals*. http://www.un.org/millennium
goals/.

## Poverty

Poverty-Environment Web site. http://www.povertyenvironment.net.

World Bank. AdePT software to make poverty analysis easier and faster.
econ.worldbank.org/programs/poverty/adept.

———. PovertyNet newsletter. http://www.worldbank.org/poverty.

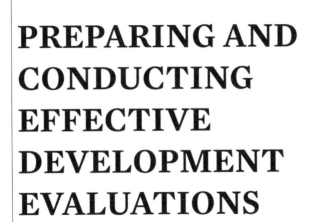

# PREPARING AND CONDUCTING EFFECTIVE DEVELOPMENT EVALUATIONS

*"Our plans miscarry because they have no aim. When a man does not know what harbor he is making for, no wind is the right wind."*

—SENECA

**Chapter 3: Building a Results-Based Monitoring and Evaluation System**

- Importance of Results-Based Monitoring and Evaluation
- What Is Results-Based Monitoring and Evaluation?
- Traditional versus Results-Based Monitoring and Evaluation
- Ten Steps to Building a Results-Based Monitoring and Evaluation System

**Chapter 4: Understanding the Evaluation Context and the Program Theory of Change**
- Front-End Analysis
- Identifying the Main Client and Key Stakeholders
- Understanding the Context
- Investigating Existing Knowledge
- Constructing, Using, and Assessing a Theory of Change.

**Chapter 5: Considering the Evaluation Approach**
- General Approaches to Evaluation
- Challenges Going Forward

**CHAPTER 3**

# Building a Results-Based Monitoring and Evaluation System

Throughout the world, governments are attempting to address demands and pressures for improving the lives of their citizens. Internal and external pressures and demands on governments and development organizations are causing them to seek new ways to improve public management. Improvements may include greater accountability and transparency and enhanced effectiveness of interventions. Results-based monitoring and evaluation (M&E) is a management tool to help track progress and demonstrate the impact of development projects, programs, and policies.[1]

**This chapter has four main parts:**

- Importance of Results-Based Monitoring and Evaluation
- What Is Results-Based Monitoring and Evaluation?
- Traditional versus Results-Based Monitoring and Evaluation
- Ten Steps to Building a Results-Based Monitoring and Evaluation System

## Importance of Results-Based Monitoring and Evaluation

There are growing pressures in developing countries to improve the performance of their public sectors. Responding to these pressures leads countries to develop performance management systems. These new systems involve reforms in budgeting, human resources, and organizational culture. To assess whether public sector efforts are working, there is also a need for performance measurement. M&E systems track the results produced (or not) by governments and other entities.

Many initiatives are pushing governments to adopt public management systems that show results. The Millennium Development Goals (MDGs) and the Heavily Indebted Poor Countries (HIPC) Initiative are two examples of these initiatives.

The strategy outlined in this chapter builds on the experiences of developed countries—especially those in the Organisation for Economic Co-operation and Development (OECD)—but it also reflects the challenges and difficulties faced by many developing countries as they try to initiate performance measurement systems. Challenges in these countries range from the lack of skill capacity to poor governance structures to systems that are far from transparent. Although the primary focus of this chapter is on improving government effectiveness and accountability using a sound monitoring and evaluation (M&E) system, the principles and strategies apply equally well to organizations, policies, programs, and projects.

A results-based M&E system provides crucial information about public sector or organizational performance. It can help policy makers, decision makers, and other stakeholders answer the fundamental questions of whether promises were kept and **outcomes** achieved. M&E is the means by which improvements—or a lack of improvements—can be demonstrated (box 3.1).

■ **Outcome:** Benefits that are achieved from a project, program, or policy (an outcome entails behavioral or organizational change and cannot be bought)

By reporting the results of various interventions, governments and other organizations can promote credibility and public confidence in their work. Providing information to the public also supports a development agenda that is shifting toward greater accountability for aid lending.

A good results-based M&E system can be extremely useful as a management and motivational tool. It helps focus attention on achieving outcomes that are important to the organization and its stakeholders, and it provides an impetus for establishing key goals and objectives that address these outcomes. It also provides managers with crucial information on whether the strategy guiding the intervention is appropriate, correct, and adequate to the changes being sought through the intervention.

A good M&E system is also an essential source of information for streamlining and improving interventions to maximize the likelihood of success. It helps identify promising interventions early on so that they can potentially be implemented elsewhere. Having data available about how well a particular project, practice, program, or policy works provides useful information for formulating and justifying budget requests. It also allows judicious allocation of scarce resources to the interventions that will provide the greatest benefits.

Once outcomes are established, indicators selected, and targets set, the organization can strive to achieve them. An M&E system can provide timely information to the staff about progress and can help identify early on any weaknesses that require corrective action. Monitoring data also provide information on outliers (sites that are performing particularly well or poorly). Evaluation can then be undertaken to find out what explains the outliers.

## What Is Results-Based Monitoring and Evaluation?

Results-based information can come from two complementary sources: a monitoring system and an evaluation system (box 3.2). Both systems are essential for effective performance measurement.

**Results-based monitoring:**
Continuous process of collecting and analyzing information on key indicators in order to measure progress toward goals

**Target:**
A quantifiable amount of change that is to be achieved over a specified time frame in an indicator

**Indicator:**
Measure tracked systematically over time that indicates progress (or the lack thereof) toward a target

**Results-based evaluation:**
Assessment of a planned, ongoing, or completed intervention to determine its relevance, efficiency, effectiveness, impact, and sustainability

**Impact:**
A long-term benefit (result) that is achieved when a series of outcomes is achieved (The Millennium Development Goals are impact statements.)

---

### Box 3.2   Difference between Results-Based Monitoring and Results-Based Evaluation

**Results-based monitoring** is the continuous process of collecting and analyzing information on key indicators and comparing actual results with expected results in order to measure how well a project, program, or policy is being implemented. It is a continuous process of measuring progress toward explicit short-, intermediate-, and long-term results by tracking evidence of movement toward the achievement of specific, predetermined **targets** by the use of **indicators**. Results-based monitoring can provide feedback on progress (or the lack thereof) to staff and decision makers, who can use the information in various ways to improve performance.

**Results-based evaluation** is an assessment of a planned, ongoing, or completed intervention to determine its relevance, efficiency, effectiveness, **impact**, and sustainability. The intention is to provide information that is credible and useful, enabling lessons learned to be incorporated into the decision-making process of recipients. Evaluation takes a broader view of an intervention, asking if progress toward the target or explicit result is caused by the intervention or if there is some other explanation for the changes picked up by the monitoring system. Evaluation questions can include the following:

• Are the targets and outcomes relevant?
• How effectively and efficiently are they being achieved?
• What unanticipated effects have been caused by the intervention?
• Does the intervention represent the most cost-effective and sustainable strategy for addressing a particular set of needs?

## Traditional versus Results-Based Monitoring and Evaluation

Governments have long engaged in traditional M&E—tracking their expenditures and revenues, staffing levels and resources, program and project activities, numbers of participants, and goods and services produced, for example. A distinction needs to be drawn, however, between traditional and results-based M&E:

• **Traditional M&E** focuses on the monitoring and evaluation of inputs, activities, and outputs (that is, on project or program implementation).
• **Results-based M&E** combines the traditional approach of monitoring implementation with the assessment of outcomes and impacts, or more generally of results.

It is this linking of implementation progress with progress in achieving the desired objectives or results of government policies and programs that makes results-based M&E useful as a public management tool. Implementing this type of M&E system allows the organization to modify and make adjustments to both the theory of change and the implementation processes in order to more directly support the achievement of desired objectives and outcomes.

## The Theory of Change

One way to view the differences between traditional and results-based M&E is to consider the theory of change. According to Kusek and Rist (2004), **theory of change** is a representation of how an intervention is expected to lead to desired results. (More information about the theory of change and definitions are provided in chapter 4.) Theory of change models typically have five main components: inputs, activities, outputs, outcomes, and impacts (table 3.1). Some theory of change models also include other features, including target groups, and internal and external factors.

■ **Traditional monitoring and evaluation:** Monitoring and evaluation that focuses on project or program implementation

■ **Results-based monitoring and evaluation:** Monitoring and evaluation that combines the traditional approach with assessment of results

■ **Theory of change:** Theory of how an initiative leads to desired results

Table 3.1  **Main Components of a Theory of Change**

| Component | Description |
|---|---|
| Inputs | Resources that go into a project, program, or policy (funding, staffing, equipment, curriculum materials, and so forth). |
| Activities | What we do. Activities can be stated with a verb ("market," "provide, " "facilitate," "deliver"). |
| Outputs | What we produce. Outputs are the tangible products or services produced as a result of the activities. They are usually expressed as nouns. They typically do not have modifiers. They are tangible and can be counted. |
| Outcomes | Why we do it. Outcomes are the behavioral changes that result from the project outputs (quit smoking, boiling water, using bed nets). Outcomes can be increased, decreased, enhanced, improved, or maintained. |
| Impacts | Long-term changes that result from an accumulation of outcomes. Can be similar to strategic objectives. |

*Source*: Kusek and Rist 2004.

**Figure 3.1 Program Theory of Change (Logic Model) to Achieve Outcomes and Impacts**

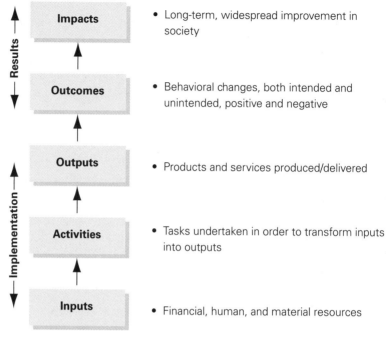

- Long-term, widespread improvement in society

- Behavioral changes, both intended and unintended, positive and negative

- Products and services produced/delivered

- Tasks undertaken in order to transform inputs into outputs

- Financial, human, and material resources

*Source*: Binnendijk 2000.

A theory of change can be depicted graphically (figure 3.1). This model can be used to frame a results-based approach to a problem such as reducing childhood morbidity with oral rehydration therapy (figure 3.2).

## Performance Indicators

Monitoring involves the measurement of progress toward achieving an outcome or impact (results). The outcome cannot be measured directly, however; it must first be translated into a set of indicators that, when regularly measured, provide information about whether or not the outcomes or impacts are being achieved. A performance indicator is "a variable that allows the verification of changes in the development intervention or shows results relative to what was planned" (OECD 2002, p. 29).

For example, if a country selects the target of improving the health of children by reducing childhood morbidity from infectious diseases by 30 percent over the next five years, it must first identify a set of indicators that

**Figure 3.2  Sample Program Theory of Change (Logic Model) to Reduce Childhood Morbidity through Use of Oral Rehydration Therapy**

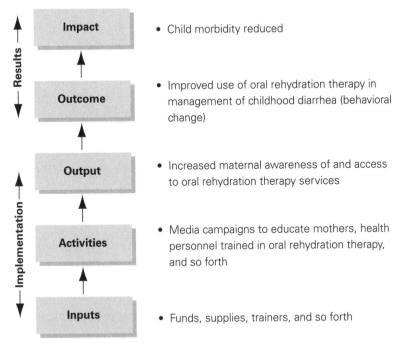

*Source*: Adapted from Binnendijk 2000.

translates changes in the incidence of childhood morbidity from infectious diseases into more specific measurements. Indicators that can help assess changes in childhood morbidity may include the following:

- the incidence and prevalence of infectious diseases, such as hepatitis (a direct determinant)
- the level of maternal health (an indirect determinant)
- the degree to which children have access to clean water.

It is the cumulative evidence of a cluster of indicators that managers examine to see if their program is making progress. No outcome or impact should be measured by just one indicator.

Measuring a disaggregated set of indicators (a set of indicators that has been divided into constituent parts) provides important information as to how well government programs and policies are working to achieve the intended outcome or impact. They are also used to identify sites that are performing better or worse than average (program outliers) and policies that are or are not performing well. If, for example, the set of indicators reveals that, over time, fewer and fewer children have clean water available to them, the government can use this information to reform programs that aim to improve water supplies or strengthen those programs that provide information to parents about the need to sanitize water before providing it to their children.

Information obtained from a monitoring system reveals the performance of only what is being measured (although it can be compared against both past performance and some planned level of present or projected performance [targets]). Monitoring data do not reveal why that level of performance occurred or provide causal explanations about changes in performance from one reporting period to another or one site to another. This information comes from an evaluation system.

An evaluation system serves a complementary but distinct function within a results-based management framework. An evaluation system allows for

- a more in-depth study of results-based outcomes and impacts
- the use of data sources other than the indicators being tracked
- examination of factors that are too difficult or expensive to monitor continuously
- investigation of why and how the trends being tracked with monitoring data are moving in the directions they are.

Data on impact and causal attribution are not to be taken lightly. They can play an important role in strategic resource allocations.

## Ten Steps to Building a Results-Based Monitoring and Evaluation System

Building a quality results-based M&E system involves 10 steps (figure 3.3):

1. conducting a readiness assessment
2. agreeing on performance outcomes to monitor and evaluate
3. selecting key indicators to monitor outcomes
4. gathering baseline data on indicators
5. planning for improvement: setting realistic targets
6. monitoring for results
7. using evaluation information
8. reporting findings
9. using findings
10. sustaining the M&E system within the organization.

The Road to Results: Designing and Conducting Effective Development Evaluations

**Figure 3.3 Ten Steps to Designing, Building, and Sustaining a Results-Based Monitoring and Evaluation System**

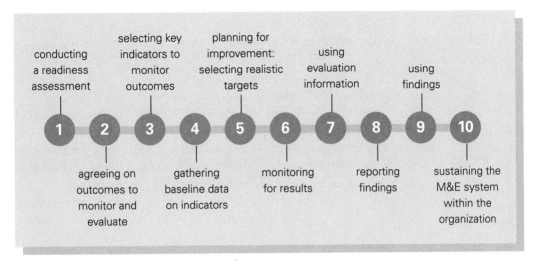

*Source*: Kusek and Rist 2004.

## Step 1: Conducting a Readiness Assessment

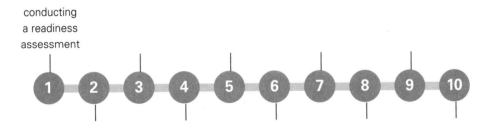

A readiness assessment is a way of determining the capacity and willingness of a government and its development partners to construct a results-based M&E system. This assessment addresses issues such as the presence or absence of champions as well as incentives, roles and responsibilities, organizational capacity, and barriers to getting started.

### *Incentives*

The first part of the readiness assessment involves understanding what incentives exist for moving forward to construct an M&E system (and what disincentives may hinder progress). Questions to consider include the following:

- What is driving the need for building an M&E system?
- Who are the champions for building and using an M&E system?
- What is motivating those who champion building an M&E system?
- Who will benefit from the system?
- Who will not benefit?

### Roles and responsibilities

Next it is important to identify who is currently responsible for producing data in the organization and in other relevant organizations and who the main users of data are. Questions to consider include the following:

- What are the roles of central and line ministries in assessing performance?
- What is the role of the legislature?
- What is the role of the supreme audit agency?
- Do ministries and agencies share information with one another?
- Is there a political agenda behind the data produced?
- Who in the country produces the data?
- Where at different levels in the government are the data used?

### Organizational capacity

A key element driving the organization's readiness for a results-based M&E system relates to the skills, resources, and experience the organization has available. Questions to consider include the following:

- Who in the organization has the technical skills to design and implement an M&E system?
- Who has the skills to manage such a system?
- What data systems currently exist within the organization, and of what quality are they?
- What technology is available to support the necessary data system? Database capacity, availability of data analysis, reporting software, and so forth should be parts of the assessment.
- What fiscal resources are available to design and implement an M&E system?
- What experience does the organization have with performance reporting systems?

### Barriers

As with any organizational change, it is important to consider what could stand in the way of effective implementation. Questions to consider include the following:

- Is there a lack of fiscal resources, political will, a champion for the system, an outcome-linked strategy, or experience?
- If so, how can such barriers be overcome?

Good practice suggests that success in establishing an effective M&E system may depend on a variety of factors, including the following:

- a clear mandate for M&E at the national level
- Poverty Reduction Strategy Papers, laws, and regulations
- strong leadership and support at the most senior levels of the government
- reliable information that may be used for policy and management decision making
- a civil society that works as a partner with government in building and tracking performance information
- pockets of innovation that can serve as beginning practices or pilot programs.

At the end of the readiness assessment, senior government officials confront the question of whether to move ahead with constructing a results-based M&E system. Essentially, the question is "go–no go?" (now, soon, or maybe later).

### Step 2: Agreeing on Performance Outcomes to Monitor and Evaluate

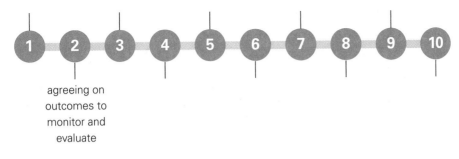

agreeing on outcomes to monitor and evaluate

It is important to generate interest in assessing the outcomes and impacts the organization or government is trying to achieve rather than simply focusing on implementation issues (inputs, activities, and outputs). After all, outcomes—such as improving coverage of preschool programs or improving learning among primary school children—are what reveal whether or not specific benefits have been realized.

Strategic outcomes and impacts should focus and drive the resource allocation and activities of the government and its development partners. These impacts should be derived from the strategic priorities of the country. Issues to consider when generating a list of outcomes include the following:

- Are there stated national/sectoral goals (for example, Vision 2016)?
- Have political promises been made that specify improved performance in a particular area?
- Do citizen polling data (such as citizen scorecards) indicate specific concerns?
- Is donor lending linked to specific goals?
- Is authorizing legislation present?
- Has the government made a serious commitment to achieving the Millennium Development Goals (MDGs)?

Agreeing on outcomes is a political process that requires buy-in and agreement from key stakeholders. Brainstorming sessions, interviews, focus groups, and surveys are used to understand their concerns.

Outcomes make explicit the intended results of an action ("know where you are going before you start moving"). They represent the results the client hopes to achieve. Before they can be achieved, they must be translated into a set of key indicators. Clearly setting outcomes—and deriving indicators based on them—is essential to designing and building results-based M&E systems.

## Step 3: Selecting Key Indicators to Monitor Outcomes

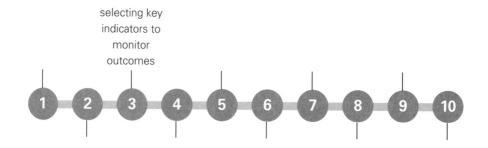

selecting key
indicators to
monitor
outcomes

What gets measured gets done. Specification of exactly what is to be measured in order to gauge achievement of outcomes not only helps track progress, it can also be a powerful motivating tool to focus efforts and create alignment within an organization if it is done early enough in the process.

An indicator is a measure that, when tracked systematically over time, indicates progress (or lack of progress) toward a target. It answers the question "How will we know success when we see it?" In new M&E systems, all indicators should be quantitative; qualitative indicators can come later, when the M&E system is more mature.

Indicator development is a core activity in building an M&E system; it drives all subsequent data collection, analysis, and reporting. The political and methodological issues in creating credible and appropriate indicators are not to be underestimated. Schiavo-Campo (1999) notes that indicators should be "CREAM," that is

- clear (precise and unambiguous)
- relevant (appropriate to the subject at hand)
- economic (available at reasonable cost)
- adequate (able to provide sufficient basis to assess performance)
- monitorable (amenable to independent validation).

Sometimes it is possible to reduce costs by using already available indicators (although evaluators should be aware of the risks of using such indicators). Before doing so, however, it is important to consider how relevant the indicators are (and will be perceived to be). Some indicators may need to be adapted or supplemented with others that are more relevant to the project, program, or policy being evaluated.

The number of indicators depends on how many are needed to answer the question "Has the outcome been achieved?" This number should range from two to seven. Once selected, these indicators are not cast in stone. New ones can be added and old ones dropped as the monitoring system is streamlined and improved over time.

The performance indicators selected and the data collection strategies used to collect information on these indicators need to be grounded in reality (Kusek and Rist 2004). Factors to consider include

- what data systems are in place
- what data can currently be produced
- what capacity exists to expand the breadth and depth of data collection and analysis.

Completing each cell in the matrix shown in table 3.2 gives an idea of the feasibility of actually deploying each indicator. Examples of indicators are shown in table 3.3.

- Evaluators need to develop their own indicators to meet the needs of the evaluation they are conducting.
- Developing good indicators takes more than one try. Arriving at final indicators takes time.
- All indicators should be stated neutrally, not as "increase in" or "decrease in."
- Evaluators should pilot, pilot, pilot!

Table 3.2    Matrix for Selecting Indicators

| Indicator | Data source | Data collection method | Who will collect data? | Frequency of data collection | Cost to collect data | Difficulty to collect | Who will analyze and report data? | Who will use the data? |
|---|---|---|---|---|---|---|---|---|
| 1. | | | | | | | | |
| 2. | | | | | | | | |
| 3. | | | | | | | | |

*Source*: Kusek and Rist 2004.

Table 3.3    Sample Performance Framework: Outcomes and Indicators

| Outcome | Indicators | Baselines | Targets |
|---|---|---|---|
| Improved coverage of preschool programs | Percentage of eligible urban children enrolled in preschool | | |
| | Percentage of eligible rural children enrolled in preschool | | |
| Improved primary school learning outcomes | Percentage of grade 6 students scoring 70 percent or better on standardized math and science tests | | |
| | Percentage of grade 6 students scoring higher on standardized math and science tests in comparison with baseline data | | |

*Source*: Kusek and Rist 2004.

## Step 4: Gathering Baseline Data on Indicators

gathering
baseline data
on indicators

The measurement of progress (or lack of it) toward outcomes begins with the description and measurement of initial conditions. Collecting baseline data essentially means taking the first measurements of the indicators to find out "Where are we today?"

A performance baseline provides information (qualitative or quantitative) about performance on an indicator at the beginning of (or immediately before) the intervention. In fact, one consideration in selecting indicators is the availability of baseline data, which allow performance to be tracked relative to the baseline.

Sources of baseline data can be either primary (gathered specifically for this measurement system) or secondary (collected for another purpose). Secondary data can come from within an organization, from the government, or from international data sources. Using such data can save money, as long as they really provide the information needed. It is extremely difficult to go back and obtain primary baseline data if the secondary source is later found not to meet the needs of the evaluation.

Possible sources of baseline data include the following:

- written records (paper and electronic)
- individuals involved with a project, program, or policy
- the general public
- trained observers
- mechanical measurements and tests
- geographic information systems.

Once the sources of baseline data for the indicators are chosen, evaluators decide who is going to collect the data and how. They identify and develop data collection instruments, such as forms for gathering information from files or records, interview protocols, surveys, and observational instruments. As they develop the collection instruments, they keep practical issues in mind:

- Are good data currently available (or easily accessible)?
- Can data be procured on a regular and timely basis to allow tracking of progress?
- Is the planned primary data collection feasible and cost-effective?

There are many ways to collect data (as discussed in chapter 9). They can be ranked from least rigorous, least formal, and least costly to most rigorous, most formal, and most costly (figure 3.4).

Table 3.4 shows the third step in developing outcomes for education policy: establishing baselines.

**Figure 3.4    Spectrum of Data Collection Methods**

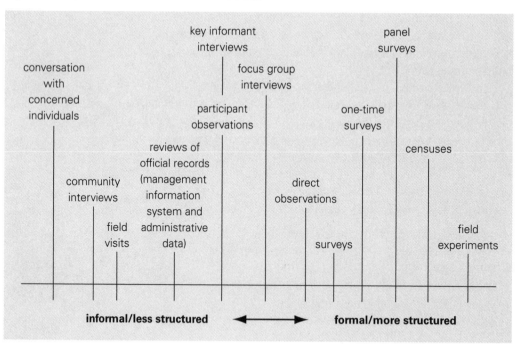

*Source*: Kusek and Rist 2004.

**Table 3.4   Sample Performance Framework: Outcomes, Indicators, and Baselines**

| Outcomes | Indicators | Baselines | Targets |
|---|---|---|---|
| Improved coverage of preschool programs | Percentage of eligible urban children enrolled in preschool<br><br>Percentage of eligible rural children enrolled in preschool | 75 percent in urban areas in 1999<br><br>40 percent in rural areas in 2000 | |
| Improved primary school learning outcomes | Percentage of grade 6 students scoring 70 percent or better on standardized math and science tests<br><br>Percentage of grade 6 students scoring higher on standardized math and science tests in comparison with baseline data | In 2002, 47 percent of students scored 70 percent or better in math, and 50 percent scored 70 percent or better in science.<br><br>In 2002, mean score for Grade 6 students was 68 percent in math and 53 percent in science. | |

*Source*: Kusek and Rist, 2004.

## Step 5: Planning for Improvements: Selecting Realistic Targets

planning for improvement: selecting realistic targets

The next step—establishing targets—is the last step in building the performance framework. According to Kusek and Rist (2004, p. 91), "In essence, targets are the quantifiable levels of the indicators that a country, society, or organization wants to achieve by a given time."

Most outcomes and nearly all impacts in international development are complex and take place only over the long term. There is, therefore, a need to establish interim targets that specify how much progress toward an outcome is to be achieved, in what time frame, and with what level of resource allocation. Measuring performance against these targets can involve both direct and proxy indicators, as well as the use of both quantitative and qualitative data.

One can think of theory of change impacts as the long-term goals the intervention is ultimately striving to achieve. Outcomes are a set of sequential and feasible targets (relative to the baseline) for the indicators one hopes to achieve along the way, within a specified, realistic (political and budgetary) time frame. Stated differently, if an organization reaches its targets over time, it will achieve its outcome (provided it has a good theory of change and successfully implements it).

When setting targets for indicators, it is important to have a clear understanding of the following:

- the baseline starting point (for example, the average of the past three years, last year, the average trend)
- a theory of change and a way of disaggregating it into a set of time-bound achievements
- the levels of funding and personnel resources over the timeframe for the target
- the amount of outside resources expected to supplement the program's current resources
- the relevant political concerns
- the organizational (especially managerial) experience in delivering projects and programs in this substantive area.

Figure 3.5 shows how to identify the targets to be achieved as one step in a chain that, over time, will lead to achievement of an outcome.

Only one target should be set for each indicator. If the indicator has never been used before, the evaluator should be cautious about setting a specific

Figure 3.5   Identifying Expected or Desired Level of Improvement Requires Selecting Performance Targets

| Baseline indicator level | | Desired level of improvement | | Target performance |
|---|---|---|---|---|
| | **+** | assumes a finite and expected level of inputs, activities, and outputs | **=** | desired level of performance to be reached within a specific time |

*Source*: Kusek and Rist 2004.

target, setting a range instead. Targets should be set for the intermediate term (no longer than three years) and include realistic time frames for achievement. Most targets are set annually, but some can be set quarterly or for longer periods.

Table 3.5 shows the last step in developing outcomes for education policy: setting performance targets. This completed matrix now becomes the performance framework. It defines the outcomes and provides a plan for determining whether the program was successful in achieving these outcomes. The framework defines the design of a results-based M&E system that will begin to provide information about whether interim targets are being achieved on the way to the longer-term outcome.

The framework helps evaluators design the evaluation. It can also assist managers with budgeting, resource allocation, staffing, and other functions. Managers should consult the framework frequently to ensure that the project, program, or policy is moving toward the desired outcomes.

Performance targeting is critical to reaching policy outcomes. Using a participatory, collaborative process involving baseline indicators and desired levels of improvement over time is key to results-based M&E.

**Table 3.5  Sample Performance Framework: Outcomes, Indicators, Baselines, and Targets**

| Outcomes | Indicators | Baselines | Targets |
|---|---|---|---|
| Improved coverage of preschool programs | Percentage of eligible urban children enrolled in preschool | 75 percent in urban areas in 1999 | 85 percent in urban areas by 2006 |
| | Percentage of eligible rural children enrolled in preschool | 40 percent in rural areas in 2000 | 60 percent in rural areas by 2006 |
| Improved primary school learning outcomes | Percentage of grade 6 students scoring 70 percent or better on standardized math and science tests | In 2002, 47 percent of students scored 70 percent or better in math, and 50 percent scored 70 percent or better in science. | By 2006, 80 percent of students will score 70 percent or better in math, and 67 percent will score 70 percent or better in science. |
| | Percentage of grade 6 students scoring higher on standardized math and science tests in comparison with baseline data | In 2002, mean score for Grade 6 students was 68 percent in math and 53 percent in science. | In 2006, mean test score will be 78 percent for math and 65 percent for science. |

*Source:* Kusek and Rist 2004.

## Step 6: Monitoring for Results

monitoring
for results

A results-based monitoring system tracks both implementation (inputs, activities, outputs) and results (outcomes and impacts). Figure 3.6 shows how each of these types of monitoring fits in with the model.

Every outcome has a number of indicators, each of which has a target. A series of activities and strategies needs to be coordinated and managed in order to achieve these targets (figure 3.7).

Linking implementation monitoring to results monitoring is crucial. Figure 3.8 provides an example for reducing child mortality.

**Figure 3.6    Key Types of Monitoring**

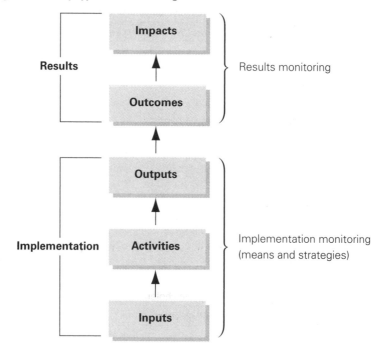

*Source*: Adapted from Binnendijk 2000.

**Figure 3.7  Links between Implementation Monitoring and Results Monitoring**

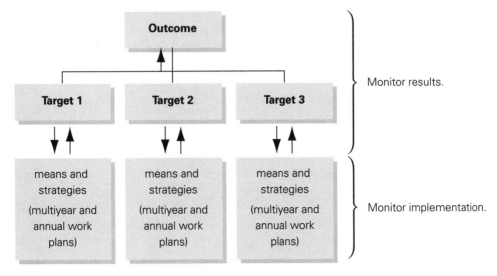

*Source*: Kusek and Rist 2004.

**Figure 3.8  Example of Linking Implementation Monitoring to Results Monitoring**

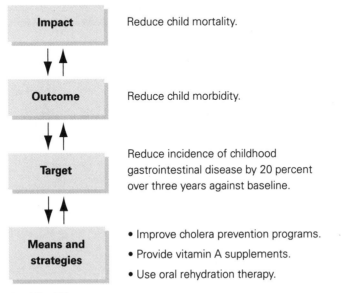

*Source*: Kusek and Rist 2004.

Working with partners is increasingly the norm in development work. Many partners at the lowest level of this hierarchy potentially contribute inputs, activities, and outputs as part of a strategy to achieve targets (figure 3.9).

Figure 3.9  **Achieving Results through Partnership**

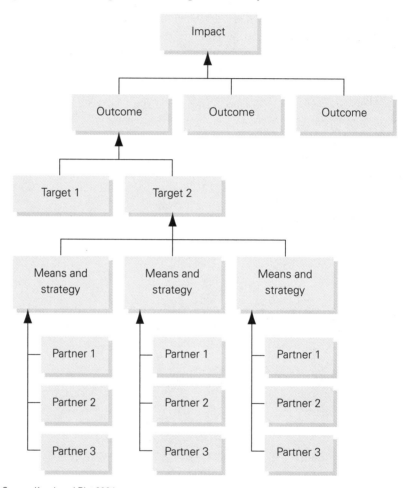

*Source*: Kusek and Rist 2004.

A strong M&E system must be supported with a budget, staffing plans, and activity planning. Building an effective M&E system involves administrative and institutional tasks, including the following:

- establishing data collection, analysis, and reporting guidelines
- designating who will be responsible for which activities
- establishing means of quality control
- establishing timelines and costs
- working through the roles and responsibilities of the government, other development partners, and civil society
- establishing guidelines on the transparency and dissemination of the information and analysis.

To be successful, every M&E system needs the following:

- ownership
- management
- maintenance
- credibility.

## Step 7: Using Evaluation Information

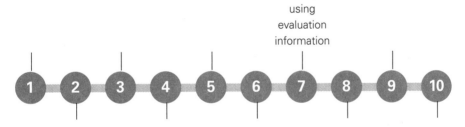

Evaluation plays an important role in supplementing information acquired by monitoring progress toward outcomes and impacts. Whereas monitoring reveals what we are doing relative to indicators, targets, and outcomes, evaluation reveals whether

- we are doing the right things (strategy)
- we are doing things right (operations)
- there are better ways of doing it (learning).

Evaluation can address many important issues that go beyond a simple monitoring system. For example, the design of many interventions is based on certain causal assumptions about the problem or issue being addressed. Evaluation can confirm or challenge these causal assumptions using theory-based evaluation and logic models (as discussed in chapter 4). Evaluation can also delve deeper into an interesting or troubling result or trend that emerges from the monitoring system (finding out, for example, why girls are dropping out of a village school years earlier than boys).

An evaluation be used in addition to monitoring

- any time there is an unexpected result or performance outlier that requires further investigation
- when resource or budget allocations are being made across projects, programs, or policies
- when a decision is being made regarding whether or not to expand a pilot
- when there is a long period with no improvement without a clear explanation as to why
- when similar programs or policies report divergent outcomes or when indicators for the same outcome show divergent trends
- when attempting to understand the side effects of interventions
- when learning about the merit, worth, and significance of what was done
- when looking carefully at costs relative to benefits.

If governments and organizations are going to rely on the information gathered from an M&E system, they must depend upon the quality and trustworthiness of the information they gather. Poor, inaccurate, and biased information is of no use to anyone.

### Step 8: Reporting Findings

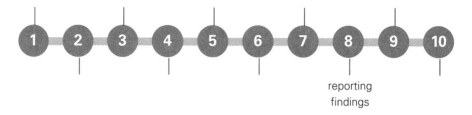

reporting
findings

Determining what findings are reported to whom, in what format, and at what intervals is a critical part of M&E. Analyzing and reporting data

- provides information on the status of projects, programs, and policies
- yields clues to problems
- creates opportunities to consider improvements in implementation strategies

- provides important information over time on trends and directions
- helps confirm or challenge the theory of change behind the project, program, or policy. (Data analysis and reporting are covered in detail in later chapters.)

The evaluator must be sure to find out what the main decision points are at the project, program, and policy levels, so that it is clear when M&E findings will be most useful for decision makers. If the data and analysis arrive too late, they will not be able to affect decisions.

All important results should be reported, whether positive or negative (table 3.6). A good M&E system should provide an early warning system to detect problems or inconsistencies, as well demonstrating the value of an intervention. Performance reports should include explanations about poor or disappointing outcomes, and they should document any steps already underway to address them.

When analyzing and presenting data, evaluators should

- compare indicator data with the baseline and targets and provide this information in an easy-to-understand graphic (see chapter 13)
- compare current information with past data, and look for patterns and trends
- be careful about drawing sweeping conclusions that are based on insufficient information (The more data collected, the more certain the evaluator can be that trends are real.)
- protect the messenger: people who deliver bad news should not be punished (Uncomfortable findings can indicate new trends or notify managers of problems early on, allowing them time needed to solve these problems.)

Table 3.6 Sample Outcomes Reporting Table

| Outcome indicator | Baseline | Current | Target | Difference (target − current) |
|---|---|---|---|---|
| Rate of hepatitis ($N = 6,000$) | 30 | 35 | 20 | −5 |
| Percentage of children with improved overall health status ($N = 9,000$) | 20 | 20 | 24 | −4 |
| Percentage of children who show 4 out of 5 positive scores on physical exams ($N = 3,500$) | 50 | 65 | 65 | 0 |
| Percentage of children with improved nutritional status ($N = 14,000$) | 80 | 85 | 83 | 2 |

*Source*: Kusek and Rist 2004.

## Step 9: Using Findings

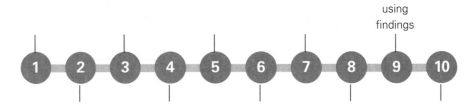

using
findings

The crux of an M&E system is not simply generating results-based information but getting that information to the appropriate users in a timely fashion so that they can take it into account (or choose to ignore it) in managing projects, programs, or policies. Development partners and civil society have important roles to play in using the information to strengthen accountability, transparency, and resource allocation procedures.

Strategies for sharing information that can be implemented at any government level include the following:

- *Empower the media.* The media can help disseminate the findings generated by results-based M&E systems. They can also be helpful in exposing corruption and calling for better governance.
- *Enact freedom of information legislation.* Freedom of information is a powerful tool that can be used to share information with concerned stakeholders.
- *Institute e-government.* E-government involves the use of information technology to provide better accessibility, outreach, information, and services. E-government allows stakeholders to interact directly with the government to obtain information and even transact business online.
- *Add information on internal and external Internet files.* Information can be shared by posting information, as well as published performance findings, on internal (agency or government) and external Web sites. Many agencies are also developing searchable databases for M&E findings.
- *Publish annual budget reports.* The best way to communicate how taxpayer money is being spent is to publish the budget. Doing so allows citizens to observe the quality and level of services being provided by the government and the priority the government gives to particular services or programs.
- *Engage civil society and citizen groups.* Engaging civil society and citizen groups encourages the groups to be more action oriented, more accountable, and more likely to agree on the information they need.
- *Strengthen legislative oversight.* Legislatures in many countries, both developed and developing, are asking for information about performance

as part of their oversight function. They are looking to see that budgets are used effectively.

- *Strengthen the office of the auditor general.* The office of the auditor general is a key partner in determining how effectively the government is functioning. As audit agencies demand more information about how well the public sector is performing, projects, programs, and policies are being implemented more effectively.
- *Share and compare findings with development partners.* As a result of the introduction of national poverty reduction strategies and similar strategies and policies, development partners (especially bilateral and multilateral aid agencies) are sharing and comparing results and findings.

Understanding the utility of performance information for various users is a key reason for building an M&E system in the first place. Key potential users in many societies, such as citizens, NGOs, and the private sector, are often left out of the information flow. M&E data have both internal (governmental) and external (societal) uses that need to be recognized and legitimated (box 3.3).

---

**Box 3.3  Ten Uses of Results Findings**

Results findings can be used to

1. respond to demands for accountability by elected officials and the public
2. help formulate and justify budget requests
3. help make operational resource allocation decisions
4. trigger in-depth examinations of what performance problems (with the theory of change or implementation) exist and what corrections are needed
5. help motivate personnel to continue making program improvements
6. monitor the performance of contractors and grantees (it is no longer enough for them to document how busy they are)
7. provide data for special, in-depth program evaluations
8. help track service delivery against precise outcome targets (are we doing things right?)
9. support strategic and other long-term planning efforts (are we doing the right things?)
10. communicate with the public to build public trust

*Source:* Hatry 1999.

---

## Step 10: Sustaining the M&E System within the Organization

sustaining the M&E system within the organization

Ensuring the longevity and utility of a results-based M&E system is a challenge. Six components are crucial to sustainability:

- demand
- clear roles and responsibilities
- trustworthy and credible information
- accountability
- capacity
- incentives.

Each component needs continued attention over time to ensure the viability of the system.

### Demand

Demand for M&E can be built and maintained in several ways:

- Build in a formal structure that requires regular reporting of performance results (an annual reporting requirement for organizational units, for example).
- Publicize the availability of this information through the media, thereby generating demand from government bodies, citizen groups, donors, and the general public.
- Make a practice of translating strategy into specific goals and targets, so that those interested in the organization's strategic direction will be able to track progress toward attaining those goals.

### Clear roles and responsibilities

One of the most important structural interventions for institutionalizing an M&E system is the creation of clear, formal lines of authority and responsibilities for collecting, analyzing, and reporting performance information. Doing so requires

- issuing clear guidance on who is responsible for which components of the M&E system and building responsibility into individuals' performance reviews
- building a system that links the central planning and finance functions with the line/sector functions to encourage a link between budget allocation cycles and the provision of M&E information, essentially a performance budgeting system
- building a system in which there is demand for information at every level of the system (that is, there is no part of the system that information simply passes through without being used).

### Trustworthy and credible information

The performance information system must be able to produce both good news and bad news. Accordingly, producers of information need protection from political reprisals. The information produced by the system should be transparent and subject to independent verification (for example, a review by the national audit office of the government or by an independent group of university professors).

### Accountability

Ways should be found to share transparent information with external stakeholders who have an interest in performance. Key stakeholder groups to consider include civil society organizations, the media, the private sector, and the government.

### Capacity

Undertaking a readiness assessment and focusing on organizational capacity is one of the first things considered in the building of an M&E system. Key elements to build on here include sound technical skills in data collection and analysis, managerial skills in strategic goal setting and organization development, existing data collection and retrieval systems, the ongoing availability of financial resources, and institutional experience with monitoring and evaluation.

### Incentives

Incentives need to be introduced to encourage use of performance information. Success needs to be acknowledged and rewarded, and problems need to be addressed. Messengers must not be punished, organizational learning must be valued, and budget savings must be shared. Corrupt or ineffective systems cannot be counted on to produce quality information and analysis.

## Concluding Comments

There is no requirement that the building of an M&E system has to be done according to these 10 steps—strategies with more or fewer steps can be developed. The challenge is to ensure that key functions and activities are recognized, clustered in a logical manner, and then implemented in an appropriate sequence.

Results-based M&E systems are powerful management tools. They can help build and foster change in the way governments and organizations operate. They can also help build a knowledge base of what works and what does not.

A results-based M&E system should be iterative. It must receive continuous attention, resources, and political commitment. It takes time to build the cultural shift to a results orientation, but the time, effort, and rewards are worth the effort.

The demand for capacity building never ends; the only way an organization can coast is downhill. Several steps can help ensure that an M&E system is set up and sustained:

- Keep champions on your side and help them.
- Convince the ministry of finance and the legislature that an M&E system needs sustained resources, just as the budget system does (the volume of resources allocated to an M&E system should be about equal to that allocated to the budget system).
- Look for every opportunity to link results information to budget and resource allocation decisions.
- Begin with pilot efforts to demonstrate effective results-based M&E.
- Begin with an enclave strategy (built, for example, around islands of innovation) rather than a whole-of-government approach.
- Monitor both progress toward implementation and the achievement of results.
- Complement performance monitoring with evaluations to ensure better understanding of public sector results.

Once the framework is developed for an evaluation (Step 7), the framework can be used to construct a theory of change, choose an approach, begin writing questions, and choose a design for the evaluation. These issues are covered in chapters 4–7.

# Summary

A results-based M&E system can be a valuable tool to assist policy makers and decision makers in tracking the outcomes and impacts of projects, programs, and policies. Unlike traditional evaluation, results-based M&E moves beyond an emphasis on inputs and outputs to focus on outcomes and impacts. It is the key architecture for any performance measurement system.

Results-based M&E systems

- use baseline data to describe a problem before beginning an initiative
- track indicators for the outcomes to be achieved
- collect data on inputs, activities, and outputs and their contributions to achieving outcomes
- assess the robustness and appropriateness of the deployed theory of change
- include systematic reporting to stakeholders
- are conducted with strategic partners
- capture information on the success or failure of partnership strategy in achieving intended results
- constantly strive to provide credible and useful information as a management tool.

Ten steps are recommended in designing and building a results-based M&E system:

1. conducting a readiness assessment
2. agreeing on performance outcomes to monitor and evaluate
3. selecting key indicators to monitor outcomes
4. gathering baseline data on indicators
5. planning for improvement: setting realistic targets
6. building a monitoring system
7. using evaluation information
8. reporting findings
9. using findings
10. sustaining the M&E system within the organization

Building and sustaining a results-based M&E system is not easy. It requires continuous commitment, champions, time, effort, and resources. There may be organizational, technical, and political challenges. The original system may need several revisions to tailor it to meet the needs of the organization. But doing so is worth the effort.

# Chapter 3 Activities

## Application Exercise 3.1: Get the Logic Right

How ready is your organization to design and implement a results-based M&E system? Rate your organization on each of the following dimensions, and provide comments to explain your rating. Discuss with a colleague any barriers to implementation and how they might be addressed.

1. Incentives (circle the appropriate rating):

   plenty of incentives          a few incentives          several disincentives

   Comments:

   Strategies for improvement:



2. Roles and responsibilities (circle the appropriate rating):

   very clear                    somewhat clear                    quite unclear

   Comments:

   Strategies for improvement:



3. Organizational capacity (circle the appropriate rating):

   excellent                     adequate                          weak

   Comments:

   Strategies for improvement:



4. Barriers (circle the appropriate rating):

   no serious barriers           very few barriers           serious barriers

   Comments:

   Strategies for improvement:

## Application Exercise 3.2: Identifying Inputs, Activities, Outputs, Outcomes, and Impacts

Identify whether each of the following statements is an input, an activity, an output, an outcome, or a long-term impact. If possible, discuss with a colleague and explain the basis on which you categorized each statement.

1. Women-owned microenterprises are significantly contributing to poverty reduction in the communities in which they are operating.
2. The government has made funds available for microenterprise loans.
3. The government approved 61 applications from program graduates.
4. The Ministry of Education identified course trainers.
5. Seventy-two women completed training.
6. Income of graduates increases 25 percent in the first year after course completion.
7. One hundred women attended training in microenterprise business management.
8. Information on availability of microenterprise program loans is provided to communities.

## Application Exercise 3.3: Developing Indicators

1. Identify a program or policy with which you are familiar. What is the main impact it is trying to achieve? What are two outcomes you would expect to see if the intervention is on track to achieve that impact?

   Impact: _____

   Outcome 1: _____

   Outcome 2: _____

2. Starting with the outcomes, identify two or three indicators you would use to track progress against each.

   Outcome 1: _____

      Indicator a: _____

      Indicator b: _____

      Indicator c: _____

Outcome 2: _____

    Indicator a: _____

    Indicator b: _____

    Indicator c: _____

Impact: _____

    Indicator a: _____

    Indicator b: _____

    Indicator c: _____

## Notes

1. This chapter, which draws heavily on Kusek and Rist (2004), explicitly addresses monitoring. The rest of this volume is devoted exclusively to evaluation.

## References and Further Reading

Binnendijk, Annette. 2000. "Results-Based Management in the Development Cooperation Agencies: A Review of Experience." Paper prepared for the OECD/DAC Working Party on Aid Evaluation, Paris, February 10–11 (revised October 2000).

Boyle, R., and D. Lemaire, eds. 1999. *Building Effective Evaluation Capacity*. New Brunswick, NJ: Transaction Books.

IFAD (International Fund for Agriculture Development). 2002. *A Guide for Project M&E: Managing for Impact in Rural Development*. Rome. www.ifad.org/evaluation/guide/.

Furubo, Jan-Eric, Ray C. Rist, and Rolf Sandahl, eds. 2002. *International Atlas of Evaluation*. New Brunswick, NJ: Transaction Books.

Hatry, Harry P. 1999. *Performance Measurement: Getting Results*. Washington, DC: Urban Institute Press.

Khan, M. Adil. 2001. *A Guidebook on Results-Based Monitoring and Evaluation: Key Concepts, Issues and Applications*. Government of Sri Lanka, Ministry of Plan Implementation, Monitoring and Progress Review Division, Colombo.

Kusek, Jody Zall, and Ray C. Rist. 2001. "Building a Performance-Based Monitoring and Evaluation System: The Challenges Facing Developing Countries." *Evaluation Journal of Australasia* 1 (2): 14–23.

———. 2003. "Readiness Assessment: Toward Performance Monitoring and Evaluation in the Kyrgyz Republic." *Japanese Journal of Evaluation Studies* 31 (1): 17–31.

———. 2004. *Ten Steps to Building a Results-Based Monitoring and Evaluation System*. Washington, DC: World Bank.

Malik, Khalid, and Christine Roth, eds. 1999. *Evaluation Capacity Development in Asia*. United Nations Development Programme Evaluation Office, New York.

Osborn, David, and Ted Gaebler. 1992. *Reinventing Government*. Boston: Addison-Wesley Publishing.

OECD (Organisation for Economic Co-operation and Development). 2002. *Glossary of Key Terms in Evaluation and Results-Based Management*. Development Co-operation Directorate and Development Assistance Committee. Paris.

Schiavo-Campo, Salvatore. 1999. "'Performance' in the Public Sector." *Asian Journal of Political Science* 7 (2): 75–87.

UNPF (United Nations Population Fund). 2002. *Monitoring and Evaluation Toolkit for Program Managers*. Office of Oversight and Evaluation. www.unfpa.org/monitoring/toolkit.htm.

Valadez, Joseph, and Michael Bamberger. 1994. *Monitoring and Evaluation Social Programs in Developing Countries: A Handbook for Policymakers, Managers, and Researchers.* Washington, DC: World Bank.

Weiss, Carol. 1972. *Evaluation Research: Methods for Assessing Program Effectiveness.* Englewood Cliffs, NJ: Prentice Hall.

Wholey, Joseph S., Harry Hatry, and Kathryn Newcomer. 2001. "Managing for Results: Roles for Evaluators in a New Management Era." *American Journal of Evaluation* 22 (3): 343–47.

World Bank. 1997. *World Development Report: The State in a Changing World.* Washington, DC.

## Web Sites

IDRC (International Development Research Centre). 2004. *Evaluation Planning in Program Initiatives.* Ottawa. http://web.idrc.ca/uploads/user-S/108549984812 guideline-web.pdf.

IFAD (International Fund for Agricultural Development). *Practical Guide on Monitoring and Evaluation of Rural Development Projects.* http://www.ifad.org/evaluation/oe/process/guide/index.htm.

Kellogg Foundation. 1998. *Evaluation Handbook.* http://www.wkkf.org/Pubs/Tools/Evaluation/Pub770.pdf.

Specialist Monitoring and Evaluation Web Sites. http://www.mande.co.uk/specialist.htm.

Uganda Communications Commission. 2005. "Monitoring and Evaluation." In *Funding and Implementing Universal Access: Innovation and Experience from Uganda.* International Development Research Centre, Ottawa. http://www.idrc.ca/en/ev-88227-201-1-DO_TOPIC.html.

World Bank. *Core Welfare Indicators Questionnaire.* Washington, DC. http://www4.worldbank.org/afr/stats/cwiq.cfm.

———.2001. *Tools: Capturing Experience Monitoring and Evaluation.* Upgrading Urban Communities Resource Framework, Washington, DC. http://web.mit.edu/urbanupgrading/upgrading/issues-tools/tools/monitoring-eval.html#Anchor-Monitoring-56567.

———. 2008. *Online Atlas of the Millennium Development Goals: Building a Better World.* Washington, DC. http://devdata.worldbank.org/atlas-mdg/.

**CHAPTER 4**

# Understanding the Evaluation Context and the Program Theory of Change

This chapter is the first of two chapters that examines evaluation planning. This chapter is about the front end of an evaluation—how to start. An evaluation that begins with a well-planned design is more likely to be completed on time and on budget and to meet the needs of the client and other stakeholders. A front-end analysis investigates and identifies lessons from the past, confirms or casts doubt on the theory behind the program, and sets the context influencing the program.

**This chapter has five main parts:**

- Front-End Analysis
- Identifying the Main Client and Key Stakeholders
- Understanding the Context
- Tapping Existing Knowledge
- Constructing, Using, and Assessing a Theory of Change

## Front-End Analysis

Where to begin? If you want to get to the correct destination, it is best to begin by finding out what direction to head in and what others have already learned about the path to that destination. You will want to collect critical information for decisions about timeframes, costs, hazards, and processes.

> ■ **Front-end analysis:** Investigation of issue or problem to determine what is known about it and how to proceed in developing an evaluative approach to it

A **front-end analysis** is an investigation of an issue or problem to determine what is known about it and how to proceed in developing an evaluative approach to it. It is what an evaluator does to figure out what to do.

In a front-end analysis, the evaluator investigates the following types of questions:

- Who is the main client for the evaluation? Who are other important stakeholders? What issues do they identify for the evaluation?
- How will the timing of the evaluation in relation to project, program, or policy implementation affect the evaluation?
- How much time is available to complete the evaluation?
- What is the nature and extent of available resources?
- Does social science theory have relevance for the evaluation?
- What have evaluations of similar programs found? What issues did they raise?
- What is the theory of change behind the project, program, or policy?
- What existing data can be used for this evaluation?

Many evaluators are impatient to get the evaluation planning finished and therefore rush into data collection. They try to do exploratory work at the same time as data collection. But completing a good front-end analysis is critical to learning about an intervention. It can save time and money on the evaluation, ensure the evaluation meets client needs, and sustain or build relationships, not only with the client but also with key stakeholders. Most important, a good front-end analysis can ensure that the evaluation is addressing the right questions to get information that is needed rather than collecting data that may never be used.

At the beginning of an evaluation, many evaluators typically make assumptions, some of which may be incorrect. They may, for example, assume that there is a rich data infrastructure when few data are actually available. They may assume that experienced consultants with extensive country knowledge will assist them with the evaluation, only to find out that the people they counted on are busy with other projects. An exploratory period is needed to learn about the availability of data and other resources.

Determining if joint evaluation is appropriate and possible should also be done at the front-end stage. If there is interest and it is appropriate, the partners will need to determine what roles each will undertake. They will also need to agree on issues such as the timing of the evaluation.

## Balancing the Expected Costs and Benefits of an Evaluation

Expected costs and benefits of the evaluation and how to balance them should be on the agenda during front-end planning. The benefits of an evaluation may include the following:

- evidence-based decision making that leads to sound decisions about what to scale up or replicate, what to improve, or what to terminate or scale back
- contribution to streams of knowledge about what works (and under what conditions) and what does not
- the building of local capacity.

Costs of evaluations are important too. They should be thought of in terms of

- the cost of the program (spending US$50,000 to evaluate a US$25,000 program does not make sense)
- the burden of the evaluation on program beneficiaries and others asked to spend time providing information or in other ways assisting evaluators
- the reputation costs to the evaluator and the evaluation community if the results are likely to be disputed because the evaluation is of a highly political, controversial program, or insufficient time is provided to conduct a comprehensive evaluation.

## Pitfalls in the Front-End Planning Process

The belief that everything can be covered up front—and that if front-end planning takes place, the evaluation will necessarily proceed smoothly—is a potential pitfall of the front-end planning process. Other pitfalls include the following:

- resistance to modifying the original plan (Leeuw 2003)
- the McDonaldization of society—"the process by which the principles of the fast-food restaurant are coming to dominate more and more sectors of American society as well as of the rest of the world" (Ritzer 1993, p. 1) (this phrase is particularly applicable when checklists, to-do lists, and frameworks replace reflective thinking)
- fixed beliefs ("truisms") that pop up while conducting front-end planning ("Randomized experiments? No way: Too complicated, too expensive, and too difficult to conduct in the development context")

- "group think" (going along with the group position to remain part of the group despite concerns about the position)
- disproportionate weighting of the views of the powerful (automatically weighing the value of suggestions by the status of those making them).

## Identifying the Main Client and Key Stakeholders

An important part of front-end analysis is identifying the main client and key stakeholders of the project, program, or policy. Identifying key stakeholders may not always be straightforward.

### The Main Client

Typically, one key stakeholder or stakeholder group sponsors or requests an evaluation and is the main recipient of its outputs. This stakeholder or stakeholder group is the main client for the evaluation. The needs of this client will have great influence on the evaluation.

The main client may be

- authorizing and funding the program
- authorizing and funding the evaluation
- accountable to the public for the intervention
- the party to which the evaluators are accountable.

There is one main client. It is important to meet with the main client (or representatives, such as a board of directors, in the case of a client group) early on to help identify issues for the evaluation from its perspective. During this meeting, evaluators should ask about the client's timing needs and intended use of the evaluation. The evaluator, who first listens to and probes the client to determine issues underlying the request for the evaluation, can return at a later date either to present the client with broad options about ways the evaluation can be approached or to propose a single recommended approach to the evaluation.

### Stakeholders

■ **Stakeholder:**
Person or organization other than the client who has stakes in the intervention

**Stakeholders** are the people and organizations other than the client with stakes in the intervention. Typically, they are those who are affected by an intervention, either during its lifetime or in subsequent years. It is important to include as stakeholders those who would not typically be asked to participate in an evaluation.

Stakeholders can include

- participants
- direct beneficiaries
- indirect beneficiaries
- development organizations that provide funding
- government officials, elected officials, and government employees with relevant interests, such as planners and public health nurses
- program directors, staff, board members, managers, and volunteers
- policy makers
- community and interest groups or associations, including those that may have a different agenda from the program officials.

Stakeholders often approach an intervention from different perspectives. A donor may be concerned that money is spent appropriately and that the intervention is effective. A program manager may be concerned that the intervention is well managed and is generating lessons learned. Program participants may want to receive more or better services. Policy makers may be most concerned with whether the intervention is having its intended impact. Others in the community may want to replicate or expand the intervention or limit what they perceive as negative consequences of the intervention. This diversity of interests is a good thing, which may be revealed in initial discussions.

The roles of each individual or group in relation to the evaluation and its potential use should be clearly identified (table 4.1).

### Identifying and involving key stakeholders

Key stakeholders can be identified by looking at documents about the intervention and talking with the main evaluation client, program sponsors, program staff, local officials, and program participants. Stakeholders can be interviewed initially or brought together in small groups. In contacting stakeholders about the evaluation, the evaluation planner must be clear about what the purpose is in talking to each stakeholder (making them aware of the upcoming evaluation, asking them to identify issues they would like the evaluation to address).

Increasing the use of an evaluation is a process that begins by meeting with the main client and engaging key stakeholders in the evaluation design. It is not something that happens when the evaluation report is complete and about to be disseminated. For some evaluations, key stakeholder meetings are held periodically, or an even more formal structure is established. The evaluation manager may set up an advisory or steering committee structure.

**Table 4.1  Roles of Stakeholders in an Evaluation**

| Stakeholder | To make policy | To make operational decisions | To provide input to evaluation | To react | For interest only |
|---|---|---|---|---|---|
| Developers of the program | | | | | |
| Funders of the program | | | | | |
| Authorizing official, board, or agency | | | | | |
| Providers of other resources (facilities, supplies, in-kind contributions) | | | | | |
| Heads of implementing agencies and senior managers | | | | | |
| Program managers responsible for implementation | | | | | |
| Program staff | | | | | |
| Monitoring staff | | | | | |
| Direct beneficiaries of the program | | | | | |
| Indirect beneficiaries of the program | | | | | |
| Potential adopters of the program | | | | | |
| People excluded from the program (by entry criteria, for example) | | | | | |
| People perceiving negative effects of the program or the evaluation | | | | | |
| People losing power as a result of the program | | | | | |
| People losing opportunities as a result of the program | | | | | |
| Members of the community or the general public | | | | | |
| Others | | | | | |

*Source*: Authors.

Engaging key stakeholders early on gives the evaluator a better understanding of the intervention, what it was intended to accomplish, and the issues and challenges it faced in doing so. The evaluation team will be better informed regarding issues to be covered in the evaluation as well as specific information needed, when the information will be needed, and who can provide it. Meeting with key stakeholders helps ensure that the evaluation will not miss major critical issues. It also helps obtain "buy-in" to the evaluation:

letting stakeholders know that the issues and questions they raise will be carefully considered is likely to increase their support of and interest in the evaluation. This is how evaluation use gets built.

The extent to which stakeholders are actively involved in the design and implementation of the evaluation depends on several factors, including resources and relationships. Stakeholders may not be able to afford to take time away from their regular duties, for example, or there may be political reasons why the evaluation needs to be as independent as possible.

### Conducting stakeholder analysis

Many guides have been developed to help with stakeholder analysis. In their Web site *A Guide to Managing for Quality,* the Management Sciences for Health and the United Nations Children's Fund (1998) lay out one such process for identifying and assessing the importance of key people, groups of people, or institutions that may significantly influence the success of an evaluation. They also suggest several other reasons for conducting stakeholder analysis:

- to identify people, groups, and institutions that can influence the evaluation (positively or negatively)
- to anticipate the kind of influence, positive or negative, these groups will have on the evaluation
- to develop strategies to get the most effective support possible for the initiative and to reduce obstacles to successful implementation of the evaluation.

Box 4.1 shows one template for conducting a stakeholder analysis. While similar to table 4.1, it emphasizes building support for and reducing opposition to the evaluation.

As important as it to be inclusive, it is also important not to be overinclusive. Efforts to involve those on the periphery may result only in irritating them.

Sometimes evaluators directly involve one or more stakeholders in planning and conducting the evaluation. (Participatory evaluations are discussed in chapter 5.) In these situations, the evaluator facilitates stakeholder involvement in

- formulating the terms of reference
- selecting the evaluation team
- analyzing data
- identifying findings and formulating conclusions and recommendations (Mikkelsen 2005).

**Box 4.1    How to Conduct a Stakeholder Analysis**

1.  Brainstorm with colleagues to identify people, groups, and institutions that will affect or be affected by the intervention. List them in the stakeholder column of the table.

2.  Identify the specific interests each stakeholder has in the evaluation. Consider issues such as the potential benefits of the evaluation to the stakeholder, the changes the evaluation may require the stakeholder to make, and the project activities that may cause damage to or conflict for the stakeholder. Record these interests in the column labeled "stakeholder interests in the project, program, or policy."

3.  Identify how important each stakeholder's interests are to the success of the evaluation. Consider both (a) the role the key stakeholder must play for the evaluation to be successful and the likelihood that the stakeholder will play this role and (b) the likelihood and impact of a stakeholder's negative response to the evaluation. For each stakeholder, record your assessment under the column labeled "assessment of potential impact" by assigning an "A" for extremely important, a "B" for fairly important, and a "C" for not very important.

4.  Consider the kinds of actions you could take to gain stakeholder support and reduce opposition. Consider how you might approach each of the stakeholders. What kind of issues will the stakeholder want the evaluation to address? How important is it to involve the stakeholder in the planning process? Are there other groups or individuals that may influence the stakeholder to support your evaluation? Record your strategies for obtaining support or reducing obstacles to your evaluation in the last column of the table.

**Box table.    Sample Format for Conducting Stakeholder Analysis**

| Stakeholder | Stakeholder interests in the project, program, or policy | Assessment of potential impact of evaluation on stakeholder and stakeholder on evaluation | Potential strategies for obtaining support or reducing obstacles |
|---|---|---|---|
|  |  |  |  |
|  |  |  |  |
|  |  |  |  |
|  |  |  |  |

*Source:* Management Sciences for Health and the United Nations Children's Fund 1998.

# Understanding the Context

A front-end analysis also investigates the relationship between program stages and the broad evaluation purpose. The life of a project, program, or policy can be thought of as a progression in which different evaluation questions are asked at different stages. For example, it would not make sense to evaluate whether the objectives of a program had been achieved just a few months after funds had been committed. A more appropriate question at this early a stage might be whether the program had obtained the inputs necessary for implementation. Pancer and Westhues (1989) present a typology for this progression of program stages and evaluation questions (table 4.2). The questions they include are only examples; many potential questions can be asked at each stage.

Another step in a front-end analysis is to determine the policy context. Research can identify evaluations conducted on similar programs. The evaluator begins by obtaining the evaluation reports and reviewing them for the issues addressed, the type of approach selected, the instruments used, and the findings. If the evaluation is for a new intervention, the evaluation may need to be designed without roadmaps from previous evaluations. This is rarely the case, however.

**Table 4.2   Questions to Ask at Different Stages of an Evaluation**

| Stage of program development | Evaluation question to be asked |
| --- | --- |
| 1. Assessment of social problem and needs | To what extent are community needs met? |
| 2. Determination of goals | What must be done to meet those needs? |
| 3. Design of program alternatives | What services could be used to produce the desired changes? |
| 4. Selection of alternative | Which of the possible program approaches is most robust? |
| 5. Program implementation | How should the program be put into operation? |
| 6. Program operation | Is the program operating as planned? |
| 7. Program outcomes/effects/impact | Is the program having the desired effects? |
| 8. Program efficiency | Are program effects attained at a reasonable cost? |

*Source*: Adapted from Pancer and Westhues 1989.

## Tapping Existing Knowledge

**■ Knowledge fund:** Body of existing theoretical and empirical knowledge about the project, program, or policy

A front-end analysis investigates the existing theoretical and empirical knowledge about the project, program, or policy. This is also known as tapping the **knowledge fund**.

The knowledge coming from evaluations and other social science research, including economic studies, increases every day. Journals contain articles synthesizing the accumulation of explanatory knowledge on a specific topic, such as the effect of class size on learning or nutritional programs for expectant mothers on infant birth weights. Problem-oriented research into how organizations function combines theories and research from such diverse disciplines as organizational sociology, cognitive psychology, public choice theory, and law and economics (Scott 2003; Swedberg 2003). Organizations such as the Campbell Collaboration (http://www.campbellcollaboration.org/) are reviewing the quality of evaluations on a given topic and synthesizing those that meet their criteria. Repositories of randomized experiments in the field of criminal justice and crime prevention, social welfare programs, and health and educational programs indicate that more than 10,000 "experiments" have been conducted (Petrosino and others 2003). In organizing and planning for an evaluation, it is crucial to identify and review the relevant knowledge fund (box 4.2).

> **Box 4.2    Tapping the Knowledge Fund on Crime Prevention**
>
> Analysis of the data on crime prevention suggests that 29 programs worked, 25 did not work, and 28 were promising (information on another 68 programs was not clear). These findings are based on a synthesis of more than 600 evaluations, including evaluation of school- and family-based crime prevention, burglary reduction programs, drug arrests, policing/hot spots, closed circuit initiatives, neighborhood wardens, mentoring programs, and types of prison sanctions and programs (anger management, training programs, cognitive programs focused on reducing recidivism, boot camps, and so forth).
>
> *Source:* Sherman and others 2002.

## Constructing, Using, and Assessing a Theory of Change

The last part of a front-end analysis is constructing a theory of change and understanding how to use and assess it. The underlying logic or theory of change is an important topic for evaluation, whether it is during the ex ante or the ex post stage of a study. This section addresses why to use a theory of change, how to construct a theory of change, and how to assess a theory of change.

Although definitions may vary (see Chapter 3), one definition of a **theory of change** states that it is "an innovative tool to design and evaluate social change initiatives," a kind of "blueprint of the building blocks" needed to achieve the long-term goals of a social change initiative (ActKnowledge and Aspen Institute 2003). A theory of change can also be viewed as a representation of how an organization or initiative is expected to achieve results and an identification of the underlying assumptions made.

A theory of change must

- depict a sequence of the inputs the project, program, or policy will use; the activities the inputs will support; the outputs toward which the project, program, or policy is budgeting (a single activity or a combination of activities); and the outcomes and impacts expected
- identify events or conditions that may affect obtaining the outcomes
- identify the assumptions the program is making about causes and effects
- identify critical assumptions that, based on the policy and environmental context and a review of the literature, the evaluation needs to examine.

Identifying the events or conditions that may affect whether an intervention obtains the desired outcomes is particularly necessary given the interrelatedness and complexity of development programs. International development institutions now provide programmatic lending, which gives developing countries greater discretion than project financing. As Pawson (2006) indicates:

> an important change in public policy in recent years has been the rise of complex, multiobjective, multisite, multiagency, multisubject programs.... The reasons are clear. The roots of social problems intertwine. A health deficit may have origins in educational disadvantage, labor market inequality, environmental disparities, housing exclusion, differential patterns of crime victimization, and so on. Decision makers have, accordingly, begun to ponder whether single-measure, single-issue interventions may be treating just the symptoms.

Pawson believes that in such cases evaluators should

- understand the underlying program theory
- examine existing evidence through research synthesis
- view a complex program as intervention chains, with one set of stakeholders providing resources (material, social, cognitive, or emotional) to other sets of stakeholders, in the expectation that behavioral change will follow.

When an evaluation is being planned, attention must be paid to the question of how the theory of change underlying the program will be constructed and tested. Visuals should be used to help overview the key components and interactions of the project, program, or policy. They should show the causes and effects of projects, programs, or policies—the links in a chain of reasoning about what causes what. The desired impact or goal is often shown as the last link in the model.

The value of a theory of change is that it visually conveys beliefs about why the project, program, or policy is likely to succeed in reaching its objectives. The theory of change also specifies the components of a program and their relationships to one another. Resources are provided to enable an organization to engage in activities in order to achieve specific objectives. These resources, activities, outputs, intended outcomes, and impacts are interrelated.

In some cases, evaluators may find that an intervention already has a theory of change. If so, they need to review it carefully. In many cases, it will be necessary to refine or rework the existing theory of change and confirm it with people directly involved. If no theory of change exists, the evaluator should create one and validate it with the program manager and staff, if possible.

With a theory of change, assumptions must also be identified. The most critical of these assumptions that the evaluation should test (based on the prevailing political and policy environment as well as a literature review) also need to be identified. Theories of change open the "black box" to show how an intervention expects to convert inputs, activities, and outputs into results (figure 4.1).

It is important to identify what is happening in the broader context— that is, the environment in which the program operates. This environment

**Figure 4.1 Moving from Inputs to Results**

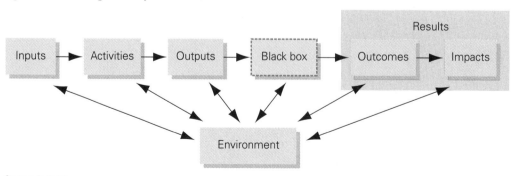

*Source*: Authors.

**Figure 4.2    Potential Environmental Influences on Program Results**

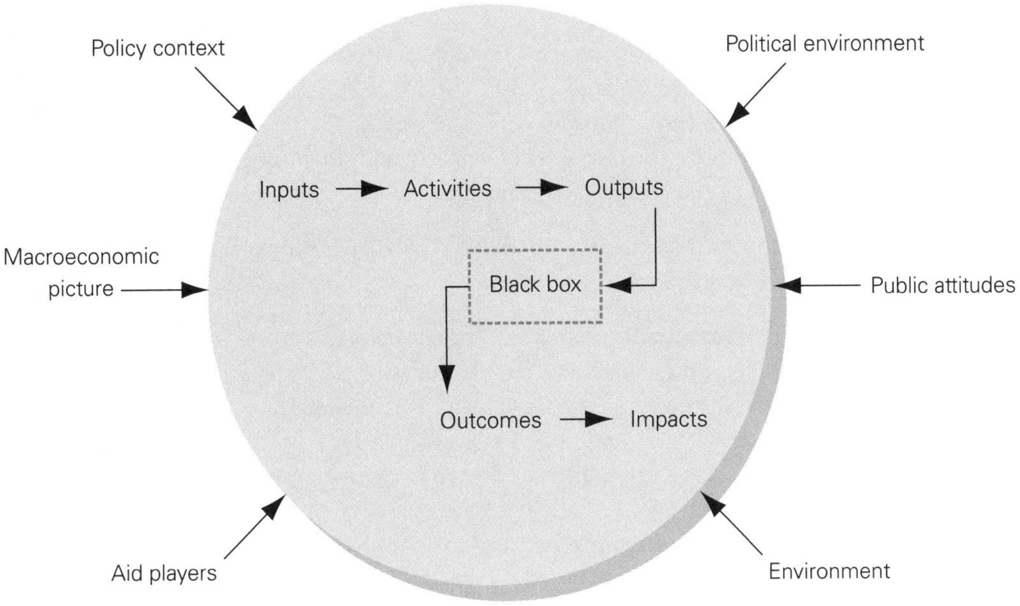

*Source*: Authors.

(political, macroeconomic, policy, and so forth) influences all parts of the system (figure 4.2).

There is a theory of change, often waiting to be articulated, behind every project, program, and policy. The theory may be visually represented in different ways, using different formats or models. These representations are sometimes called *theory models, logic models, change frameworks, logical frameworks, results chain models,* and *outcome models.* Each is a variation on a theme depicting the theory of change. The theory of change should lay out a casual chain, show influences, and identify key assumptions.

## Why Use a Theory of Change?

A theory of change is valuable to both evaluators and stakeholders because it allows them to work together to build "a commonly understood vision of the long-term goals, how they will be reached, and what will be used to measure progress along the way" (ActKnowledge and Aspen Institute 2003).

A theory of change can also be used to report the results of an evaluation. A report by the Kellogg Foundation (2004) discusses the importance of communication in reporting a program's success and sustainability. It identifies three primary ways a depiction of a theory of change can support strategic marketing efforts:

- describing programs in language clear and specific enough to be understood and evaluated
- focusing attention and resources on priority program operations and key results for the purposes of learning and program improvement
- developing targeted communication and marketing strategies.

In sum, articulating the theory of change for a project, program, or policy has several benefits:

- It helps identify elements of programs that are critical to success.
- It helps build a common understanding of the program and expectations among stakeholders based on a common language.
- It provides a foundation for the evaluation.
- It identifies measures for determining progress on intervening variables on which outcomes depend.
- It identifies assumptions that being made, which may become one basis for identifying evaluation questions.

## Constructing a Theory of Change

Managers often develop a theory of change as they conceptualize a project, program, or policy. During this process they may include stakeholders. The theory of change is not always made explicit, however, and it is not always or necessarily consistent from start to finish for a given intervention. For other interventions, a theory of change may not exist. In this case, the evaluator will need to construct one. Examining the theory of change should form the basis of every evaluation.

Before beginning to review or construct a theory of change, evaluators must have a clear understanding of the purpose and goals of the project, program, or policy. Three main questions should be considered:

- Do research and evaluation underlie the project, program, or policy?
- What is the logic or results chain of the project, program, or policy?
- What are the key assumptions being made?

The process begins with learning as much as possible about related interventions and evaluations. With the new information, the process of drawing out the logic of the program and the key assumptions begins. As the logic is identified, it is placed in a chain of events and mapped or drawn. Key assumptions are then identified (figure 4.3).

**Figure 4.3  Process for Constructing a Theory of Change**

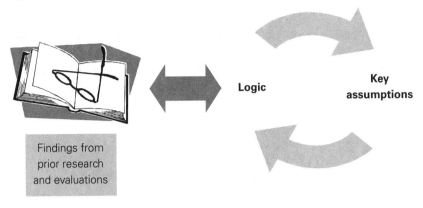

Logic

**Key assumptions**

Findings from prior research and evaluations

*Source:* Authors.

### *Do findings from prior research and evaluations underlie the program?*

Developing a theory of change begins by identifying and reviewing the research and evaluation literature. For example, prior research may show that when other factors are controlled for, a positive relationship is found between student academic performance and parental involvement in the child's homework. Or an evaluation of an earlier education program in an urban area of a developing country may have reported moderately successful findings for a program component involving teacher visits to student homes. Once the literature search is complete and any relevant findings identified, a theory of change can be constructed to predict what will take place as the result of a similar intervention. It may be necessary to construct theories of change without the benefit of findings from prior research or evaluations. In this case, the theories will necessarily be weaker.

A review of the evaluation literature should begin with a broad identification of possible sources of research and evaluative information. Sources include the following:

- evaluative studies conducted by one's own organization
- the Organisation for Economic Co-operation and Development/Development Assistance Committee (OECD/DAC) repository of publications and documents or information by country
- evaluation studies conducted by development organizations, development banks, nongovernmental organizations (NGOs), and others
- articles in evaluation journals
- applied research reported in journals in psychology, sociology, education, and other fields on specific topics
- research on theories of development.

Evaluators in a development organization have been asked to evaluate an education program in Africa whose goal is to improve the achievement of students in the classroom. Evaluators were told that home visits by primary school teachers in a neighboring country were associated with higher student achievement. The evaluators began by exploring the research and evaluation literature. They first looked for research on primary school education and achievement to see what findings were available on similar interventions. They focused on the *International Journal of Educational Research*, the *American Education Research Journal*, *Early Childhood Research and Practice*, and the *Journal of Educational Research*. They also checked the Development Gateway, the DAC Evaluation Resource Centre, and Education Resources Information Center for evaluations. Through this process, the evaluators found some related research and several projects and programs that seemed similar. The evaluation team read the research and evaluation literature to learn as much as they could about issues and findings from similar programs in other countries.

*Source*: Authors.

Executive summaries and conclusions or lessons learned are a good place to determine the relevance of evaluation reports. For research articles, abstracts can be read quickly. With limited time available, evaluators should scan to find important information. Once evaluators locate relevant research and evaluation findings, they need to examine them carefully (box 4.3).

### What is the logic of the program?

The logic of a program, policy, or project looks at the purpose and the goals of an intervention and posits "If *X* happens, then *Y* should happen." Details about the nature of the desired change—the target population, the level of change required to signal success, the timeframe over which such change is expected to occur—are specified. A chain of "if-then" statements—the theory of change—is then created. Small pieces of paper or cards can be used to record statements in the chain of activities. They can easily be moved around, added, or removed as the chain builds.

Evaluators often work backward from the long-term goal, identifying the logical chain of events until they return to the current situation. If a theory of change has already been constructed, the evaluator must go through a similar process to reconstruct the theory of change.

Consider the example of an intervention to train people in the techniques of development evaluation (figure 4.4). The expected results of this intervention would be the production of higher-quality evaluations and the making of better evidence-based decisions by decision makers. (The ultimate goal would be improvements in development, but as so many factors influence development, evaluators do not try to measure this ultimate outcome.) A simple chain for this intervention may include the following: if evaluators are better trained, then they will conduct better evaluations, which then should result in useful information for policy makers, which then will lead to evidence-based decision making. The useful information should result in better decisions by decision makers.

What has been presented so far is a linear model. A good theory of change does not assume simple linear cause-and-effect relationships; it shows complex relationships by using boxes and arrows that link back to earlier—or ahead to later—parts of the theory or change. They also detail key assumptions underlying the model, including the major contextual or environmental factors or events that will likely influence the intervention.

### *What are the key assumptions?*
Initial logic chains often appear linear. When evaluators consider the many factors that interact with their projects, programs, and policies, the theory of change becomes more complex. When identifying the logic of the program, they must also identify the assumptions they are making about the change process. The assumptions that are highest risk for the success of the intervention (the key assumptions) can then be examined and tested as part of the evaluation.

**Figure 4.4   A Simple Theory of Change for Improving Decision Making by Training Evaluators**

*Source*: Authors.

Assumptions usually fall into one of four groups:

- assertions about the connections between long-term, intermediate, and early outcomes on the map
- substantiation for the claim that all of the important preconditions for success have been identified
- justification of the links between program activities and the outcomes they are expected to produce
- implicit or explicit understandings of the contextual or environmental factors that will likely support or hinder progress toward results and the extent to which results are attained.

Evaluators study the emerging logic and investigate their assumptions. Possible questions to ask include the following:

- Is this theory of change plausible? Is the chain of events likely to lead to the long-term goal?
- Is this theory of change feasible? Are the capabilities and resources to implement the strategies possible to produce the outcomes?
- Is this theory testable? Are the measurements of how success will be determined specified? (Anderson 2004)

They also ask this:

- What else is going on in the environment that might help or hinder the intervention?

The assumptions are written down and then included in the chain of events. Small pieces of paper can be used so that they can be reorganized to match the emerging theory.

Not all assumptions should be identified—if they were, the list would be very long. However, key assumptions—those presenting the greatest risk to the program success if found to be false—must be identified.

In the example of the training program, key assumptions may include the following:

- Evaluators do not have readily available sources of training that meet their needs.
- Evaluators can obtain the financial resources for training participation.
- The training is appropriate for the needs of the evaluators.
- Evaluators value the training and are motivated to learn.
- Evaluators will be given the support and other resources they need so they can put into practice what they learn in the training.

- Evaluators will have the report-writing skills needed to communicate the information effectively to the government agency.
- Government decision makers will use the results of the evaluations to make better evidence-based decisions.

For this chain to be effective, the critical assumptions must be addressed. They can be listed along with the theory of change diagram or drawn into the theory of change diagram (figure 4.5).

### Theory of change template

The Kellogg Foundation (2004) suggests evaluators use a template to help them explain the theory of change (figure 4.6).

To use the theory of change template, the Kellogg Foundation suggests that evaluators begin in the middle of the model (Problem or Issue). This is the heart of the template and the core of the theory of change. In this space, the evaluator writes a clear statement of the problem or issue the intervention is to address.

In the second step, Community Needs/Assets, the evaluator specifies the needs and assets of the community or organization. If a needs assessment has been conducted or if the needs of the community or organization have been prioritized, that information should be included here.

In the third step, Desired Results, Kellogg suggests that the evaluator identify what the intervention is expected to achieve in both the near and

Figure 4.5 Simple Theory of Change Diagram with Key Assumptions Identified

*Source*: Authors.

**Figure 4.6 Theory of Change Template**

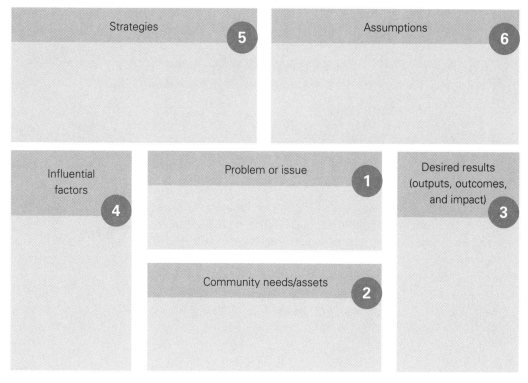

*Source*: Kellogg Foundation 2004.

the long term. This may be mostly a vision of the future. The entries in this box will become the outputs, outcomes, and impacts.

In the fourth step, Influential Factors, Kellogg asks the evaluator to list the potential barriers and supports that may affect the desired change. These may be risk factors, existing policy environment, or other factors. (They may come from the review of the research and evaluation literature or other sources.)

In the fifth step, Strategies, the evaluator is to list general successful strategies the research has identified that helped similar communities or organizations to achieve the kinds of results the project, program, or policy is attempting to elicit ("best practices").

In the last step, Assumptions, Kellogg asks the evaluator to state the assumptions regarding how and why the identified change strategies will work in the community or organization. These may be principles, beliefs, or ideas. The theory of change template can then be used to draw out the graphic representation of the theory of change.

If a group of people is involved in constructing the theory of change, each person (or group) can be given a blank template to complete. When all of the templates are completed, the group can discuss them and come to agreement.

This is one example of a template. It might be revised or adjusted to meet specific organizational needs or practices. For example, an evaluator might want to indicate not only successful strategies but also unsuccessful ones (to avoid).

### Examples of constructing a theory of change

Two examples illustrate how an evaluator constructs a theory of change. The first describes a program to improve academic performance by having teachers visit students' homes. The second describes a program that uses participatory workshops to reduce government corruption.

*Improving student performance through teachers' visits to students' homes.* Consider the following situation. A mature program is due for an evaluation, but it does not have a theory of change. The evaluator needs to begins constructing one by going through the research and evaluation literature (as described in box 4.3). The desired goal of the program is to improve the academic performance of students. The intervention is teachers visiting students' homes. The logic of the situations is as follows: if teachers (input) visit (activity) the homes of their students (input) and talk to parents (output), they will be more empathetic to the child (outcome). Parents will better understand the school's need for homework to be completed on time and for children to attend school every day (output); as a result, they will make sure both happen (outcomes). Because the child does homework, attends school regularly, and has an empathetic teacher, then the child's achievement will increase (impact).

The evaluator creating the theory of change begins with the intended result—higher achievement in reading—and places it at the bottom of the diagram, in this case (figure 4.7). Next, the evaluator identifies the intervention by writing "visits by teachers to student's home" at the top. From there, the evaluator identifies three possible results from home visits:

- Teachers gain an understanding of the home culture of the student.
- Parents gain information about what the school expects of students.
- Both teachers and parents are able to address problems that keep the student from doing well at school.

From each of these three possible results, the evaluator identifies other results, creating chains of results and interacting results. For example, from

**Figure 4.7  Theory of Change for Program to Improve Student Achievement in Reading through Home Visits by Teachers**

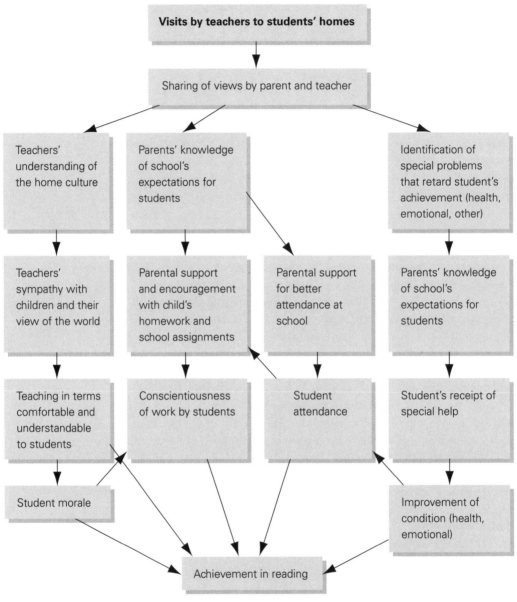

*Source*: Weiss 1972, 50.

the result "teachers' understanding of the home culture," the evaluator identifies a chain of results that includes the following:

- Then teachers gain sympathy for their students and their view of the world.
- Then teachers begin to teach in ways that are more comfortable to the student.
- Then student morale improves.
- Then student achievement in reading improves.

The evaluator then identifies other possible results from each of the original possibilities, all ending with achievement in reading. Some of the chains of results also interact with other possible results.

This theory of change also identifies several assumptions. In this case, they are listed instead of being drawn into the diagram. The assumptions the evaluator identifies are as follows:

- Children come from two-parent families with homes.
- Parents are available and in their homes when the teachers are available.
- Teachers are willing to make the visits.
- Parents will welcome teachers into their homes.
- Parents will feel comfortable discussing their views of educating their children.
- Teachers will better understand the home culture and so will be more empathetic to their students.
- Teachers will adjust their teaching and teaching styles using what they learn from the home visits.
- Parents want to be involved in student learning and want their children to attend school, do their homework, and achieve academically.
- Parents do not need for their children to work.
- Nothing else is going on in the school or home environment that might cause an improvement in student achievement.

The evaluation would be constructed to address those assumptions that the literature or stakeholders have identified as critical.

*Using participatory workshops to combat corruption.* Consider a different example. A program is attempting to introduce participatory workshops to reduce government corruption. To construct the theory of change, the evaluator begins by writing the long-term goal of reducing corruption at the bottom of the diagram and writing the intervention at the top of the diagram. The main events predicted to occur are placed in a chain of events between the two (figure 4.8) (Haaruis 2005).

**Figure 4.8 Theory of Change for Program to Use Participatory Workshops to Reduce Government Corruption**

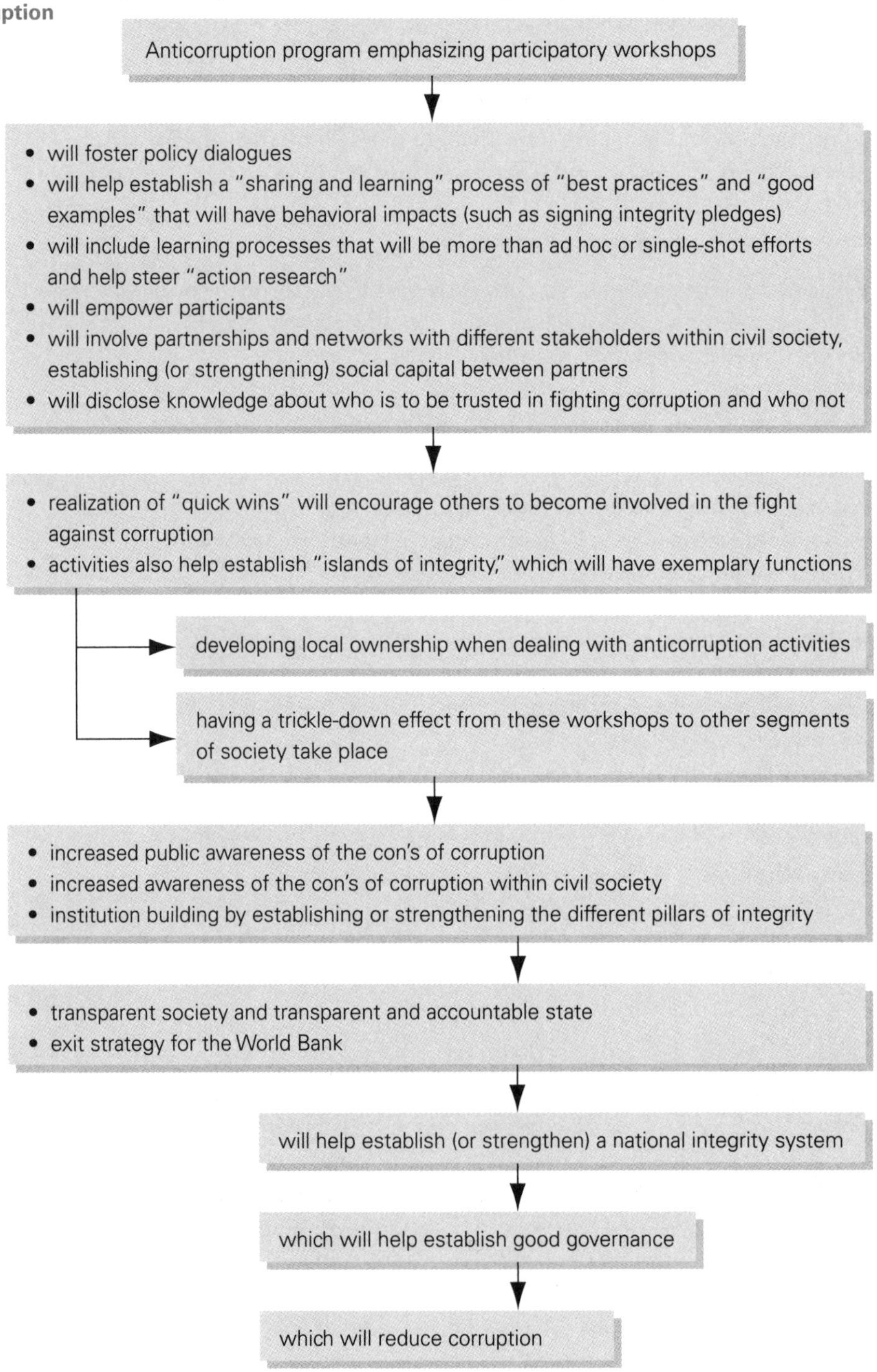

Anticorruption program emphasizing participatory workshops

- will foster policy dialogues
- will help establish a "sharing and learning" process of "best practices" and "good examples" that will have behavioral impacts (such as signing integrity pledges)
- will include learning processes that will be more than ad hoc or single-shot efforts and help steer "action research"
- will empower participants
- will involve partnerships and networks with different stakeholders within civil society, establishing (or strengthening) social capital between partners
- will disclose knowledge about who is to be trusted in fighting corruption and who not

- realization of "quick wins" will encourage others to become involved in the fight against corruption
- activities also help establish "islands of integrity," which will have exemplary functions

developing local ownership when dealing with anticorruption activities

having a trickle-down effect from these workshops to other segments of society take place

- increased public awareness of the con's of corruption
- increased awareness of the con's of corruption within civil society
- institution building by establishing or strengthening the different pillars of integrity

- transparent society and transparent and accountable state
- exit strategy for the World Bank

will help establish (or strengthen) a national integrity system

which will help establish good governance

which will reduce corruption

*Source*: Leeuw, Gils, and Kreft 1999.

Although many assumptions have been identified, the evaluator limits the assumptions to be investigated by the evaluation to three key ones, which are based on the literature review and stakeholder and client discussions:

- The participatory workshops are effective and meet the needs of learners and the program.
- Learners have the skills, attitude, and motivation to participate in the workshops.
- Learners will develop a sense of "local ownership," creating a trickle-down effect.

## Terminology and Graphic Representations of Theory of Change

As program theory has grown to become a major force in evaluation, confusion has arisen over terminology, including terms such as *logic models, outcome models,* and *theory models.* Patton (2002), for example, distinguishes a logic model from a theory of change, stating that the only criterion for a logic model is that it portrays a reasonable, defensible, and sequential order from inputs through activities to outputs, outcomes, and impacts. In contrast, a theory of change must also specify and explain assumed, hypothesized, or tested causal linkages. Regardless of the specific terminology or format used, all theory of change depictions should lay out a casual chain, show influences, and identify key assumptions.

Theory of change models can be presented visually in flow charts in different ways. This section illustrates a few formats.

### *Standard flow chart*

Flow charts are the most common format used to illustrate theory of change. A **flow chart** illustrates the sequence of results that flow (or result) from activities and outputs (figure 4.9). It is a very flexible logic model as long as the core components—inputs, activities, outputs, and results—are presented. Different result levels (immediate, intermediate, final) can be shown to ensure that the flow chart indicates how final results are achieved. When using this format, evaluators need to list their assumptions, including factors in the external environment that could affect the extent to which the intervention achieves its intended results.

The cause–effect linkages can be explained by using "if–then" statements. For example, "if the activity is implemented, then these outputs will be produced. If the outputs are achieved, then they will lead to the first level of immediate results."

■ **Flow chart:** Chart that illustrates the sequence of results that result from activities and outputs

**Figure 4.9   Standard Flow Chart**

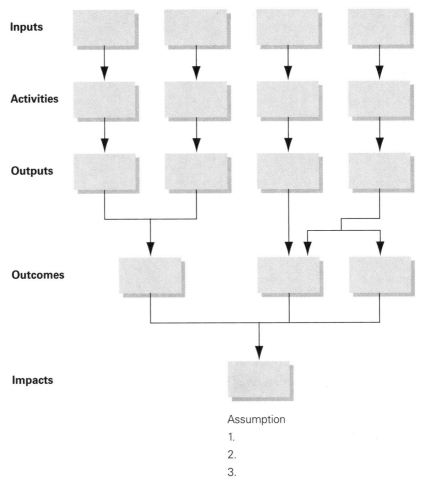

Inputs

Activities

Outputs

Outcomes

Impacts

Assumption
1.
2.
3.

*Source*: Authors.

■ **Results
chain:** Causal
sequence for a
development
intervention that
stipulates the
necessary sequence
to achieve desired
objectives,
beginning with
inputs, moving
through activities
and outputs, and
culminating in
outcomes, impacts,
and feedback

### *Standard flow chart with emphasis on assumptions*

Another design for a theory of change is shown in figure 4.10. This model includes assumptions as the principles behind the design of the initiative.

### *Standard results chain*

A **results chain**—also referred to as a *performance chain*—is similar to a flow chart, but it does not necessarily match specific activities with specific outputs or results. Because it does not show the same detail as a flow chart with respect to the causal sequence of activities, outputs, and results, the user

**Figure 4.10   Flow Chart Emphasizing Assumptions**

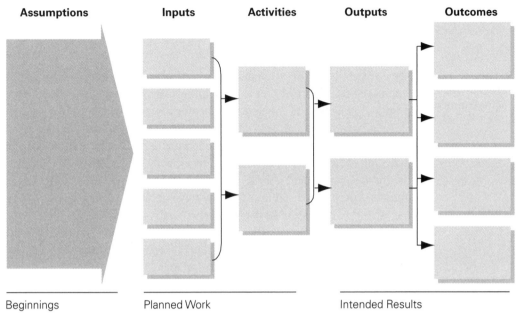

Beginnings                Planned Work                    Intended Results

*Source*: Adapted from Kellogg Foundation 2004.

needs to check that "simplistic" does not replace "standard." As in other
visual depictions, the influence of external factors is explicitly considered.
Inputs, activities, and outputs are often used as measures of efficiency; the
results are used to determine program effectiveness (figure 4.11).

**Figure 4.11   Standard Results Chain**

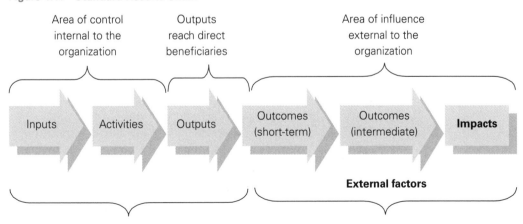

*Source*: Canadian Department of Foreign Affairs and International Trade 2005.

Many examples of completed models are available on the University of Wisconsin Extension Web site. Links to the site are given at the end of this chapter.

### Logical framework (logframe)

■ **Logical framework (logframe):**
Matrix that links the activities, results, purpose, and objectives of a program, policy, or project in a hierarchy

A variant of the theory of change model is the **logical framework,** or as it is commonly called, the logframe. A logframe links the activities, results, purpose, and objectives of a program, policy, or project in a hierarchy. For each of the program, project, or policy components, the evaluator identifies the performance indicators that are needed, the sources of information for each indicator, and the assumptions. Logframes clarify the objectives of a project, program, or policy and identify the causal links between inputs, processes, outputs, outcomes, and impact. Many development organizations require the use of logframes and have trained their staff in using them.

The logframe is essentially a 4 × 4 matrix that summarizes the critical elements of a project, program, or policy. The approach addresses key questions in a methodical manner, using causal logic.

The logframe can be used for a variety of purposes:

- improving the quality of a project, program, or policy design by requiring the specification of clear objectives, the use of performance indicators, and the assessment of risks
- summarizing the design of complex activities
- assisting staff in preparing detailed operational plans
- providing an objective basis for activity review, monitoring, and evaluation (World Bank 2004).

The logframe has been closely critiqued. Important criticisms include the following:

- When developing a logframe, an evaluator can get lost in the details and lose sight of the bigger picture.
- Baseline data are not emphasized.
- Logframes are often too simple, even for simple project designs. As Gasper (1997) notes, "Not everything important can be captured in a one-to-three-page, four-or-five-level diagram."
- Many logframe users fail to recognize that a frame includes some things and leaves others out. A framework is intended as an aid to conducting an evaluation, not a substitute for an evaluation.
- The logframe does not look for unintended outcomes; its scope is limited to stated objectives.
- After a logframe has been prepared, it tends to be fixed and not updated, thus becoming a "lock-frame" (Gasper 1997).

A logframe for a well-baby clinic could include immunizations as one of its activities, with a target result of immunizing 50 percent of all children under age six in a particular district (table 4.3). If this target is achieved, the incidence of preventable childhood diseases should decrease. This decline should achieve the overall objective of reducing the number of deaths of children under age six.

The second column in table 4.3 identifies the indicators that verify the extent to which each objective has been achieved. The third and fourth columns specify where the data will be obtained in order to assess performance against the indicators, and any assumptions made about the nature and accessibility of those data.

## Assessing a Theory of Change

Once the theory of change is constructed, evaluators need to step back and assess the quality of the theory from different viewpoints. These viewpoints or frameworks include assessment

- in relation to social needs
- of logic and plausibility
- by comparing with research and practice
- by comparing the program theory of change with one or more relevant scientific theories
- via preliminary observation (adapted from Rossi, Freeman, and Lipsey 1999).

The theory of change should be able to answer the following questions:

- Is the model an accurate depiction of the program?
- Are all elements well defined?
- Are there any gaps in the logical chain of events?
- Are elements necessary and sufficient?
- Are relationships plausible and consistent?
- Is it realistic to assume that the program will result in the attainment of stated goals in a meaningful manner?

The Kellogg Foundation (2004) developed a checklist to asses the quality of a logic model. The following list of criteria is adapted from that checklist:

- Major activities needed to implement the program are listed.
- Activities are clearly connected to the specified program theory.
- Major resources needed to implement the program are listed.
- Resources match the type of program.
- All activities have sufficient and appropriate resources.

**Table 4.3   Logical Framework for Program to Reduce Child Mortality**

| Component | Performance indicators | Verification | Assumptions |
|---|---|---|---|
| *Goal:* Improve the economic and social welfare of women and their families | Improvements in family income × percentage of participating families. Improvements in measures of health status, nutritional status, and educational participation | Household surveys of the economic, social, and health condition of all family members | Other family members maintain or improve their employment and earnings. Economic conditions remain stable or improve. |
| *Objective:* Provide women with opportunities to earn and learn while their children are cared for in home day care centers | • Day care homes functioning, providing accessible, affordable care of adequate quality during working hours and thus allowing shifts in women's employment and education activities | From surveys: changes in women's employment and education and their evaluations of care provided. Evaluations of quality of care provided on basis of observation | Family conditions allow home day care mothers to carry through on their agreements to provide care. |
| *Outputs*<br>• Trained caregivers, supervisors, and directors<br>• Day care homes upgraded and operating<br>• Materials developed<br>• Administrative system in place<br>• Management information system (MIS) in place | • Caregivers trained<br>• Homes upgraded and operating<br>• Materials created and distributed<br>• Functioning MIS | Data from MIS on trainees, homes, and materials. Evaluations of trainees After initial training and during course of continuous training | |
| *Activities*<br>• Select caregivers and supervisors and provide initial training.<br>• Upgrade homes.<br>• Develop materials.<br>• Develop administrative system.<br>• Deliver home day care.<br>• Provide continuous training and supervision.<br>• Develop an MIS. | *Resources*<br>Budget<br>Technology<br>Human resources | Plan of action, budgets, and accounting records. Studies showing that the chosen model and curriculum work. Evaluations to determine that activities were carried out well | |

*Source:* Inter-American Development Bank (http://www.iadb.org/sds/soc/eccd/6example.html#ex1).

## Summary

Evaluators must resist the urge to rush into an evaluation without a plan. A front-end analysis is a valuable part of planning that helps evaluators get a larger picture of the project, program, or policy. The front-end analysis can answer important questions about the evaluation, including timing, time to complete, people involved, resources, design, program theory and logic, and existing knowledge.

One part of the front-end analysis is identifying people or groups involved in the intervention. Stakeholder analysis is one way to identify the key evaluation stakeholders and determine what they know about, what they can contribute to, and what they expect from the evaluation.

Another part of front-end analysis is looking at the context of the intervention. Evaluators must identify and learn from related research and from evaluations of similar interventions. Evaluators ask different questions at different stages of the life cycle of an intervention, so identifying the stage of the intervention is important.

Constructing a theory of change underlying an intervention helps evaluators and stakeholders visualize the intervention and determine the assumptions underlying the program that will need to be examined in the evaluation. While there are different ways to graphically depict a theory of change, all should be based on the findings of related research and evaluations, depict the logical flow, identify events that may influence the results, and show a causal chain of events. Typically, theories of change depict inputs, activities, outputs, and results, as well as their interrelationships with one another and the environment in which they take place.

# Chapter 4 Activities

### Activity 4.1: Applying the Theory of Change

Consider a microlending program that aims to promote new livelihoods and improve household well-being by helping women, particularly poor rural women, enter the labor force and build entrepreneurial skills, thereby increasing household income. The long-term goal is to promote private sector development and increase economic growth. Loans average US$225, with a maximum size of US$500. They are provided as lump sums for working capital or investment in a microenterprise. Loan maturities range from 1 to 10 years, with an average maturity of 2–3 years. A grace period of one year is provided. The associated capacity building component covers basic bookkeeping and financial management. Figure A shows a simplified logic model depicting the microlending program. Figure B shows a more detailed graphical depiction of the theory of change for the same microlending program. The circled items in figure B show some major factors in the environment that may influence attainment of the program's goal. Think about the assumptions underlying this program.

List five key assumptions underlying this program:

1. _____

2. _____

3. _____

4. _____

5. _____

### Figure A  Simple Theory of Change for a Microlending Program

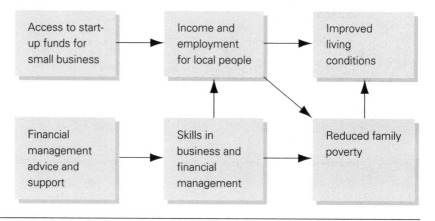

**Figure B   More Complex Theory of Change for a Microlending Program**

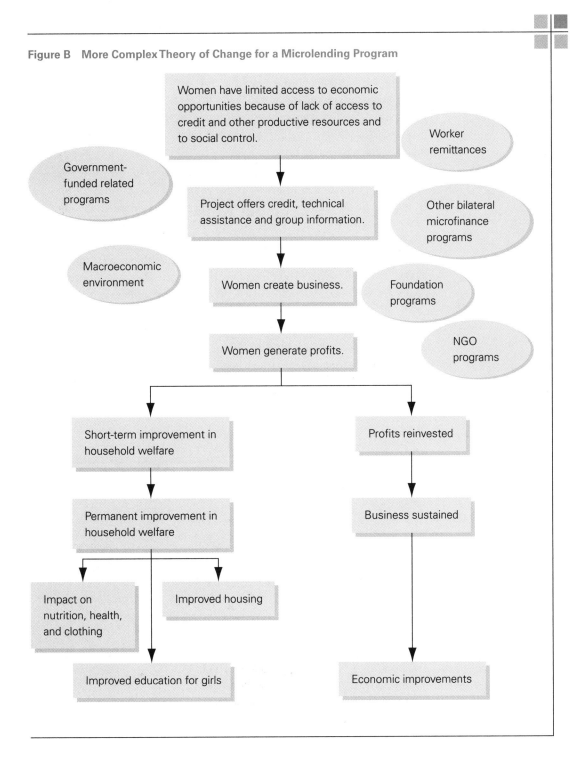

Women have limited access to economic opportunities because of lack of access to credit and other productive resources and to social control.

Worker remittances

Government-funded related programs

Project offers credit, technical assistance and group information.

Other bilateral microfinance programs

Macroeconomic environment

Women create business.

Foundation programs

Women generate profits.

NGO programs

Short-term improvement in household welfare

Profits reinvested

Permanent improvement in household welfare

Business sustained

Impact on nutrition, health, and clothing

Improved housing

Improved education for girls

Economic improvements

## Application Exercise 4.2: Analyzing Your Program

Consider a program or project you are currently working with or one with which you are familiar but not directly involved. Develop a graphic showing the theory of change for this program or project. Be sure to identify the assumptions underlying the program or project, especially those related to external environmental factors.

## References and Further Reading

ActKnowledge and Aspen Institute. 2003. *Theory of Change*. Roundtable on Community Change.
http://www.theoryofchange.org/.

Anderson, Andrea, A. 2004. "The Community Builder's Approach to Theory of Change: A Practical Guide to Theory Development." Presentation at the Aspen Institute Roundtable on Community Change, New York.
http://www.aspeninstitute.org/atf/cf/ percent7BDEB6F227-659B-4EC8-8F84-8DF23CA704F5 percent7D/rcccommbuildersapproach.pdf.

Bell, P. 1997. "Using Argument Representations to Make Thinking Visible for Individuals and Groups." In *Proceedings of CSCL '97: The Second International Conference on Computer Support for Collaborative Learning*, eds. R. Hall, N. Miyake, and N. Enyedy, 10–19. Toronto: University of Toronto Press.

Bruning, R. H., G. J. Schraw, M. M. Norby, and R. R. Ronning. 2004. *Cognitive Psychology and Instruction*. 4th ed. Upper Saddle River, NJ: Pearson Merrill Prentice-Hall.

Canadian Department of Foreign Affairs and International Trade. 2005. *Six Easy Steps to Managing for Results: A Guide for Managers*. April. Evaluation Division, Ottawa.

CIDA (Canadian International Development Agency). 2005. *Case Study #1: Jamaica Environmental Action Program ENACT*. Caribbean Division, Americas Branch.
http://www.acdi-cida.gc.ca/CIDAWEB/acdicida.nsf/En/EMA-218131811-PHY#1.

Eggen, P., and D. Kauchak. 1999. *Educational Psychology: Windows on Classrooms*. 4th ed. Upper Saddle River, NJ: Merrill: Prentice-Hall.

Fitzpatrick, Jody L., James R. Sanders, and Blaine R. Worthen. 2004. *Program Evaluation: Alternative Approaches and Practical Guidelines*. New York: Person Education.

Funnell, S. 1997. "Program Logic: An Adaptable Tool for Designing and Evaluating Programs." *Evaluation News and Comment* 6 (1): 5–7.

Gagne, R. M., and W. D. Rohwer Jr. 1969. "Instructional Psychology." *Annual Review of Psychology* 20: 381–418.

Gasper, D. 1997. "Logical Frameworks: A Critical Assessment Managerial Theory." Pluralistic Practice Working Paper 264, Institute of Social Studies, The Hague.

———. 2000. "Evaluating the 'Logical Framework Approach' towards Learning-Oriented Development Evaluation." *Public Administration Development* 20 (1): 17–28.

Haarhuis, Carolien Klein. 2005. "Promoting Anticorruption Reforms: Evaluating the Implementation of a World Bank Anticorruption Program in Seven African Countries." http://igitur-archive.library.uu.nl/dissertations/2005-0714-200002/full.pdf.

Healy, A. F, and D. S. McNamara. 1996. "Verbal Learning Memory: Does the Modal Model Still Work?" *Annual Review of Psychology* 47: 143–72.

Heubner, T. A. 2000. "Theory-Based Evaluation: Gaining a Shared Understanding Between School Staff and Evaluators." In *Program Theory in Evaluation: Challenges and Opportunities,* eds. Patricia J. Rogers, T. A. Hacsi, A. Petrosino, and T. A. Huebner, 79–90. New Directions for Evaluation No. 87. San Francisco, CA: Jossey-Bass.

Kassinove, H., and M. Summers. 1968. "The Developmental Attention Test: A Preliminary Report on an Objective Test of Attention." *Journal of Clinical Psychology* 24 (1): 76–78.

Kellogg Foundation. 2004. *Logic Model Development Guide.* Battle Creek, MI. http://www.wkkf.org/Pubs/Tools/Evaluation/Pub3669.pdf.

Leeuw, Frans, Ger Gils, and Cora Kreft. 1999. "Evaluating Anti-Corruption Initiatives: Underlying Logic and Mid-Term Impact of a World Bank Program." *Evaluation* 5 (2): 194–219.

Leeuw, Frans L. 1991. "Policy Theories, Knowledge Utilization, and Evaluation." *Knowledge and Policy* 4: 73–92.

———. 2003. "Reconstructing Program Theories: Models Available and Problems to Be Solved." *American Journal of Evaluation* 24 (1): 5–20.

Mikkelsen, B. 2005. *Methods for Development Work and Research: A New Guide for Practitioners.* Thousand Oaks, CA: Sage Publications.

MSH (Management Sciences for Health), and UNICEF (United Nations Children's Fund). 1998. "Quality Guide: Stakeholder Analysis." In *Guide to Managing for Quality.* http://ERC.MSH.org/quality.

Newman, David Kent. 2007. "Theory: Write-up for Conceptual Framework." http://deekayen.net/theory-write-conceptual-framework.

Ormrod, J. E. 2006. *Essentials of Educational Psychology.* Upper Saddle River, NJ: Pearson Merrill Prentice-Hall.

Owen, J. M., and P. J. Rogers. 1999. *Program Evaluation: Forms and Approaches.* Thousand Oaks, CA: Sage Publications.

Pancer, S. Mark, and Anne Westhues. 1989. "A Developmental Stage Approach to Program Planning and Evaluation." *Evaluation Review* 13 (1): 56–77.

Patton, M. Q. 2002. *Qualitative Research and Evaluation Methods.* 3rd ed. Thousand Oaks, CA.: Sage Publications.

Pawson, Ray. 2006. *Evidence-Based Policy: A Realistic Perspective.* New Brunswick, NJ: Sage Publications.

Petrosino, Anthony, Robert A. Boruch, Cath Rounding, Steve McDonald, and Iain Chalmers. 2003. "The Campbell Collaboration Social, Psychological, Educational, and Criminological Trials Register C2OSPECTR." http://www.campbellcollaboration.org/papers/unpublished/petrosino.pdf.

Porteous, Nancy L., B. J. Sheldrick, and P. J. Stewart. 1997. *Program Evaluation Tool Kit: A Blueprint for Public Health Management.* Ottawa-Carleton Health Department, Ottawa. http://www.phac-aspc.gc.ca/php-psp/tookit.html.

———. 2002. "Introducing Program Teams to Logic Models: Facilitating the Learning Process." *Canadian Journal of Program Evaluation* 17 (3): 113–41.

Prensky, Marc. 2001. "Digital Natives, Digital Immigrants." *On the Horizon* 9 (5). http://www.marcprensky.com/writing/Prensky percent20-percent20Digital percent20Natives,percent20Digital percent20Immigrants percent20-percent20Part1.pdf.

Ritzer, George. 1993. *The McDonaldization of Society.* Rev. ed. Thousand Oaks, CA: Pine Forge Press.

Rogers, Patricia J., T. A. Hacsi, A. Petrosino, and T. A. Huebner, eds. 2000. *Program Theory in Evaluation: Challenges and Opportunities.* New Directions in Evaluation No. 87. San Francisco: Jossey-Bass Publishers.

Rossi, P., H. Freeman, and M. Lipsey. 1999. *Evaluation: A Systematic Approach.* Thousand Oaks, CA: Sage Publications.

Scott, M. 2003. "The Benefits and Consequences of Police Crackdowns." *Problem-Oriented Guides for Police, Response Guide 1.* U.S. Department of Justice, Office of Community-Oriented Policing Services, Washington, DC.

Scriven, Michael. 2007. *Key Evaluation Checklist.* http://www.wmich.edu/evalctr/checklists/kec_feb07.pdf.

Shadish, W. R. Jr., T. D. Cook, and L. C. Leviton. 1991. *Foundations of Program Evaluation.* Thousand Oaks, CA: Sage Publications.

Sherman, L. W., D. Farrington, B. C. Welsh, and D. L. MacKenzie, eds. 2002. *Evidence-Based Crime Prevention.* London: Routledge.

Stufflebeam, Daniel L. 2001. *Evaluation Models.* New Directions for Evaluation No. 89. San Francisco, CA: Jossey-Bass.

Stufflebeam, D. L., G. F Madaus, and T. Kellaghan, eds. 2000. *Evaluation Models.* 2nd ed. Boston: Kluwer Academic Publishers.

Suthers, D. D., and A. Weiner. 1995. *Belvédère.* http://lilt.ics.hawaii.edu/belvedere/index.html.

Suthers, D. D., E. E. Toth, and A. Weiner 1997. "An Integrated Approach to Implementing Collaborative Inquiry in the Classroom." In *Proceedings of CSCL '97: The Second International Conference on Computer Support for Collaborative Learning,* eds. R. Hall, N. Miyake, and N. Enyedy, 272–79. Toronto: University of Toronto Press.

Swedberg, Richard. 2003. *Principles of Economic Sociology.* Princeton, NJ: Princeton University Press.

Taylor-Powell, Ellen. 2005. *Logic Models: A Framework for Program Planning and Evaluation*. University of Wisconsin Extension, Program Development and Evaluation. http://www.uwex.edu/ces/pdande/evaluation/pdf/nutritionconf05.pdf.

U.S. GAO (General Accounting Office). 1991. *Designing Evaluations*. Washington, DC. http://www.gao.gov/special.pubs/10_1_4.pdf.

Weiss, Carol H. 1997. *Evaluation: Methods for Studying Programs and Policies*. Upper Saddle River, NJ: Prentice-Hall.

World Bank. 1996. *World Bank Participation Sourcebook*. Washington, DC: World Bank. http://www.worldbank.org/wbi/sourcebook/sbhome.htm.

———. 2004. *Monitoring and Evaluation: Some Tools, Methods and Approaches*. Operations Evaluation Department/Evaluation Capacity Development, Washington, DC. http://lnweb18.worldbank.org/oed/oeddoclib.nsf/b57456d58aba40e585256ad 400736404/a5efbb5d776b67d285256b1e0079c9a3/$FILE/MandE_tools_ methods_approaches.pdf.

Worthen, Blaine. R., James R. Sanders, and Jody L. Fitzpatrick. 1997. *Program Evaluation*. New York: Longman.

## Web Sites

Campbell Collaboration. http://www.campbellcollaboration.org/.

Community Toolbox. *A Framework for Program Evaluation: A Gateway to Tools*. http://ctb.lsi.ukans.edu/tools/EN/sub_section_main_1338.htm.

Evaluation Center, Western Michigan University. *The Checklist Project*. http://www .wmich.edu/evalctr/checklists/checklistmenu.htm#mgt.

IDRC (International Development Research Centre). 2004. *Evaluation Planning in Program Initiatives* Ottawa, Ontario, Canada. http://web.idrc.ca/uploads/ user-S/108549984812guideline-web.pdf.

Suthers, D., and A. Weiner. 1995. *Groupware for Developing Critical Discussion Skills*. http://www-cscl95.indiana.edu/cscl95/suthers.html.

University of Wisconsin-Extension. *Logic Model*. http://www.uwex.edu/ces/ pdande/evaluation/evallogicmodel.html.

———. *Examples of Logic Models*. http://www.uwex.edu/ces/pdande/evaluation/ evallogicmodelexamples.html.

## Theories of Change

Audience Dialogue. 2007a. "Enhancing Program Performance with Logic Models." http://www.uwex.edu/ces/lmcourse/, http://www.wkkf.org/pubs/tools/ evaluation/pub3669.pdf.

———. 2007b. "Program Logic: An Introduction." http://www.audiencedialogue.org/ proglog.htm.

AusAid. 2005. "Section 3.3: The Logical Framework Approach and Section 2.2: Using the Results Framework Approach." http://www.ausaid.gov.au/ausguide/default.cfm.

BOND. 2001. *Guidance Notes Series I: Beginner's Guide to Logical Framework Analysis.* http://www.ngosupport.net/graphics/NGO/documents/english/273_BOND_Series_1.doc.

Davies, Rick. 2003. "Network Perspective in the Evaluation of Development Interventions: More than a Metaphor." Paper presented at the EDAIS Conference "New Directions in Impact Assessment for Development: Methods and Practice," November 24–25. http://www.enterprise-impact.org.uk/conference/Abstracts/Davies.shtml and http://www.mande.co.uk/docs/nape.doc.

Department for International Development. 2002. *Tools for Development: A Handbook for Those Engaged in Development Activity Performance and Effectiveness.* http://www.dfid.gov.uk/pubs/files/toolsfordevelopment.pdf.

den Heyer, Molly. 2001a. *A Bibliography for Program Logic Models/Logframe Analysis.* Evaluation Unit, International Development Research Centre. http://www.idrc.ca/uploads/user-S/10553606170logframebib2.pdf and http://www.mande.co.uk/docs/Phillips.ppt.

———. 2001b. "The Temporal Logic Model™: A Concept Paper." http://www.idrc.ca/uploads/user-S/10553603900tlmconceptpaper.pdf.

Inter-American Development Bank. http://www.iadb.org/sds/soc/eccd/bexample.html#ex1.

International Fund for Agricultural Development. 2003. *Annotated Example of a Project Logframe Matrix.* http://www.ifad.org/evaluation/guide/3/3.htm and http://www.ifad.org/evaluation/guide/annexb/index.htm.

JISC infoNet. 2001. *Engendering the Logical Framework.* http://www.jiscinfonet.ac.uk/InfoKits/project-management/InfoKits/infokit-related-files/logical-framework-information.

———. 2004. *Logical Framework (LogFRAME) Methodology.* http://www.jiscinfonet.ac.uk/InfoKits/project-management/InfoKits/infokit-related-files/logical-framework-information.

Kellogg Foundation. 2004. *Evaluation Logic Model Development Guide: Using Logic Models to Bring Together Planning, Evaluation, and Action.* http://www.wkkf.org./Pubs/Tools/Evaluation/Pub3669.pdf.

Knowledge and Research Programme on Disability and Healthcare Technology. 2004. *Constructing a Logical Framework.* http://www.kar-dht.org/logframe.html.

McCawley, Paul F. 1997. *The Logic Model for Program Planning and Evaluation.* University of Idaho Extension. http://www.uidaho.edu/extension/LogicModel.pdf.

NORAD (Norwegian Agency for Development Cooperation). 1999. *The Logical Framework Approach: Handbook for Objectives-Oriented Planning.* 4th ed. http://www.norad.no/default.asp?V_ITEM_ID=1069.

PPM&E Resource. 2005. *Logical Framework Approach.* portals.wdi.wur.nl/ppme/index.php?Logical_Framework_Approach.

Rugh, Jim. "The Rosetta Stone of Logical Frameworks." http://www.mande.co.uk/docs/Rosettastone.doc.

SIDA (Swedish International Development Agency). 2004. *The Logical Framework Approach: A Summary of the Theory behind the LFA Method.* http://www.sida .se/shared/jsp/download.jsp?f=SIDA1489en_web.pdf&a=2379.

Usable Knowledge, USA. 2006. Online Logic Model Training: An Audiovisual Presentation. http://www.usablellc.net/Logic percent20Modelpercent20percent 28Online percent29/Presentation_Files/index.html.

Weiss, Carol. 1972. *Evaluation Research: Methods for Assessing Program Effectiveness.* Englewood Cliffs, New Jersey: Prentice Hall.

Wikipedia. 2006. "Logical Framework Approach." http://en.wikipedia.org/wiki/ Logical_framework_approach.

## Critiques of the Logical Framework

Bakewell, Oliver, and Anne Garbutt. 2006. *The Use and Abuse of the Logical Framework Approach A Review of International Development NGOs' Experiences.* Swedish International Development Agency. http://www.sida.se/shared/jsp/ download.jsp?f=LFA-review.pdf&a=21025.

MISEREOR. 2005. *Methodological Critique and Indicator Systems.* http://www .misereor.org/index.php?id=4495.

## Alternative Versions of the Logical Framework

Broughton, Bernard. 2005. *A Modified Logframe for Use in Humanitarian Emergencies.* http://www.mande.co.uk/docs/EmergencyLogframeBroughton.doc.

Shaikh, Partha Hefaz. 2005. *Intertwining Participation, Rights-Based Approach and Log Frame: A Way Forward in Monitoring and Evaluation for Rights-Based Work.* http://www.mande.co.uk/docs/PIFA_Article_PDF.pdf. SIDA Civil Society Centre. 2006. *Logical Framework Approach, with an Appreciative Approach.* http://www.sida.se/shared/jsp/download.jsp?f=SIDA28355en_LFA_web .pdf&a=23355.

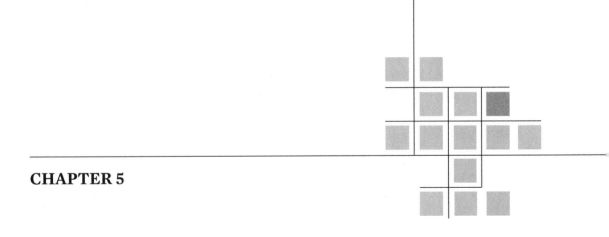

**CHAPTER 5**

# Considering the Evaluation Approach

Development has moved from focusing on projects to focusing on programs and policies, with an emphasis on sustainability. A wide variety of approaches to designing and conducting evaluations has been used to address these broader and more complex subjects. This chapter looks at some of these approaches.

**This chapter discusses the following:**

- General Approaches to Evaluation
- Their Strengths and Challenges

# General Approaches to Evaluation

Since the 1990s, the international community has been moving slowly from projects to programs to partnership approaches to development assistance (see table 1.3). Partnership approaches include a larger number of stakeholders, who are involved to a greater extent in more complex operations, such as sectorwide funding approaches. Evaluations of large programs have consequently become more participatory and jointly conducted, although joint evaluations are yet the norm. Renewed calls for increased untied funding to governments—such as those voiced in Accra in 2008—imply greater evaluation challenges for the future.

A variety of approaches has been developed to meet the changing nature of development evaluation. The choice of evaluation approach depends partly on the context. Approaches are not necessarily mutually exclusive, and evaluations may combine elements of two or more approaches. The approaches include the following:

- prospective evaluation
- evaluability assessment
- goal-based evaluation
- goal-free evaluation
- multisite evaluation
- cluster evaluation
- social assessment
- environmental and social assessment
- participatory evaluation
- outcome mapping
- rapid assessment
- evaluation synthesis and meta-evaluation
- other approaches.

Whatever approach is chosen, the same planning steps must be taken: defining evaluation questions, identifying measures, collecting and analyzing data, and reporting and using findings.

## Prospective Evaluation

■ **Prospective evaluation:** Evaluation of the likely outcomes of a proposed project, program, or policy

A **prospective evaluation** is conducted ex ante—that is, a proposed program is reviewed before it begins, in an attempt to analyze its likely success, predict its cost, and analyze alternative proposals and projections. Prospective evaluations have been conducted by evaluation organizations within legislative branches. An example is the U.S. Government Accountability Office

**Table 5.1 Types of Forward-Looking Questions and Ways of Addressing Them**

| Purpose of question | Critique others' analysis | Conduct own analyses |
|---|---|---|
| Anticipate the future | How well has the administration projected future needs, costs, and consequences? | What are future needs, costs, and consequences? |
| Improve future actions | What is the likely success of an administration or congressional proposal? | What course of action has the greatest potential for success? |

*Source*: U.S. GAO 1990.

(GAO)—renamed as such in 2004—which reports to the U.S. Congress. GAO evaluators sometimes assist government decision makers by providing analytical information on issues and options on potential programs (U.S. GAO 1990).

The GAO is often asked about the likely success of proposed new programs. It reviews information on alternative proposals and analyzes the results of similar programs that may be ongoing or completed. Table 5.1 identifies four kinds of forward-looking questions the GAO is asked to investigate.

Most prospective evaluations involve the following kinds of activities:

- a contextual analysis of the proposed program or policy
- a review of evaluation studies on similar programs or policies and synthesis of the findings and lessons from the past
- a prediction of likely success or failure, given a future context that is not too different from the past, and suggestions on strengthening the proposed program and policy if decision makers want to go forward (GAO 1990).

(Resources on and examples of various types of assessments are provided in the list of Web sites at the end of this chapter.)

## Evaluability Assessment

An **evaluability assessment** is a brief preliminary study undertaken to determine whether an evaluation would be useful and feasible. This type of preliminary study helps clarify the goals and objectives of the program or project, identify data resources available, pinpoint gaps and identify data that need to be developed, and identify key stakeholders and clarify their information needs. It may also redefine the purpose of the evaluation and the methods for conducting it. By looking at the intervention as implemented on

■ **Evaluability assessment:** Brief preliminary study undertaken to determine whether an evaluation would be useful and feasible

the ground and the implications for the timing and design of the evaluation, an evaluability assessment can save time and help avoid costly mistakes.

Wholey and his colleagues developed the evaluability assessment approach in the early 1970s to address their belief that many evaluations failed because of discrepancies between "rhetoric and reality" (Nay and Kay 1982, p. 225). They saw evaluability assessment as a means of facilitating communication between evaluators and stakeholders. They proposed using evaluability assessment as a means for determining whether a program was "evaluable" and for focusing the evaluation (Fitzpatrick, Sanders, and Worthen 2004). Evaluability assessment was originally developed as a precursor to summative evaluation; its role has since expanded to include clarifying the purposes of a formative study or to function as a planning tool (Smith 1989).

In an evaluabilty assessment, evaluators perform preliminary work to determine if an evaluation can be conducted. If, for example, a goal-based (or objectives-based) evaluation is proposed, the lack of clear program objectives or agreement among stakeholders may be problematic. Until there is clarification and agreement, evaluation may be premature. Sometimes measures are unavailable or inaccessible. In this case, they need to be developed before the intervention can be evaluated.

Evaluability assessment thus focuses on the feasibility of conducting an evaluation. If it is not feasible to design an evaluation from available information or the intervention lacks a coherent theory of change, more preliminary work needs to be done. An evaluability assessment can help clarify the intervention and the desired results. It often creates a dialogue on the goals and objectives, outputs, target population, and intended outcomes of an intervention so that agreement can be reached on what is to be achieved.

Evaluability assessments are often conducted by a group, including stakeholders, such as implementers, and administrators, as well as evaluators. To conduct an evaluability assessment, the team

- reviews materials that define and describe the intervention
- identifies modifications to the intervention
- interviews managers and staff on their perceptions of the intervention's goals and objectives
- interviews stakeholders on their perceptions of the intervention's goals and objectives
- develops or refines a theory of change model
- identifies sources of data
- identifies people and organizations that can implement any possible recommendations from the evaluation.

One of the potential benefits of evaluability assessment is that it can lead to a more realistic and appropriate evaluation. Smith (1989) and Wholey (1987) also point out that it can improve

- the ability to distinguish between intervention failure and evaluation failure
- the estimation of longer-term outcomes
- stakeholder investment in the intervention
- intervention performance
- intervention development and evaluation skills of staff
- the visibility of and accountability for the intervention
- administrative understanding of the intervention
- policy choices
- continued support for the intervention.

## Goal-Based Evaluation

A **goal-based (or objectives-based) evaluation** measures the extent to which a program or intervention attains clear and specific objectives (Patton 1990). The focus of the evaluation is on the stated outcomes (the goals or objectives) of the project, program, or policy. This is the typical evaluation with which most people are familiar; it is the basis of most development organizations' project evaluation systems.

■ **Goal-based evaluation:** Evaluation that measures the extent to which a program or intervention attains clear and specific objectives

One criticism of the goal-based approach is that it concentrates on the economical and technical aspects instead of the social and human aspects (Hirschheim and Smithson 1988). A second criticism is that such evaluations focus only on stated goals. Achievement of other important goals—which may be implicit rather than explicit or may have been discussed during board meetings or division meetings but not included in the stated project goals—is not evaluated. A third related criticism is that they do not look for unintended effects (positive or negative).

These may be serious oversights. An evaluation of a new water treatment plant, for example, may focus on the stated project objectives of building, operating, and maintaining a water treatment facility to produce clean water at a certain volume each day to meet the needs of a certain number of households or communities. The effects on the people living on the land who need to be relocated before construction can begin are often overlooked. Failure to articulate a goal or objective for the relocation that leaves people with improved, sustainable livelihoods represents a serious omission. The evaluation compounds the problem if it does not ask questions about the relocation because it was not a formal, explicit project objective.

The evaluation should look for unanticipated positive or negative effects of the intervention. Though no specific objective may have been articulated, it may be useful for the evaluation to document reduced incidence of water-borne diseases in the communities now receiving potable water.

Results-based evaluation, the method advocated in this text, looks for results—whether or not they were articulated as goals or objectives. Goal-based evaluations can be strengthened by being open to unexpected positive or negative results.

### Goal-Free Evaluation

Goal-free evaluation was developed as a reaction to goal-based (or objectives-based) evaluation. Scriven (1972b), who first proposed goal-free evaluation, has been a major advocate of this approach.

**Goal-free evaluation:** Evaluation in which evaluators make a deliberate attempt to avoid all rhetoric related to program goals, basing evaluation solely on degree to which it meets participants' needs

In **goal-free evaluation**, the evaluator makes a deliberate attempt to avoid all rhetoric related to program goals. Evaluators do not discuss goals with staff or read program brochures or proposals. They evaluate only the program's observable outcomes and documentable effects in relation to participant needs (Patton 2002). As Scriven (1972b, p. 2) notes:

> It seemed to me, in short, that consideration and evaluation of goals was an unnecessary but also a possibly contaminating step.... The less the external evaluator hears about the goals of the project, the less tunnel-vision will develop, the more attention will be paid to looking for actual effects (rather than checking on alleged effects).

Goal-free evaluations gather data on the effects and effectiveness of programs without being constrained by a narrow focus on goals or objectives. Such evaluations capture the actual experiences of program participants in their own terms. They require that evaluators suspend judgment about what a program is trying to do in order to focus instead on finding out what is actually occurring. For these reasons, it is especially compatible with qualitative inquiry, although it can employ both quantitative and qualitative methods.

Scriven (1997) proposes conducting separate goal-free and goal-based evaluations in order to maximize the strengths and minimize the weaknesses of each approach.

Wholey, Harty, and Newcomer (1994) describe the following characteristics of goal-free evaluation:

- The evaluator avoids becoming aware of the program goals.
- Predetermined goals are not permitted to narrow the focus of the evaluation study.
- The evaluator has minimal contact with the program manager and staff.
- The focus is on actual rather than intended program outcomes.

It is generally difficult in the development context to avoid knowing an intervention's goals and objectives. It may not be feasible or desirable for the evaluator to have minimal contact with program staff. Nonetheless, by taking a results-based approach, the evaluator can use many of the elements of a goal-free evaluation.

## Multisite Evaluations

In a large-scale intervention, it is often necessary to look at interventions implemented at a variety of locations. These are called **multisite evaluations.** The intervention may have been implemented in the same way in all locations or implemented somewhat differently in some locations. A multisite evaluation provides information about the overall experience of the intervention as well as a deeper understanding of the variations that occurred. It may answer questions such as the following:

■ **Multisite evaluation:** Evaluation that examines interventions implemented at a variety of locations

- What features of the intervention implementation are common to all locations?
- Which features vary and why?
- Are there differences in outcomes based on those variations?

Obtaining in-depth information is key. To do so, evaluators often use case studies for multisite evaluation. Sites are generally selected for study because they represent certain characteristics (for example, size, ethnicity, socioeconomic status) that may result in systemic differences in intervention implementation and results. Of course, it may be difficult to determine whether it was the variations in the interventions that caused the difference. In some cases, interventions show impacts because of unique differences in a setting, such as strong leadership or an active citizenry. In other cases, changes may be explained by systematic differences, such as regional differences. These differences may have implications for replication.

A multisite evaluation must capture the climate in which the interventions operate, as well as any cultural, geographic, economic, size or other systematic differences that may affect variation in experiences and outcomes. Stakeholder participation is important, because stakeholders can help the evaluator better understand the local situation.

A multisite evaluation is typically stronger than an evaluation of a single intervention in a single location. It can more credibly summarize across a larger population, because it includes a larger sample and a more diverse set of intervention situations. It can address "within" as well as "between" site analyses. Overall findings, as well as consistent findings across interventions, provide stronger evidence of intervention effectiveness than that obtained from a single site.

Comparison of an intervention across sites is likely to provide a range of lessons and strategies for dealing with a variety of situations. Good practices may also emerge from a multisite evaluation. It is important, however, to keep in mind that sites selected on the basis of the evaluator's judgment, even if selected to represent certain characteristics, are not statistically representative of the population and do not necessarily reveal all good practices.

In a conducting a multisite evaluation, evaluators must ensure that data collection is as standardized as possible. The same data must be collected in much the same way if comparisons are to be meaningful. This collection requires well-trained staff, the availability of the same data at every site, and sufficient information ahead of time to design the data collection instruments.

Each location is different. Some indicators may be comparable, but each site may have a slightly different focus. Political, social, economic, and historical contexts can shape project implementation and therefore evaluation (Johnston and Stout 1999).

### Cluster Evaluation

■ **Cluster evaluation:** Evaluation that looks at groups of similar or related interventions

A **cluster evaluation** is similar to a multisite evaluation, but the intention is different. It generally looks at groups of similar or related interventions that together represent a set of interventions. It looks at this "cluster" of interventions in one or more settings. Like a multisite evaluation, a cluster evaluation focuses on interventions that share a common mission, strategy, and target population. Unlike a multisite evaluation, a cluster evaluation is not intended to determine whether an intervention works or to ensure accountability. It does not evaluate the success or failure of individual interventions or identify interventions to be terminated. Its intent is to learn about what happened across the clusters and to ascertain common themes and lessons learned. Information is reported only in aggregate, so that no one project is identified. As in multisite evaluations, stakeholder participation is key.

Cluster evaluations differ from multisite evaluations in that they are not concerned with generalizability or replicability. Variation is viewed as positive, because individual projects are adjusting to their contexts. A cluster evaluation is more focused on learning than on drawing overall conclusions about program quality or value.

While there is no specific methodology for cluster evaluations, such evaluations often use qualitative approaches to supplement quantitative data. It is possible to think of cluster evaluations as multiple case studies, with sharing of information across cases through networking conferences as a significant characteristic of this approach.

A disadvantage of cluster evaluations is that they do not show results for individual sites or take into account planned or unplanned variation. The data show only aggregate information.

## Social Assessment

Social assessment has become an important part of many evaluations. A social assessment looks at social structures, processes, and changes within a group or community. It can also look at trends that may affect the group.

A **social assessment** is the main instrument used to ensure that social impacts of development projects, programs, and policy are taken into account. It is used to understand key social issues and risks and to determine the social impacts of an intervention on different stakeholders. In particular, social assessments are intended to determine whether a project is likely to cause adverse social impacts (such as displacing residents to make way for a power plant). Strategies can be put into place to mitigate adverse impacts if they are known and acknowledged; these mitigation strategies can then be monitored and assessed as part of the evaluation.

■ **Social assessment:** Assessment that looks at social structures, processes, and changes within a group or community

The *World Bank Participation Sourcebook* (1996) identifies the following purposes of social assessment:

- Identify key stakeholders and establish an appropriate framework for their participation in the project selection, design, and implementation.
- Ensure that project objectives and incentives for change are acceptable to the range of people intended to benefit and that gender and other social differences are reflected in project design.
- Assess the social impact of investment projects; where adverse impacts are identified, determine how they can be overcome or at least substantially mitigated.
- Develop ability at the appropriate level to enable participation, resolve conflict, permit service delivery, and carry out mitigation measures as required.

The *Participation Sourcebook* identifies the following common questions asked during social assessment:

- Who are the stakeholders? Are the objectives of the project consistent with their needs, interests, and capacities?
- What social and cultural factors affect the ability of stakeholders to participate or benefit from the operations proposed?
- What is the impact of the project or program on the various stakeholders, particularly women and vulnerable groups? What are the social risks

(lack of commitment or capacity and incompatibility with existing conditions) that may affect the success of the project or program?
- What institutional arrangements are needed for participation and project delivery? Are there adequate plans for building the capacity required for each?

Social assessment tools and approaches include the following:

- stakeholder analysis
- gender analysis
- participatory rural appraisal
- observation, interviews, and focus groups
- mapping, analysis of tasks, and wealth ranking
- workshops focusing on objective-oriented project planning.

Examples of key indicators for social impact monitoring include the following:

- participation rates by social groups in voluntary testing
- participation rates by social groups in counseling activities
- reports of increased use of condoms
- percentage of community members participating in care for people with HIV/AIDS and their families.

Box 5.1 provides an example of the incorporation of social assessment into a project.

## Environmental and Social Assessment

Increasingly, development organizations are recognizing the need for programs and projects to address environmental and social issues and to evaluate the attainment of environmental and social objectives. Most development organizations adhere to a set of core environment and social standards and identify potential environmental and social impacts as part of a program or project approval process. If the project or program is approved, these potential impacts are monitored during implementation and assessed at program or project completion. Environmental and social assessments are being viewed as inseparable.

Development organizations now recognize the role local people must play in designing, implementing, and monitoring interventions that have implications for the environment and natural resources. Local people and other stakeholders are partners in conservation and natural resource management.

Environmental and social evaluation may be the sole purpose of an evaluation or it may be one component of the evaluation. Environmental and

## Box 5.1    Social Assessment of the Azerbaijan Agricultural Development and Credit Project

The Farm Privatization Project, which provided more flexible and adaptable loans, was implemented to restore Azerbaijan's farming areas to former levels of productivity. The project focused on real estate registration, the development of land markets, and the provision of credit and information to rural women and men, especially those with low incomes.

The purpose of the social assessment was to ensure that the proposed intervention was based on stakeholder ownership (commitment) and that the anticipated benefits were socially acceptable. The information gained from the assessment helped program managers design a participatory monitoring and evaluation process.

The first phase of the social assessment included the following components:

- review of secondary data, including earlier assessments
- surveys of households and women in three of the six regions, following a qualitative rapid assessment
- semistructured interviews of individuals (farmers, farm managers, unemployed workers, community leaders, women's groups, local associations, technicians, government officials)
- on-site observation by staff (a member of the team lived with a farming family to conduct an in-situ observation of the impact of farm privatization)
- five focus groups with homogeneous groups of stakeholders
- consultations with policy makers and administrators as well as local and international NGOs
- discussions with former managers of state farms and community leaders
- a stakeholder seminar.

The assessment was organized around four pillars:

- *Social development*: Key concerns focused on poverty, gender, and social exclusion.
- *Institutions*: The power base of the rural areas was changing, making it difficult to identify key stakeholders. There was limited research about the social organizations and lack of analysis of the impacts of rural migration.
- *Participation*: Confusion and ambiguities in the land reform process were reported. Land distribution had reduced poverty, curtailed the influence of former farm managers, and helped empower the rural population. Access to credit had increased, but interest rates remained high (15–18 percent).
- *Monitoring/evaluation*: Performance indicators were used to monitor implementation. Indicators linked the project's inputs and activities with quantified measure of expected outputs and impacts.

The assessment also looked at impacts, in the form of increased productivity, increased income, reduced poverty, and participant satisfaction.

*Source*: Kudat and Ozbilgin 1999.

social assessments should be conducted not only on projects with obvious environmental effects (pulp and paper mills, oil pipelines) but also on interventions such as the building of a new school or the funding of a credit line.

If an organization lacks environmental and social standards, evaluators can draw on the standards of the country in which the organization functions, the Equator Principles, ISO 14031, and *Sustainable Development Strategies: A Resource Book* (Dalal-Clayton and Ba 2002).

### The Equator Principles

■ **Equator Principles:** Industry approach for determining, assessing, and managing environmental and social risk in private sector project financing

The **Equator Principles** are a set of principles that assist financial institutions in determining, assessing, and managing environmental and social risk in project financing for projects with total capital costs of at least US$10 million (revised from $50 million in 2006). The principles are intended to serve as a common baseline and framework for the implementation of individual, internal, environmental, and social procedures and standards for development projects.

### ISO 14031

■ **ISO 14031:** Set of international standards for environmental management developed by the International Organization for Standardization

The International Organization for Standardization (ISO) developed and maintains international standards for environmental management, known as **ISO 14031.** The standard, first released in 1999, is an internal management process and tool designed to provide management with reliable and verifiable information on an ongoing basis. It helps determine whether an organization's environmental performance is meeting the criteria set by the organization's management. Environmental performance evaluation and environmental audits help management assess the status of its environmental performance and identify areas for improvement (ISO 1999).

Environmental performance evaluation assists by establishing processes for

- selecting indicators
- collecting and analyzing data
- assessing information against environmental performance criteria (objectives)
- reporting and communicating
- periodically reviewing and improving this process.

### Sustainable Development Strategies: A Resource Book

A resource book published by the Organisation for Economic Co-operation and Development (OECD) and the United Nations Development Programme (UNDP) provides flexible, nonprescriptive guidance on how to develop, assess, and implement national strategies for sustainable development in line with the principles outlined in the guidelines on strategies for sustainable development (Dalal-Clayton and Ba 2002). It contains ideas and case studies on the main tasks in the strategy processes. Its guidelines are intended for countries, organizations, and individuals concerned with sustainable development at the national or local levels, as well as international organizations concerned with supporting such development.

## Participatory Evaluation

**Participatory evaluation** takes the notion of stakeholder involvement to a new level. It involves sharing the responsibilities for evaluation planning, implementing, and reporting by involving stakeholders in defining the evaluation questions, collecting and analyzing the data, and drafting and reviewing the report.

Paulmer (2005, p. 19) describes participatory evaluation as

> a collective assessment of a program by stakeholders and beneficiaries. They are also action-oriented and build stakeholder capacity and facilitate collaboration and shared decision making for increased utilization of evaluation results. There can be different levels of participation by beneficiaries in an evaluation.

There are two primary objectives to participation and participatory approaches:

- participation as product, where the act of participation is an objective and is one of the indicators of success
- participation as a process by which to achieve a stated objective.

According to Patton (1997), the basic principles of participatory evaluation are the following:

- Evaluation process involves participants' skills in goal setting, establishing priorities, selecting questions, analyzing data, and making decisions on the data.
- Participants own (commit to) the evaluation, as they make decisions and draw their own conclusions.
- Participants ensure that the evaluation focuses on methods and results they consider important.
- People work together, facilitating and promoting group unity.
- All aspects of the evaluation are understandable and meaningful to participants.
- Self-accountability is highly valued.
- Facilitators act as resources for learning; participants act as decision makers and evaluators.

■ **Participatory evaluation:** Evaluation in which responsibilities for planning, implementing, and reporting are shared with stakeholders, who may help define evaluation questions, collect and analyze data, and draft and review the report

Conventional research has developed and documented guidelines for specific techniques in an attempt to increase the reliability and validity of their data. Participatory evaluation does not operate by clear-cut rules handed down to data collectors by experts. Instead, the guidelines for data collection are developed and evolve through consensus, reflection, dialogue, and experience (Narayan 1996).

The participatory evaluation approach is receiving increased attention in the development context. It is being used more often for development projects, especially community-based initiatives. Participatory evaluation is another step in the move away from the model of independent evaluation or evaluator as expert.

The participatory approach identifies and then involves the people, agencies, and organizations with a stake in an issue. The people include children, women, and men in communities, especially those from marginalized groups. They also include agency staff, policy makers, and all those affected by the decisions made through the participatory research process (Narayan 1996).

In participatory evaluation, stakeholders may be asked to keep diaries or journals of their experiences with an intervention. They may help interview others in the community. They may also be involved in analyzing data, interpreting findings, and helping develop recommendations.

Planning decisions, such as identifying the questions, measures, and data collection strategies, are made together with participants. It is a joint process rather than a traditional top-down process (table 5.2).

The participatory approach usually increases the credibility of the evaluation results in the eyes of program staff, as well as the likelihood that the results will be used. Advocates of participatory evaluation see it as a tool for empowering participants and increasing local capacity for engaging in the development process.

Table 5.2 Features of Participatory and Traditional Evaluation Techniques

| Participatory | Traditional |
| --- | --- |
| • Participant focus and ownership | • Donor focus and ownership |
| • Focus on learning | • Focus on accountability and judgment |
| • Flexible design | • Predetermined design |
| • More informal methods | • Formal methods |
| • Outsiders as facilitators | • Outsiders as evaluators |

*Source*: Authors.

Participatory evaluation poses considerable challenges. It involves higher transaction costs than a traditional evaluation, because holding meetings and making sure that everyone understands what is expected is time consuming and requires considerable skill. Groups tend to go through a process in which differences are reconciled and group norms develop before the group focuses on achieving the tasks at hand. This group dynamic process is sometimes referred to as "forming, storming, norming, and performing." After the forming, it is natural to hit a period of conflict (storming). If the group works through these conflicts, it will establish more specific agreements about how they will work together (norming). Once these agreements are established, they will move onto performing the tasks at hand (performing).

There may also be challenges in creating an egalitarian team in a culture in which different members have a different status in the community. The evaluator wanting to conduct a participatory evaluation must have facilitation, collaboration, and conflict management skills (or have someone with those skills take the lead). He or she must also have the ability to provide just-in-time training on the basic skills and techniques associated with evaluation and group processes inherent in participation.

People trained in and conducting traditional evaluations may be concerned that a participatory evaluation will not be objective. There is a risk that those closest to the intervention may not be able to see what is actually happening if it is not what they expect to see. The evaluation may indeed become "captured" and lose objectivity. Participants may be fearful of raising negative views, because they fear that others in the group may ostracize them or the intervention will be terminated, resulting in loss of money for the community, or that they will never get the development organization to work with them again. Approaching participatory evaluations from a learning perspective may help in reducing these fears. Evaluators should consider the degree to which credibility may be compromised (in the view of outsiders) by choosing a participatory rather than an independent evaluation approach.

Gariba (1998) describes how the word *evaluation* causes mixed reactions among donors and implementers. Donors may worry about how the evaluation will affect a project (that is, cause it to be extended or terminated). Project implementers may fear that an evaluation may vilify their approaches to project management.

Gariba describes how participatory evaluation can be a successful and systematic way of learning from experience. With participatory evaluation, partners in the development intervention can draw lessons from their interaction and take corrective actions to improve the effectiveness or efficiency of their ongoing future activities.

Gariba (1998) describes three critical elements of participatory evaluation:

- *Evaluation as a learning tool*: This principle forms the main paradigm of choice. The purpose is not to investigate but to create an opportunity for all stakeholders, including donors included, to learn from their roles in the development intervention exercise.
- *Evaluation as part of the development process*: The evaluation activity is not discrete and separable from the development process itself. The results and corresponding tools become tools for change rather than historical reports.
- *Evaluation as a partnership and sharing of responsibility*: In the participatory impact assessment methodology, all actors have more or less equal weight (this is in sharp contrast to the tendency for evaluators to establish a syndrome of "we" the professionals and "they" the project actors and beneficiaries). The evaluator is transformed from an investigator to a promoter and participant.

According to the Canadian International Development Agency Guide (CIDA 2004), if stakeholders participate in the development of results, they are more likely to contribute to the implementation of the intervention. CIDA believes that participatory evaluation also

- builds accountability within communities
- gives a more realistic orientation to evaluation
- increases cooperation
- empowers local participants by getting them involved in the evaluation process.

Box 5.2 illustrates one technique used in participatory evaluation.

### Outcome Mapping

The Canadian International Development Research Centre (IDRC) has developed an innovative approach to evaluation. Its outcome mapping approach attempts not to replace more traditional forms of evaluation but to supplement them by focusing on related behavioral change.[1]

■ **Outcome mapping:**
Mapping of behavioral change

**Outcome mapping** focuses on one specific type of result: behavioral change. The focus is on outcomes rather than the achievement of development impacts, which are considered too "downstream" and which reflect many efforts and interventions. Trying to accurately assess any one organization's contribution to impact, IDRC argues, is futile. Instead, outcome mapping seeks to look at behaviors, resulting from multiple efforts, in order to help improve the performance of projects, programs, and policies.

Under outcome mapping, boundary partners—individuals, groups, and organizations that interact with projects, programs, and policies—are identified. Outcome mapping assumes that the boundary partners control change. It also assumes that it is their role as an external agent that provides them with access to new resources, ideas, or opportunities for a certain period of time. The most successful programs, according to advocates of outcome mapping, are those that transfer power and responsibility to people acting within the project or program.

The focus of outcome mapping is people. It represents a shift away from assessing the development impact of a project or program toward describing changes in the way people behave through actions either individually or within groups or organizations. Outcome mapping provides a way to model what a program intends to do. It differs from most traditional logic models because it recognizes that different boundary partners operate within different logic and responsibility systems.

Outcome mapping offers a method for monitoring changes in the boundary partners and in the program as an organization. It encourages the program to regularly assess how it can improve its performance. Outcome mapping can also be used as an end-of-program assessment tool when the purpose of the evaluation is to study the program as a whole.

Advocates of outcome mapping believe that many programs, especially those focusing on capacity building, can better plan for and assess their contributions to development by focusing on behavior. For example, a program objective may be to provide communities with access to cleaner water by installing purification filters. A traditional method of evaluation might evaluate results by counting the number of filters installed and measuring the changes in the level of contaminants in the water before and after they were installed. An outcome mapping approach would focus on behavior. It would start with the premise that water does not remain clean if people do not maintain its quality over time. The outcomes of the program would then be evaluated by focusing on the behavior of those responsible for water purity—specifically, changes in their acquisition and use of the appropriate tools, skills, and knowledge. Outcome mapping would evaluate how people monitor contaminant levels, change filters, or bring in experts when required.

A song about outcome mapping, written by Terry Smutylo, the former director of evaluation of the International Development Research Centre, summarizes some of the problems it seeks to address. (A link to a recording of Terry Smutylo performing "The Output Outcome Downstream Impact Blues" appears in the Web site list at the end of this chapter.)

### The Output Outcome Downstream Impact Blues

*Outputs, Outcomes, Impacts : For Whom, by Whom, Says Who?*

Coda
Don't look for *impact* with attribution (4×)
Well there's a nasty little word getting too much use
In development programs it's prone to abuse
It's becoming an obsession now we're all in the act
Because survival depends on that elusive *impact*.

REFRAIN I
Because it's *impact* any place, *impact* any time
Well you may find it 'round the corner or much farther down the line
But if it happens in a way that you did not choose
You get those *Output Outcome Downstream Impact Blues*.

Now when donors look for *impact* what they really wanna see
Is a pretty little picture of their fantasy
Now this is something that a good evaluator would never do
Use a word like *impact* without thinking it through.

But now donors often say this is a fact
Get out there and show us your *impact*
You've got to change peoples' lives and help us take the credit
Or next time you want funding—huh hmm
You may not just get it.

REFRAIN I

Because it's *impact* any place, *impact* any time
Well you can find it 'round the corner or much farther down the line
But if it happens in a way that you did not choose
You get those *Output Outcome Downstream Impact Blues.*

Well recipients are always very eager to please
When we send our evaluators overseas
To search for indicators of measurable *impact*
Surprising the donors what, what they bring back.

Well, *impact* they find when it does occur
Comes from many factors and we're not sure
Just what we can attribute to whom
Cause *impact* is the product of what many people do.

REFRAIN II

Because it's *impact* any place, *impact* any time
Well you can find it 'round the corner or much farther down the line
But if you look for attribution you're never going to lose
Those *Output Outcome Downstream Impact Blues.*

So donors wake up from your impossible dream
You drop in your funding a long way upstream
Then in the waters they flow, they mingle, they blend
So how can you take credit for what comes out in the end.

REFRAIN II

Because it's *impact* any place, *impact* any time
Well you can find it 'round the corner or much farther down the line
But if you look for attribution you're never going to lose
Those *Output Outcome Downstream Impact Blues.*

Coda (4× then fade)


## Rapid Assessment

Rapid assessments meet the need for fast and low-cost evaluations. They are especially useful in the developing country evaluation context, where time and other resource constraints—lack of baseline data, low levels of literacy that make administered questionnaires necessary, and limited evaluation budgets, to name a few—often make it difficult to conduct a more thorough evaluation.

**■ Rapid
assessment:**
Systematic,
semistructured
evaluation
approach that is
administered in the
field, typically by a
team of evaluators

While there is no fixed definition as to what a **rapid assessment** is, it is generally described as a bridge between formal and informal data collection—a "fairly quick and fairly clean" approach rather than a "quick and dirty" one. It can be described as a systematic, semistructured approach that is administered in the field, typically by a team of evaluators. Ideally, the team is diverse, so that a variety of perspectives is reflected.

Rapid assessment is best used when looking at processes rather than outcomes or impacts. Generally, it seeks to gather only the most essential information—the "must know" rather than the "nice to know"—obtained through both quantitative and qualitative approaches. Its basic orientation in development evaluation is to "seek to understand," because a nonjudgmental approach will be more likely to elicit open and honest conversations.

Site visits are made, because observation of an intervention within its setting can provide clues as to how well it is working. A key task is to identify people for interviewing who have a range of experiences and perspectives, especially those who would most likely be overlooked in an evaluation. A small but highly diverse group of key informants can be very effective in obtaining a holistic view of the situation. Listening skills are essential.

Rapid assessment can use the same data collection and data analysis methods as any other type of evaluation. The difference is usually one of scope. Typically, rapid assessments are small in scope, contacting a few key people in a small number of locations. More than one source of information must be used, because multiple sources increase credibility, reduce bias, and provide a holistic perspective. Interview data from key informants should therefore be supplemented with information from previous reports and studies, records, and documents as well as from data collected through observation, focus groups, group interviews, and surveys. The more consistent the information from these sources is, the stronger the confidence in the findings.

To the extent that qualitative methods are used, strong note-taking skills are essential. It helps if the evaluator maintains a journal to note observations, themes, hunches, interpretations, and any incidents that happen during the field visit. These need to be shared with other team members to help identify common themes.

In conducting a rapid assessment, evaluators should keep the following tips in mind:

- Review secondary data before going into the field.
- Once in the field, observe, listen, ask, and record.
- Maintain good notes throughout the process; not only are good notes essential for the report, they also help make sense of the information gathered by different team members.

Strategies and lessons learned in conducting rapid appraisals indicate that the following should be considered before undertaking a rapid appraisal:

- Create a diverse, multidisciplinary team made up of both men and women.
- When possible, recruit both insiders (who are familiar with the intervention and the local area) and outsiders (who will see things in a fresh way).
- Use small rather than large teams to maximize interactions.
- Divide time between collecting data and making sense out of it.
- Be willing to go where needed (fields, market places, areas off the main road), not just where it is convenient to go.
- Maintain flexibility and adaptability, because new information can change the evaluation plan (FAO 1997).

## Evaluation Synthesis

An **evaluation synthesis** is a useful approach when many evaluations of the results of similar interventions have already been conducted. It enables the evaluator to look across interventions addressing a similar issue or theme to identify commonalities. It is useful when the evaluation seeks to find out the overall effectiveness of an intervention.

■ **Evaluation synthesis:** Approach in which an evaluator looks across interventions addressing a similar issue or theme to identify commonalities

Chelimsky and Morra (1984) brought the method to a wider policy context when they applied the technique to predominantly qualitative as well as quantitative evaluations of interventions. Until they did so, evaluation synthesis had been used with evaluations that lent themselves to predominantly quantitative analysis, such as effects of nutritional programs for young women on infant birthweight and mortality or the effects of class size on student educational performance.

The concept behind evaluation synthesis is that while individual evaluations may provide useful information about a specific intervention, each is often too qualified and context specific to allow for a general statement about intervention impact. However, when the results of many studies are combined, it is possible to make general statements about the impact of an intervention (and even a policy).

One advantage of an evaluation synthesis is that it uses available research, making it less expensive to conduct than other types of evaluations. Another advantage is that it creates a larger base for assessing an intervention impact, increasing confidence in making general statements about impact. The challenges are locating all relevant studies, published and unpublished; determining the quality of each evaluation; and, when applicable, obtaining the data sets to combine for the secondary analysis.

An evaluation synthesis should include the following:

- clearly stated procedures for identifying evaluations and defining their scope
- transparent quality criteria for making decisions about including or excluding evaluations from the synthesis
- procedures for applying the quality criteria (often done by a panel instead of an individual)
- citations for all evaluations reviewed
- summary descriptions of each evaluation included in the synthesis and the findings on the themes or variables of interest
- gaps or limitations of the synthesis.

Sometimes only some elements of an evaluation synthesis are used. In the case described in box 5.3, for example, the reports do not appear to have been screened for quality, casting some doubt on the synthesis findings.

The terms *evaluation synthesis* and *meta-evaluation* are sometimes used interchangeably in the evaluation literature. We distinguish between the two. As used here, evaluation synthesis refers to an analytic summary of results across evaluations that meet minimum quality standards. In contrast,

---

**Box 5.3 Using an Evaluation Synthesis to Measure Environmental Benefits**

In 2000, the U.K. Department for International Development (DfID) published an evaluation synthesis study on the environment. DfID had successfully managed a substantial portfolio of environmental projects in the 1990s, but it had the sense that the environmental benefits were "generally assumed rather than critically examined" (p. 1). The environmental synthesis study was commissioned to examine 49 DfID–supported projects in five countries in order to assess the implementation and impact of DfID bilateral project support for environmental improvement and protection. The projects were not primarily environmental projects but covered a wide range of environmental interventions (energy efficiency, industrial, forestry, biodiversity, agriculture, and urban improvement).

After looking through the 49 studies, the evaluators concluded that there was a "gap between high policy priority attached by DfID to environmental issues . . . and what has actually been delivered in terms of positive environmental impact."

*Source:* DfID 2000, 1.

---

**meta-evaluation** refers to an expert review of one or more evaluations against professional quality standards.

## Other Approaches

Other approaches, theories, and models are also used in development evaluations. Most are variations on the theme of participatory evaluation. Readers will find elements of some of the models in the results-based evaluation promoted in this volume, such as reliance on specifying and testing a theory of change and focusing on utilization from the beginning and throughout the evaluation process by identifying and involving key stakeholders.

This section describes the following approaches:

* utilization-focused evaluation
* empowerment evaluation
* realist evaluation
* inclusive evaluation
* beneficiary evaluation
* horizontal evaluation.

### *Utilization-focused evaluation*
**Utilization-focused evaluation** proposes that an evaluation should be judged by its utility and how it is actually used. Patton (2002, p. 173), whose main book on utilization-focused evaluation is now in its fourth edition (2008), describes it as beginning with "identification and organization of specific, relevant decision makers and information users (not vague, passive audience) who will use the information that the evaluation produces." It is evaluation focused on intended use by intended users. The intended users are those who have responsibility to apply the evaluation findings and implement their recommendations. Utilization-focused evaluation helps the primary intended users select the most appropriate evaluation model, content, and methods for their particular situation.

### *Empowerment evaluation*
**Empowerment evaluation** is the use of evaluation concepts, techniques, and findings to foster improvement and self-determination (Fetterman, Kaftarian, and Wandersman 1996). It acknowledges a deep respect for people's capacity to create knowledge about their own experience and find solutions to problems they face. By helping people achieve their goals as individuals and members of a community and improving their lives, empowerment can create a sense of well-being and positive growth (Fetterman and Wandersman 2004).

Fetterman and Wandersman (2004) describe the role of an empowerment evaluator as that of a "critical friend." They advocate that community members remain in charge of the evaluation; the evaluator should play the role of facilitator, influencing rather than controlling the evaluation.

Empowerment evaluation shares some characteristics of utilization-focused evaluation. Both approaches are designed to be helpful, constructive, and useful at every stage of the evaluation (Fetterman and Wandersman 2004). But Patton (1997) indicates his view that while empowerment evaluation overlaps participatory approaches in concern for ownership, relevance, and capacity building, its defining focus is fostering self-determination. Empowerment evaluation goes beyond most participatory evaluation in that the evaluator-facilitator is an advocate of the disempowered and promotes a political change agenda.

In describing the difference between empowerment and participatory evaluation, Alkin and Christie (2004, p. 56) state:

> Since participatory evaluation emerges from a utilization framework, the goal of participatory evaluation is increased utilization through these activities [design, implementation, analysis, and interpretation] as opposed to empowering those that have been oppressed, which is political or emancipatory in nature.

### Realist evaluation

Pawson and Tilley (2004, p. 1) describe **realist evaluation** as a "species of theory-driven evaluation." They relate it to theory of change and program theory. To build the theory, one has to understand the overall context in which the intervention takes place, how the intervention works in the particular context, and whether it works.

According to Pawson and Tilley (2004, p. 22), realist evaluation provides a "coherent and consistent framework" for the way evaluations engage with programs. It recognizes the importance of stakeholders to program development and delivery, but it steers a course between disregarding stakeholders (because of their self-interested biases) and viewing them as omniscient and infallible (because of their inside knowledge). Stakeholders are treated as fallible experts whose understanding needs to be formalized and tested (Pawson and Tilley 2004).

Realist evaluation is derived from a wide range of research and evaluation approaches. It draws on parts or all of other approaches. Realist evaluation can be qualitative or quantitative; it often combines both methods, but does not determine a causal relation between an intervention and an outcome by experimentation. The causal relationship is determined by delineating

■ **Realist evaluation:** A theory-driven evaluation that provides a coherent and consistent framework for the way evaluations engage programs, treats stakeholders as fallible experts, and draws on other approaches to evaluation.

the theory behind how the intervention works. The steps are then placed in a logical sequence to test the hypothesis to determine what might work for whom in what circumstances. Pawson and Tilley (2004) indicate that Realist evaluation can be challenging. because no simple formula provides simple recipes for delivering findings.

### Inclusive evaluation

**Inclusive evaluation** focuses on involving the least advantaged members of a population as part of a systematic investigation of the merit or worth of a project, program, or policy. Inclusive evaluation is data based, but the data are generated from the least advantaged stakeholders, those who have been traditionally underrepresented. An inclusive evaluation does not include those who have been traditionally included in evaluations (Mertens 1999). Like empowerment evaluation, inclusive evaluation is a transformational paradigm.

An inclusive evaluation would ask questions such as the following:

- What are the important differences within the population to be served?
- How are services delivered within different subgroups?
- What are the values underlying the distribution of services?

### Beneficiary assessment

**Beneficiary assessment** is "a qualitative research tool used to improve the impact of development operations by gaining the views of intended beneficiaries regarding a planned or ongoing intervention" (Salmen 1999, p. 1). Like inclusive evaluation, this approach seeks to involve groups that are often overlooked. This project-focused approach was developed by the World Bank in the late 1980s to complement its more technical and financial evaluation focus. It has generally been applied to projects with a service delivery component.

Beneficiary assessment involves the ultimate client, the project beneficiaries. The rationale is that increased participation by beneficiaries in helping shape project design, providing monitoring feedback, and providing their views on impacts increases their ownership, making them key players in producing the needed and desired changes in their own development.

The objective of beneficiary assessment is to assess the value of an activity as perceived by project beneficiaries and to integrate those findings into project activities. Beneficiary assessment plays a central part in social assessment by helping bridge between culture with decision making (Salmen 1999).

■ **Inclusive evaluation:** Evaluation that includes the least advantaged members of a population

■ **Beneficiary assessment:** Tool used to improve the impact of development operations by gaining the views of intended beneficiaries regarding a planned or ongoing intervention

## Horizontal evaluation

**Horizontal evaluation** is a relatively new evaluation approach that combines an internal assessment process with an external review by peers. The combination was designed to neutralize "lopsided power relations that prevail in traditional external evaluations, creating a more favorable atmosphere for learning and subsequent program improvement" (Thiele and others 2006, p. 1).

Horizontal evaluation has often been used to learn about and improve research and development methodologies that are under development. The approach has been used in an Andean regional program developing new research and development methodologies and in Uganda to assess the participatory market chain approach (Thiele and others 2006, p. 1).

The key to the horizontal evaluation approach is two separate groups of stakeholders. The first are local participants, who present and critique the process under investigation and make recommendations on how to improve it. The second are visitors (peers from other organizations or projects who work on similar themes), who assess the process, identify strengths and weaknesses, and make suggestions for improvement (Thiele and others 2006). A component of horizontal evaluation is a workshop that allows the two groups to come together.

## Summary

An evaluation approach is a way of looking at or conceptualizing an evaluation in a general way. It often incorporates a philosophy and a set of values. Some approaches have been in use for years, while others have been developed relatively recently or applied more recently to development evaluation. Key features of the evaluation approaches are summarized in table 5.3.

The approaches described have been used largely at the level of the single intervention. Chapter 11 addresses complex evaluations of complex development interventions, which increasingly are the norm.

**Table 5.3 Purpose, Characteristics, Strengths, and Challenges of Different Evaluation Approaches**

| Evaluation approach | Purpose/philosophy | Characteristics/activities | Strengths | Challenges |
|---|---|---|---|---|
| Prospective | Reviews intervention before it begins<br><br>Answers forward-looking questions about likely success | Provides contextual analysis of project, program, or policy<br><br>Reviews completed evaluations of similar programs to identify lessons and issues<br><br>Predicts success or failure and suggests ways to strengthen proposed intervention if it goes forward | Use of secondary analysis keeps cost of evaluation down<br><br>Can address and resolve issues and strengthen a program before it begins | Can rely on body of evaluation reports on closely related programs |
| Evaluability assessment | Determines if evaluation would be useful and feasible<br><br>Facilitates communication between evaluators and stakeholders<br><br>Clarifies purpose of formative study or functions as planning tool | Reviews materials and available data<br><br>Checks for shared understanding of program goals and objectives<br><br>Interviews intervention managers, stakeholders, and people and organizations that can implement recommendations<br><br>Develops theory of change model | Can lead to more realistic and appropriate evaluation and better designed programs<br><br>Can build stakeholder support and improve understanding of goals and objectives<br><br>Can prevent expenditures on evaluations that are not able to answer questions posed because of data gaps | Can delay evaluation unnecessarily if applied to all programs before evaluation is conducted |
| Goal-based | Measures whether goals and objectives have been met<br><br>Serves as basis of most donor project evaluation systems | Identifies goals and objectives<br><br>Assesses whether intervention reaches goals and objectives (normative evaluation) | Can simplify evaluation in clear methodology comparing actual and standards | Can miss important effects that are not explicitly stated as goals or objectives |
| Goal-free | Opens option of gathering data on effects and effectiveness of programs without being constrained by narrow focus of stated goals or objectives | Seeks to prevent evaluators from becoming captured by program goals and objectives by limiting contact with program manager and staff | Increases likelihood that unanticipated side effects will be noted | Allows limited contact with the program staff; evaluators may find it difficult to avoid becoming aware of program goals and objectives |

*continued*

Table 5.3 *continued*

| Evaluation approach | Purpose/philosophy | Characteristics/activities | Strengths | Challenges |
|---|---|---|---|---|
| Multisite | Investigates interventions with standard implementation in all locations or planned variations, to determine conditions under which program best achieves its goals and objectives<br><br>Must capture climate in which interventions operate, as well as cultural, geographic, economic, size, or other systemic differences that may affect variations | Builds stakeholder participation<br><br>Gathers deeper information than some other approaches<br><br>Selects sites to represent certain characteristics that may result in systematic differences in intervention implementation and results<br><br>Describes and compares interventions within their contexts to provide range of lessons and strategies for dealing with variety of situations | Can often lead to identification of good practices<br><br>Obtains stronger findings than evaluation of single intervention in single location<br><br>Can address within- and between-site analyses | Requires standardized data collection<br><br>Requires a well-trained staff, access to all sites, and sufficient information ahead of time to design data collection instruments<br><br>Can measure highly context-specific findings per site that are not representative |
| Cluster | Looks at groups of similar or related interventions that together represent a set of interventions<br><br>Examines the "cluster" of interventions in one or multiple settings. | Builds stakeholder participation<br><br>Deemphasizes generalizability and replicability<br><br>Views variation as positive<br><br>Uses multiple case studies, with sharing of information across cases | Focuses on learning rather than drawing overall conclusions about program quality or value | Shows aggregate results, not results on individual sites |
| Social assessment | Looks at various social structures, processes, and changes within a group or community<br><br>Acts as main instrument to ensure that social impacts of development interventions are taken into account | Investigates consistency between objectives of intervention and stakeholders' needs, interests, and capacities<br><br>Addresses effects of social and cultural factors on ability of stakeholders to participate in or benefit from intervention<br><br>Investigates differential impact of intervention on subsets of stakeholders | Identifies potential adverse social impacts, so that mitigation strategies can be put in place | Can lose focus on interactions with environmental issues by addressing only one part of equation |
| Environmental and social assessment | Evaluates attainment of environmental and social objectives | Focuses on social and environmental aspects of all interventions, not only those focusing solely on the environment or social inequities<br><br>Is useful when environmental and social assessment is sole purpose of evaluation | Emphasizes overriding importance of social and environmental aspects of interventions | Can require technical expertise |

The Road to Results: Designing and Conducting Effective Development Evaluations

| Approach | Description | Strengths | Challenges |
|---|---|---|---|
| Participatory | Shares with stakeholders responsibility for evaluation planning, implementing, and reporting<br><br>Looks at participation as a product where the act of participation is an objective and is one of the indicators of success<br><br>Considers participation also as a process by which to achieve stated objective | Involves participants in goal setting, establishing priorities, selecting questions, analyzing data, and making decisions on data<br><br>Facilitates group cooperation, group unity, and self-accountability<br><br>Changes role of evaluator to facilitators and guides, with participants as decision makers and evaluation leads | Increases credibility of evaluation results in eyes of program staff and likelihood that results will be used<br><br>Empowers participants and increases local capacity | Requires evaluators with good facilitation, collaboration, and conflict management skills, as well as skills to train participants in evaluation techniques<br><br>Often viewed as not independent |
| Outcome mapping | Supplements more traditional forms of evaluation by focusing on related behavioral change; focus is on people and outcomes rather than achievement of development impacts | Looks at behaviors resulting from multiple efforts to help improve performance of projects, programs, or policies by providing new tools techniques, and resources<br><br>Identifies boundary partners to assess their influences on change<br><br>Describes changes in way people behave through actions as individuals or within groups or organizations | Gets out of the "Downstream Outcome Blues" (see text) | Has demand for impact evaluation with independence and accountability |
| Rapid assessment | Meets need for fast and low-cost evaluations; generally seeks to gather only the most essential information to provide indications on performance | Typically uses systematic, semistructured approach<br><br>Typically uses documents analysis, interview, and short site visit<br><br>Must use more than one source of information<br><br>Requires good listening and note-taking skills | Serves as bridge between formal and informal data collection; is best used when looking at processes and issues | Is typically small in scope<br><br>Provides limited, mostly descriptive information |
| Evaluation synthesis | Locates and rates quality of all relevant evaluations and combines or summarizes their results; is useful when many evaluations about an intervention have already been conducted | Locates all relevant studies<br><br>Establishes criteria to determine quality of studies<br><br>Includes only quality studies<br><br>Combines results or otherwise synthesizes findings across studies on key measures<br><br>May be used with qualitative or quantitative data | Uses available evaluation and research, making it less costly<br><br>Creates larger and stronger base for assessing impact | May have difficulty locating all relevant studies and obtaining data<br><br>Carries some risk of bias in selecting "quality" evaluations, (these risks can be mitigated by panel use) |

*continued*

**Table 5.3** *continued*

| Evaluation approach | Purpose/philosophy | Characteristics/activities | Strengths | Challenges |
|---|---|---|---|---|
| Utilization-focused | Judges intervention by its utility and how it is actually used | Begins with identification and organization of specific, relevant decision makers and information users (not vague, passive audience) who will use information evaluation produces | Builds in use of evaluation by focusing from the start on intended use by intended users | Emphasizes primary client; may not be inclusive of other stakeholders |
| Empowerment | Uses evaluation concepts, techniques, and findings to foster improvement and self-determination | Goes beyond participatory evaluation by acknowledging deep respect for people's capacity to create knowledge about their own experience and develops solutions to problems they face | Champions disempowered groups | Changes role of evaluator to advocate (evaluation may be viewed as political and biased) |
| Realist | Provides coherent and consistent framework for evaluating programs through context description; looks at how a program should work and whether there is a causal relation between program and intended outcome | Derived from wide range of research and evaluation approaches; draws on parts or all of other approaches; Uses qualitative research, quantitative research, or both | Delineates underlying theory behind how intervention might work, under what conditions, and for whom | Knows that each program's model has to be individually determined |
| Inclusive | Involves least advantaged stakeholders as part of systematic investigation of merit or worth of a project, program, or policy | Generates data from least advantaged stakeholders; does not include those who have traditionally been included in evaluations | Focuses on least advantaged stakeholders and differences in delivery of services | Changes role of evaluator to advocate (evaluation may be viewed as political and biased) |
| Beneficiary | Improves impact of development operations by gaining views of intended beneficiaries regarding a planned or ongoing intervention | Involves project beneficiaries, increasing their sense of ownership | Uses collaborative approach that builds ownership and capacity and improves value of evaluation by capturing beneficiary views | Separates consideration of environmental issues and their social consequences |
| Horizontal | Combines internal assessment process with external review by peers to neutralize lopsided power relations that prevail in traditional external evaluations | Used to learn about and improve evaluation and development methodologies under development | Combines the strengths of self-evaluation and external peer review | Understands that peer reviews may be mutually positive |

*Source:* Authors.

The Road to Results: Designing and Conducting Effective Development Evaluations

**Application Exercise 5.1: Choosing the Most Appropriate Evaluation Approach**

Select an evaluation approach for analyzing each of the assignments described below. Describe the approach, list the benefits it provides and the challenges it presents, and explain your rationale for choosing it.

1.  Assess the strategic focus of technical assistance to a country on the basis of the findings of five country studies completed by different development organizations.
2.  Identify successful educational interventions that have been implemented in your organization's projects and programs in order to improve the educational systems in the region.
3.  Evaluate the most significant issues concerning a country's natural resources and environment sector.
4.  Assess the development of the rice sector in a country, including the importance of rice in the current cultural, social, and economic contexts; rice production systems; constraints facing rice farmers; research conducted and technologies developed; and future priorities for further rice development.
5.  Evaluate the evaluations completed by a development organization that has received millions of dollars in funding for international agriculture research over the past 30 years.

## Notes

1. Much of the information in this section is adapted from Earl, Carden, and Smutylo (2001).

## References and Further Reading

Alkin, Marvin, and Christina Christie. 2004. "An Evaluation Theory Tree." In *Evaluation Roots: Tracing Theorist Views and Influences*, ed. M. Alkin. 12–65, Thousand Oaks, CA: Sage Publications.

Chambers, R. 1991. "Shortcut and Participatory Methods for Gaining Social Information for Projects." In *Putting People First: Sociological Variables in Rural Development,* 2nd ed., ed. M. M. Cernea, 515–37. Washington, DC: World Bank.

Chelimsky, E., and L. G. Morra. 1984. "Evaluation Synthesis for the Legislative User." In *Issues in Data Synthesis,* ed. W. H. Yeaton and P. M. Wortman, 75–89. New Directions for Program Evaluation No. 24. San Francisco: Jossey-Bass.

Christie, Christina, and Marvin Alkin. 2004. "Objectives-Based Evaluation." In *Encyclopedia of Evaluation*, ed. Sandra Mathison. 281–85. Thousand Oaks, CA: Sage Publications.

CIDA (Canadian International Development Agency). 2004. *CIDA Evaluation Guide 2004.* Ottawa.

Cousins, J. B., and L. M. Earl, eds. 1995. *Participatory Evaluation in Education.* Bristol, PA: Falmer Press.

Dalal-Clayton, Barry, and Stephen Ba. 2002. *Sustainable Development Strategies: A Resource Book.* Sterling, VA: Earthscan Publications. http://www.nssd.net/res_book.html#contents.

DFID (Department for International Development). 2000. *Environment: Mainstreamed or Sidelined?* Environmental Evaluation Synthesis Study EV626, January, London. http://www.dfid.gov.uk/aboutdfid/performance/files/ev626s.pdf.

Duignan, Paul. 2007. *Introduction to Strategic Evaluation: Section on Evaluation Approaches, Purposes, Methods, and Designs.* http://www.strategicevaluation.info/se/documents/104f.html.

Earl, Sarah, Fred Carden, and Terry Smutylo. 2001. *Outcome Mapping: Building Learning and Reflection into Development Programs.* International Development Research Centre, Ottawa. http://www.dgroups.org/groups/pelican/docs/Mapping_M&E_capacity_080606.pdf.

ECDPM (European Centre for Development Policy Management). 2006. *Study on Capacity, Change and Performance: Mapping of Approaches Towards M&E of Capacity and Capacity Development.* Maastricht.

Eerikainen, Jouni, and Roland Michelevitsh. 2005. "Environmental and Social Sustainability. Methodology and Toolkit: Various Approaches." International Program for Development Evaluation Training (IPDET) presentation, Ottawa, July.

FAO (Food and Agriculture Organization of the United Nations). 1997. "Rapid Rural Appraisal." In *Marketing Research and Information Systems Marketing and Agribusiness*. Rome.
http://www.fao.org/docrep/W3241E/w3241e09.htm.

Fetterman, David M. 2001. *Foundations of Empowerment Evaluation*. Thousand Oaks, CA: Sage Publications.

Fetterman, David M., S. Kaftarian, and A. Wandersman, eds. 1996. *Empowerment Evaluation: Knowledge and Tools for Self-Assessment and Accountability*. Thousand Oaks, CA: Sage Publications.

Fetterman, David M., and Abraham Wandersman. 2004. *Empowerment Evaluation Principles in Practice*. New York: Guilford Publications.

——. 2007. "Empowerment Evaluation: Yesterday, Today, and Tomorrow." *American Journal of Evaluation* 28 (2):179–98.
http://homepage.mac.com/profdavidf/documents/EEyesterday.pdf.

Fitzpatrick, Jody L., James R. Sanders, and Blaine R. Worthen. 2004. *Program Evaluation: Alternative Approaches and Practical Guidelines*. New York: Pearson.

Gariba, Sulley. 1998. "Participatory Impact Assessment: Lessons From Poverty Alleviation Projects in Africa." in *Knowledge Shared: Participatory Evaluation in Development Cooperation*, ed. Edward T. Jackson and Yussuf Kassam, 64–81. Bloomfield, CT: Kumarian Press.

Gill, M., and A. Spriggs. 2002. *The Development of Realistic Evaluation Theory through the Evaluation of National Crime Prevention Programmes*.
http://www.evaluationcanada/distribution/20021010_gill_martin_spriggs_angela. pdf.

Glass, Gene V., and Mary Lee Smith. 1979. "Meta-Analysis of Research on Class Size and Achievement." *Educational Evaluation and Policy Analysis* 1 (1): 2–16.

Hirschheim, R., and S. Smithson. 1988. "A Critical Analysis of Information Systems Evaluation." In *IS Assessment: Issues and Changes*, eds. N. Bjorn-Andersen and G. B. Davis. Amsterdam: North-Holland.

ISO (International Organization for Standardization). 1999. *Environmental Management: Performance Evaluation Guidelines*. ISO 14301, Geneva.

Johnston, Timothy, and Susan Stout. 1999. *Investing in Health: Development in Health, Nutrition, and Population Sector*. World Bank, Operations Evaluation Department, Washington, DC.
http://wbln0018.worldbank.org/oed/oeddoclib.nsf/6e14e487e87320f7852568080 06a001a/daf8d4188308862f852568420062f332/US$FILE/HNP.pdf.

Khon Kaen University. 1987. *Proceedings of the 1985 International Conference on Rapid Rural Appraisal*. Rural Systems Research and Farming Systems Research Projects, Khon Kaen, Thailand.

Kretzmann, John P., John L. McKnight, and Deborah Puntenney. 1996. A Guide to Massing Local Business Assets and Modulizing Local Business Capabilities. Skokie, IL: ACTA Publications.

Kudat, Ayse, and Bykebt Ozbilgin. 1999. *Azerbaijan Agricultural Development and Credit Program*.

http://lnweb18.worldbank.org/ESSD/sdvext.nsf/61ByDocName/Azerbaijan
AgriculturalDevelopmentandCreditProject/US$FILE/AzerbaijanAgricultural
DevelopmentandCreditProject424KbPDF.pdf.

Kumar, Krishna, ed. 1993. *Rapid Appraisal Methods.* Washington, DC: World Bank.

Light, R. J., and D. B. Pillemer. 1984. *Summing Up: The Science of Reviewing Research.* Cambridge, MA: Harvard University Press.

Mertens, D. 1999. "Inclusive Evaluation: Implications of Transformative Theory for Evaluation." *American Journal of Evaluation* 20 (1): 1–14.

Narayan, Deepa. 1996. *Toward Participatory Research.* World Bank Technical Paper 307, World Bank, Washington, DC. http:// www-wds.worldbank.org/external/default/WDSContentServer/WDSP/ IB/1996/04/01/000009265_3980625172923/Rendered/PDF/multi0page.pdf.

Nay, J., and P. Kay. 1982. *Government Oversight and Evaluability Assessment.* Lexington, MA: Heath.

OECD (Organisation for Economic Co-operation and Development). 1997. *Searching for Impact and Methods: NGO Evaluation Synthesis Study.* Development Assistance Committee, Paris. http://www.eldis.org/static/DOC5421.htm.

Patton, Michael Q. 1990. *Qualitative Evaluation and Research Methods.* 2nd ed. Thousand Oaks, CA: Sage Publications.

———. 1997. *Utilization-Focused Evaluation: The New Century Text.* Thousand Oaks: CA: Sage Publications.

———. 1997. "Toward Distinguishing Empowerment Evaluation and Placing It in a Larger Context." *Evaluation Practice* 18 (2):147–63.

———. 2002. *Qualitative Evaluation and Research Methods*, 3rd ed. Thousand Oaks, CA: Sage Publications.

———. 2008. *Utilization-Focused Evaluation.* 4th ed. Thousand Oaks, CA: Sage Publications.

Paulmer, Hubert E. 2005. "Evaluation Guidelines of International Development Aid Agencies: A Comparative Study." International Rural Planning and Development, School of Environmental Design and Rural Development, University of Guelph, Ontario.

Pawson, Ray, and Nick Tilley. 2004. "Realistic Evaluation." In *Encyclopaedia of Evaluation*, ed. Sandra Matthieson, 359–67. Thousand Oaks, CA: Sage Publications.

Picciotto, Robert. 2007. "The New Environment for Development Evaluation." *American Journal of Evaluation* 28: 509–21.

Preskill, Hallie, and Darlene Russ-Eft. 2005. *Building Evaluation Capacity: 72 Activities for Teaching and Training.* Thousand Oaks, CA: Sage Publications.

Salmen, Lawrence F. 1999. *Beneficiary Assessment Manual for Social Funds.* World Bank, Social Protection Team Human Development Network, Washington, DC. http://lnweb18.worldbank.org/ESSD/sdvext.nsf/07ByDocName/Beneficiary AssessmentManualforSocialFunds/US$FILE/ percent5BEnglish percent5D+ Beneficiary+Assessment+Manual.pdf.

Sanders, J. R. 1997. "Cluster Evaluation." In *Evaluation for the 21st Century: A Handbook,* eds. E. Chelimsky and W. R. Shadish Jr., 396–401. Thousand Oaks, CA: Sage Publications.

Scrimshaw, N., and G. R. Gleason. 1992. *Rapid Assessment Procedures: Qualitative Methodologies for Planning and Evaluation of Health Related Programs.* Boston: International Nutrition Foundation for Developing Countries.

Scriven, Michael. 1972a. "Objectivity and Subjectivity in Educational Research." In *Philosophical Redirection Educational Research: The Seventy-First Yearbook of the National Society for the Study of Education,* ed. L. G. Thomas. Chicago: University of Chicago Press.

———. 1972b. "Pros and Cons about Goal-Free Evaluation." *Evaluation Comment* 3: 1–7.

———. 1991. *Evaluation Thesaurus.* 4th. ed. Thousand Oaks, CA: Sage Publications.

Smith, M. F. 1989. *Evaluability Assessment: A Practical Approach.* Boston: Kluwer Academic Press.

Smith, Mary Lee, and Gene V. Glass. 1980. "Meta-Analysis of Research on Class Size and Its Relationship to Attitudes and Instruction." *American Educational Research Journal* 17: 419–33.

Smith, Nick L., and Paul R. Brandon, eds. 2007. *Fundamental Issues in Evaluation.* New York: Guilford Press.

Smutylo, Terry. "The Output Outcome Downstream Impact Blues." http://www.idrc.ca/en/ev-65284-201-1-DO_TOPIC.html.

Thiele, G., A. Devaux, C. Velasco, and D. Horton. 2007. "Horizontal Evaluation: Fostering Knowledge Sharing and Program Improvement within a Network." *American Journal of Evaluation* 28 (4): 493–508.

Thiele, G., A. Devaux, C. Velasco, and K. Manrique. 2006. "Horizontal Evaluation: Stimulating Social Learning among Peers." International Potato Center, Papa Andina Program, Lima, Peru. Draft of May 18. http://www.dgroups.org/groups/pelican/docs/Hor_Evaln_18_05.doc?ois=no.

Tilley, Nick. 2000. *Realistic Evaluation: An Overview.* Paper presented at the Founding Conference of the Danish Evaluation Society, Nottingham Trent University, September. http://www.danskevalueringsselskab.dk/pdf/Nick percent20Tilley.pdf.

Turpin, R. S., and J. M. Sinacore, eds. 1991. *Multisite Evaluations.* New Directions for Program Evaluation No. 50. San Francisco, CA: Jossey-Bass.

U.S. GAO (General Accounting Office) 1990. *Prospective Evaluation Methods: The Prospective Evaluation Synthesis.* Washington, DC. http://www.gao.gov/special.pubs/10_1_10.PDF.

———. 1992. *The Evaluation Synthesis.* Washington, DC. http://www.gao.gov/special.pubs/pemd1012.pdf.

Wandersman, A., J. Snell-Johns, B. E. Lentz, D. M. Fetterman, D. C. Keener, M. Livet, P. S. Imm, and P. Flaspoler. 2005. "The Principles of Empowerment Evaluation." In *Empowerment Evaluation Principles in Practice,* eds. D. M. Fetterman and A. Wandersman, 27–41. New York: Guilford.

Wholey, J. S. 1987. "Evaluability Assessment: Developing Program Theory." In *Using Program Theory in Evaluation,* ed. L. Bickman, 77–92. New Directions for Program Evaluation No. 33. San Francisco: Jossey-Bass.

Wholey, J. S., H. P. Hatry, and K. E. Newcomer, eds. 1994. *Handbook of Practical Program Evaluation*. San Francisco: Jossey-Bass.

World Bank. 1996. *World Bank Participation Sourcebook*. Washington, DC. http://www.worldbank.org/wbi/sourcebook/sba108.htm#D.

———. 2004. "Social Assessment." In *Turning Bureaucrats into Warriors*. 135–38. Washington, DC. http://www.worldbank.org/afr/aids/gom/manual/GOM-Chapter percent2024 .pdf.

## Web Sites

Equator Principles. http://www.equator-principles.com/, http://www.ifc.org/ ifcext/equatorprinciples.nsf/Content/ThePrinciples.

Frechtling, Joy, and Laure Sharp Westat, eds. 1997. *User-Friendly Handbook for Mixed-Method Evaluations*. Washington, DC: National Science Foundation. http://www.nsf.gov/pubs/1997/nsf97153/start.htm.

IFC (International Finance Corporation). *Environmental and Social Policies and Guidelines*. http://www.ifc.org/ifcext/enviro.nsf/Content/PoliciesandGuidelines.

ISO (International Organization for Standardization). *ISO 14031*. http://www.iso .org/iso/catalogue_detail?csnumber=23149, http://www.iso-14001.org.uk/ iso-14031.htm, and http://www.altech-group.com/ftp/EPEarticle.pdf.

IUCN (World Conservation Union). *Sustainability Assessment*. http://www.iucn .org/themes/eval/search/iucn/sustassess.htm.

World Bank. 2009. *Social Analysis*. http://web.worldbank.org/WBSITE/ EXTERNAL/TOPICS/EXTSOCIALDEVELOPMENT/EXTSOCIALANALYSIS/ 0,,menuPK:281319~pagePK:149018~piPK:149093~theSitePK:281314,00.html.

### Cluster Evaluation

AusAid. 2004. *Governance in PNG: A Cluster Evaluation of Three Public Sector Reform Activities*. Evaluation and Review Series 35, Sydney. http://www.ausaid .gov.au/publications/pdf/governance_in_png_qc35.pdf.

### Empowerment Evaluation

Empowerment Evaluation Blog. http://www.eevaluation.blogspot.com/.

### Environment and Social Assessment

Lanco Amarkantak Thermal Power. *Environmental & Social Review*. Report prepared for the IFC Board of Directors. http://www.ifc.org/ifcext/spiwebsite1 .nsf/1ca07340e47a35cd85256efb00700ceeC126975A64D3306E852572A00048 07BD.

## Evaluability Assessment

Lewin Group. 1997. *An Evaluability Assessment of Responsible Fatherhood Programs.* http://fatherhood.hhs.gov/evaluaby/intro.htm.

## Evaluation Synthesis

Kruse, S. E., T. Kyllönen, S. Ojanperä, R. C. Riddell, and J. Vielaj. *Searching for Impact and Methods: NGO Evaluation Synthesis Study.* Institute of Development Studies, University of Helsinki. http://www.eldis.org/static/DOC5421.htm.

## Goal-Based Evaluation

IFAD (International Fund for Agricultural Development). *Country Program Evaluation of the People's Republic of Bangladesh.* http://www.ifad.org/evaluation/public_html/eksyst/doc/country/pi/bangladesh/bangladesh.htm.

## Goal-Free Evaluation

Evaluation Center, Western Michigan University. http://www.wmich.edu/evalctr/project-pub.html.

## Meta-evaluation

Campbell Collaboration Online Library. http://www.campbellcollaboration.org/frontend.aspx.

## Multisite Evaluation

Australian HIV Test Evaluation Group. 1995. *Multisite Evaluation of Four Anti-HIV-1/HIV-2 Enzyme Immunoassays.* http://www.ncbi.nlm.nih.gov/entrez/query.fcgi?cmd=Retrieve&db=PubMed&list_uids=7882108&dopt=Abstract/.

SRI International. 2001. *A Multisite Evaluation of the Parents as Teachers (PAT) Project.* http://policyweb.sri.com/cehs/projects/displayProject.jsp?Nick=pat.

## Outcome Mapping

African Health Research Fellowship Program. *Strengthening Leadership Capacity to Improve the Production and Use of Health Knowledge in Africa.* http://www.idrc.ca/fr/ev-34425-201-1-DO_TOPIC.html.

## Participatory Evaluation

Contra Costa Health Services. 2009. *Preventing Chronic Disease: A Participatory Evaluation Approach.* http://www.cchealth.org/groups/chronic_disease/guide/evaluation.php.

Community Integrated Pest Management. 2001. *Picturing Impact: Participatory Evaluation of Community IPM in Three West Java Villages.* http://www .communityipm.org/docs/Picturing percent20Impact/Picturing percent20 Impact percent20top percent20page.html.

## Prospective Evaluation

Glewwe, Paul, Michael Kremer, and Sylvie Moulin. 1998. *Textbooks and Test Scores: Evidence from a Prospective Evaluation in Kenya.* http://www.econ.yale .edu/~egcenter/infoconf/kremer_paper.pdf.

## Rapid Assessment

UNICRI (United Nations Interregional Crime and Justice Research Institute), and ACI (Australian Institute of Criminology). *Global Programme against Trafficking in Human Beings, Rapid Assessment: Human Smuggling and Trafficking from the Philippines.* http://www.unodc.org/pdf/crime/trafficking/RA_UNICRI.pdf.

## Social Assessment

World Bank. 1996. "Morocco: Fez Medina Rehabilitation Project." In *World Bank Participation Sourcebook.* Washington, DC: World Bank. http://www.worldbank .org/wbi/sourcebook/sba108.htm#D.

## Utilization-Focused Evaluation

Evaluation Center, Western Michigan University. *Utilization-Focused Evaluation Checklist.* http://www.wmich.edu/evalctr/checklists/ufechecklist.htm.

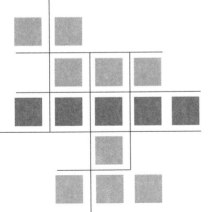

# DESIGNING AND CONDUCTING

*"There's no limit to how complicated things can get, on account of one thing always leading to another."*

—E. B. White

**Chapter 8: Selecting and Constructing Data Collection Instruments**
- Data Collection Strategies
- Characteristics of Good Measures
- Quantitative and Qualitative Data
- Tools for Collecting Data

**Chapter 9: Choosing the Sampling Strategy**
- Introduction to Sampling
- Types of Samples: Random and Nonrandom
- Determining the Sample Size

**Chapter 10: Planning for and Conducting Data Analysis**
- Data Analysis Strategy
- Analyzing Qualitative Data
- Analyzing Quantitative Data
- Linking Quantitative Data and Qualitative Data

# CHAPTER 6

# Developing Evaluation Questions and Starting the Design Matrix

This is the first of five chapters that discuss specific steps in designing an evaluation. This chapter discusses the types of evaluation questions and explains when to use each type. The chapter also covers how to write and structure good questions.

**This chapter has five main parts:**

- Sources of Questions
- Types of Questions
- Identifying and Selecting Questions
- Developing Good Questions
- Designing the Evaluation

## Sources of Questions

Why is choosing evaluation questions so important? One reason is that questions give direction to the evaluation and the evaluation design selected (we cover these implications more fully in chapter 6). Evaluation questions are the critical element that helps key individuals and groups improve efforts, make decisions, and provide information to the public. Careful reflection and investigation are needed to complete the critical process of identifying and defining the questions to be answered by an evaluation (Fitzpatrick, Sanders, and Worthen 2004).

Evaluators ask evaluation questions to learn about the project, program, or policy being evaluated. A frequent problem in developing questions is assuming that everyone involved shares the same understanding of the intervention's goals. If, for example, the question is "Did the program assist participants?" different stakeholders may interpret the words *assist* and *participants* differently. Obtaining agreement on the theory of change, discussed in the previous chapter, can remedy this problem.

Fitzpatrick, Sanders, and Worthen (2004) list the sources evaluators should use in order to ensure that they obtain diverse viewpoints:

- questions, concerns, and values of stakeholders
- evaluation models
- frameworks and approaches, including heuristic (trial and error) approaches
- research and evaluation findings and important issues raised in the literature
- professional standards, checklists, guidelines, instruments, or criteria developed or used elsewhere
- views and knowledge of expert consultants
- the evaluator's own professional judgment.

Chapter 4 covered identifying and working with stakeholders to solicit their views on issues they believe are important to evaluate. It also covered the importance of reviewing previous research and evaluation studies for question identification. Emphasis was placed on developing and using theory of change models to help identify areas of focus for the evaluation. Questions come from the major assumptions underlying the model.

Figure 6.1 shows the types of evaluation questions that should be asked at different points in a causal chain. The generic questions at the bottom of the diagram show that formative questions can be drawn from activities and outputs and summative questions from intermediate and long-term results. Questions derived from short-term results can be written as either formative

**Figure 6.1   Using a Logic Model to Frame Evaluation Questions**

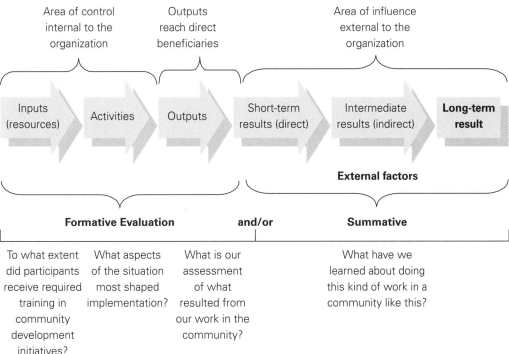

or summative questions. Questions should flow from the major assumptions being made in the logic model about how the program will work and what benefits or outcomes will be achieved. Questions will also come from the review of research of completed evaluations of similar programs, as well as stakeholders' diverse perspectives on the project, program, or policy, as discussed in chapter 4.

## Types of Questions

Many questions can be considered in planning an evaluation. All must be clearly defined in measurable ways.

Questions can be grouped into three categories: descriptive questions, normative questions, and cause-and-effect questions. The types of questions asked—along with the data, time, and money available to conduct the evaluation—will drive the type of design selected.

## Descriptive Questions

**Descriptive questions** seek to determine what is. They may describe aspects of a process, a condition, a set of views, or a set of organizational relationships or networks. Patton (2002) refers to descriptive questions as the foundation of evaluations.

Descriptive questions

- seek to understand or describe a program or process
- provide a "snapshot" of what is
- are straightforward (who, what, where, when, how, how many)
- can be used to describe inputs, activities, and outputs
- are frequently used to gather opinions from program clients.

Examples of descriptive questions include the following:

- What are the goals of the program from the perspectives of different stakeholders?
- What are the primary activities of the program?
- How do people get into the program?
- Where has the program been implemented?
- What services does the program provide to men? What services does it provide to women?
- What effects does the program have on participants?
- To what extent does the program design reflect lessons learned from past similar programs?
- To what extent are there differences across sites in how the program has been implemented?
- What are the qualifications of service providers?
- When was the program implemented?
- How many women participated in the program?
- How does the cost of the program compare with the costs of similar programs?
- What are the informal communication channels inside the organization?
- How useful did participants find the program?

Evaluative questions about policy making are often descriptive questions. Rist (1994) identifies a "policy-cycle" process with three phases, during which distinct questions are asked (table 6.1).

## Normative Questions

**Normative questions** compare what is with what should be. They compare the current situation with a specified target, goal, or benchmark. These questions are similar in compliance orientation to those often asked in performance auditing. They ask the following:

- Are we doing what we are supposed to be doing?
- Are we hitting our target?
- Did we accomplish what we said we would accomplish?

If the program has a results-based monitoring system, with indicators and targets and timeframes for achieving them, normative questions can be used to answer questions about inputs, activities, and outputs.

Sometimes a program has objectives but no apparent criteria for determining how they will be measured or attained. No indicators or targets have been established. In such a case, the evaluator has several options, some better than others (box 6.1).

The search for standards or criteria generally begins with the criteria found in program authorizing documents, such as legislation or governing board approval documents. Criteria may also be specified as indicators with specific targets in results-based management systems. Other sources that

■ **Normative question:** Question that compares what is with what should be

Table 6.1 Qualitative Questions to Pose During Different Policy-Cycle Phases

| Phase | Examples |
| --- | --- |
| Policy formulation | • What has taken place previously in response to this condition or problem? |
| | • What is known about previous efforts that would help a decision maker choose among current options? |
| Policy implementation | • What information about the problem or condition prompted the policy or program response? |
| | • What efforts did the organization or institution make to respond to the initiative? |
| | • What are the qualifications of those responsible for the implementation effort? |
| | • To what extent has interest been shown by management and staff? |
| | • What controls are in place regarding the allocation of resources? |
| | • Does the organizational structure adequately reflect the demands on the organization to respond to this initiative? |
| | • What means exist in the organization for deciding among competing demands? |
| | • What kinds of feedback systems are in place to assist managers ? |
| Policy accountability | • What relevance does the program or policy have to present circumstances? |
| | • How sharp was the focus on accountability? |

*Source:* Adapted from Rist 1994.

> **Box 6.1    Evaluating an Intervention That Has No Standards**
>
> Consider a multisector program whose objectives include the following:
>
> - Improve the reading scores of children in selected school districts.
> - Raise awareness of HIV/AIDS and methods of preventing it in a region.
> - Increase the number of microenterprises in a village, and increase their profits.
>
> The evaluator would like to know exactly what these objectives mean (what proportion of children will improve their reading scores, whose awareness of HIV/AIDS will increase and how will we know, how many microenterprises will expand and by how much?), but the program has not defined its objectives in these terms. What can the evaluator do in such circumstances?
>
> One approach is to work with the program's "owners"—the officials responsible administratively for the program or its implementation. These officials should be able to indicate a reasonable level of performance for this program to attain.
>
> A concern with this approach is that one group may not accept the standards another group has set. Staff members with oversight responsibility, for example, may not agree with the standard proposed by the program implementers. They may argue that the standards have been set too low.
>
> Another approach is to bring in one or more experts and have them agree on a standard that could be used. A potential problem with this approach is that the standard may reflect the personal biases of the expert. This criticism can be diminished by using several experts. In such a case, it is important that the expert group be viewed as politically neutral or balanced and that the experts have no previous involvement with the program.
>
> The weakest and riskiest alternative is for the evaluator to set the standard. This approach should be avoided, as it sets the evaluator up for difficulties. Those within the program can argue that the standards are too high or too low or that such standards cannot be set after the fact and used to judge their performance.
>
> *Source*: Authors.

may establish the standards are accreditation systems, blue-ribbon panels, professional organizations, and other commissions.

Examples of normative questions include the following:

- Did we spend as much as we had budgeted?
- Did we reach the goal of admitting 5,000 students a year?

- Did we vaccinate 80 percent of children, as required?
- Did we meet the objective of draining 100,000 hectares of land?
- Was the process for selecting participants fair and equitable?

## Cause-and-Effect Questions

**Cause-and-effect questions** determine what difference the intervention makes. Often referred to as *outcome, impact,* or *attributional questions,* they attempt to measure what has changed because of the intervention. Cause-and-effect questions seek to determine the effects of a project, program, or policy. They are the "so what" questions. Cause-and-effect questions ask whether the desired results have been achieved as a result of the program.

Program theory of change models depict the desired outcomes and impacts of an intervention, but outcomes may or may not be stated as cause-and-effect questions. For example, in a program to introduce farmers to a new and improved seed, an outcome question may be whether the grain yield increased. As stated, this would be a descriptive question—it asks, simply, how much did the crop increase? If the evaluation is asking whether the crop increased as a result of the program—and not, for example, as a result of unusually ideal weather for the grain crop—then it is asking a clear cause-and-effect question. Cause-and-effect questions imply a comparison of performance on one or more measures or indicators not only before and after the intervention but also with and without it.

Examples of cause-and-effect questions include the following:

- Was the three-country partnership strategy effective in preserving the biodiversity of the affected area while sustaining livelihoods?
- As a result of the job training program, do participants have higher-paying jobs than they otherwise would have?
- Did the microenterprise program reduce the poverty rate in the townships in which they operated?
- Did the increased tax on gasoline improve air quality?
- Did the government's increase in financial penalties for violating firms reduce the use of under-age children in the garment industry?
- What other impacts or side effects (positive or negative) did this intervention have on the wider community?

Evaluators need to pose such questions in terms of cause and effect. Because many activities are occurring at the same time, it is difficult to demonstrate that the outcomes are solely, or at least primarily, the result of the intervention. When coming up with designs to answer cause-and-effect questions, evaluators need to exercise great care to eliminate other possible explanations for whatever changes they measure.

Chapter 7 discusses designs that can be used to answer cause-and-effect questions and examines the kinds of analysis needed to attribute a causal relationship. Because it is more difficult to answer cause-and-effect questions than descriptive or normative questions, it is important to be quite sure that this form of question is intended and needed.

Many evaluations use only descriptive and normative questions, particularly if they are formative evaluations that focus on implementation of an intervention. Evaluations focusing on impact ask cause-and-effect questions, but they typically also include some descriptive and normative questions. Box 6.2 illustrates how an evaluation may include different types of questions.

---

**Box 6.2 Evaluating Policies and Interventions Using Question-and-Answer Questions**

*Improving Preventative Health Care*

Policy: Ensure that all children receive preventative health care.

Goal: To reduce infant and preschool child mortality.

Evaluation questions:

1. What percentage of children have received preventative health care since the program began? (descriptive question)
2. Have the intended groups of low-income children received preventative health care? (normative question)
3. Have child mortality rates decreased as a result of the program? (cause-and-effect question)

*Training Secondary-School Students for the Job Market*

Policy: Ensure that secondary schools teach the knowledge and skills needed for employment in local markets.

Goal: To ensure that graduates are able to obtain well-paying skilled jobs.

Evaluation questions:

1. How are secondary schools preparing students for jobs in the local market? (descriptive question)
2. After one year, are graduates receiving higher wages than those who dropped out of the program? (descriptive question)
3. To what extent are secondary schools making market-based decisions on areas in which to train, as required? (normative question)
4. How much more are graduates earning than they would have absent the program?

### Providing Free Measles Immunization

Intervention: Family clinics provide free immunization against measles to all children under the age of five in three regions of the country in one year.

Evaluation questions:

1. How did the clinics reach parents to inform them about the free immunization for their children? (descriptive question)
2. Did the program meet the target of providing immunization against measles to 100 percent of all children under the age of five in the three regions last year? (normative question)
3. Did the program use innovative methods to reach the children most at risk? (descriptive question)
4. Did the proportion of children contracting measles decrease as a result of the program? (cause-and-effect question)
5. Has there been a decline in child mortality from measles-related complications as a result of this program? (cause-and-effect question)

### Introducing a Market-Based Curriculum

Intervention: Three secondary schools within three cities implement a market-based curriculum.

Evaluation questions:

1. How different is the curriculum from that used by nonparticipating schools? (descriptive question)
2. Was the curriculum market-based as required? (normative question)
3. To what extent did graduates of these schools obtain high-paying jobs? (descriptive question)
4. As a result of the intervention, are graduates of schools using market-based curricula obtaining higher-paying jobs than they otherwise would have? (cause-and-effect question)

*Source*: Authors.

### Relationship between Question Types and Theories of Change

How do question types fit with the theories of change discussed in the previous chapter? Questions about whether program inputs have been obtained and output targets reached are usually normative questions: did the funds spent procure the required number of goods and delivery of services over the time specified? Questions concerning attainment of targeted outcomes are also normative questions. Asking to what extent reading scores increased over a period of time is a descriptive question; asking if reading scores increased to the target set out by program managers is a normative question. Questions that seek to test relationships posited in theory of change models that, because of an intervention, gains were made that would not otherwise have been made are cause-and-effect questions. Questions about these gains leading to other intermediate outcomes or impacts are also cause-and-effect questions.

Frequently, questions about changes in outcomes are either descriptive questions or poorly worded cause-and-effect questions. If meant to be cause-and-effect questions, they may need to be rewritten to indicate that the question is not only what change occurred but also whether the change can be attributed to the intervention (that is, the change is greater than it would have been absent the intervention). Other outcomes and impacts may also be attributed to the intervention, as posited in the theory of change.

## Identifying and Selecting Questions

How does the evaluator decide which of many potential questions to pose? Cronbach (1982) suggests using two phases for identifying and selecting questions, the divergent phase and the convergent phase.

### The Divergent Phase

■ **Divergent phase:** Phase of an evaluation in which the evaluator develops a comprehensive list of potentially important questions and concerns

In the **divergent phase**, the evaluator develops a comprehensive list of potentially important questions and concerns. Few questions are eliminated; many sources are consulted. Cronbach (1982) summarizes the divergent phase of planning an evaluation as follows:

> The first step is opening one's mind to questions to be entertained at least briefly as prospects for investigation. This phase constitutes an evaluative act in itself, requiring collection of data, reasoned analysis, and judgment. Very little of this information and analysis is quantitative. The data come from informal conversations, casual observations, and review of extant records.

Naturalistic and qualitative methods are particularly suited to this work because, attending to the perceptions of participants and interested parties, they enable the evaluator to identify hopes and fears that may not yet have surfaced as policy issues. . . .

The evaluator should try to see the program through the eyes of the various sectors of the decision making community, including the professionals who would operate the program if it is adopted and the citizens who are to be served by it.

At some point, no new questions are being generated. At that time, the evaluator should stop and examine the list of questions and begin to organize them.

## The Convergent Phase

In the **convergent phase**, the evaluator narrows the list of questions generated in the divergent phase in order to identify the most critical questions. How does the evaluator decide which questions are most critical? Fitzpatrick, Sanders, and Worthen (2004) propose the following criteria for determining which proposed evaluation questions should be investigated:

- Who would use the information? Who wants to know? Who would be upset if this evaluation question were dropped?
- Would an answer to the question reduce uncertainty or provide information not now readily available?
- Would the answer to the question yield important information? Would it have an impact on the course of events?
- Is this question merely of passing interest to someone, or does it focus on critical dimensions of continued interest?
- Would the scope or comprehensiveness of the evaluation be seriously limited if this question were dropped?
- Is it feasible to answer this question, given financial and human resources, time, methods, and technology?

This list of criteria can be put into a matrix to help the evaluator and client narrow down the original list of questions into a manageable set (table 6.2).

The evaluator should pay particular attention to the questions the client and key stakeholders pose. If there are disagreements on questions, it is usually important to resolve them at this early stage. The process helps the evaluator and client, as well as other key stakeholders, establish a sense of shared ownership or partnership that can be valuable during later stages of the evaluation.

■ **Convergent phase:** Phase of an evaluation in which the evaluator narrows the list of questions generated in the divergent phase in order to identify the most critical questions

**Table 6.2  Matrix for Selecting and Ranking Evaluation Questions**

| | Evaluation question | | | | | | | | | |
|---|---|---|---|---|---|---|---|---|---|---|
| *Would the evaluation question* | 1 | 2 | 3 | 4 | 5 | 6 | 7 | 8 | 9 | 10 |
| be of interest to key audiences? | | | | | | | | | | |
| reduce present uncertainty? | | | | | | | | | | |
| yield important information? | | | | | | | | | | |
| be of continuing (not fleeting) interest? | | | | | | | | | | |
| be critical to the study's scope and comprehensiveness? | | | | | | | | | | |
| have an impact on the course of events? | | | | | | | | | | |
| be answerable given the financial and human resources, time, methods, and technology available? | | | | | | | | | | |

*Source:* Adapted from Fitzpatrick, Sanders, and Worthen 2004.

## Developing Good Questions

To develop good evaluation questions, the evaluator begins by identifying the major issues being addressed by the project, program, or policy. As noted earlier, major issues are generally identified through a review of the related literature, including evaluations of similar programs, the theory of change, and program documents, as well as through discussions with program stakeholders and the client funding the evaluations.

Examples of major issues to be addressed by an evaluation of a program that aims to reduce infant mortality include the following:

- multiple causes of infant mortality
- competing ongoing programs
- effectiveness of methods used to reach low-income mothers
- extent and nature of use of food supplements for unintended purposes.

Once these issues have been identified, the evaluator can ask the questions that will help determine if the issues have been affected by the policy or intervention. Sample questions to learn about issues include the following:

- What outreach methods has the program used?
- Which outreach methods have been the most effective?

- What was the incidence of life-threatening infant diseases during the time the program was operational?
- By how much have mortality rates decreased?
- What other related efforts to improve maternal health have been ongoing?

Questions that include more than one issue—such as "how many women have received health screenings and nutritional supplements?"—should be avoided. Instead, the question should be separated into two questions ("How many women have received health screenings? How many women have received nutritional supplements?").

Questions about an issue can be addressed using all three question types by adjusting the wording. An evaluation of a program intended to reduce injury and death from land mines, for example, could ask the following questions:

- Where do most involving land mines occur? (descriptive)
- Did the project reach the goal of eliminating 1,000 land mines in the area within the given time? (normative)
- Has the number of people injured or killed from land mines decreased as a result of the intervention? (cause and effect)

The following suggestions can help evaluators write better questions.

- Establish a clear link between each evaluation question and the purpose of the study.
- Make sure that the evaluation questions address the issues of greatest concern.
- Make sure that all questions are answerable.
- Set a realistic number of questions.
- Focus on the important questions, the ones that must be answered as opposed to those that would be nice to investigate.
- Make sure that questions are answerable given the evaluation's time-frame and available resources.
- Consider the timing of the evaluation relative to the program cycle. Questions about impact, for example, are best answered after the intervention has been fully operational for a few years.

The evaluation questions may relate to a project, a program, an overarching policy issue, a specific policy, or a specific intervention associated with a policy. For example, if the overall concern (the policy issue) is reducing poverty, a number of program interventions may be launched. Each policy gets translated into action through an intervention designed to achieve specific objectives. Ultimately, if the policy and the interventions are carried out effectively and the theory of change is correct, then the overall outcomes should be attained. If they are not, then both the interventions and policy need to be reassessed. One or both may need to be changed.

## Designing the Evaluation

Much like an architect designs a building, an evaluator designs an evaluation. An evaluation design is the plan for what the evaluation will include. It is not the full work plan for the study.

An evaluation design consists of

- the major evaluation issue or question
- the general evaluation approach
- specific evaluation questions and subquestions
- the operationalization (measures or indicators), data sources, and methodological strategies for the type of data collection to be used
- the analysis planned
- the dissemination strategy.

Patton (1997) distinguishes between two kinds of design issues: conceptual issues and technical issues. Conceptual issues focus on how the people involved think about the evaluation. They include such issues as determining the purpose of the evaluation and its primary stakeholders, as well as political issues that should be taken into account.

Technical issues concern the plan for collecting and analyzing the data. These technical issues are the heart of the design matrix that should be developed for any evaluation. For each question or more typically subquestion, the design matrix requires:

- determining the type of question or subquestion being asked (descriptive, normative, cause and effect)
- specifying the measure (indicator or variable) by which the question or subquestion will be answered (for example, percentage growth in local housing or number of children vaccinated)
- identifying the methodological design that will provide appropriate information for answering the descriptive, normative, or cause-and-effect question
- identifying the sources of data for each question or subquestion
- determining if a sampling framework is needed and, if so, what kind will be used

- identifying the type of data collection instrument(s) that will be used for each question or subquestion
- identifying how the data will be analyzed and presented.

Sometimes the measure by which the question will be answered is an agreed-on indicator with a clear target and date by which it will be achieved. This is the ideal situation; it is most often the case when a monitoring and evaluation framework has been developed for the intervention or the intervention is part of a larger monitoring system for a sector or government ministry, for example. Whether or not a target is set, the presence or absence of a baseline must be indicated.

The completed evaluation matrix represents the evaluation design. This is not the complete work plan: it does not indicate all the tasks or identify who will perform each task and when. The complete work plan is covered in chapter 12.

## Stages in the Evaluation Design Process

Ideally, the evaluation process begins ex ante, with the initial program design. It then proceeds in several distinct and important stages.

### Stage 1: Planning for or scoping the evaluation

The initial planning or scoping phase clarifies the nature and scope of the evaluation. During this phase, the main purpose of the evaluation, the stakeholders to be consulted, the person who will conduct the evaluation, and the time frame for the results are established. This is an exploratory period. Key issues are identified from the perspective of the main client and other stakeholders, the literature review, and related interventions that may influence the program. The theory of change and assumptions underlying it are developed or refined.

### Stage 2: Designing the evaluation

At the end of the initial planning or scoping phase, there should be enough knowledge of the context for the evaluation that a general approach may be decided. The heart of the evaluation planning is the evaluation design phase, which culminates in the evaluation design matrix. A flawed overall design will limit the ability to draw conclusions about the performance of the intervention.

It is generally a good practice to present and discuss the overall design with the evaluation sponsor (client) and other key stakeholders before finalizing the evaluation design. Doing so ensures that there are no surprises, and it builds buy-in and support of the evaluation. An advisory group and peer reviewers are also good sounding boards to ensure the soundness of the evaluation design. In high-profile cases, draft designs can be posted on a Web site for comment.

The design matrix can be used as the basis for developing the terms of reference (TOR). The TOR may serve as the basis for a request for proposal or as a guide for the evaluation team if the evaluation is conducted internally. When the scoping and background work for the evaluation are to be conducted by an external consultant, it is wise to put the matrix as a deliverable for this work. Subsequently, another TOR can be developed for implementation of the evaluation design.

### Stage 3: Conducting the evaluation

The "doing phase" of the evaluation involves the gathering and analysis of the data. Typically, if different kinds of data are to be collected (or similar data collected from different sources), different instruments must be developed and tested. Analysis is often conducted concurrently with data collection.

About two-thirds of the way through data collection, the evaluation team should hold a story conference to examine the findings to date and identify emerging themes and main messages. A **story conference** is a useful way to reach early agreement on the three to five main messages. The purpose of the story conference is to ensure early agreement on the major themes and check that the main issue or question behind the evaluation has been addressed. (While the report outline may have been organized around the evaluation questions, organizing the final report and communicating with decision makers by message or theme may be more effective, as not all the evaluation questions are likely to be of equal interest.)

■ **Story conference:** Meeting at which the evaluation team discusses and agrees on a major theme and checks that the main issue behind the evaluation has been addressed

### Stage 4: Reporting the evaluation's findings

In the reporting phase, initial findings or statements of fact can be shared and discussed with the program "owners" so that any factual errors can be corrected and any new information considered before a report is drafted and recommendations developed. Once the analysis is completed, the results are written up, drafts are reviewed, comments are incorporated as appropriate, and a final report is presented to the client and key stakeholders.

A report typically provides background and context for the evaluation, indicates the purpose of the evaluation, describes the evaluation's scope and methodology, and reports findings (including both intended and unintended outcomes). It generally also includes information about lessons learned and recommendations. Understanding what does not work well and why is as important as understanding what works and why; both should be clear. The report should be written with its audience in mind; it should be free of jargon and easy to read. (Report writing is discussed in chapter 13.)

### Stage 5: Disseminating and following up on the evaluation's findings

Planning the evaluation means planning for communication along the way, not only with the client and key stakeholders but also within the evaluation team. An evaluation is not complete until its dissemination is complete: development of a dissemination plan is, therefore, part of the planning process. Findings do not always need to be presented in printed form. Briefings are especially useful for communicating findings while the evaluation is ongoing, especially when the findings are unexpected or critical.

Many evaluations result in action to

- modify an intervention
- remove barriers identified in the evaluation
- inform future policy or interventions (modify the theory of change)
- show others the way in relation to lessons learned
- reshape thinking about the nature of the problem.

Many organizations have follow-up systems to track formal recommendations and summarize lessons. The capability to search such databases by theme, sector, locality, and date increases their utility. Whether or not such systems are in place, evaluators should consider sending a read-only electronic copy of the report to relevant evaluation knowledge bases. They may also want to consider presenting their findings at evaluation conferences or submitting an article on the evaluation for publication in a professional journal.

### Relationship between stages

The various stages are summarized in box 6.3. The relationship between the different components is shown in figure 6.2.

Figure 6.2 illustrates the centrality of promoting evaluation use to the entire evaluation process. Rather than something thought about at the end of the evaluation, promoting evaluation use is the center of the evaluation, with other evaluation processes or stages guided by it.

**Box 6.3   The Five Stages of the Evaluation Process**

*Stage 1: Planning for or Scoping the Evaluation*

Gain a thorough understanding of the program, project, or policy.

- Meet with the main client for the evaluation.
- Identify and meet with other key stakeholders.
- Explore program context and gather background materials.
- Search for related relevant evaluations.
- Review previous evaluations to identify issues, designs, and data collection strategies used.
- Meet with program staff (if external to the program).
- Review and refine or develop a theory of change for the program.

*Stage 2: Designing the Evaluation*

Determine the questions and issues.

- Meet the client, and identify the main purpose of the evaluation, issues of concern, and critical timing needs.
- Identify and meet with other key stakeholders to identify issues and concerns for possible inclusion in the evaluation.
- Determine resources available for the evaluation, such as budget for consultants and travel, team members, and skill mix.
- Assess stakeholders' needs, including timing.

Prepare terms of reference and evaluation matrix.

- Identify the type of evaluation.
- Identify specific evaluation questions and subquestions.
- Select measures for each question or subquestion.
- Identify data sources for addressing each question or subquestion.
- Identify an appropriate design for each question or subquestion.
- Develop a data collection strategy, including the instruments and sampling methods to be used for each question or subquestion.
- Develop a strategy for analyzing the data.
- Determine resource and time requirements.

*Stage 3: Conducting the Evaluation*

- Brief the client and key stakeholders on the evaluation design.
- Prepare a work plan, including reviewing and testing the methodology, including pretest instruments, training data collectors, and developing protocol.

- Gather the data.
- Prepare the data for analysis by developing table shells (if not conducted as part of the evaluation design) and cleaning the data.
- Analyze the data.
- Develop graphics.
- Formulate the findings.

### Stage 4: Reporting the Evaluation's Findings

- Hold a story conference.
- Identify major findings and themes: what works, what does not, and what needs improvement.
- Write the report.
- Brief the client on findings and statements of fact.
- Brief program officials and key stakeholders on findings and statements of fact, and make corrections as needed.
- Allow program officials to review and comment on the draft report.
- Develop recommendations that are clear and specific and indicate who should do what and when.
- Check that recommendations are linked to evidence.

### Stage 5: Disseminating and Following Up on the Evaluation's Findings

- Determine who will receive what kind of study dissemination product (for example, a briefing, a two- to four-page summary, the full report, an in-depth workshop) and implement the plan.
- Identify lessons and mechanisms for sharing and retaining them.
- Follow up on formal recommendations to determine implementation.
- Deposit electronic file in read-only form in evaluation knowledge repositories.
- Consider further dissemination through professional organizations and journals.

*Source*: Authors.

**Figure 6.2 Approach to Development Evaluation**

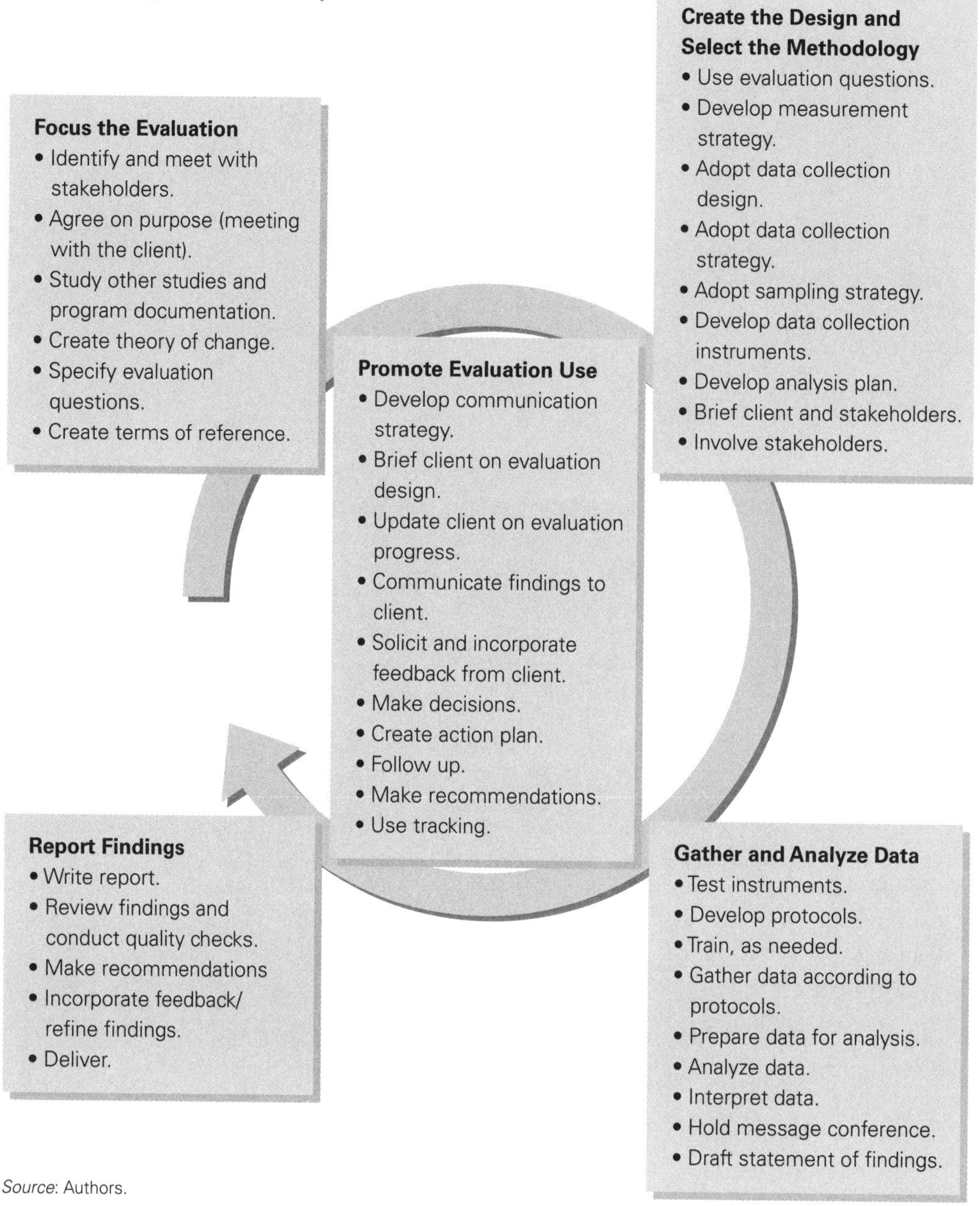

**Focus the Evaluation**
- Identify and meet with stakeholders.
- Agree on purpose (meeting with the client).
- Study other studies and program documentation.
- Create theory of change.
- Specify evaluation questions.
- Create terms of reference.

**Create the Design and Select the Methodology**
- Use evaluation questions.
- Develop measurement strategy.
- Adopt data collection design.
- Adopt data collection strategy.
- Adopt sampling strategy.
- Develop data collection instruments.
- Develop analysis plan.
- Brief client and stakeholders.
- Involve stakeholders.

**Promote Evaluation Use**
- Develop communication strategy.
- Brief client on evaluation design.
- Update client on evaluation progress.
- Communicate findings to client.
- Solicit and incorporate feedback from client.
- Make decisions.
- Create action plan.
- Follow up.
- Make recommendations.
- Use tracking.

**Report Findings**
- Write report.
- Review findings and conduct quality checks.
- Make recommendations
- Incorporate feedback/ refine findings.
- Deliver.

**Gather and Analyze Data**
- Test instruments.
- Develop protocols.
- Train, as needed.
- Gather data according to protocols.
- Prepare data for analysis.
- Analyze data.
- Interpret data.
- Hold message conference.
- Draft statement of findings.

*Source*: Authors.

## The Evaluation Design Matrix

An **evaluation design matrix** is a highly recommended organizing tool to help plan an evaluation. It organizes the evaluation questions and the plans for collecting information to answer the questions. The matrix links descriptive, normative, and cause-and-effect questions to the design and methodologies. Beyond its immediate usefulness as a planning tool, the matrix can help promote the use of the evaluation and enhance cooperation between evaluators and program staff members.

Evaluators need a tool to identify the necessary pieces of the evaluation and to ensure that they connect clearly at every step. Which tool they use to help think about a program; what its context, measurable objectives, and data collection and analysis are; and which strategies to use will vary. Some evaluators may decide to create their own tools.

The purpose of the design matrix is to organize the evaluation purpose and questions and to match what is to be evaluated with the appropriate data collection techniques. A design matrix usually includes the following linked elements:

- main evaluation issue
- general approach
- questions and subquestions
- type of questions and subquestions
- measures or indicators
- targets or standards (if normative)
- presence or absence of baseline data
- design strategy
- data sources
- sample or census
- data collection instrument
- data analysis and graphics
- comments.

Data collection protocols and evaluation on work assignments and schedules, terms of references, and communication plans may be added or remain as separate but linked tools.

The data collection method may address more than one question, or several data collection methods may be used to address a single question. The design matrix incorporates known and planned sources of information. As the process moves from planning to implementation, sources can be expanded and clarified.

■ **Evaluation design matrix:** Matrix that organizes evaluation questions and plans for collecting information to answer them

The evaluation matrix is not cast in stone. Like any other planning tool, it undoubtedly will need modification as the evaluation progresses. During the evaluation, evaluators can review the matrix, update it, and use it as a guide for implementing the evaluation. While up-front planning should minimize the surfacing of problems, the best of planning cannot prevent surprises. The template for a design matrix is shown in figure 6.3.

In the design matrix, questions are broken down into as many subquestions as needed. For each, specification should be made of the type of subquestion (descriptive, normative, or cause-and-effect), the measure (think variable or indicator) used to answer it; the target or standard that it will be compared to IF a normative subquestion; the indication if baseline data exist; the data source or sources for answering the subquestion; the actual design strategy that will be used to answer the subquestion; the specification of whether a sample will be taken and if so, what type; the data collection instrument to be used; the analysis to be performed; and any comments noted. Examples of comments include notes to check the quality of a dataset, to indicate limitations of the design, and to develop a graphic from the data.

The matrix is often presented on legal-size paper or by piecing two pieces of paper together side-by-side. Some evaluators prefer to work the matrix vertically for each subquestion. Whatever format is used, evaluators must fill in all cells for each subquestion.

A completed design matrix will run multiple pages. It is this document that lets a decision maker understand what needs to be done and how the evaluation questions will be answered. The next chapters discuss the filling in of the columns in detail.

At this point, readers who are trying to apply the matrix to design an evaluation of a program, policy, or project can identify the questions and subquestions and can indicate the type of subquestion. The columns for presence or absence of baseline data, measure or indicator, and target (if the subquestion is normative) can also be filled in.

Subquestions for descriptive questions will be descriptive. Subquestions for a normative question may be descriptive, but at least one subquestion must be normative. Cause-and-effect questions must have at least one cause-and-effect subquestion but may include descriptive or normative subquestions. An example of a completed design matrix is in Appendix B.

Figure 6.3　Design Matrix Template

**Design matrix for:** _____　　**General evaluation approach:** _____
**Main evaluation issue:** _____

| Question | Subquestion | Type of subquestion | Measure or indicator | Target or standard (normative) | Baseline data? | Data source | Design | Sample or census | Data collection instrument | Data analysis | Comments |
|---|---|---|---|---|---|---|---|---|---|---|---|
| | | | | | | | | | | | |
| | | | | | | | | | | | |
| | | | | | | | | | | | |
| | | | | | | | | | | | |
| | | | | | | | | | | | |

## Summary

Evaluators need to work with the main client and key stakeholders to identify possible questions. After completing the background research and meeting with the client and key stakeholders, developing the program theory of change, and identifying major assumptions underlying the program, the evaluator can begin to generate and then select evaluation questions from the long list of those generated. Evaluation questions should be checked against the major evaluation issue to confirm that it is being addressed.

Evaluators use descriptive questions, normative questions, and cause-and-effect questions. The wording of each question is important, because it helps determine the means for finding the answers to the question.

The recommended way to organize the evaluation is to use a design matrix. The matrix helps to organize the questions, designs, and data collection and analysis strategies, among other things. The following chapters provide a step-by-step guide to completing the design matrix.

**Application Exercise 6.1: Types of Questions**

Identify whether each of the following questions about a rural women's pre-ventative health initiative is a descriptive, normative, or cause-and-effect question. If some questions need to be rewritten to make their type clearer, do so (this is often the case in real life).

1. Did the initiative provide the required advice, support, and other services to 30 rural women in its first month of operation, as planned?
2. Were services delivered at a location and time that maximized the number of women who could participate?
3. What were the best methods for reaching women in remote areas and making the program accessible to them?
4. Were health problems among rural women detected earlier among those who participated in the women's health initiative?
5. Since the program's inception, how many women have received what types of services?
6. How effective is the women's health initiative compared with other interventions for improving the health of rural women?
7. What is the impact of the health initiative on the women, their families, and the wider rural community in which they live?
8. How satisfied are participants with the advice, information, support, and other services they receive?
9. Is the rural women's health initiative meeting the government's required efficiency standards?
10. What do participants say are the impacts of the program on them?
11. To what extent did women receiving services meet eligibility requirements?
12. Did the program meet its objective of increasing women's knowledge of preventative techniques?

**Application Exercise 6.2: Modifying Question Types**

Write one descriptive, one normative, and one cause-and-effect question for each of the following programs:

1. A vocational training program that trains young men
2. A road-building program that links three communities to a central market

# References and Further Reading

Cronbach, L. J. 1982. *Designing Evaluations of Educational and Social Programs*. San Francisco: Jossey-Bass.

Feuerstein, M. T. 1986. *Partners in Evaluation: Evaluating Development and Community Programs with Participants*. London: MacMillan, in association with Teaching Aids at Low Cost.

Fitzpatrick, Jody L., James R. Sanders, and Blaine R. Worthen. 2004. *Program Evaluation: Alternative Approaches and Practical Guidelines*. New York: Pearson Education Inc.

Human Rights Resource Center. 2000. "Questions about Evaluation." In *The Human Rights Education Handbook: Effective Practices for Learning, Action, and Change*. University of Minnesota, Minneapolis. http://www1.umn.edu/humanrts/edumat/hreduseries/hrhandbook/part6B.html.

Lawrence, J. 1989. "Engaging Recipients in Development Evaluation: The 'Stakeholder' Approach." *Evaluation Review* 13 (3): 243–56.

OECD (Organisation for Economic Co-operation and Development). 2007. *Criteria for Evaluating Development Assistance*. Development Assistance Committee. http://www.oecd.org/document/22/0,2340,en_2649_201185_2086550_1_1_1_1,00.html.

Patton, Michael Quinn. 1997. *Utilization-Focused Evaluation*. 3rd ed. Thousand Oaks, CA: Sage Publications.

———. 2002. *Qualitative Research and Evaluation Methods*. 3rd ed. Thousand Oaks, CA: Sage Publications.

Rist, R. C. 1994. "Influencing the Policy Process with Qualitative Research." In *Handbook of Qualitative Research*, ed. N. K. Denzin and Y. S. Lincoln, 545–57. Thousand Oaks, CA: Sage Publications.

Shadish, William 1998. "Some Evaluation Questions." *Practical Assessment, Research & Evaluation* 63. http://PAREonline.net/getvn.asp?v=6&n=3. Also available from ERIC/AE Digest at http://www.ericdigests.org/1999-2/some.htm.

## Web Sites

Kellogg Foundation. 2004. *Evaluation Logic Model Development Guide*. http://www.wkkf.org/pubs/tools/evaluation/pub3669.pdf.

World Bank. 1996. *Participation Sourcebook*. http://www.worldbank.org/wbi/sourcebook/sbhome.htm.

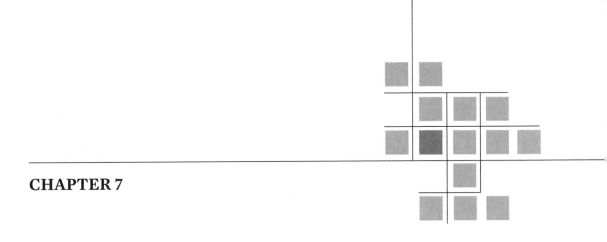

**CHAPTER 7**

# Selecting Designs for Cause-and-Effect, Descriptive, and Normative Evaluation Questions

After choosing the evaluation questions, the evaluator next selects the evaluation design approach that is most appropriate given each question. This chapter presents some guidelines on design and identifies the strengths and weaknesses of various design options. It is important to keep in mind, however, that every situation is unique. There is no perfect design choice and thus no "one and only" way to address an evaluation question.

**This chapter has five main parts:**

- Connecting Questions to Design
- Designs for Cause-and-Effect Questions
- Designs for Descriptive Questions
- Designs for Normative Questions
- The Need for More Rigorous Designs.

# Connecting Questions to Design

When we evaluate, we seek to answer questions. In chapter 6, we indicated there were three main types of questions: descriptive, normative, and cause-and-effect questions The design selected should be appropriate to the type of questions being asked. If, for example, cause-and-effect questions are posed, a design that can answer cause-and-effect questions must be adopted.

Development organizations seek to find solutions to questions about development issues, just as villagers might seek to learn how to solve a problem plaguing their village (box 7.1). In attempting to answer questions, however, neither evaluators nor villagers have always taken the right steps.

The first potential misstep in answering a question is to begin by choosing a strategy for collecting data. To answer the young girl's question on the elephants, the village elder might say, "Let's conduct a survey and find out what villagers say makes the elephants leave." Leading with a data collection strategy is almost certainly not going to provide the information needed.

The second potential misstep is to think that each evaluation has a single design. Typically, an evaluation seeks to address several questions, each of which requires an appropriate design. An evaluation will usually need to address descriptive and normative questions and sometimes cause-and-effect questions. The evaluator needs to avoid applying the "method in search of an application" technique (what questions can we answer by conducting a survey or focus groups?) or thinking that if one is addressing a cause-and-effect question, one does not also have to address descriptive and normative questions.

In the elephant example, it is possible that an in-depth case study of the elephants' movements would show that neither the pot banging nor the dust

---

**Box 7.1  What Makes Elephants Go Away?**

Twice each year, from opposite directions, elephants rampaged through an African village. All of the villagers were involved in driving the elephants away. Some banged pots and pans; others whistled, shouted, or screamed. Others kicked up dust and moved around in an effort to establish their ownership of the land.

After the elephants left the village, one young girl asked, "Why did the elephants leave?" The villagers answered, "Because we drove them away." The girl then asked, "But what was it that made them leave, the sound of banging on pots, whistling, or other loud noises, or the dust in the air?"

made the elephants leave the village. The village may instead have simply been in the elephants' migrating path.

## Broad Categories of Design

Evaluators have three broad categories of designs from which to select: experimental designs, quasi-experimental designs, and nonexperimental designs. Each is described below.

### *Experimental design*

Many evaluators consider an **experimental design**—also called a *randomized* or *true experiment*—the strongest and most robust design for an evaluation. But many others disagree. As we argue in chapter 6, evaluators should strive for as much rigor as possible, but the right design is the one that is most appropriate for answering the evaluation question. In a true experimental design, evaluators must show that if the intervention had not occurred, the desired result would not have been achieved. Using the elephants in the village example, the evaluator must prove that if the villagers had not banged on pots, whistled, and made other noises, the elephants would not have left the village.

To show that the intervention is the cause of an outcome, an experimental design compares the results of two groups—one that receives an intervention and one that does not. The main criterion for distinguishing experimental designs from other designs is random assignment to groups. Through random assignment, those assigned to groups should be similar in terms of background, gender, context, timeframe, and so forth.

Here our elephant analogy breaks down, because the villagers have no way to separate the elephants into two or three randomly assigned groups that could be subjected to different interventions or no intervention. But to carry the example forward, let us say that the national government is aware of 30 villages in the rural province that report problems with elephants causing destruction of village homes and crops. The government wants to help solve this problem in a manner that lets the elephants and villagers live in harmony. An animal behavior expert is hired but can work with only 20 villages at a time. It is decided that the 20 villages to receive the expert's help will be randomly selected and that the 10 villages not randomly selected will serve as a control group. Surveys are administered to the adult villagers in all 30 villages to provide baseline data for treatment and control groups on attitudes toward the elephants and estimates of crop loss and other damages. For selection of the villages to receive the intervention, the names of all 30 villages are written on slips of paper and placed into a bowl. The village

■ **Experimental design:**
A type of ex ante evaluation design requiring random assignment of a population to at least two groups such that each and every member of the population of interest has an equal chance of being assigned to an intervention (treatment group) or to a nonintervention group (control group).

elders are brought together, and the 10 most senior are asked in turn to select (blindly) one of the folded pieces of paper from the bowl. As each name on the papers is read, the village name is written on a blackboard. When 10 have been identified, the control group has been finalized. The objective of the behaviorist intervention is to decrease the problem, improve attitudes, and reduce damages and associated cost. After a predetermined period of time, there should be differences between the treatment and control villages on these measures, if the behaviorist is effective and all else remains constant. In this example, the behaviorist is the intervention.

### Quasi-experimental design

■ **Quasi-experimental design:**
A type of evaluation design where intervention and nonintervention or comparison groups are formed either ex ante or ex post, but without random assignment to groups or where repeated measures are taken over time

A **quasi-experimental design** is similar to an experimental design, but it does not randomly assign individuals to groups. Such designs are often more feasible than experimental designs, because true experimental designs are often difficult to execute and quasi-experimental designs do not require randomization but rather the creation of comparison groups.

A quasi-experimental design can be used to compare groups that are similar but not equivalent. The groups may exist in different but similar villages, or the same group may be used at different times (before and after). In the elephants in the village story, for example, a quasi-experimental design could choose two villages in the same region, with the same climate, the same number of elephants in the area, similar numbers of villagers, the same number of homes, and so forth. One village would receive the treatment (banging pots); the other would not.

Alternatively, the two groups could be selected by changing the behavior of the villagers when the elephants arrive. The first time the elephants arrive in the village, the villagers bang their pots. The second time the elephants arrive at the village, they do not bang their pots. One then has two instances in which to compare the reactions of the elephants.

■ **Nonexperimental (descriptive) design:**
A type of evaluation design where no attempt is made to create intervention and nonintervention groups, and the emphasis is on description

In both examples, the two groups are similar but not equivalent. In the first example, differences between the two groups and their environments may affect the results. In the second example, the difference between the two situations is the behavior of the villagers. With a quasi-experimental design, evaluators cannot definitively link the intervention to the solution or show a cause-and-effect link with the certainty that comes with true randomization, but they can learn a great deal and postulate about the likely cause and effect.

### Nonexperimental design

**Nonexperimental,** or **descriptive, designs** do not compare one group with another. Instead, they provide an extensive description of the relationship

**Table 7.1  Two Key Characteristics of Experimental, Quasi-Experimental, and Nonexperimental Experiments**

| Type of evaluation design | Randomly assigned control group | Non-random comparison group | Repeated measures |
|---|---|---|---|
| Experimental | Yes | No | Yes |
| Quasi-experimental | No | Likely | Likely |
| Nonexperimental | No | No | No |

*Source:* Authors.

between an intervention and its effects. With a nonexperimental study, an evaluator chooses, for example, when to sample, whom to sample, and where to sample. No effort is made to create two or more equivalent or similar samples.

A nonexperimental evaluation may, for example, use an analysis of existing data or information, a survey, or a focus group to gather appropriate data that are relevant to the evaluation questions. Nonexperimental designs tend to look at characteristics, frequency, and associations (Project STAR 2006).

Annex 7.1 summarizes three of the key features of each of the three design categories.

## Design Notation

Evaluation designs are sometimes represented using Xs and Os. In these representations, an X represents an intervention or treatment, and an O represents an observation. Each treatment and observation is given a subscript to identify it. For example, the notation for an evaluation design that has one treatment followed by one observation is

$$X O_1$$

The notation for an evaluation design that has one observation followed by the treatment followed by two observations would be

$$O_1 X O_2 O_3$$

Each group in the design is given a separate line. The following notation shows the notation for an evaluation design that has two groups, one that received the treatment and one that does not. Both groups are observed once before treatment is administered to the test group and twice afterward:

$$O_1 X O_2 O_3$$

$$O_1 O_2 O_3$$

# Designs for Cause-and-Effect Questions

Cause-and-effect questions pose the greatest challenge; answering them requires a particularly well thought-out design. In evaluations that include cause-and- effect questions—that is, questions about the impacts and causes of these observed impacts—the evaluation design attempts to rule out feasible explanations for the observed results other than the intervention in order to conclude that it was the invention that made the impact. In short, the challenge is to decide whether or not to attribute the observed changes (impacts) to the intervention or to some other cause.

When one addresses cause-and-effect questions, evaluation designs can also be framed to address the question "What would the situation have been if the intervention had not taken place?" It may not be possible to measure the counterfactual of no intervention precisely, but it is possible to estimate what might have happened if there was no intervention.

## Experimental Designs

The experimental model has its roots in medical research, where it is often used to test drugs and treatment protocols. In applying this design to a health-related evaluation question, a development organization that seeks to reduce the incidence of malaria in a region might pose the question "What is the best way to reduce the incidence of malaria in the region?" A subquestion might be "Do treated bed nets reduce the incidence of malaria in this region?"

The experimental design takes a question and turns it into a proposition. In the case of the malaria example, the proposition would be as follows: if people in the region are given treated bed nets, then there will be fewer cases of malaria in the region.

As was presented in chapter 4, a theory of change should be developed for the proposition. Randomization is the most important factor in an experimental design. A group of patients may be selected from among volunteers for random trials who have the same stage and type of disease, the same gender, and so forth. Individuals are then randomly assigned to one of several drug regimens. One subgroup may be taking the drug that represents current knowledge; another subgroup may receive another promising new drug. In a double-blind experiment, neither the study participants nor the medical staff members are aware of which drug is being administered to which patients.

There is a slight but growing trend in development evaluation toward using experimental designs. The movement in this direction comes from a frustration with the perceived lack of sufficient knowledge, despite many years of evaluation, of what works in the development context and under what conditions.

A classic experiment has six steps:

1. Formulate a hypothesis.
2. Obtain a baseline (that is, measure the dependent variable).
3. Randomly assign cases to intervention and nonintervention (control) groups.
4. Introduce the treatment or independent variable in the intervention.
5. Measure the dependent variable again (posttest).
6. Calculate the differences between the groups and test for statistical significance.

In the malaria example, the question is whether treated bed netting reduces the incidence of malaria in a region. The six steps would be as follows:

1. *Form a hypothesis:* Households' use of bed nets treated with mosquito repellent reduces the incidence of malaria.
2. *Obtain a baseline:* During a two-month period, the number of new cases of malaria in the region was 172.
3. *Randomly assign cases to intervention and nonintervention (control) groups.*
4. *Introduce treatment:* Give bed nets to one group (the treatment group) and not the other (the control group).
5. *Measure the dependent variable again:* After two months of the intervention, the number of new malaria cases was 65 among the test group and 118 among the control group.
6. *Calculate the difference between the two groups:* The test group had 53 fewer new cases than the control group.

The design notation for the classic experiment with one treatment group and one control group looks like this:

$$O_1 \, X \, O_2$$

$$O_1 \, O_2$$

In some cases, evaluators also use an R in front of the line for each group to show that the group had random assignment. For an experimental design like the one described above (randomly assigning some participants to receive a bed net), the notation would look like this:

$$R \, O_1 \, X \, O_2$$

$$R \, O_1 \, O_2$$

Humans are complex, and social situations are difficult to analyze. The experimental design works well when testing drugs on human bodies, which are relatively similar. When looking at complex human behavior, one needs to be alert for false positives and false negatives. False positives occur when the study indicates the intervention was the cause of the effect when in fact it was not. False negatives occur when a study shows no link between an intervention and success when, in fact, the intervention is actually linked to the success.

A false positive may appear because household data are self-reported. People in the region may be aware of the experiment and the treatment households and underreport cases of malaria to please government officials.

False negative may be more common. No difference may be found between the two groups because the postintervention two-month measurement period was taken in the dry season, when the incidence of malaria is low. A false negative may occur because treatment group households fail to use the bed nets every night or because those in the no-intervention groups purchase nets themselves.

If this study asked no additional questions, it would be hard to interpret results even in this simple random-assignment intervention. For one to explain the results, it would have been helpful if the evaluators had also asked some of the following questions:

- What information did households receive on the use of bed netting?
- How was the composition of the "household" determined, and who actually slept under the bed net?
- What implementation issues were raised by intervention and nonintervention groups?
- How did the incidence of malaria in the region compare historically for the two two-month periods?
- Were any other malaria prevention efforts going on in the region at the time of this intervention?

All of these questions are descriptive questions, which require simpler designs to answer.

### Control groups

An experimental design attempts to rule out or control for other factors that may represent competing explanations for the results in the experiment. When using experimental design, evaluators compare equivalent groups. The **control group** is the group that is exposed to the usual conditions; its members are not exposed to or provided the intervention. The group exposed to the intervention may be called the **treatment group.** Using a

■ **Control group:** Group in an experiment whose members are not exposed to or given an intervention

■ **Treatment group:** Group in an experiment whose members are exposed to or given an intervention

control group allows groups that were exposed to the intervention to be compared with groups that were not exposed to the treatment.

Control groups often involve withholding an intervention from some of those in need. Sometimes withholding the intervention is justified because there are not enough resources to serve all those in need. Only partial coverage of a population with an intervention is possible, or the program will be phased in over time. In other cases, the intervention is unproven, so it is uncertain that something of value is being withheld. If an intervention is shown to be effective, it can be difficult to explain why some people are being denied access to it (Patton 2008).

### Random assignment

Experimental design involves randomly assigning potential program participants to intervention and nonintervention groups in order to maximize the probability that the groups are identical (there was no bias for group assignment) in terms of factors that could influence the program or intervention results. These factors could include participants' age, gender, education, attitudes, history, and other factors.

In the ideal world, one would be able to randomly decide who receives and who does not receive an intervention. A real-world problem in evaluation is to identify a credible control group that does not receive the intervention. One way to do so is by allocating the project or program resources in a random manner. The project or program beneficiaries are then a random sample of the population as a whole. This sample can then be compared with those of another randomly drawn sample of nonbeneficiaries (the control group) (White 2007).

Random assignment may enable the use of a strong design to measure impact. It may also be more equitable than assignment by a different method—no bias or favoritism is in play when assignment to the treatment or control groups is based on random chance.

Although random assignment is more applicable to development interventions than might be thought, it is not always an option. As in medical testing, it is sometimes unethical to withhold an intervention to create a control group, but there may not be sufficient resources to accommodate all who apply to participate, thus resulting in withholding the treatment from some. A project manager may want to assign those with the best chance of benefiting from the intervention to participate. This may be a way to get the most benefit from limited program dollars. From an evaluation perspective, however, if the best people are assigned to the program, the results will be biased, because the samples were not created in an unbiased randomized manner.

When random selection is not possible, one option is to collect data about factors that may differ between the two groups and that seem likely to affect outcomes. These variables can then be built into the data analysis as control variables. Using **control variables** allows the evaluator to rule out some alternative explanations even when random assignment is not possible.

When selecting groups, evaluators need to consider the problem of selection bias. In **selection bias,** a difference between the participants and nonparticipants may be based on unobservable differences between the groups rather than the effects of the intervention.

The process of randomization ensures that before the intervention takes place the treatment and control groups are statistically equivalent, on average, with respect to all characteristics. Randomized experiments solve the problem of selection bias by generating an experimental control group of people who would have participated in a program but who were randomly denied access to the program or treatment. The random assignment does not remove the selection bias but instead balances the bias between the participant (treatment) and nonparticipant (control) groups, so that it cancels out when calculating the mean impact estimate. Any differences in the average outcomes of the two groups after the intervention can be attributed to the intervention (World Bank 2008.)

Selection bias can occur in two ways. First, participants may self-select into a program. Second, program managers may select the participants most likely to succeed. For example, consider the treated bed netting program. If the program intervention were to introduce treated bed nets into the market at a very low cost, there would be selection bias, because only those who both could afford to purchase and did purchase the bed netting would be in the treatment group; those who could not afford the netting or those who did not learn about treated bed netting would not be in the treatment group. Moreover, it would be very difficult to compare the treatment and control groups, because there may be no record of who used bed netting and who did not.

To reduce the possibility of being mislead into thinking that something that is not true is true (a false positive), evaluators borrow from social science methods. Using an experimental evaluation design, evaluators do all they can to control the implementation of a program, policy, or project and the environment in which it is delivered. When the evaluation can reasonably control everything but the intervention, evaluators can be fairly certain that any observed differences are the result of that intervention.

Consider an evaluation of an intervention that applies fertilizer in order to increase the crop yield of corn. The project operates a greenhouse where villagers control the temperature, water, and soil conditions. As part of the evaluation design, two separate growing areas are created within the greenhouse. One is randomly assigned to receive fertilizer; the other serves as a control area. Both areas receive the same temperature, sunlight, and water, and the corn is planted in exactly the same soil mixture. At harvest, the yields are measured. If the test area has a higher yield than the control area, the evaluator can conclude that the fertilizer made a difference.

Now think about what happens when the intervention is applied in the field instead of in the controlled environment of the greenhouse. What happens if the two areas are close together and fertilizer runs off into the nontest area? The nontest area could be moved to a different part of the field—but the soil, light, temperature, or rainfall might be slightly different there. The two fields may also receive different amounts of attention. While the evaluation could still measure impact, it would likely be more tentative about concluding that the fertilizer alone caused higher yields.

In the complex world in which development interventions take place, it becomes difficult to determine attribution in the midst of other factors. In the agricultural case, suppose an irrigation intervention was implemented during a time of ideal weather and strong demand for crops. The income in the area in which the irrigation intervention was implemented increased over previous years. But is the higher income a result of the intervention? Or is it caused by other factors, such as increased rainfall, good economic times, or an unusual period of political stability? Ideally, one would take those eligible for the water irrigation intervention within a defined area and randomly assign some to the intervention and some to the nonintervention group. But what are the options when random assignment is not possible and the experimental design is thus not an option?

In many such cases, quasi-experimental designs are used for attribution. In quasi-experimental designs, there is comparison but without random assignment of groups. Chatterji (2007), Patton (2007), and Bamberger and White (2007) have excellent papers on the limitations of experimental designs in the real world.

### Internal validity

When we talk about eliminating other possible explanations, we are talking about internal validity. **Internal validity** refers to the design's ability to rule out other explanations for the observed results. An evaluation design with strong internal validity increases evaluators' confidence in their conclusion that the intervention did or did not cause the observed results. A design with weak internal validity makes it harder to convince others that the intervention caused the observed results. Internal validity is raised here, because in the absence of randomization, the validity of the evaluation findings can be compromised in a variety of ways.

■ **Interval validity:** Ability of a design to rule out all other potential alternate factors or explanations for the observed results other than the intervention

These threats to the internal validity of the evaluation findings are just possible rival explanations; they may not actually exist. Thus internal validity is context related. Quasi-experimental designs need to address threats to internal validity.

The United Kingdom Evaluation Society (2003) defines internal validity in this way:

> The confidence one can have in one's conclusions about what the intervention actually did accomplish. A threat to internal validity is an objection that the evaluation design allows the causal link between the intervention and the observed effects to remain uncertain. It may be thought of as a question of the following nature: could not something else besides the intervention account for the difference between the situation after the intervention and the counterfactual?

In a classic text, Cook and Campbell (1979) identify several common threats to internal validity:

- history
- maturation
- repeated testing
- selection bias
- mortality
- regression to the mean
- instrumentation.

■ **History effect:** Effect of events unrelated to an intervention on its results

*The history effect.*   The **history effect** refers to the possibility that events that occurred during the course of the intervention or between repeated measures that are not part of the intervention may have influenced the results. History will always be a threat in longitudinal research. It is perhaps the most difficult threat to detect, because the evaluator must investigate events that occurred during the intervention that may have affected the results. When one looks at the results for an individual, historical events that affect the results are quite probable. Personal history involves a succession of events, some of which may be trait changing. For a group of individuals, a historical threat to internal validity must identify an event that simultaneously affected most or at least some of the individuals enough to appreciably change the measured trait. As Brossart, Clay, and Willson (2002) note:

> If all individuals are members of some group, the search for this event may be conducted through interview or observation; if the participants are independent, the likelihood of such an event simultaneously changing the trait will be small unless the event occurs in a common setting where all participants are located, such as a hospital.

Say, for example, that during the course of a program aimed at high-risk youth, a heinous crime is committed by a juvenile offender. The situation brings about an outcry for tougher responses to high-risk juveniles. The situation may alter the types of people referred to the program and presumably affect the results. Attitude surveys are particularly subject to influences of this type, because opinions may be heavily influenced by recent events and media presentation of topical issues (Office of Juvenile Justice and Delinquency Prevention 1989).

Consider an intervention such as the introduction of a new seed or improved cultivation training for farmers in a province. The dependent variable or outcome measure may be increased income from crops relative to the previous year. But it could be that farmers stuck to their old ways of cultivation and tried and true seed, even though their income increased on average. Deeper investigation may show a year of excellent climate for crop production. Climate rather than the intervention was the cause of the results. Events outside the intervention influenced the results. Before-and-after designs often suffer from the history effect.

*The maturation effect.* The **maturation effect** occurs when results are caused by aging or development. As people age, they mature. As they mature, they may feel or respond differently to situations. Changes that naturally occur as a result of the passage of time include growing older, getting smarter, and gaining experience. This effect occurs among individuals and groups. Children, for example, are likely to become better readers over a two-year period even without additional training. Organizations also develop and change. These changes may be part of a natural cycle of growth and development and have nothing to do with the intervention. Before-and-after designs often are weak because of the maturation effect.

■ **Maturation effect:** Effect of aging or development on results

Maturation may be conceived as occurring in two forms: short or long term. Short-term maturation is demonstrated by fatigue and learning. Long-term maturation deals with psychophysical development, cultural changes, and environmental changes that can affect psychological constructs. When measurements are made several months apart, long-term maturation is potentially important.

For example, an evaluation may investigate the effects of a two-year reading program on reading scores for primary school children. After two years, the children's cognitive skills will increase with or without the reading program. How can the evaluator be sure the increased reading scores reflected the reading program and not the maturation of the students?

*The repeated testing effect.* The **repeated testing effect** (short-term) occurs when subjects are given the same test before and after the intervention or multiple times. The subjects may learn how to respond to the questions, marring the validity of the results.

■ **Repeated testing effect:** Effect on results caused by exposure of subjects to a test multiple times

Consider, for example, an intervention that is attempting to improve the skills of teachers in rural schools. Teachers are given performance tests at the end of each month. They are evaluated by members of the evaluation committee using a checklist and provided with monthly feedback on their performance. The teachers may improve on skills measured on the standard checklist just by repeated skill testing.

*Selection bias.* **Selection bias** is created when a group of people that self-selects into a program is compared with a group of people that did not self-select into the program. The two groups are not equivalent, because self-selecting individuals are more likely to improve their skills or change their attitudes even without the program intervention than those who did not choose to participate. Selection bias may even be present in those who choose to complete a survey versus those who do not respond. Self-selection bias is possible in any program in which people or firms find out about and sign up for a program. This is a risk for quasi-experimental design.

*The mortality effect.* The **mortality effect** refers to dropouts from an intervention. Losing participants can create a false treatment effect that appears to be the result of the intervention. Just as selection can be a source of bias, so can the differential dropout rate among participants. While there is a strong temptation to present results only on those who successfully complete the program, doing so will result in a biased group, because those who drop out from a program likely had worse performance than those completing it. While completing a program and obtaining the full treatment effect are important inputs to an evaluation, they should not cloud the comparison with the performance of a comparison group.

Consider, for example, a teacher education program with 400 participants that used graduation rates as one way to determine the success of the program. After the three-year program, 25 of the participants had died of AIDS. The loss of these participants artificially lowered the graduation rate, creating the impression that the program was less successful than it may actually have been.

Consider another example, using the same teacher education program. Suppose the teachers' college sponsoring the program had a policy that pregnant women could not attend classes or sit for examinations. Pregnant women would then not be included in graduation rates.

*The regression to the mean effect.* The phenomenon of regression shows a natural tendency for individuals who score either very high or very low to score closer to the middle when retested. This effect is known as **regression**

---

**■ Selection bias:** Distortion of evidence or data about the results of a program intervention due to systematic differences in the characteristics of the subset of the population receiving the intervention and those in the same population not receiving the intervention

**■ Mortality effect:** Effect of drop-outs on the measurement of results of an intervention

**to the mean.** If a measure is not reliable, there will be some variation between repeated measures. The chances are that the measurements will move toward the middle instead of toward extremes. Thus, in programs selecting individuals or groups based on their extreme scores, changes in performance could be expected as the "extreme" group regresses toward the mean, whether it benefited from the program or not.

Say, for example, a program to improve bookkeeping skills in a microcredit intervention chooses participants based on test scores on a test of arithmetic ability, with those with the very highest scores selected to participate in the program. If these participants were given the same arithmetic test after the intervention, their scores may decrease, because they would move closer to the mean score.

*The instrumentation effect.* The **instrumentation effect** occurs if the reliability of the instrument changes. Changes can reflect changes in measurement cause (as the result, for example, of calibration errors). For example, an evaluation of a program trying to increase adult weights by providing nutritional information may show no significant effect if the scales used to measure body weight have not been calibrated or if they vary in how and when they were calibrated.

## Quasi-Experimental Designs

**Quasi-experimental design** methods can be used to carry out an evaluation when it is not possible to construct treatment and control groups using random assignment. Quasi-experimental designs include those designs using comparison groups with similar characteristics and those designs using multiple measures but no comparison groups, the evaluator constructs groups that are as equivalent on important characteristics (gender, income, socioeconomic background) as possible. The performance of these equivalent groups, sometimes called *comparison groups,* is then compared (box 7.2). Sometimes the evaluator can create a comparison group by matching key characteristics. Other times, the evaluator will find a comparison group that is not exactly the same as the group that received the intervention but similar enough to provide some comparison.

Selecting a quasi-experimental design ex ante is not necessary, but it is preferred. It generally results in a stronger design if a comparison group can be identified rather than sole reliance on multiple measures of the same group over time. Ideally, baseline data on the comparison group are obtained at the same time as they are obtained for the group receiving the intervention and prior to program intervention. In ex post quasi-experimental designs, the comparison group is identified after the start of the program,

■ **Regression to the mean:** Natural tendency for individuals who score either very high or very low to score closer to the middle when retested

■ **Instrumentation effect:** Effect on results of an evaluation caused by lack of reliability of the instrument used to measure them

■ **Quasi-experimental design:** Design in which groups with similar characteristics are compared or multiple measures of the same group are taken over time

**Box 7.2 Do Community-Managed Schools Work? An Evaluation of El Salvador's EDUCO Program**

El Salvador's Community-Managed Schools Program (EDUCO) aimed to expand rural education rapidly following a civil war. The evaluation of the program was intended to measure the effects of decentralizing educational responsibility to communities and schools on student outcomes.

The question was whether quick expansion to rural areas came at the expense of learning. The evaluation compared outcome measures (results based on standardized tests in math and language) of third graders in EDUCO and traditional schools, controlling for student characteristics and selection bias using statistical controls. Because test scores may be unresponsive in the short term, the evaluators also looked at school days missed because of teacher absence.

Differences in educational outcomes can be affected by a variety of factors. The evaluators needed to determine whether test score differences reflected differences in the type of school or other factors, such as household characteristics (education, family size, income); student characteristics (gender, age, number of siblings); school characteristics (enrollment, teacher quality, school facilities and finances); and teacher characteristics (educational background, years of experience).

The evaluators used data collected by surveys administered by the Ministry of Education to construct a model that would measure the independent impact of the type of school while controlling for other factors. Using complex statistical modeling that controlled for all of the above factors, the evaluators concluded that the achievement scores of children in EDUCO and traditional schools were about the same. The rapid expansion did not have an adverse impact on learning. In other words, the community-managed schools were as effective as regular schools.

perhaps even after it has ended. This is obviously a much more challenging situation for an evaluator.

The notation for a quasi-experimental design is the same as for an experimental design. The difference is that there is a nonequivalent assignment of subjects to groups for quasi-experimental designs. In some cases, at the start of the line for nonequivalent groups an N is indicated. Thus, a basic quasi-experimental design in which there are treatment and comparison groups would be written as follows:

$$N \, O_1 \, X \, O_2$$

$$N \, O_1 O_2$$

To determine whether an intervention made a difference, the evaluation has to show that performance on the key measures or indicators changed as a result of the intervention. There are many quasi-experimental designs; some are stronger than others. Eight of these quasi-experimental evaluation designs are discussed below:

- before-and-after design without comparison group
- pre- and post-nonequivalent comparison design
- post-only nonequivalent comparison design
- interrupted time series comparison design
- longitudinal design
- panel design
- correlational design using statistical controls
- propensity score matching.

### Before-and-after design without comparison group

**Before-and-after design** is one way to measure change. It is done by comparing key measures after the intervention began with measures taken before the intervention began. Pretests and posttests are common before-and-after measures (the "before" measure often is called the baseline). The collection of baseline data is sometimes called a baseline study.

The simple before-and-after design is a weak quasi-experimental design in that it is a design with only one before-and-after measure that is insufficient by itself to demonstrate that the intervention alone caused the change. It could be that people changed their behavior because they were being observed or that something else that occurred at the same time as the intervention was the real cause of the changes we observed.

Where there is little change in measured performance, evaluators should be hesitant to conclude that the intervention did not work. Consider, for example, an intervention to reduce poverty. The target area was so poor that everyone was eligible to receive the intervention, so there was no comparison group. At the end of 10 years, the proportion of people in poverty had not changed. The evaluator cannot conclude that the poverty reduction intervention did not work, because it may that without the intervention (here again is a question framed as asking about the counterfactual), a larger proportion of people would have been in poverty.

Before-and-after measures are not usually regarded as yielding credible answers to questions, because they do not control for other factors affecting the outcomes; they compare only the before-and-after conditions. There is no comparison with and without the intervention. This design element should therefore be used only with other design elements.

■ **Before-and-after design:** Design in which measures after the intervention began are compared with measures taken before the intervention began

The notation for a before-and-after design is written as follows:

$$O_1 \, X \, O_2$$

### Pre- and post-nonequivalent comparison design

Although subjects in quasi-experimental designs are not assigned randomly to groups, a comparison group can still be used. These comparison groups can then be called *nonequivalent groups*. The groups can still be compared, but evaluators need to carefully consider the threats to internal validity discussed above.

To make groups more equivalent, evaluators try to match the groups as closely as they can. Matching can be done using, for example, demographic characteristics, skills tests, performance tests, judgment scores, and other means. Evaluators may give all subjects a pretest and then select groups by using their scores on the test. In an intervention to improve awareness on gender issues, for example, a pretest covering concepts and principles of gender awareness was administered. The scores were ranked from highest to lowest. Of the two highest scores, one was placed in one group and the other in the second group. This procedure was then used until all students had been assigned to one of two groups, one of which then received additional training. At some point, the two groups were measured again to see if the group that received the additional training had different scores than from the group that did not.

The notation for a matched, nonequivalent comparison be written as follows:

$$\begin{array}{ccc} N \, O_1 & X & O_1 \\ N \, O_2 & & O_2 \end{array}$$

### Post-only nonequivalent comparison design

The post-only nonequivalent comparison design is a weaker design than the pre- and post- nonequivalent comparison design. As with the pre- and post-nonequivalent comparison design, a comparison group exists. Thus, post-intervention data exist. While this is preferable to having no comparison group, a major problem is that the treatment or intervention group and the comparison group may not have started at the same place. So while we know where the two groups ended, we do not know where they began. Differences between the intervention group and the comparison group may reflect differences in where they began rather than the effect of the intervention. Still this may be the best design the ex post situation allows.

$$\begin{array}{ccc} N \, O_1 & X & O_2 \\ N & & O_2 \end{array}$$

### Interrupted time series comparison design

An interrupted time series comparison design measures the performance of one group multiple times before the intervention, administers the intervention, and then measures the same group for performance multiple times after the intervention. The notation for an interrupted time series design within a group would look like the following:

$$O_1\ O_2\ O_3\ X\ O_4\ O_5\ O_6$$

The use of the term *interrupted* comes from the fact that while there is continuous measurement of one or more indicators over time, the measurement is interrupted by the introduction of the intervention. Multiple measures both before and after the intervention are what distinguish this design from a classic before-and-after design. It can also be used with one or more comparison groups.

### Longitudinal design

In a **longitudinal design,** a form of time series, subjects are assessed at several points over a long period of time. The purpose of the design is to see how things change over time. The health care field, for example, may be interested in investigating long-term health concerns for children born to mothers with HIV/AIDS who received drugs to prevent transmission of the virus. A longitudinal study would track the children over time. The results would be examined to determine whether there were any similarities in health problems among these children.

Longitudinal studies can provide a wealth of information that cannot be found using other designs. They are expensive and difficult to conduct, however, and they suffer from attrition problems (as subjects die or lose contact with evaluators).

The notation for a longitudinal design is written as follows:

$$X\ O_1\ O_2\ O_3\ldots$$

> **Longitudinal design:** Design in which individuals are tracked at several points over a long period of time

### Panel design

One form of a longitudinal design is a **panel design.** Instead of following individuals, as in a longitudinal study, a panel design follows the same sample of subjects over time. For example, a program may be investigating the shifting attitudes and patterns of behavior about gender over time among students at a particular school. The panel design would collect information about gender attitudes for each member of one class from grade 1 to grade 6.

The notation for a panel design is written as follows:

$$X\ O_1\ O_2\ O_3\ O_4\ O_5\ O_6\ldots$$

> **Panel design:** Design in which a panel is tracked at several points over a long period of time

### Correlational design using statistical controls

■ **Correlational design:**
Examines the relationship between two or more variables that cannot be manipulated

Ethical and practical problems sometimes make it impossible to use an experimental design for evaluation. At its simplest level, a **correlational design** looks for relationships between two or more variables that cannot themselves be manipulated and is considered a nonexperimental design. It is with these simple correlation designs that the phrase "correlation does not equal causation" is often associated. But it is important to keep in mind that two variables must be related for there to be a cause and effect. Today, sophisticated analytic techniques using forms of multiple regression are used widely. Correlation techniques are often used to create comparison groups statistically so that they can be compared. Johnson (2002) indicates that such comparison groups are used to answer questions about relationships, associations, or causes and effects. Coordination of a longitudinal design with partial correlation methods is one powerful way to begin to separate causal inferences.

For example, a correlation might be investigated between amount of homework completed and test performance, if all members of the population of interest had the same motivation. The task is to correlate the part of homework completion not related to motivation with the part of test scores not related to motivation. If one can link or predict the dependent variable with three independent variables then a causal link is maintained (Garbin 2009; psych.unl.edu/psycrs/942/q2/control.ppt).

Consider, for example, an evaluation that seeks to find out whether the percentage of women in political office is correlated with more honest government. Data on the proportion of women in political office in different areas in a country and the amount of reported corruption could be collected to determine if the two variables are correlated. Of course, correlational evidence alone cannot establish causality; even if governments with more women in office are correlated with less corruption, it would still be necessary to rule out any plausible alternative explanations for the relationship.

Because a correlational design can be set up in different ways, its notation can appear in several forms. The first notation (a) below shows a design with three groups and one observation. The second notation (b) shows two groups, one receiving the treatment. The third notation (c) shows three different treatments (X, Y, and Z), each followed by an observation.

| (a) | $O_1$ | (b) | $O_1$ | (c) | X | $O_1$ |
|-----|-------|-----|-------|-----|---|-------|
| | $O_2$ | | $X\,O_2$ | | Y | $O_2$ |
| | $O_3$ | | | | Z | $O_3$ |

## Propensity score matching

**Propensity score matching** is used to measure a program's effect on project participants relative to nonparticipants with similar characteristics (White and Masset 2005). To use this technique, evaluators must first collect baseline data. They must then identify observable characteristics that are likely to link to the evaluation question (for example, "Do girls living near the school have higher graduation rates than those who walk more than five kilometers to school?"). The observable characteristics may include gender, age, marital status, distance from home to school, room and board arrangements, number of siblings graduating from secondary school, and birth order. Once the variables are selected, the treatment group and the comparison group can be constructed by matching each person in the treatment group with the one in the comparison group that is most similar using the identified observable characteristics. The result is pairs of individuals or households that are as similar to one another as possible, except on the treatment variable (White 2007).

Software tools are available to help implement the matching of propensity scores. Stata is the most commonly used tool (Aliendo and Kopeinig 2005).

## Nonexperimental Designs

### Simple cross-sectional design

A **simple cross-sectional design** shows a snapshot at one point in time. This kind of design is often used with a survey. Evaluators are interested in subgroup responses within the overall sample. The subgroups may be based on subgroup characteristics such as age, gender, income, education, ethnicity, or amount of intervention received. The point of this design is to systematically disaggregate the subgroups within the sample so that evaluators can examine them in detail.

A cross-sectional survey selects a sample of citizens, intervention beneficiaries, or former intervention participants at one point in time. It then gathers data from them and reports what they said (box 7.3). Sometimes a question may seek to determine the current status of people who participated in an intervention a few years ago.

A simple cross-sectional design may answer questions such as the following:

- Do participants with different levels of education have different views on the value of the training?
- Did women and men receive different training services?

For example, an evaluation question could focus on whether subgroups of citizens or beneficiaries of an intervention are satisfied with the

---

■ **Propensity score matching:** a design used to measure an intervention's effect on project participants relative to nonparticipants by predicting the probability of group membership e.g., treatment vs. control group—based on observed predictors, usually obtained from logistic regression to create a counterfactual group. Also used for matching or as covariates—alone or with other matching variables or covariates."

■ **Nonexperimental Designs:** A type of evaluation design where no attempt is made to create intervention and non-intervention groups and the emphasis is on description

■ **Simple cross-sectional design:** A design that provides a picture or snapshot, fixed in time and at a single point in time, of the characteristics of a subset of a population; sometimes called a "one-shot" design

services they received or why they do not use services. Evaluators would use this design to learn how the subgroups compare on variables such as services received, use of services, or opinions of services at a single point in time.

The notation for cross-sectional design is written as follows:

$$X \quad O_1$$
$$O_2$$
$$O_3$$
$$"$$

### One-shot design

■ **One-shot design:** Design that looks at a group receiving an intervention at a single point in time after the intervention

A **one-shot design** looks at a group receiving an intervention at a single point in time after the intervention. One can think of a one-shot design such as a photograph that has the date printed on it. This design can be used to answer questions such as "How many women were trained?" or "How many participants received job counseling during a specified period?"

Evaluators may use one-shot designs (a) to ask program participants questions about how much they liked a program or (b) to determine how they found out about the services offered. The notation for one-shot designs is written as follows:

$$X\, O_1$$

### Causal tracing strategies

Many of the strategies for determining whether observed changes are caused by an intervention require a structured and quantitative data collection strategy. For the evaluator who is conducting a rapid assessment or evaluating a very small or new intervention, such strategies may be neither practical nor advisable. Although it is best to choose a strong evaluation design whenever possible, in situations like those described here, a weaker design using causal tracing strategies may be the only option.

What options are available when the sample size is small, the data collection strategies are largely open ended, or sophisticated statistical analysis is not feasible? One or more of eight logical arguments can be made to rule out rival hypotheses. The arguments have to do with presenting the logic around causality and are called **causal tracing strategies.**

1. *Causal list inference:* We know that a particular outcome is almost always caused by A, B, C, or D. On one occasion, neither B, C, nor D occurred, so we can be almost sure that the cause was A. While we cannot apply randomization, we can draw from studies that did.

   In the example in box 7.1, the villagers know that the elephants ran away when the villagers blew whistles (A), hit pots and pans (B), shouted (C), and ran around kicking up dust (D). If the villagers do only A and are successful in getting the elephants to leave, they can almost be sure that blowing whistles makes elephants flee.

2. *Modus operandi inference:* This technique is useful if more than one possible cause occurred. Say that we know that an outcome is almost always caused by A, B, C, or D and that on this occasion neither C nor D occurred, narrowing the cause down to A or B. In addition, only the characteristic causal chain/modus operandi/telltale pattern of events for A was present. This inference is strengthened if the modus operandi for A is very different from that for B.

   If the villagers learn from another village that elephants there did not flee when the villagers chased them and ran around kicking up dust, they can be almost sure that the cause of the elephants leaving was blowing whistles. This result is strengthened by the fact that blowing whistles is very different from kicking up dust.

3. *Temporal precedence:* The observed effect happened only after the intervention began, not before.

   If the elephants arrived, then the villagers began blowing the whistles, and then the elephants left the village, the villagers can believe there may

■ **Causal tracing strategies:** Type of nonexperimental design that consists of arguments for causal relationships based on theory of change models and logically ruling out alternative or rival explanations

be some connection between blowing the whistles and driving the elephants away. If the villagers were blowing whistles before the elephants came and the elephants still came to the village, then the whistle blowing probably did not cause the elephants to depart.

4. *Constant conjunction:* The effect was observed everywhere the intervention was implemented.

   Say the villagers met with villagers from the entire region and shared their hypothesis that blowing whistles causes elephants to flee. Other villages try this technique and find that the elephants leave. One can then be almost sure that blowing whistles causes elephants to leave villages.

5. *Strength of association:* The observed change was much stronger where the program was implemented than it was where other possible causes were present.

   If the villages in the region use many different techniques to drive elephants from their villages and those villages that used whistle blowing were most successful in driving the elephants away, one can associate the elephants' leaving with whistle blowing.

6. *Biological gradient:* The more treatment received, the larger the observed change.

   Say the villagers used more than one technique to drive the elephants away from the village. When they blow multiple whistles very loudly, the elephants leave. When they blow only one whistle, the elephants do not leave. One could then associate the elephants' leaving the village with loud whistle blowing.

7. *Coherence:* The relationship between the intervention and the observed change fits logically with other things we know about the intervention and the outcome.

   Dangerous animals such as hippopotami, crocodiles, and hyenas leave the village when villagers blow whistles. One could logically conclude that whistle blowing drives dangerous animals out of villages and could apply the strategy to elephants.

8. *Analogy:* The pattern between the intervention and the observed changes resembles the well-established pattern between a related intervention and its effects.

   Villagers hear a story about a village in South America that uses the sound of loud high-pitched whistles whenever they hear a puma in the area. The South American villagers believe that the noise keeps the puma away. The African villagers could draw an analogy with their problem and could conclude that loud, sharp noises may drive elephants away.

In each of these cases, the principle is the same: the researcher systematically rules out alternative explanations, one by one, until convinced that it is most likely that the changes observed are or are not caused (primarily or at least substantially) by the intervention.

When designing a data collection strategy, evaluators should determine which of the above pieces of evidence it is feasible and necessary to gather and then plan how to obtain them. Not all are needed to be able to make causal attributions; evaluators gather the pieces that make the most sense and that together will give sufficient certainty about the findings, given the decisions that will be based on the evaluation. But establishing that more than one of these causal tracing strategies is present can strengthen the basis for inferring causality.

### Case study design

A **case study** is a nonexperimental design. It does not use random selection or control and comparison groups. A case study design is frequently used when the evaluator wants to gain in-depth understanding of a process, event, or situation and explain why results occurred. It is useful when the question deals with how something works or why something happens. It is especially useful when the intervention is innovative or experimental or not well understood. Case studies emphasize more than descriptions; they also include interpretations of situations by those most knowledgeable about them.

> ■ **Case study:**
> A nonexperimental design that provides an in-depth comprehensive description and understanding of an intervention as a whole and in its context

Case studies are frequently used in evaluating development interventions. The case study design is particularly useful for describing what implementation of the intervention looked like on the ground and why things happened the way they did. A descriptive case study may be used to examine program extremes or a typical intervention.

Case studies can use qualitative methods, quantitative methods, or both to collect data. They can consist of a single case or multiple cases. Their intention and objective is to focus on in-depth understandings of the effects of an intervention on organizations, communities, programs, cities, or countries.

To evaluate public transportation in a country, for example, one could simply track key indicators against the baseline and targets. A national study could be conducted if the indicators are the number of miles covered by public transportation, the number of people who use the system, and revenues received. However, if other kinds of questions were relevant that require more in-depth data collection, one would opt for a case study.

For instance, if asked to evaluate a program to improve transportation to rural areas, an evaluator might investigate people's choices about using public transportation. The design could stipulate that data be gathered directly from people in rural areas. More resources would be required to collect these data on a national scale. It is more manageable to gather them within a more narrowly defined geographic area (a single case).

Alternatively, evaluators could opt for multiple case studies, in which several rural areas may be selected. Cases may be randomly selected or purposively selected based on some specific criteria (best case, typical case, worst case, including only isolated rural areas, also including rural areas near large cities). The same data collection strategies used in the single case study can be used in multiple case studies.

Case studies make sense in development where the intention is to understand a specific situation in order to make or adjust policy or practice. Not only are case studies more practical than large national studies, they also provide in-depth information that is often helpful to decision makers (box 7.4). A comparative case study of the use of free immunization clinics, for example, might help explain why one approach is more successful than another.

The notation for a case study design is written as follows:

$$O_1$$

$$O_2$$

$$O_3$$

## Designs for Descriptive Questions

Descriptive questions include questions such as "how many?" or "how much?" They may solicit perceptions or opinions. Descriptive questions generally use descriptive or nonexperimental designs. When used to answer

---

**Box 7.4    Example of Case Study Design for Descriptive Questions**

A study investigating a microlending program in India wanted to explore ways that the women involved conceptualized and initiated their marketing ideas. The case study method chose five women and their projects and followed their progress for three years.

---

descriptive questions, these designs do not involve a comparison group that did not receive the intervention. They focus only on those who receive the intervention. Some of the designs used for descriptive questions are the same as those used for cause-and-effect questions.

To answer descriptive questions, the most common designs include the following:

- simple cross-sectional
- one-shot
- before-and-after
- interrrupted time series
- longitudinal
- case studies.

Here we discuss how some of these designs work with descriptive questions.

## Before-and-After Design

Before-and-after designs were introduced in a previous section discussing designs for cause-and-effect questions. These designs can also be used to answer descriptive questions. In a before-and-after design, often called a *predesign and postdesign,* evaluators ask about group characteristics before and after the intervention; there is no comparison group (box 7.5.) For example, one might ask whether program participants increased their knowledge of parenting techniques and then test them at program entry and following program completion. The notation for before-and-after designs is written as follows:

$$O_1 \, X \, O_2$$

---

**Box. 7.5   Using a Before-and-After Design to Answer Descriptive Questions**

A before-and-after design might look at the wages of a sample of vocational training program participants before their training intervention and two years following the program to address the question of how much, on average, wages increased. This design could easily be transformed into a cross-sectional before-and-after design by asking questions of subgroups of people with different occupations in order to study the relation of wage increases to different types of vocations.

---

### Interrupted Time Series Design

Interrupted time series designs were introduced earlier under designs for
cause-and-effect questions. An interrupted time series design can also be
used to answer descriptive questions (box 7.6). Interrupted time series
designs look for changes over time, generally in order to identify trends.
When they are used to answer descriptive questions, the purpose is to
explore and describe changes over time both before and after the intervention. Thus interrupted time series designs can be used to discern trends. The
notation for an interrupted time series design is written as follows:

$$O_1 \, O_2 \, O_3 \, X \, O_4 \, O_5 \, O_6 \ldots$$

### Longitudinal Design

■ **Longitudi-
nal design:**
Interrupted time
series design in
which repeated
measures of the
same variable are
taken from same
subjects

A **longitudinal design** is a type of interrupted time series design in which
repeated measures of the same variable are taken from the same subjects.
When used for descriptive questions, a longitudinal design may be used to
find out, for example, whether children attending an enrichment program
maintain learning gains over time.

A panel design can also be used to answer descriptive questions. A
panel design is a special type of longitudinal design in which a smaller
group of the same people are tracked at multiple points in time and their
experiences recorded in considerable detail. Panel designs almost always
use qualitative techniques (open-ended survey questions, in-depth interviews, observation) as well as quantitative data. Panel designs can give a
deeper perspective on any changes people may be experiencing as a result
of an intervention. The notation for a longitudinal design is written as
follows:

$$X \, O_1, \, O_s, \, O_3 \ldots$$

## Designs for Normative Questions

The logic for normative questions is similar to that for descriptive questions, except that normative questions are always assessed against a criterion or standard. Findings are compared with that standard, which may include indicators and targets. Generally, the same designs work for normative questions as descriptive questions.

Performance auditing addresses some aspects of performance of an organization (Mayne 2005, 2006). Performance audits can be very similar to normative evaluations. Barzelay (1997) identifies seven types of performance audits, which are based on a survey of Organisation for Economic Co-operation and Development (OECD) member countries. Table 7.2 shows four of the most relevant ones.

Box 7.7 illustrates a point made earlier—that when it is not possible to create an experimental evaluation design with randomized control groups, turning to a quasi-experimental evaluation design with comparison groups is acceptable.

### Designs for Cause-and-Effect Questions

Experimental designs are generally used to address cause-and-effect questions (see page 252).

## The Need for More Rigorous Evaluation Designs

What designs work for cause-and-effect questions?

Leaders in the field of international development evaluation have been debating the need for more rigorous program evaluation (Davidson 2006;

**Table 7.2 Four Types of Performance Audits**

| Type | Unit of analysis | Focus |
|---|---|---|
| Efficiency audit | Organization or jurisdiction; process or program element | Identify opportunities to reduce budgetary cost of delivering program outputs. |
| Effectiveness audit | Policy, program, or major program element | Assess impact of public policies; evaluate policy or program effectiveness. |
| Performance management capacity audit | Organization or jurisdiction public management issue | Assess capacity of systems and procedures of a jurisdiction, organization, or program to achieve intended goals. |
| Performance information audit | Organization | Attest to quality of performance information provided by organization. |

*Source:* Adapted from Barzelay 1997.

Scriven 2006; Bamberger and White 2007). They note that most evaluations conducted by official development agencies are process evaluations, which focus on how well a program is operating. The increase in participatory evaluations added more opinions from beneficiaries, but it "did not produce data amenable to quantitative analysis of impact" (Bamberger and White 2007, p. 58).

Results-based approaches and the focus on the Millennium Development Goals (MDGs) have resulted in greater calls to demonstrate impact. Calls for impact evaluations, which are concerned with the results caused by a project, program, or policy, have come from a variety of sources, including the following:

- the 2002 Monterrey Conference on Financing for Development, which called for more use of results-based management in development agencies
- the 2005 Paris Accords, which encouraged multidonor cooperation in the promotion of impact evaluations

- the Poverty Action Lab, which promotes the use of randomized designs and offers training programs for developing countries on these designs
- the Center for Global Development (CGD), which advocates strongly for more rigorous evaluation designs, notably in the publication *When Will We Ever Learn?* (CGD 2006). The CGD has also issued a call to action by independent evaluation agencies to ensure more independence and rigor in development evaluations (Bamberger and White 2007).

Pushing the bounds of current thinking about international development and development evaluation is spurring the use of impact evaluation. The efforts of the government of Spain illustrate this new thinking and the push toward more rigorous evaluation designs (box 7.8). Often "rigorous" is defined as an experiment involving use of a randomized control group. Ravallion, director of the World Bank's research department, notes that randomization is not always the answer it may first appear to be, especially in the development context (Ravallion 2009). For example, one can only randomize some interventions relevant to development. How does one randomize the location of infrastructure projects and related programs? Ravallion discusses how randomized experiments can have severe generalizability problems as they are often done only for narrow and discrete project interventions under certain conditions. He also describes "spillover" effects. That is, those selecting randomized designs often assume that non-participants are unaffected by the program. But it is known that spillover effects are pervasive in development applications. Spillover stems from movement of subjects in and out of a treatment area; long-term imitation, because as one group will copy another group's practices if they seem to work and local governments stepping in and using resources freed by the development organizations to provide the same intervention to a designated control group.

### Box 7.8  Spain's Support of Rigorous Evaluation Designs

Spain is seeking to improve aid effectiveness by promoting results-based management in its own development agency and in partner countries. It has implemented a new program to support the World Bank in evaluating the impact of innovative programs to improve human development outcomes. The program—the Spanish–World Bank Trust Fund for Impact Evaluation (SIEF)—is the largest trust fund ever established at the World Bank focused on impact evaluation and results (World Bank 2007).

Evaluation designs must be appropriate for each situation and to each type of evaluation question being asked. Patton (2007) discusses matching designs to different kinds of development interventions, noting that "different impact situations and different evaluation purposes have different implications for methods" (p. 1). Evaluators need to begin by clarifying the situation; the design will emerge from the situation. As Patton notes, "There are multiple development impact situations and therefore diverse approaches to impact evaluation" (p. 2).

Bamberger and Patton (2007) offer the following suggestions for strengthening an evaluation design and addressing time and budget constraints:

1. Build the evaluation design on a sound program theory model. Doing so can help explain links in the causal chain and identify assumptions. It can also identify local economic, political, institutional, environmental, and sociocultural factors to explain differences in performance and outcomes.

2. Adopt a good mixed-method design, and combine qualitative and quantitative approaches:
   • Use qualitative data for triangulation to provide additional evidence in support of the quantitative results, help frame the research, and help interpret quantitative results.
   • Make maximum use of secondary data, including project monitoring data.
   • Whenever time and budget permit, collect data at additional points in the project cycle.

3. Simplify data collection instruments.

4. Use secondary data creatively, using data from completed surveys for baseline data or control or comparison groups.

5. Consider reducing the sample size if the sample is a judgmental one.

6. Reduce the costs of data collection by using less expensive interviewers, using direct observation rather than household surveys, and piggybacking on or synchronizing with other evaluations by adding to another planned survey.

Evaluators must explore the options for each design in an attempt to provide the most robust results (table 7.3). Choosing the right design is critical, because "different methods can produce quite different findings. The challenge is to figure out which design and methods are most appropriate, productive, and useful in a given situation" (Patton 2002, p. 255).

Evaluation is both an art and a science. In making design decisions, evaluators should keep in mind that there is no perfect design; all evaluations involve trade-offs in terms of time, cost, and practicality. These trade-

**Table 7.3  Advantages and Disadvantages of Common Experimental Designs**

| Type of design | Advantages | Disadvantages |
|---|---|---|
| **Experimental** | | |
| Comparison | Controls for internal threats to validity | Difficult to conduct in public sector |
| | Useful in looking at differences between groups; controls for history and maturation if comparison group is close match | Selection and attrition that are threats |
| **Quasi-experimental** | | |
| Before-and-after | Useful in providing context for measuring change | Testing, instrumentation, regression to the mean, attrition, history, and maturation effects that may be threats |
| **Nonexperimental** | | |
| One-shot | Useful for addressing descriptive and normative questions; multiple one-shot designs begin to build a case | Very weak for cause-and-effect questions |

*Source:* Authors.

offs should be acknowledged by providing some assessment of their likely impact on the results and conclusions.

As implied by Ravallion (2009), let the evaluation questions drive the approach. The most important questions may be "Who gains and who loses from the intervention? Does the intervention look on the ground like it did on paper? What is the variability in implementation? Which variations should be built on? For whom and under what conditions does the intervention seem to work?

In sum, each evaluation question needs a design that is experimental, quasi-experimental, or nonexperimental. An experimental design attempts to control all factors in the "experiment" to determine or predict what may occur. An experimental design uses randomized assignment of subjects into at least two groups, the treatment group and the control group.

Quasi-experimental design is similar to experimental design in that it uses two or more groups, but it does not randomly assign subjects to each group. A comparison group usually is created to allow the study of one group with the intervention and a similar group without the intervention. Nonexperimental designs are more descriptive. They use neither randomized assignment nor a comparison group.

For most development interventions, it is difficult to create a design that answers cause-and-effect questions because of the complexity of the situation. It is difficult to "prove" that an intervention causes the observed effect.

Evaluation designs can help determine the impact of a program to the extent that they give the evaluator control over the implementation and measurement of the program. The intent is to eliminate other possible explanations for what is observed.

For cause-and-effect questions, the evaluator should consider one or more of these types of evaluation designs:

- matched and nonequivalent comparison design
- interrupted time series design
- correlational design using statistical controls
- longitudinal design
- panel design
- before-and-after
- cross-sectional design
- propensity score matching
- causal tracing.

Descriptive questions are generally evaluated using descriptive or nonexperimental designs. Designs for descriptive questions focus only on answering questions that do not address attribution or match performance to some criteria. Some of the designs used for descriptive questions are the same as those for cause-and-effect questions.

To answer descriptive questions, the evaluator should consider one or more of these types of evaluation designs:

- one-shot
- cross-sectional
- before-and-after
- interrupted time series
- longitudinal design
- case studies.

The logic for normative questions is similar to that of descriptive questions, except that normative questions are always assessed against a standard or criterion.

Many leaders in international development evaluation are calling for more rigor in evaluation design. As projects, programs, and policies move toward results-based management, one would expect to see more designs for evaluations that attempt to address issues of attribution.

### Application Exercise 7.1: Selecting an Evaluation Design

You have been asked to measure the impact of building a community health clinic to teach parents how to treat common family illnesses and identify problems that may be serious. The goals of the program are to increase the number of parents with basic understanding of preventative health care, first aid, and early treatment strategies and to reduce the number of children and elderly people whose illnesses become serious.

1. What are the desired outcomes?
2. Write a cause-and-effect question, a normative question, and a descriptive question for this evaluation.
3. What design would you use to investigate these questions? What are the strengths and limits of this design? Why is the design you chose better than other possible designs?

### Application Exercise 7.2: Choosing an Evaluation Design and Data Collection Strategy

You have been asked to create an evaluation design for a six-month study to assess the effectiveness of a preventative health information campaign in your country. The campaign is to consist of two-day seminars conducted by health professionals in communities throughout the country. The purpose of your evaluation is to determine whether the information campaign resulted in improved health practices. You have a moderate-size budget and six research assistants to help you design and conduct the evaluation.

1. Is your primary evaluation question a descriptive, a normative, or a cause-and-effect question? Explain.
2. Should your data collection strategy be structured, open-ended, or a combination of both? Why?
3. How would you identify the most important outcomes to measure, and how would you measure them?
4. What evaluation design would you use?
5. What are the strengths and weaknesses of your design?

| IPDET Terms | Design types | Visual representation | Key advantages | Key disadvantages |
|---|---|---|---|---|
| **Experimental** | Experimental designs are characterized by random assignment to control and intervention groups. | | | |
| | *Randomized* Comparison group | $O_1$ X $O_2$ <br> $O_1$ $O_2$ | strong internal validity, identifies change over time both with and without intervention | costly, ethical considerations, difficult to generalize |
| | After only *Randomized* Comparison group No before test | $O_3$ <br> X <br> $O_4$ | good internal validity, slightly more practical, useful for comparing outcome | does not identify change over time |
| **Quasi-experimental** | **All quasi-experimental designs are slightly weaker than experimental designs with respect to validity or have a low internal validity. Quasi-experimental designs involve comparisons but without random assignments.** | | | |
| Before-and-After without comparison | Within Group Before & After Design | $O_1$ X $O_2$ | practical, context must be considered | testing, instrumentation and regression threats |
| Pre- and Post-Nonequivalent comparison | Before-and-after Between Groups (non-equivalent) comparison | N $O_1$ X $O_1$ <br> N $O_2$ $O_4$ | context must be considered, greater confidence than with group comparison | rules out the effect of history, difficult to control for all variables which make groups non-equivalent |
| Post-only nonequivalent comparison | Only compares data on post-intervention | N $O_1$ X $O_2$ <br> N $O_2$ | may be the best design for ex post situation | do not know where the treatment or intervention group began |
| | Post only with Non-equivalent Comparison Group | $O_1$ <br> X $O_2$ | practical, context must be considered, control of effects of testing, instrumentation, regression, history | ethical considerations, selection threatens validity |
| | Post only with Different Treatments Design | X $O_1$ <br> Y $O_2$ <br> Z $O_3$ | can compare interventions, must take context into consideration | many threats remain |

| Design | Description | Notation | Strengths | Weaknesses |
|---|---|---|---|---|
| Interrupted Time Series comparison (good for descriptive questions) | Time Series (within group) | $O_1O_2O_3XO_4O_5O_6$ | threat of history partially controlled, maturation controlled | threat of testing bias |
| | Time Series Between Groups (non-equivalent) Comparison | | rules out threats of history, regression toward mean reduced | costly, time consuming, difficult to keep track of people over time |
| Longitudinal | No Baseline | $X\ O_1O_2O_3\cdots$ | follows individuals over time | costly, difficult to keep track of individuals over time |
| Panel | Follows same group over time | $X\ O_1O_2O_3O_4O_5\cdots$ | in depth information | can be costly |
| Correlational using Statistical Controls | | $O_1$ $O_2$ $O_3$ | uses statistics to determine correlations between cases to isolate potential threats determines important relationships and potentially confounding variables | requires large sample sizes, no statement about cause can be made, speculative |
| Propensity Score Matching | Intervention participants compared to similar non-participants | | use for evaluation of voluntary programs—more reliable assessment of the project or program effect on the participants | requires large datasets and computing capabilities |
| **Nonexperimental** | **Ideal for Description**  All nonexperimental designs are weaker than experimental designs. | | | |
| Cross Sectional | Within and Between | $X$ $O_1$ $O_2$ $O_3$ $=$ | clear picture of a point in time | no clear indication of what is happening over time |
| One shot | | $X$ $O_1$ | ease, practicality | many threats to validity, weak design |
| Causal Tracing Strategies | Argues for causal relationships based on theory of change models and logic | | | |
| Case Study | | $O_1$ $O_2$ $O_3$ | in depth contextual information | time consuming, little internal validity |

# References and Further Reading

Aliendo, Marco, and Sabine Kopeinig. 2005. *Some Practical Guidance on the Implementation of Propensity Score Matching.* Discussion Paper 1588, IZA, Institute for the Study of Labor, Bonn.
http://ftp.iza.org/dp1588.pdf.

Bamberger, Michael, and Howard White. 2007. "Using Strong Evaluation Designs in Developing Countries: Experience and Challenges." *Journal of Multidisciplinary Evaluation* 4 (8): 58–73.

Barzelay, M. 1997. "Central Audit Institutions and Performance Auditing: A Comparative Analysis of Organizational Strategies in the OECD." *Governance: An International Journal of Policy and Administration* 103: 235–60.

Boruch, Robert. 2004. "Ethics and Randomized Trials." International Program for Development Evaluation Training (IPDET) presentation, Ottawa.

Brossart, Daniel F., Daniel L. Clay, and Victor L. Willson. 2002. "Methodological and Statistical Considerations for Threats to Internal Validity in Pediatric Outcome Data: Response Shift in Self-Report Outcomes." *Journal of Pediatric Psychology* 27 (1): 97–107.

Brown, Randall S., and Ellen Eliason Kisker. 1997. "Nonexperimental Designs and Program Evaluation." *Children and Youth Services Review* 19 (7): 541–66.
http://www.aei.org/publications/pubID.17770/pub_detail.asp.

Campbell, D. T., and J. C. Stanley. 1963. "Experimental and Quasi-Experimental Designs for Research." In *Handbook of Research on Teaching,* ed. N. L. Cage. Chicago: Rand-McNally.

CGD (Center for Global Development). 2006. *When Will We Ever Learn? Improving Lives through Impact Evaluation.* Washington, DC.

Chatterji, M. 2007. "Grades of Evidence: Variability in Quality of Findings in Effectiveness Studies of Complex Field Interventions." *American Journal of Evaluation* 283: 239–55.

Cohen, M. 2001. "Evaluating Microfinance's Impact: Going Down Market." In *Evaluation and Poverty Reduction,* eds. O. N. Feinstein and R. Picciotto, 193–203. New Brunswick, NJ: Transaction Publishers.

Cook, T. D., and D. T. Campbell. 1979. *Quasi-Experimentation: Design and Analysis for Field Settings.* Boston: Houghton Mifflin.

Davidson, E. J. 2000. "Ascertaining Causality in Theory-Based Evaluation." *New Directions for Evaluation* 87: 17–26.

———. 2006. "The RCT's Only Doctrine: Brakes on the Acquisition of Knowledge?" *Journal of Multidisciplinary Evaluation* 6: ii–v.

Garbin, Cal. 2009. *Statistical Control.* Lincoln, NE: University of Nebraska. psych.unl.edu/psycrs/942/q2/control.ppt.

Grembowski, D. 2001. *The Practice of Health Program Evaluation.* Thousand Oaks, CA: Sage Publications.

Homer-Dixon, Thomas. 1995. *Strategies for Studying Causation in Complex Ecological Political Systems.* Occasional Paper; Project on Environment, Population, and

Security. American Association for the Advancement of Science, Washington, DC, and the University of Toronto. http://www.library.utoronto.ca/pcs/eps/method/methods1.htm.

Mayne, John. 2005. "Ensuring Quality for Evaluation: Lessons from Auditors." *Canadian Journal of Program Evaluation* 20 (1): 37–64.

———. 2006. "Audit and Evaluation in Public Management: Challenges, Reforms, and Different Roles." *Canadian Journal of Program Evaluation* 21 (1): 11–45.

Miles, M. B., and A. M. Huberman. 1994. *Qualitative Data Analysis: An Expanded Sourcebook*. 2nd ed. Thousand Oaks, CA: Sage Publications.

NIOSH (National Institute for Occupational Safety and Health). 1999. *A Model for Research on Training Effectiveness TIER*. Centers for Disease Control, Atlanta. http://www.cdc.gov/niosh/99-142.html.

Office of Juvenile Justice and Delinquency Prevention. 1989. *Evaluating Juvenile Justice Programs: A Design Monograph for State Planners*. Report prepared for the U.S. Department of Justice, Office of Juvenile Justice and Delinquency Prevention by Community Research Associates, Inc.

Patton, Michael Q. 2002. *Qualitative Research and Evaluation Methods*. 3rd ed. Thousand Oaks, CA: Sage Publications.

———. 2005. "The Debate about Randomized Controls in Evaluation: the Gold Standard Question." International Program for Development Evaluation Training (IPDET) presentation, Ottawa, July.

———. 2007. *Design Options and Matching the Type of Impact Evaluation and Attribution Issue to the Nature of the Intervention: Background Discussion on Impact Evaluation for International Development Efforts*. November.

———. 2008. "The Logic of Experimental Designs and 10 Common Criticisms: The Gold Standard Debate." In *Utilization-Focused Evaluation*. 4th ed. Thousand Oaks, CA: Sage Publications.

Powell, Keith D. 2004. "Research Methods on Psychological Science: Psychology 242." Powerpoint presentation, November 8. Department of Psychology, University of Chicago, Chicago, IL.

Prennushi, Giovanna, Gloria Rubio, and Kalanidhi Subbarao. 2002. *PRSP Sourcebook Core Techniques*. Washington, DC: World Bank. http://go.worldbank.org/3I8LYLXO80.

Project STAR. 2006. *Study Designs for Program Evaluation*. Aguirre Division, JBS International, Inc. Bethesda, MD. http://www.nationalserviceresources.org/filemanager/download/performance Measurement/Study_Designs_for_Evaluation.pdf.

Ravallion, Martin. 2009. "Should the Randomistas Rule?" *The Economists Voice* 6(2): 1–5.

Schweigert, F. J. 2006. "The Meaning of Effectiveness in Assessing Community Initiatives." *American Journal of Evaluation* 27: 416. http://aje.sagepub.com/cgi/content/abstract/27/4/416.

Scriven, Michael. 2006. "Converting Perspective to Practice." *Journal of Multidisciplinary Evaluation* 6: 8–9.

———. 2007. *Key Evaluation Checklist*. February.
http://www.wmich.edu/evalctr/checklists/kec_feb07.pdf.

Stake, R. E. 1995. *The Art of Case Study Research*. Thousand Oaks, CA: Sage
Publications.

Stufflebeam, Daniel L. 2004. *Evaluation Design Checklist*. Western Michigan University, Evaluation Center, Kalamazoo, MI.
http://www.wmich.edu/evalctr/checklists/evaldesign.pdf.

Stufflebeam, D. L., G. F. Mdaus, and T. Kellaghan, eds. 2000. *Evaluation Models:
Viewpoints on Educational and Human Services Evaluation*. Boston: Kluwer.

Trochim, W. M. "The Research Methods Knowledge Base. http://www.socials
researchmethods.net/kb.

Trochim, W., and D. Land. 1982. "Designing Designs for Research." *Researcher* 1 (1):
1–16.
http://www.socialresearchmethods.net/kb/desdes.htm.

United Kingdom Evaluation Society. 2003. *Glossary of Evaluation Terms*.
http://www.evaluation.org.uk/Pub_library/Glossary.htm.

Wadsworth, Y. 1997. *Everyday Evaluation on the Run*. St. Leonards, New South
Wales, Australia: Allen and Unwin.

White, Howard. 2007. "Challenges in Evaluating Development Effectiveness."
Working Paper, World Bank, Washington DC.

White, Howard, and Edoardo Masset. 2005. "Quasi-Experimental Evaluation."
PowerPoint presentation, February 16.

World Bank. 1998. *Do Community-Managed Schools Work? An Evaluation of El
Salvador's EDUCO Program*. Impact Evaluation of Education Reforms Paper 8,
Development Research Group, Washington, DC.

———. 2004. *PovertyNet: Evaluation Designs*. Washington, DC: World Bank.
http://web.worldbank.org/WBSITE/EXTERNAL/TOPICS/EXTPOVERTY/
EXTISPMA/0,,contentMDK:20188242~menuPK:412148~pagePK:148956~piPK:
216618~theSitePK:384329,00.html.

———. 2006a. *Conducting Quality Impact Evaluations under Budget, Time, and Data
Constraints*. Independent Evaluation Group, Washington, DC.

———. 2006b. *Impact Evaluation: The Experience of the Independent Evaluation
Group of the World Bank*. Independent Evaluation Group, Washington, DC.

———. 2007. PowerNet. Spanish Impact Evaluation Fund.
http://web.worldbank.org/WBSITE/EXTERNAL/TOPICS/EXTPOVERTY/
EXTISPMA/0,,contentMDK:21419502~menuPK:384336~pagePK:148956~piPK:
216618~theSitePK:384329,00.html.

———. 2008. *PovertyNet: Impact Evaluation, Methods and Techniques, Evaluation
Designs*. Washington, DC: World Bank.
http://web.worldbank.org/WBSITE/EXTERNAL/TOPICS/EXTPOVERTY/
EXTISPMA/0,,contentMDK:20188242~menuPK:415130~pagePK:148956~piPK:
216618~theSitePK:384329,00.html.

Yin, R. K. 1984. *Case Study Research*. Thousand Oaks, CA: Sage Publications.

## Web Sites

Campbell Collaboration. http://www.campbellcollaboration.org/.

Schweigert, F. J. 2006. "The Meaning of Effectiveness in Assessing Community Initiatives." *American Journal of Evaluation* 27: 416. http://aje.sagepub.com/cgi/content/abstract/27/4/416.

Scriven, Michael 2007. *Key Evaluation Checklist.* http://www.wmich.edu/evalctr/checklists/kec_feb07.pdf.

Stufflebeam, Daniel L. 2004. *Evaluation Design checklist.* Western Michigan University, Evaluation Center, Kalamazoo, MI. http://www.wmich.edu/evalctr/checklists/evaldesign.pdf.

University of Northern Iowa, Department of Psychology. http://www.psych.uni.edu/psycrs/457/e2/control.ppt.

World Bank. *Doing Impact Evaluation Series.* http://web.worldbank.org/WBSITE/EXTERNAL/TOPICS/EXTPOVERTY/EXTISPMA/0,,menuPK:384336~pagePK:149018~piPK:149093~theSitePK:384329,00.html#doingIE.

**CHAPTER 8**

# Selecting and Constructing Data Collection Instruments

Previous chapters discussed evaluation questions and evaluation designs to match these questions. This chapter looks at how to collect the data to answer evaluation questions.

**This chapter has four main parts:**

- Data Collection Strategies
- Characteristics of Good Measures
- Quantitative and Qualitative Data
- Tools for Collecting Data

# Data Collection Strategies

Data can be collected from many sources, including existing records, electro-mechanical measurements, observations, surveys, focus groups, and expert judgment. No single way is the best way. As illustrated in table 8.1, the decision about which method to use depends on

- what you need to know
- where the data reside
- the resources and time available
- the complexity of the data to be collected
- the frequency of data collection
- the intended forms of data analysis.

The choice of methods hinges partly on the evaluation question to be answered, partly on how well the intervention is understood, and partly on the time and resources available. There is a trade-off between the in-depth understanding that comes from a case study (intensive data collection), for example, and the validity of the results yielded from a survey (extensive data collection). Intensive data collection generally uses semistructured approaches that permit flexible responses. Extensive data collection generally requires structured approaches that allow for efficiency across many respondents.

**Table 8.1　Sample Decision Table for Data Collection Method**

| If you need to know | Then consider |
|---|---|
| Whether villagers with low literacy levels who participated in the program write better than those with low literacy levels who did not participate | • Collecting samples of writing before and after the intervention<br>• Using test results from before and after the intervention |
| Whether participants are more actively engaged in their children's education | • Observing parent–child interactions before and after the intervention<br>• Asking children, parents, and teachers about parent involvement before and after the intervention |
| Whether program participants were satisfied with the quality of the literacy workshops and follow-up | • Using a structured interview of participants<br>• Conducting a survey to determine if literacy levels are high enough |

*Source:* Authors.

To determine which type of data to collect, evaluators need to determine what is most important to the main client for the evaluation. Is the client more interested in numerical data on the condition of the nation's schools or a more in-depth understanding of the situation in the poorest urban areas? Sometimes both are important, but resource availability requires that one must be assigned priority. Whichever types of data are used, evaluators should apply certain rules (box 8.1).

## Structured Approach

A **structured data collection approach** requires that all data be collected in exactly the same way. This is particularly important for multisite and cluster evaluations. In these evaluations, evaluators need to be able to compare findings at different sites in order to draw conclusions about what is working where (box 8.2). Structure is also important when comparing alternative interventions to determine which is most cost-effective.

Structured data collection approaches are used to collect quantitative data when the evaluator:

- needs to address extent questions
- has a large sample or population
- knows what needs to be measured
- needs to show results numerically
- needs to make comparisons across different sites or interventions.

■ **Structured data collection approach:** Data collection approach in which all data are collected in exactly the same way

**Box 8.2    Taking a Structured Approach to Evaluating an Agricultural Intervention**

Consider the example of an evaluation of an agricultural intervention. To address one question, evaluators decide to use the moisture content of the soil as a measure of successful land drainage. They then plan to collect measures of moisture content from multiple sites in the region, before and after the drainage, over the same period of time (and under the same weather conditions).

To address a second question, evaluators use a structured interview guide to ask affected farmers their views of the project's effects. Drawing on the interviews, they report the percentage of respondents reporting various views (such tabulated results are known as frequency counts). The questions for a structured interview should be narrowly focused and precisely worded, and a set of multiple choice responses should be provided. All respondents should be asked the same questions in exactly the same way and asked to choose from exactly the same set of responses.

To investigate a third question, evaluators plan to use records of crop production and prices over time, before the intervention and after it, in the drained area and in a similar area in the region where the land has not been drained. To investigate a fourth question, they will ask a sample of 100 of the 2,600 participants about their views about the project and its effects. For these interviews, the evaluators plan to use semistructured questions to guide the interviews. They intend to probe responses as needed to understand the views.

*Source:* Authors.

### Semistructured Approach

■ **Semistructured data collection approach:**
Data collection approach in which data are not collected in the same way every time

A **semistructured data collection approach** may be systematic and follow general procedures, but data are not collected in the same way every time. Semistructured interviews are often based on a predetermined set of broad questions, but the order of presenting them may depend on circumstances. Moreover, some responses provided are probed with additional questions developed during the interview. These approaches are more open and fluid than structured approaches. They allow respondents to tell evaluators what they want in their own way.

Semistructured data collection methods are generally qualitative. They are used when an evaluator

- is conducting exploratory work in a new development area
- seeks to understand themes or issues
- wants participant narratives or in-depth information
- wants in-depth, rich, "backstage" information
- seeks to understand results of structured data collection that are unexpected and not well understood or simply to have rich examples to supplement the findings from a structured data collection effort.

In an evaluation of a community-driven development project, for example, evaluators might choose a semistructured approach to data collection. Because such programs give control of planning decisions to local groups, it is appropriate for the evaluator to use a semistructured approach to learn more about how decisions are made as well as to solicit community members' views of the process and project outcomes.

## Characteristics of Good Measures

Evaluators measure beliefs, attitudes, opinions, knowledge, skills, performance, and habits. In determining how to measure the variable of interest and collect data on it, evaluators should keep four key issues in mind:

- Is the measure relevant? Does it measure what really matters as opposed to what is easiest to measure?
- Is the measure credible? Will it provide information about the actual situation?
- Is the measure valid? Will the measure reflect what the evaluator set out to measure?
- Is the measure reliable? If data on the measure are collected in the same way from the same source using the same decision rules every time, will the same results be obtained?

*Relevant* refers to the extent to which what is measured matters. Evaluators should avoid measuring what is easy to measure instead of what is needed. They should also avoid trying to measure too much. The design matrix is a tool for making sure the data collected will be relevant.

*Credible* is the term used to indicate how trustworthy or believable the data collected are to the intended audiences of the evaluation report. Teachers' opinions, for example, may not be viewed as the most credible measure for learning why dropout rates are high. The opinions of the dropouts themselves or their friends may be viewed as more credible measures.

*Validity* is the term used to indicate whether a measurement actually measures what it is supposed to measure. Do the questions yield accurate information? Waiting lists, for example, have little validity as a measure of demand for certain early childhood education programs, because they are frequently out of date and parents place their children on multiple waiting lists. When children are placed, their names are not necessarily removed from other waiting lists.

Two kinds of validity are face validity and content validity:

**Face validity:** Extent to which content of test or procedure looks as if it measures what it is supposed to measure

- *Face validity* addresses the extent to which the content of the test or procedure looks as if it measures what it is supposed to measure. For example, if an evaluation is measuring physical fitness, the measure of how fast one runs 100 meters may look like one valid measure of physical fitness.

**Content validity:** Extent to which content of a test or procedure adequately measures the variable of interest

- *Content validity* addresses the extent to which the content of a test or procedure adequately measures the variable of interest. If, for example, evaluators are trying to develop a measure of health status, they might consult with health professionals to ensure that the measure selected has a high content validity. A measure of an individual's actual proportion of body fat, for example, is generally a more valid measure of the person's fitness than a self-report of healthy eating habits. A test of knowledge of healthy eating habits may be more valid than the self-report data. It may not be a measure with high validity, however, because a respondent may not apply knowledge of healthy eating habits to his or her own eating. Results could show a rosier picture than is the actual case.

**Reliability:** Degree to which a measurement measures the same thing, in the same way, in repeated tests

*Reliability* is the term used to describe the stability of the measurement—the degree to which it measures the same thing, in the same way, in repeated tests. The measurement tools for sporting events, for example, need to be highly reliable. The tape that measures the distance of a jump must measure the distance in the same way every time it is used. If it does, it is considered a reliable measure. If it does not, the measure may be flawed and the results of the event could be questioned.

Birth weights of newborn babies are an example of a reliable measure, assuming the scales are calibrated properly. Attendance rates at schools are an example of a measure with low reliability, because they vary depending on when in the school year the measure is taken.

## Quantitative and Qualitative Data

**Quantitative data:** Data in numerical form

**Qualitative data:** Data in nonnumerical form

Data can be classified as quantitative or qualitative. **Quantitative data** are data in numerical form. **Qualitative data** are data in nonnumerical form.

Quantitative data are data that can be precisely measured. Examples include data on age, cost, length, height, area, volume, weight, speed, time, and temperature.

Qualitative data deal with descriptions. They are data that can be observed, or self-reported, but not necessarily precisely measured. Examples of qualitative data are data on relationships and behavior.

Consider an evaluation of a microlending program. Quantitative data for this program may include the number of participants, by gender, age, and number of children; income; inventory of product; cost of product; and sales. Qualitative data for this program may include descriptions of products, family relationships, demeanor of participants, relationships with the community, and feelings of control.

Patton (2002) identifies three data collection methods that may produce qualitative findings:

- in-depth, open-ended interviews
- direct observations (using narrative descriptions)
- analysis of written documents.

He describes the kinds of information evaluators learn from each of the three methods:

- Open-ended interviews yield direct quotations about experiences, opinions, feeling, and knowledge.
- Direct observations can provide detailed descriptions of activities, behaviors, actions, and the full range of interpersonal interactions and organizational processes.
- Document analysis can yield excerpts, quotations, or entire passages from records, memoranda and correspondence, official publications and reports, diaries, and open-ended written responses to questionnaires and surveys.

Most qualitative data collection comes from spending time in the setting under study. The evaluator makes firsthand observations of activities and interactions, sometimes engaging in activities as a participant observer. The extensive notes from the data collection are the raw data. These data are then organized into readable narrative descriptions with major themes, categories, and illustrative case examples (Patton 2002).

The quality of the qualitative data collected depends on the evaluator. According to Patton:

> Systematic and rigorous observation involves far more than just being present and looking around. Skillful interviewing involves much more than just asking questions. Content analysis requires considerably more than just reading to see what's there. Generating useful and credible qualitative findings through observation, interviewing, and content analysis requires discipline, knowledge, training, practice, creativity, and hard work. (2002, p. 5)

Patton (1987) developed a checklist of 20 questions to help evaluators decide whether or not qualitative methods are an appropriate evaluation strategy (box 8.3). If the answer to any question is "yes," then the collection of at least some qualitative data is likely to be appropriate.

### Box 8.3  Patton's 20-Question Qualitative Checklist

1. Does the program emphasize individual outcomes—that is, are different participants expected to be affected in qualitatively different ways? Is there a need or desire to describe and evaluate these individualized client outcomes?

2. Are decision makers interested in elucidating and understanding the internal dynamics of programs—program strengths, program weaknesses, and overall program processes?

3. Is detailed, in-depth information needed about certain client cases or program sites (for example, particularly successful cases, unusual failures, or critically important cases) for programmatic, financial, or political reasons?

4. Is there interest in focusing on the diversity among, idiosyncrasies of, and unique qualities exhibited by individual clients and programs (as opposed to comparing all clients or programs on standardized, uniform measures)?

5. Is information needed about the details of program implementation: What do clients in the program experience? What services are provided to clients? How is the program organized? What do staff members do? Do decision makers need to know what is going on in the program and how it has developed?

6. Are the program staff and other stakeholders interested in collection of detailed, descriptive information about the program for the purpose of improving the program (that is, is there interest in formative evaluation)?

7. Is there a need for information about the nuances of program quality—descriptive information about the quality of program activities and outcomes, not just levels, amounts, or quantities of program activity and outcomes?

8. Does the program need a case-specific quality assurance system?

9. Are legislators or other decision makers or funders interested in having evaluators conduct program site visits so that the evaluations can be the surrogate eyes and ears for decision makers who are too busy to make such site visits themselves and who lack the observing and listening skills of trained evaluators? Is legislative monitoring needed on a case-by-case basis?

10. Is the obtrusiveness of evaluation a concern? Will the administration of standardized measuring instruments (questionnaires and tests) be overly obtrusive in contrast to data-gathering through natural observations and open-ended interviews? Will the collection of qualitative data gen-

erate less reactivity among participants than the collection of quantitative data? Is there a need for unobtrusive observations?

11. Is there a need and desire to personalize the evaluation process by using research methods that emphasize personal, face-to-face contact with the program—methods that may be perceived as "humanistic" and personal because they do not label and number the participants, and they feel natural, informal, and understandable to participants?

12. Is a responsive evaluation approach appropriate—that is, an approach that is especially sensitive to collecting descriptive data and reporting information in terms of differing stakeholder perspectives based on direct, personal contact with those different stakeholders?

13. Are the goals of the program vague, general, and nonspecific, indicating the possible advantage of a goal-free evaluation approach that would gather information about what effects the program is actually having rather than measure goal attainment?

14. Is there a possibility that the program may be affecting clients or participants in unanticipated ways and/or having unexpected side effects, indicating the need for a method of inquiry that can discover effects beyond those formally stated as desirable by program staff (again, an indication of the need for some form of goal-free evaluation)?

15. Is there a lack of proven quantitative instrumentation for important program outcomes? Is the state of measurement science such that no valid, reliable, and believable standardized instrument is available or readily capable of being developed to measure quantitatively the particular program outcomes for which data are needed?

16. Is the evaluation exploratory? Is the program at a preevaluation stage, where goals and program content are still being developed?

17. Is an evaluability assessment needed to determine a summative evaluation design?

18. Is there a need to add depth, detail, and meaning to statistical findings or survey generalizations?

19. Has the collection of quantitative evaluation data become so routine that no one pays much attention to the results anymore, suggesting a possible need to break the old routine and use new methods to generate new insights about the program?

20. Is there a need to develop a program theory grounded in observations of program activities and impacts, and the relationship between treatment and outcomes?

*Source:* Patton 1987.

Data collection usually includes both quantitative and qualitative data, but one approach may be dominant. The two approaches can be characterized in the following ways. A quantitative approach

- is more structured
- emphasizes reliability
- is harder to develop
- is easier to analyze.

A qualitative approach

- is less structured
- is easier to develop
- can provide "rich data" (idiosyncratic data on each unit being studied)
- demands more labor intensivity to collect and analyze data
- emphasizes validity.

The approach used will depend on the goals of the evaluation (table 8.2).

In practice, quantitative and qualitative data are related. According to Trochim (2006), "All quantitative data [are] based upon qualitative judgments, and all qualitative data can be described and manipulated numerically." Indeed, computerized analysis (content analysis) of written documents focuses on the frequency of various words, types of words, and structures, turning qualitative data into quantitative data.

■ **Obtrusive method:**
Method used to observe participants with their knowledge

Data can be collected obtrusively or unobtrusively. **Obtrusive methods** are observations made with the participants' knowledge. Such methods are used to measure perceptions, opinions, and attitudes through interviews, surveys, and focus groups. Observations made with the knowledge of those being observed are also obtrusive.

**Table 8.2 When to Use a Quantitative and a Qualitative Approach**

| If you | Then use this approach |
|---|---|
| Want to conduct statistical analysis | |
| Want to be precise | Quantitative |
| Know what you want to measure | |
| Want to cover a large group | |
| Want narrative or in-depth information | |
| Are not sure what you are able to measure | Qualitative |
| Do not need to quantify the results | |

*Source:* Authors.

If an evaluation uses questionnaires to collect data, subjects know they are being studied, which may produce artificial results. According to Patton (1987, p. 33), "The instrument itself can create a reaction which, because of its intrusiveness and interference with normal program operation and client functioning, fails to reflect accurately what has been achieved in the program."

Those being studied may change their behavior or responses. A teacher whose lesson is being observed by the school system's top administrator, for example, may teach quite differently than when the top administrator is not observing.

**Unobtrusive methods** are observations made without the knowledge of the participant. Examples of unobtrusive methods include using data from documents or archives and observing participants without their knowledge (box 8.4).

■ **Unobtrusive method:** Method used to observe participants without their knowledge

## Tools for Collecting Data

The data collection technique chosen will depend on the situation. No matter which method is chosen to gather data from people, all the information gathered is potentially subject to **bias.** Bias means that when asked to provide information about themselves or others, respondents may or may not tell the whole truth, unintentionally or intentionally. They may distort the truth because they do not remember accurately or fear the consequences of providing a truthful answer. They may also be embarrassed or uncomfortable about admitting things they feel will not be socially acceptable. All self-reported data are vulnerable to this problem.

■ **Bias:** The intentional of unintentional distortion of data in terms of collecting, analyzing, or reporting

Respondents may be embarrassed about responding truthfully to questions about the use of protection during sexual intercourse or the date of their last visit to a doctor, for example. They may describe what they think the evaluator wants to hear rather than the truth.

Selection bias—the fact that the people who choose to participate in a program may be different from those who choose not to participate—may also exist (this issue was discussed in chapter 5). This is often an issue in surveys, interviews, and focus groups. Those who volunteer to participate may be systematically different from those who do not.

Typically, more than one data collection approach is used to answer different evaluation questions or to provide multiple sources of data in response to a single evaluation question. The evaluation may, for example, collect available data from farmers' crop yield records, interview buyers of farm produce, and survey farmers. Sometimes evaluators use focus groups or conduct case studies to help develop themes for a questionnaire or to make sense of survey results.

Collecting the same information using different methods in order to increase the accuracy of the data is called a ***triangulation of methods.*** Evaluators use method triangulation to strengthen findings. The more information gathered using different methods that supports a finding, the stronger the evidence is.

Method triangulation is not the only type of triangulation. Denzin (1978) identifies several types of triangulation, including the **triangulation of sources. Evaluator triangulation,** in which multiple evaluators are involved in an investigation, is another type of triangulation.

Subjects of a study are not the only people who may affect the results of an evaluation. Evaluators and the evaluation setting may also have effects. Women, for example, may respond differently to a male interviewer than to a female interviewer; they may respond differently if they are interviewed alone or with their spouses.

The next sections describe nine data collection tools:

- Tool 1: Participatory data collection
- Tool 2: Analysis of records and secondary analysis
- Tool 3: Observation
- Tool 4: Surveys and interviews
- Tool 5: Focus groups
- Tool 6: Diaries, journals, and self-reported checklists
- Tool 7: Expert judgment
- Tool 8: Delphi technique
- Tool 9: Other measurement tools.

■ **Triangulation of methods:** Collection of the same information using different methods in order to increase the accuracy of the data

■ **Triangulation of sources:** Collection of the same information from a variety of sources in order to increase the accuracy of the data

■ **Evaluator triangulation:** Collection of the same information from more than one evaluator in order to increase the accuracy of an evaluation

## Tool 1: Participatory Data Collection

Participatory data collection approaches involve groups or communities heavily in data collection. Examples of participatory data collection techniques are community meetings, mapping, and transect walks.

### Community meetings

One of the most common methods of participatory data collection is through community meetings. These meetings allow members of the community to ask questions, make comments, and discuss issues of importance to the community.

For meetings to yield usable data, they must be well organized. The evaluator and stakeholders should agree on the purpose of the meeting and commit to being present for it. Before the meeting, the evaluator should establish and announce ground rules. Items to consider are how to identify speakers, how much time to allot to speakers, and the format for questions and answers. If the population has sufficient literacy, the ground rules should be put in writing and made available for latecomers.

The community meeting should be widely publicized, through flyers, newspaper ads, and radio station announcements. Community members can also be responsible for spreading the word. Evaluators should not rely primarily on local officials to invite people, because they may invite a biased selection that reflects their own views. The location for the meeting should be chosen with the idea of encouraging community participation while still meeting the comfort, access, and safety needs of participants (Minnesota Department of Health 2007).

Holding community meetings has several advantages:

- The meetings can raise the credibility of the process by enhancing openness and inclusion.
- Holding community meetings is inexpensive and relatively easy to arrange.
- Community meetings allow for broad participation.
- Their more relaxed setting may increase community participation.
- Community meetings can raise the level of awareness and understanding of the evaluation and build support for it.
- They can increase the evaluator's knowledge of important program issues.
- They may reveal issues that warrant further investigation.

Community meetings have pitfalls as well (table 8.3). For example, community members who choose to participate may not be representative of

**Table 8.3    Advantages and Challenges of Community Meetings**

| Advantages | Allow members of the community to learn about the intervention and to discuss issues |
| --- | --- |
| | Can raise awareness and credibility |
| | Is inexpensive |
| | Can increase evaluator's knowledge of important issues |
| Challenges | May not accurately represent the community, because of issues of gender and power |

*Source:* Authors.

the community, and some people with good ideas or a clear understanding of the issues may not like to attend or to speak at such events. Those who do attend may be those who feel most strongly (positively or negatively) about the program. Those who speak may be those who hold power positions in the community. Depending on the time the meeting is held, gender issues may affect attendance. Attendance and participation of women is likely to be related to the culture. Because of these issues, community meetings should never be the primary data collection method for the evaluation.

### Mapping

■ **Mapping:**
Drawing of or use of existing maps as part of data collection

The drawing of or use of existing maps—a process called **mapping** when applied to data collection—can be used to generate discussions about local development priorities and the extent to which they have been met. It can be used to verify secondary sources of information. Mapping can also capture changes or perceived changes over time (before and after an intervention, for example). While the process of mapping is often applied to the planning of interventions, it can also be used in evaluations.

Mapping can be done with individuals or groups. As a group tool, it is useful for participatory evaluations involving stakeholders, because it provides a way for them to work together. At the same time, mapping can increase everyone's understanding of the community. This is especially important when people may have different understandings of the community based on their status and experience. Mapping is also a useful data collection tool for use with groups where literacy is an issue.

Types of mapping include the following:

- resource mapping
- historical mapping
- social mapping
- health mapping
- wealth mapping
- land use mapping
- demographic mapping.

Resource mapping is often used to collect and plot information on the distribution, access, and use of resources within a community. It may be used before and after an intervention to identify changes.

Maps can be developed in many ways. For a water supply and sanitation program, for example, evaluators may develop simple paper and pencil drawings showing known water sources, toilet sites, primary ecological features, and settlement patterns. Evaluators may then ask villagers to use other materials they provide, such as thread, straw, ribbon, and rope, to demarcate which families use which water sources for drinking water or toilet sites. Colored pencils, ink, or crayons can be used to draw dots to indicate the distribution of special groups, such as poor women, the rich, or leaders (Narayan 1996).

Examples of using mapping in a participatory manner include the following:

- asking school children to map their community by drawing their homes and those of their neighbors
- asking a group of men and women to use locally available materials—clay, grass, mud, stones, and sticks—to make a model of their community and mark all water (or other) resources
- initiating discussion and involving people in the process of developing a map of the community during a group meeting (Narayan 1996).

**Social mapping** involves "drawing" a conceptual picture of the elements that make up a community, including its resources and assets, and how they interact with one another. Social mapping can be used to present information on village layout, infrastructure, demography, ethnolinguistic groups, community facilities, health patterns, wealth, and other community issues. This approach brings together community members in order to better understand the community and how the intervention fits (or does not fit) within it. It can be used as part of any approach if appropriate to the evaluation questions. It can also be used for before the intervention and after the intervention comparisons.

■ **Social mapping:** The "drawing" of a conceptual picture of the elements that make up a community, including its resources and assets, and how they interact

Other mapping tools include aerial photography, including Google Earth (box 8.5); land surveys; maps prepared by professional cartographers; and maps prepared by field workers who walk through a community and seek assistance from key local people. Information obtained in this way can be used in planning multicommunity activities (Narayan 1996).

### Transect walks

Walking through an area that is being studied is very different from looking at an aerial image. Instead of using a camera, a walker uses his or her observation skills to develop an understanding of the area. Following dirt

paths that community members take can reveal why women fetch water only once a day or switch to different paths when the rains begin. A walk may lead to an understanding of social divisions in the community, such as power and caste divisions. It may also help identify spatial organization, architectural styles, use of space, environmental sanitation, overuse or underuse of facilities, and activities around water and sanitation facilities (Narayan 1996).

■ **Transect walk:** Walk taken in order to observe a community's people, surroundings, and resources

A **transect walk** is a type of walk an evaluator might take around a community in order to obtain a representative observation of its people, surroundings, and resources. Transect walks are a kind of spatial data-gathering tool. A transect walk can take as little as an hour or as long as a day.

The transect walk is planned by drawing a "transect line" through a map of a community. The line should go through, or transect, all zones of the community in order to provide a representative view of the community.

The evaluator, accompanied by several community members, walks along the area represented by the transect line on the map. He or she talks to the community members while observing conditions, people, problems, and opportunities (Academy for Educational Development 2002).

The following are examples of aspects of a community that can be observed during a transect walk:

- housing conditions
- presence of street children
- nature of children's labor
- informal street commerce and prostitution
- availability of public transportation
- types of nongovernmental organizations (NGOs) and church organizations
- types of stores
- types of food sold in open markets
- sanitary conditions
- interactions between men and women
- presence of health facilities
- community facilities (Academy for Educational Development 2002).

Transect walks provide an evaluator with a "big picture" view of the community. They help identify issues that need further investigation.

## Tool 2: Analysis of Records and Secondary Data

Sometimes data that have already been collected can be used to answer evaluation questions. When using data sets gathered by others, it is necessary to understand how the data were collected, how variables were defined, and how the data were coded and cleaned, including how missing data, non-responses, and low response rates were treated. Secondary data sources include not only data sets from prior data collection activities but also newspaper articles, television shows, Web pages, blogs, and Internet discussion groups.

### Using records

Government agencies, clinics, schools, associations, and development organizations are but a few of the organizations that produce records. These records can be a mainstay of evaluations.

Organizational records are a common source of evaluation information. Most organizations have already collected and organized data from clients and communities. They may also have summarized and reported the information, in the form of internal management reports, budget documents, reports to the public or funding agencies, or evaluation or monitoring reports.

McCaston (2005) presents a sampling of types of secondary data and information commonly associated with poverty analysis:

- demographic (population, population growth rate, rural/urban, gender, ethnic groups, migration trends)
- discrimination (by gender, ethnicity, age)
- gender equality (by age, ethnicity)
- the policy environment
- the economic environment (growth, debt ratio, terms of trade)
- poverty levels (relative and absolute)
- employment and wages (formal and informal; access variables)
- livelihood systems (rural, urban, on-farm, off-farm, informal)
- agricultural variables and practices (rainfall, crops, soil types and uses, irrigation)
- health (malnutrition, infant mortality, immunization rate, fertility rate, contraceptive prevalence rate)
- health services (number, level, facility-to-population ratio; access by gender, ethnicity)
- education (adult literacy rate, school enrollment rate, drop-out rates, male-to-female ratio, ethnic ratio)
- schools (number and level, school-to-population ratio, access by gender, ethnicity)
- infrastructure (roads, electricity, telecommunication, water, sanitation)
- environmental status and problems
- harmful cultural practices.

The above information can be found in

- files and records
- computer data bases
- industry reports
- government reports
- other reports, including previous evaluations
- census and household survey data
- electronic mailing lists and discussion groups
- documents (budgets, policies and procedures, organizational charts, maps)
- newspapers and television reports.

To extract information from paper-based documents, evaluators develop a data collection instrument that specifies exactly what data to collect from the file or record and how to code it. The objective is to develop an instrument that is simple and clear. Once the instrument is developed, it should be pretested.

Consider, for example, an evaluation of whether critical care nurses trained in a government-sponsored training program are more effective than other critical care nurses. A data collection instrument could be used to systematically gather relevant data in their files (figure 8.1). Evaluators could select a sample of critical care clinics in which one or more nurses were trained through the government program and review the records of all the nurses. These records include their educational background, the length of time they have been nursing, and their performance ratings.

When working with documents that describe current activities or practices, the evaluator should verify that the documents accurately reflect practice. Observations (if the program is still ongoing) and interviews can help do

**Figure 8.1   Sample Data Collection Instrument**

Date _____

                                                    ID #:_____
1.  Highest level of education completed: _____
2.  Registered nurse?                Yes _____ No _____
3.  Completed government training? Yes _____ No _____
4.  If yes, year completed training?       _____
5.  How many years nursing at this clinic? _____
6.  How many years nursing elsewhere?      _____
7.  performance ratings for the past five years:
              Year: _____ Rating: _____
              Year: _____ Rating: _____
              Year: _____ Rating: _____
              Year: _____ Rating: _____
              Year: _____ Rating: _____
8.  Performance award received during past five years:
              ____Yes ____No
    If yes, number of awards received in past five years: _____
9.  Gender:     ___Male___Female

10. Comments: _____
    _____
    _____

*Source:* Authors.

so. For example, when using documents describing a training program, the evaluator might check if classes were actually held five days a week, materials were available, and participants were as diverse as documents indicate. This verification could come from a few interviews of people knowledgeable about the program, its history, and implementation. Depending on the case, it might be important to seek out people who have different roles, including budget staff and clients, whose perspectives could shed light on the information obtained and provide insights into the unwritten history. When neither observations nor interviews are feasible, the evaluator might verify information by identifying and reviewing other supporting documents that report similar information.

It is usually necessary to read and analyze official documents in addition to files. In evaluating a program to improve the responsiveness of government officials to telephone calls by citizens, for example, evaluators would look at official documents to determine the following:

- When was the program authorized?
- What goals and objectives were presented for the program in the authorizing document?
- How many government workers were to be involved?
- What agencies or departments were to be involved?
- Over what period was the program to be implemented?
- What performance measures or indicators were implied or specified?
- What was the budget for the program?
- What activities were to be implemented?

### Using existing data sets

Electronic data sets collected by one organization are often obtained and reanalyzed by another to answer new questions. This type of analysis is called **secondary data analysis.** Evaluators often use large computer databases containing, for example, household survey data or loans made by a financial intermediary to small and medium-size enterprises. In performing secondary data analysis, evaluators must stay focused on the purpose and design of the evaluation.

■ **Secondary data analysis:** Analysis of data obtained from another source rather than collected by evaluators

Key issues to consider in determining whether to obtain and use data for secondary analysis include the following:

- Are the available data valid?
- Are the available data reliable?
- Are the available data accurate?
- What are the response and missing data rates?

McCaston (2005) suggests also checking on

- the credentials of the organization holding the database
- the methods and decision rules used to clean the data
- the age of the information in the database (current or out of date?)
- whether the data make sense and are consistent with data from other sources.

Consider, for example, an evaluation unit that is considering using data from a large computerized management information system with data about university loans obtained under a major government program. As a requirement of this program, the student's income must have been under a required level. The evaluators considering using these data must check that the data show that students who were not eligible for funding did not receive funding. If they find that ineligible students did receive funding, they then need to determine whether the problem is one of incorrectly entered data (accuracy) or improper implementation of the requirements. The evaluators must also check that eligible students were not denied funding or that students did not receive more than one loan. The evaluators may first perform data runs to determine the nature and extent of these problems in the database. To verify the data, they may phone a sample of the students to confirm that they both received the funding and attended school. The evaluators could also check with the schools to determine if their records show that the students attended and received funding from the program.

The following process should be followed in using secondary data:

- Find out what is needed to transfer the data to your computer. Sometimes the organization holding the database will prefer to conduct the analysis for you, and this is the only option. (If possible and practical, it is preferable to transfer the file.)
- Check for viruses before transferring data to your computer.
- Obtain the database structure, data dictionary, and coding schemes.
- Verify the accuracy of the data through testing and cross-validation.
- Transfer the data in a way that prevents new errors from being introduced (no retyping). Manually check some of the data to ensure that they were transferred as planned.
- Properly reference all secondary data (publication date, proper citation of authors).

Table 8.4 summarizes the advantages and challenges of using available data.

**Table 8.4  Advantages and Challenges of Using Available Data**

| | |
|---|---|
| Advantages | Data are usually less expensive and faster than collecting original data. |
| Challenges | Data may not be exactly what is needed. |
| | May be difficult to sustain long-term access to data |
| | Validity and reliability of data need to be verified and coding errors corrected. |

*Source:* Authors.

### Tool 3: Observation

Observation can be a powerful data collection tool. By just using one's eyes, one can observe, for example, traffic patterns, land use patterns, the layout of city and rural environments, the quality of housing, the condition of roads, or who comes to a rural health clinic for medical services.

Observation is a useful data collection tool when the purpose of the evaluation is to collect benchmark and descriptive data or to document program activities, processes, and outputs. It is appropriate in a variety of situations (table 8.5).

Observations can be structured or semistructured:

- Structured observations determine before the observation precisely what will be observed over what time interval. Observers usually use a checklist to count events or instances or a stopwatch to time activities.
- Unstructured observations select the method depending on the situation, without preconceived ideas or a plan on what to observe or how long to observe. The observer watches and records as the situation unfolds.
- Semistructured observations are conducted when the evaluator has a general idea of what to observe but no specific plan. The evaluator may simply note what he or she finds interesting, typical, unusual, or important. The evaluator may engage in continuous note taking about transactions as they occur or focus on specific actions.

#### *Structured observation*

Using a structured approach to observation, Stake (1995) developed an issue-based observation form (figure 8.2). Many forms for structured observation use abbreviations and symbols to allow more room on the form for collecting data. Forms can be modified to meet the needs of particular evaluations.

Figure 8.3 shows another example of a form used for structured observation. This tool is used to collect observation data on children's communication skills.

**Table 8.5  Reasons for Using and Examples of Observation**

| Reason for using observation | Examples |
|---|---|
| To gain direct information | Making random visits to schools, homes, farms, or other sites and observing rather than only asking people |
| | Observing operations and procedures in offices, schools, hospitals, or other sites rather than relying solely on reports |
| | Unobtrusively recording numbers of occurrences, such as ethnic, gender, or age groups involved in a particular activity |
| To understand an ongoing behavior, process, unfolding situation, or event | Observing and describing what is done in each phase of project or program |
| | Observing children interacting with other children on the playground, parents dealing with children, teachers dealing with students, health care workers dealing with patients, and managers dealing with employees |
| | Observing managers conducting business meetings before and after officer training programs |
| To examine physical evidence, products, or outputs | Observing food and other items sold in the market |
| | Periodically observing the coastline of a lake involved in a cleanup program |
| | Having a team of experts inspect the quality of grasses and legumes in a pasture |
| | Inspecting gardens, newsletters, project books, and so forth |
| To provide an alternative when written or other data collection procedures may be infeasible or inappropriate | Having several participants volunteer to observe and report on program delivery rather than having all participants fill out questionnaires |
| | Observing dynamics and concerns expressed during a workshop for new immigrants |
| | Having trainers observe one another's classes; noting dynamics, questions, and level of participation |

*Source:* Adapted from the University of Wisconsin Cooperative Extension 1996.

**Figure 8.2  Sample Issue-Based Observation Form**

| Observer: | | School: | Date: | Time of Observation: From    To |
|---|---|---|---|---|
| Teacher: Male Female | | Age 25 35 50 65 | Grade: | Time of write-up: |
| Teacher Experience: 0 - - Months | | Direct instruction Low - - High | # Students: | Subject |
| Synopsis of lesson, activities: | | | Comments on science education issues: 1 response to budget cuts 2 locus of authority 3 teacher prep 4 hands-on materials | |
| Description of room | Pedagogic orientation | Teacher aim | Reference made to | |
| learning place L - - H | textbook L - - H | didactic L - - H | sci method 0 - - M | |
| science place L - - H | stdzd testing L - - H | heuristic L - - H | technology 0 - - M | |
| compet'n place L - - H | prob solving L - - H | philetic L - - H | ethics, relig 0 - - M | |

*Source:* Adapted from Stake 1995.

**Figure 8.3 Sample Structured Observation Form**

# Early Communication Indicator (ECI)

Early Childhood
Research Institute
**on Measuring
Growth and
Development**

Child name or #_____ Test Date_____(MM/DD/YY)
Test duration _____ - _____
           Min   Sec
Form: House or Barn Condition Change (see list below): ____
Primary Coder: _____ Assessor:_____
Location (circle one): Home Center Other (explain in notes)
Language of administration: _____
If reliability, reliability coder's name: _____
Notes:

| | Gestures | Vocalizations | Single words | Multiple words |
|---|---|---|---|---|
| Begin 0:00 Sec. | G | V | W | M |
| 1:00 Sec. | G | V | W | M |
| 2:00 Sec. | G | V | W | M |
| 3:00 Sec. | G | V | W | M |
| 4:00 Sec. | G | V | W | M |
| 5:00 Sec. | G | V | W | M |
| 6 min End Total | G | V | W | M |

**Condition List**
interpreter
language intervention toolkit
medical intervention (e.g., tubes)
mental health consultant
milieu or incidental teaching
none
nutritionist
other
physical therapist
primary care provider
registered nurse
responsive interaction
social worker
speech/language therapist

| | Gestures | Vocalizations | Single words | Multiple words | Total |
|---|---|---|---|---|---|
| Primary coder | | | | | |
| Reliability coder | | | | | |
| Agreement | | | | | |
| Disagreement | | | | | |
| Percent | | | | | |

Overall percent

Agreement

A/A D

Determining reliability:

1. Record primary coder scores in first line.
2. Record reliability coder scores in second line.
3. Record number on which they agreed on third line.
4. Record number on which they disagreed on fourth line.
5. Calculate percent agreement for each key element category.
6. Calculate overall percent agreement using total scores.
7. Calculate average percent agreement across categories (add agreements and disagreements across categories (third and fourth lines).

*Source:* Early Childhood Research Institute on Measuring Growth and Development 2008.

### Semistructured observation

A semistructured observation may not have a specific plan. Instead, it may identify what kinds of things to observe (table 8.6).

### Recording observations

Observations can be recorded in at least three ways:

- *Observation guide:* Printed form that provides space for recording observations. (Examples for observation guides can be found in Stake (1995), University of Wisconsin Cooperative Extension (1996), and Yin (2003).)
- *Recording sheet or checklist:* Form used to record observations in yes/no form or on a rating scale. Recording sheets are used when there are specific, observable items, actors, or attributes to observe.

Table 8.6   **Uses of Semistructured Observation**

| Observation of | Examples |
|---|---|
| Characteristics of participants (individually and as a group) | Gender, age, profession/vocation, dress, appearance, ethnicity |
| | Attitude toward subject, toward others, about self |
| | Skills, habits, and knowledge |
| Interactions | Level of participation, interest |
| | Power relationships, decision making |
| | General climate for learning, problem-solving |
| | Levels of support, cooperation versus conflict |
| Nonverbal behavior | Facial expressions |
| | Gestures |
| | Postures |
| Program leaders, presenters | Clarity of communication |
| | Group leadership skills, encouraging participation |
| | Awareness of group climate |
| | Flexibility, adaptability |
| | Knowledge of subject, use of aids, other teaching/learning techniques |
| | Sequence of activities |
| Physical surroundings | Room (space, comfort, suitability) |
| | Amenities (beverages and so forth) |
| | Seating arrangements |
| Products of a program | Demonstrations, facility, plan |
| | Brochures, manuals, newsletters |

*Source:* Cloutier and others 1987.

- *Field notes:* Least structured way to record observations. Observations are recorded in a narrative, descriptive style when the observer notices or hears something important.

**Field notes** contain "the ongoing data that are being collected. They consist of descriptions of what is being experienced and observed, quotations from the people observed, the observer's feelings and reactions to what is observed, and field-generated insights and interpretations" (Patton 2002, p. 305).

According to Lofland (1971, p. 102), field notes are "the most important determinant of bringing off a qualitative analysis. Field notes provide the observer's raison d' être. If . . . not doing them, [the observer] may as well not be in the setting."

Patton (2002) discusses techniques for keeping field notes for observations. He describes the importance of describing everything that the observer believes to be worth noting and not trusting anything to future recall. As soon as possible, the observer should record any information that has helped understand the context, the setting, and what went on. The field notes should contain descriptive information that during analysis will allow an evaluator to mentally return to the observation to experience that observation. Patton suggests recording basic information, such as where the observation took place, who was present, what the physical setting was like, what social interactions occurred, and what activities took place.

He notes the importance of using specific rather than general terms: words such as *poor, angry,* and *uneasy* are not sufficiently descriptive. "Such interpretive words conceal what actually went on rather than reveal the details of the situation," according to Patton.

### Training and preparing observers

Patton (2002, p. 260) points out that just because a person is "equipped with functioning senses does not make that person a skilled observer." He discusses the importance of training and preparing observers, identifying six components of training for observers:

- Learn to pay attention, see what there is to see, and hear what there is to hear.
- Practice writing descriptively.
- Acquire discipline in recording field notes.
- Know how to separate detail from trivia to achieve the former without being overwhelmed by the later.
- Use rigorous method to validate and triangulate observations.
- Report the strengths and limitations of one's own perspective, which requires both self-knowledge and self-disclosure.

> ■ **Field notes:**
> Descriptions of what is being experienced and observed, quotations from the people observed, the observer's feelings and reactions to what is observed, and field-generated insights and interpretations

**Table 8.7  Advantages and Challenges of Observational Data Collection**

| | |
|---|---|
| Advantages | Collection is of data on actual behavior rather than self-reports or perceptions. |
| | Collection is of data in real time rather than retrospectively. |
| Challenges | Sampling as well as recording and interpreting the data can be difficult. |
| | Collecting data can be labor intensive. |

*Source:* Authors.

Whenever feasible, more than one observer should be used. All observers should be trained so that they observe according to agreed upon procedures.

The observation data collection procedure should be test piloted before it is used for the evaluation. To do this, at least two observers must go to the same area and complete their field notes on coding forms and rating sheets. After they complete their sheets, the sheets should be compared. If there are large differences, more training and clarification should be provide. If there is little difference, the procedure can be adopted.

Table 8.7 summarizes the advantages and challenges of collecting observational data.

### Tool 4: Surveys and Interviews

Surveys are excellent tools for collecting data about people's perceptions, opinions, and ideas. They are less useful in measuring behavior, because what people say they do may not reflect what they actually do.

Surveys can be structured or semistructured, administered in person or by telephone, or self-administered by having people respond to a mailed or Web form. Surveys can poll a sample of the population or all of the population (for a discussion of sampling, see chapter 9).

#### *Structured surveys and semistructured surveys*

■ **Structured survey:** Survey that includes a range of response choices, one or more of which respondents select

**Structured surveys** are surveys that include a range of response choices, one or more of which respondents select. All respondents are asked exactly the same questions in exactly the same way and given exactly the same choices to answer the questions.

How many response options should be used? For nominal responses, such as region of the country, primary occupation, or age group, the number of responses needs to cover the number of possible responses. When using scales to indicate responses, the number of response options should generally be an odd number (3, 5, or 7) so that the neutral response is readily apparent to the respondent. (Sometimes even-numbered scales are used, to require the respondent to make a choice between a "satisfactory" and "partly unsatisfactory" rating.) Semistructured surveys ask the same general set of questions, but they allow opened-ended responses to all or most questions (box 8.6).

**Semistructured surveys** are surveys that ask predominantly open-ended questions. They are especially useful when the evaluator wants to gain a deeper understanding of reactions to experiences or to understand the reasons why respondents hold particular attitudes. Semistructured surveys should have a clearly defined purpose. It is often more practical to interview people about the steps in a process, the roles and responsibilities of various members of a community or team, or a description of how a program works than to attempt to develop a written survey that captures all possible variations. If potential respondents feel good rapport and are posed

■ **Semistruc-tured survey:** Survey, often administered, that asks predominantly open-ended questions

---

### Box 8.6   Structured and Semistructured Survey Questions

Examples of structured questions include the following:

1. Has this workshop been useful in helping you to learn how to evaluate your program?
   - Little or no extent
   - Some extent
   - Moderate extent
   - Great extent
   - Very great extent
   - No opinion
   - Not applicable
2. Do all people in the village have a source of clean water within 500 meters of their homes?
   - Yes
   - No

Examples of semistructured questions include the following:

1. What have you learned from the program evaluation workshop that you have used on the job?
2. Where are the sources for clean water for the villagers?

---

**Table 8.8 Advantages of Structured and Semistructured Surveys**

| Structured surveys | Semistructured surveys |
|---|---|
| Harder to develop: survey needs to cover all possible pieces of information | Easier to develop: survey can include broad open-ended questions that capture anything missed in the structured sections, reducing the danger of leaving something out |
| Easier to complete: checking a box takes less time than writing a narrative response | More difficult to complete: burdensome for people to complete self-administered questionnaires |
| Easier to analyze | Harder to analyze but provide richer source of data; interpretation of open-ended responses subject to bias |
| More efficient when working with large numbers of people | |

*Source:* Authors.

interesting questions, they may be willing to be interviewed for an hour or more. In contrast, few people would be willing to spend an hour filling out a questionnaire. Ideally, two people should conduct each interview, so that interviewers can compare notes. Using two interviewers also can help resolve disputes about what was said.

Table 8.8 highlights the advantages of structured and semistructured surveys.

### Modes of survey administration

The most frequent means of conducting surveys are

- telephone questionnaires
- self-administered questionnaires distributed by mail, e-mail, or the Web
- administered questionnaires (common in the development context).

Telephone surveys are useful for understanding experiences, opinions, or individual personal descriptions of a process. In-person and telephone surveys are similar; they differ only in the mode of delivery.

Self-administered questionnaires can be delivered to respondents in person or by mail, by e-mail, or over the Web. Respondents answer the questions on a form and then return the completed form to the interviewer. Self-administered surveys should be short and take no more than 20 minutes to complete (shorter is better). Of all the approaches, research suggests that people are most likely to give honest responses to sensitive questions in an anonymous self-administered survey.

Using the mail, e-mail, or the Web is much less expensive than administering surveys in person. Surveys can be sent to any area where potential respondents have access to these methods of distribution. If an area does not receive postal access regularly or has limited telephone or Internet capability, it would not have good participation in the survey, yielding a major source of bias. Low levels of literacy make these approaches inappropriate in many development contexts.

Administered surveys, which are typical in the development context, can be structured, semistructured, or mixed. These written surveys are read by a data collector, who records the responses. It is generally preferable to use closed-ended questions but to include one or two open-ended questions at the end. These open-ended questions often make people feel comfortable, as they can add anything they feel the survey missed or comment on the survey itself. One or two open-ended questions are all that is needed; more may be burdensome. These open-ended responses can be time consuming to analyze, but they can provide some useful insights and quotations to illustrate major themes of the evaluation.

**Computer-assisted telephone interviewing** (CATI) uses an interactive computer system that aids interviewers as they ask questions over the phone. The interviewer begins the interview, and the computer program controls branching to or skipping among questions. The choice of questions is based on the answers to other questions, allowing more personalized and sophisticated interviews than are possible with paper questionnaires. During the interview, interviewers enter data along with simple coding directly into the computer system. Most questions are in a multiple choice format, so the interviewer simply clicks on the correct answer; the computer system translates the data into a code and stores it in a data base (UNESCAP 1999).

Table 8.9 summarizes the advantages and challenges of using surveys.

■ **Computer-assisted telephone interviewing (CATI):** Interviewing that uses interactive computer system to help interviewers as they ask questions over the phone

Table 8.9 **Advantages and Challenges of Surveys**

| | |
|---|---|
| Advantages | Respondents indicate what they think, believe, or perceive. |
| Challenges | People may not accurately recall their behavior or may be reluctant to reveal their behavior, particularly if it is illegal or stigmatized. |
| | What people think they do or say they do is not always the same as what they actually do. |

*Source:* Authors.

### Developing survey questions

Developing survey questions involves

- choosing the questions
- wording the questions and responses
- sequencing the questions
- choosing a layout for the survey
- reviewing, translating, and pretesting the questions.

*Choosing the questions.* Evaluators can use open-ended or closed-ended questions. Open-ended questions cannot be answered with a simple response or selection. Respondents are often uncomfortable or unwilling to answer open-ended questions in writing.

Closed-ended questions can be answered with one simple piece of information. The question "What is your date of birth?" is a close-ended question because it can be answered with just the date of birth, no details, just a simple piece of information. A second form of closed-ended question is a dichotomous question, such as a yes/no or true/false question. A third form of closed-ended question is a multiple choice question. Many experts advise using mostly closed-ended questions but including one or two open-ended questions at the end of the survey (Burgess 2001) or leaving a space for a comment after each question.

Using too many different forms of questions can be confusing for respondents. Jackson and Agrawal (2007) suggest using no more than three forms of questions in most surveys.

According to the Living Standards Measurement Survey Study (LSMS) (World Bank 1996), it is helpful to develop survey questions in levels (table 8.10). In this way, a well-balanced questionnaire is obtained.

Distinguishing the type of question forces the evaluator to be clear about what is being asked and helps the respondent to respond appropriately. Patton (2002) describes six kinds of questions:

- *Experience and behavior questions:* What a person does, or aims to do, to elicit behaviors, experience, action, and activities
- *Opinion and values questions:* Aimed at understanding the cognitive and interpretive processes of people (rather than actions and behaviors)
- *Feeling questions:* Aimed at eliciting emotions of people to experiences and thoughts, looking for adjective responses, such as anxious, happy, afraid, intimidated, and confident. The question should cue the person being interviewed that the question is asking for opinions, beliefs, and considered judgments, not feelings.

**Table 8.10    Levels of Refinement in Determining Questionnaire Content**

| Level | Description |
|---|---|
| Define overarching objectives | Define objectives (to study poverty; to understand the effects of government policies on households). |
| Determine balance between sections | Define which issues are most important (incidence of food price subsidies, effect of changes in the accessibility or cost of government health and education services, effect of changes in the economic climate as a result of structural adjustment or transition from a centrally planned to a market economy. |
| Determine balance within sections | Within the education sector, for example, define which of the following are the most important for the country and moment: the levels and determinants of enrollment, poor attendance, learning, and differences in male and female indicators; the impact of number of years of schooling on earnings in formal sector and agriculture and how or if they differ; which children have textbooks or receive school lunches or scholarships; how much parents have to pay for schooling. |
| Write questions to study specific issues or programs | In a study on access to textbooks, for example, the evaluator would need to know how many subjects textbooks cover; if books are to be given to each child or to be shared; if books can be taken home or used only in the classroom; if books are to be used for only one year or several; if books are to be paid for or provided free of charge; when the books are supposed to be available; and whether textbooks bought from bookshops are better or worse than those provided by the school. |

*Source:* World Bank 1996.

- *Knowledge questions:* Questions that inquire about the respondent's factual information—what the respondent knows
- *Sensory questions:* Questions about what is seen, heard, touched, tasted, and smelled
- *Background/demographic questions:* Age, education, occupation, and other characteristics of the person being interviewed.

*Wording questions and response choices.*    Each of Patton's six types of questions can be asked in the present, past, or future. For example, an evaluator can ask:

- What did you know about HIV/AIDS treatment five years ago? (past tense)
- What did you learn today from the presentation about HIV/AIDS? (present tense)
- What would you like to learn about HIV/AIDS? (future tense) (Patton 2002).

Evaluation questions must be clear (box 8.7). If they are not, the respondent may feel uncomfortable, ignorant, confused, or hostile. Evaluators
must learn the terms used by people being surveyed when talking about the
project, program, or policy and must use these words when constructing
the survey.

The evaluator must be careful not to lead the respondent into giving a
desired answer. Consider, for example, the following questions:

"To what extent, if any, have your profits increased since the training?"

"If profits have increased to a slight, moderate, substantial, or great
extent, do you attribute the increase to the training?"

Clearly, these questions "lead the witness" down the path the evaluator wants to go. It would be better to ask about trends in profits over a
longer period of time and then ask, if there was an increase, to what it was
attributed.

Slight changes in the way questions are worded can have a significant
impact on how people respond.

Several investigators have looked at the effects of modifying adjectives and
adverbs. Words like *usually, often, sometimes, occasionally, seldom,* and *rarely*
are "commonly" used in questionnaires, although it is clear that they do not

mean the same thing to all people. Some adjectives have high variability and others have low variability. The following [phrases] have highly variable meanings and should be avoided in surveys: *a clear mandate, most, numerous, a substantial majority, a minority of, a large proportion of, a significant number of, many, a considerable number of,* and *several.* Other [phrases] produce less variability and generally have more shared meaning. These are *lots, almost all, virtually all, nearly all, a majority of, a consensus of, a small number of, not very many of, almost none, hardly any, a couple,* and *a few* (StatPac 2007).

Frary (1996) offers several suggestions for designing effective question-naires. Among his suggestions for rated responses are the following:

- Order the responses from a lower level to a higher order from left to right: *1) Never 2) Seldom 3) Occasionally 4) Frequently.*
- Consider combining response categories if responders would be very unlikely to mark "never" and if "seldom" would connote an almost equiv-alent level of activity: *1) Seldom or never 2) Occasionally 3) Frequently.*
- Ask responders to rate both positive and negative stimuli (responses from both ends of the scale). In this way, respondents must evaluate each response rather than uniformly agree or disagree with all of the responses.
- If possible, reduce the number of possible responses. For example, if the opinions of the respondents are likely to be clear, use a simple *1) Agree 2) Disagree.* When many respondents have opinions that are not strong or well-formed, use more options: *1) Agree, 2) Tend to Agree, 3) Tend to Disagree, 4) Disagree.*

After writing the questions, the evaluator should read each question and response to check for language and logic. Is the grammar correct? Does the response follow the question logically?

Writing survey questions is hard to do, because they have to be under-standable to everyone. Words have multiple meanings and connotations. If a question is asked in a way that people do not understand or understand in a variety of ways, they will be responding to a different question. There is also a risk of collecting useless data. For example, an agency head may want to find out how much computer training people in his organization have had. The following questions could be asked:

- Have you had any training in the past three months?
- Have you had any training in the past six months?
- Have you had any training in the past year?

The problem with asking this set of questions is that everyone who had training within the past three months will answer "yes" to all three questions.

A better-designed question would ask, "How many training courses have you attended in each of the following time periods?

a. Within the past 1–3 months: _____
b. Within the past 4–6 months: _____
c. Within the past 6–9 months: _____
d. Within the past 10–12 months: _____
e. Within the past 12–24 months: _____

Poorly worded questions may frustrate respondents, causing them to guess at answers or even throw the survey away. Because poorly constructed questions cannot be salvaged in analysis, questions need to be well written. Evaluators should therefore leave plenty of time for review and pretesting of the survey.

Both confidentiality and anonymity should be ensured and protected. Confidentiality is an ethical principle that protects information by allowing it to be accessed only by those who are authorized. Anonymity means that the personal identity or personal information about a person will not be shared. Many evaluators include a statement such as, "Your responses will be treated with confidence and at all times data will presented in such a way that your identity cannot be connected with specific published data" (Burgess 2001).

*Sequencing the questions.*    Sequencing questions in the following order can improve the chances that a survey is completed:

- Begin with questions that are of interest to the respondent.
- Keep the flow of questions logical and avoid complex branching.
- Group similar or related questions together, and try to establish a logical sequence for the questions (Burgess 2001).
- Move from easy and interesting to difficult and uncomfortable, from general to specific (Jackson and Agrawal 2007).
- Set questions in chronological order (Jackson and Agrawal 2007).
- Ask the most important questions by two-thirds of the way through the survey, because some respondents may not complete the survey (Jackson and Agrawal 2007).
- Put personal or confidential questions at the end of the survey—if they are placed at the beginning, some respondents may not continue (Frary 1996).
- Prioritize questions and consider dropping low-priority questions (Jackson and Agrawal 2007).

Jackson and Agrawal (2007) suggest that most self-administered surveys run no longer than a single page. For respondents with university education, a survey can run two pages.

*Choosing a layout for the survey.*    The layout of the printed survey deserves consideration:

- The survey should have a title and version date.
- It should be uncluttered and free of unnecessary headings.
- It should include contact and return information.
- It should include a brief introductory statement (in case the cover letter is misplaced) that indicates the purpose of the survey and explains how it will be used.
- Questions and response choices should be formatted and worded consistently. Each question should be numbered.
- The survey should include instructions on how to answer the questions. Instructions should indicate how many responses may be chosen (just one or all that apply) and how to indicate one's selection (tick a box, circle the answer, write a short answer) (Burgess 2001).

Jackson and Agrawal (2007) suggest placing check-off boxes or lines for responding, with enough space between them that the evaluator can identify which selection was made. They also discuss the importance of giving the survey a professional look.

A cover letter should accompany the survey. This letter identifies the sponsor and gives the participants information about the purpose of the questionnaire. Jackson and Agrawal (2007) suggest that the cover letter identify the following:

- The purpose of the survey (and why it is in the respondent's interest to complete it)
- How the person was selected for the survey
- How the data will be used
- Whether anonymity will be maintained
- The length of time needed to complete the survey
- Any incentives
- Contact information for more information or clarification.

If the survey is being sent by mail, a self-addressed stamped envelope should be included or another procedure established for returning the survey.

*Reviewing, translating, and pilot testing the questions.*   The process of survey development is an iterative one. Once the initial version of the survey is drafted, the interested parties should review the draft closely. During their review, they should make notes and share their criticisms and suggestions. Revisions are then made to the survey. This process may have to be repeated several times before the survey is ready for pilot testing.

Where more than one language is needed to collect data, the survey must be translated. Those responsible for the survey need to make sure that the instruments have been accurately translated. When translating surveys, a trained person who knows both languages and is familiar with the subject of the questionnaire should do the first translation (see Behling and Law 2000). Once the survey is translated into the local language, another person should translate it back to the original. This process checks for gaps or misunderstanding in what was translated. This is the only way to ensure an accurate translation. Lack of agreement on all parts of the survey need to be reconciled before any pilot testing can be done.

In most cases, surveys are printed only in the official language(s) of the country, and teams of interviewers with skills in communicating in a number of local languages are used to collect data. In these cases, a few key questions or phrases are translated into local languages and presented in the survey manual. Local interpreters may be needed to survey respondents who speak other languages.

Survey questions should always be worded in simple terms in the language that is commonly spoken. Questions should not be written in an academic or formal language style. In local languages, the gap between the spoken and written languages and the difficulty of balancing simplicity and precision may be great. This is especially true for languages that are not commonly used in writing.

Once the survey is agreed upon, it should be field or pilot tested with a small number of subjects. According to the results of the field test, additional revisions are likely needed. If the first field test suggests many changes, another field test may be needed, covering some or all of the survey, especially if there were problems with multiple translations.

With all surveys and interviews, it is essential to field or pilot test (pretest) the data collection instrument early on. This means asking a small but representative sample of potential respondents to take the survey and highlight areas where clarification is needed. One useful strategy is to sit down with respondents as they complete the survey and to ask them to reason aloud as they fill it out. This exercise can yield insights into how potential respondents interpret questions. Often things considered crystal clear turn out to be confusing or ambiguous in ways that were never anticipated. If respondents misunderstand a question, the evaluators need to revise the question and retest it before implementing the instrument.

The goal of a field test is to ensure that the survey is capable of collecting the information it is aimed to collect. A good pilot test will look at the survey at three levels:

- *As a whole:* Are all parts of the survey consistent? Are there areas that ask the same question?
- *Each section:* If the survey has more than one section, does the information looked for in each section collect the intended information? Are all major activities accounted for? Are there any questions that are not relevant?
- *Individual questions.* Is the wording clear? Does the question allow ambiguous responses? Are there alternative interpretations?

When conducting a field or pilot test, it is important to test the survey among people from diverse areas and all major language and socioeconomic groups. This may include rural and urban residents, people employed in the formal and informal sectors, and people speaking all key language groups.

If the pilot test is administered in only one language, it usually takes about one week to complete. If the final survey is to be conducted in more than one language, it will take more time to pilot it, because a version in each language should be field tested.

At the end of the pilot test, one or two weeks should be set aside to review the results. The team(s) working on the field test should meet to discuss and agree on changes needed. In a typical large-scale survey, three cycles of pilot testing are generally done.

Boxes 8.8 and 8.9 provide guidelines for conducting surveys. The first emphasizes the administration process. The second focuses on writing good questions.

### Citizen report cards

A **citizen report card,** sometimes called a *citizen score card,* is a type of survey that measures the performance of public services. It is being increasingly used in development. In Bangalore, India, for example, a group of private citizens is using them to address problems with public services (Paul and Thampi 2008). Citizen report cards have been used for many years in the United States to grade the performance of public agencies.

■ **Citizen report card:** Type of survey that measures the performance of public services

**Box 8.8   General Guidelines for Conducting Surveys**

The following are general guidelines for conducting surveys:

- Keep it simple, clear, easy, and short.
- Locate other people who have conducted the kind of evaluation you are interested in. Find and study surveys similar to the one you think you want to conduct.
- Make sure people know why you are asking them to participate (but in a way that is unlikely to bias their responses).
- Ask questions that are easy to answer, and do not frustrate the respondent's desire to be clear.
- Do not ask respondents for information that requires them to go to a file or other source. If you must do this, you need to let them know in advance so the material can be assembled before the survey is administered.
- Respect respondents' privacy. Treat surveys confidentially, and have procedures in place to ensure privacy. Never promise confidentially unless it can be delivered.
- Respect respondents' time and intelligence.
- Tell respondents how they were selected and why their participation is important.
- Do no harm: keep responses confidential. In your report, use aggregate responses. Assign an identification number to the data, and destroy the link to the person's name.
- Let respondents know if they will receive a copy of the final report that uses the questionnaire results.

*Source:* Authors.


**Box 8.9   Tips for Writing Questionnaires**

The following tips can help evaluators write questionnaires:

1. If possible, use an existing questionnaire as a guide. Modify as needed to fit your situation. It is easier to modify than it is to create one from scratch.
2. Follow the following basic guidelines:
   - Use simple, clear language that is appropriate for respondents.
   - Ask only one question at a time, for example: "To what extent, if at all, is the material clear" rather than "To what extent, if at all, is the material clear and helpful." (If the material is clear but not helpful, there is no way the person can give an accurate answer.)

- Write your questions so that all respondents feel their responses are acceptable. Lead into your question by giving the range: "To what extent, if at all," Or "How important or unimportant are...."
- Provide appropriate response categories that are mutually exclusive. If asking age groups, make categories; 20–30, 31–40, 41–50 rather than 20–30, 30–40, 40–50.
- When possible, write questions so that responses range from negative to positive:

  "To what extent, if at all, was ... Very Unhelpful ← ... → Very Helpful."

- Avoid yes/no responses when the answer is not dichotomous. Instead, try to capture a range of views by asking respondents to answer along a scale. For example, provide a five-point point scale ranging from a "little or no extent" to "very great extent."
- Avoid absolutes at either end of the scale (few people are absolute about anything). Soften the ends by using "always or almost always" at one end of the scale and "never or almost never" at the other end of the scale.
- Ask questions about the current situation. Memory decays over time.
- Leave exits (use "no basis to judge" and "no opinion" categories). If you do not provide an exit, respondents may make meaningless responses.
- Avoid using double negatives.

3. Make the survey easy to complete. Provide boxes to check. Provide sufficient instructions so that respondents know what they are to do: indicate "check only one" or "check all that apply" when appropriate.
4. Ask general questions first, then more specific questions, then one or two final open-ended questions, such as "any comments or anything else we should know?"
5. Ask only about demographic information you will use. Be sensitive that some people can be identified by demographics. Place demographic questions toward the end of the survey.
6. Have draft questions reviewed by experts.
7. If the questions need to be translated, have that done, and then have them translated back to the original language to check the translation.
8. Pretest, pretest, pretest! Have typical respondents answer the questionnaire rather than just read it. Then go back through each question to get their feedback. Is each question clear? Did they understand what was being asked? Are there unknown words or unclear phrases? Is there a better way to ask each question?

*Source:* Authors.

Citizen report cards are used to

- collect citizen feedback on public services from actual users of a service
- assess the performance of individual service providers or compare performance across providers
- generate a database of feedback on services that can then be placed in the public domain (ADB and ADBI 2004).

Table 8.11 shows an example of a citizen report card reporting overall satisfaction with services.

Citizen reports collect feedback on the following factors:

- availability of service
- access to service
- reliability of service
- overall quality of service
- satisfaction with service
- responsiveness of service provider
- hidden costs
- corruption and support systems
- willingness to pay (World Bank 2006).

Citizen report cards can be used in many ways (table 8.12). They can also be administered at different levels of government.

Table 8.13 summarizes the advantages and challenges of citizen report cards for data collection.

### Interviews

An interview is a dialogue between a skilled interviewer and the person being interviewed. The goal is to elicit information that can be used to answer evaluation questions (box 8.10). The quality of the information

Table 8.11   Citizen Report Card Results on Satisfaction with Infrastructure Services

| Agency | Number of users among respondents (thousands) | Percent users satisfied | Percent users dissatisfied |
|---|---|---|---|
| Power | 1,024 | 43 | 15 |
| Water | 775 | 41 | 19 |
| Telephone | 203 | 87 | 12 |
| Police | 98 | 45 | 36 |

*Source:* Authors.

**Table 8.12   Uses of Citizen Report Cards**

| Type of study or project | Example |
|---|---|
| Studies of satisfaction with urban service studies | Seven Indian cities; Kampala, Uganda |
| Studies of provincial and national satisfaction with service delivery | India, the Philippines, Uganda |
| Sector studies | Public hospitals in Bangalore, India |
| Program evaluations | Rural food security in Tamil Nadu, rural water and sanitation in Maharashtra, India |
| Governance reform projects | Bangladesh, Peru, the Philippines, Sri Lanka, Ukraine, Vietnam |

*Source:* World Bank 2006.

**Table 8.13   Advantages and Challenges of Citizen Report Cards for Data Collection**

| Advantages | • Provide summative feedback on performance |
|---|---|
| | • Are structured for simple communication |
| | • Help reduce bias in data collection |
| Challenges | • Require capacity to understand this kind of assessment |
| | • Are limited to comparing across services |
| | • Require large sample for heterogeneous population for services used by only a small percentage of population |
| | • Lacks predictability about how government officials will respond |

*Source:* Authors.

obtained depends largely on the interviewer's skill and personality (Lofland and Lofland 1995). The key to a good interview is being a good listener and good questioner.

Every culture has its own values and customs: a question or gesture may offend people from one culture and not another. Cultural competence is therefore a must for the interviewer, who must pay attention to respondents' reactions during the interview to ensure that he or she does not inadvertently cause offense (box 8.11).

In dealing with people from all cultures, interviewers should keep in mind the following:

- Every person appreciates being treated with respect.
- Even people who come from cultures noted for self-sacrifice and community thinking have a sense of self-value and appreciate being treated as individuals.
- Every person appreciates feeling as if his or her opinion matters to you.

## Box 8.10    Tips for Conducting Interviews

The following tips can help evaluators conduct interviews:

1. Let interviewees know
   * what the purpose and timing of the study is
   * why they are being interviewed
   * how they were selected
   * how the data will be used
   * whether the interview is confidential
   * how long the interview will take
   * what the content is of the interview (by sharing questions in advance)
   * whether you may want to talk to them again
   * whether they will receive a copy of the final report
   * whether a summary of your notes will be made available to them if desired.
2. Try to pick a time and place that is quiet and free of distractions.
3. Ideally, have a second person help take notes.
4. Consider tape recording the interview. If you do, be sure to check with the interviewee and get permission before recording.
5. Stick to your script. If asking close-ended questions, ask them exactly the way they were written. If asking open-ended questions, "go with the flow" rather than always directing it.
6. Be aware of cultural norms, such as eye contact, direct questions, and gender issues.
7. Maintain balance: if you ask respondents about what they think are the major supports to a project, for example, follow with what they think are the major barriers.
8. Try to avoid asking "why" questions, if doing so is seen as aggressive or critical.
9. Accept whatever respondents say with empathy and without judgment.
10. Take good notes without distracting from the conversation.
    * Maintain eye contact while writing.
    * Write key words or phrases, not a verbatim account of the interview.
    * If the interviewee is saying something you want to capture, ask the person to repeat it or finish what you are writing before asking the next question.
    * If the interviewee says something quotable, ask if you may use his or her exact words.
11. Write up the interview.
    * Keep in mind that every word and idea is potentially valuable.
    * Take the time to write up your notes as carefully and in as much depth as possible.
    * Conduct at least a brief clean-up of your notes immediately after the interview (leave sufficient time between interviews).
    * Write up full notes within a day of the interview.
12. In sensitive situations, consider sharing notes with respondent to check recollection of responses and agree on what was said.

*Source:* Authors.

## Box 8.11 Tips for Conducting Interviews across Cultures

The following tips may help evaluators conduct interviews in developing settings:

1. Before each interview, learn more about the culture of the person you will be interviewing.
2. Discuss interview techniques with someone familiar with the culture or use an interviewer from the same culture as the interviewee.
3. Find out as much as possible about cultural characteristics such as
   - the amount of physical space to leave between yourself and the interviewee
   - the amount of eye contact that is appropriate
   - the significance of voice inflections, head movements, and other body language during a conversation
   - the appropriate way to dress
   - the appropriate form of greeting
   - gender roles.

Gender issues are particularly important. In some cultures, for example, it may be inappropriate for a male interviewer to be alone in a room with a woman who is being interviewed. In certain cultures men may clam up when interviewed by a woman. Using same-sex interviewers or having an opposite-sex witness present is a necessary procedure in such situations.

Table 8.14 summaries the advantages and challenges of interviews.

**Table 8.14  Advantages and Challenges of Interviews**

| | |
|---|---|
| Advantages | • Can be structured, semistructured, unstructured, or a combination, but are generally semistructured |
| | • Can explore complex issues in depth |
| | • Are forgiving of mistakes: unclear questions can be clarified during the interview and changed for subsequent interviews |
| | • Can last an hour or more, depending on importance and interest |
| | • Can provide evaluators with an intuitive sense of the situation |
| Challenges | • Can be expensive, labor intensive, and time-consuming |
| | • May not indicate why different people have different viewpoints |
| | • As a result of selective hearing by the interviewer, may miss information that does not conform to preexisting beliefs |
| | • Requires cultural sensitivity, particularly with respect to gender issues. |

*Source:* Authors.

*Response rates*

■ **Response rate:** Percentage of people who participate in a survey divided by total number asked to do so

The **response rate** is the percentage of people who actually participate divided by the total number asked to do so. A good evaluation provides the number of people (or units, such as organizations) surveyed; the number who responded; the response rate; and a description of efforts made to increase the response rate (follow-up telephone calls, letters).

Low response rates may suggest a biased (self-selected) sample. This is a problem because people who choose to participate may be different from those who choose not to. Say, for example, an organization conducts an employee attitude survey of all employees but just 30 percent respond. If the most dissatisfied employees tended to complete the survey while those who were satisfied did not, the data will not reveal the views of all types of employees. It would be a mistake to make decisions based on these results without collecting more information on who responded and who did not. Surveys with response rates under 70 percent should not be reported unless the evaluator has analyzed response bias and demonstrated the survey's validity (Jackson and Agrawal 2007).

An evaluator can look at the demographics of the survey respondents to see if they match the larger population in terms of such characteristics as age and gender. If they do, the evaluator may proceed, but only with appropriate qualifying of the results. In some cases, the evaluator may follow up directly with some nonrespondents to determine if there are patterns. If the demographics of those responding and not responding are different, the survey results must be qualified appropriately. Evaluators should report such analyses of nonrespondents and how they potentially affect the findings.

Survey results with low response rates must always be reported in terms of the number of respondents, recognizing that these results may or may not accurately reflect the larger group. That is, the data should be expressed as "of the 87 respondents" or "75 percent ($N = 60$) of the survey respondents reported. . . ." Percentages should not be used if the total number of those sent the survey is less than 50. A proportion such as "75 percent of those responding" when applied to a total number of 45 respondents is quite different from 75 percent of 3000 respondents.

■ **Focus group:** Qualitative evaluation methodology in which small groups of people are brought together to discuss specific topics under the guidance of a moderator

## Tool 5: Focus Groups

A **focus group** is a qualitative evaluation methodology in which small groups of people are brought together to discuss specific topics under the guidance of a moderator. The structure of the focus group may appear informal, but, in fact, it uses a script that includes a set of open-ended questions. A trained moderator leads the discussions and probes or asks additional questions as warranted by the situation.

The group process tends to elicit more information than individual interviews, because people express different views and engage in dialogue with one another. But a focus group is not simply a group interview. The moderator facilitates the dialogue and explores members' reasons and feelings. The conversation is often nonlinear; participants may bring up information or different perspectives at any time.

Focus groups are used to collect data on the following:

- group interaction
- complexity of resources
- "how" and "why" rather than "whether" and "how much"
- contextual responses, not yes/no responses
- immediate feedback
- complexity of behaviors and motivations
- intensity of opinions
- views on sensitive topics (Billson and London 2004).

It can be used to triangulate methods. It is also useful when respondents are not comfortable with "paper and pencil" methods.

Focus groups should not be used to gather statistical data. They are also inappropriate where

- language barriers are insurmountable
- the evaluator has little control over the group
- trust cannot be established
- free expression cannot be ensured
- confidentiality is critical (Billson 2004).

A focus group generally includes 6–12 people. The composition of the group depends upon its purpose. Most focus groups are homogeneous, including people of similar status (teachers in one group, students in another; supervisors in one group, employees in another group). Who should and should not be in the same focus group depends on the situation and the cultures involved. The selection of participants must not bias the evaluation results in any predictable way. No category of potential participants should be overlooked if their responses can be expected to alter or expand the results. In this case of potential additional groups of relevance, another focus group should be held.

Focus groups should provide

- comfortable, safe surroundings (essential)
- refreshments (essential)
- monetary incentives (optional)
- transportation or childcare arrangements (optional)
- a skilled moderator (essential)
- a note taker (optional).

Sessions are tape recorded, and, ideally, a verbatim transcript is prepared for each session. The focus group begins with a clear explanation of

- what the purpose is of the focus group
- why participants' views are important
- how participants were selected
- what a focus group is
- what the rules are of the process, including the key rule: what is said in this room stays in this room.

The moderator guides the process, keeps the group focused, and makes sure all participants have the opportunity to voice their views and that a few people do not dominate the conversations. The moderator asks a small number of questions, using a guide developed specifically for the session. All questions are open ended. The conversation progresses from easy, conversational questions to more serious questions. It ends with summary and wrap-up questions that allow for impressions to be corrected if necessary and any additional comments and ideas to be recorded.

Evaluators are responsible for all aspects of the focus group, including

- who should be in it
- how many sessions should be conducted
- where the sessions are conducted
- when the sessions are conducted
- what to ask participants
- how to analyze and present the data.

A typical focus group project requires six to eight weeks' lead time. The length of time depends on logistical factors, the complexity or urgency of the project, the accessibility of decision makers, and the ease with which participants can be recruited.

Focus group evaluation works best if conducted in the following way (Billson 2004):

- Step 1: Clarify the key evaluation questions. If clients and evaluators are not clear about the key questions the focus groups are supposed to answer, the entire process will be frustrating.
- Step 2: Design the evaluation approach. Using the evaluation purpose and key questions, design the general approach and flow of topics to get at the key questions.
- Step 3: Develop the moderator's guide, which must include all of the needed protocol (structure or code of behavior) for the evaluation in a way that does not bias responses but directs the group toward key issues.
- Step 4: Recruit participants.
- Step 5: Specify the moderation techniques. Identify and use good moderation techniques during the focus group sessions.
- Step 6: Debrief observers, evaluators, and clients and record additional information. Immediately after each focus group, when the data are fresh, share insights generated during the focus group with clients and other interested parties. Record additional information not openly discussed (impressions, conclusions, and so forth) for use in the next step.
- Step 7: Analyze the data. If the focus group has worked well, it will produce a mountain of words and ideas. These qualitative data require special analytical techniques, particularly content analysis (see chapter 10).
- Step 8: Present the findings. Report findings in a way that is meaningful and useful to others, particularly the client. Use oral, written, or video formats, or a combination of any of them.

Focus group sessions normally last one to two hours. For most projects, 100 minutes allows time to follow through on each major line of questioning without exhausting or boring the participants or the moderator (Billson 2004). Focus groups should be not be overscheduled. Two or three focus group sessions in one day are the maximum a moderator can handle.

Focus groups should be held in a neutral setting, if possible. The location should also be easily accessible. Typically, participants sit around a table or chairs arranged in a circle, to facilitate conversation among participants. It is possible for a few observers to be present in the room while the focus group is conducted. They should be introduced at the beginning of the session and the reason for their presence explained.

Audio or video recorders are extremely useful in providing an accurate transcript of a session. Most participants soon forget they are being taped. If the session is not taped, two note-takers should be present to document the sessions. Taking notes on a laptop computer can speed up the initial data analysis and report writing. The moderator should not take notes.

There is no fixed rule about how many focus group sessions to conduct. The general rule is to conduct them until the same themes emerge or no new information emerges. This usually happens after three to six sessions. It may be useful to ask a core set of questions of every focus group and then add different questions or probes that are more extensive once it becomes clear that the themes are consistent. Evaluators should debrief one another after each session so that decisions can be made about adjustments to the protocols in subsequent sessions.

The daily activities of participants should be considered: evaluators must be sensitive to demands on participants' time, including commuting time; participation in a session may take half a day or more. A focus group scheduled in the late afternoon may interfere with the preparation of an evening meal, limiting the number of people who are willing to participate.

Focus groups require considerable preparation and lead time. Box 8.12 provides tips on writing focus group questions.

The focus group session can be broken into four distinct phases. These and the steps under each phase are laid out in table 8.15.

The focus group questions in box 8.13 are meant to illustrate the types of questions that the evaluator may want to ask when using this tool.

---

**Box 8.12   Tips for Designing Focus Group Questions**

The following tips can help evaluators get the most out of focus group sessions:

- Think first about how the information gleaned from the focus group will be used. Make sure all questions will lead, directly or indirectly, to usable information.
- Avoid vague, confusing wording.
- Ask one question at a time.
- Ask open-ended questions.
- Avoid assumptions that are leading or misleading.
- Avoid questions that introduce bias, skewing the responses.
- Avoid supplying alternative responses.
- Make it interesting. Mechanical questions elicit mechanical responses.
- Use the "protocol funnel," which begins with questions about broad conceptual issues and ends with probing questions.

**The Protocol Funnel**

Broad conceptualization
Key evaluation questions
General questions
Specific questions
Probes

*Source:* Billson 2004: 29.

---

**Table 8.15  Four Phases of Focus Group and Moderator Actions**

| Phase | Actions |
|---|---|
| I. Preamble or opening statement | Moderator puts participants at ease by beginning with ice-breaking questions. |
| | Moderator explains purpose of focus group. |
| | Moderator provides ground rules. |
| | Everyone in the room introduces himself or herself. |
| II. Introductions and warmup | Participants relate experience and roles to the topic. |
| | Moderator stimulates group interaction and thinking about the topic. |
| | Moderator starts with the least threatening and simplest questions. |
| III. Main body of group discussion | Moderator moves to more threatening or sensitive and complex questions. |
| | Moderator elicits deep responses. |
| | Emergent data are connected to create a complex, integrated basis for analysis. |
| | Broad participation is ensured. |
| IV. Closure | Moderator ends with closure-type questions. |
| | Moderator summarizes and refines key themes. |
| | Moderator presents theories, impressions, and hunches to group members for reaction, confirmation, or clarification and correction. |
| | Moderator invites participants to provide a round of final comments or insights ("key lessons learned"), plus "last thoughts," anything missed, and anything else participants would like evaluation team to know. |
| | Moderator thanks participants and distributes any incentive they were promised. |

*Source:* Authors.

---

**Box 8.13  Sample Focus Group Questions**

The following script may be useful in modeling questions to ask during a focus group.

*Introductions:* Let us start by asking you to introduce yourselves. Please mention your title and where you work, as well as the nature of your experience in receiving services from this health clinic program, including why you went there.

*On perceptions:* Critics of the free health clinic program argue that they provide low-quality care. What was your experience in receiving services from the free clinics?

*On governance:* Recent surveys suggest that the current budgets to districts do not reach local clinics. What is your assessment of these problems based on your experience receiving services from the clinics?

*Source:* Adapted from Billson 2004.

**Table 8.16 Advantages and Challenges of Focus Groups**

| | |
|---|---|
| Advantages | Can be conducted relatively quickly and easily |
| | May take less staff time than in-depth, in-person interviews |
| | Allows flexibility to make changes in process and questions |
| | Can explore different perspectives |
| | Can be fun for participants |
| Challenges | Analysis is time-consuming. |
| | Participants may not be representative of the population, possibly biasing the data. |
| | Group may be influenced by moderator or dominant group members. |

*Source:* Authors.

Table 8.16 summarizes the advantages and challenges of focus groups.

### Tool 6: Diaries and Self-Reported Checklists

Another method of collecting data is to use diaries or self-reported checklists.

#### *Diaries or journals*

■ **Diary:** Written self-report by a participant, usually maintained daily

A **diary** (or journal) is a written self-report by a participant, usually maintained daily. Diaries are used to capture detailed information about events in people's daily lives. They can be used to study such phenomena as social networks; health, illness, and associated behavior; diet and nutrition; farm work; study habits; contraception use; and child-rearing practices. In addition to capturing the activities of interest over a particular timeframe, diaries may include some characterizations of the activities. For example, smokers enrolled in a smoking cessation program might be asked to use diaries to record when they get a strong urge to smoke, where they were, and what they were doing at that time. The idea is that if the patterns are known, participants can take action on them. If the end of a meal is a trigger for, they can break the pattern by quickly getting up from the table after eating.

Diaries have been used on a broad national scale as well as in smaller programs (Stafford 2006). Diaries are useful tools with which to supplement other data sources (table 8.17). Keeping a diary generally requires literacy and the willingness to take the time to maintain the diary. In some cases, however, diaries can use a checklist format to decrease needs for literacy. For example, a pictorial diary has been used to collect data on household

**Table 8.17   Guidelines for Using Diaries or Journals**

| Action | Details |
|---|---|
| Recruit people face-to-face | Encourage participation using highly motivated, personal interviewers. |
| | Appeal to altruism, helpfulness. |
| | Ensure confidentiality. |
| | Provide incentive for completing. |
| Provide booklet to each participant | Begin with clear instructions on how to fill in diary. |
| | Include example of completed diary entry. |
| | Include short memory-joggers. |
| | Explain all terms, such as *event* or *session*. |
| | On last page, ask whether this was a typical or atypical time period and for any comments or clarifications. |
| | Include a calendar, indicating when an entry is due. |
| Consider the time period for collecting data. | If period is too long, it may become burdensome or tedious for participants. |
| | If period is too short, diary may miss a behavior or event. |

*Source:* Authors.

consumption and expenditure in Tanzania and The Gambia (Wiseman, Conteh, and Matovu 2005).

What is the right period of time to use a checklist? In general, at least one week is needed to get large enough a sample of behaviors and more than one month is too long. After that, the keeping of the diary becomes tedious, and record-keeping declines.

Typically, participants are given booklets that provide a clear set of instructions as well as an example of a completed diary entry. Any unusual terms are explained. The last page of the booklet asks whether the diary covers a typical or atypical period. It also provides an opportunity for participants to share any comments not included in the daily entries.

### Self-reported checklist

A **self-reported checklist** is a cross between a questionnaire and a diary. Participants are asked to keep track of a specific set of activities or events, which are listed, so that the respondents can easily check them off. Checklists can be completed on a daily or weekly basis or every time a particular

■ **Self-reported checklist:** List of specific set of activities or events that respondents check off as applicable

event or activity occurs. A checklist could be used, for example, to capture the times for taking malaria pills or to track the number and times of trips to a water connection.

Self-reported checklists were used in a study of midwives in Indonesia (Abdallah 2002). The project was based on the theory that providers need reinforcement after training for behavior change. The objective was to improve the quality of midwives' counseling on family planning. Participating midwives completed one self-assessment a week on specific interpersonal communication skills to increase their understanding of their own communication patterns, analyze them, and take actions to improve them.

A self-reported checklist is easier to complete and analyze than a diary. Creating a checklist, however, requires that the evaluator understand the situation very specifically.

Table 8.18 summarizes the advantages and challenges of diaries and self-reported checklists.

### Tool 7: Expert Judgment

Sometimes it makes sense to engage experts as the source of information or opinion. Consider the role of a book or movie critic. People use their judgments to help inform their own decisions or choices. Government task forces are a form of expert judgment.

**Table 8.18  Advantages and Challenges of Diaries and Self-Reported Checklists**

| | |
|---|---|
| Advantages | Can capture in-depth, detailed data ("rich data") that may otherwise be forgotten |
| | Can collect data on how people use their time |
| | Can collect sensitive information |
| | Can supplement interviews, provide richer data |
| Challenges | Require some literacy |
| | May change behavior, because people know their behavior is being observed |
| | Require commitment and self-discipline, accurate and honest recording of information by participant; participant who may not accurately recall behaviors |
| • | Data recorded that may be incomplete, or participant may have waited to record information and did not remember correctly ("tomorrow diaries") |
| | Reading people's handwriting that may be difficult |
| | Phrases in diaries that may be difficult to understand. |

*Source:* Authors.

**Expert judgment** can be obtained from an individual expert or a panel of experts. A panel of experts may perform a hospital review conducted as part of the accreditation process. This group of experts visits the hospital to investigate its programs, facilities, and staff. An individual expert (such as a school inspector) may visit schools to evaluate the school, the administration, and teachers.

■ **Expert judgment:** Opinion of individual expert or panel of experts

Expert judgment can use preestablished professional criteria and procedures, or it can be done ad hoc. When expert judgment uses established criteria, the criteria are usually published standards and instruments that ensure that the experts ask questions and evaluate in a consistent manner. For example, a funding agency may want to evaluate the quality of a training program for which a curriculum was established, with stated goals, objectives, and outcomes. An expert who is fully versed in the curriculum, goals, objectives, and outcomes examines the training program and bases the evaluation on documentation.

Ad hoc reviews are done on an irregular schedule, as circumstances indicate. They are usually conducted for a specific purpose. Such reviews usually have no predetermined standards for experts to use. The experts determine the standards for judging. An example of an ad hoc review is a program director visiting the site of a water treatment program to get an idea of how the program is proceeding.

Selection of experts should pass the reasonable person test: would a reasonable person think this expert or group of experts is credible? The experts should reflect a diverse set of views, experiences, and roles.

It is important to establish criteria for selecting experts based not only on recognition as an expert but also on the following types of criteria:

- areas of expertise
- diverse perspectives
- diverse political views
- diverse technical expertise.

The rationale for the selection of all experts should be indicated in the evaluation report.

The International Council on Security and Development (2006) used an expert panel to review the effectiveness of the International Narcotics Control Board. In this case, it was particularly important not only to have recognized experts but also to make sure that they were drawn from diverse parts of the world, especially those with recognized large narcotics problems.

While an expert panel is not considered a strong evaluation approach, under some circumstances, it may be the best approach given time and resource constraints. Expert panels are more appropriate at the program or project design and early to mid-implementation stages than for impact evaluations. They are especially useful in rapid assessments.

#### Table 8.19  Advantages and Challenges of Expert Judgment

| Advantages | Fast, relatively inexpensive |
|---|---|
| Challenges | Weak for impact evaluation |
| | May be based largely on perceptions |
| | Value of data collected depends on how credible the group is perceived to be |

*Source:* Authors.

Table 8.19 shows the advantages and challenges of expert judgment.

### Tool 8: Delphi Technique

■ **Delphi technique:** Technique that elicits information and judgments from participants in order to facilitate problem-solving, planning, and decision making without bringing participants face to face

The **Delphi technique** enables experts who live in different locations to engage in dialogue and reach consensus through an iterative process. Experts are asked specific questions; their answers are sent to a central source, summarized, and fed back to the experts. The experts then comment on the summary. They are free to challenge particular points of view or to add new perspectives by providing additional information. Because no one knows who said what, conflict is avoided.

The Delphi technique elicits information and judgments from participants in order to facilitate problem-solving, planning, and decision making without bringing participants face to face (Dunham 1996). Experts share information by mail, fax, or e-mail. This method can help groups reach consensus on issues, strategies, and priorities. It has been used to predict tourism potential in South Africa (Kaynak, Bloom, and Leibold 1994); reach consensus on the priorities for national drug policies in developing countries (Rainhorn, Brudon-Jakobowicz, and Reic 1994); and establish priorities for eradicating schistosomiasis (snail fever) in Kenya (Kirigia 1997).

The Delphi technique requires a coordinator, who identifies experts as participants, organizes requests for information, summarizes information received, and communicates with participants. The coordinator's job can take substantial time. Coordinating the Delphi technique by email with 20 participants and three rounds of questionnaires could take 30–40 hours of the coordinator's time.

The Delphi technique process involves the following steps:

1. Identify and invite experts to participate. Determine the criteria needed in experts, usually a group with diverse expertise. Invite the experts to join.
2. Identify the issue and solicit ideas. For example, ask, "What action could be taken to provide faster response to patient inquiries between visits?" Prepare and send the first questionnaire, which asks each participant to

engage in individual brainstorming to generate as many ideas as possible for dealing with the issue.

3. Have participants complete the first questionnaire. Ideas need not be fully developed—in fact, it is preferable to have each idea expressed in a single sentence or phrase, with no attempt at evaluating or justifying these ideas. Participants then return the list to the coordinator.

4. Create and send the second questionnaire. The coordinator prepares and sends a second questionnaire to participants that contains all of the ideas sent in response to the first questionnaire. (Only the coordinator knows which expert contributed which ideas.) Space is provided for participants to refine each idea, comment on each idea's strengths and weaknesses, and identify new ideas.

5. Collect responses to the second questionnaire. Participants anonymously record their responses to the second questionnaire and return them to the coordinator.

6. Create and send the third questionnaire. The coordinator creates and sends a third questionnaire that summarizes the input from the previous step and asks for additional clarifications, strengths, weaknesses, and new ideas.

7. Continue the process. If desired, the coordinator performs iterations of the process until no new ideas emerge and all strengths, weakness, and opinions have been identified.

8. Achieve resolution. Resolution may occur in one of two ways.
   - If a consensus emerges around dominant ideas that have been evaluated, the exercise is declared finished. The end product is a list of ideas, with their strengths and weaknesses indicated.
   - If there is no consensus, the coordinator conducts a formal assessment of the group's opinions of the merits of the ideas. There are a number of ways to conduct a formal evaluation. One approach is to have the coordinator prepare a questionnaire that lists all the ideas and asks participants to rate each one. A seven-point scale could be used that ranges from 0 (no potential for dealing with the issue) to 7 (very high potential for dealing with the issue). If this approach is used, participants send the rating forms to the coordinator, who compiles the results and rank-orders the ideas based on the evaluations. A second approach is to have the coordinator ask each member to identify the top five ideas and assign five points to the most promising idea, four points to the next most promising, and so forth. The votes are returned to the coordinator, who tallies the results and prepares a report. The report notes the rank order of the ideas based on the total number of points received and indicates the number of people who voted for each idea (Dunham 1996).

**Table 8.20 Advantages and Challenges of the Delphi Technique**

| Advantages | Allows participants to remain anonymous |
|---|---|
| | Is inexpensive |
| | Is free of social pressure, personality influence, and individual dominance |
| | Is conducive to independent thinking and gradual formulation |
| | Allows sharing of information and reasoning among participants |
| Challenges | May not be representative |
| | Has tendency to eliminate extreme positions and force a middle-of-the-road consensus |
| | Requires skill in written communication |
| | Requires time and participant commitment |

*Source:* Michigan State University Extension 1994.

Table 8.20 shows the advantages and challenges of the Delphi technique.

### Tool 9: Other Measurement Tools

For some projects or programs, evaluators will encounter other measurement tools, such as electronic, chemical, and mechanical devices. Tools such as paper and pencil tests and skill tests or assessments may be used to collect data for some projects and programs. The following are examples of some of the other tools used in data collection.

Many projects and programs (especially those in the health sector) require measurement of physiological status to determine the effects of interventions. Scales are used to collect data on the weight of subjects. Height, length, and circumference of appendages may be measured using tape measures, measuring sticks, or other devices. Stopwatches can be used to determine the length of time to complete a task. In some cases, specialized tools are used to collect additional physiological data on cholesterol, blood pressure, blood sugar, body composition, lung capacity, aerobic capacity, muscular strength, joint flexibility, and other variables.

Chemical tests of well water and soils may be used to determine the quality of the water or soil. Other tests can measure melting point, vapor pressure, and the bioconcentration factors to determine the physical and chemical properties of each specific chemical. Tests such as these help identify environmental and health hazards (U.S. EPA 2007). When one is using measurement devices, it is important to check the calibration of the instruments and make corrections when needed. Projects and programs dealing with nutrition may use assessments of the chemical or nutritional components of food.

Aptitude or achievement tests may be used to assess knowledge and facts. They are commonly used for training and education programs but are applicable in many others fields as well.

In the past, many tests were administered using paper and pencil. They can now also be administered electronically, including over the Internet.

Before choosing a test, it is important to understand the kind of test that best measures what the evaluator wants to learn. There are four approaches to achievement testing:

- norm referenced
- criterion referenced
- objectives referenced
- domain referenced (Fitzpatrick, Sanders, and Worthen 2004).

Norm-referenced tests are used primarily to compare students' performance with that of other students taking the same test. Norm-referenced tests are often used to assess progress. Many school districts use norm-referenced testing to compare their students with students in other school districts on commonly accepted knowledge and skills. A weakness in norm-referenced testing is identifying "commonly accepted knowledge and skills." Different cultures, societies, and environments may have very different instructional objectives (Fitzpatrick, Sanders, and Worthen 2004).

Criterion-reference tests are used to measure performance against some absolute criterion. A country may establish criteria against which to judge the performance of schools or school districts (not individual students) and to use them to determine how schools or districts compare. Criteria are often used to assess a curriculum or program (Fitzpatrick, Sanders, and Worthen 2004).

Objectives-reference tests are based on the objectives or outcomes identified by an educational or training program. The items for the test are based on the stated objectives or outcomes. Objectives-referenced tests are used to provide formative evaluation feedback to help teachers or trainers examine areas that meet the objectives or outcomes and those that may need improvement (Fitzpatrick, Sanders, and Worthen 2004).

Domain-referenced tests are linked to a content domain being measured, such as knowledge of history or mathematics. These tests are costly to develop, but they can offer valuable information such as "How much do our students know about world geography?" or "How much do our trainees know about gender?" (Fitzpatrick, Sanders, and Worthen 2004).

Norm-referenced and criterion-referenced tests provide standards for judging performance. Objectives-referenced and domain-referenced tests do not provide standards. They provide descriptive data about student performance without judging students or schools (Fitzpatrick, Sanders, and Worthen 2004).

Many standardized tests are available on the Internet (see the links at the end of this chapter). They can help assess personality, vocational interest, aptitude, achievement, development, intelligence, reading, and study skills.

Some stakeholders may want to know more about an intervention than the scores of participants on a standardized knowledge test. Skill performance can be evaluated using simulation devices, portfolio development, oral presentations, and debates. It is important to match the skill needed with the test that best demonstrates the performance desired.

Skill tests may be useful when evaluating any intervention that seeks to introduce new skills (sanitation practices to mothers, agricultural practices to farmers, recordkeeping practices to government employees). Development evaluations often try to assess whether the new practice was used, but they may not assess whether it was used skillfully. Experts who are trained to observe performances can be used to observe and evaluate skills. Criteria are established and subjects rated on how well they meet the criteria. Photography or videography can be used to document performance.

## Summary

There is no single best way to collect data. Which of the many methods described in this chapter should be used depends on the needs of the evaluation and the specific questions being addressed.

Evaluations should use more than one data collection technique. Decisions about which data collection techniques to use should be based on

- what the evaluator needs to know
- where the data are
- what resources and time are available
- how complex the data to be collected are
- the frequency of data collection.

## Application Exercise 8.1: Collecting Information from Files

You are asked to use admission files to determine the qualifications and experience of students admitted to a horticultural training workshop. Develop a short form of five questions that can be used to collect data from these files.

## Application Exercise 8.2: Collecting Information from Interviews

You have been asked to develop questions for a short interview to evaluate participants' reactions to the quality of a workshop on the basis of a conference you have recently attended. Develop five open-ended questions that address the content, level, and delivery of the workshop. If possible, find a partner who attended the same workshop or conference. Interview your partner, and let your partner interview you using the instrument you developed. Then write an in-depth summary of the interviews. Have your partner critique it for accuracy, readability, and coverage.

## Application Exercise 8.3: Collecting Information from Focus Groups

You have been asked to design a focus group to evaluate the impact of a series of workshops and a financial assistance package to help women start and run their own small businesses. Develop a set of five questions for a focus group that would be appropriate to ask women who completed the program six months ago. Be sure to find out what intended effects the program had and how it affected participants' lives, friends, and family.

# References and Further Reading

Abdallah, H. 2002. *Cost-Effectiveness of Self-Assessment and Peer Review in Improving Family Planning Provider-Client Communication in Indonesia.* Quality Assurance Project Case Study. Study conducted for the U.S. Agency for International Development by the Quality Assurance Project, Bethesda, MD.

Academy for Educational Development, Population Communication Services. 2002. "Session 10 Transect Walks and Observation." *Empowering Communities: Participatory Techniques for Community-Based Programme Development,* vol. 2, *Participant Handbook.* Washington, DC: Academy for Educational Development. http://pcs.aed.org/manuals/cafs/handbook/sessions10-12.pdf.

ADB (Asian Development Bank), and ADBI (Asian Development Bank Institute). 2004. *Improving Local Governance and Service Delivery: Citizen Report Card Learning Tool Kit.* http://www.citizenreportcard.com/index.html#.

BBC (British Broadcasting Corporation). 2008. "Data Validation and Verification." *GCSE Bitesize.* http://www.bbc.co.uk/schools/gcsebitesize/ict/databases/3datavalidationrev1 .shtml.

Behling, Orlando, and Kenneth S. Law. 2000. *Translating Questionnaires and Other Research Instruments: Problems and Solutions.* Quantitative Applications in the Social Sciences, Series 07-133. Thousand Oaks, CA: Sage Publications.

Billson, Janet Mancini. 2002. *The Power of Focus Groups for Social and Policy Research.* Barrington, RI: Skywood Press.

———. 2004. *The Power of Focus Groups: A Training Manual for Social, Policy, and Market Research: Focus on International Development.* Barrington, RI: Skywood Press.

Billson, Janet, and N. T. London. 2004. "The Power of Focus Groups." International Program for Development Evaluation Training (IPDET) presentation, Ontario, July.

Burgess, Thomas F. 2001. *Guide to the Design of Questionnaires,* ed. 1.1. University of Leeds, United Kingdom. http://www.leeds.ac.uk/iss/documentation/top/top2/top2-5.html.

Cloutier, Dorothea, Bill Lilley, Devon Phillips, Bill Weber, and David Sanderson. 1987. *A Guide to Program Evaluation and Reporting.* University of Maine Cooperative Extension Service, Orono.

CNCSTE (Chinese National Centre for Science and Technology Evaluation), and IOB (Policy and Operations Evaluation Department). 2006. *Country-Led Joint Evaluation of the ORET/MILIEV Programme in China.* Amsterdam: Aksant Academic Publishers.

Cnossen, Christine. 1997. *Secondary Research.* Learning Paper 7, School of Public Administration and Law, Robert Gordon University, Aberdeen, United Kingdom.

Dawson, Susan, and Lenor Manderson. 1993. *Methods for Social Research in Disease: A Manual for the Use of Focus Groups.* International Nutrition Foundation for Developing Countries, Boston. http://www.unu.edu/Unupress/food2/UIN03E/uin03e00.htm.

Denzin, K. 1978. *The Research Act.* New York: McGraw-Hill.

Dunham, Randall B. 1996. *The Delphi Technique.*
http://www.medsch.wisc.edu/adminmed/2002/orgbehav/delphi.pdf.

Early Childhood Research Institute on Measuring Growth and Development. 2008.
*Early Communication Indicator (ECI).* http://cehd.umn.edu/ceed/projects/ecri/.

EuropeAid Co-operation Office. 2005. *Evaluation Methods.*
ec.europa.eu/europeaid/evaluation/methodology/egeval/index_en.htm.

Fitzpatrick, Jody L., James R. Sanders, and Blaine R. Worthen. 2004. *Program Evaluation: Alternative Approaches and Practical Guidelines.* New York: Pearson.

Foddy, William. 1993. *Constructing Questions for Interviews and Questionnaires.* New York: Cambridge University Press.

Fowler, Floyd J. Jr. 2002. *Applied Social Research Methods Series,* vol. 1 *Survey Research Methods.* 3rd. ed. Thousand Oaks, CA: Sage Publications.

Frary, Robert B. 1996. "Hints for Designing Effective Questionnaires." *Practical Assessment, Research & Evaluation* 5 (3).
http://PAREonline.net/getvn.asp?v=5&n=3.

Hofstede, G. 2001. *Culture's Consequences.* 2nd ed. Thousand Oaks, CA: Sage Publications.

Jackson, Gregg, and Rashmi Agrawal. 2007. "Guidelines for Developing Survey Instruments as a Part of the Designing and Conducting Surveys Workshop." International Program for Development Evaluation Training (IPDET) presentation, Ottawa, Ontario.

Kaynak, Erdener, Jonathan Bloom, and Marius Leibold. 1994. "Using the Delphi Technique to Predict Future Tourism Potential." *Marketing Intelligence and Planning* 12 (7): 18–29.
http://www.emeraldinsight.com/Insight/viewContentItem.do;jsessionid=372
EF38765D6F8133CDF8DABFB2071B4?contentType=Article&hdAction=lnkpdf
&contentId=854271.

Kirigia, J. M. 1997. *Economic Evaluation in Schistosomiasis Using the Delphi Technique to Assess Effectiveness.*
http://www.ncbi.nlm.nih.gov/entrez/query.fcgi?cmd=Retrieve&db=PubMed&
list_uids=9107365&dopt=Abstract.

Krueger, R. A., and M. A. Casey. 2000. *Focus Groups.* 3rd ed. Thousand Oaks, CA: Sage Publications.

Kellogg Foundation. 2008. *"Tips on Using Tests and Assessments." Evaluation Toolkit.*
http://www.wkkf.org/Default.aspx?tabid=90&CID=281&ItemID=2810034&NID
=2820034&LanguageID=0.

Lofland, John. 1971. *Analyzing Social Settings.* Belmont, CA: Wadsworth.

Lofland, John, and L. H. Lofland. 1995. *Analyzing Social Settings: A Guide to Qualitative Observation and Analysis.* 3rd ed. Belmont, CA: Wadsworth Publication.

McCaston, M. Katherine. 2005. *Tips for Collecting, Reviewing, and Analyzing Secondary Data.* Partnership and Household Livelihood Security Unit.
http://pqdl.care.org/pv_obj_cache/pv_obj_id_8F453F01C87B8BB24774628B95B
42BBCBD020200.

McNamara, Carter. 2007. *General Guidelines for Conducting Interviews.*
http://www.managementhelp.org/evaluatn/intrview.htm#anchor615874

Michigan State University Extension. 1994. *Delphi Technique*.
http://web1.msue.msu.edu/msue/imp/modii/iii00006.html.

Miles, Matthew B., and A. Michael Huberman. 1994. *Qualitative Data Analysis an Expanded Sourcebook*. Thousand Oaks, CA: Sage Publications.

Minnesota Department of Health. 2007. *Community Engagement: Community Forums and Public Hearings*.
http://www.health.state.mn.us/communityeng/needs/needs.html.

Narayan, Deepa. 1996. *Toward Participatory Research*. World Bank Technical Paper 307, Washington, DC.
http://www-wds.worldbank.org/external/default/WDSContentServer/WDSP/IB/1996/04/01/000009265_3980625172923/Rendered/PDF/multi0page.pdf.

O'Brien, G. 2001. *Data Flow, Application of Data Quality Flags, and Data Validation Processes for CCAQS*. Preliminary draft.
http://www.arb.ca.gov/airways/Documents/reference percent20tables/March percent2006, percent202001/DataFlow_PrelimDraft.pdf.

Patton, Michael Q. 1987. *How to Use Qualitative Methods in Evaluation*. Thousand Oaks, CA: Sage Publications.

———. 2002. *Qualitative Evaluation and Research Methods*. 3rd ed. Thousand Oaks, CA. Sage Publications.

Paul, Samuel, and Gopakumar K. Thampi. 2008. "Monitoring Public Service Delivery: Citizen Report Cards Score in India." *Capacity.org*. 35 (December). United Nations Development Programme, New York.
http://www.capacity.org/en/journal/tools_and_methods/citizen_report_cards_score_in_india.

Phuyal, Kamal. 2006. "Sharing Some Practical Experiences on Participatory Appreciative Planning Approach (PAPA): An Appreciative Approach to Working in Partnership with Community People." Paper presented at the international workshop on "Action Learning: Lessons from the Field," organized by the Faculty of Policy Studies, Chuo University, Tokyo, October.
http://www.scn.org/cmp/modules/emp-papa.htm.

Porteous, Nancy L., B. J. Sheldrick, and P. J. Stewart. 1997. *Program Evaluation Tool Kit: A Blueprint for Public Health Management*. Ottawa: Ottawa-Carleton Health Department.

Rainhorn, J.-D. P. Brudon-Jakobowicz, and M. R. Reich. 1994. "Priorities for Pharmaceutical Policies in Developing Countries: Results of a Delphi Survey." Bulletin of the World Health Organization 72(2): 257–64. 72 (2): 257–64.
http://74.125.47.132/search?q=cache:D1zbVUz7oG0J:whqlibdoc.who.int/bulletin/1994/Vol72-No2/bulletin_1994_72(2)_257-264.pdf+Use+of+the+delphi+technique+in+developing+countries&cd=3&hl=en&ct=clnk&gl=us&client=firefox-a.

Sanders, J. R. 2000. *Evaluating School Programs*. 2nd ed. Thousand Oaks, CA: Sage Publications.

Stafford, Frank P. 2006. *Timeline Data Collection and Analysis: Time Diary and Event History Calendar Methods*. Department of Economics, University of Michigan, Ann Arbor.
http://www.atususers.umd.edu/wip2/papers_i2007/Stafford_Diaries.pdf.

Stake, Robert E. 1995. *The Art of Case Study Research.* Thousand Oaks, CA: Sage Publications.

StatPac. 2007. *Survey Software, Question Wording.* http://www.statpac.com/surveys/index.htm#toc.

Sue, Valerie M., and Lois A. Ritter. 2007. *Conducting Online Surveys.* Thousand Oaks, CA: Sage Publications.

TC Evaluation Center. 2007. *Wording Questions: Some General Guidelines.* University of California, Davis. http://ucce.ucdavis.edu/files/filelibrary/5715/27621.pdf.

Trochim, William M. K. 2006. *Types of Data, Research Methods Knowledge Base.* http://www.socialresearchmethods.net/kb/datatype.php.

UNESCAP (United Nations Economic and Social Commission for Asia and the Pacific). 1999. *Guidelines on the Application of New Technology to Population Data Collection and Capture.* http://www.unescap.org/stat/pop-it/pop-guide/capture_ch04.pdf.

University of Wisconsin, Cooperative Extension. 1996. *Program Development and Evaluation, Collecting Evaluation Data: Direct Observation.* http://learningstore.uwex.edu/pdf/G3658-5.pdf.

U.S. EPA (U.S. Environmental Protection Agency). 2007. *CTSA-Chapter 2: Data Collection.* http://www.epa.gov/dfe/pubs/lithography/ctsa/ch02/ch02.html.

Wadsworth, Y. 1997a. *Do It Yourself Social Research.* 2nd ed. St. Leonards, New South Wales, Australia: Allen and Unwin.

———. 1997b. *Everyday Evaluation on the Run.* St. Leonards, New South Wales, Australia: Allen and Unwin.

Wengraf, Tom. 2001. *Qualitative Research Interviewing: Biographic Narrative and Semi-Structured Methods.* Thousand Oaks, CA: Sage Publications.

Wiseman, V., L. Conteh, and F. Matovu. 2005. "Using Diaries to Collect Data in Resource-Poor Settings: Questions on Design and Implementation." Health Policy and Planning 20 (6): 394–404. http://heapol.oxfordjournals.org/cgi/reprint/20/6/394.

World Bank. 1996. "A Manual for Planning and Implementing the Living Standards Measurement Study Survey." Working Paper 126, Washington, DC.

———. 2006. "Citizen Report Cards: A Presentation on Methodology." Participation and Civic Engagement Group, Social Development Department, Washington, DC. http://info.worldbank.org/etools/docs/library/94360/Tanz_0603/Ta_0603/CitizenReportCardPresentation.pdf.

———. 2007. "Community-Driven Development." Washington, DC. http://web.worldbank.org/WBSITE/EXTERNAL/TOPICS/EXTSOCIALDEVELOPMENT/EXTCDD/0,,menuPK:430167~pagePK:149018~piPK:149093~theSitePK:430161,00.html.

Yin, Robert K. 2003. *Case Study Research: Design and Methods.* 3rd ed. Thousand Oaks, CA: Sage Publications.

## Web Sites

*Alphabetical List of Aptitude or Achievement Tests.* http://www.yorku.ca/psycentr/tests/alpha.html.

Evaluation Portal. http://www.evaluation.lars-balzer.name/.

International Council on Security and Development. 2006. "Think tank announces expert panel to review effectiveness of International Narcotics Control Board." http://www.icosgroup.net/modules/press_releases/narcotics_control_board.

Measurement Group. *Evaluation/Research Tools.* http://www.themeasurementgroup.com/evalbttn.htm.

Nielsen, J. 1997. *The Use and Misuse of Focus Groups.* http://www.useit.com/papers/focusgroups.html.

Standardized Monitoring and Assessment of Relief and Transitions. *Instruments and Tools.* http://www.smartindicators.org/IT.php?page=80.

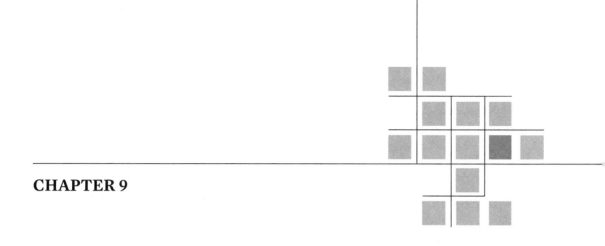

# Choosing the Sampling Strategy

This chapter discusses how to determine how much data to collect.
It also addresses how to select the sources of data so that they closely
reflect the population and help answer the evaluation questions.

**This chapter has three main parts:**

- Introduction to Sampling
- Types of Samples: Random and Nonrandom
- Determining the Sample Size

## Introduction to Sampling

**Population:** Total set of units about which the evaluator wants to make inferences

**Census:** Collection of data from an entire population

**Sample:** Subset of a population on which data are collected

Once evaluators have decided to collect data from a particular **population** (of people, health clinics, schools, or other units), they need to decide whether to collect data from all units of interest or a subset of those units. Data collection from all units is called a ***census.*** Data collection from a subset of all units is called a ***sample.*** If the population is small and the cost of data collection is low, a census is generally preferred. When the population is large or the cost of data collection high, it is usually necessary to collect data on a sample. Sampling is also sometimes used to minimize the burden on respondents.

People use samples all the time. When you have a blood test to check your health, for example, the laboratory takes a sample rather than all of your blood. Tests are run using that sample, and it is assumed that what is found in the sample accurately reflects what is in all of your blood.

Sampling is not just something that applies to large, quantitative studies. Even when conducting a highly qualitative, one-week field visit to assess a program that is spread out over a large geographic region, for example, evaluators still need to think carefully about which areas of that region to investigate. Biases may be introduced if program officials, who are eager to show the best picture, select the sites and participants to be studied. Those biases could be avoided with a randomly selected sample. An understanding of the basic concepts of sampling can enhance the extent to which an evaluation accurately reflects what is really going on in a program.

## Types of Samples: Random and Nonrandom

When data cannot be collected from every country, every person, or every farm, evaluators select a subset, or sample, to study. Samples can be random or nonrandom.

**Random sample:** Sample in which each unit in the population has an equal chance of being selected

**Selection bias:** Distortion of evidence caused by way in which data are collected

### Random Sampling

**Random samples** are samples in which each unit in the population has an equal chance of being selected. A lottery is an example of a random sample, because every number has an equal change of being selected as the winning number.

One advantage of random sampling is that it eliminates **selection bias** or the distortion of data arising from the way the data are collected. If not taken into account, selection bias may result in any conclusions drawn from the data being wrong. Because everyone or everything has an equal chance of being selected, selection bias is removed. There are different forms of selection bias. A common one is self-selection bias, which itself has several forms. Self-selection bias occurs in any program for which people volunteer and even is found in people who voluntarily respond to a survey. The source of bias is that volunteers and responders often share characteristics that are not found in those who do not volunteer or respond.

A random sample should be representative of the population as a whole. Such a sample enables evaluators to generalize to the population from which the sample was drawn.

A complete list of every unit in the population of interest, called a ***sampling frame,*** is needed to select a random sample. Each unit in the population needs to be assigned a unique identification number. Units are then selected from the total population using a random schedule such as a random number table. This is a table with sets of digits (i.e., 0, 1, 2, 3 ... ) arrayed in random order. Web sources for random number tables are provided in the references for this chapter. Many people use a Web-based random number generator to produce random numbers. Sources such as Stattrek ask how many random numbers are needed and which minimum and maximum values are needed, then the random numbers are generated.

■ **Sampling frame:**
Complete set of units from which a sample is drawn

There are six types of random samples:

- simple random samples
- random interval samples
- random-start and fixed-interval samples
- stratified random samples
- random cluster samples
- multistage random samples.

### Simple random samples

A simple random sample is the most common and simplest type of random sample. It is used when the primary objective is to make inferences about the whole population rather than about specific subpopulations.

Simple random samples are good for drawing samples of 50–500 from homogenous populations or larger samples from more heterogeneous populations (Jackson 2008). They can be drawn in a variety of ways. For example, evaluators interested in observing classroom activities to measure the amount of time students spend doing hands-on learning activities could randomly select classrooms, times of day, or days of the week. Evaluators wanting to observe the volume of traffic on the road from the village to a major town could randomly select times or days of the week, times of year, or observation points along the road.

The procedure for drawing a simple random sample is as follows (Jackson 2008):

1. Define the population carefully, indicating what it includes and excludes.
2. Find or generate a sampling frame that lists all of the units in the population assigns each a unique number. The numbers do not have to be contiguous (using each consecutive number), but drawing the sample will go faster if there are not large gaps between the assigned numbers.
3. Decide on the size of the sample.
4. Determine the number of digits in the largest assigned number.
5. Acquire a random number table.
6. Decide on any fixed pattern for reading the numbers (for example, top to bottom and then right to the next column, reading the first digits).
7. Blindly select a starting point in the table.
8. Read the numbers in the selected pattern, always reading the number of digits determined in step 4 above.
9. Each time you read a digit that corresponds with the number of a unit in your sampling frame, mark that unit for selection.
10. Continue until you have selected the number of units you need.
11. If you come upon a random number that is the same as the one already used, go on to the next number. You cannot select the same unit twice.

Or, for example, an evaluation team selects 100 files from a population of 500. All the files have been consecutively numbered from 001 to 500 and filed in numerical order. The team can then use a random number generator, indicating that 100 numbers are needed and that the minimum value is 001 and the maximum value is 500.

### Random-interval and random-start and fixed-interval samples

■ **Random interval sample:** Sample chosen using randomly determined distances between numbers

**Random-interval sampling** can be used when there is a sequential population that is not already enumerated and would be difficult or time consuming to enumerate. Like a simple random sample, a random interval sample uses a random number table. However, instead of using the table to select the units for the sample, it uses the table to select the interval (the count between numbers) over which to select the units.

The following steps can be used to draw a random-interval sample (Jackson 2008):

1. Estimate the number of units in the population.
2. Determine the desired sample size.

3. Divide the estimated number of units by the desired sample size. Round this number off to two decimal places to get the average random interval length needed to yield the desired sample size when sampling the entire population.

4. Multiply the result of step 3 by one-fifth and round to two decimal places to get the "multiplier."

5. Blindly designate a starting point in the population.

6. Use a random number table to select a single-digit random number, multiply it by the multiplier, round to the nearest whole number, count from the starting point down that many places, select that unit for the sample, and place a marker where it was drawn.

7. Take the next single-digit random number, multiply it by the multiplier, round it to the nearest whole number, and count that many more places.

8. Continue in the same manner through the entire population until you reach the point where you started.

9. WARNING: If it is important to return the units to their original positions, make sure that you mark each place from which you draw a file with a file identifier, so that you can return the files to their proper places.

Random interval samples can also be generated using computer programs.

Sometimes it is not possible to conduct a truly random selection. In this case, a systematic sampling technique can be used, starting from a random place and then selecting every *n*th case.

**Random-start and fixed-interval samples** are sometimes considered quasi-random samples, because the starting point is random but the interval is not. While this sampling technique is somewhat simpler than random interval sampling, it has a serious weakness under particular conditions. Consider, for instance, an evaluation that requires you to sample daily records of a marketplace that is open every day of the week. The population is estimated to be 700 records, and you need a sample of 100. In this case, the fixed interval will be every seventh record, which would result in all your records being drawn for the same day of the week. That is not likely to be representative of all the days in the week. To avoid such a situation, if there is any chance that a fixed interval may yield a biased sample, use the random interval sampling procedure.

A random-start and fixed-interval sample is selected in the following way:

■ **Random-start and fixed-interval sample:** A systematic sampling technique in which the starting point is random, but then every nth case is selected

1. Estimate the number of units in the population.

2. Determine the desired sample size.

3. Divide step (1) by step (2) to get the interval.
4. Blindly designate a starting point in the population.
5. Count down the specified interval and select that unit for the sample.
6. Continue counting down the same interval and selecting the units until you return to where you started.

### Stratified random samples

Frequently, it is important to include specific groups in a sample that might be poorly represented by using a simple random sample. To ensure that such groups are sampled, evaluators can divide the population into strata based on some meaningful characteristic, such as gender, age, ethnicity, or other characteristic and sample. This kind of sample is called a ***stratified random sample.***

Say evaluators want to look at the effects of an intervention on both urban and rural residents. If rural residents represent only a small proportion of the total population in the area, a simple random sample may not include enough of them to allow meaningful analysis to be conducted.

A stratified random sample is drawn by dividing the population into non-overlapping groups (strata) ($n_1, n_2, n_3, ... n_i$, such that $n_1 + n_2 + n_3 + ... n_i$, = $n$). and drawing a simple random sample within each stratum. The number selected from each stratum should be equivalent to the stratum's proportion of the total population.

■ **Stratified random sample:** Sample in which the sampling frame is divided into two or more strata (subpopulations) from which participants are randomly selected

### Random cluster samples

A **random cluster sample** is a sample drawn from naturally occurring clusters of the unit of analysis. Households (or homes) are clusters of people, towns are clusters of households. Clusters should be mutually exclusive and collectively exhaustive. Cluster samples are often used in the following situations:

■ **Random cluster sample:** Sample drawn from naturally occurring clusters of the unit of analysis

• There is not a complete list of everyone in the population of interest, but there is a complete list of the clusters in which they occur.
• There is a complete list, but the names on the list are so widely dispersed that it would be too time-consuming and expensive to send data collectors out to conduct a simple random sample.

In a random cluster sample, the cluster is randomly sampled and data collected on all target units. This technique is particularly useful when the target units are located far from one another (box 9.1)

The main drawback of random cluster samples is that they are likely to yield less accurate estimates of the population parameter (characteristic) than simple random samples or stratified random samples of the same number of units of interest. It is possible that the clinics selected in box 9.1 serve clients who differ in economic or religious characteristics from the ones not included in the sample. If this is the case, the results of the sample will yield biased estimates of the full population of AIDS patients served by the region's clinics.

### Multistage random samples

**Multistage random sampling** combines two or more forms of random sampling. The process usually begins with random cluster sampling and then applies simple random sampling or stratified random sampling. In the example shown in box 9.1, a multistage random sample would initially draw a cluster sample of eight clinics. It would then draw a simple random sample of 25 patients from each clinic. This technique would provide a sample of 200 patients, just as in the above example, but they would come from a larger number of clinics.

It is possible to combine nonrandom and random sampling in a multistage sample. For instance, the clinics in box 9.1 could be sampled nonrandomly and the AIDS patients then sampled randomly from each clinic.

The drawback of multistage and cluster samples is that they provide somewhat less precise estimates of the population than simple random sampling. In the example of the AIDS clinics, for example, only 8 clinics are randomly sampled from the total of 25 clinics; they may not be fully representative of the 25.

■ **Multistage random sample:** Sample in which two or more random sampling procedures are used sequentially

## Nonrandom Sampling

When random sampling is not possible, a different approach must be used. Nonrandom samples are commonly classified into three types: purposeful, snowball, and convenience.

Nonrandom sampling techniques allow evaluators only limited ability to generalize findings to the larger population. Such samples can nevertheless strengthen the results of an evaluation.

■ **Purposeful sample:** Sample in which selections are made based on predetermined criteria

■ **Typical-case (median) sample:** Purposeful sample in which units are drawn from the middle range of the distribution

■ **Maximum variation (heterogeneity) sample:** Purposeful sample in which units are drawn to represent full range of a parameter

■ **Quota sample:** Purposeful sample in which specific number of different types of units are selected

■ **Extreme-case sample:** Purposeful sample in which units are drawn from the left and right ends of a distribution

### *Purposeful samples*

In a **purposeful sample** (also called a *judgment sample*), selections are made to meet the specific purposes of a study. Selection is based on predetermined criteria that, in the judgment of the evaluators, will provide the data needed.

The following are the most widely used forms of purposeful samples (Jackson 2008):

- *Typical-case (median) sample:* Units are deliberately drawn from the typical or most common characteristics of a population (those in the middle range of a bell curve). The purpose of the study is to closely look at the typical items, not those that are atypical.
- *Maximum variation (heterogeneity) sample:* Units are drawn to represent the full range of a characteristic of interest. They are taken from all parts of a bell curve.
- *Quota sample:* Units are drawn so that there are equal numbers or an equal proportion from each stratum. For example, the evaluator chooses five units from the top third, five units from the middle third, and five units from the lower third of a distribution.
- *Extreme-case sample:* Units are drawn from the extreme cases of a distribution. The units would be selected from the left and right ends of a bell curve. Extreme case samples look at the least common units.
- *Confirming and disconfirming cases sample:* Units are drawn from cases that are known to confirm or contradict conventional wisdom, principle, or theory (for example, from well-prepared projects that succeeded and well-prepared projects that failed).

### *Snowball samples*

**Snowball samples** (also known as *chain referral samples*) are used when evaluators do not know who or what to include in a sample. They are used when the boundaries of the population are unknown and there is no sampling frame.

The Road to Results: Designing and Conducting Effective Development Evaluations

Snowball samples are often used in interviews. Evaluators using this kind of purposive sampling ask people who meet the criteria for study inclusion whom else they should talk with.

Snowball samples contain serious potential biases in relying on a referral claim. One example of their use is described in Nambiar (2008). They should be used cautiously.

### Convenience samples

In a **convenience sample,** selections are made based on the convenience to the evaluator. Common examples of convenience samples in development evaluation include the following:

- visiting whichever project sites are closest to an airport
- interviewing those project managers available the day of the evaluator's visit
- observing whichever physical areas project officials choose to show
- talking with whichever nongovernmental organization (NGO) representatives and town leaders are encountered (Jackson 2008).

Convenience samples are an extremely weak means of inferring any type of evidence or pattern from the data, because there is no way to know how different these samples are from the relevant population as a whole.

### Shortcomings of nonrandom sampling

While nonrandom samples have legitimate uses in development evaluation, they also have several shortcomings:

- Policymakers sometimes perceive them as less credible than random samples.
- Because they do not meet the assumptions of inferential statistics, tests of statistical significance and computations of confidence intervals should never be applied to nonrandom samples.
- Nonrandom samples can be subject to all types of bias.

Without random sampling, one cannot generalize to a larger population. The data may be very useful, however, and may be the best available given constraints.

## Combined Sampling

Random and nonrandom sampling methods can be combined. An evaluation team collecting data on schools, for example, might select two schools from the poorest communities and two from the wealthiest communities. From these four schools, they might then randomly select students for their sample.

■ **Confirming and disconfirming cases sample:** Purposeful sample in which units are drawn from cases known to confirm or contradict conventional wisdom, principle, or theory

■ **Snowball sample:** Sample drawn by asking interviewees whom else to interview

■ **Convenience sample:** Sample chosen on the basis of convenience to evaluator

# Determining the Sample Size

Even when using a random sample, there is some possibility of error; the sample may be different from the population. Statistics are used to estimate the probability that the sample results are representative of the population as a whole. Statisticians have developed theories and formulas for making these estimates and determining the appropriate sample size. This section focuses on understanding the basic concepts of statistical analysis and how to apply them to designing evaluations.

■ **Sample size:**
Number of observations in a sample

In choosing the **sample size,** evaluators must decide how confident they need to be that the sample results accurately reflect the entire relevant population. The confidence level generally used is 95 percent. A 95 percent confidence level means that 95 times out of 100, sample results will accurately reflect the population as a whole. If evaluators are willing to be 90 percent certain, they will be able to use a smaller sample. If they want to be 99 percent confident, they will need a larger sample.

Having chosen the sample size, evaluators next need to determine how precise they need their estimates to be. Unlike bias, the sampling error can be calculated. It is the average difference between all estimates for all possible samples and the value obtained if the total population had been studied. This is sometimes called **sampling error** or margin of error. A poll may report that 48 percent of the population favor raising taxes and 52 percent oppose raising taxes, with a sampling error of +/–3 percentage points. What this means is that if everyone in the population were surveyed, the actual proportions would be 45–51 percent (48 +/–3) in favor of and 49–55 percent (52 +/– 3) opposed to raising taxes. The ± 3 percentage points is called a *confidence interval* (not to be mistaken with a confidence level). Note that the two intervals partially overlap. That means that one cannot be sure, at the 95 percent confidence level, that more people in the population oppose raising taxes than favor raising them. The results from the sample are too close to call.

■ **Sampling error (or margin of error):** Estimate of error caused by observing a sample rather than the whole

■ **Confidence interval:**
Range within which the true population value lies with a given probability

Sample size is a function of the size of the population of interest, the desired confidence level, and the desired level of precision. The appropriate sample size can be determined in two ways. The first is to use a formula. The second is to use a table that shows the sample size needed for a given level of confidence (table 9.1).

The smaller the population, the larger the size of the sample relative to the population as a whole. If the population is 300, for example, a sample size of 169—just over half the total population—is needed to obtain a confidence level of 95 percent. A population of 900 would require a sample size of 269—less than a third of the population. If the population exceeds

**Table 9.1** Minimum Sample Size Needed at the 95 Percent Confidence Level with a 5 Percentage Point Margin of Error

| Population size | Sample size | Population size | Sample size |
|:---:|:---:|:---:|:---:|
| 10 | 10 | 550 | 226 |
| 20 | 19 | 600 | 234 |
| 40 | 36 | 700 | 248 |
| 50 | 44 | 800 | 260 |
| 75 | 63 | 900 | 269 |
| 100 | 80 | 1,000 | 278 |
| 150 | 108 | 1,200 | 291 |
| 200 | 132 | 1,300 | 297 |
| 250 | 152 | 1,500 | 306 |
| 300 | 169 | 3,000 | 341 |
| 350 | 184 | 6,000 | 361 |
| 400 | 196 | 9,000 | 368 |
| 450 | 207 | 50,000 | 381 |
| 500 | 217 | 100,000+ | 385 |

*Source:* Krejcie and Morgan 1970.

100,000, a sample of 385 —just 0.385 percent of the total population—would be needed.

When sampling units (such as districts, schools, teachers, parents, or citizens) for voluntary participation in an evaluation, there is no assurance that all those selected will be found (even with the most up-to-date of sampling frames), respond to a request for participation, or respond affirmatively to participate in the evaluation. Because of this phenomenon, many evaluators oversample, that is, they select a larger sample than is actually needed in order to end up with the sample size they need. When the actual response rate differs from the planned by 10 percent or more, the likelihood of **response bias** is high and requires analysis (see Chapter Data Collection Instruments).

■ **Response rate:** Percentage of intended sample from which data are actually collected

Table 9.2 shows the sample sizes for very large populations (1 million and larger). Many national surveys use samples of about 1,100, which leaves a margin of error of +/– 3 percentage points with a 95 percent confidence level.

Tools available on the Internet identify the population size needed to achieve a given confidence level and margin of error. Links to these sources are given at the end of this chapter.

**Table 9.2 Sampling Sizes for Populations of 1 Million and More**

| Margin of error (percent) | Confidence level | | |
|---|---|---|---|
| | **99 percent** | **95 percent** | **90 percent** |
| ± 1 | 16,576 | 9,604 | 6,765 |
| ± 2 | 4,144 | 2,401 | 1,691 |
| ± 3 | 1,848 | 1,067 | 752 |
| ± 5 | 666 | 384 | 271 |

*Source:* Jackson 2007.

To summarize:

- Accuracy and precision can be improved by increasing the sample size. To increase accuracy and reduce the margin of error, increase the sample size.
- The standard to aim for is a 95 percent confidence level (margin of error of +/–5 percent).
- The larger the margin of error, the less precise the results are.
- The smaller the population, the larger the ratio of the sample size to the population size.

If an evaluation requires a complex multistage sampling strategy, evaluators may want to consider asking for assistance. The American Statistical Association has a directory of statistical consultants. The Alliance of Statistics Consultants offers assistance for data management, data analysis, and thesis consultation, as well as statistics training and tutoring. HyperStat Online provides links to many other resources that provide assistance with statistics. Links to these Web pages appear at the end of this chapter.

## Summary

It is usually impossible or impractical to collect data from every data source. For this reason evaluators collect from a sample of sources.

There are two forms of sampling, random sampling and nonrandom sampling. Random samples are samples in which each unit in the population has an equal chance of being selected. Random sampling examines a subset of the population and then generalizes the results to the larger population.

There are six types of random samples:

- simple random samples
- random interval samples
- random-start and fixed-interval samples
- stratified random samples
- random cluster samples
- multistage random samples.

There are three types of nonrandom samples:

- purposeful samples
- snowball samples
- convenience samples.

Evaluations need not use only one kind of sampling. They can use combinations of sampling techniques.

Sample size is a function of the size of the population of interest, the desired confidence level, and the desired level of precision. Even when using a random sample, there is some possibility of error. Evaluators use various statistical approaches to determine the confidence level and confidence interval.

# Chapter 9 Activities

### Application Exercise 9.1: Sampling

The town you are studying has a population of 300, all of whom are registered in the town's record, each with a unique identification number. You have the time and resources to sample up to 50 townspeople. You would like to make generalizations from the sample to the entire population of 300. Will this be possible? What type of sample would you choose? Justify your decision.

### Application Exercise 9.2: Using a Random Number Table

The small village you are studying has 90 homes. You have a numbered list of the homes from which you want to select a simple random sample of 10. How might you use the random number table below to select the sample?

| | | | | | | | | | | | | | | |
|---|---|---|---|---|---|---|---|---|---|---|---|---|---|---|
| 44 | 14 | 12 | 12 | 03 | 12 | 73 | 72 | 62 | 33 | 35 | 62 | 80 | 34 | 77 |
| 69 | 59 | 54 | 90 | 01 | 50 | 04 | 93 | 76 | 69 | 43 | 95 | 47 | 60 | 80 |
| 23 | 95 | 24 | 95 | 24 | 55 | 69 | 89 | 41 | 18 | 12 | 94 | 43 | 21 | 43 |
| 40 | 76 | 50 | 38 | 18 | 05 | 44 | 23 | 72 | 61 | 58 | 67 | 99 | 05 | 75 |
| 54 | 05 | 51 | 52 | 04 | 34 | 25 | 64 | 90 | 95 | 02 | 86 | 51 | 14 | 37 |
| 36 | 82 | 03 | 65 | 38 | 93 | 49 | 64 | 06 | 93 | 01 | 30 | 62 | 05 | 68 |
| 96 | 19 | 97 | 24 | 16 | 26 | 94 | 14 | 17 | 45 | 22 | 51 | 09 | 92 | 16 |
| 75 | 85 | 18 | 50 | 50 | 60 | 80 | 52 | 42 | 11 | 05 | 70 | 89 | 53 | 38 |
| 57 | 78 | 12 | 98 | 55 | 51 | 48 | 77 | 54 | 07 | 66 | 15 | 33 | 44 | 64 |
| 58 | 20 | 10 | 51 | 62 | 06 | 25 | 56 | 63 | 67 | 73 | 73 | 79 | 05 | 65 |
| 55 | 84 | 17 | 67 | 52 | 38 | 16 | 29 | 05 | 24 | 12 | 05 | 35 | 87 | 31 |
| 92 | 44 | 84 | 04 | 17 | 47 | 18 | 78 | 54 | 40 | 02 | 59 | 74 | 06 | 73 |
| 86 | 96 | 79 | 86 | 75 | 67 | 31 | 41 | 40 | 20 | 87 | 17 | 85 | 98 | 70 |
| 78 | 84 | 03 | 69 | 43 | 38 | 43 | 98 | 90 | 75 | 56 | 49 | 88 | 52 | 78 |
| 25 | 05 | 76 | 72 | 06 | 59 | 37 | 56 | 24 | 36 | 95 | 05 | 30 | 62 | 02 |
| 26 | 67 | 04 | 13 | 77 | 37 | 21 | 57 | 77 | 41 | 82 | 30 | 32 | 80 | 09 |

## Application Exercise 9.3: Sampling Strategy

Working in small groups if possible, identify an appropriate measure or statistic for each of the following evaluation questions. Then decide which sampling strategy you would use for each of these situations and explain why you chose it.

1. What is the quality of the roads in villages in northwest Cambodia immediately after the rainy season?
2. What proportion of children in Tamil Nadu contract malaria at least once before the age of 10?
3. What are the demographic characteristics of the people who visit rural health clinics in Sri Lanka?

# References and Further Reading

Easton, V. J., and J. H. McColl. 2007. *Statistics Glossary: Sampling.* http://www.stats.gla.ac.uk/steps/glossary/sampling.html.

Guba, E., and Y. S. Lincoln. 1989. *Fourth Generation Evaluation.* Thousand Oaks, CA: Sage Publications.

Henry, G. T. 1990. *Practical Sampling.* Thousand Oaks, CA: Sage Publications.

Jackson, Gregg B. 2007. *Sampling for IEG Managers.* Presentation at George Washington University, Washington, DC, December 18.

——. 2008. *Sampling in Development Evaluations.* International Program for Development Evaluation Training (IPDET) presentation, Ottawa, June 30 and July 1.

Kish, L. 1995. *Survey Sampling.* New York: John Wiley & Sons.

Krejcie, R. V., and D. W. Morgan. 1970. "Determining Sample Size for Research Activities." *Educational and Psychological Measurement* 30: 607–10.

Kumar, R. 1999. *Research Methodology: A Step-by-Step Guide for Beginners.* Thousand Oaks, CA: Sage Publications.

Laws, S., with C. Harper and R. Marcus 2003. *Research for Development: A Practical Guide.* Thousand Oaks, CA: Sage Publications.

Levy, P., and S. Lemeshaw. 1999. *Sampling of Populations.* 3rd ed. New York: John Wiley & Sons.

Lipsey, M. W. 1990. *Design Sensitivity: Statistical Power for Experimental Research.* Thousand Oaks, CA: Sage Publications.

Lohr, S. 1998. *Sampling: Design and Analysis.* Pacific Grove, CA: Duxbury Press.

Nambiar, Devaki. 2008. "The Delhi Snowball: Sampling Escapades in Urban India." Paper presented at the Annual Meeting of the International Communication Association, Montreal, May 22–26.

Neuman, W. Lawrence. 2006. *Social Research Methods: Qualitative and Quantitative Approaches.* 6th ed. Boston: Allyn and Bacon.

Patton, M. Q. 2002. *Qualitative Research and Evaluation Methods.* Thousand Oaks, CA: Sage Publications.

Scheyvens, R., and D. Storey, eds. 2003. *Development Fieldwork: A Practical Guide.* Thousand Oaks, CA: Sage Publications.

Stattrek. http://stattrek.com/tables/randon.asph.

Tryfos, P. 1996. *Sampling Methods for Applied Research.* New York: John Wiley & Sons.

## Web Sites

Alliance of Statistics Consultants. http://www.statisticstutors.com/#statistical-analysis.

American Statistical Association Directory. http://www.amstat.org/consultant directory/index.cfm.

Dr. Drott's Random Sampler. http://drott.cis.drexel.edu/sample/content.html.

HyperStat Online. "Chapter 11: Power." http://davidmlane.com/hyperstat/power.html.

HyperStat Online: Help with Statistics: Statistical Consultants and Tutors. http://davidmlane.com/hyperstat/consultants.html.

Probability Sampling. http://www.socialresearchmethods.net/kb/sampprob.htm.

Power Analysis. http://www.statsoft.com/textbook/stpowan.html.

Research Randomizer. http://www.randomizer.org.

StatPages.net. Web Pages that Perform Statistical Calculations, http://www.Stat Pages.net.

Survey Research Methods Section. http://www.fas.harvard.edu/~stats/survey-soft/survey-soft.html.

The Survey System: Sample Size Calculator. http://www.surveysystem.com/sscalc.htm.

UCLA Statistics Calculator: http://calculators.stat.ucla.edu.

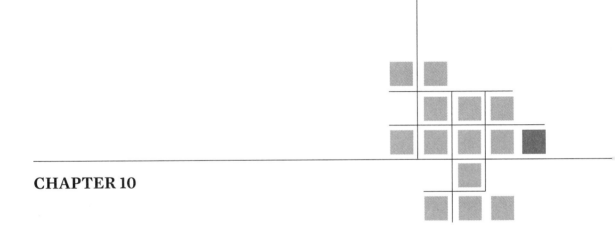

**CHAPTER 10**

# Planning for and Conducting Data Analysis

Once the data have been collected, evaluators need to examine them to find meaning. This process begins with a data analysis strategy. Qualitative and quantitative data demand different strategies and techniques.

**This chapter has four main parts:**

- Data Analysis Strategy
- Analyzing Qualitative Data
- Analyzing Quantitative Data
- Linking Quantitative Data and Qualitative Data

# Data Analysis Strategy

Developing the data analysis strategy is an important part of the planning process. Evaluators should be aware of the options for data analysis—and their respective strengths and weaknesses—as they plan the evaluation. In the design matrix, the objective should be specific and indicate the analysis and graphics that will result from the information collected. A common mistake is collecting vast amounts of data that are never used.

Whether the evaluation design emphasizes mostly qualitative data or quantitative data, data collection and data analysis will overlap. At the start of data collection, a small amount of time is spent in data analysis, especially if a pilot test is being conducted first. As the evaluation continues, more time is spent on data analysis and less on data collection.

Qualitative analysis is appropriate in situations in which, for example, a semistructured interview guide is used to gain in-depth insight into an intervention. It would be used to analyze responses to questions such as the following:

- What are some of the difficulties faced by staff?
- Why do participants say they dropped out early?
- What is the experience like for participants?

Quantitative analysis would be used to answer questions for which structured data collection instruments, such as a survey, were used. It might be used to answer questions such as the following:

- What are the mean scores for the different groups of participants?
- How do participants rate the relevance of the intervention on a scale of one to five?
- How much variability is there in the responses to the item?
- Are the differences between the two groups statistically significant?

## Analyzing Qualitative Data

**Qualitative data analysis** is used to make sense of nonnumerical data collected as part of the evaluation. Analyzing semistructured observations, open-ended interviews, written documents, and focus group transcripts all require the use of qualitative techniques.

Qualitative data analysis begins while still in the field, when insights may emerge. Part of fieldwork is recording and tracking analytical insights that occur during data collection. Data collection and analysis should overlap, as

■ **Qualitative data analysis:** Procedure used to analyze information gathered in nonnumeric form, such as narrative written or taped responses to semistructured interviews and observations or other documents and media, to understand and interpret behavior and situations; the procedure involves the identification of themes.

long as the evaluator takes care not to allow initial interpretations to confine analytical possibilities (table 10.1). As Patton (2002, p. 436) notes:

[F]or data collection based on surveys, standardized tests, and experimental designs, the lines between data collection and analysis are clear. But the fluid and emergent nature of naturalistic inquiry makes the distinction between data gathering and analysis far less absolute. In the course of fieldwork, ideas about directions for analysis will occur. Patterns take shape. Possible themes spring to mind. Hypotheses emerge that inform subsequent fieldwork. While earlier stages of fieldwork tend to be generative and emergent, following wherever the data lead, later stages bring closure by moving toward confirmatory data collection—deepening insights into and confirming (or disconfirming) patterns that seem to have appeared.

Sometimes gaps or ambiguities are found during analysis. If the schedule, budget, and other resources allow, an evaluator may return to the field to

**Table 10.1  Tips for Collecting and Analyzing Qualitative Data**

| Task | Tips |
|------|------|
| Collect data. | • Keep good records. |
| | • Write up interviews, impressions, and notes from focus groups immediately after data are collected. |
| | • Make constant comparisons as you progress. |
| | • Meet with team regularly to compare notes, identify themes, and make adjustments. |
| Summarize data. | • Write one-page summary immediately after each major interview or focus group. |
| | • Include all main issues. |
| | • Identify most interesting, illuminating, or important issue discussed or information obtained. |
| | • Identify new questions to be explored. |
| Use tools to keep track. | • Create a separate file for your own reactions during the study, including your feelings, hunches, and reactions. |
| | • Record your ideas as they emerge. |
| | • Keep a file of quotations from the data collection process for use in bringing your narrative to life when you write your report. |
| Store data. | • Make sure all of your information is in one place. |
| | • Make copies of all information, and place originals in a central file. |
| | • Use copies to write on, cut, and paste as needed. |

*Source:* Authors.

collect more data in order to clarify responses or make new observations. In collecting data, members of a team often confer daily or weekly to discuss emerging themes and adapt protocols, if indicated.

### Taking Good Notes

When collecting qualitative data, it is important to accurately capture all observations; good notes are essential. This means paying close attention to what people say and how they say it. While taking notes, evaluators should try not to interpret what people say. Instead, they should write down what they observe, including body language and anything potentially relevant that happens during data collection (for example, interruptions during the interview). Evaluators should capture immediate thoughts, reactions, and interpretations and should keep them in a separate section of their notes.

It is important to provide evaluators time immediately after an interview, observation, mapping exercise, or focus group to review, add to, and write up their notes so that they will be able to make sense of them later on. It is surprising how difficult it is to understand notes taken even just a day earlier if they are not clearly written.

Even if the session is tape-recorded, evaluators should invest at least a small amount of time in a preliminary write-up while the session is still fresh. Doing so can save hours of listening to or watching tapes or poring over transcripts.

**Triangulation** is the use of three or more theories, sources, types of information, or types of analysis to verify and substantiate an assessment by cross-checking results. Triangulation is useful in qualitative data analysis. Consider, for example, the following examples of mixed sources of data:

- interviews, focus groups, and questionnaires
- questionnaires, existing data, and expert panels
- observations, program records, and mapping
- interviews, diaries, and existing data.

The combination of findings from any three sources makes for evidence of a pattern.

■ **Triangulation:** Use of three or more data, sources, types of information, or types of analysis to verify and substantiate an assessment by cross-checking results

### Organizing Qualitative Data for Analysis

After collecting qualitative data, the evaluator will have many pages of notes and transcriptions of observations, interviews, and other data sources. Organizing and making sense of this information can be challenging.

Guidelines have been established for how data should be organized. Documenting this process is important to demonstrate the validity of the findings (IDRC 2008).

To begin organizing, evaluators should

- check to make sure that all of the data are complete
- make several copies of all data
- organize the data into different files (IDRC 2008).

The evaluator can organize files in different ways, using hard copies or electronic files, some of which may be of scanned documents. Some evaluators create four files: a first in which they store data in chronological order, a second in which they keep analytical files or journal notes, a third in which they keep relevant notes about research methodology, and a fourth that contains a copy of all notes (IDRC 2008).

Patton (2002) presents other options for organizing and reporting qualitative data. Patton reminds evaluators that data analysis should stem from the evaluation questions. The choice of the organization of data should strive to answer the evaluation questions.

- Storytelling approaches present data either chronologically (telling the story from start to finish) or as a flashback (starting at the end and then working backward to describe how the ending emerged).
- Case study approaches present information about people or groups; critical incidents are usually presented in order of appearance.
- Analytical frameworks include descriptions of processes, illumination of key issues (often equivalent to the primary evaluation questions), organization of questions, and discussion of key concepts, such as leadership versus followership.

### Reading and Coding Qualitative Data

Identifying and using the categories for organizing information are beginning steps. The next step is to read through the data. After several readings the evaluator should begin seeing potential themes. Patton (2002) notes that coming up with the most central topics is like constructing an index for a book or labels for a filing system. He suggests that evaluators look at what is there and give each topic a name or label. Once the data have been organized into topics, they need to be coded (box 10.1). "Codes are "efficient data-labeling and data-retrieval devices. They empower and speed up analysis" (Miles and Huberman 1994, p. 65).

Coding is an iterative process. While creating a list of codes before fieldwork begins is helpful, evaluators will need to review, revise, redefine, add to, and sometimes discard codes as the evaluation progresses, as field notes suggest more empirically driven labels.

**■ Content analysis:**

A type of systematic analysis of qualitative data that identifies and notes through codes the presence of certain words, phrases, or concepts within text, speech, and/or other media

### Conducting Content Analysis

Analysis of qualitative data is called **content analysis.** It identifies and codes the presence of certain words, phrases, or concepts within text, speech, or other media. It is a systematic approach that identifies and summarizes the messages hidden in the data.

Content analysis refers to the analysis of books, brochures, transcripts, news reports, other written documents, speeches, and visual media. It is applied to narratives such as diaries and journals as well as to qualitative responses to open-ended questions in surveys, interviews, and focus groups. Content analysis could be used, for example, to examine children's textbooks to determine whether they cover the necessary material for learning a particular subject, impart the material at the appropriate reading level, and present it in a way that is consistent with the context in which the children live and study. A deeper analysis might examine whether the textbooks convey a specific political agenda or biased interpretation of history.

Content analysis generally starts with data coding. The process assumes that the words and phrases mentioned most often are those reflecting important concerns. Therefore, content analysis starts with word frequencies, space measurements (column centimeters in the case of newspapers), time counts (for radio and television time), and keyword frequencies.

Content analysis extends far beyond mere word counts. So one can analyze content, words are coded and organized into manageable categories. These new coded categories are examined for frequency of response and relationships (box 10.2).

Content analysis can be classified into two types, conceptual analysis and relational analysis. A **conceptual content analysis** looks at the frequency of the occurrence of selected terms within a text. A **relational content analysis** goes beyond determining frequency to explore relationships among the concepts identified (Busch and others 2005).

■ **Conceptual concept analysis:** Analysis that looks at the frequency of the occurrence of selected terms within a text

■ **Relational concept analysis:** Analysis that goes beyond determining frequency to explore relationships among the concepts identified

---

**Box 10.2   Using Content Analysis to Identify the Perceived Benefits of Hand Pumps**

To learn how villagers perceive the use of hand pumps for pumping water, evaluators interview 100 villagers. They analyze the results using the following process:

1. Read every other answer, and write down each response.
2. Pick the most frequent responses, and state each briefly. Group each major response into a category. If, for example, responses include "hand pumps are so much easier to use" and "the water is always clean and the pump has never broken down," the evaluator could identify the following categories: ease of use, provision of clean water, reliability.
3. Ensure that all categories are mutually exclusive and that coders will be able to identify which responses fall into which category.
4. Complete the coding procedure.
5. Tabulate frequencies for each response.

*Source:* Narayan 1996.

For example, a concept analysis might identify categories using the following list:

- shared language on the topic (what was taken for granted and what needed clarification by other participants)
- beliefs and myths about the topic that are shared, taken for granted, and challenged
- arguments participants call upon when their views are challenged
- sources of information participants call upon to justify their views and experiences and how others respond to them
- arguments, sources, and types of information that stimulate changes of opinion or reinterpretation of experience
- tone of voice, body language, and degree of emotional engagement involved when participants talk to each other about the topic (Catterall and Maclaran 1997).

According to Kripendorff (2004), content analysis must address six questions:

- Which data are analyzed?
- How are the data defined?
- What is the population from which the data are drawn?
- What is the context relative to which the data are analyzed?
- What are the boundaries of the analysis?
- What is the target of the inferences?

Once these questions are addressed, choices can be made about relevant and irrelevant data.

Neuendorf (2006) presents a flowchart showing the process of content analysis (figure 10.1). It begins by considering the theory and rationale for the analysis.

Content analysis is challenging to do well. Evaluators should be aware of potential issues in its application (table 10.2).

### Computer-assisted content analysis

If computers are to be used to perform content analysis, all information must be in files a computer program can read. Evaluators may need to type in, scan, or recreate data files.

Many software packages can help organize data derived from observations, interviews, or focus groups. These include text-oriented database managers, word processors, and automatic-indexing software. These programs were developed specifically for working with text applications. Some of the content analysis software programs can be used with other types of media.

**Figure 10.1   Flowchart for Content Analysis Research**

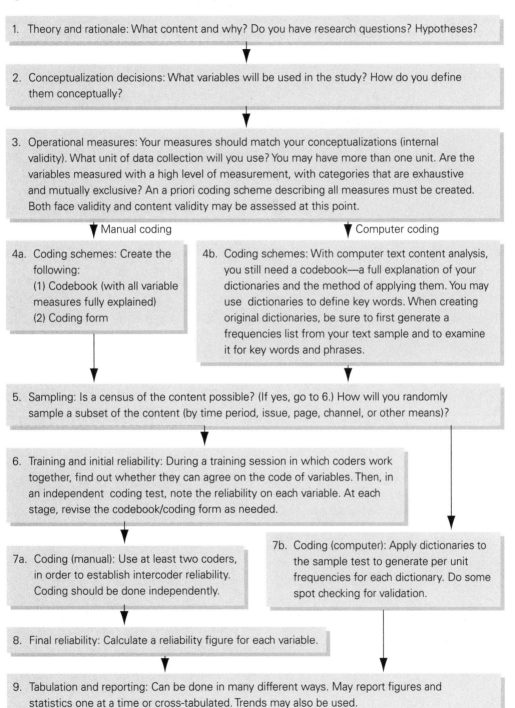

1. Theory and rationale: What content and why? Do you have research questions? Hypotheses?

2. Conceptualization decisions: What variables will be used in the study? How do you define them conceptually?

3. Operational measures: Your measures should match your conceptualizations (internal validity). What unit of data collection will you use? You may have more than one unit. Are the variables measured with a high level of measurement, with categories that are exhaustive and mutually exclusive? An a priori coding scheme describing all measures must be created. Both face validity and content validity may be assessed at this point.

Manual coding                                    Computer coding

4a. Coding schemes: Create the following:
   (1) Codebook (with all variable measures fully explained)
   (2) Coding form

4b. Coding schemes: With computer text content analysis, you still need a codebook—a full explanation of your dictionaries and the method of applying them. You may use dictionaries to define key words. When creating original dictionaries, be sure to first generate a frequencies list from your text sample and to examine it for key words and phrases.

5. Sampling: Is a census of the content possible? (If yes, go to 6.) How will you randomly sample a subset of the content (by time period, issue, page, channel, or other means)?

6. Training and initial reliability: During a training session in which coders work together, find out whether they can agree on the code of variables. Then, in an independent coding test, note the reliability on each variable. At each stage, revise the codebook/coding form as needed.

7a. Coding (manual): Use at least two coders, in order to establish intercoder reliability. Coding should be done independently.

7b. Coding (computer): Apply dictionaries to the sample test to generate per unit frequencies for each dictionary. Do some spot checking for validation.

8. Final reliability: Calculate a reliability figure for each variable.

9. Tabulation and reporting: Can be done in many different ways. May report figures and statistics one at a time or cross-tabulated. Trends may also be used.

*Source:* Neuendorf 2006.

**Table 10.2    Potential Strengths and Challenges of Content Analysis**

| Potential Strengths | Potential Challenges |
|---|---|
| Looks directly at communication using texts or transcripts and hence gets at the central aspect of social interaction | Can be extremely time-consuming |
| | Is subject to error, particularly when relational analysis is used to attain a higher level of interpretation |
| Can allow for both quantitative and qualitative operations | |
| | Is often devoid of theoretical base or attempts to draw meaningful inferences about the relationships and impacts implied in a study too liberally |
| Can provide valuable historical/cultural insights over time through analysis of texts | |
| Can be used to interpret texts for purposes such as the development of expert systems (because knowledge and rules can be coded in terms of explicit statements about the relationships among concepts) | Is inherently reductive, particularly when dealing with complex texts |
| | Tends too often to consist simply of word counts |
| | Often disregards the context that produced the text, as well as the state of things after the text is produced |
| Is an unobtrusive means of analyzing interactions | |
| Provides insight into complex models of human thought and language use | Can be difficult to computerize |

*Source:* Busch and others 2005.

■ **Computer-assisted qualitative data analysis software (CAQDAS):** Use of computer to search, organize, categorize, and annotate data

**Computer-assisted qualitative data analysis software (CAQDAS)**—also referred to as qualitative data analysis software (QDAS or QDA software)—searches, organizes, categorizes, and annotates textual and visual data (box 10.3). Programs of this type allow evaluators to visualize relationships and theoretical constructs and help them build theories. Packages include Ethnograph, Qualpro, Hyperqual, Atlas-ti, QSR's N6 (formerly NUD*IST) and NVivo 8, AnSWR, HyperRESEARCH, Qualrus, and others.

The American Evaluation Association's Web site has a public section on resources. One of the categories under resources is "qualitative data analysis software." Under this category are brief descriptions of available software, often including costs and scope or type of media addressed, as well as links to software provider sites. The descriptions also note availability of free downloads or free trial downloads.

### Manual analysis of qualitative data

Porteous, Sheldrick, and Stewart (1997) provide valuable suggestions for analyzing qualitative data manually. Of course, if large amounts of data have been collected, then computer-assisted software is preferred. Begin by having the following materials available:

- several highlighters (a different color for each evaluation question)
- a worksheet for each evaluation question (figure 10.2)

**Box 10.3 Strategies for Coding Data Electronically**

The following tips are useful in using CAQDAS:

- Memos are the most basic way to annotate data. Small electronic stick-up notes allow users to attach memos to data.
- Free coding allows evaluators to mark and attach a code to sections of data.
- Automatic coding procedures work in various ways. The most common way is to have the computer program automatically code the search results. Data can also be automatically recoded based on previously specified queries.
- Software-generated coding suggestions are a novel feature of Qualrus, in which an algorithm suggests codes on the basis of previously occurring codes.
- Multimedia coding is offered by N6, HyperRESEARCH, and Qualrus. These programs allow coding sequences of audio or video files and parts of pictures. Some other CAQDAS programs allow linking to external multimedia files.

*Source:* Loughborough University Department of Social Sciences 2007.

**Figure 10.2 Blank Worksheet for Qualitative Data Analysis**

| Topic/number of references | Quotations | Findings |
|---|---|---|
| | | |
| | | |
| | | |
| | | |
| | | |
| | | |
| | | |
| | | |

*Source:* Porteous, Sheldrick, and Stewart 1997.

- data, including notes, transcripts, and tapes from interviews or focus groups
- collection tools for self-completed questionnaires, registration forms, observations, or chart reviews.

Use at least one worksheet for each evaluation question. Write each evaluation question in the space provided at the top of each worksheet. For each question, choose a code to identify the data. It might be the color of a pen, pencil, or highlighter, or it might be a symbol. Record your color or symbol in the second space at the top of each worksheet.

To fill in the worksheets, go through the notes and materials collected thus far and code the information, using the following procedure:

- Read all completed tools or notes and transcripts in one sitting.
- Use highlighters of different colors to mark the parts that deal with each evaluation question.
- Go back and carefully read all of the data that pertain to the first evaluation question.
- In the "Topics" column of the worksheet, write down each opinion, idea, or feeling that pertains to the expectations for that evaluation question.
- Leave a space between each topic, leaving room to keep track of how frequently each point is raised.
- Keep a tally of the number of times an opinion, idea, or feeling is mentioned.

Address the rest of the worksheet in the following way (figure 10.3):

- From the notes, extract and insert quotations that best represent each topic.
- Make a preliminary conclusion about specific points, and write them in the "Findings" column.
- Organize the findings by type or category.
- Use numbers of responses ($N = x$) to give precision and a sense of magnitude.

When one uses note cards when analyzing qualitative data, the goal is to summarize what has been seen or heard in common words, phrases, themes, or patterns. New themes may appear later and earlier material may need to be reread to check if the theme was actually there from the beginning but was missed because at the time its significance was not clear.

When identifying words, issues, themes, or patterns, mark where they are located in order to be able find them again if needed to verify quotations or context. This may be tedious the first time it is done; with experience, it becomes easier to locate potentially important information more quickly.

**Figure 10.3    Completed Worksheet for Qualitative Data Analysis**

| Topic/number of references | Quotations | Findings |
|---|---|---|
| Parents<br><br>//// //// //// //// //// //// //// //// | Narrative: I think the process of deciding would be valuable. | There was a strong feeling that parents should be more involved in the choice of topics. |
| Cover several topics per session<br><br>//// //// //// /// | Sometimes we just got into a topic and then it was time to leave or move to something else. | Many participants (38 of 52 interviewed) thought there should be more time for discussion. |
| Not enough time spent on each topic<br><br>//// //// //// /// | We need more time to discuss. | |

*Source:* Porteous, Sheldrick, and Stewart 1997.

Occasionally, the minority view is important and needs to be reported. Use your judgment, but always make it clear that only one or a few respondents expressed that opinion. As the University of the West of England Web site on data analysis notes:

> Life is rarely neatly packaged up into tidy bundles. There are always cul-de-sacs, themes which peter out or are inconsistent with one another. The temptation in qualitative research is to ignore the odd categories that do not fit neatly into the emerging theory. These oddments are like the solo socks you find in your drawers, hence the sock bag phenomenon. All qualitative research projects will have oddments that defy characterization; rather than air brush them from the picture, they need to be acknowledged as part of the whole.

## Interpreting Qualitative Data

Evaluators describe data and interpret them. Before qualitative data can be analyzed, they need to be presented clearly, in a descriptive way. Interpreting data means finding possible causal links, making inferences, attaching meanings, and dealing with cases that contradict the analysis.

Many people are afraid of using statistics. Consequently, there is a tendency to think that using qualitative methods is somehow the easier option. In fact, good qualitative data analysis requires more than meets the eye of the casual observer. Analyzing qualitative data can be labor intensive and time-consuming, but it can reveal insights about behaviors or processes that are not obtainable from quantitative data. Evaluators need to plan enough time to do it well.

**■ Inductive analysis:**
Analysis of data involving discovery of patterns, themes, and categories

**■ Deductive analysis:**
Analysis of data using existing framework

Qualitative methods can be powerful tools for examining causality. (An excellent resource with a step-by-step guide for conducting systematic qualitative data analysis is Miles and Huberman 1994.) Patton (2002) describes two kinds of qualitative analysis: inductive and deductive. **Inductive analysis** involves discovering patterns, themes, and categories in the data. **Deductive analysis** involves analyzing data using an existing framework. Typically, qualitative data are analyzed inductively in the early stages (figuring out categories, patterns, and themes). Once these categories, patterns, and themes are established, deductive analysis may be performed. The deductive phase involves testing and affirming the authenticity and appropriateness of the inductive analysis.

There is some risk of bias in working with qualitative data (if not using software for content analysis); people often see what they want to see and miss things that do not conform to their expectations. It helps (but does not always completely remedy the situation) to have another person analyze the data. By comparing the two analyses, evaluators may identify new themes or find different ways of understanding the data.

When one reports qualitative data, it is not always possible or meaningful to present a count of how many or what percent said or did something. Because all participants were not asked the same question, it is difficult to know how everyone felt about that question Another way to control for bias is to have two coders review the same documents and code them in terms of themes. If the evaluators are well trained and the operational definitions and rating systems are clear and agreed upon in advance, both evaluators would have a high rate of agreement in their ratings of the material. A high level of interrater reliability would be an indicator of credibility. A low rate of interrater reliability would indicate a need to revise the operational definitions, the rating systems, or both.

Table 10.3 summarizes suggestions for organizing and interpreting qualitative data.

### Reporting Qualitative Data

Many evaluations use both qualitative and quantitative data. If using mixed-method (qualitative and quantitative) data collection approaches, evaluators will want to find comments that clarify and illuminate some of the quantitative data. If, for example, 55 percent of respondents were dissatisfied with the accessibility of an intervention, it is useful to include a representative mix of comments that illustrates the sources of the dissatisfaction.

The evaluator will want to capture "quotable quotes." Statements by participants should be chosen because they clearly present a theme or

**Table 10.3  Organizing and Interpreting Qualitative Data**

| Task | Suggestion |
|---|---|
| Develop categories. | • Use recurrent themes, ideas, words, and phrases.<br>• Use categories that are large enough to capture a range of views but not so large as to be meaningless.<br>• Create categories that are distinct from one another. |
| Code the categories. | • Develop a coding scheme.<br>• Develop decision rules for coding that are exhaustive and unambiguous.<br>• Train coders to use the coding scheme. |
| Check for reliability when using more than one observer. | • Conduct a pretest with a small sample of qualitative data.<br>• Check for interrater reliability—do people measuring the same thing, in the same way, obtain the same results?<br>• If problems exist, fix them; then pretest again. |
| Analyze the data. | • Bring order to the data.<br>• Consider placing data on cards.<br>• Consider placing data on a spreadsheet.<br>• Consider using a computer to assist with data analysis.<br>• Sort the data to reveal patterns and themes. |
| Interpret the data. | • When possible, have teams of at least two people review and categorize the data in order to compare their findings and to review and revise them if they differ.<br>• Look for meaning and significance in the data.<br>• Link themes and categories to processes of the program, outcomes, or both. Are some themes more prevalent when respondents discuss process issues? Are some themes more relevant when respondents discuss outcome issues? Look for alternative explanations and other ways of understanding the data. |
| Share and review information. | • Share information early and often with key informants.<br>• Have others review early drafts with the intention of obtaining information, questions, other ways of interpreting the data, and other possible sources of data. |
| Write the report. | • Describe major themes (thematic approach) or present material as it reflects what happened over time (natural history approach).<br>• Highlight interesting perspectives even if noted by only one or two people<br>• Stay focused; with large amounts of data it is easy to get lost.<br>• Include only important information. Ask yourself whether information answers the evaluation questions and will be information useful to stakeholders? |

*Source:* Adapted from Porteous 2005.

important point worth emphasizing. There is power in these words: many report readers will remember a quotation but not a page of description. To avoid bias, evaluators should include quotations that show a range of issues and perspectives about the same theme.

## Analyzing Quantitative Data

Quantitative data analysis summarizes numerical information collected as part of an evaluation. Evaluators enter the data into a computer data file to help organize the data or to use software packages that analyze the data as they are entered.

### Coding the Data

Quantitative data need to be coded for analysis, but doing so is simpler than conducting content analysis of qualitative data. Coding of quantitative data is used when data need to be transformed into a numeric response. Coding allows the data to be processed in a meaningful way. Data on such characteristics as height, weight, age, and number of days absent from school do not need coding, because they are already numerical. Other types of data—such as whether or not a respondent has a bank account—need numeric codes to allow for analysis. An evaluator can code the responses using 1 for yes and 2 for no.

Other data may be collected in ranges or opinions. Say, for example, the question is "To which age group do you belong?" Each of the age groups can be given a code (under 18 = 1, 18–15 = 2, 26–35 = 3, and so forth). Some tips for maintaining quantitative data should be helpful (box 10.4).

---

**Box 10.4  Tips for Maintaining Quantitative Data**

- Always be sure data variables are labeled.
- Make sure the data dictionary is updated for any changes made to data labels or response codes. Good documentation is essential!
- Create a backup of the data set in case of emergency. Create temporary and permanent data sets wisely. Think about what needs to be done if the data are lost.
- Always keep a copy of the original data set.

*Source:* Child and Adolescent Health Measurement Initiative 2009.

---

Each person or record is called a "case." Data files are made up of variables and values for each variable. Variables are each of the items to be analyzed.

It is extremely important for evaluators to indicate how each variable is coded and in what category it is placed. The codes should be recorded in a codebook (sometimes called a *data dictionary*). Coders must have access to the codebook and be trained to use it.

### Cleaning the Data

**Data cleaning** (also called *data cleansing* or *data scrubbing*) is the process of removing errors and inconsistencies from data in order to improve their quality (Rahm and Do 2000). Data with errors or inconsistencies are often called "dirty data." Data analysts estimate that up to half of the time needed for analysis is spent cleaning the data. Typically, this time is underestimated. Once the dataset is clean, the analysis is straightforward (P.A.N.D.A. 2000).

Common sources of errors in a database include the following:

- missing data
- "not applicable" or blank responses
- typing errors on data entry
- incorrectly formatted data
- column shift (data for one variable column are entered under the adjacent column)
- fabricated data
- coding errors
- measurement and interview errors
- out-of-date data (P.A.N.D.A. 2000).

In some cases, respondents do not know the answer to a question or refuse to answer it. In other cases, a respondent may inadvertently skip a question. One convention many evaluators use for these responses is as follows:

- do not know = 8
- refused or missing data = 9.

Consider, for example, data that have been entered into a database by several different people. One coder typed all of the data using capital letters, another entered the first letter of last names in capital letters and all other letters in lower-case letters. One coder entered each address as one entry, another entered the street address as one entry, the township as another entry, and the country as another entry. In addition, data were merged with data from an evaluation conducted 10 years earlier. The new survey instrument included more questions than the older ones, so the older data include no responses for many of the questions.

> **Data cleaning:** Process of removing errors and inconsistencies from data in order to improve their quality

Another problem with the data is that many respondents were confused by some of the questions. The people recording the answers made their best guesses on how to deal with these responses, but each data recorder used different rules for coding. In several cases, respondents asked to select from a scale of 1 to 5 used decimal figures (for example, 2.5). Some coders rounded such figures down to the nearest integer, others rounded down to 2, and yet others treated the responses as missing data.

All of these problems are caused by human error in responding to items or in entering the data. Many of these problems can be minimized if rules for coding data for data entry are established and strictly enforced. However, there will always be errors in data entry. For this reason, data entry needs to be checked. Evaluators need to set up rules for coding responses and keeping track of original questionnaires (to refer to when possible errors are identified). Evaluators will need to inspect the data and try to identify any dirty data.

Once data are entered, they should be screened and cleaned before they are analyzed. Consider, for example, data based on school records. For questions about gender, there are just two possible responses: 1 for male and 2 for female. If other responses are found, they must be considered errors. For a question about having a physical exam, the only possible values would be 1 for yes, 2 for no, 8 for do not know, and 9 for missing or refused. Any other responses should be considered coding errors. To detect possible errors in height data, the evaluator can look at entries that are far above or below those expected for the age of the student (O'Rourke 2000b). If there is a concern about the accuracy of the data, the evaluator can go back to the original data sheets to verify the accuracy (or inaccuracy) of the coded data. (Chapman [2005] offers a useful primer on principles and methods of data cleaning. He references several on-line resources and available software. While specifically addressing biodiversity issues, much of the information provided is of general use. To demonstrate data cleaning techniques, Cody [n.d.] provides an exercise. A link to this exercise is given at the end of this chapter.)

Computer software programs are available to help clean data. The programs check for out-of-range data. One example is WinPure. It is crucial to maintain a record of data cleansing decisions made.

## Using Statistics

Quantitative data are analyzed using statistics. This section introduces some of the most important statistical concepts that people conducting or reading development evaluations need to know.

Statisticians divide statistics into two large categories:

- **descriptive statistics,** which (in its narrowest definition) describe and summarize quantitative data
- **inferential statistics,** which are typically used to analyze random sample data by predicting a range of population values for a quantitative or qualitative variable, based on information for that variable from the random sample. Part of the prediction includes a reliability statement, which states the probability that the true population value lies within a specified range of values.

### Descriptive statistics

Typically, data are summarized using two kinds of descriptive statistics:

- **measures of central tendency:** way of describing a group of data to indicate the central point
- **measures of dispersion:** way of describing a group of data to indicate how spread out the data are.

*Measures of central tendency.* The three measures of central tendency are sometimes called the three Ms.

A group of data is often arrayed in a graphical form called a frequency distribution to summarize it such that the frequency of each variable in the group is indicated. The central value is then determined using one or more of the three measures of central tendency: the mean, the median, and the mode.

*Mode:* Most frequent response.

*Median:* Midpoint or middle value in a distribution; half of all values in the distribution larger and half are smaller. In even-numbered data sets, the median is defined as the average of the two middle cases.

*Mean:* The sum of all collected values divided by the number of values collected (sample size).

The two most commonly used statistics are the mean and the median.

Table 10.4 presents data on the proportion of population in 16 countries that is urban. Suppose you wanted to summarize this information and report the mean urbanicity (average) for this group of countries. The mean would be the sum of the urban proportions divided by the number of countries: $(90 + 64 + 84 \ldots + 93)/16 = 1141/16 = 71.3$. The two middle cases below which and above which 50 percent of the cases fall are 71 and 73, which makes the median 72 $(73 + 71 = 144/2 = 72)$. The mode is 47.6. Notice in this case that the mean and median are close but the mode is much different.

■ **Descriptive statistics:**
Statistics used to describe and summarize quantitative data

■ **Inferential statistics:**
Statistics used to draw inferences about a population from a sample

■ **Measures of central tendency:**
Statistical measures that show how similar characteristics are

■ **Measures of dispersion:**
Statistical measures that show how different characteristics are

Table 10.4 **Percent of Urbanicity by Country for Latin America and Central America**

| Country | Percent of Population Living in an Urban Area in 2007 | Country | Percent of Population Living in an Urban Area in 2007 |
|---------|-----------------------------------------------------|---------|-----------------------------------------------------|
| Argentina | 90 | Honduras | 47 |
| Bolivia | 64 | Mexico | 76 |
| Brazil | 84 | Nicaragua | 59 |
| Chile | 88 | Panama | 71 |
| Colombia | 73 | Paraguay | 59 |
| Costa Rica | 62 | Peru | 73 |
| Ecuador | 63 | Uruguay | 92 |
| Guatemala | 47 | Venezuela | 93 |

*Source:* World Bank. World Development Indicators 2008, 162–64.

■ **Nominal data:** Data that that fit into one of multiple non-overlapping categories, such as gender, religion, or country of origin

■ **Ordinal data:** Data that can be placed on a scale that has an order to it

■ **Interval/ ratio data:** Data with a zero point and fixed intervals, like a ruler, that can be divided and compared with other ratio numbers

■ **Range:** Difference between highest and lowest values of a variable

Which measure of central tendency to use depends on the type of data: nominal, ordinal, or interval/ratio data (table 10.5).

• **Nominal data,** sometimes called *categorical data,* are data that fit into one of multiple nonoverlapping categories, such as gender, religion, or country of origin.
• **Ordinal data** are data that can be placed on a scale that has an order to it, but the "distance" between consecutive responses is not necessarily the same. Scales that go from "most important" to "least important" or "strongly agree" to" strongly disagree" illustrate ordinal data. Ordinal data lack a zero point.
• **Interval/ratio data** are real numbers. These data have a zero point and fixed intervals, like a ruler, and can be divided and compared with other ratio numbers.

For interval/ratio data, the choice will also depend on the distribution. If the distribution is bell shaped, the mean, median, and mode should be very close. In this case, the mean would be the best measure of central tendency. In contrast, if the scores include a few very high scores or a few very low scores, the mean will no longer be close to the center. In this situation, the median would be a better measure of central tendency.

*Measures of dispersion.* Two measures are commonly used to measure the spread of quantitative variables: the range and the standard deviation. The **range** is the difference between the highest and lowest value of a variable.

Using the data in table 10.4, the range for the percent urban population is 93 – 47 = 46.

The range is not very revealing, because it is determined exclusively by two observations; all other cases are ignored. When the two end values are extreme, the range gives no sense of where all other scores lie.

The most commonly used measure of dispersion for interval or ratio data is the standard deviation. Standard deviation is a measure of the spread of the scores on either side of the mean. The more the scores differ from the mean, the larger the standard deviation will be.

For one to better understand the notion of standard deviation, it is important to understand the **normal distribution** (figure 10.4), sometimes called the *bell curve* because of its bell shape. In a normal distribution, the majority of the data fall in the middle of the distribution. There are fewer and fewer data at either end of the distribution.

Data do not always have normal distributions. Some distributions have flatter curves, others have steeper curves or curves that rise at one end or the other (figure 10.5).

The standard deviation measures how closely the data cluster around the mean. It measures distance from the mean. In a normal distribution, one standard deviation from the mean in either direction on the horizontal axis accounts for about 68 percent of the data (figure 10.6). Two standard deviations from the mean account for roughly 95 percent of the data. Three standard deviations from the mean account for about 98 percent of the data.

Table 10.5   Preferred Measures of Central Tendency by Type of Data

| Type of data | Best measure of central tendency |
|---|---|
| Nominal | Mode |
| Ordinal | Mode or median |
| Interval/ratio | Mode, median, or mean |

*Source:* Authors.

■ **Normal distribution:** Continuous probability distribution that describes data that cluster around a mean

Figure 10.4   The Normal Distribution

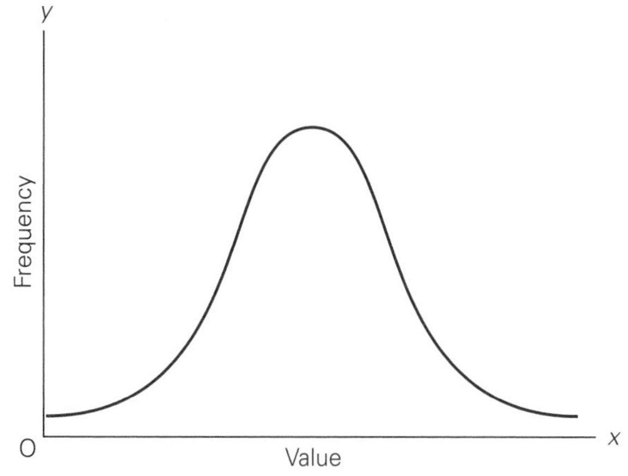

*Source:* Authors.

**Figure 10.5   Nonnormal Distributions**

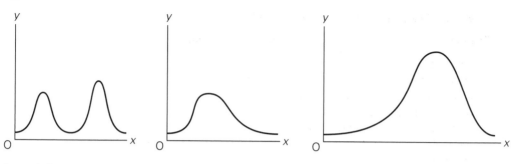

*Source:* Authors.

**Figure 10.6   Standard Deviations in a Normal Distribution**

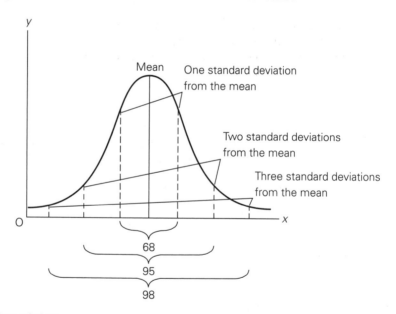

*Source:* Authors.

If the curve from a data set were flatter, the standard deviation would be larger. The value of the standard deviation indicates how spread out the data are from the mean (box 10.5).

If everyone scores 75 on a test, the mean would be 75, and the standard deviation would be 0. If everyone scores between 70 and 80, with a mean

The Road to Results: Designing and Conducting Effective Development Evaluations

The standard deviation of a distribution is calculated as follows:

1. Calculate the mean for the data.
2. Subtract the mean from each data point to find the deviation.
3. Square each of the deviation scores.
4. Sum all of the squares of deviations.
5. Subtract 1 from the number of data points.
6. Divide the sum of all the squares of deviations by the result of step five (number of items in the list minus 1).
7. Take the square root of the result of step 6.
   The formula for calculating standard deviation is as follows:

$$\sigma = \sqrt{\frac{\sum(x - \bar{x})}{N - 1}}$$

where $\sigma$ = standard deviation, $\sum$ = the sum of, and $\bar{x}$ = the mean.

Even with a small sample, calculating the standard deviation is time-consuming. Thankfully, most statistical programs, including Excel and SPSS for Windows, can perform the calculations.

score of 75, the standard deviation would be smaller than if everyone scores between 40 and 90 (with a mean of 75). Put another way:

Small standard deviation = not much dispersion.

Large standard deviation = lots of dispersion.

Standard deviation is superior to range, because it allows every case to have an impact on its value.

*Frequently used descriptive measures.* Sometimes a question asks for specific counts ("How many goats do you own? How often do you use a bank?") Responses to such questions are reported absolutely and in terms of percentages.

Other times, people are asked to give opinions along a scale. For example, an evaluator might ask whether respondents were able to apply what they learned, giving them a five-point scale ranging from "not at all" to "a lot." When analyzing this type of data, establish a decision rule: concentrate on the percentage who answered at the extreme ends of the scale, on those who answered on either side of the middle category, or on the average response. Although there are no firm rules here, some guidelines may be helpful (box 10.6).

Consider a survey of clients of a health center (table 10.6). One way to analyze these data is to report that half the respondents agree or strongly agree that they receive good health care and 55 percent agree or strongly agree that clinic staff is willing to answer questions. However, 60 percent agree or strongly agree that they wait a long time before being seen. In this analysis, the evaluator decided to report the combined percentages of agree and strongly agree.

If the data were different, the evaluator might use a different strategy. Consider, for example, the results presented in table 10.7.

The analysis in this case might note that 80 percent of respondents agree or strongly agree that they receive good health care and 70 percent agree or strongly agree that they wait a long time before being seen. The greatest strength appears to be the willingness of staff members to answer questions, with 95 percent of respondents reporting that they strongly agree or agree that they receive good health care.

*Describing two variables at the same time.* At times evaluators want to describe two variables at the same time. Suppose, for example, they want to

**Table 10.6   Client Views on Health Care Services at the Local Clinic (percentage of respondents)**

1. Considering your experiences with the local health clinic, do you agree or disagree with the following statements?

| Statement | Strongly disagree | Disagree | Neither agree nor disagree | Agree | Strongly agree |
|---|---|---|---|---|---|
| I wait a long time before being seen. | 10 | 20 | 10 | 35 | 25 |
| The staff members are willing to answer my questions. | 5 | 10 | 30 | 30 | 25 |
| I receive good health care at the clinic. | 15 | 25 | 10 | 25 | 25 |

*Source:* Authors.

*Note:* N = 36.

**Table 10.7   Client Views on Health Care Services at the Local Clinic (percentage of respondents)**

1. Considering your experiences with the local health clinic, do you agree or disagree with the following statements?

| Statement | Strongly disagree | Disagree | Neither agree nor disagree | Agree | Strongly agree |
|---|---|---|---|---|---|
| I wait a long time before being seen. | 50 | 20 | 10 | 15 | 5 |
| The staff members are willing to answer my questions. | 0 | 5 | 0 | 30 | 65 |
| I receive good health care at the clinic. | 0 | 20 | 0 | 55 | 25 |

*Source:* Authors.

*Note:* N = 36.

describe the composition of hands-on classes and lecture classes. For each class, they want to know the percentage of boys and the percentage of girls. Analysis of the data shows that the hands-on classes consist of 55 percent boys and 45 percent girls, while the traditional lecture classes consist of 55 percent girls and 45 percent boys.

**■ Cross-tabulation:**
Joint distribution of two or more variables, usually presented in a table

A **cross-tabulation** (or "cross-tab") displays the joint distribution of two or more variables, usually presented in a matrix format. Whereas a frequency distribution provides the distribution of one variable, a contingency table describes the distribution of two or more variables simultaneously. Each cell shows the percentage and the number of respondents who give a specific combination of responses.

The data on class enrollment could be interpreted as follows: in this sample, boys are somewhat more likely (55 percent) than girls (45 percent) to take the hands-on classes. This finding suggests a relationship between gender and class enrollment. But how strong is it? When looking at measures of association it is important to understand the concepts of independent and dependant variables.

**■ Independent variable:** Variable that explains a change in another (dependent) variable

**Independent variables** are variables that explain a change in another (dependent) variable. In an evaluation of a training course, for example, the independent variables might include the experience of the instructors, the backgrounds of the participants, the curriculum used, the length of the training, the modality used, and so forth.

**■ Dependent variable:**
Variable to be explained

**Dependent variables** are the variables to be explained. For a training course, the dependent variables might be scores on a knowledge test, grades on a design matrix for an evaluation, or improved evaluation designs.

Evaluators are often interested in whether there is a difference in the average values of a quantitative variable for a pair of samples. They might, for example, be interested in investigating questions such as the following:

- Are average crop yields higher after an irrigation project than they were before the project?
- Do surveys of patients at an older hospital and patients at a hospital built under a development project reveal differences in the percentage of patients who are satisfied with their care?

Evaluators need to determine whether any apparent differences indicate actual differences in the population means or random variation in the samples taken from the two populations. In a statistical test, it is commonly assumed that there is no difference between the two population means (or proportions). This issue is addressed in the section below on inferential statistics.

**■ Measures of association:**
Measures that indicate how strongly variables are related

**Measures of association** (or relationship) indicate how strongly variables are related. Simple association does not prove cause. It can only generally suggest the possibility of a causal relationship if the measure is association is strong.

Measures of association are usually reported in terms of a scale that ranges from –1 to +1. A measure with a positive sign means that the variables change in the same direction: both go up or both go down. This is called a **direct relationship.** A perfect positive relationship would score +1.

A negative sign indicates that the variables have an **inverse relationship,** meaning that they move in opposite directions (for example, as age increases, health status decreases). A perfect negative relationship would score –1. The closer the measure is to zero, the weaker the relationship (a relationship showing no association at all would score 0); the closer the measure is to +1 or –1, the stronger the relationship.

### Inferential statistics

Inferential statistics enable evaluators to make an estimate about a population based on a random sample selected from that population. The major fear in using a random sample is that the results reflect some quirkiness of the sample and, therefore, do not reveal an accurate picture of the population. If the evaluators had picked a different sample, would their results be fairly similar or quite different?

Statistical significance tests measure the probability of getting the same results if there really was no difference in the population as a whole. Evaluators call this the null hypothesis; it is always based on zero difference in the population.

Suppose a survey based on a random sample of people in Pakistan shows that there was a 5,000 rupee difference in annual income between men and women. The test might be expressed in this way: if there really is no difference in the population, what is the probability of finding a 5,000 rupee difference in a random sample? If there is a 5 percent chance (0.05) or less, we conclude that the sample results are an accurate estimate of the population, that there is a difference of about 5,000 rupees, and that the difference is statistically significant.

A *p*-value (for probability of error) of 5 percent means that the evaluator is 95 percent certain that the sample results are not due to chance. It means that the results are statistically significant at the 0.05 level.

All tests of statistical significance are partly based on sample size. If the sample is very large, small differences are likely to be statistically significant. Evaluators need to decide whether the differences are important, given the nature of their research. Three often-used statistical tests are the chi-square test, the *t*-test, and the analysis of variance test. Each is briefly described next.

*Chi-square test.* Although it is not the strongest measure of association, the **chi-square test** is one of the most popular statistical tests, because it is easy to calculate and interpret. The purpose of the chi-square test is to determine

▪ **Direct relationship:** Relationship in which variables move in the same direction (both go up or down)

▪ **Inverse relationship:** Relationship in which variables move in opposite directions

▪ **Chi-square test:** Statistical test used to determine whether the observed frequencies differ markedly from the frequencies one would expect by chance

whether the observed frequencies differ markedly from the frequencies one would expect by chance. This test is used to compare two nominal values (for example, marital status and religious affiliation). It is also used to compare two ordinal variables (scaled responses) or a combination of nominal and ordinal variables.

The chi-square statistic is the sum of the contributions from each of the individual cells in a data table. Every cell in the table contributes something to the overall chi-square statistic. If a given cell differs markedly from the expected frequency, then the contribution of that cell to the overall chi-square statistic is large. If a cell is close to the expected frequency for that cell, then the contribution of that cell to the overall chi square is low. A large chi-square statistic indicates that—somewhere in the table—the observed frequencies differ markedly from the expected frequencies. It does not tell which cell (or cells) is causing the high chi-square, only that they are there. Chi square measures whether two variables are independent of one another based on observed data

The chi-square test measures the significance of cross-tabulations. Chi-square values should not be calculated for percentages. The cross-tabs must be converted back to absolute counts (numbers) before performing the test. The chi-square test is also problematic when any cell has a frequency of less than five (For an in-depth discussion of this issue, see Fienberg 1980.)

*t-test.   When looking at the differences between scores for two groups, evaluators have to judge the difference between their means relative to the spread or variability of their scores. A **t-test** does just that.* It is used to determine whether one group of numerical scores is statistically higher or lower than another group of scores. This analysis is appropriate whenever the means of two groups is compared. Evaluators use *t*-statistics to compare the mean scores of a group affected by a project with the mean scores of a control group.

■ **t-test:**
Statistical test used to determine whether one group of numerical scores is statistically higher or lower than another

*Analysis of variance (ANOVA).   The t-test is very cumbersome to use when three or more groups are compared.* When an evaluation needs to compare the means of several different groups at one time, it is best to use **analysis of variance (ANOVA)**.

ANOVA is a statistical technique for assessing the differences between data sets. Using EXCEL, it is used to make simultaneous comparisons between two or more means to determine if the observed change is due to chance variation or likely a factor or combination of factors tested. ANOVA thus assesses how nominal independent variables influence a continuous dependent variable. It assumes that the populations for all groups being

■ **Analysis of variance (ANOVA):**
Statistical technique for assessing the difference between data sets

compared have equal standard deviations (assumption of the homogeneity of variance) and that the samples are randomly selected from the population. It is important to check that these assumptions hold before using ANOVA. The tests in an ANOVA are based on the F-ratio—the variation due to an experimental treatment or effect divided by the variation due to experimental error. The null hypothesis is that this ratio equals 1.0 (that is, the treatment effect is the same as the experimental error). This hypothesis is rejected if the $F$-ratio is large enough that the possibility of it equaling 1.0 is smaller than some preassigned level, such as 0.05 (1 in 20).

## Linking Qualitative Data and Quantitative Data

Miles and Huberman (1994) discuss how qualitative and quantitative data can be linked. They begin their discussion with a quotation from Fred Kerlinger, a highly regarded quantitative researcher: "There's no such thing as qualitative data. Everything is either 1 or 0." They then offer an opposing view: all data are basically qualitative.

The argument over quantitative versus qualitative data has raged for many years in the United States; it has not generally been an issue in development, however. Development evaluation uses both quantitative and qualitative data to understand the world: "quantities are of qualities, and a measured quality has just the magnitude expressed in its measure" (Miles and Huberman 1994). Qualitative methods provide more context; quantitative approaches allow generalization of the findings to other situations.

Miles and Huberman note that linking quantitative and qualitative data in a study design allows evaluators to

- confirm or corroborate each kind of data via triangulation
- elaborate or develop analysis, providing richer detail
- initiate new lines of thinking through attention to surprises or paradoxes, "turning ideas around" and providing fresh insight.

Greene, Caracelli, and Graham (1997) describe the epistemological and political value of mixing methods in evaluation:

- epistemological: we can know something better if we bring multiple ways of knowing to bear on it
- political: all ways of knowing are partial, hence multiple, diverse ways of knowing are to be valued and respected.

They note that "good mixed-method evaluation actively invites diverse ways of thinking and valuing to work in concert toward better understanding" and "different kinds of methods are best suited to learning about different kinds of phenomena."

Hawkins (2005) lists the following benefits of using an integrated mixed-method approach to evaluation:

- Consistency checks can be built in with triangulation procedures that permit two or more independent estimates to be made for key variables.
- Different perspectives can be obtained. For example, while evaluators may consider income or consumption to be the key indicators of household welfare, case studies may reveal that women are more concerned about vulnerability, powerlessness, or exposure to violence.
- Analysis can be conducted on different levels. Survey methods can provide good estimates of individual, household, and community-level welfare, but they are much less effective for analyzing social processes (for example, social conflict) or conducting institutional analysis (for example, how effectively public services operate or are perceived by the community to operate). Many qualitative methods are designed to analyze issues such as social processes, institutional behavior, social structure, and conflict.
- Opportunities can be provided for feedback that can help evaluators interpret findings. Survey reports frequently include references to apparent inconsistencies in findings or interesting differences between groups that cannot be explained by analysis of the data. In most quantitative evaluations, once the data collection phase is completed, it is not possible to return to the field to gather additional data.
- Survey evaluators frequently refer to the use of qualitative methods to check on outliers. In many cases, the analyst has to make an arbitrary decision as to whether a respondent who reports conditions that are significantly above or below the norm should be excluded.
- The perceived benefits of integrated approaches depend on the evaluator's background. From the perspective of the quantitative evaluator, a qualitative component will help identify key issues to be addressed in the evaluation; refine questions to match the views of respondents; and provide information about the social, economic, and political context within which the evaluation takes place. It is also possible to return to the field to follow up on interesting findings.
- Qualitative evaluators can benefit from using quantitative methods. Sampling methods can be used to allow findings to be generalized to the wider population. Sample selection can be coordinated with ongoing or earlier survey work so that findings from qualitative work can be compared with survey findings. Statistical analysis can be used to control for household characteristics and the socioeconomic conditions of different study areas, thereby eliminating alternative explanations of the observed changes.

Hawkins (2005) discusses when and when not to use a mixed-method approach. According to him, mixed methods should be used under the following circumstances:

- An in-depth understanding of the intervention and its context is required.
- There is a limited budget and significant time constraints, and triangulation can help validate information collected from different sources using different methods and small samples.

Mixed methods should not be used under the following circumstances:

- Questions can be answered using a single-method approach.
- The generalizability of the findings is required, and the indicators/measures are straightforward.
- Evaluators with expertise in the chosen methods are not available for the whole study (better to use only those methods for which expertise is available).
- Key stakeholders' commitment to a particular paradigm to the exclusion of all others is so strong that they will remain unconvinced by a mixed-method approach no matter how good it is.
- Time available at the analysis and interpretation stage is very limited.

## Summary

Qualitative data analysis is used for nonnumerical data. Qualitative data can be gathered, for example, using unstructured observations, open-ended interviews, analysis of written documents, and focus group transcriptions. Notes taken during the collection of qualitative data are extremely important, so they must be detailed.

Content analysis is a process for analyzing qualitative data. Analyzing qualitative data is labor intensive and time-consuming, but doing so can reveal valuable information.

After collecting qualitative data, evaluators need to organize them. The data can be sorted so that patterns and commonalities appear. Once sorted (either manually or electronically), the data can be coded and then interpreted.

Quantitative data are analyzed using descriptive and inferential statistics. Descriptive statistics summarize the data and describe the central value through the 3 Ms—the mean, median, and mode. Common measures of dispersion are the range and the standard deviation. Other commonly used descriptive statistics include frequency distributions, percentages, rates, ratios, and rates of change.

Inferential statistics enable evaluators to make estimates about a population based on a random sample selected from that population. Common inferential statistical tools are chi-square tests, $t$-tests, and ANOVA.

Evaluators usually use both qualitative and quantitative methods. Using more than one method has many benefits in many cases. In cases in which only a few questions are posed that are relatively easy to answer, a single approach is usually recommended.

## Application Exercise 10.1: Coding and Analyzing Qualitative Data

Collect several lengthy newpaper articles about a development issue. Using these articles set up a table or handwritten grid, labeling the columns "article" and "excerpt." Next, enter excerpts from the articles that you find important. As you identify themes from the articles, enter them as additional column headings. Then mark the appropriate cell where an excerpt contains each theme. Write a narrative summarizing the findings from the articles.

## Application Exercise 10.2: Avoiding Common Mistakes in Interpreting Quantitative Data

1. Eighty percent of survey respondents indicate that they found a program helpful. Which would be the better way to report the findings, "The program is helpful" or "Participants found the program helpful"? Survey respondents were asked to identify the barriers and supports to the program. What is the problem with reporting the results in terms of pros and cons?
2. A survey asked students to rate various components of a course. Most students rated each of the components positively. What is the problem with reporting that most (70 percent) of the students felt the course was a success?
3. Forty percent of women and 30 percent of men favor curriculum changes. Is it accurate to report that a majority of women favored curriculum changes?
4. Fifty-one percent of respondents favor changing the curriculum. Is it accurate to report that more than half of respondents favored curricular change?
5. The survey was completed by 5 of the course's 20 instructors. All 5 reported that they were well prepared to tech the course. Is it accurate to say that all of the instructors were well prepared? Is it accurate to say that 25 percent of the instructors were well prepared?
6. The number of women in political office rose from 2 to 4 seats in the 50-person legislature. Is it accurate to report a 100 percent increase?
7. Participants in a training program earned 20 percent more than those not in the program. Is it accurate to report that the program caused a 20 percent increase in salary?

Complete this survey, and have at least two colleagues complete it. Collect the surveys and tally the results. Working alone or with others, summarize the results in narrative form, drawing some conclusions about the overall findings.

1.  To what extent would you say that you currently have the analytical capacity to do each of the following?

| Skill | Little or no extent | Some extent | Moderate extent | Great extent | Very great extent |
|---|---|---|---|---|---|
| a. Design an evaluation. | | | | | |
| b. Analyze data. | | | | | |
| c. Develop a survey. | | | | | |
| d. Conduct a focus group. | | | | | |
| e. Facilitate a stakeholders' meeting. | | | | | |
| f. Write an evaluation report. | | | | | |
| g. Prepare an oral briefing. | | | | | |

2. At this point in this training program, would you agree or disagree with each of the following statements:

| Statement | Strongly disagree | Disagree | Neither agree nor disagree | Agree | Strongly agree |
|---|---|---|---|---|---|
| a. The material is new to me. | | | | | |
| b. The material is interesting. | | | | | |
| c. The amount of time devoted to lectures is sufficient. | | | | | |
| d. The amount of time devoted to class discussion is sufficient. | | | | | |
| e. The exercises are helpful. | | | | | |
| f. I am learning material I can use in my job. | | | | | |

3. Please provide any comments you may have about the course.

# References and Further Reading

Babbie, E., F. Halley, and J. Zaino. 2000. *Adventures in Social Research*. Thousand Oaks, CA: Pine Forge Press.

Busch, Carol, Paul S. De Maret, Teresa Flynn, Rachel Kellum, Sheri Le, Brad Meyers, Matt Saunders, Robert White, and Mike Palmquist. 2005. *Content Analysis*. Writing@CSU, Colorado State University, Department of English, Fort Collins, CO.
http://writing.colostate.edu/guides/research/content/.

Child and Adolescent Health Measurement Initiative (CAHMI). 2006. "Promoting Healthy Development Survey: Implementation Guidelines." Portland, OR: Oregon Health and Science University, Department of Pediatrics.

———. 2009. "Step 4: Monitor Survey Administration and Prepare for Analysis." http://www.cahmi.org.

Catterall, M., and P. Maclaran. 1997. "Focus Group Data and Qualitative Analysis Programs: Coding the Moving Picture as Well as the Snapshots." *Sociological Research Online* 2 (1).
http://www.socresonline.org.uk/socresonline/2/1/6.html.

Chapman, Arthur D. 2005. *Principles and Methods of Data Cleaning: Primary Species-Occurrence Data*. Report for the Global Biodiversity Information Facility, Version 1.0, Copenhagen.
http://www2.gbif.org/DataCleaning.pdf.

Cody, Ronald. n.d. "Data Cleaning 101." Robert Wood Johnson Medical School, Piscatawy, NJ.
http://www.ats.ucla.edu/stat/sas/library/nesug99/ss123.pdf.

Constable, Rolly, Marla Cowell, Sarita Zornek Crawford, David Golden, Jake Hartvigsen, Kathryn Morgan, Anne Mudgett, Kris Parrish, Laura Thomas, Erika Yolanda Thompson, Rosie Turner, and Mike Palmquist. 2005. *Ethnography, Observational Research, and Narrative Inquiry*. Writing@CSU, Colorado State University, Department of English, Fort Collins, CO.
http://writing.colostate.edu/guides/research/observe/.

Dehejia, Rajeev H., and Sadek Wahba. 2002. "Propensity Score-Matching Methods for Nonexperimenal Causal Studies." *Review of Economics and Statistics* 84 (1): 151–61.
http://www.nber.org/~rdehejia/papers/matching.pdf.

Denzin, N., and Y. Lincoln, eds. 2000. *Handbook of Qualitative Research*. 2nd ed. Thousand Oaks, CA: Sage Publications.

Fienberg, S. E. 1980. The *Analysis of Cross-Classified Categorical Data*. 2nd ed. Cambridge, MA: MIT Press.

Firestone, W. 1987. "Meaning in Method: The Rhetoric of Quantitative and Qualitative Research." *Educational Researcher 16* (7): 16–21.
http://edr.sagepub.com/cgi/content/abstract/16/7/16.

Gao, Jie, Michael Langberg, and Lenard J. Schulman. 2006. *Analysis of Incomplete Data and an Intrinsic-Dimension Helly Theorem*.
http://www.cs.sunysb.edu/~jgao/paper/clustering_lines.pdf.

Glass, G., and K. Hopkins. 1996. *Statistical Methods in Education and Psychology*. 3rd ed. Boston: Allyn and Bacon.

Greene, J. C., and V. J Caracelli. 1997. *Advances in Mixed Method Evaluation: The Challenges and Benefits of Integrating Diverse Paradigms*. New Directions for Evaluation No. 74. San Francisco: Jossey-Bass.

Greene, J. C., V. J. Caracelli, and W. F. Graham. 1989. "Toward a Conceptual Framework for Mixed-Method Evaluation Designs." *Educational Evaluation and Policy Analysis* 11 (3) 255–74.

Hawkins, Penny. 2005. "Thinking about Mixed Method Evaluation." International Program for Development Evaluation Training (IPDET) presentation, Ottawa, July.

IDRC (International Development Research Centre). 2008. *Qualitative Research for Tobacco Control, Module 6: Qualitative Data Analysis*. Ottawa, Canada. http://www.idrc.ca/en/ev-106563-201-1-DO_TOPIC.html.

Jaeger, R. M. 1990. *Statistics: A Spectator Sport*. 2nd ed. Thousand Oaks, CA: Sage Publications.

Krippendorf, Klaus. 2004. *Content Analysis: An Introduction to Its Methodology*. 2nd ed. Thousand Oaks, CA: Sage Publications.

Loughborough University Department of Social Sciences. 2007. *New Methods for the Analysis of Media Content. CAQDAS: A Primer*. Leicestershire, United Kingdom. http://www.lboro.ac.uk/research/mmethods/research/software/caqdas_primer.html#what.

Miles, Mathew. B., and A. Michael Huberman. 1994. *Qualitative Data Analysis an Expanded Sourcebook*. 2nd ed. Thousand Oaks, CA: Sage Publications.

Morse, Janice M., and Lyn Richards. 2002. "The Integrity of Qualitative Research." In *Read Me First for a User's Guide to Qualitative Methods,* ed. J. M. Morse and L. Richards, 25–46. Thousand Oaks, CA: Sage Publications.

Narayan, Deepa. 1996. "Toward Participatory Research." World Bank Technical Paper 307, Washington, DC. http://www-wds.worldbank.org/external/default/WDSContentServer/WDSP/IB/1996/04/01/000009265_3980625172923/Rendered/PDF/multi0page.pdf.

NCSTE (Chinese National Centre for Science and Technology Evaluation), and IOB (Policy and Operations Evaluation Department. 2006. *Country-Led Joint Evaluation of the ORET/MILIEV Programme in China*. Amsterdam: Aksant Academic Publishers.

Neuendorf, Kimberly A. 2006. *The Content Analysis Guidebook Online*. http://academic.csuohio.edu/kneuendorf/content/index.htm.

O'Rourke, Thomas W. 2000a. "Data Analysis: The Art and Science of Coding and Entering Data." *American Journal of Health Studies* 16 (3): 164–66. http://Findarticles.com/p/articles/mi_m0CTG/is_3_16/ai_72731731.

———. 2000b. "Techniques for Screening and Cleaning Data for Analysis." *American Journal of Health Studies* 16: 217–19. http://Findarticles.com/p/articles/mi_m0CTG/is_4_16/ai_83076574.

P.A.N.D.A. (Practical Analysis of Nutritional Data). 2000. "Chapter 2: Data Cleaning." http://www.tulane.edu/~panda2/Analysis2/datclean/dataclean.htm.

Patton, Michael. Q. 2002. *Qualitative Research and Evaluation Methods*. 3rd ed. Thousand Oaks, CA: Sage Publications.

Porteous, Nancy. 2005. "A Blueprint for Public Health Management: The ToolKit's Approach to Program Evaluation." Presentation at the International Program for Development Evaluation Training, June–July 2005. Ottawa, Ontario.

Porteous, Nancy L., B. J. Sheldrick, and P. J. Stewart. 1997. *Program Evaluation Tool Kit: A Blueprint for Public Health Management*. Ottawa-Carleton Health Department, Ottawa.
http://www.phac-aspc.gc.ca/php-psp/tookit.html.

Rahm, Erhard, and Hong Hai Do. 2000. "Data Cleaning: Problems and Current Approaches." University of Leipzig, Germany.
http://homepages.inf.ed.ac.uk/wenfei/tdd/reading/cleaning.pdf.

Rossman, G. B., and B. L. Wilson. 1994. "Numbers and Words Revisited: Being 'Shamelessly Methodologically Eclectic.'" *Quality and Quantity* 28: 315–27.

Sieber, S. D. 1973. "The Integration of Fieldwork and Survey Methods." *American Journal of Sociology* 78 (6):1335–59.

Smith, J. A. 1991. *The Idea Brokers: Think Tanks and the Rise of the New Policy Elite*. New York: Free Press.

StatSoft. 2008. *Electronic Textbook*. http://www.statsoft.com/textbook/glosp.html.

Stemler, Steve 2001. "An Overview of Content Analysis." *Practical Assessment, Research & Evaluation* 7 (17).
http://PAREonline.net/getvn.asp?v=7&n=17.

Swimmer, Gene. 2006. "Qualitative Data Analysis, Part I." *IPDET Handbook 2005*. International Program for Development Evaluation Training (IPDET) presentation, Ottawa, July.

University of the West of England. 2006. *Analysis of Textual Data*. Bristol.
http://hsc.uwe.ac.uk/dataanalysis/qualTextData.asp.

U.S. GAO (General Accounting Office). 1996. *Content Analysis: A Methodology for Structuring and Analyzing Written Material*. GAO/PEMD-10.3.1. Washington, DC. (Available free of charge.)

Washington State University. 2000. A *Field Guide to Experimental Designs: What Is an ANOVA?* Tree Fruit Research and Extension Center. Wenatchee, WA.
http://www.tfrec.wsu.edu/ANOVA/basic.html.

Weber, Robert Philip 1990. *Basic Content Analysis*. 2nd ed. Thousand Oaks, CA: Sage Publications.

Weiss, Christopher, and Kristen Sosulski. 2003. *Quantitative Methods in Social Science: QMSS E-lessons*. Columbia Center for New Media Teaching and Learning, Columbia University, New York.
http://www.columbia.edu/ccnmtl/projects/qmss/anova_about.html.

Wolcott, H. F. 1990. "On Seeking—and Rejecting—Validity in Qualitative Research." In *Qualitative Inquiry in Education: The Continuing Debate,* eds. E. W. Eisner and A. Peshkin, 121–52. New York: Teachers College Press.

# Web Sites

## Online Texts and Tutorials

CAQDAS (Computer-Assisted Qualitative Data Analysis Software). 2008. http://caqdas.soc.surrey.ac.uk/.

Lane, D. M. *Hyperstat Online Textbook*. http://davidmlane.com/hyperstat/index.html.

Statistics at Square One. http://bmj.bmjjournals.com/collections/statsbk/index.shtml.

Stat Primer. http://www2.sjsu.edu/faculty/gerstman/Stat Primer.

## Computer Software for Qualitative Data

AEA (American Evaluation Association). http://www.eval.org/Resources/QDA.htm.

AnSWR. http://www.cdc.gov/hiv/topics/surveillance/resources/software/answr/index.htm (developer site), http://www.cdc.gov/hiv/software/answr/ver3d.htm (free download site).

Atlas-ti. http://www.atlasti.com/.

CDC EZ-Text. http://www.cdc.gov/hiv/topics/surveillance/resources/software/ez-text/index.htm (developer site), http://www.cdc.gov/hiv/software/ez-text.htm (free trial download site)

Ethnograph. http://www.qualisresearch.com/default.htm.

Friese, Susanne. 2004. *Overview/Summary of Qualitative Software Programs*. http://www.quarc.de/software_overview_table.pdf.

Hyperqual. http://home.satx.rr.com/hyperqual/.

QSR Software. NVivo 8. http://www.qsrinternational.com/.

Qualpro. http://www.qualproinc.com/.

## Computer Software

SPSS. http://www.spss.com.

OpenStat. Version 4. http://www.statpages.org/miller/openstat/.

Tutorial for SPSS v. 11.5. http://www.datastep.com/SPSSTraining.html/.

Getting Started with SPSS for Windows. http://www.indiana.edu/~statmath/stat/spss/win/.

WinPure. Data Cleaning Software. http://www.winpure.com.

## Examples of Data Analysis

Carleton University. *Canadian Foreign Policy Journal*. http://www.carleton.ca/npsia/cfpj.

IISD (International Institute for Sustainable Development). http://www.iisd.org/measure/default.htm.

IMF (International Monetary Fund). http://www.imf.org/external/pubs/res/index
.htm.

——. http://www.imf.org/external/np/sta/index.htm.

North-South Institute. http://www.nsi-ins.ca/ensi/research/index.html.

OECD (Organisation for Economic Co-operation and Development). http://www
.oecd.org/dac/.

UNDP (United Nations Development Programme). *Human Development Report
2002*. http://www.undp.org/hdr2002.

UNEP (United Nations Environmental Programme). http://www.grid.unep.ch.

UNESCO (United Nations Educational, Scientific, and Cultural Organization).
http://www.uis.unesco.org/en/stats/stats0.htm.

UNHCR (United Nations High Commission for Refugees). http://www.unhcr.ch/
cgi-bin/texis/vtx/home.

UNSD (United Nations Statistics Division). http://unstats.un.org/unsd/databases
.htm.

USAID (U.S. Agency for International Development.) http://www.usaid.gov/educ_
training/ged.html.

——. http://www.dec.org/partners/eval.cfm.

U.S. Census Bureau. http://www.census.gov/ipc/www/idbnew.html.

WHO (World Health Organization). http://www.who.int/health-systems-
performance.

——. Statistical Information System (WHOSIS). http://www.who.int/topics/
statistics/en/.

World Bank. http://www.worldbank.org/data.

——. *World Development Indicators 2005*. http://worldbank.org/data/wdi2005.

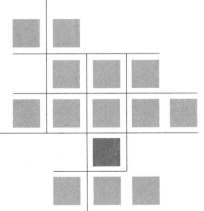

# MEETING CHALLENGES

*"When we do the best we can, we never know what miracle is wrought in our life, or in the life of another."*

—HELEN KELLER

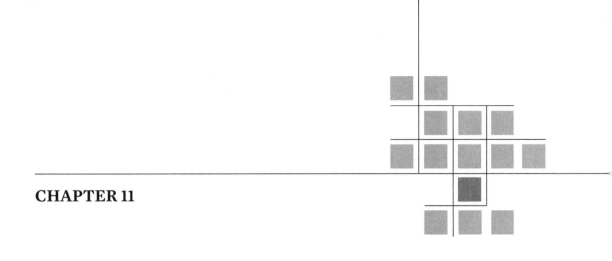

**CHAPTER 11**

# Evaluating Complex Interventions

Development interventions are becoming more complex, creating new challenges, expectations, paradigms for dealing with poverty, methods, and clients for evaluators. This chapter discusses evaluation at the joint, country, thematic, sector, and global levels.

**This chapter has six main parts:**

- Big-Picture Views of Development Evaluation
- Joint Evaluations
- Country Program Evaluations
- Sector Program Evaluations
- Thematic Evaluations
- Evaluation of Global and Regional Partnership Programs

# Big-Picture Views of Development Evaluation

Evaluation must sometimes take a big-picture view. Doing so means going beyond evaluating a single project, program, or policy to also evaluate related projects, programs, and policies.

A big-picture view may address the overall experience and impact of development interventions within a sector, such as health, education, or transportation. A ministry, for example, may want to determine the overall impact of and lessons to be learned from interventions aimed at improving the well-being of children or women; a donor may want to examine the effectiveness of its education sector strategy.

Increasingly, as a response to the Paris Declaration and Accra Accord, donor-lending programs are being based on sectorwide approaches (SWAps). Complex economic, political, and social factors affect development activities and evaluations. Development and development evaluation are increasingly becoming pluralistic enterprises, including the involvement of nongovernmental actors, such as the private sector, not-for profit implementation and advocacy agencies, and civil society as a whole.

Development interventions do not proceed along a linear chain. While there is an "if–then" reasoning behind development interventions, many factors—economic, political, climatic, and social—interact with a program and may affect its outcomes. Evaluators need to identify these factors and design evaluations that tease out their influence.

As the complexity of evaluation increases, the interaction of these factors also becomes more complex. Countries and their partners are seeking to determine the cumulative effects of bringing about changes in a sector, in a country, or on cross-cutting thematic issues such as climate change.

Evaluators have to manage evaluations in the face of this complexity. But complexity of evaluation is not simply increasing because of the broadening scope of what is being evaluated. With increased awareness of the burden of evaluations on fledgling or weak country capacities, the Paris Declaration and Accra Accord have reinforced the need for multipartner evaluations of the quality of assistance in a country and the results of that assistance.

Development has evolved toward a more comprehensive agenda, increasingly addressing country policy reforms, capacity building, and global concerns. In turn, evaluation has expanded, by

- reorienting its focus from just the project, program, or activity level to the country, sector, thematic, regional, or global level

- determining how best to aggregate outcomes of interventions at the activity and country level in order to assess global or programwide results
- finding ways to assess the influence of program design, partnership approach, and governance on overall results
- seeking replicability at a higher level and applicability at the system level (Heath, Grasso, and Johnson 2005).

Country evaluations are one way to gain an overall understanding of what is happening and to provide insights about the overall effect and experience of development within a country. But how these should be conducted is not always clear. Sector or thematic evaluations—on a single country or multiple countries—can also reveal the big picture. They are likely to use multiple methods, including some combination of available data, interviews, field visits, surveys, and focus groups.

This chapter looks at five types of big-picture views:

- joint evaluations
- country program evaluations
- sector program evaluations
- thematic evaluations
- evaluation of global and regional partnership programs.

## Joint Evaluations

**Joint evaluations** are evaluations in which more than one organization participates.

> There are various degrees of "jointness," depending on the extent to which individual partners cooperate in the evaluation process, merge their evaluation resources and combine their evaluation reporting. Joint evaluations can help overcome attribution problems in assessing the effectiveness of programs and strategies, the complementarity of efforts supported by different partners, the quality of aid coordination, and so forth. (OECD 2002, p. 26)

Joint evaluations have been conducted since the early 1990s. Joint evaluations have increased in number and quality since the issuing of the Paris Declaration in 2005 and the Accra Accord in 2008. However, the concept envisioned, of relying on country systems for results-based data, is still weak. Evaluation of the Paris Declaration indicates that joint evaluations are increasing, and they are increasingly seen as of better quality and more useful. Nevertheless, donors, unable to count on robust country systems for

■ **Joint evaluation:** Evaluation in which more than one organization participates

data, still face pressure to report on results under their own systems. Joint evaluations can be conducted by

- donor + donor
- donor + partner country
- multidonor + multipartner
- partner + partner (Chen and Slot 2007).

Breier (2005) identifies a typology for joint evaluations based on the mode of work. Under a classic multipartner arrangement, participation is open to all interested partners, who participate and contribute actively and on equal terms. Under a qualified multipartner arrangement, participation is open only to those who meet certain requirements, such as belonging to a particular group (such as the European Union) or having a strong stake in the issue being evaluated.

Planning for a joint evaluation is critical to its success. According to Breier:

> One of the near-universal lessons learned from recent experience with joint evaluations is that it is imperative to allow sufficient time at the beginning of the process to develop and agree on this framework of common understanding about the proposed evaluation's purpose, objectives, focus and scope. When this is not done with the necessary time and patience, as is the case in a number of the evaluations analyzed, there is a strong chance that the evaluation process will run into difficulties later on. (2005, p. 40)

When a joint evaluation involves only a few agencies, the management structure can be simple:

- Evaluators may decide to meet regularly and to share in all management decisions.
- Evaluators may decide to have all agencies equally involved in the management but to place one or more agencies in a leadership role.
- Evaluators may decide to delegate management responsibility to one agency, allowing the other agencies to review key outputs (OECD 2006).

For larger joint evaluations, the most common management structure is a

> two-tier system, consisting of (a) a broad membership steering committee and (b) a smaller management group that runs the day-to-day business of the evaluation. Within this structure there is significant leeway for deciding whether some agencies will participate as silent partners, at what level of detail the steering committee should be involved in decision making, and how many partners should be on the management group and how much responsibility should be delegated. (OECD 2006, p. 20)

Another option is a flexible or decentralized approach. Each agency may manage discrete subcomponents of the overall evaluation in a sort of jigsaw puzzle fashion. It is also possible to adopt a mixed approach, in which some parts are undertaken jointly and others are undertaken by specific partners (OECD 2006).

Both decentralized and centralized structures have strengths and weaknesses. Decentralizing management of an evaluation by issue makes it easier to delegate or divide responsibilities, resulting in a more efficient management process. Decentralized structures, however, may also create duplication of efforts or cause important issues to be missed. Using a centralized management structure enables each partner to have input on, and influence over, all components of the evaluation process, but it lacks the sense of ownership and urgency that comes with a decentralized strategy. Partners need to consider the pluses and minuses of each structure and then decide which best fits the need of the evaluation.

The DAC identifies the following key areas on which evaluation partners must reach agreement:

- ground rules for managing the evaluation
- terms of reference for the evaluation
- techniques for collecting and analyzing data
- means of selecting the evaluation team (bidding and contracting)
- budgeting, costing, and financing
- reporting findings, including disclosure rules (OECD 2006).

Breier (2005) discusses ways of coping with legal issues for joint evaluation. These issues include the following:

- contractual needs of different partners
- agreed-upon procedures that normally reflect the legal system, the requirements, and the established practice of the agency that is taking the lead on behalf of the group
- lump-sum agreements versus negotiated contracts, including cancellation clauses (for poor performance)
- stipulation to submit progress reports showing that funds are being put to proper use.

Once the formal structure is in place and ground rules established, the leadership of the joint evaluation has to turn to operational and management issues. Freeman (2007) describes 16 rules for organizing and managing an external evaluation team (table 11.1).

Another valuable resource is the DAC's *Guidance for Managing Joint Evaluations*. (A link to the guide's Web site is provided at the end of this chapter.)

**Table 11.1 Selecting, Organizing, and Managing an External Evaluation Team and Reporting Its Results**

| Issue | Rule |
|---|---|
| Selecting the external evaluation team | • Ensure that the core expertise in complex, large-scale evaluations of development cooperation is as solid as possible.<br>• Keep the organization as simple as possible, and, whenever possible, work with organizations you have worked with before.<br>• Integrate national consultants into the international competitive bidding process, and include them in the methodology selection and design.<br>• In multicountry studies, have each field team combine resources from different organizations in the consortia rather than having each organization specialize geographically or institutionally. |
| Managing the external evaluation team | • Make commitment to the evaluation clear at the board level of the main external evaluation organization.<br>• Hold evaluation team workshops to develop a common approach to measurement and reporting.<br>• Wherever possible, create a management group that reports to the overall evaluation steering committee.<br>• Allow sufficient time at steering committee meetings for full discussions and the working out of a common position.<br>• In joint evaluations, ensure that external evaluators operate openly and transparently and directly link methods to evidence gathered to findings, conclusions, and recommendations.<br>• In negotiations for additional resources, when needed, have the evaluation team and the management group begin by agreeing on the division of labor that should be undertaken as a result of the original contract (and using the original resource envelope) and the work that is the result of new issues and interests or arises from unforeseeable circumstances. Doing so will require the team to prepare detailed, costed, and timebound plans for any new work required. |
| Organizing the external management team | • Ensure that the lead organization in the consortium has a strong commitment and track record in the evaluation of international development cooperation. The project should be a natural fit with its core business and markets.<br>• Ensure that stakeholders maintain a strong positive orientation throughout the exercise.<br>• Ensure that the external evaluation team that deals with all members of the steering committee avoids demonstrating institutional bias and behaves as if all were equal.<br>• Invest a substantial proportion of the budget in dissemination and follow-up activities. |
| Reporting the results of the external management team | • Present preliminary findings before presenting the draft report itself.<br>• Have evaluators and steering committee members discuss drafts with an open attitude toward improvements that can be made, while ensuring that evaluators are able and willing to maintain their objective responsibility for evaluation findings and conclusions. |

*Source:* Based on Freeman 2007.

# Country Program Evaluations

Big-picture views often focus on country assistance. A **country program evaluation** (sometimes called country assistance evaluations or country program evaluations) evaluates the entire aid program to a country.

■ **Country program evaluation:** Evaluation of entire aid program to a country

A country program evaluation is largely a normative study that compares what is being done with what was planned. It may seek to

- assess the strategic relevance of the country assistance program relative to the country's needs
- test the implementation of agencywide outcomes to determine whether the intended outcomes were obtained
- identify the successes and failures in different sectors or of different approaches used in the country, and identify the factors contributing to the performance
- identify the effectiveness of the donor's aid to a given country (OECD 1999).

Country assistance evaluations usually focus on the DAC criteria of relevance, efficiency, impact, and sustainability. They can look at donor performance, country performance, or both (box 11.1).

Country program evaluations may face substantial challenges:

- Overall country assistance may lack coherent goals and well-articulated outcomes, instead reflecting an opportunistic approach.
- Similar development interventions may be funded by several sources, making attribution difficult. (Note: co-funding is one issue; donors funding similar interventions is another.)
- There is usually no mapping of in-country assistance, making it difficult to know what others are doing in the area of the intervention.
- As in any evaluation, "[T]here are reputations at stake and fears of the consequences can threaten the morale and commitment of programme and partner staff. Country Program Evaluation, like any evaluation, must proceed with sensitivity." (OECD, 1999, p. 18).

The DAC Network on Development Evaluations proposes the following recommendations:

- A greater proportion of evaluations should be undertaken jointly, with full and active participation of the aid recipients and other partners.
- Developing countries should show greater initiative in taking the lead in planning, coordinating, and scheduling evaluations.
- Developing countries should be supported to build their institutional capacity for initiating and leading joint evaluations.

### Box 11.1 Example of Country Program Evaluation Methodology

Since 1995, the Independent Evaluation Group (IEG) of the World Bank has undertaken more than 70 country program evaluations and developed a clearly articulated methodology (World Bank 2008). The IEG evaluation methodology is a bottom-up and top-down approach. For each of the main objectives, the Country Assistance Evaluation evaluates:

- the relevance of the objective
- the relevance of the Bank's strategy toward meeting the objective, including the balance between lending and nonlending instruments
- the efficacy with which the strategy was implemented
- the results achieved.

The evaluation is conducted in two steps. The first is a top-down review of whether the Bank's program achieved a particular Bank objective or planned outcome and had a substantive impact on the country's development. The second is a bottom-up review of the Bank's products and services (lending, analytical and advisory services, and aid coordination) used to achieve the objectives. Together these two steps test the consistency of findings from the products and services and the development impact dimensions. Subsequently, assessment is made of the relative contribution to the results achieved by the Bank, other donors, the government, and exogenous factors.

When IEG evaluates the expected development impact of an assistance program, it gauges the extent to which the major strategic objectives were relevant and achieved. Typically, programs express their goals using higher-order objectives, such as the Millennium Development Goals (MDGs) and poverty reduction. The Country Assistance Strategy may also establish intermediate goals, such as improved targeting of social services or promotion of integrated rural development. It may also specify how the programs are expected to contribute to achieving the higher-order objective.

The evaluation seeks to validate whether the intermediate objectives produced satisfactory net benefits and whether the results chain specified in the Country Assistance Strategy was valid. Where causal linkages were not specified, the evaluator must try to reconstruct this causal chain from the evidence. The evaluator also needs to assess the relevance, efficacy, and outcome of the intermediate and higher-order objectives.

Evaluators also assess the degree to which clients demonstrate ownership of international development priorities. Examples of such priorities include the MDGs, safeguards for human rights, democratization, gender, and the environment. Ideally, these issues are identified and addressed by the Country Assistance Strategy, allowing the evaluator to focus on whether the approaches adapted for this assistance were appropriate. The strategy may have glossed over certain conflicts or avoided addressing key client development constraints, potentially reducing program relevance and client ownership and increasing unwelcome side effects, such as safeguard violations. All of these factors must be taken into account in judging program outcomes. The important point is that even if the World Bank's projects performed well, if the country did not do well, the assistance could be judged unsatisfactory or vice versa.

- Better coordination and knowledge sharing is needed among the various partners within aid recipient countries. National monitoring and evaluation networks and professional associations need to be built and expanded.
- When a large joint evaluation is undertaken with the participation of several developing countries, the developing countries should be facilitated to meet together to coordinate their views and inputs. (OECD 2005, p. 7).

The Evaluation Cooperation Group of the Multilateral Development Banks has recently published good practice standards for country evaluations. These standards are intended to further harmonize evaluation criteria, processes, and procedures and to make results of evaluations more comparable. A link to a Web site for the 2003 version of these standards can be found at the end of this chapter (Evaluation Cooperation Group 2008).

The country program evaluation should start with a clearly defined terms of reference developed jointly by the country and the development organization to determine exactly what stakeholders expect. The time period to be covered should be specified. The terms of reference should

- clearly state the purpose of the evaluation, the evaluation criteria, and the way in which the findings will be used
- specify the organization's original priorities for the country program (for example, poverty reduction, increased crop production)
- specify reporting, dissemination, and follow-up procedures; full disclosure of findings is ideal.

Because of the difficulty of finding a counterfactual, benchmarking is important in country program evaluations. Comparisons are usually made with similar countries, usually in the same region. As more country program evaluations are publicly disclosed, more cross-organizational comparisons will be feasible. As pointed out in the GPS, the complexity of country evaluations is increasing. In response to the Paris Declaration and Accra Accord, for example, there is need for multipartner evaluations of country assistance to extend beyond that of the MDBs and to include all sources of external assistance, for which the evaluation challenges are significantly greater.

## Sector Program Evaluations

**Sector program evaluations** are evaluations conducted on major program sectors, such as education, health, housing, or transportation. The International Organization for Migration (IOM) Evaluation Guidelines define a sector evaluation as "an evaluation of a variety of aid actions all of which are located in the same sector, either in one country or cross-country. A sec-

■ **Sector program evaluation:** Evaluation conducted on a major program sector, such as education, health, housing, or transportation

tor covers a specific area of activities such as health, industry, education, transport, or agriculture" (IOM 2006, p. 30).

Because sector program evaluations look at many projects with different objectives and different donors, they are more complex than project evaluations; they can be as complex as country program evaluations (or more so, if conducted across countries). As with evaluations of country programs, sector evaluations are generally normative.

It is useful to compare country program evaluations and sector program evaluations at IEG. At the country level, IEG typically conducts a review of the entire portfolio of World Bank Group projects over the relevant time period for the country. In sector evaluations, IEG conducts a portfolio review of all projects in the sector over the relevant period across selected countries. However, in the case of sector reviews, IEG often has definitional issues. If, for example, a project is multisectoral, does IEG include only projects for which the sector of interest was the main sector, or does it also include those for which it was a secondary or tertiary issue? If IEG takes the broader set, does it weight results by the percentage of resources going to that sector as opposed to others? Thus, although both country and sector evaluations include portfolio reviews, the issues can be more complex for sector reviews.

Similar issues can be raised about evaluation design and methods. For the World Bank Group, and increasingly for other lenders and donors, country evaluation methods have become more standardized. By contrast, sector evaluations tend to be more sui generis, with design and methods determined by the specific evaluation questions and the resources available for the study. While most include country case studies, this is not a necessity. Where case studies are used, there are important questions of case selection and methods that have to be resolved.

Ownership and partner responsibility are key issues in sector program evaluations (Danish Ministry of Foreign Affairs 1999). Both development organizations and partner institution are concerned with improving the delivery of aid, accountability, and sustainability in the sector. The brief description of the joint evaluation of Tanzania's health sector highlights these key concerns (box 11.2).

■ **Thematic evaluation:**
Evaluation of selected aspects or themes in a number of development activities

## Thematic Evaluations

**Thematic evaluations** deal with "selected aspects or themes in a number of development activities" (Danish Ministry of Foreign Affairs 1999, p. 30). These themes emerge from policy statements. The development

### Box 11.2 Joint External Evaluation of Tanzania's Health Sector, 1999–2006

During the 1990s, Tanzania's health sector faced a period of stagnation. Local health services were characterized by severe shortages of essential drugs, equipment, and supplies, as well as deteriorating infrastructure, poor management, lack of supervision, and lack of staff motivation. The sector faced stagnating or deteriorating hospital care. There was little cooperation in health service delivery between the public sector, faith-based organizations, and private service providers. Health services were severely underfunded, with public health sector spending at US$3.46 per capita. There was also little evidence of coordination of support to the health sector by development partners.

The government of Tanzania and its development partners (Belgium, Canada, Denmark, Germany, the Netherlands, and Switzerland) responded to this situation in a process beginning with a joint planning mission convened by the government mid-decade. By 1999, this process resulted in the first major health sector strategic plan, the Health Sector Program of Work (POW), and an agreement that support to the health sector would take place in the framework of a sectorwide approach (SWAp). The POW and subsequent Health Sector Strategic Plan 2 (HSSP2) articulated a process of health sector reform aimed at addressing the evident deficiencies in the sector and achieving specific goals and targets in health as set out in the Millennium Development Goals (MDGs) and the National Strategy for Growth and Reduction of Poverty (NSGRP)/MKUKUTA).

The POW and HSSP2 identified several priority areas of strategic intervention:

- strengthening district health services and reforming and strengthening regional and national referral hospitals
- transforming the role of the central Ministry of Health and Social Welfare into a facilitative policy organization
- improving central support systems (including infrastructure, health management information systems, drug supplies, transport, and communications and information technology)
- adopting and implementing a national strategy for combating HIV/AIDS as an explicit element of the HSSP2
- improving government and development partner relations to improve harmonization and alignment of external and Tanzanian resources in a more effective partnership.

*continued*

**Box 11.2** *continued*

The evaluation focused on four areas:

- the relevance of health sector strategic and implementation plans to achievement of the MDGs in health and to the NSGRP health sector goals and targets and the appropriateness and relevance of external support
- the extent of progress and achievements under each of the nine strategic priorities of the health sector reform process
- achievements in improving access, service quality, and health outcomes during the evaluation period
- changes in partnership during the evaluation period, including the evolution of efforts at harmonization and alignment and the use of different aid modalities.

The evaluation was conducted from December 2006 to September 2007 by a team of eight international health and evaluation consultants, three of whom were nationals of Uganda and Malawi. The main methodologies used included the following:

- an extensive document review
- key informant interviews at the national level
- district self-assessments carried out by Ministry of Health and Social Welfare staff in 16 districts in Tanzania
- in-depth case studies in six districts (including discussions with community members) carried out by the evaluation team
- analysis of financial and other resource flows to the health sector at the national, regional, and council levels
- a review of national health outcomes data.

Evaluation information from all the methodologies used was tested and triangulated to identify similarities and strengthen the validity of findings and conclusions.

*Source:* Danish Ministry of Foreign Affairs 2007.

organization may decide, for example, that all projects or programs will address a specific issue or issues—gender, environmental and social sustainability, or poverty alleviation. Each of these issues must be addressed at all stages of the project or program and for all forms of aid.

As with country and sector evaluations, the approach to thematic evaluations is bottom up and top down. Themes are evaluated on a project by project basis; the information in these evaluations provides a wealth of information for thematic evaluations. In addition, thematic evaluations go beyond the project level to look across all projects; they also generally select countries for in-depth study (case studies). A thematic evaluation looks at many different kinds of information (box 11.3). It then extracts aggregate information from these sources.

One of the key findings of the thematic evaluation on child scavenging was the role of gender: most of the children involved were girls, and almost all of the adults involved were women. This study distinguished itself by the sensitivity it demonstrated to gender-related issues.

---

**Box 11.3  Example of Thematic Evaluation of Assessment of Child Scavenging in Africa, Asia, and Europe**

WASTE is an organization that works toward sustainable improvement in the living conditions of the urban poor and the urban environment in general. The International Labour Organisation (ILO) contracted it to carry out a thematic evaluation of child labor in waste picking. The purpose of the evaluation was to provide guidance to the ILO on how best to address the exploitation of children in this sector.

The thematic evaluation identified and critically assessed scavenging and various approaches to addressing the problem of child labor in relation to waste picking. The information was drawn from the various projects carried out in this sector by the International Programme on the Elimination of Child Labour as well as from similar efforts by other agencies, institutions, or governments. The evaluation resulted in a strategic assessment and recommendations for the ILO. (The evaluation, *Addressing the Exploitation of Children in Scavenging (Waste Picking): A Thematic Action Agenda on Child Labour,* can be downloaded from the ILO Web site.)

WASTE field researchers in Egypt, India, Romania, Tanzania, and Thailand wrote additional reports based on their key findings. In Tanzania, for example, the report included review of relevant documents, interviews with project management and staff, interviews with other stakeholders, a field visit to two transfer points in the city and the main dump site in Dar es Salaam, and interviews with waste pickers and representatives from an association of waste pickers.

*Source:* Duursma 2004; WASTE 2005.

---

The distinguishing characteristics of a gender-responsive approach are

- a conceptual framework that recognizes the gendered nature of development and the contribution of gender equity to economic and social development
- the creation of a gender data base at the national, sectoral, or local level that synthesizes gender-relevant data and identifies the key gender issues to be addressed in the design and thematic evaluation of projects.

The lack of gender-disaggregated data is often used to justify the lack of attention to gender. Where data are not disaggregated by gender, it is important to define strategies for developing the appropriate data bases to make it possible to conduct better gender analysis in the future. Such strategies include the following:

- ensuring that data collection methods generate information on both women and men and that key gender issues (such as the gender division of labor, time-use analysis, control of resources, and decision making at the household and community levels) are incorporated into the research design
- ensuring that information is collected about, and from, different household members and that the "household head" (usually defined as a male) is not the only source of information
- complementing conventional data collection methods with gender-inclusive methods where appropriate
- ensuring that the research team includes a balance between men and women
- ensuring that stakeholders are consulted during the design, analysis, and dissemination of the evaluation and that consultations include groups representing both men and women (World Bank 2007e).

Development planning and evaluation frequently use "gender neutral" approaches, which assume that men and women have the same development needs. In most societies, men tend to dominate community and household decision making, so that "gender-neutral" approaches respond largely to male priorities. Ignoring women's needs and capacities will significantly reduce the efficiency and equity of policies and programs. The way in which many development planning and evaluation tools are applied is not gender responsive, so that even when community consultations or household surveys are intended to capture the views of all sectors of the community, women's concerns are often not fully captured.

# Evaluation of Global and Regional Partnership Programs

**Global and Regional Partnership Programs (GRPPs)** are an increasingly important modality for channeling and delivering development assistance to address pressing global or regional issues. Most GRPPs are specific to a sector or theme, such as agriculture, environment, health, finance, or international trade.

GRPPs are programmatic partnerships in which

- partners contribute and pool (financial, technical, staff, and reputational) resources in order to achieve agreed-upon objectives over time
- the activities of the program are global, regional, or multicountry in scope
- partners establish a new organization with a governance structure and management unit to deliver these activities (World Bank 2007f).

A new GRPP is usually established after a group of global or regional actors identifies a problem or opportunity that requires public action but that crosses national sovereign boundaries. The actors may be donors or recipients and may come from the public or private sector.

Consider the example of water resource management in the Mekong or Nile River basins. Issues or opportunities cannot be addressed effectively solely at a single-country level, because many countries—6 in the Mekong basin, 19 in the Nile basin—are involved in basin management. Moreover, substantial economies result from collective action at the global or regional level (generation of new technologies or good practices relevant to development in many countries).

GRPPs often focus on production or preservation of global public goods (for example, research that yields improved seed technology or increases biodiversity) or reduction of global public problems (for example, HIV/AIDS, or pollution). Global public goods are goods that are nonrival (provision to one person or country does not decrease supply to another) and nonexcludable (once provided to one person or country, all benefit) and whose benefits extend beyond national boundaries.

Partners to GRPPs usually have differing perspectives and incentives. A formal governance structure is set up that sets out formal objectives, criteria on membership or participation, decision-making procedures, and sometimes allocation criteria.

About 150 multipartner GRPPs have been established. The level of disbursements ranges from a few million dollars to more than US$1 billion a

■ **Global and Regional Partnership Program (GRPP):** Programmatic partnership in which partners contribute and pool resources to achieve agreed-upon objectives that are global, regional, or multicountry in scope

year. Their activities may be limited to knowledge sharing and networking, or they may also encompass technical assistance, investment, and market/ trade activity. Examples of GRPPs include the Consultative Group for International Agricultural Research, the West Africa HIV/AIDS and Transport Program, the Global Water Partnership, the Integrated Framework for Trade, and the Medicines for Malaria Venture.

Features of GRPPs that make them complex to evaluate include the following:

- The nature of the programs as partnerships has two implications. First, the differing perspectives of different partners may need to be taken into account. Second, the effectiveness of the governance structure itself needs to be evaluated, both on intrinsic criteria related to good practice in partnership and in terms of its contributions to program results (positive or negative).
- Unlike projects, GRPPs do not have a fixed timeframe in which to achieve objectives. Indeed, objectives and strategies often evolve as funding increases (or decreases), the donor or partnership composition changes, or external conditions change.
- Costs are incurred and benefits accrued at different levels (local, country, and global). An evaluation of effectiveness needs to consider the contributions of and interdependence across different levels; this makes the construction of the results chain complex and poses a results aggregation problem.
- The global and regional public good dimension of GRPPs means that there is a divergence between the costs and benefits captured at the national and global levels. This makes evaluation of cost-effectiveness complex and assessment of the effectiveness of global-country coordination and linkages essential.
- Because of the open-ended and longer timeframe, evaluators are often asked to consider progress toward complex medium-term strategic goals, such as resource mobilization aimed at scaling up, devolution to local implementers, independence from host agency, closure or exit, or changed patterns of collaboration with new emerging global programs.

Given the growing participation of the World Bank Group in GRPPs and their increasing importance in achieving global sustainable development results, in 2006 the World Bank's Independent Evaluation Group (IEG) launched two new activities to support continued examination and improvement of their performance. First, in response to a request from the OECD/ DAC Evaluation Network (supported by the United Nations Evaluation Group [UNEG] and Multilateral Development Bank Evaluation Cooperation

Group), IEG led an effort to develop consensus principles and standards for evaluating GRPPs. The first product of this work was the *Sourcebook for Evaluating Global and Regional Partnership Programs* (World Bank 2007f). Work is ongoing on research that will contribute to publication of an accompanying report giving more detailed guidelines and examples.

Second, IEG began reviewing independent evaluations of GRPPs in which the Bank is involved in order to assess the quality of the evaluation and give feedback, provide an independent assessment of the findings and recommendations, and assess the performance of the Bank as partner. Seven of these global program reviews have been released to the public, and lessons are emerging.

The evaluation and global program review of the Medicines for Malaria Venture (MMV) is an example of such a review. Established in 1999, MMV seeks to reduce the burden of malaria in disease-endemic countries by discovering, developing, and delivering new affordable antimalarial drugs through effective public-private partnerships. Cumulative contributions were US$151 million through 2006. The Secretariat of the program, which is organized as an independent nonprofit organization under Swiss law, is in Geneva, and there is a satellite office in New Delhi. MMV's board of directors consists of 11 distinguished individuals from industry, academia, the World Health Organization, and the Bill & Melinda Gates Foundation, which provides 60 percent of its funding.

MMV's donors commissioned an external evaluation in 2005. The board cooperated with the evaluation, although it did not commission it. The evaluation was carried out by a four-person team, led by a distinguished African public health professor.

The terms of reference called for use of the standard evaluation criteria, with the evaluation questions drilling down to more detail on aspects specific to GRPPs in general and the nature of the activities funded by MMV in particular. The following discussion illustrates how such criteria are applied in complex GRPP evaluations:

*Relevance.* Questions were posed regarding the relevance of the objectives of the program: was there an international consensus on the problem being resolved and the need for the program to address it? The evaluation pointed out the relevance of the program to achieving the MDG of preventing the spread of communicable diseases, which is also a global public good. The evaluation's assessment of relevance also applied the subsidiarity principle criterion, which states that programs should be implemented at the most local level possible. The evaluation asked, does the program provide services that cannot be provided at the country or local level? Because of the global public good being addressed, the evaluation concluded that the program met the subsidiarity principle.

The evaluation considered MMV's value added relative to other sources of supply and services (considering both other programs dealing with malaria and purely private sector drug development programs). It also assessed the relevance of the objectives of the program to beneficiaries' needs. The program was judged relevant by this criterion, because it addresses not only drug development but also delivery and access issues.

The evaluation also asked the following questions: Is the program strategy and design relevant? Was the choice of interventions relevant and appropriate? What was the geographical scope and reach? How were public–private partnerships used? Would an alternative design to guide program strategy have been more relevant?

*Efficacy (achievement of objectives).* The evaluation examined both outputs and outcomes achieved, relative to expectations, as well as the factors that helped or hindered the achievement of objectives. This aspect of the evaluation was highly dependent on the quality of the monitoring and evaluation (M&E) framework and data collection. The contributions of the following factors were assessed:

- stakeholder involvement
- effectiveness of portfolio management
- effectiveness of public–private partnership management
- use of a scientific approach
- effectiveness of key approaches to product
- unintended outcomes.

*Efficiency.* Though not called for explicitly as a separate criterion in the terms of reference, the evaluators recognized the important of considering opportunity costs of more efficient means of delivering services. They analyzed the costs of management and administration relative to program expenditures and trends over time and compared them to benchmarks such as the cost of development of drugs for other diseases and the costs of a typical product development process in a large private pharmaceutical company.

*Governance.* The evaluation assessed the legitimacy of MMV governance by looking at the representation of endemic countries on the governing body; the use of scientific expertise, such as that of researchers from the World Health Organization and endemic countries; evidence of confidence of the partners in successful resource mobilization campaigns; and reactions to evaluations. The evaluation also assessed the effectiveness of governance in performing the following important functions:

- setting strategy (how well did the governance structure inform deliberations on the new direction of addressing drug access at the country level?)
- collaboration with other agencies with similar mandates (the evaluation recommended more attention to this aspect)
- resource mobilization (the evaluation recommended acting more proactively to raise needed resources and diversify donor support).

*Sustainability/medium-term strategic questions.* The evaluation examined whether the benefits of the program were likely to be sustained under current conditions, addressing sustainability in terms of both financing needs and sustained advocacy and support of objectives. It also assessed whether changes could be made to make conditions more favorable for sustainability. (Should the scale of the program be changed? Could relationships with other organizations be made more effective? Should alternative organizational or governance arrangement be considered?) The evaluation also addressed improvement of M&E. The terms of references called for the evaluators to test a template proposed by donors for assessing the effectiveness of public–private partnerships. In addition, the evaluators made recommendations on improving monitoring to support future monitoring and evaluation initiatives. The methodology of the evaluation involved a review of documents about the program, extensive interviews with stakeholders at both the program and activity levels, observation of a scientific advisory committee meeting, and in-country site visits.

The Global Program Review assessed the independence and quality of the evaluation. It considered who commissioned the evaluation and how the evaluation was managed, in order to judge the degree of independence. It examined whether the evaluation covered all aspects of work, in accordance with the terms of reference. And it looked at the quality of the evaluation and its ultimate impact (the degree to which program management implemented the recommendations). The review provided an independent assessment of the findings of the evaluations. It confirmed that it provided a sound basis for follow-up actions by program management and the Bank.

The Global Program Review assessed the World Bank's performance as a partner, considering its use of convening power to help establish the program; its subsequent financial support, which was initially important but shrank over time relative to other donors; and the Bank's participation in deliberations of the governing bodies and committees. It identified issues concerning the Bank's role in the program that it deemed likely to arise in the future. The review summarized lessons from the evaluation and the review, including those for the program itself (the need to establish an appropriate monitoring and evaluation framework), those applicable to other GRPPs (the need for effective coordination and consultation with other key players at the global and country level), and those applicable to other aid instruments (lessons for projects that rely on public–private partnerships to deliver services).

## Summary

Recently, evaluators have been attempting to investigate the effects of many interventions with a conceptual focus on a sector, a country, or a theme. These approaches are trying to determine how interventions are affecting a larger picture. The more complex approaches look at multiple projects, programs, or policies to identify interactions and ways to share resources. Such evaluations include joint evaluations, country program evaluations, sector program evaluations, thematic evaluations, and global or regional partnership program evaluations.

# References and Further Reading

ADB (Asian Development Bank). 2006a. *Indonesia: Capacity Building Project in the Water Resources Sector.* Project Performance Evaluation Report for Indonesia. http://www.adb.org/Documents/PPERs/INO/26190-INO-PPER.pdf.

———. 2006b. *Private Sector Development and Operations: Harnessing Synergies with the Public Sector.* http://www.oecd.org/dataoecd/6/59/39519572.pdf.

AfDB (African Development Bank). 2005. *Morocco: Evaluation of Bank Assistance to the Education Sector.* http://www.oecd.org/dataoecd/36/19/37968449.pdf.

Bamberger, Michael. 2005. *IPDET Handbook for Evaluating Gender Impacts of Development Policies and Programs.* International Program for Development Evaluation Training, Ottawa.

Bamberger, Michael, Mark Blackden, Lucia Fort, and Violeta Manoukian. 2001. "Integrating Gender into Poverty Reduction Strategies." In *The PRSP Sourcebook.* 335–74. Washington, DC: World Bank. http://povlibrary.worldbank.org/files/4221_chap10.pdf.

Breier, Horst. 2005. *Joint Evaluations: Recent Experiences, Lessons Learned and Options for the Future.* Draft report to the Development Assistance Committee Network on Development Evaluation, Organisation for Economic Co-operation and Development, Paris.

Chen, Jhaoying, and Hans Slot. 2007. "Country-Led Joint Evaluation: Dutch ORET/ MILIEV Programme in China." Presentation at the sixth meeting of the Development Assistance Committee Network on Development Evaluation, Paris, June. http://www.oecd.org/dataoecd/63/28/38851957.ppt.

Compton, Donald W., M. Baizerman, and S. H. Stockdill, eds. 2002. *The Art, Craft, and Science of Evaluation Capacity Building.* New Directions for Evaluation 93 (Spring) (publication of the American Evaluation Association).

Danish Ministry of Foreign Affairs. 1999. *Evaluation Guidelines.* 2nd ed. Copenhagen. http://www.um.dk/NR/rdonlyres/4C9ECE88-D0DA-4999-9893-371CB351C 04F/0/Evaluation_Guidelines_1999_revised.pdf.

———. 2006. *Evaluation Guidelines.* Copenhagen.

———. 2007. *Joint External Evaluation: The Health Sector in Tanzania 1999–2006.* http://www.oecd.org/dataoecd/53/46/39837890.pdf.

Duursma, M. 2004. *Child Labour in Scavenging, Tanzania, Dar es Salaam.* Updated August 16, 2005. http://www.waste.nl/page/724.

"Evaluation of the Implementation of the Paris Declaration. Synthesis Report.: 2008, 26.

Freeman, Ted. 2007. "Joint Evaluations." International Program for Development Evaluation Training (IPDET) presentation, Ottawa, June–July.

Fullan, M. 1993. *Change Forces.* London: Falmer Press.

GTZ (Gesellschaft für Technische Zusammenarbeit). 2004. *National Monitoring of Sustainable Poverty Reduction Strategy Papers PRSPs.* Eschborn, Germany.

http://siteresources.worldbank.org/INTISPMA/Resources/Training-Events-and-Materials/summary_MainReport.pdf.

Heath, John, Patrick Grasso, and John Johnson. 2005. *World Bank Country, Sector, and Project Evaluation Approaches.* International Program for Development Evaluation Training (IPDET) presentation, Ottawa, July.

House, Ernest R. *Guiding Principles for Evaluators.* 1995. New Directions for Program Evaluation No. 66. San Francisco: Jossey-Bass.

IOM (International Organization for Migration). 2006. *IOM Evaluation Guidelines.* Office of the Inspector General. http://www.iom.int/jahia/webdav/site/myjahiasite/shared/shared/mainsite/about_iom/eva_techref/Evaluation_Guidelines_2006_1.pdf.

Johnson, John. 2007. "Confronting the Challenges of Country Assistance Evaluation." International Program for Development Evaluation Training (IPDET) presentation, Carleton University, Ottawa, June 26–27.

Kusek, Jody Zall, and Ray C. Rist. 2004. *Ten Steps to a Results-Based Monitoring and Evaluation System.* World Bank, Washington, DC. http://www.oecd.org/dataoecd/23/27/35281194.pdf.

Mackay, Keith. 1999. *Evaluation Capacity Development: a Diagnostic Guide and Action Framework.* ECD Working Paper 6 (January), World Washington, DC. http://lnweb18.worldbank.org/oed/oeddoclib.nsf/a4dd58e444f7c611852568080 06a0008/7f2c924e183380c5852567fc00556470?OpenDocument.

———. 2006. *Institutionalization of Monitoring and Evaluation Systems to Improve Public Sector Management.* World Bank, Independent Evaluation Group, Washington, DC. http://siteresources.worldbank.org/INTISPMA/Resources/ecd_15.pdf.

———. 2007. *How to Build M&E Systems to Support Better Government.* World Bank, Washington, DC. http://www.worldbank.org/ieg/ecd/docs/How_to_build_ME_gov.pdf.

Mertens, D. M. 1994. "Training Evaluators: Unique Skills and Knowledge." *New Directions for Program Evaluation* 62: 17–27.

MLB (Multilateral Development Bank), EC (Evaluation Cooperative Group), and WGEC (Working Group on Evaluation Criteria and Ratings for Public Sector Evaluation). 2003. *Good Practice Standards for Evaluation of MDB Supported Public Sector Operations.* http://www.ifc.org/ifcext/oeg.nsf/AttachmentsByTitle/MDB-ECG/US$FILE/MDB-ECG_Good-Practice.pdf.

OECD (Organisation for Economic Co-operation and Development). 1999. "Evaluating Country Programmes," Development Assistance Committee, Vienna Workshop, March 11–12. http://www.oecd.org/dataoecd/41/58/35340748.pdf.

———. 2002. *OECD Glossary of Key Terms in Evaluation and Results Based Management.* Development Assistance Committee, Paris.

———. 2005. Workshop on "Challenging the Conventional Wisdom: The View from Developing Country Partners," Network on Development Evaluations, Development Assistance Committee, Nairobi, April 20–21. http://www.oecd.org/dataoecd/20/44/34981186.pdf.

———. 2006. *DAC Evaluation Series: Guidance for Managing Joint Evaluations.* Development Assistance Committee, Paris. http://www.oecd.org/dataoecd/29/28/37512030.pdf.

Porteous, Nancy L., Barbara J. Sheldrick, and Paula J. Stewart. 1999. "Enhancing Managers' Evaluation Capacity: A Case Study for Ontario Public Heath." *Canadian Journal of Program Evaluation.* Special Issue: 137–54. http://www.phac-aspc.gc.ca/php-psp/pdf/toolkit/enhancing_managers_evaluation%20_capacity%20_CJPE_1999.pdf.

UNFPA (United Nations Population Fund). 2005. *State of World Population 2005.* http://www.unfpa.org/swp/2005/english/notes/index.htm.

WASTE. 2005. *Thematic Evaluation on Child Labour in Scavenging Africa, Asia, and Europe Assessment.* Gouda, the Netherlands. http://www.waste.nl/page/720.

World Bank. 2001a. *Design Paper for a Multipartner Evaluation of the Comprehensive Development Framework.* Comprehensive Development Framework Secretariat, Washington, DC. http://www.worldbank.org/evaluation/cdf/cdf_evaluation_design_paper.pdf.

———. 2001b. *Engendering Development—through Gender Equality in Rights, Resources and Voice.* Washington, DC: World Bank.

———. 2001c. *The PRSP Sourcebook.* http://web.worldbank.org/WBSITE/EXTERNAL/TOPICS/EXTPOVERTY/EXTPRS/0,,menuPK:384207~pagePK:149018~piPK:149093~theSitePK:384201,00.html.

———. 2005. *Evaluation of World Bank's Assistance to Primary Education.* Operations Evaluation Department, Washington, DC. http://www.worldbank.org/oed/education/evaluation_design.html.

———. 2007a. *Country Assistance Evaluation: CAE Retrospective.* Independent Evaluation Group, Washington, DC. http://www.worldbank.org/ieg/countries/cae/featured/cae_retrospective.html.

———.2007b. *Global Program Review: Medicines for Malaria Venture.* Independent Evaluation Group, Washington, DC. http://lnweb18.worldbank.org/oed/oeddoclib.nsf/24cc3bb1f94ae11c85256808006a0046/d591aea3bbb897de852573130077a0cb?OpenDocument.

———. 2007c. *Impact Evaluations: Bangladesh Maternal and Child Health.* Independent Evaluation Group, Washington, DC. http://www.worldbank.org/oed/ie/bangladesh_ie.html.

———. 2007d. *Poverty Monitoring Systems.* http://web.worldbank.org/WBSITE/EXTERNAL/TOPICS/EXTPOVERTY/EXTPAME/0,,contentMDK:20203848~menuPK:435494~pagePK:148956~piPK:216618~theSitePK:384263,00.html.

———. 2007e. *PRSP Sourcebook.* Washington, DC. http://web.worldbank.org/WBSITE/EXTERNAL/TOPICS/EXTPOVERTY/EXTPRS/0,,contentMDK:20175742~pagePK:210058~piPK:210062~theSitePK:384201,00.html.

———. 2007f. *Sourcebook for Evaluating Global and Regional Partnership Programs: Indicative Principles and Standards.* Independent Evaluation Group, Washington, DC.
http://siteresources.worldbank.org/EXTGLOREGPARPRO/Resources/source-book.pdf.

———. 2008. *CAE Methodology.* Independent Evaluation Group, Washington, DC.
http://web.worldbank.org/WBSITE/EXTERNAL/EXTOED/EXTCOUASSEVA/
0,,contentMDK:21107046~menuPK:3098030~pagePK:64168445~piPK:64168309
~theSitePK:2832047,00.html.

## Web Sites

International Labour Organization. http://www.ilo.org.

Stufflebeam, D. L. 1999. *Evaluation Plans and Operations Checklist.* http://www
.wmich.edu/evalctr/checklists/plans_operations.htm.

———. 2001. *Guiding Principles Checklist.* http://www.wmich.edu/evalctr/checklists/
guiding_principles.pdf.

World Bank. *ADePT: Stata Software Platform for Automated Economic Analysis.*
http://econ.worldbank.org/programs/poverty/adept.

———. *Core Welfare Indicators Questionnaire (CWIQ).* http://www4.worldbank.org/
afr/stats/cwiq.cfm.

———. *Global and Regional Partnership Programs.* http://www.worldbank.org/ieg/
grpp.

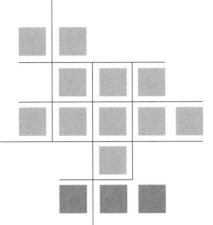

# LEADING

*"Action should culminate in wisdom."*

—BHAGAVAD GITA

**Chapter 14: Guiding the Evaluator: Evaluation Ethics, Politics, Standards, and Guiding Principles**

- Ethical Behavior
- Politics and Evaluation
- Evaluation Standards and Guiding Principles

**CHAPTER 12**

# Managing an Evaluation

Evaluations can be complicated undertakings; keeping everyone on task, meeting deadlines, and performing high-quality work can be challenging. This chapter discusses ways evaluators can plan, manage, meet quality standards, and share results so that their evaluations are used by policy makers to effect change.

**This chapter has four main parts:**

- Managing the Design Matrix
- Contracting the Evaluation
- Roles and Responsibilities of Different Players
- Managing People, Tasks, and Budgets

## Managing the Design Matrix

The key to successful development evaluations is planning. If the evaluation is poorly planned, no amount of later analysis—no matter how sophisticated it is—will save it. According to a Chinese adage, even a thousand-mile journey must begin with the first step. The likelihood of reaching one's destination is much enhanced if the first step and subsequent steps take the traveller in the right direction. Wandering about without a clear sense of purpose or direction consumes time, energy, and resources—not only of the traveler, but also of the evaluator. It also diminishes the possibility that one will ever arrive. It is, therefore, wise to be prepared for a journey by collecting the necessary maps; studying alternative routes; and making informed estimates of the time, costs, and hazards one is likely to confront.

As shown in earlier chapters, the evaluation design matrix is a visual way of mapping out an evaluation. It focuses on each of the major components in designing an evaluation. The matrix template is not cast in stone; it can be adapted to best suit the needs of the evaluation. Like any plan, it will likely go through an iterative process of updates and revisions. As new information is acquired, revisions will be needed to some ideas and approaches.

A good evaluation design matrix is not all that is needed to conduct a good evaluation. The best designs may result in a low-quality evaluation if, for example, people without the needed skills try to implement it, the evaluation is delivered too late to affect a critical decision, or the budget runs out during data collection.

## Contracting the Evaluation

The evaluation manager is responsible for identifying and remedying skill gaps in the staff available to conduct an evaluation. Staff with evaluation skills may be in short supply and high demand. For this reason, development evaluations are often contracted out to consulting firms or individual consultants. Some institutions, such as the European Union, contract out most or all of their evaluations to specialists. To ensure that their objectivity is not compromised, consultants should have no previous involvement with the program being evaluated.

Using contractors has advantages and disadvantages. Advantages include the fact that the contractor may have in-depth knowledge of the sector and type of program being evaluated; speak the local language and have local knowledge; and, if a competitive process was used, be the most cost-effective evaluator available. Disadvantages include the fact that contracting is expensive (the tender process can cost more than the contract itself) and means that in-house capacity is not increased.

## Requests for Proposals

The process of hiring a consulting firm, and sometimes individual consultants, generally begins by developing a **request for proposals** (RFP). Depending on the organization and contract rules and procedures, the contract may be awarded on a sole-source basis, from invitations to a few contractors to bid, or from open competition. The winning proposal may be selected by the evaluation manager or by an appointed panel that makes its recommendation based on prespecified criteria.

■ **Request for proposal:**
Invitation to bid on a project

Hawkins (2005) suggests that the RFP include the following items:

- purposes of the evaluation
- background and context for the study
- key information requirements
- evaluation objectives
- deliverables required
- time frame
- criteria for tender selection
- contract details for the project manager
- deadline for proposals
- budget and other resources.

Selection of the winning proposal should be done by a panel of people with evaluation knowledge and experience, knowledge of the program area, knowledge of the culture, and ownership of the findings and their uses. This panel should select the proposal using the criteria in the RFP. Good records should be kept concerning the selection process.

Hawkins advises using the following criteria for selecting a consultant:

- Has the RFP been adequately addressed?
- Is there a detailed explanation of how the evaluation will be implemented?
- What communication and reporting strategy is being proposed?
- Is there evidence of competence? What is the record of accomplishment?
- What is the cost? Is it specified in detail?

Once a contractor is hired, the evaluation manager still has responsibilities toward the contractor and the evaluation. These include the following

- keeping goals and objectives clear
- maintaining ownership of the study
- monitoring the work and providing timely feedback
- making decisions—in good time
- being open to negotiation with the contractor if changes to the contract are required.

### Terms of Reference

**Terms of reference (TOR):** Statement of the background, objectives, and purpose of an evaluation; the individual duties and responsibilities of members of an evaluation team; and timelines for deliverables

The **terms of reference** (TOR) is a statement of the background, objectives, and purpose of an evaluation; individual duties and responsibilities of members of an evaluation team; and timelines for deliverables. A TOR usually describes the overall evaluation and establishes the initial agreements. It may be an agreement between a client and an evaluation manager, an evaluation manager and a contractor, or an evaluation manager and the evaluation staff. All members of the evaluation team should have a clear, written understanding of their specific responsibilities for the evaluation, usually written as TORs.

The TOR should realistically define what needs to be accomplished in a defined period of time.

The TOR may include the design matrix, or development of the design matrix may be one of the first deliverables. It may also reflect agreements on ethics and standards in conducting and reporting the evaluation (see chapter 14 for a discussion of ethics and standards).

The process for developing the overall TOR can be useful in ensuring that stakeholders are included in the discussion and in decision making about what evaluation issues will be addressed. The TOR establishes the basic guidelines, so that everyone involved understands the expectations for the evaluation (box 12.1).

According to the *Glossary of Key Terms in Evaluation and Results-Based Management* (OECD 2002), a TOR for an evaluation is a written documentation that presents

- the purpose and scope of the evaluation
- the methods to be used
- the standard against which performance is to be assessed or analyses are to be conducted
- the resources and time allocated
- reporting requirements.

**Box 12.1    Tips for Writing Terms of Reference for an Evaluation**

The following tips can be useful in writing the TOR for an evaluation:

- State clearly the objectives of the evaluation and identify the following:
  - the general issues and preliminary evaluation questions to be addressed
  - key stakeholders and their expected uses of the evaluation
  - the overall evaluation approach to be adopted
  - the products expected from the evaluation, when each needs to be submitted, and how each will be used
  - the expertise required from members of the evaluation team
  - logistical arrangements.
- Do not simply state the objectives in technical or process terms. Be clear on how the evaluation is expected to help the organization.
- Focus on preliminary questions to be addressed.
- Avoid choosing too many questions. It is better to have an evaluation examine a few issues in depth than to look into a broad range of issues superficially.

*Source:* Adapted from UNDP 2006.

The TOR typically includes the following:

- a short and descriptive title
- a description of the project or program
- the reasons for and expectations of the evaluation
- a statement of the scope and focus of the evaluation (issues to be addressed, questions to be answered)
- identification of stakeholder involvement (who will be involved, who will do what, accountability process)
- a description of the evaluation process (what will be done)
- a list of deliverables (an evaluation work plan, interim report, final report, presentations)
- identification of necessary qualifications (education, experience, skills, abilities required)
- cost projection, based on activities, time, number of people, professional fees, travel, and any other costs.

The TOR is written in addition to, not in lieu of, the evaluation design matrix. The TOR focuses on responsibilities. The design matrix is a plan for conducting the evaluation.

## Roles and Responsibilities of Different Players

Many people work on an evaluation. They have different capacities and fill different roles and responsibilities. The key roles are those of the client (requestor), stakeholders, evaluation manager, and evaluator (contract or staff). People engaged in limited roles include data analysts, advisors, peer reviewers, and data collectors. The roles and responsibilities of everyone involved in the evaluation need to be clearly defined and agreed to.

### The Main Client

An evaluation may have many stakeholders, but it usually has just one main client who requests and usually funds the evaluation. The specific issues the client wants to have addressed, the client's planned use of the evaluation, and the corresponding timing implications generally frame the evaluation.

Evaluators are encouraged to meet early with the client to discuss the following issues:

- the nature and context of the request
- the need, issue, or interest leading to the evaluation request
- critical timing needs for the evaluation findings
- questions of major importance for the evaluation to address
- the communication schedule and frequency.

Scriven's (2007) Key Evaluation Checklist describes the importance of meeting with the client before beginning the evaluation to identify the details of the request as the client sees them or to encourage the client to clarify thinking on details. Scriven suggests asking questions such as the following:

- Exactly what should be evaluated?
- How much context should be included?
- Is the evaluator evaluating the effects of the program as a whole or the contribution of each of its components? Is he or she evaluating the client's theory of how the components work?
- Should the evaluation consider impact in all relevant respects or just some respects?
- Is the evaluation to be formative, summative, and/or descriptive?

As discussed in chapter 4, the evaluation team manages its relationship with the main client in part by developing a communication plan.

A communication plan helps evaluators work with the client, as well as with key stakeholders, the media, and the public. It defines the why, what, where, and how for giving and receiving information. It establishes a plan for communicating, which usually involves different media for different audiences. Establishing a communication plan is especially important if the evaluation involves sensitive information.

Evaluators often think of communication as something that happens at the end of the process, when a report has been produced. In fact, communication and development of a communication strategy need to be addressed up front and refined throughout the process. Communication should be used to build support for the evaluation, improve the evaluation and its methodology, help obtain buy-in, and promote the use of the findings.

## Stakeholders

As defined in chapter 4, stakeholders are the people and organizations other than the client with stakes in the intervention. Typically, they are those who are affected by an intervention, either during its lifetime or in subsequent years.

Stakeholders may be internal or external to the organization. Their roles in an evaluation may range from identifying issues and questions for the evaluation to providing data.

In participatory evaluations, stakeholders can take on responsibilities at various levels for the evaluation. Such evaluations may include selected stakeholders as part of the evaluation team, involving them in question development, data collection, and analysis. Stakeholders are more likely to support the evaluation and to act on results and recommendations if they are involved in the evaluation process. (For a discussion of participatory evaluations, see chapter 5.)

It can be beneficial to engage critics of the project, program, or policy being evaluated in the evaluation. To the extent that they identify issues that are important for the evaluation to address (and could actually discredit the evaluation if not addressed), participation of critics strengthens the evaluation process (CDC 2001).

The World Bank's *Participation Sourcebook* provides useful guidance on involving stakeholders that is particularly relevant for participatory evaluations (World Bank 1996). Once stakeholders have been identified, their participation needs to be enlisted. Evaluators have sought to work with stakeholders through a variety of approaches. Special measures are often needed to ensure that groups that are normally excluded from the decision-making process have a voice. To achieve this, evaluators have to first organize the "voiceless," arrange for their representation, hold participatory sessions with them, and use techniques that allow stakeholders at all levels to be heard.

To many stakeholders, an outsider bringing offers of "participatory evaluation" may seem suspect. Experience with public agencies, public servants, and donor projects may have created negative impressions that need to be rectified. Trust can be built by sharing information, working through intermediaries, and starting early and broadly. One way to build trust is to share information about what is intended by the evaluation. Evaluators can do this through individual meetings or large groups such as town meetings. During these meetings, evaluators can share information about the hows and whys of the evaluation. The participants in the meeting have the opportunity to express their expectations and concerns. If the evaluation is participatory, once trust is established, participants can be invited to form their own committees to work on the evaluation.

Posting approach papers on Web sites and inviting comment is a way of opening communication with the academic and research community, nongovernmental organizations (NGOs), and concerned citizens. Of course, this must be done when new input can still be considered and revisions made. It is most effective when evaluators post responses summarizing comments and actions taken (or reasons for not including suggestions).

In some instances, distrust is so great that intermediaries may be required to bridge the gap between evaluators and stakeholders. In such cases, a party that is respected by stakeholders may be able to use its position to bring evaluators and stakeholders together.

Evaluators should also visit stakeholders, especially those directly affected by the intervention. They can introduce themselves and ask if stakeholders have heard about the evaluation and what they think of it. This informal feedback can be compared with what the evaluator hears through other conduits. It serves as a way of verifying consistency and checking for biases.

Giving stakeholders a voice in designing their collective evaluation increases the chances of differences being resolved and consensus emerging around issues. Early engagement with stakeholders can thus be a conflict-avoidance measure. For those who perceive a loss for themselves in the evaluation design, outright opposition may appear to be the only possible stance; the greater the loss, the stronger the opposition is likely to be. Once opposition mobilizes, it is difficult—if not impossible—to resolve the matter.

### The Evaluation Manager

The **evaluation manager** is the person who manages the design, preparation, implementation, analysis, reporting, dissemination, and follow-up of an evaluation. He or she may manage several evaluations at the same time. In some cases, an evaluator will both manage and conduct the evaluation.

■ **Evaluation manager:** Person who manages the design, preparation, implementation, analysis, reporting, dissemination, and follow-up of an evaluation

Evaluation managers' responsibilities can be grouped into three stages: preparation, implementation, and follow-up (UNFPA 2007). *Preparation* includes the up-front work of defining the evaluation and developing RFPs, TORs, and the evaluation design matrix and of dealing with logistics. It requires that managers do the following:

- Determine the purpose, and identify the users of the evaluation results.
- Determine who needs to be involved in the evaluation process.
- Meet with key stakeholders.
- Define the evaluation scope and approach and the design matrix, including questions.
- Draft the TOR for the evaluation, and indicate the timeframe for the evaluation.
- Identify the mix of skills and experiences required to conduct the evaluation.
- Oversee the development and pretesting of data collection instruments and the collection of existing information. Use selectivity and ensure that existing sources of information are reliable and of sufficiently high quality to yield meaningful evaluation results; information gathered should be manageable.
- Select, recruit, and brief evaluators on the purpose of the evaluation, the matrix, and the work plan, and then train as needed.
- Ensure that the background documentation/materials compiled are submitted well in advance of the evaluation exercise so that the evaluation team has time to digest the materials.
- Oversee the field visit plan.
- Ensure the availability of funds to carry out the evaluation.

*Implementation* is the actual conduct of the evaluation, including analysis, drafting, and reporting. It requires that managers do the following:

- Ensure that evaluators have full access to files, reports, publications, and all other relevant information.
- Follow the progress of the evaluation; provide feedback and guidance to evaluators during all phase of implementation.
- Assess the quality of the evaluation reports, and discuss strengths and limitations with evaluators to ensure that the draft report satisfies the

TOR, evaluation findings are defensible, and recommendations are realistic.

- Arrange for a meeting with evaluators and key stakeholders to discuss and comment on the draft report.
- Approve the end product, and ensure presentation of evaluation results to stakeholders.

The final stage, *follow-up,* refers to assessing performance, disseminating results, tracking recommendations, and conducting a postmortem. During this stage, managers' responsibilities include the following:

- Evaluate the performance of evaluators, and place it on record.
- Disseminate evaluation results to key stakeholders and other audiences.
- Promote the implementation of recommendations and the use of evaluation results in present and future programming; monitor regularly to ensure that recommendations are acted upon.
- Lead the team in a learning review to identify what went well and should be repeated and what, in hindsight, might have been done differently.

During all three stages, the evaluation manager may serve as a facilitator during team meetings, enabling all participants to share their views and ideas. As a facilitator, the manager is responsible for

- setting an agenda
- helping the group stick to the agenda
- ensuring that all views are heard
- overseeing a process for decision making (consensus or a voting process).

### The Evaluator

Evaluators are the people who perform the main work in an evaluation. The number of evaluators depends on the size and scope of the evaluation, the budget, and the number of people available.

The United Nations Development Programme (UNDP 2006) identifies the following characteristics of a good evaluator:

- expertise in the specific subject matter
- knowledge of key development issues, especially those relating to the main goals, or the ability to see the "big picture"
- familiarity with the organization's business and the way such business is conducted
- evaluation skills in design, data collection, data analysis, and report preparation
- skills in the use of information technology.

The United Nations Population Fund (UNFPA 2007) identifies several potential responsibilities of evaluators:

- Provide inputs regarding evaluation design; bring refinements and specificity to the evaluation objectives and questions.
- Conduct the evaluation.
- Review information/documentation made available.
- Design/refine instruments to collect additional information as needed; conduct or coordinate additional information gathering.
- Undertake site visits; conduct interviews.
- In participatory evaluations, facilitate stakeholder participation.
- Provide regular progress reporting/briefing to the evaluation manager.
- Analyze and synthesize information, interpret findings, develop and discuss conclusions and recommendations, and draw lessons learned.
- Participate in discussions of the draft evaluation report; correct or rectify any factual errors or misinterpretations.
- Guide reflection/discussions to facilitate the presentation of evaluation findings in a seminar/workshop setting.
- Finalize the evaluation report, and prepare a presentation of evaluation results.

Many organizations are attempting to establish professional competency criteria for individuals who engage in evaluation. Discussions are also underway to establish certification for evaluators. (Competencies and certification for evaluators are examined in chapter 15.)

## Managing People, Tasks, and Budgets

Many comparisons have been made in describing project management. Some compare project management with juggling, because the project manager must keep an eye on many things at the same time (people, tasks, time, budget, quality). Others compare project management with directing an orchestra, because the manager stands at a distance and directs many competent people with different skills.

### Managing People

Ensuring that an evaluation team works well together requires a variety of skills. This section describes conflict resolution and team building skills managers need to master.

Managers also have to manage the fears of program "owners." Some people may be concerned that the evaluation will focus on the negative as that is what gets attention. They may fear that some negative evaluation findings may be detrimental to an overall good program. Fears may also arise that lack of difficult-to-measure program impact may result in the erroneous conclusion that the program is ineffective, with negative consequences for its funding.

One way that evaluators can address program owners' fears of evaluation is by involving them in identifying the issues the evaluation might address. Evaluators also need to provide them with opportunities to review evaluation work plans, findings, and recommendations.

### Conflict resolution skills

Conflicts often occur among people working in groups. The two skills most needed in resolving conflict are communication skills and listening skills. Important communication skills include using "I" statements instead of "you" language. Listening skills include confirming that the listener has correctly understood the speaker ("I hear you saying . . . Is that correct?").

Not all conflicts should end up with a winner and a loser. The most constructive conflicts end up with both parties "winning" (box 12.2).

---

**Box 12.2   Tips for Resolving Conflicts**

Managers can help resolve conflicts in a variety of ways:

- Bring those in conflict to a meeting. Allow each side to briefly summarize its point of view, without interruption. If one person does not allow the other to finish or begins to criticize, stop him or her.
- Allow people to discuss their feelings. Doing so goes a long way toward reducing conflict.
- Ask each person involved to describe the actions he or she would like to see the other person take.
- Listen to both sides. Ask yourself if there is anything about the work situation that is causing this conflict. If there is, consider ways of changing the work situation to solve the conflict.
- Do not choose sides. Remind the participants of the goal or objective of the evaluation and strive to find a way to help both sides reach the goal.
- Expect participants to work to solve their dispute. Allow them to continue to meet to address the conflict. Set a time to review their progress.

---

## Teambuilding skills

Working on a team requires a variety of skills. These skills include the following:

- *Listening:* Team members should develop and use good active listening skills. These skills can be a team's most valuable asset.
- *Questioning:* Team members should ask questions to clarify and elaborate on what others are saying.
- *Persuading:* Team members may need to exchange ideas, elaborate, defend, and rethink their ideas.
- *Respecting:* Team members should respect the opinions of others and encourage and support their ideas and efforts.
- *Helping:* Team members should help one another by offering assistance when it is needed.

Managing a team requires some additional skills (box 12.3).

A variety of techniques can be used to get the most out of teams. **Brainstorming** is used to gather ideas from a group of people in a short time. Each person contributes an idea for an evaluation question, which is written on a flip chart. One person gives one idea, and another person gives another idea. The facilitator keeps circling the group until no more ideas are offered. The basic rule is that every idea goes up on the flip chart— there are no bad ideas. No discussion of ideas occurs. In this way, all ideas

■ **Brainstorming:** Technique used to gather ideas from a group of people in a short time

---

**Box 12.3   Tips for Improving Teamwork**

The following tips help managers improve the way in which team members work together:

- Communicate the purposes and importance of specified work.
- Engage in active listening, helping others voice their thinking through effective paraphrasing.
- Collaborate with colleagues and others in positive inquiry practices, valuing each person's unique contribution and viewpoint.
- Put aside personal biases for the sake of seeking answers to hard questions for the good of the people affected by the project, program, or evaluation.
- Put aside defensive postures in the face of evaluation findings.

*Source:* NEIR TEC 2004.

are heard. The group as a whole then begins to identify common ideas, and a new list is created.

**Concept mapping** is a facilitated group process used to solicit ideas from all participants and to group and rank them by importance. It begins by generating ideas, through brainstorming or affinity diagramming. Each idea is written on a separate index card and taped to the wall.

When no more ideas are offered, participants are asked to look at all the ideas and arrange the cards into groups that seem to represent a similar concept or theme. Participants then identify the appropriate label for each concept/theme. The facilitator then leads a discussion of the importance of each and why each is or is not important. Some relatively unimportant concepts or themes may drop out at this stage; the ideas under them may be dropped or moved to other rubrics. As participants review the groupings on the wall, they may ask the facilitator to move other ideas to other categories as well.

When participants are satisfied with the concepts/themes and the groupings under them, the facilitator moves on to ranking them. Each participant is given a number of stickers, depending on the number of concepts/themes the facilitator wants selected as important. If five, then each participant receives five sticker dots. Participants are asked to put a dot next to each of the five concepts/themes they consider most important. The facilitator then identifies the five concepts/themes with the largest number of dots and ranks them by the number of dots received. The process can be repeated with ideas under each concept/theme, if desired.

## Managing Tasks

Managing tasks sometimes looks easier than managing people, but this process has its own challenges. Staying focused on the evaluation goal and the most important tasks is key.

A **task map** can help by listing everyone's assignments along with the start and completion dates (table 12.1). A **Gantt chart** can also be used (figure 12.1). A Gantt chart is a useful monitoring tool. The bar of each task can be filled in to show actual progress against what was planned. The chart can also show the dependency of one task on completion of another task or a bottleneck where too many task completions converge. Many software packages have Gantt chart templates.

Activities must be monitored to ensure that assignments are completed on schedule. If expected progress is not being made, the evaluator needs to

**Table 12.1  Sample Task Map**

| Task | Person or people responsible | Start date | Due date |
|---|---|---|---|
| Conduct review of external literature, and identify related internal and external issues. | Anna, Miguel, and Kabir | 7/1 | 7/4 |
| Review program/project documents (for example, board paper, decision paper, supervision reports) specific to intervention. | Kabir | 7/5 | 7/23 |
| Schedule and hold meeting with client. | Anna | 7/15 | 7/31 |
| Identify key stakeholders, and schedule meetings. | Kabir and Miguel | 7/15 | 7/17 |
| Write up summary of meeting with client and decisions made. | Anna | 8/1 | 8/3 |
| Conduct stakeholder meetings, and summarize issues. | Anna and Miguel | 8/5 | 8/15 |
| Draft initial design of evaluation. | Anna | 7/1 | 8/31 |

*Source:* Authors.

**Figure 12.1  Sample Gantt Chart**

| Task | Week 1 | Week 2 | Week 3 | Week 4 | Week 5 | Week 6 | Week 7 |
|---|---|---|---|---|---|---|---|
| Conduct literature review. | △▬▬▬▬▬▬▬▬▬▬▬▬▬▬▬▲ | | | | | | |
| Hold stakeholder meetings. | | △▬▬▬▬▬▬▬▬▬▬▬▬▲ | | | | | |
| Draft theory of change. | | | △▭▭▭▭▭▭▭▭▭▭▭▭▭▭▭▭▭▬ | | | | |

*Source:* Authors.

identify the barriers and determine how to remove them. It is important that team members feel safe to report problems, as it is often easier to fix a problem that is detected early.

While it is important to have a plan, it is also important to remain flexible in the face of obstacles. Adjustments can be made by allocating more time or resources or reducing the number of tasks included.

## Managing Budgets

According to Sanders (1983), an evaluation budget usually includes 10 categories:

- evaluation staff salary and benefits
- consultants
- travel and per diem (for staff and consultants)
- communication (postage, telephone calls, and so forth)
- printing and duplication
- data processing
- printed materials
- supplies and equipment
- subcontracts
- overhead (facilities, utilities).

Horn (2001) provides a detailed checklist for establishing an evaluation budget. The checklist breaks down the elements of costing under the types of categories listed above. An evaluation manager can calculate the cost for each of the categories to estimate total evaluation costs.

If the budget for the evaluation comes in high, it may be necessary to think about some cost-saving measures developed by Fitzpatrick, Sanders, and Worthen (2004):

- Use volunteers or low-cost workers.
- Use local specialists for data collection to reduce travel costs.
- Train less-costly personnel to perform selected tasks.
- Borrow equipment, people, materials, and supplies.
- Seek in-kind contributions from the organization in which the external evaluator is employed.
- Reduce the scope of the evaluation (perhaps deferring some parts for the future).
- Use existing measures, data, or reports.
- Use inexpensive data collection when precision can be sacrificed without severe consequences.
- Use public media to disseminate results.
- Increase efficiency through good management.

The proportion of a program or project budget devoted to an evaluation depends on many factors, including the visibility of the project or program, the planned scope of the evaluation, and the reputational risk if the evaluation leaves gaps. The Kellogg Foundation's *Evaluation Toolkit* (1998) indicates that an evaluation budget should represent 5–10 percent of a project's total budget. Other evaluation specialists suggest that 1–3 percent of the cost of the program or project should be earmarked for evaluation (the percentage is smaller for larger projects).

## Managing Projects

Project management is about managing all facets of a project—including the timing, scope, cost, and resources available—at the same time. Project management is a process, involving various phases. There are many project management models and several certification programs in project management. Michael Greer (2001), one authority on project management, has developed a model that emphasizes actions and results. His model divides project management into five phases:

- initiating
- planning
- executing
- controlling
- closing.

Each phase is divided into steps, which Greer calls *actions*. He identifies 20 actions to be performed across the 5 phases (table 12.2).

**Table 12.2   Greer's 20 Project Manager Activities**

| Phase/action | Results of successful performance |
|---|---|
| **Initiating phase** | |
| 1. Demonstrate project need and feasibility. | • Document confirming need for project deliverables and describing, in broad terms, the deliverables, means of creating the deliverables, costs of creating and implementing the deliverables, and benefits to be obtained by implementing the deliverables |
| 2. Obtain project authorization. | • "Go–no go" decision by sponsor. |
| | • A project manager is assigned who formally recognizes project and authorizes project manager to apply resources to project activities; A project charter is created that (a) formally recognizes the project, (b) is issued by a manager external to the project and at high enough organizational level so that he or she can apply resources to project needs, and (c) authorizes the project manager to apply resources to project activities |
| 3. Obtain authorization for phase. | • "Go–no go" decision is made by the sponsor, authorizing project manager to apply organizational resources to activities of particular phase |
| | • Written approval of the phase, which is created and that (a) formally recognizes the existence of the phase and (b) is issued by a manager external to project and at a high enough organizational level so that he or she can meet project needs |
| **Planning phase** | |
| 4. Describe project scope. | • Statement of project scope |
| | • Scope management plan |
| | • Work breakdown structure |
| 5. Define and sequence project activities. | • List of activities that will be performed |
| | • Updates to work breakdown structure |
| | • Project network diagram |
| 6. Estimate durations for activities and resources required. | • Estimate of time required for each activity and assumptions related to each estimate |
| | • Statement of resource requirements |
| | • Updates to activity list |
| 7. Develop a project schedule. | • Supporting details, such as resource usage over time, cash flow projections, order/delivery schedules, and so forth |
| 8. Estimate costs. | • Cost estimates for completing each activity |
| | • Supporting detail, including assumptions and constraints |
| | • Cost management plan describing how cost variances will be handled |

| Phase/action | Results of successful performance |
|---|---|
| 9. Build budget and spending plan. | • Cost baseline or time-phased budget for measuring/ monitoring costs<br>• Spending plan, telling how much will be spent on what resources at what time |
| 10. Create formal quality plan (optional). | • Quality management plan, including operational definitions<br>• Quality verification checklists |
| 11. Create formal project communications plan (optional). | • Communication management plan, including collection structure, distribution structure, description of information to be disseminated, schedules listing when information will be produced, method for updating communications plan |
| 12. Organize and acquire staff. | • Role and responsibility assignments<br>• Staffing plan<br>• Organizational chart, with detail as appropriate<br>• Project staff<br>• Project team directory |
| 13. Identify risks and plan to respond (optional). | • Document describing potential risks, including sources, symptoms, and ways to address them |
| 14. Plan for and acquire outside resources (optional). | • Procurement management plan describing how contractors will be hired<br>• Statement of work or statement of requirements describing the item (product or service) to be procured<br>• Bid documents<br>• Evaluation criteria (means of scoring contractors' proposals)<br>• Contract with one or more suppliers of goods or services |
| 15. Organize project plan. | • Comprehensive project plan that pulls together all outputs of preceding project planning activities |
| 16. Close out project planning phase. | • Project plan that has been approved, in writing, by the sponsor ("green light" to begin work on project) |
| 17. Revisit project plan and replan if needed. | • Confidence that detailed plans to execute a particular phase are still accurate and will effectively achieve results as planned |

*continued*

**Table 12.2** *Continued*

| Phase/action | Results of successful performance |
|---|---|
| **Executing phase** | |
| 18. Execute project activities. | • Work results (deliverables)<br>• Change requests (based on expanded or contracted project)<br>• Periodic progress reports<br>• Assessment and improvement (if necessary) of team performance<br>• Solicitation of bids/proposals for deliverables, selection of contractors (suppliers), and re-establishment of contracts<br>• Administration of contracts to achieve desired work results |
| **Controlling phase** | |
| 19. Control project activities. | • Decision to accept inspected deliverables<br>• Corrective actions, such as rework of deliverables, adjustments to work process, and so forth<br>• Updates to project plan and scope<br>• List of lessons learned<br>• Improved quality<br>• Completed evaluation checklists (if applicable) |
| **Closing phase** | |
| 20. Close project activities. | • Formal acceptance, documented in writing, that sponsor has accepted product of this phase or activity<br>• Formal acceptance of contractor work products and updates to contractor's files<br>• Updated project records prepared for archiving<br>• Plan for follow-up and/or hand-off of work products |

*Source:* Greer 2001. Reprinted with permission.

## Summary

Planning is essential to ensure that evaluations meet their objectives. Each evaluator working on an evaluation needs to understand his or her role and responsibilities in relation to others working on the evaluation. Terms of reference put these responsibilities in print for all to review.

In addressing questions of personnel, time, tasks, and costs, managers must keep the goal of the evaluation in mind. Every decision should be based on reaching the evaluation's goal.

# Chapter 12 Activities

## Application Exercise 12.1: Terms of Reference

Read the following terms of reference, and follow the instructions that appear after it.

> At the suggestion of the World Trade Organization (WTO), the interagency group that manages the Integrated Framework program asked the World Bank to take the lead in conducting a review of the implementation of the program over the past two years. A joint undertaking of several agencies, the Integrated Framework seeks to help least-developed countries take advantage of opportunities offered by the international trade system. It provides trade-related assistance, from seminars on WTO rules to improvement of ports and harbors. It functions by helping individual countries to identify their needs and then bringing a program of requested assistance to a roundtable meeting for support from donors.
>
> The review should cover the following topics:
>
> - perceptions of the objectives of the Integrated Framework (achieved by exploring the views of involved parties)
> - review of trade-related assistance (institution-building, building of human and enterprise capacity and infrastructure)
> - policy considerations, including the enlargement of the Integrated Framework and the trade and macroeconomic policy environment
> - administration of the Integrated Framework
> - recommendations for the future.
>
> In covering these topics, the consultant should assess the relevance of the Integrated Framework's operations to its objectives. They should also assess the cost-effectiveness of the Framework in achieving its objectives and the effectiveness of coordination among the core agencies that oversee the Framework, the roundtables, and other activities.
>
> The consultant is expected to examine documentation on implementation, conduct interviews with operational staff of all agencies involved, and seek out the reviews of the representatives of the least developed countries as well as government and business representatives in at least two least developed countries that have benefited from the Integrated Framework, one of which should be from Africa (Botswana and Uganda are proposed). Representatives of the key donor should also be consulted. The report should be about 20 pages long, not including annexes as needed.

Working in pairs if possible, review and critique the terms of reference and answer the following questions:

1. Do the terms of reference include all the necessary elements?
2. Which elements are complete?
3. Which elements could be improved?

### Application Exercise 12.2: Are You Ready to Be a Manager?

Read through this list of characteristics of a manager (Reh 2007). Identify the skills you have and those you need to improve.

**As a person**

- You have confidence in yourself and your abilities. You are happy with who you are, but you are still learning and getting better.
- You are something of an extrovert. You do not have to be the life of the party, but you cannot be a wallflower. Management is a people skill—it is not the job for someone who does not enjoy people.
- You are honest and straightforward. Your success depends heavily on the trust of others.
- You are an "includer," not an "excluder." You bring others into what you do. You don't exclude others because they lack certain attributes.
- You have presence. Managers must lead. Effective leaders have a quality about them that makes people notice when they enter a room.

**On the job**

- You are consistent but not rigid; dependable but can change your mind. You make decisions but easily accept input from others.
- You are a little bit crazy. You think out of the box. You try new things, and, if they fail, you admit the mistake but don't apologize for having tried.
- You are not afraid to "do the math." You make plans and schedules and work toward them.
- You are nimble and can change plans quickly, but you are not flighty.
- You see information as a tool to be used, not as power to be hoarded.

# References and Further Reading

Bemelmans Videc, M. L., R. C. Rist, and E. Vedung. 1997. *Sticks, Carrots, and Sermons: Policy Instruments and Their Evaluation.* Piscataway, NJ: Transaction Publishers.

Billson, Janet Mancini. 2004. *The Power of Focus Groups: A Training Manual for Social, Policy, and Market Research: Focus on International Development.* Burlington, RI: Skywood Press.

CDC (U.S. Centers for Disease Control and Prevention). 2001. *Introduction to Program Evaluation.*
http://www.cdc.gov/tobacco/tobacco_control_programs/surveillance_evaluation/evaluation_manual/00_pdfs/Chapter1.pdf.

Chelimsky, E. 1987. "The Politics of Program Evaluation." *Social Science and Modern Society* 25: 24–32.

de Regt, Jacomina. 1996. "Mozambique: Country Implementation Review." In *World Bank Participation Sourcebook,* 83–88. Washington, DC: World Bank.
http://www.worldbank.org/wbi/sourcebook/sb0211.pdf.

ESRC (Economic and Social Research Council). 2007. "Welcome to ESRC Today. Top Ten Tips."
http://www.esrc.ac.uk/ESRCInfoCentre/Support/Communications_toolkit/communications_strategy/index.aspx.

Feuerstein, M. T. 1986. *Partners in Evaluation: Evaluating Development and Community Programs with Participants.* London: MacMillan, in association with Teaching Aids at Low Cost.

Fitzpatrick, Jody L., James R. Sanders, and Blaine R. Worthen. 2004. *Program Evaluation: Alternative Approaches and Practical Guidelines.* New York: Pearson Education.

Greer, Michael. 2001. "20 Key Project Manager Actions and Results." In *The Project Manager's Partner.* Amherst, MA: HRD Press.
http://www.michaelgreer.com/20-actns.htm.

———. 2008. *Michael Greer's Project Management.* http://www.michaelgreer.com.

Hawkins, Penny. 2005. "Contracting Evaluation." International Program for Development Evaluation Training (IPDET) presentation, Ottawa, June 30–July 1.

Horn, Jerry 2001. *A Checklist for Developing and Evaluating Evaluation Budgets.*
http://www.wmich.edu/evalctr/checklists/evaluationbudgets.pdf.

Kellogg Foundation. 1998. *Evaluation Handbook.* Battle Creek, MI.
http://www.wkkf.org/Pubs/tools/Evaluation/Pub770.pdf.

King, Jean A., Laurie Stevahn, Gail Ghere, and Jane Minnema. 2001. "Toward a Taxonomy of Essential Evaluator Competencies." *American Journal of Evaluation* 222: 229–47.
http://www.nbowmanconsulting.com/Establishing percent20Essentialpercent 20Programpercent20Evaluator percent20Competencies.pdf.

Kirkhart, K. E. 2000. "Reconceptualizing Evaluation Use: An Integrated Theory of Influence." In *The Expanding Scope of Evaluation Use,* ed. V.J. Caracelli and H. Preskill, 5–24. New Directions for Evaluation No. 88. San Francisco: Jossey-Bass.

Kusek, Jody Zall, and Ray C. Rist. 2004. *Ten Steps to a Results-Based Monitoring and Evaluation System.* Washington, DC: World Bank.

Lawrence, J. 1989. "Engaging Recipients in Development Evaluation: The 'Stake-holder' Approach." *Evaluation Review* 13 (3): 243–56.

Leeuw, Frans. 1991. "Policy Theories, Knowledge Utilization and Evaluation." *OECD World Forum on Statistics: Knowledge and Policy,* vol. 4, 73–91. Organisation for Economic Co-operation and Development, Paris.

McNamara, C. 1999. *Checklist for Program Evaluation Planning.* http://www.managementhelp.org/evaluatn/chklist.htm.

Muir, Edward. 1999. "They Blinded Me with Political Science: On the Use of Non–Peer Reviewed Research in Education Policy." *Political Science and Politics* 32 (4): 762–64.

NCSTE (Chinese National Centre for Science and Technology Evaluation), and IOB (Policy and Operations Evaluation Department [the Netherlands]). 2006. *Country-Led Joint Evaluation of the ORET/MILIEV Programme in China.* Amsterdam: Aksant Academic Publishers.

NEIR TEC (Northeast and the Islands Regional Technology in Education Consortium). 2004. *Gathering Together and Planning: Exploring Useful Skills for Educators to Develop Through Collaborative Evaluation.* http://www.neirtec.org/evaluation/PDFs/Gathertogether3.pdf.

OECD (Organisation for Economic Co-operation and Development). n.d. *DAC Evaluation Quality Standards for Test Phase Application.* Development Assistance Committee, Paris. http://www.oecd.org/dataoecd/30/62/36596604.pdf.

———. 2002. *OECD Glossary of Key Terms in Evaluation and Results-Based Management.* Development Assistance Committee, Paris.

Patton, Michael Q. 1977. "In Search of Impact: An Analysis of the Utilization of Federal Health Evaluation Research." In *Using Social Research in Public Policy Making,* ed. C. H. Weiss, 141–64. Lexington, MA: Lexington Books.

———. 1997. *Utilization-Focused Evaluation.* 3rd ed. Thousand Oaks, CA: Sage Publications.

———. 2005. "Qualitative Methods and Analysis for Development Evaluation." International Program for Development Evaluation Training (IPDET) presentation, Ottawa, June 27–29.

Reh, F. John. n.d. "How to Be a Better Manager." http://management.about.com/cs/midcareermanager/a/htbebettermgr.htm.

———. 2007. "Management Tips." http://management.about.com/cs/generalmanagement/a/mgt_tips03.htm.

Rist, Ray C., and N. Stame. 2006. *From Studies to Streams: Managing Evaluative Systems.* Piscataway, NJ: Transaction Publishers.

Rossi, Peter Henry, Howard E. Freeman, and Mark W. Lipsey. 1999. *Evaluation: A Systematic Approach.* Thousand Oaks, CA: Sage Publications.

Rutman, L. 1980. *Planning Useful Evaluations: Evaluability Assessment.* Thousand Oaks, CA: Sage Publications.

Sanders, James R. 1983. "Cost Implications of the Standards." In *The Cost of Evaluation,* eds. M. C. Alkin and L. C. Solman, 101–17. Thousand Oaks, CA: Sage Publication.

Schwartz, R. 1998. "The Politics of Evaluation Reconsidered: A Comparative Study of Israeli Programs." *Evaluation* 4: 294–309.

Schwartz, R., and J. Mayne. 2004. *Quality Matters: Seeking Confidence in Evaluating, Auditing, and Performance Reporting.* Piscataway, NJ: Transaction Publishers.

Scriven, Michael. 2007. "Key Evaluation Checklist." http://www.wmich.edu/evalctr/checklists/kec_feb07.pdf/.

Stufflebeam, Daniel L. 1999. "Evaluations Plans and Operations Checklist." http://www.wmich.edu/evalctr/checklists/plans_operations.pdf.

Tilley, Nick. 2004. *Applying Theory-Driven Evaluation to the British Crime Reduction Programme: The Theories of the Programme and of Its Evaluations.* Thousand Oaks, CA: Sage Publications.

UNFPA (United Nations Population Fund). 2007. "Tool No. 5: Planning and Managing an Evaluation." *Programme Manager's Planning, Monitoring and Evaluation Toolkit.* New York. http://www.unfpa.org/monitoring/toolkit/5managing.pdf.

Weiss, Carol H. 1973. "Where Politics and Evaluation Research Meet." *Evaluation* 1: 37–45.

———. 2004. *Identifying the Intended Uses of an Evaluation.* International Program for Development Evaluation Training (IPDET) presentation, Ottawa, July. http://www.idrc.ca/ev_en.php?ID=58213_201&ID2=DO_TOPIC.

Wholey, J. S. 1979. *Evaluation: Promise and Performance.* Washington, DC: Urban Institute.

———. 1994. "Assessing the Feasibility and Likely Usefulness of Evaluation." In *Handbook of Practical Program Evaluation,* eds. Joseph S. Wholey, Harry P. Hatry, and Kathryn E. Newcomer, 15–39. San Francisco: Jossey-Bass.

Widavsky, A. 1972. "The Self-Evaluating Organization." *Public Administration Review* 32: 509–20.

World Bank. 2006. *The World Bank Participation Sourcebook.* Washington, DC: World Bank. http://www.worldbank.org/wbi/sourcebook/sbhome.htm.

## Web Sites

Canadian Evaluation Society. *Professional Designation Project.* http://www.evaluationcanada.ca/site.cgi?s=5&ss=6&_lang=EN.

Conflict Resolution Information Source. http://www.crinfo.org/index.jsp.

Conflict Resolution Network. http://www.crnhq.org/.

EIB (European Investment Bank Group). 2008. "What Is the EIB Group?" http://www.eib.org/attachments/general/whatis_eibgroup_2008_en.pdf.

ESRC (Economic and Social Research Council). "ESRC Society Today: Communication Strategy." http://www.esrc.ac.uk/ESRCInfoCentre/Support/Communications_toolkit/communications_strategy/index.aspx.

Europe Aid Co-operation Office. 2005. *Evaluation Methods.* http://ec.europa.eu/europeaid/evaluation/methodology/index_en.htm.

———. 2006. *Methodological Bases.* http://ec.europa.eu/europeaid/evaluation/methodology/methods/mth_en.htm.

European Commission. 2008. *Evaluation Network*. http://ec.europa.eu/regional_policy/sources/docgener/evaluation/tech_en.htm.

Evalnet. 2000. http://www.evalnet.co.za/services/.

IBSTPI (International Board of Standards for Training, Performance, and Instruction). *Competencies for Internal Staff and External Consultants Conducting Evaluations in Organizational Settings*. http://www.ibstpi.org/Competencies/evaluatorcompetencies.htm.

IDRC (International Development Research Centre). 2004. *Evaluation Planning in Program Initiatives*. http://web.idrc.ca/uploads/user-S/108549984812guideline-web.pdf.

MSH (Management Sciences for Health), and UNICEF (United Nations Children's Fund). "Quality Guide: Stakeholder Analysis." In *Guide to Managing for Quality*. http://bsstudents.uce.ac.uk/sdrive/Martin percent20Beaver/Week percent 202/Quality percent20Guide percent20- percent20Stakeholder percent20 Analysis.htm.

Treasury of Board of Canada Secretariat. 2005. *Improving the Professionalism of Evaluation*. http://www.tbssct.gc.ca/eval/dev/Professionalism/profession_e.asp.

UNDP (United Nations Development Programme). 2006. *Planning and Managing an Evaluation Website*. http://www.undp.org/eo/evaluation_tips/evaluation_tips.html.

UNFPA (United Nations Population Fund). 2004. *Programme Manager's Planning, Monitoring and Evaluation Toolkit*. http://www.unfpa.org/monitoring/toolkit/5managing.pdf.

Weiss, Carol. *Identifying the Intended Use(s) of an Evaluation*. International Development Research Centre. http://www.idrc.ca/ev_en.php?ID=58213_201&ID2=DO_TOPIC.

Western Michigan University Evaluation Center. *Evaluation Checklists*. http://www.wmich.edu/evalctr/checklists/checklistmenu.htm.

——. *The Checklist Project*. http://evaluation.wmich.edu/checklists.

## Examples of Terms of Reference

ADB (Asian Development Bank). 2008. *Model Terms of Reference Diagnostic City Water Assessment* (Links). http://www.adb.org/Water/tools/City-Water-Assessments.asp.

CIDA (Canadian International Development Agency). *Model for Evaluation Terms of Reference*. http://www.acdicida.gc.ca/INET/IMAGES.NSF/vLUImages/Performancereview4/US$file/tor_sample_text.pdf.

FAO (Food and Agriculture Organization of the United Nations). *FAO Model Terms of Reference for a Joint Evaluation Mission*. http://www.fao.org/pbe/pbee/common/ecg/233/en/torseng.doc.

UNDP (United Nations Development Programme). 2002. *Handbook on Monitoring and Evaluating for Results*. http://www.undp.org/eo/documents/HandBook/ME-HandBook.pdf.

**CHAPTER 13**

# Presenting Results

Once data collection and analysis are largely completed, it is time to share preliminary results and to make plans to communicate the final results. Sharing what has been learned is one of the most important parts of an evaluation. It is a critical precondition to effecting change. Presenting results can be done in writing (through memos and reports) or orally (through briefings and presentations).

This chapter has four main parts:
- Crafting a Communication Strategy
- Writing an Evaluation Report
- Displaying Information Visually
- Making an Oral Presentation

## Crafting a Communication Strategy

An evaluation that is not used to inform decisions is of little value. When one designs an evaluation, it is critical to keep in mind the goal of providing useful information to stakeholders that leads to decisions. Evaluation does not seek knowledge for knowledge's sake. This is the key difference between evaluation and research. It is essential that the results of an evaluation be communicated clearly, accurately, and in way that allows the audience to best make use of the information.

A communication strategy is an essential component of development evaluation. We have emphasized throughout this text that good communication starts at the very beginning and continues throughout the evaluation. It is not an activity that takes place only at the end of an evaluation. The client and the main stakeholders should be involved not only in planning the evaluation but also in developing the process and means for communicating its findings and for soliciting feedback.

The communication strategy should be developed right from the start. It should identify

- who needs to receive information on the evaluation
- what information is needed
- what format the information should be in
- when the information should be provided
- who is responsible for providing it.

A good communication strategy covers all phases and products of the evaluation. It uses multiple forms of communication tailored to the needs of particular stakeholders.

The communication strategy for an evaluation might start with an exploratory discussion of the issues with the evaluation requestor, followed by discussions with local stakeholder groups (table 13.1). The discussion with the requestor might be followed with a formal briefing on the preliminary design for the evaluation. Local stakeholder groups might receive an e-mail notification that the preliminary design is on a Web site for public comment. Informal communications are valuable during the evaluation. Clients and key stakeholders can, for example, be kept informed of the progress of the evaluation with telephone calls or e-mails.

Final results may be disseminated to different parties in different forms. A donor, for example, might receive an in-depth briefing on the evaluation findings, followed by the formal final report. Local program staff might receive an overview report and a briefing.

**Table 13.1 Sample Communication Strategy Checklist for Preliminary and Design Phases of Evaluation**

| Audience | Action | Form of communication | Who is responsible | Due date |
|----------|--------|----------------------|-------------------|----------|
| **Preliminary work** | | | | |
| Client | Discuss program issues and timing needs. | Meeting | Team leader | 6/1 |
| National and local nongovernmental organization | Discuss program issues. | Meetings | Team member B | 6/5 |
| Program staff | Discuss program issues. | Meetings | Team member C | 6/11 |
| Local government officials | Discuss program issues. | Meeting | Team member B | 6/10 |
| Advisory board | Identify and send invitation letters. | E-mail | Team member A | 6/14 |
| | Plan and hold preliminary meeting on issues. | Advisory board meeting | Team member B | 6/25 |
| Development evaluation community | Invite comments on issues. | E-mail notices about open evaluation Web site | Team member C | 6/25 |
| **Design** | | | | |
| Advisory board | Review and discuss draft design. | Advisory board meeting | Team member A | 7/15 |
| | Provide final design. | E-mail | Team member A | 7/30 |
| Client | Share final design. | Oral briefing | Team leader | 7/22 |
| Development evaluation community | Review draft design. | Web site (comments monitored) | Team member B | 7/31 |

*Source:* Authors.

For the final report, evaluators can use briefings, presentations, and written reports. Press releases can be used to disseminate information to a wider audience. If a press release or press conference is planned, its timing and handling should be discussed with the main stakeholders.

It is important to include a feedback process to bring stakeholders and evaluators together to discuss the findings, insights, alternative actions, and next steps. If large group discussions will be held, evaluators should identify any challenges to communicating results simultaneously to different groups of stakeholders.

Even writers of technical evaluation reports concede that they may not be the most effective way of communicating evaluation findings (Torres, Preskill, and Piontek 1997). Evaluators may need to use alternative communication tools, such as brochures, videos, issue papers, and short summaries with charts and graphs, to get their messages out (box 13.1).

---

**Box 13.1    Using Innovative Communication Techniques to Increase Interest in Evaluation Results**

To disseminate their results to stakeholders, Lawrenz, Gullickson, and Toal (2007) used a variety of innovative techniques.

1. They wrote a reflective case narrative, which they disseminated through a variety of outlets, including the Internet, to meet the needs of their audience. The case narrative described site visits to 13 projects by teams of evaluators. It considered not just the needs of the client but also the needs of others who might benefit from the findings.
2. They organized the evaluation results into nine issue papers (addressing collaboration, dissemination, materials development, professional development, program improvement, recruitment and retention, sustainability, advisory committees, and evaluation) and posted them on their Web site. These papers synthesized the site visit reports, survey data, and previous research by issue.
3. To build interest in the issue papers, they created a brochure as a teaser. The brochure stirred so much interest in the issue papers that they published the full set of issue papers in a journal, disseminating the results to a wider audience than original planned.
4. They put their site visit handbook, containing the procedures used to conduct the site visits, on line. After posting it on their Web page, they found that many organizations and other researchers were interested in it.
5. They developed a brochure with key action steps for the sustainability of the program they studied, which they posted on their Web site in PDF format. This brochure was well received by the field, because it was easy to use and provided pertinent information about improving projects.
6. They held a videoconference to provide in-depth discussion of some of their ideas.
7. They hyperlinked the videoconference proceedings to their Web site. Information on the site included links to information about the study authors, key presenters in the videoconference, and supporting documents and video materials. All of this information was posted on the Web site and made available on compact disc.

---

# Writing an Evaluation Report

The purpose of a report is to communicate with readers. To do so, consider the following tips:

- Keep your purpose and audience in mind as you write the report. Learn as much as possible about the audience, and write the report in a way that is best suited to reach it.
- Use words that are
  - simple
  - active
  - positive
  - familiar
  - culturally sensitive.
- Avoid abbreviations and acronyms to the maximum extent possible.
- Limit background information to that needed to introduce the report and to make its context clear. Additional context can be included as an annex if necessary.
- Provide enough information about the evaluation design and methods so readers have confidence in the report's credibility but recognize its limitations. Warn readers about interpreting the findings in ways that may not be valid. Again, details can be put in an annex.
- Write an executive summary (described next).
- Organize the material in the body of the report into sections that address major themes or answer key evaluation questions.
- Place major points first in each section, with minor points later in the section. Open each paragraph by stating the point it addresses.
- Support conclusions and recommendations with evidence.
- Place technical information, including the design matrix and any survey instruments, in an appendix.
- Leave time to revise, revise, and revise!!
- Find someone who has not seen any of the material to proofread the draft. Ask the proofreader to identify anything that was left out or is not clear.
- If possible, have an external reviewer with expertise on the issues and knowledge of evaluation methodology review the final draft and suggest changes to the document as necessary. If peer review is not feasible, ask a colleague who is not associated with the evaluation to review the report.

## Executive Summary

The **executive summary** of a report identifies the evaluation questions addressed; describes the methodology used; and summarizes the report's

■ **Executive summary:** A short summary of a report that identifies the evaluation questions addressed; describes the methodology used; and summarizes the report's findings, conclusions, and recommendations

findings, conclusions, and recommendations. It provides a way for the reader to quickly grasp the major messages of the report. The executive summary is not simply a condensed version of the conclusions section of the report. It is not a teaser that promises to reveal information later. It must serve as a stand-alone document for readers too busy to read the main report.

According to Scriven (2007, p. 1), the aim of the executive summary is to summarize the results, not just the process:

> Through the whole process of evaluation, keep asking yourself how the overall summary is going to look, based on what you have learned so far, and how it relates to the client's and stakeholders' and audiences' needs; this helps you to focus on what still needs to be done to learn about what matters most.

The executive summary should be short: two pages is great; more than four is too much. This point bears repeating: two single-spaced pages is great, and more than four single-spaced pages is too much!

An executive summary should include the following components:

- A brief overview or introductory paragraph stating the purpose of the study and the issue of concern, written in a way that grabs the reader's attention.
- A description of the evaluation, stating the major questions addressed, plus a brief statement about the evaluation's scope and methodology.
- Enough background information to place the study in context.
- A summary of the report's major findings. Use judgment in determining which findings are most important to the audience.
- A way to refer readers to page numbers of information in the text.
- Major conclusions and recommendations.

## Body of the Report

The body of an evaluation report should contain the following components, usually divided into chapters (sections in a shorter report):

- introduction
- description of the evaluation
- findings
- conclusions
- recommendations.

The introduction to the report includes the following components:

- purpose of the evaluation
- background information

- program goals and objectives, depicted through a theory of change model
- evaluation questions.

The brief description of the evaluation includes the following components:

- purpose
- scope
- questions
- methodology
- limitations
- people involved (advisory board, consulting firm).

The findings follow the description of the evaluation. In writing this section, evaluators should

- present findings in a way that the audience can clearly understand
- include only the most important findings
- organize the findings around study questions, major themes, or issues
- use charts, tables, and other graphic elements to highlight major points.

The last parts of the report are the conclusions and recommendations, which readers often read first. Evaluators often have difficulty distinguishing findings from conclusions. Findings describe what was found in the evaluation. They may relate to whether a criterion was or was not met. Findings should be supported by evidence.

Conclusions are based on professional assessment of the findings. They should be made about each evaluation subobjective as well as the overall objective of the project, program, or policy. No new information should be presented in the conclusions section

Recommendations advocate action. They indicate what the report wants the client or other key stakeholders to do. Recommendations are often difficult to draft. They should not be overly prescriptive, thus reducing management's prerogative to identify specific solutions to the problems identified. An evaluation might, for example, recommend developing a pricing policy for technical assistance activities. It would not draft the policy or specify in detail the policy's requirements. It might, however, specify key components that should be included in the pricing policy.

At the same time, recommendations cannot be so general that they have no teeth. Recommendations should be clear and specific enough so that all understand what needs to be done to satisfy them, what organization or unit needs to take action, and when it should be done.

Reports should not include "laundry lists" of recommendations. Evaluators should limit the number of major recommendations to three or four. It is better to group recommendations so that they are a manageable number (three to four) with subparts, as needed. The tone of the recommendations should be considered. It is important to remember that reports do not make decisions; people do.

Recommendations serve little purpose if not acted upon. One way to follow up recommendations is to establish a recommendation tracking system. Such a system allows stakeholders to monitor the implementation of evaluation recommendations. It tracks each recommendation from an evaluation and the progress being made to implement the recommendation, including

- date of the recommendation
- who is responsible for taking action
- response/progress.

Table 13.2 shows a simple matrix that can be used for a recommendation tracking system. In this matrix, the evaluators can fill out the first two columns, but managers keep track and ensure that recommendations are followed up by their designate.

The International Finance Corporation (IFC), the private-sector arm of the World Bank, provides another example. The IFC has its own recommendation tracking system. Evaluation reports prepared by IFC's Independent Evaluation Group (IEG) include recommendations for IFC Management and IFC's Management Response. These recommendations are discussed at the IFC Board's Committee on Development Effectiveness (CODE). CODE expects periodic status reports on recommendations including their level of adoption and status. The IEG, with IFC Management, developed the Management Action Tracking Record (MATR, pronounced "matter").

The MATR is designed to maintain the integrity of the reporting process, wherein neither IEG nor IFC can change finalized ratings. Figure 13.1 illustrates the two stages of the MATR. In the first stage, IEG and IFC agree on indicators to assess the implementation of each new recommendation. In the second stage, the status and level of adoption of each active recommendation is periodically updated and reported to CODE. IEG and IFC ratings

**Table 13.2    Recommendation Tracking System**

| Recommendation | Source | Date | Who is responsible | Response/progress |
|---|---|---|---|---|
| 1. | | | | |
| 2. | | | | |
| 3. | | | | |
| 4. | | | | |

*Source:* Authors.

**Figure 13.1   IFC's Two-Stage MATR to Track Recommendations**

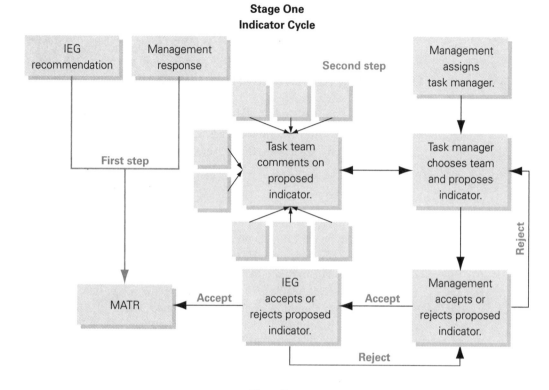

### Stage One
### Indicator Cycle

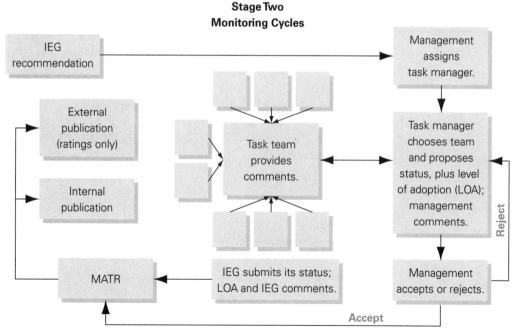

### Stage Two
### Monitoring Cycles

*Source:* Independent Evaluation Group of the International Finance Corporation  2008.

need not be the same. When recommendations are implemented, superseded, or no longer relevant, they are made inactive. The IEG recommendations that are not accepted by IFC management are not tracked.

## Displaying Information Visually

Visual information can make a report interesting, communicate information more clearly than text, and attract readers' eyes to particular points. Using graphics effectively can, therefore, increase the impact of an evaluation report.

### Illustrations

Illustrations can help illuminate points made in the text. They should always be used for a reason, however, never just for decoration. Illustrations on the cover of the report can relate to the overall theme; illustrations within the report should have a specific and concrete reason for being there.

All illustrations should be called out in the text, which should indicate what the reader is supposed to see in the picture. Examples of illustrations that can be used in an evaluation include maps, sketches, line drawings, and photographs. Where necessary, permissions should be obtained to use the illustrations.

#### *Maps*
Maps can be used in reports to

- indicate the location of a program
- provide context
- indicate the geographic reach or spread of a program
- show the basis for drawing a sample
- indicate rates or levels across the topography of an area using patterns or isolines (Cummings 2003).

    Making the most of maps requires

- making sure they are easy to read and understand (patterns and shading must be readily distinguishable)
- using the most current version
- identifying the source
- including a compass arrow indicating the scale, where appropriate.

### Sketches and line drawings

As a part of data collection, evaluators sometimes ask participants to make sketches (illustration 13.1). Such sketches can be used to

- add interest to a report
- personalize a report
- reflect a methodological approach
- replace more sophisticated illustrations if the technical capacity does not exist to create such illustrations
- introduce humor
- allow participants' impressions to be viewed directly.

Line drawings can be used to illustrate how something works or how one object relates to another. They are very useful when describing a process or situation is much more difficult than depicting it.

### Photographs

Photographs can be useful additions to reports. They can

- provide context
- indicate the extent of field work (progress)
- capture direct observations (for example, house types, crowded conditions in a neighborhoods)
- familiarize the audience with the field situation
- provide evidence (Cummings 2003).

Like other types of illustrations, photographs should never be used for mere decoration. Levin, Anglin, and Carney (1987) reviewed and summarized information about using pictures and illustrations in materials. They

**Illustration 13.1   Child's Impression of Village before and after Intervention**

*Source:* Cummings 2003.

concluded two things about the effects that pictures have on the process of learning from prose:

- When the illustrations are relevant to the content, then moderate to substantial gains can be expected in learning.
- When illustrations are NOT relevant to the content, or even worse, conflicting, expect NO gain in learning and maybe even confusion.

Thus, photographs and other pictures used within the report should have a specific and concrete reason for being there.

### Charts and Graphs

Charts and graphs provide visual representations of data. Ideally, they tell a story on their own, without the need for narrative.

#### *Organization chart*

■ **Organization chart:** Chart illustrating the hierarchy and reporting structure within an organization

An **organization chart** illustrates the hierarchy within an organization (figure 13.2). Such charts clearly and concisely identify responsibilities and reporting structures.

Organization charts are often included in evaluation reports, because understanding an entity's structure may be the first step to understanding it. Most word-processing programs have a feature that allows such charts to be created.

Figure 13.2 **Example of Organization Chart**

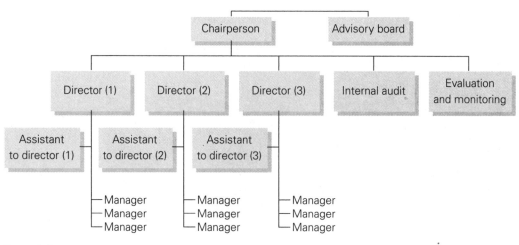

*Source:* Authors.

### Gantt chart

**Gantt charts** are often used for planning (figure 13.3). They are particularly useful for project management, especially the planning of a project.

### Graphs

A **graph** should convey a clear message with little scrutiny.

Every graph must have a title, a number, and a source line. The title of the graph should indicate the year of the data (if applicable) (table 13.3).

At least four types of graphs or charts are useful for presenting data. Each serves a different purpose (table 13.4).

*Line graph.* A **line graph** usually depicts how a variable (or variables) change over time (figures 13.4 and 13.5). For example, evaluators might use a line graph to show costs for food rising or falling over the months of the year, population changes over many years, or student grades each day over a six-week term.

Line graphs can show one item or multiple items as they change over the same period of time. Line graphs are a good way to show continuous data, that is, data that are interval or ratio data. Interval data are data that are divided into ranges and in which the distance between the intervals is meaningful. Examples of interval data are counts, such as counts of income, years of education, or number of votes. Ratio data are interval data that also have a true zero point. Income is ratio because zero dollars is truly "no income."

■ **Gantt chart:** Chart used to illustrate a project schedule

■ **Graph:** Visual representation of the relationship between two or more pieces of data

■ **Line graph:** Graph created by connecting a series of data points together with a line; usually used to show changes over time

**Figure 13.3  Example of Gantt Chart**

| Task | Week 1 | Week 2 | Week 3 | Week 4 | Week 5 | Week 6 | Week 7 |
|---|---|---|---|---|---|---|---|
| Conduct literature review. | △▬▬▬▬▬▬▬▬▬▬▬▬▲ | | | | | | |
| Hold stakeholder meetings. | | △▬▬▬▬▬▬▬▬▬▬▲ | | | | | |
| Draft theory of change. | | | △▢▢▢▢▢▢▢▢▢▢▢▢ | | | | |

*Source:* Authors.

**Table 13.3    Parts of Graphs**

| Name of Part | Description |
|---|---|
| Title | All graphs and charts should have **titles** so that the audience knows the message of the graph immediately |
| Horizontal or x axis | The **horizontal or x axis** is the horizontal line of a line or bar chart, representing one variable (e.g., time) |
| Vertical or y axis | The **vertical or y axis** is the vertical line of a line or bar chart, representing a second variable (e.g., costs) |
| Origin | The **origin** is the point where the vertical and horizontal axes meet. |
| Grid lines | Many charts include **grid lines** to help compare data by clearly showing levels. Only a limited number of grid lines should be used to avoid a cluttered look. |
| Axis titles | The **x-axis and y-axis titles** are very important. They identify what is being measured and the units of measurement (years, meters, pounds, square miles, cubic tons, dollars, degrees). For example:<br><br>• Costs (in US$)<br>• Distance (in km) |
| Axis scales | The x axis and y axis need appropriate **scales** to show values. Chose your scale carefully to include the full range of values of your data. Chose the proportions between axis scales to best illustrate the relationship between the variables. |
| Actual values | Many graphs and charts also include the **actual values** for the entries, shown as additional text within the graphic. These additions are helpful to the reader in grasping the real situation. |
| Coordinate | A **coordinate** is the point on a graph where the x value of the data meets the y value. How this is represented (a point, a peak, the top of a bar) will depend on the type of graphic you choose. |

*Source:* Authors.

**Figure 13.4    Average Temperature Declines in Province A, February–June 2008**

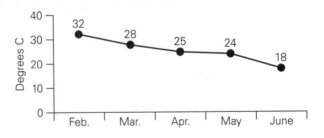

Table 13.4 Types and Purposes of Different Types of Graphs

| Type of graph | Example | Purpose |
|---|---|---|
| Line graph | | Show trends over time. |
| Single bar chart | | Compare linear or one-dimensional characteristics. |
| Multiple bar chart | | Compare two or more characteristics with the values of a common variable. |
| Pie chart | | Show parts of a whole. |
| Scatter diagram | | Show trends or relationships. |

*Source:* Authors.

Figure 13.5 Reading Scores Differ in Three Schools in District, 2004/05

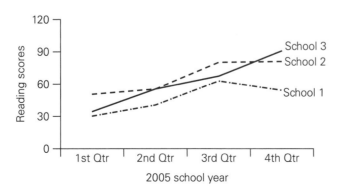

**■ Bar graph:**
Type of graph in which horizontal or vertical rectangles are used to represent and compare quantities

*Bar graph.* **Bar graphs** use bars (elongated rectangles) to represent quantities and let us compare numbers. They should be carefully titled to ensure that the reader understands what factors are being represented.

There are two kinds of bar graphs: single bar graphs that show information about a single variable and multiple bar graphs that give information for more than one variable. The bars can be formatted vertically or horizontally.

Use a multiple bar graph to compare two or more groups' data on the same variable. For example, an evaluation wants to compare rate of land mine recovery in three different regions of a country. They might use a multiple bar graph to depict the information. In another example, double bar graphs might be used to compare the responses of boys and girls to a questionnaire.

Bar graphs are often used to show nominal or categorical data. Nominal or categorical data have no order, and the assignment of numbers to categories is purely arbitrary (1 = East, 2 = North, 3 = South). These categories must be clearly explained in the legend.

The following are examples of bar graphs. Figure 13.6 shows the score earned as a parenting test given to four pregnant women. A **single bar graph** shows data on a particular variable for a single group (figure 13.6). A **multiple bar graph** provides data on a particular variable for more than one group (figure 13.7).

**■ Pie chart:**
Circular chart divided into sections in which each section shows the relative magnitude of the element depicted

*Pie chart.* A **pie chart** can be useful when the number of sections is small (figure 13.8). It should not be used when the number of sections exceeds about eight or is less than three.

**Figure 13.6 Scores on Parenting Test Vary by Region**

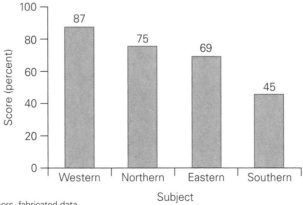

*Source:* Authors, fabricated data.

**Figure 13.7  Assistants and Directors Differ in Responses to Questions**

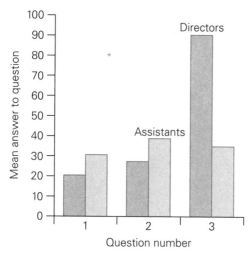

Source: Authors, fictitious data.

**Figure 13.8  Third Quarter Shows Highest Electricity Costs in Canadian Dollars, 2008**

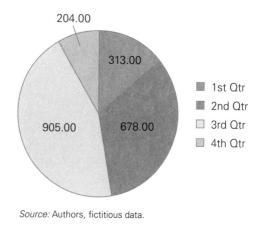

Source: Authors, fictitious data.

*Scatter diagram.*   A **scatter diagram** is a graph that plots the relationship of a set of data points by plotting them on a horizontal and vertical axis (figure 13.9). If the variables are correlated, a line or curve will be evident. The better the correlation, the closer the data points will be to the line or curve. A scatter diagram that shows no particular pattern indicates that there is no clear relationship between the two variables.

**Figure 13.9   Mean Scores Comparing Test Score and Grade Level**

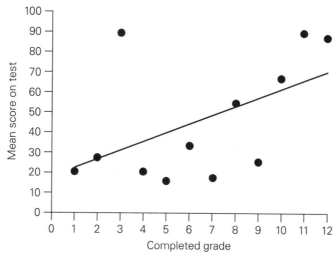

Source: Authors, fictitious data.

## Tables

Tables can be used to present information in an organized manner. There are two types of tables to consider using in a report: data tables and classification tables (matrices).

### Data tables

It can be useful to present numerical information in tables, called data tables only if the data sets are small (Tufte 1983). Larger data tables generally provide the basis for presenting data in other formats, such as line and bar charts, and are usually put in annexes.

As with pictures and illustrations, the audience will not automatically know what to look for in a table. It is helpful if the title of a table describes what they should see and how they can relate the information. A short description of what to see should also be included in the narrative of the report. Whenever presenting data in a table, include the sources of the data and the year in which the data were collected.

Eherenburg (1977) summarizes principles to guide the design of tables to present information.

- Round off numbers to no more than two significant digits. This helps audience make comparisons. [Note: We suggest rounding to whole numbers; the audience rarely wants the decimal point level of detail.]
- Provide sums and means of rows and columns (as appropriate) to help audience make comparisons of individual cell entries.
- Put the most important data into columns because it allows the reader to easily make comparisons.

When deciding on the format of the table, keep in mind that too many lines (dividing cells of the table) will make it difficult to read. This is shown in the next two tables, where table 13.5 gives an example of data in a table with many lines. Table 13.6 shows the same data in a table with fewer lines. Notice how the data becomes the focus in the second table, not the lines. Also, notice that the last row of the table shows the means for the columns with data.

### Classification tables (matrices)

A classification table, or matrix, has a layout that shows how a list of things has been organized according to different factor (table 13.7). At least two sorting factors indicate similarity or difference among the things that are

Table 13.5    Example of Data in a Table with Many Lines

**Demographic Information on Participants**

| Participant number | Height | Weight | Age | District |
|---|---|---|---|---|
| 1 | 44 | 30 | 7.2 | North |
| 2 | 46 | 35 | 7.1 | East |
| 3 | 40 | 20 | 7.6 | North |
| 4 | 32 | 22 | 7.2 | South |
| 5 | 29 | 23 | 7.0 | South |
| 6 | 50 | 38 | 7.8 | North |
| 7 | 44 | 30 | 7.3 | West |
| 8 | 44 | 28 | 7.3 | West |
| 9 | 42 | 30 | 7.5 | East |
| 10 | 48 | 45 | 7.9 | South |
| Mean | 38.09 | 27.36 | 6.72 | |

Table 13.6    Example of Data in a Table with Few Lines

**Demographic Information on Participants**

| Participant number | Height | Weight | Age | District |
|---|---|---|---|---|
| 1 | 44 | 30 | 7.2 | North |
| 2 | 46 | 35 | 7.1 | East |
| 3 | 40 | 20 | 7.6 | North |
| 4 | 32 | 22 | 7.2 | South |
| 5 | 29 | 23 | 7.0 | South |
| 6 | 50 | 38 | 7.8 | North |
| 7 | 44 | 30 | 7.3 | West |
| 8 | 44 | 28 | 7.3 | West |
| 9 | 42 | 30 | 7.5 | East |
| 10 | 48 | 45 | 7.9 | South |
| Mean | 38 | 27 | 7.0 | |

*Source:* Authors (fabricated data).

*Note:* N = 10.

Table 13.7 Example of Classification Table

**Poverty Reduction Strategies: Case Study Countries**

| County | Start Date | Years of Implementation | Review Complete |
|---|---|---|---|
| Ethiopia | 17 Sept. 2002 | 4.7 | Yes |
| Guinea | 25 July 2002 | 4.9 | Yes |
| Mauritania | 6 Feb. 2001 | 6.3 | Yes |
| Mozambique | 25 Sept. 2001 | 5.7 | Yes |
| Tanzania | 30 Nov. 2000 | 6.3 | Yes |

*Source:* Adapted from World Bank 2004.

*Note:* Data are as of May 2007:

classified. Classification tables can also help illustrate complex information. A design matrix is a classification table.

## Improving the Effectiveness of Visual Information

According to Edward Tufte, an expert on the display of visual information, graphical displays should achieve the following:

- Show the data.
- Induce the viewer to think about the substance of the graphic rather than the methodology, graphic design, technology of graphic production, or anything else.
- Avoid distorting what the data have to say.
- Represent many numbers in a small space.
- Make sense of large data sets.
- Encourage the eye to compare different pieces of data.
- Reveal the data at several levels of detail, from a broad overview to the fine structure.
- Be closely integrated with the statistical and verbal descriptions of the data (Tufte 1983).

Tufte refers to the amount of ink used to present the data themselves as "data ink." Most ink used to create a graphic should be data ink; as little ink as possible should go toward grid lines, labels, or other distractors (box 13.2). He refers to decoration that does not add additional information as "chartjunk."

Figure 13.10 shows an example of a figure loaded with chartjunk. The shading and gridlines do nothing to enhance the message of the figure. The data labels at the top of each column distract the reader from seeing the patterns. Figure 13.11 shows the same figure without chartjunk. Most of the ink in this figure is data ink.

Figure 13.10 **Example of Unnecessarily Cluttered Figure**

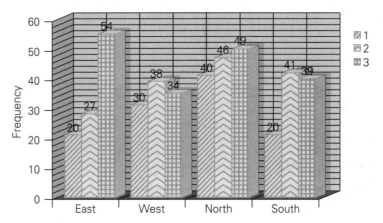

*Source:* Authors.

Figure 13.11 **Example of Streamlined Figure Graph that Maximizes Data Ink**

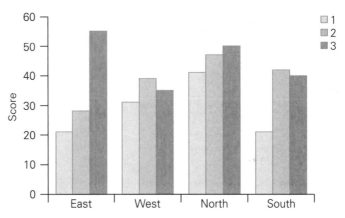

*Source:* Authors.

## Making an Oral Presentation

Many people have tremendous fear of speaking in public. Fear of public speaking can be eased by being well prepared and by practicing a presentation ahead of time.

In planning a presentation, consider the following questions:

- Who is in the audience? What do they expect? How much detail do they want?
- What is the point of my presentation? What are the three most important messages I want the audience to remember? What do I want the audience to do with the information I present?
- Are there language or technical challenges to communicating this information to this audience?
- How can I find out ahead of time how the audience may respond to my presentation?
- How much time will I have to give my presentation?
- What audiovisual resources will I be able to use (slides, overhead projections)?

When preparing a presentation, keep the audience in mind, focus on the main messages, and respect the simple time-proven rule "Tell them what you will tell them, tell them, and then tell them what you told them."

One of the best ways to improve the quality of a presentation is to practice. Rehearse the presentation alone before rehearsing in front of others. Solicit feedback after the rehearsal, and adjust the presentation accordingly. Make sure that the presentation fills the time allocated and does not run over.

During the presentation, talk to the audience, not to your notes. Make eye contact with many people in the audience. If you are using a projector and screen, print out a copy of all slides and place them in front of you so that you are never standing with your back to the audience and reading off the screen.

## Using Visual Aids

Visual elements can enhance a presentation. They can be presented as slides, overhead projections, poster boards, and handouts. (If slides or overheads are to be used, be sure to have a backup plan in case the electricity or equipment fails.)

Written information reinforces information conveyed orally. For this reason, especially when presenting to people whose native language may be different, it is often a good idea to distribute a small number of handouts at the beginning of the presentation (box 13.3). Doing so also has the advantage of allowing people to add their notations to the copy. Without handouts, it is not unusual to see people frantically trying to write down the presentation! The disadvantage of distributing handouts at the beginning of the presentation is that people tend to look ahead at the handouts, instead of focusing on what the presenter is saying. If for this reason handouts will be held until the end of the presentation, it is important to let the audience know that they will be coming. If the presentation includes complex data or tables, consider handing these tables out as the topic is presented.

## Using Presentation Programs

Presentation programs, such as PowerPoint, can make visuals look more professional. They should be used judiciously, however, lest they turn a talk into a mere slide show. To keep a presentation interesting, the speaker should limit the number of slides, using them to convey only the most important points (box 13.4).

Excessive use of slides can make a presentation deadly. It also risks "turning everything into a sales pitch" and "setting up a speaker's dominance over the audience" (Tufte 2003). As Tufte notes:

> Audiences consequently endure a relentless sequentiality, one damn slide after another. When information is stacked in time, it is difficult to understand

context and evaluate relationships. Visual reasoning usually works more effectively when relevant information is shown side by side. Often, the more intense the detail, the greater the clarity and understanding. This is especially so for statistical data, where the fundamental analytical act is to make comparisons. (Tufte 2003)

## Summary

Communicating the results of an evaluation is as critical as conducting the evaluation itself: if an evaluation's messages are not communicated, there is little point in having conducted the evaluation in the first place. Whether the evaluation is presented in writing or orally, it must be tailored to meet the needs of the audience.

Both written and oral reports can be enhanced by the use of graphics. By respecting the principles delineated in this chapter, evaluators can increase the impact their evaluations will have.

## Chapter 13 Activities

### Application Exercise 13.1: Improving an Evaluation Report

Develop a list of criteria for assessing how well an evaluation report conveys its methodology, findings, conclusions, and recommendations to its intended audience. Using these factors, assess a report that was recently written in your field. Give it a grade based on your assessment of each criterion (A for excellent, B for very good, C for adequate, and NI for needs improvement). Identify improvements that could be made to the report so that it more effectively communicates its messages.

### Application Exercise 13.2: Tailoring a Report to an Audience

For the report you reviewed in the previous exercise, identify the various audiences that might be interested in its findings or methodology. Consider which aspects of the evaluation would be of most interest to each audience, the level of detail that would be of interest to each audience, and the best way to communicate the report's main messages to meet each group's needs and preferences. Using your analysis, create a checklist to show which audiences should receive which kind of communication, when, and from whom.

# References and Further Reading

Busuladzic, Dino, and James Trevelyan. 1999. *Demining Research: An Ergonomic Aspect of Humanitarian Demining.* University of Western Australia, Perth. http://www.mech.uwa.edu.au/jpt/demining/tech/dino/ergonomics.html.

Cummings, Harry. 2003. "Using Graphics in Development Evaluations." International Program for Development Evaluation Training (IPDET) presentation, Carleton University, Ottawa, June 16–July 11.

Druker, Phil 2006. *Advanced Technical Writing.* University of Idaho, Moscow, Idaho. http://www.class.uidaho.edu/adv_tech_wrt/week14/conclusion_recommendation_final_report.htm.

Ehrenberg, A. S. C. 1977. "Rudiments of Numeracy." *Journal of the Royal Statistical Society* 140: 277–97.

Independent Evaluation Group of the International Finance Corporation. 2008. *Enhancing Monitoring and Evaluation for Better Results: Biennial Report on Operations Evaluation in IFC 2008.* Washington D.C.: World Bank. http: www.ifc.org/.../BROE2008_FullReport/$FILE/BROE+for+disclosure-final+V8-final.pdf.

Kaplan, Craig S. 2003. "Presentation Tips." Craig Web Experience. http://www.cgl.uwaterloo.ca/~csk/presentations.html.

Lawrenz, Frances, Arlen Gullickson, and Stacie Toal. 2007. "Dissemination: Handmaiden to Evaluation Use." *American Journal of Evaluation* 28 (3): 275–89.

Lentz, Michelle 2007. "Tufte and Visual Presentation." http://www.writetech.net/2007/02/presentation_st.html.

Lester, P. M. 2000. *Visual Communication: Images with Messages.* 2nd ed. Kentucky: Wadsworth Cengage Learning.

Levin, J. R., G. J. Anglin, and R. N. Carney. 1987. "On Empirically Validating Functions of Pictures in Prose." In *the Psychology of Illustration,* vol. 1, eds. D. A. Willows and H. A. Houghton, 51–85. London: Springer-Verlag.

MIGA. 2007. *Annual Report 2007–08.* http://www.miga.org/documents/IEG_MIGA_2007_Annual_Report.pdf.

Scriven, Michael. 2007. "Key Evaluation Checklist." http://www.wmich.edu/evalctr/checklists/kec_feb07.pdf.

Taylor, Dave. 2007. "Use PowerPoint to Enhance Your Presentation, Not Cripple It." http://www.intuitive.com/blog/use_powerpoint_to_enhance_your_presentation_not_cripple_it.html.

Torres, R., H. S. Preskill, and M. E. Piontek. 1997. *Evaluation Strategies for Communicating and Reporting.* Thousand Oaks, CA: Sage Publications.

Tufte, Edward R. 1983. The *Visual Display of Quantitative Information.* Cheshire, CT: Graphics Press.

———. 1990. *Envisioning Information.* Cheshire, CT: Graphics Press.

———. 1997. *Visual Explanations: Images and Quantities, Evidence and Narrative.* Cheshire, CT: Graphics Press.

——. 2003. "PowerPoint Is Evil: PowerPoint Corrupts. PowerPoint Corrupts Absolutely." *Wired* 11.09, September. http://www.wired.com/wired/archive/11.09/ppt2.html.

——. 2006. *Beautiful Evidence.* Cheshire, CT: Graphics Press.

——. 2008. The *Work of Edward Tufte.* http://www.edwardtufte.com/tufte/.

Wallgren, Anders, Britt Wallgren, Rolf Persson, Ulf Jorner, and Jan-Aage Haaland. 1996. *Graphing Statistics and Data.* Thousand Oaks, CA: Sage Publications.

World Bank Operations Evaluation Department. 2004. "The Poverty Reduction Strategy Initiative: An Independent Evaluation of the World Bank's Support through 2003." World Bank, Washington, DC.

## Web Sites

Statistics Canada. *Using Graphs.* http://www.statcan.ca/english/edu/power/ch9/using/using.htm.

Torok, George. *Presentation Skills Success.* http://www.presentationskills.ca/.

**CHAPTER 14**

# Guiding the Evaluator: Evaluation Ethics, Politics, Standards, and Guiding Principles

Evaluators have many tasks, including planning, organizing, and designing evaluations and collecting, analyzing, and presenting data. They also have to deal with internal and external pressures. They may be asked to make changes to the plan, organization, or reporting of the evaluation to meet the needs of others. Sometimes proposed modifications are welcome; at other times, they may raise ethical or political considerations.

Ethics and politics are issues for all evaluators, especially for those working in countries with poor governance and a history of corruption. Internal pressures within a development organization can also create ethical issues. This chapter discusses ethical issues and political considerations in evaluations.

**This chapter has three main parts:**

- Ethical Behavior
- Politics and Evaluation
- Evaluation Standards and Guiding Principles

## Ethical Behavior

Ethics are a set of values and beliefs that guide choices. Ethics considers big questions, such as "How should we live?" Think about this question. Who defines "how" (method), "should" (ambition), "we" (a group seeking consensus), and "live" (beings with bodies) (World IQ 2008)? Ethics depends on the people making the decisions. It is based on their view of what is right, wrong, good, and bad.

Laws are written in an attempt to identify and control ethical behavior, but laws cannot cover every possible situation. Moreover, behavior can be legal but still unethical (for example, taking a small gift from someone who is about to be evaluated or changing the tone of a report to make it more positive or negative despite the strength of the evidence behind it).

Evaluators are often faced with situations in which the right thing to do is not clear; there are many gray areas. But they are always expected to conduct evaluations ethically. Because the grounds for deciding what is ethical are based on values and beliefs, different cultures establish different laws. For this reason, it is important to be aware of what is legal as well as what is considered ethical in the country in which the evaluation is being conducted.

Evaluators should also be aware of any laws requiring reporting of a crime or suspected crime. In the United States, for example, sexual harassment is a crime. It is defined broadly as unwelcome sexual advances, requests for sexual favors, and other verbal or physical conduct of a sexual nature when submission to or rejection of the conduct implicitly or explicitly affects a person's employment or work performance or creates an intimidating, hostile, or offensive work environment (U.S. Equal Employment Opportunity Commission 2002.) Failure to report suspected sexual harassment could create legal liability.

Evaluators should be aware of the laws in the country in which they work as well as the guidance and standards of their own organization. Many development organizations have developed and issued ethical standards or guidelines.

### Evaluation Corruptibility and Fallacies

Evaluators have to be able to "speak truth to power." An independent, questioning, and analytic mindset is a must. Fitzpatrick, Sanders, and Worthen (2004) present five forms of "evaluation corruptibility":

- willingness to twist the truth and produce positive findings, as a result of conflict of interest or other perceived payoffs or penalties (such willingness may be conscious or unconscious)

- intrusion of unsubstantiated opinions because of sloppy, capricious, or unprofessional evaluation practices
- "shaded" evaluation "findings" as a result of intrusion of the evaluator's prejudices or preconceived notions
- inducements to clients or participants to cooperate by making promises that cannot be kept
- failure to honor commitments that could have been honored.

House (1995) looks at corruptibility from a slightly different perspective. He indicates that evaluators may simply misunderstand their responsibilities. He identifies five "evaluation fallacies":

- *Clientism:* the fallacy that doing whatever the client requests or whatever will benefit the client is ethically correct
- *Contractualism:* the fallacy that the evaluator must follow the written contract without question, even if doing so is detrimental to the public good
- *Methodologicalism:* the belief that following acceptable inquiry methods ensures that the behavior of the evaluator will be ethical, even when some methodologies may actually compound the evaluator's ethical dilemmas
- *Relativism:* the fallacy that all opinion data the evaluator collects from various participants must be given equal weight, as if there is no basis for appropriately giving the opinions of peripheral groups less priority than that given to more pivotal groups
- *Pluralism/elitism:* the fallacy of allowing powerful voices to be given higher priority because the evaluator believes they hold more prestige and potency than the powerless or voiceless.

## Identifying Ethical Problems

Morris and Cohn (1993) surveyed the members of the American Evaluation Association about their views on ethical issues. The following list of ethical problems is modified from their survey:

- The client decides what the findings should be before the evaluation takes place or plans to use the findings in an ethically questionable fashion.
- The client declares certain research questions off limits in the evaluation, despite their relevance.
- The client deliberately modifies findings before they are released.
- The client pressures the evaluator to alter the presentation of findings.
- The client suppresses or ignores findings.
- The client pressures the evaluator to violate confidentiality.
- The client makes unspecified misuse of findings.

- Legitimate stakeholders are omitted from the planning process.
- The evaluator discovers behavior that is illegal, unethical, or dangerous.
- The evaluator is reluctant to present findings fully, for unspecified reasons.
- The evaluator is unsure of his or her ability to be objective or fair in presenting findings.
- Although not pressured by the client or stakeholders to violate confidentiality, the evaluator is concerned that reporting certain findings could represent such a violation.
- Findings are used as evidence against someone.

In addition to these ethical problems are ethical issues associated with the design of an evaluation. Ethical issues can emerge in randomized designs in deciding who receives the intervention and who is placed in a control group. If, during the course of a project, an intervention proves promising, those not receiving the intervention may demand access to it. Granting such access changes the evaluation design and the evaluation.

If evaluations are to be useful to managers, development organizations, participants, and citizens, they must be honest, objective, and fair. It is the evaluator's job to ensure that the data are collected, analyzed, and reported honestly and fairly.

Influence at the beginning of an evaluation may be subtle. Sometimes there is pressure to avoid asking certain kinds of evaluation questions or to steer the evaluation onto less sensitive grounds. Certain issues may not be brought up that might reflect negatively on the organization or the program. Clients may say, "We know and you know we have a problem to fix and we have already started corrective action, but we do not need to make this public and jeopardize the program's support." There may be resistance to surveying staff, program participants, or citizens because sensitive (negative) issues might be revealed. In other situations, certain people may be excluded from meetings or interviews, or field trips may be limited because of "time constraints." The evaluator should strive to raise issues that are being avoided, avoid being co-opted, and make sure that all points of view are heard or considered.

Attempts to influence an evaluation often also occur during the course of an evaluation. While most evaluators would quickly recognize a bribe, they may not always recognize subtle forms of influence. Offers of friendship, dinner, or recreational activities can be a welcome gesture to someone who is far from home. They can also be an attempt to influence the evaluator's perspective and ultimately the report.

Sometimes someone provides an evaluator with leads about corruption or fraud. The evaluator should not attempt to sort out whether this information is an attempt to direct focus away from other issues, an attempt by the informant to get even with someone, or actual corruption or fraud. Evaluators are not trained as special investigators. They should, therefore, not investigate to determine if the allegations are true. Rather, they should report the allegation to the appropriate authority for investigation.

In most development organizations, procedures exist for reporting suspected misconduct or fraud. At the World Bank, for example, the Department of Institutional Integrity investigates allegations of staff misconduct as well as allegations of fraud and corruption in Bank operations. Such departments often have "hotlines" for reporting misconduct, fraud, or abuse.

Evaluation team members must be familiar with their organizations' policies and standards for handling allegations of fraud, abuse, and misconduct. These procedures may be part of a staff manual, special brochure, or contract of employment. Evaluators need to keep in mind that they are bound by their organization's policies and standards.

The motto "do no harm" certainly applies to evaluation. Except when fraud or abuse are suspected and reported for investigation, evaluations should not harm participants. This means that people who participate should never be identified or placed in threatening situations.

If confidentiality of participants is ensured and names are later divulged, harm is done. Protecting confidentiality is essential, but there may be situations where it is difficult. Say, for instance, that evaluators of an education program are told by several interviewees that the director is spending program money for personal benefit. What should the evaluators do? Revealing these findings runs the risk of exposing those who reported them in confidence. Not disclosing the incident to special investigations leads to potential complicity in the act. This situation illustrates the benefits of anonymous hotlines. It also may be helpful to talk with a supervisor or manager (not involved in the allegation) about the situation and options.

Evaluators should be particularly careful when asked to respond to reporters, program managers, or even board members "off the record." At a minimum, they should clarify what "off the record" means to the person asking them to go off the record. Evaluators should be sure they are comfortable with the definition given before proceeding.

## Politics and Evaluation

Evaluation is always carried out in a political context; the mere fact that an evaluation is being conducted may be used to advance a personal or institutional agenda. It is often said that knowledge is power; evaluation provides knowledge that can be used as a carrot or a stick to leverage behavior. It is an activity that often creates winners and losers.

Politics can undermine the integrity of an evaluation. It can determine how and the extent to which an evaluation is used. Positive evaluations can help secure more funds, expand pilot projects into full-scale programs, enhance reputations and influence, and build the careers of those involved in the intervention. Evaluations that identify serious problems can improve interventions and future results, but they may result in reduced program budgets or the cancellation of programs and the loss of face, power, and influence of those involved in the intervention.

## Causes of Politics in Evaluation

Evaluation is a form of organizational knowledge. Power struggles over definitions of reality are, therefore, inherent in the evaluation process.

Murray (2002) argues that the reason why politics are inevitable in evaluation is that there is so much room for subjectivity. Subjectivity leads to differences among the people involved in the evaluation. Evaluators gather perceptions of reality from stakeholders and from people being evaluated. Perceptions may differ, often causing disagreements at different stages of the evaluation and giving rise to political behavior.

Murray (2002 p. 2) ascribes the basis for the disagreements to "inherent problems with technical elements of evaluation methods and very common frailties in many human beings." He also describes technical and human weakness in evaluations that can have political effects. Each type of weakness is described below.

### Technical weaknesses

Most evaluations work best when measured against stated goals, objectives, and standards. But evaluators, clients, and other stakeholders may find it difficult to agree on what to measure. In addition, it can be difficult to determine the focus of the evaluation. A good evaluation identifies the theory of change and underlying assumptions of the program. If developed with program stakeholders, the theory of change can ensure a common understanding of the program's goal and objectives, activities, and the results for which the program should be accountable. Thus a theory of change can help avoid potential conflicts over the understanding of the program before they become political problems.

Murray (2002) identifies a second common technical problem that leads to political problems: evaluating one level of an organization and generalizing the findings to another. This causes problems when the links between the performance of the individuals, programs, or functions and the organization as a whole are not clearly established. Again, a theory of change is one way to help identify the underlying assumptions.

### Human weaknesses

Humans often do what is in their self-interest. They may have unconscious biases that affect how they conduct an evaluation or analyze its results.

Cutt and Murray (2000) identify three human factors that can affect evaluation:

- the "look good–avoid blame" (LGAB) mindset
- the "subjective interpretation of reality" (SIR) phenomenon
- trust factors.

The LGAB mindset identifies a common human characteristic: people want to succeed and want to avoid being associated with failure. Most evaluations have the intent of revealing both successes and failures. However, evaluators may fail to report the full extent of failures for fear that they will be associated with the failure. In an LGAB situation, people will go to great lengths to explain negative results as beyond their control. Alternatively, they may challenge the evaluation scope and approach (one reason up-front agreements on evaluation design are so important).

The SIR phenomenon arises during the interpretation of evaluation data. Two people witnessing the same event may describe it as "a teacher losing control of a classroom" or "a teacher who has fully engaged a class on an issue." Evaluators have preexisting beliefs and attitudes about what works. Evaluation results may be subjectively interpreted based on those beliefs and attitudes. For example, the evaluator who believes that a good teacher is one who has children in their seats, speaking one at a time when called upon, may be more likely to see the events as chaos or loss of control. The evaluator whose own child is in an "open classroom" may be more likely to see the same event as an example of a teacher engaging students.

The SIR phenomenon is one of the reasons this text indicates that evaluators need to conduct literature reviews to learn about what works and what issues evaluations have identified in similar programs. Another way to reduce the bias of subjective reality is to use multiple data collection methods, such as questionnaires, interviews, and structured observations, with multiple sources as a triangulation strategy.

Another factor identified by Cutt and Murray is the trust factor. It can trigger (or cause) the LGAB and SIR factors. Trust is the belief in the integrity or ability of a person. If people feel another person lacks integrity or ability, they may mistrust that person. They may fear that this person can do them harm. Trust is measured in degrees, varying from partial trust (only in certain contexts or about certain matters) to full trust (in all situations). When distrust occurs, it is likely that the LGAB or SIR phenomenon will cause politics to enter into the relationship. Previous chapters have suggested various strategies for building trust, from involving stakeholders in evaluation design to specific trust-building techniques.

### Identifying Political Games

It is impossible to keep evaluation completely separate from politics. The challenge is to manage the political situation in which evaluators find themselves. To help evaluators do so, Murray (2002) classifies games according to the roles of the people involved. Understanding these games helps evaluators manage the situation.

#### *Political games played by people being evaluated*
People being evaluated often want to avoid unwanted formal scrutiny of their activities. They may respond by

- denying the need for an evaluation
- claiming the evaluation would take too much time away from their normal or especially heavy workload and asking that it be postponed
- claiming evaluation is a good thing but engaging in delaying tactics
- seeking to form close personal relationships with evaluators in order to convince them to trust them.

Once the evaluation has begun and the data are being collected, other political games. Providers of information may

- omit or distort the information evaluators ask them to provide, so that they will not look bad
- provide evaluators with huge amounts of information, making it difficult for evaluators to sort out what is relevant and what is not
- come up with new data toward the end of the evaluation.

Once the data have been collected and evaluators are ready to interpret them, people being evaluated may respond by

- denying the problem exists
- downplaying the importance of the problem, claiming that they already knew about it and are implementing changes, or attributing it to others or forces beyond their control
- arguing that the information is irrelevant because things have changed.

### Political games played by other stakeholders

Other stakeholders may also affect the politics of an evaluation. Different stakeholders have different agendas and concerns.

If stakeholders were not involved in identifying the evaluation's major questions, they may decide that the evaluation looked at the wrong things. In addition, they may try to get others, such as the media, to criticize the organization and indicate how the evaluation should have been conducted.

### Political games played by evaluators

Evaluators can also play evaluation games. During data collection, some evaluators may subvert the process by collecting their own information "off the record." This informal information can then enter the interpretation phase of the evaluation.

Most evaluator game playing occurs during the interpretation phase of the evaluation. These games include

- shifting or not stating the measurement standards
- applying unstated criteria to decision making
- applying unstated values and ideological filters to the data interpretation, such as deciding that one source of data is not to be trusted
- ignoring data that are not consistent with the evaluator's conclusion.

## Managing Politics in Evaluations

Because politics in evaluation is inevitable, it is important to learn how to manage it. Throughout the evaluation process, the evaluator should build trust. Ideally, during each phase of an evaluation, open discussions are held that give all players involved a chance to discuss their concerns and at least agree to disagree about their differences. Murray (2002) discusses the importance of making sure that all parties involved in the evaluation fully understand the underlying logic. He suggests the theory of change (or logic model) is one way to articulate the logic so that there is little room for misunderstanding.

In what other ways does one build trust? It usually takes time and many encounters. Murray suggests involving all interested parties in the evaluation process, particularly those who are to be evaluated.

## Balancing Stakeholders with Negotiation

One of the greatest challenges for evaluators is dealing with multiple stakeholders. Evaluators need strong negotiating skills to manage multiple stakeholders' interests and often competing agendas. Markiewicz (2005) sets forth useful principles and practices for negotiating an evaluation.

### Principles for negotiating evaluation

The following is adapted from Markiewicz's (2005) list of principles for negotiating evaluations:

- Recognize the inherently political nature of evaluation.
- Value the contribution of multiple stakeholders.
- Assess stakeholder positions and plan the evaluation.
- Ensure that the evaluator is an active player within the stakeholder community.
- Develop the skills of the evaluator as negotiator responding to conflict.
- Develop skills in managing conflict with multiple stakeholders.

One key strategy is to organize stakeholders into reference groups, steering committees, or advisory committees to oversee the evaluation process. This approach is consistent with the "evaluator as facilitator" model (it is not usually applicable for independent evaluations whose main purpose is evaluating accountability). It is important that these groups have clearly defined roles and functions. The groups or committees need to establish ground rules defining how active the members are to be in the evaluation process.

According to Markiewicz (2005), once the evaluator establishes a level of credibility and acceptance with the stakeholders, he or she needs to negotiate areas of conflict or dispute among them. The evaluator needs to act as a catalyst that helps stakeholders arrive at their own solutions. To do this, the evaluator needs strong communication skills, which include the ability to listen actively and reflectively, ask appropriate questions, and check understanding. The evaluator also needs to keep the negotiation process focused and to facilitate and encourage interaction among all stakeholders.

Evaluators need to develop negotiating skills. In some cases evaluators may arrange for additional training and practice in negotiating skills (the evaluator as facilitator model). Another way for evaluators to develop negotiating skills is to work with peers to share experiences (both successful and unsuccessful) of conflict resolutions.

Patton (1997) suggests that at least four meetings take place (more for longer-term projects):

- first meeting: focus of the evaluation
- second meeting: methods and measurement tools
- third meeting: instrumentation developed before data collection
- fourth meeting: review of data to find agreement on interpretations that will lead to findings.

This is similar to the steps recommended in this volume.

Markiewicz discusses the active role evaluators should play with stakeholders. Two characteristics she describes as valuable are being both responsive and flexible, in order to allow stakeholders to engage in the process. She also discusses the difficulties that arise if the evaluator becomes too close and has too much interpersonal interaction with the stakeholders.

Patton suggests remaining focused on the empirical process and assisting stakeholders to do so as well. Doing so helps keep relationships objective and avoids the intrusion of bias or the misuse of findings.

### Practice of negotiating evaluation

Markiewicz (2005) identifies three stages in evaluation negotiation:

- Initial stage: Positions are put on the table
- Middle stage: Active negotiation takes place
- Last stage: Steps are taken to reach consensus.

To use this model, the evaluation negotiator needs to have a range of skills that are both empathetic and assertive. The empathetic skills create a climate that is conducive to negotiation. The assertive skills provide structure to the process.

Empathy can be defined as "the process of demonstrating an accurate, nonjudgmental understanding of the other side's needs, interest, and positions" (Mnookin, Peppet, and Tulumello 2000, p. 46). It includes two components: the ability to see the world through the eyes of the other and the ability to express that viewpoint in words. Empathy involves translating the understanding of the experience of the other into a shared response.

Markiewicz (2005) believes that empathy is an important characteristic for acquiring information about other goals, values, and priorities. It becomes the catalyst for inspiring openness in others and becomes a persuasive tool for negotiating.

Once the evaluator has a good understanding of the views of each stakeholder, he or she needs to paraphrase that understanding for all stakeholders present (Hale 1998). The evaluator should then ask the parties if that understanding was correct and have them clarify any differences. Active and reflective listening help the evaluator understand what is being said, ask appropriate questions, and check the understanding of what the stakeholders say.

Assertiveness is the ability to express and advocate for one's own needs, interest, and positions (Mnookin, Peppet, and Tulumello 1996). In negotiating evaluations, it can be described as facilitator authority. Balancing between empathy and assertiveness can be difficult. Mnookin, Peppet, and Tulumello (1996) see empathy and assertiveness as two interdependent dimensions of negotiation behavior. When used together, they can produce substantial benefits in negotiation and a better understanding of stakeholders' needs.

## Evaluation Standards and Guiding Principles

Professional associations develop standards or guidelines to help their members make ethical decisions. Professional associations in North America, Europe, and Australia have established ethical codes for evaluators.

The American Evaluation Association (AEA) has developed a set of standards and principles, laid out in two documents, the *Program Evaluation Standards* and *Guiding Principles for Evaluators*. These standards and principles have often served as the platform for other groups, which have modified and adapted them to their local circumstances or situations.

The AEA developed the *Guiding Principles for Evaluators* to provide guidance for evaluators in their everyday practice. The biggest difference between the AEA standards and the principles is their purpose. The standards are concerned with professional performance, while the guiding principles are concerned with professional values. The standards focus on the product of the evaluation, while the guiding principles focus on the behavior of the evaluator. Both documents provide guidance on ethical and appropriate ways to conduct evaluations.

### Program Evaluation Standards

The AEA Program Evaluation Standards are grouped into four categories:

- utility
- feasibility
- propriety
- accuracy.

Propriety includes eight specific standards:

- *Service orientation:* Addresses the need for evaluators to serve not only the interests of the agency sponsoring the evaluation but also the learning needs of program participants, community, and society.
- *Formal agreements:* Includes such issues as following protocol, having access to data, clearly warning clients about the evaluation limitations, and not promising too much.
- *Rights of human subjects:* Includes such things as obtaining informed consent, maintaining rights to privacy, and ensuring confidentiality.
- *Human interactions:* An extension of the rights of human subjects, it holds that evaluators must respect human dignity and worth in all

interactions and that no participants in the evaluation should be humiliated or harmed.

- *Complete and fair assessment:* Aims to ensure that both the strengths and weaknesses of a program are portrayed accurately. The evaluator needs to ensure that he or she does not tilt the study to satisfy the sponsor or appease other groups.
- *Disclosure of findings:* Deals with evaluator's obligation to serve the broader public who benefit from both the program and its accurate evaluation, not just the clients or sponsors. Findings should be publicly disclosed.
- *Conflict of interest:* Deals with need for evaluators to make their biases and values explicit in as open and honest a way as possible, so that clients are alert to biases that may unwittingly creep into the work of even the most honest evaluators.
- *Fiscal responsibility:* Includes need to make sure that all expenditures—including time and effort spent providing, collecting, and facilitating the collection of information requested by evaluators and explaining evaluations to various constituencies—are appropriate, prudent, and well documented.

The AEA maintains that its program evaluation standards are uniquely American and may not be appropriate for use in other countries without adaptation. In 2000, the W. K. Kellogg Foundation funded a meeting of regional and national evaluators in Barbados. Several international evaluation organizations were represented at the meeting. One of the issues discussed was whether and how the AEA program evaluation standards relate to other countries.

One result of the meeting was the publication of occasional papers discussing this issue (Russon 2000). In the first occasional paper, Taut (2000) claims that the Program Evaluation Standards developed by the AEA are values based and that values differ across cultures. She investigates how differing values affect the usability of the AEA standards outside the United States.

Taut compares the values in the standards with cultural value dimensions identified in cross-cultural literature. The cultural value dimensions she identifies as the most important are

- individualism versus collectivism
- hierarchy versus egalitarianism (or power distance)
- conservatism versus autonomy
- mastery versus harmony
- uncertainty avoidance.

Other differences she notes across cultures are direct versus indirect communication, high context versus low context, and the importance of seniority.

Taut concludes that "what is useful and ethical differs to a greater extent across cultures than what is feasible and accurate . . . . [I]t becomes clear that Propriety Standard issues are highly dependent on both political and cultural influences" (2000, p. 24). She recommends that evaluators describe their societies with regard to the cultural dimensions discussed in her paper. She also recommends that they consult with colleagues for their perceptions and with cultural experts to guide their analysis.

### Guiding Principles for Evaluators

The AEA strives to promote ethical practice in the evaluation of programs, personnel, and policy. Toward that end, it developed guiding principles (1995) to assist evaluators in their professional practice. They include the following:

- systematic inquiry
- competence
- integrity/honesty

- respect for people
- responsibility for general and public welfare.

The AEA Ethics Committee oversaw a major review and update of the Principles in 2004. (This publication and more information about the Guiding Principles and the Program Evaluation Standards can be found on the AEA Web site. Links to both documents are given at the end of this chapter in the "Evaluation Organizations" section.)

Other evaluation organizations with draft or finalized guidelines or standards available on the Internet include the following:

- the African Evaluation Association (draft evaluation standards and guidelines)
- the Australasian Evaluation Society (ethical guidelines)
- the Canadian Evaluation Society Guidelines for Ethical Conduct
- the German Society for Evaluation (standards)
- the Italian Evaluation Association (guidelines)
- the Swiss Evaluation Society (standards)
- the U.K. Evaluation Society (good practice guidelines).

In addition to guidelines for practitioners, the U.K. good practice guidelines established guidelines for commissioners and participants in the conduct of evaluations.

### Evaluation Ethics for the UN System

The United Nations Evaluation Group (UNEG) addresses evaluation ethics in its *Ethical Guidelines* (UNEG 2008). These guidelines are based on "commonly held and internationally recognized professional ideals" (UNEG 2008,

p. 3). They apply to the conduct of evaluation by staff members, external consultants, and evaluators from partner organizations in all UN agencies.

The following is an outline of the ethical principles of these guidelines:

- intentionality of evaluation, which includes the following:
  - utility
  - necessity
- obligations of evaluators
  - independence
  - impartiality
  - credibility
  - conflicts of interest
  - honesty and integrity
  - accountability
- obligations to participants
  - respect for dignity and diversity
  - rights
  - confidentiality
  - avoidance of harm
- evaluation process and product
  - accuracy, completeness, and reliability
  - transparency
  - reporting
  - omissions and wrongdoing (UNEG 2008).

UNEG has also established Standards for Evaluation in the UN system. Its standards for ethics include the following:

- Evaluators should be sensitive to beliefs, manners, and customs and act with integrity and honesty in their relationships with all stakeholders.
- Evaluators should ensure that their contacts with individuals are characterized by the same respect with which they would want to be treated.
- Evaluators should protect the anonymity and confidentiality of individual informants.
- Evaluators are responsible for their performance and their products.

## DAC Standards

Chapter 1 of this volume discussed the OECD Development Assistance Committee Network on Development Evaluation, the main group for development evaluation norms and standards. An updated summary of the DAC key norms and standards is available at http://www.oecd.org/dac/evaluationnetwork.

Of particular relevance for this chapter are the DAC's draft evaluation quality standards, which provide guidance on evaluation process and product. These standards will be finalized in 2009–10 following a three-year test phase. Section 6 of the guidelines focuses on the independence of evaluators and the extent to which the evaluation team is able to work freely and without interference. Section 7 is devoted to evaluation ethics. This draft guidance indicates that the evaluation process, and hence the evaluator, "show sensitivity to gender, beliefs, manners, and customs of all stakeholders and is undertaken with integrity and honestly. The rights and welfare of participants in the evaluation are protected. Anonymity and confidentiality of individual informants should be protected when requested and/or as required by law" (p. 22).

### Conflict of Interest

Explicit or implicit conflict of interest is a major issue potentially affecting the credibility of evaluators and the soundness of the evaluation. For each evaluation, evaluators should indicate whether they are free from conflict of interest or appearance of conflict of interest.

Some organizations have developed guidelines governing conflict of interest. The Operations Evaluation Group of the Asian Development Bank, for example, prohibits staff members or consultants from evaluating works they were involved in. This is a good practice for evaluation units.

## Summary

Ethics are a set of values and beliefs that guide choices. Evaluators can violate ethical standards by conducting evaluations despite conflicts of interest, engaging in sloppy or unprofessional evaluation practices, allowing prejudice to affect their work, making promises they cannot keep, or failing to honor commitments. Misunderstanding—in the form of clientism, contractualism, methodologicalism, relativism, or pluralism/elitism—can also cause unethical behavior to occur.

The OECD Development Assistance Committee Network on Development Evaluation, the United Nations Evaluation Group, the AEA, and other agencies and associations have developed standards, guidelines, and norms to help define and measure quality, ethics, and norms. Development evaluators need to become familiar with the relevant standards, guidelines, and norms and model their practices.

# Chapter 14 Activity

## Application Exercise 14.1: Ethics: Rosa and Agricultural Evaluation

*Rosa Marquez tells you the following story and asks for your advice. What are the major ethical issues, and how would you advise Rosa to address them?*

Rosa met with local officials, program officials, and landowners to brief them on an upcoming evaluation of a local agricultural program. Over the years, the community has received a substantial amount of money to build irrigation systems, buy fertilizer, build roads, and purchase equipment.

This was Rosa's first visit to the area. The local team member, Eduardo, had visited the area several times and knew many of the landowners. He suggested that they all go out to dinner to begin to build rapport.

During the dinner, Rosa listened to the conversation between Eduardo and the landowners. The landowners appeared to have a close relationship with Eduardo, presenting him with a box of cigars. They discussed the needs of the area. The landowners felt that they needed more resources to effectively use the land. They wanted to bring in more equipment to replace some of the farm workers. They also wanted to use more fertilizer than environmental laws permitted. Eduardo agreed with the landowners and told them the upcoming evaluation could help, because it could recommend that they be granted an exception.

The dinner ended with an invitation for Rosa to join one of the landowners for a tour of the area, followed by lunch with his family. Rosa felt it would be rude not to accept and made plans to meet the next day. She briefly spoke with Eduardo after the dinner and asked why he agreed with the landowner. Eduardo said that he believed it would make the landowners more cooperative if they felt they would get something positive from the evaluation.

During the tour the next day, the landowner explained how hard they had worked and how much progress they had made against great odds. He told Rosa that he counted on her to support their efforts. If the evaluation was negative, he and his family could not survive. As a token of his appreciation, he gave her a necklace that he said had been in his family for generations.

After the tour and lunch with the landowner's family, Rosa met with the program manager. He had mapped out a schedule indicating whom she was to meet during the three remaining days. He also set up two community meetings. These meetings included the landowners, agricultural extension workers, members of the business community that sell agricultural equipment and fertilizer, and exporters of agricultural products. When she asked why none of the farm workers and their families were included, Rosa was told they did not have anything of value to contribute to an evaluation of the effectiveness of the project. She asked whether there were others in the community whom she should talk to. She was told that the program manager had taken pains to make sure that all the right people were included so that she would have an easy job assessing the program.

# References and Further Reading

Cutt, James, and Vic Murray. 2000. *Accountability and Effectiveness Evaluation in Nonprofit Organizations.* London: Routledge.

Fitzpatrick, Jody L., James R. Sanders, and Blaine R. Worthen. 2004. *Program Evaluation: Alternative Approaches and Practical Guidelines.* New York: Pearson Education Inc.

Hale, K. 1998. "The Language of Co-Operation: Negotiation Frames." *Mediation Quarterly* 16 (2):147–62.

House, E. R. 1995. "Principles Evaluation: A Critique of the AEA Guiding Principles." In *Guiding Principles for Evaluators,* eds. R. Shadish, D. L. Newman, M. A. Scheirer, and C. Wye, 27–34. New Directions for Program Evaluation No. 66. San Francisco: Jossey-Bass.

JCSEE (Joint Committee on Standards for Educational Evaluation). 1994. *The Program Evaluation Standards: How to Assess Evaluations of Educational.* Programs Thousand Oaks, CA: Sage Publications.

Markiewicz, Anne. 2005. "'A Balancing Act': Resolving Multiple Stakeholder Interests in Program Evaluation." *Evaluation Journal of Australasia* 4 (1–2): 13–21.

Molund, Stefan, and Göran Schill. 2004. *Looking Back, Moving Forward: SIDA Evaluation Manual.* Stockholm: Swedish International Development Cooperation Agency.

Mnookin, Robert H., Scott R. Peppet, and Andrew S. Tulumello. 1996. "The Tension between Empathy and Assertiveness." *Negotiation Journal* 12 (3): 20–35.

———. 2000. *Beyond Winning: Negotiating to Create Values in Deals and Disputes.* Cambridge, MA: Harvard University Press.

Morris, M., and R. Cohn. 1993. "Program Evaluators and Ethical Challenges: A National Survey." *Evaluation Review* 17: 621–42.

Murray, Vic V. 2002. *Evaluation Games: The Political Dimension in Evaluation and Accountability Relationships.* http://www.vserp.ca/pub/CarletonEVALUATIONGAMES.pdf.

Patton, M. Q. 1997. *Utilization-Focused Evaluation: The New Century Text.* 3rd ed. Thousand Oaks, CA: Sage Publications.

Russon, Craig. 2000. The *Program Evaluation Standards in International Settings.* http://www.wmich.edu/evalctr/pubs/ops/ops17.pdf.

Stufflebeam, D. L. 1986. "Standards of Practice for Evaluators." Paper presented at the annual meeting of the American Educational Research Association, San Francisco, April.

Tassie, A. W., V. V. Murray, J. Cutt, and D. Gragg. 1996. "Rationality or Politics: What Really Goes on When Funders Evaluate the Performance of Fundees?" *Nonprofit and Voluntary Sector Quarterly* 25 (3): 347–63.

Taut, Sandy. 2000. "Cross-Cultural Transferability of the Program Evaluation Standards." In *The Program Evaluation Standards in International Settings,* ed. Craig Russon. Occasional Papers Series, Western Michigan University, Evaluation Center, Kalamazoo. http://www.wmich.edu/evalctr/pubs/ops/ops17.pdf.

UNEG (United Nations Evaluation Group). 2005. *Norms for Evaluation in the UN System.*
http://www.uneval.org/index.cfm?module=UNEG&Page=UNEGDocuments
&LibraryID=96.

———. 2008. *Ethical Guidelines.*
http://www.uneval.org/papersandpubs/documentdetail.jsp?doc_id=102.

U.S. Equal Employment Opportunity Commission. 2002.
http://www.eeoc.gov/facts/fs-sex.html.

World IQ. 2008. "Simple View of Ethics and Morals."
http://www.wordiq.com/definition/Simple_view_of_ethics_and_morals.

## Web Sites

Department for International Development. http://www.keysheets.org/red_7_
swaps_rev.pdf.

Evaluation Center, Western Michigan University. http://www.wmich.edu/evalctr/

Human Rights Education. http://www.hrea.org/pubs/EvaluationGuide/.

Institute of Development Studies. 1998. *Participatory Monitoring and Evaluation: Learning from Change,* IDS Policy Briefing 12 (November). http://www.ids
.ac.uk/ids/bookshop/briefs/PB12.pdf.

Inter-American Development Bank. 2004. *Proposal for Sectorwide Approaches (SWAps).* http://enet.iadb.org/idbdocswebservices/idbdocsInternet/IADB
PublicDoc.aspx?docnum=509733.

MEASURE Evaluation Project. *Monitoring and Evaluation of Population and Health Programs.* University of North Carolina, Chapel Hill. http://www.cpc.unc.edu/
measure.

National Aeronautics and Space Act of 1958. http://www.hq.nasa.gov/office/pao/
History/spaceact.html.

Treasury Board of Canada. *Linkages between Audit and Evaluation in Canadian Federal Developments.* http://www.tbs-sct.gc.ca/pubs_pol/dcgpubs/TB_h4/
evaluation03_e.asp.

United Nations Population Fund. *UNFPA List of Evaluation Reports and Findings.*
http://www.unfpa.org/publications/index.cfm.

World Bank. *The World Bank Participation Sourcebook.* Washington, DC: World
Bank. http://www.worldbank.org/wbi/sourcebook/sbhome.htm.

## Evaluation Organizations

African Evaluation Association. http://www.geocities.com/afreval/.

American Evaluation Association. http://www.eval.org.

Australasian Evaluation Society. http://www.aes.asn.au/.

Canadian Evaluation Society. http://www.evaluationcanada.ca.

European Evaluation Society. http://www.europeanevaluation.org.

German Society for Evaluation. http://www.degeval.de/.

Government and Nongovernmental Organizations. http://www.eval.org/ Resources/govt_orgs_&_ngos.htm.

Institute of Internal Auditors. http://www.theiia.org.

International Organization of Supreme Audit Institutions. http://www.gao.gov/ cghome/parwi/img4.html.

Italian Evaluation Association. http://www.valutazioneitaliana.it/aiv/news.php.

Swiss Evaluation Society. http://www.seval.ch/en/.

United Kingdom Evaluation Society. http://www.evaluation.org.uk/.

## Standards and Guiding Principles

American Evaluation Association. 2004. *Guiding Principles*. http://www.eval.org/ Publications/GuidingPrinciples.asp. (Abbreviated version in brochure form: http://www.eval.org.)

———. 2005. *Program Standards*. http://www.eval.org/EvaluationDocuments/ progeval.html.

Asian Development Bank. *Guidelines*. Operations Evaluation Group. http://www .adb.org/documents/guidelines/evaluation/independent-evaluation.pdf.

Australasian Evaluation Society. *Ethical Guidelines for Evaluators*. http://www.aes .asn.au/about/Documents%20-%20ongoing/guidelines_for_the_ethical_ conduct_of_evaluations.pdf.

Canadian Evaluation Society. *Guidelines for Ethical Conduct*. http://www .evaluationcanada.ca.

German Society for Evaluation. *Standards*. http://www.degeval.de/standards/ standards.htm.

Italian Evaluation Association. *Guidelines*. http://www.valutazioneitaliana.it/ statuto.htm#Linee).

Organisation for Economic Co-operation and Development. *Principles for Evaluation of Development Assistance*. Development Assistance Committee. http:// www.oecd.org/dataoecd/31/12/2755284.pdf.

———. *DAC Criteria for Evaluating Development Assistance*. Development Assistance Committee. http://www.oecd.org/document/22/0,2340,en_2649_34435_ 2086550_1_1_1,00.html.

———. DAC Network on Development Evaluation. *Evaluating Development Co-Operation: Summary of Key Norms and Standards*. http://www.oecd.org/dac/ evaluationnetwork.

United Kingdom Evaluation Standards. 2008. http://www.mfcr.cz/cps/rde/xbcr/ mfcr/EvalStandards_UK.pdf and http://www.evaluation.org.uk/resources/ guidelines.aspx.

**CHAPTER 15**

# Looking to the Future

The previous 14 chapters described "the road to results." They discussed the foundations of development evaluation; how to prepare, design, and conduct an evaluation; and how to act professionally. These chapters brought us to today. This chapter briefly reviews where we have been and where we are today before looking at what the future may hold for development evaluation.

**This chapter has two main parts:**
- Past to Present
- The Future

## Past to Present

Changes in development are soon reflected in development evaluation. The 2000 gathering of world leaders to endorse the Millennium Development Declaration and to define development as a global partnership for poverty reduction turned attention to measuring results. Development evaluation responded, but a long road still lies ahead.

This book is dedicated to increasing the use of evaluative knowledge for decision making. Seven critical steps can improve the usefulness of evaluation in determining development effectiveness:

1. *Shift to results-based evaluation.* More attention is being paid to achieving results beyond output measures, but doing so is still not routine for development or development evaluation. Without knowing what success of an intervention should look like in the short, medium, and long term, organizations will continue to reward delivery of required goods or services without being sure that they will cause changes in behavior and result in the desired sustainable institutional improvement.

2. *Identify the theories of change behind development interventions.* The essential first question in addressing impact is not "What was the intervention's impact?" but rather "Was the intervention actually needed, and why would we expect it to have the impact it did?" This kind of analysis needs to become standard practice. Theories of change need to graphically depict the logic of the link between an intervention and its intended results, the key assumptions being made about how and why it will work, and the other major competing events in the environment that may account for changes observed.

3. *Promote the appropriate use of counterfactuals in evaluation designs.* Counterfactuals are often necessary to establish the link between an intervention and outcomes and impacts. But while experimental (and quasi-experimental) designs are strong designs, they are not "gold standards." Development evaluation needs to focus on the questions that need to be answered and to select designs appropriate to the questions. It may be more useful, for example, to learn about the marginal impact of longer duration of a program or the variance of an intervention in implementation as the result of contextual factors or participant characteristics than to learn about differences in impact among treatment and nontreatment groups. While understanding experimental and quasi-experimental designs must be part of any impact evaluation training, such training must also include nonexperimental designs, such as case studies.

4. *Use mapping, contribution, and additionality at the country level instead of searching for attribution.* Attribution of development results to a single development entity is difficult at the project level; it is generally fruitless in more complex evaluations, such as those at the sector or country level. With recognition of development as a global partnership, a shift of paradigms is needed. A first step for development evaluation is mapping the activities of the main donors, lenders, and nongovernmental organizations (NGOs) in a given country. Preferably, this analysis would be done by the country itself and then used as the basis for evaluating aid coordination and determining an individual development organization's contribution through additionality.

5. *Reduce the costs and increase the benefits of project-level evaluation.* Despite much rhetoric, most evaluation resources are still tied to project evaluation. More use should be made of cluster evaluations of related projects one to three years after the last funding disbursement. These evaluations could look for outcome patterns and test whether there are participant characteristics or contextual variables that are critical to success.

6. *Build evaluation capacity.* The increased emphasis on measuring results has itself led to increased demand for development evaluation specialists. The Paris Declaration and Accra Accord have helped focus attention on the capacity-building needs of developing countries and donors are responding with increased funding, but building evaluation capacity will be a long-term effort. Donors also need to address the issue of building demand for evaluators in ministries and other agencies in developing countries. This end of the equation on building demand cannot be ignored.

    Multilateral development banks, bilateral development banks, and other aid organizations must address the building of evaluation capacity by their own staffs. Their dedicated evaluation staffs, generally drawn from the internal ranks of development project officers, often lack solid evaluation backgrounds. Sometimes they are economists or researchers from other backgrounds, who, while trained in generally applicable social science research methods and econometrics, may lack training on qualitative methods.

    Training and other evaluation capacity building efforts need their own evaluation to ensure quality programs. When demand outstrips supply, low-quality programs can be a problem. Claims of expertise in evaluation training need verification.

7. *Use evaluative knowledge.* None of the previously listed steps makes much of a difference unless the findings from sound evaluation are used to inform development of the next intervention. Evaluation serves not

just the purpose of accountability but that of learning. This has long been the mantra of evaluators. Much is known about how to increase the likelihood of use of evaluation in the development evaluation context. It is past time to place emphasis on translating this knowledge into action. (Rist and Stame 2006).

## The Future

None of us has a crystal ball into which we can gaze to accurately predict the future. We can, however, develop informed views of the future trends and challenges for development evaluation. We close the book with some thoughts on this.

First and foremost, we see the continuing rise of monitoring and evaluation (M&E) in just about every developing country. An interesting development is study tours to developing countries to learn more about their M&E systems. These tours are for people from developing and developed countries. We believe that similar efforts will occur not only in government ministries and offices but also in parliaments, foundations, churches, associations, other voluntary organizations, and the private sector.

The demand for accountability for results is not going away. Its chief threat is death by overloaded monitoring indicator systems that are fed too much data, with the result that the level of effort is unsustainable.

### Internal and External Evaluation

Development evaluation largely sat out the quantitative–qualitative methods debate that raged through the American Evaluation Association (AEA) in the 1990s. Indeed, use of mixed methods has been common in the development community.

More problematic for development evaluation has been the issue of whether to perform external or internal evaluations and where, organizationally, to locate evaluation units. While monitoring systems and M&E staff members are clearly viewed as internal, evaluation has given more pause. This is a particularly important issue for those who start from scratch rather than from an inherited framework.

Will development evaluation tend to be internal and a combined function for those managing results-based monitoring systems? Or will development evaluation turn more to the strategy of the European Commission and favor contracting out evaluations to external individuals and firms?

Our prediction is that continued strong demand for results will mean that development evaluation flourishes not only within management M&E units but also in requests for evaluations conducted by external consultants and firms. We also foresee increased calls and necessity for independent evaluation.

Externally conducted evaluation is not necessarily independent evaluation. If the evaluation is conducted externally but is funded by and under the general oversight of those who manage the program, it is an internal evaluation and should not be deemed independent. Independent evaluations, independent evaluation units, and independent evaluators should meet principles for independence, such as those established by the multilateral development banks' Evaluation Cooperation Group (see chapter 1), irrespective of the reputation or ethics of the entity conducting the evaluation.

An independent evaluation function may be located inside a development organization (an example is the Independent Evaluation Group of the World Bank Group). It may be part of a parliament or other legislative organization. Wherever it is located, however, the independent evaluation unit will need to formally assess its attainment of the principles of independence, using a rating scale such as that presented in chapter 1.

## Development of Evaluation Capacity

Increased demand for M&E must go hand in hand with the building of evaluation capacity. An evaluation function that relies on a few external experts is not likely to meet long-term needs. Evaluation capacity at all levels within a country must generally be developed. We predict a continued increase in evaluation capacity building efforts in developing countries.

Development of evaluation capacity encompasses multiple actions to build and strengthen M&E systems in developing countries. It focuses on the national and sector levels. It encompasses many related concepts and tools, including capacities to keep score on development effectiveness, specification of project and program objectives and result chains, performance information (including basic data collection), program and project M&E, beneficiary assessment surveys, sector reviews, and performance auditing (Kusek and Rist 2004; Mackay 2007).

Evaluation capacity development assists countries in determining where to start in building evaluation capacity (box 15.1). Various diagnostic instruments have been developed (see, for example, World Bank 1999].

**Box 15.1   Key Issues for Diagnosing a Government's
M&E Systems**

1. Genesis of the existing M&E system: role of M&E advocates or champions, key events that created the priority for M&E information (for example, election of reform-oriented government, fiscal crisis).
2. The ministry or agency responsible for managing the M&E system and planning evaluations. Roles and responsibilities of the main parties to the M&E system (the finance ministry, the planning ministry, the president's office, the sector ministries, the legislature). Incentives for stakeholders to take M&E seriously (strength of demand for M&E information). Possible existence of several uncoordinated M&E systems at the national and sectoral levels. Importance of federal/state/local issues to the M&E system.
3. The public sector environment and whether it makes it easy or difficult for managers to perform to high standards and to be held accountable for their performance. Existence of public sector reforms—such as a poverty reduction strategy, performance budgeting, the strengthening of policy analysis skills, creation of a performance culture in the civil service, improvements in service delivery (such as customer service standards), government decentralization, greater participation by civil society, or an anticorruption strategy—that might benefit from a stronger emphasis on the measurement of government performance.
4. The main aspects of public sector management that the M&E system supports strongly, such as budget decision making, national or sectoral planning program management, and accountability relationships (to the finance ministry, president's office, parliament, sector ministries, civil society).
5. The role of M&E information at the various stages of the budget process (policy advising and planning, budget decision making, performance review and reporting) and the possible disconnect between the M&E work of sector ministries and the use of such information in the budget process. The existence of any disconnect between the budget process and national planning. Opportunities to strengthen the role of M&E in the budget.
6. The extent to which the M&E information commissioned by key stakeholders (for example, the finance ministry) is used by others (such as sector ministries). Identification of barriers to use (if any). Evidence concerning the extent of utilization by different stakeholders (for example, a diagnostic review or a survey). Examples of major evaluations that have been highly influential with the government.

7. Types of tools emphasized in the M&E system (regular performance indicators, rapid reviews or evaluations, performance audits, rigorous in-depth impact evaluations). Scale and cost of each of these types of M&E. Manner in which evaluation priorities are set (are they focused on "problem programs,'" pilot programs, high-expenditure or high-visibility programs, or are they based on a systematic research agenda to answer questions about program effectiveness?).

8. Responsibility for collecting performance information and conducting evaluations (ministries themselves, academics, or consulting firms). Problems with data quality or reliability or with the quality of evaluations that have been conducted. Strengths and weaknesses of local supply of M&E. Key capacity constraints and the government's capacity-building priorities.

9. Extent of donor support for M&E in recent years. Donor projects that support M&E at whole-of-government, sectoral, or agency levels (provision of technical assistance, other capacity building, and funding for the conduct of major evaluations, such as rigorous impact evaluations).

10. Conclusions regarding overall strengths and weaknesses of the M&E system, including its sustainability in the face of a change in government. Dependence of system on donor funding or other support. Current plans for future strengthening of the M&E system.

*Source:* World Bank 2006.

Evaluation capacity development ensures that evaluation findings are available to assist countries in four key areas:

- Allocating government resources in planning, decision making, and prioritization, particularly in the budget process.
- Understanding the performance of ongoing activities at the sector, program, and project levels so that learning and improvement can occur.
- Holding managers accountable for the performance of the activities they manage, so that government can be held accountable for performance. The notion of accountability encompasses the recognition that economic governance and a sound public sector are central to national economic competitiveness. Markets reward countries that are able to manage and screen public expenditures; evaluation offers a tool to help governments do so.
- Demonstrating the extent to which development activities have been successful. This is proving to be increasingly important for countries in attracting external resources, particularly given the pressures on

international development assistance agencies to channel their assistance to countries where past development efforts have been successful. Moreover, the increasing emphasis by development assistance agencies on a whole-of-government approach to development increases the premium on having countrywide measures of performance available.

Developing evaluation capacity requires convincing policy makers that evaluation is helpful; it cannot be imposed on a government. It requires an information infrastructure that allows data to be routinely collected and results disseminated and used. Building useful evaluation systems usually takes a long time, because doing so requires political and institutional changes (Schaumberg-Müller 1996). It took the United States, for example, 10 years to fully implement the Government Performance and Results Act (GPRA) and all of the M&E systems within it (Kusek and Rist 2004). Institutions need to believe that evaluations are not control systems but tools to improve performance and decision making.

What can be done to motivate evaluation capacity development? What incentives and constraints exist? Toulemonde (1999) discusses the importance of using both incentives (carrots) and evaluation by demand (sticks). The first incentive he identifies is budgetary. Evaluations cost money, which must be available for evaluation capacity development to occur. The second incentive is a good career path for those who choose to become evaluators.

Toulemonde identifies ways of creating evaluation demand by constraints. The first is compulsory evaluation. Where organizations are required to conduct evaluations, they must be given the right to ask questions. They must have full access to field data and be required to make use of the evaluation results.

Toulemonde admits that "laws and rules are meaningless on their own" (1999, p. 159). They must be enforced, and power must be exerted. He goes on to discuss the value of mixing both incentives and constraints.

## Professionalism of Development Evaluators

Anyone can decide to take on the identity of development evaluator. There are as yet no standard competencies to be met through training or practice, no credentialing or certifying process that one needs to go through before one can call oneself a development evaluator. Many people learn on the job without formal training. Managing or directing evaluation units also requires no special credentials: evaluative knowledge and experience are not prerequisites.

The time-honored method of learning on the job should not be discounted; managers without formal training can grow into the job. The lack of credentialing, however, makes it difficult for purchasers of development evaluation services to identify expertise.

As development evaluation demand continues to grow, we believe that increasing calls for professionalism are likely in response to poorly conceived or conducted evaluations. The International Development Evaluation Association (IDEAS) is playing a growing role in the global professionalization of development evaluation.

### Establishing Core Competencies

One major issue within and outside of development evaluation is whether core evaluator competencies, such as those shown in box 15.2, should be established. The American Evaluation Association (AEA) has chosen not to endorse such competencies, after initial investigation. In contrast, the Canadian Evaluation Society (CES) is pursuing "professional designations," a form of credentialing. It is simultaneously seeking to increase graduate training in evaluation. The New Zealand Evaluation Association is currently thinking of developing competencies.

The Treasury Board of Canada is calling for certification for heads of the evaluation units that have been mandated for Canadian agencies. A report prepared by its Secretariat presents the results of a study to "investigate optional approaches to increase the professionalism of evaluation in the federal government" (Treasury of Board of Canada Secretariat 2005). An International Board of Standards for Training, Performance, and Instruction has developed competencies for internal staff and external consultants conducting evaluations in organizational settings (the link to this Web site is given at the end of this chapter).

The CES's Professional Designations Project believes credentialing should be based on a combination of education and experience. It views certification as requiring an examination. Therefore it is choosing a nonexam-based credentialing approach. Many of the tasks required to establish credentialing are well under way, including the establishment of credentialing requirements, grandparenting mechanisms for those who are already practitioners, a credentialing board, and a dispute mechanism. A demonstration project is expected to begin in 2009 (AEA 2008). The link to the CES at the end of this chapter presents more information on this effort.

What about standards for those engaged in development evaluation? IDEAS is beginning to explore this issue for development evaluators. The extensive efforts of and background work done by the Canadian Evaluation Society will provide a strong starting point. Work by the Evaluation Capacity Development Task Force of the United Nations Evaluation Groups (UNEG)—which developed core competencies for the evaluation staff at

**Box 15.2    Essential Competencies for Program Evaluators**

*1.0    Professional practice*

1.1    Applies professional evaluation standards

1.2    Acts ethically and strives for integrity and honesty in conducting evaluations

1.3    Conveys personal evaluation approaches and skills to potential clients

1.4    Respects clients, respondents, program participants, and other stakeholders

1.5    Considers the general and public welfare in evaluation practice

1.6    Contributes to the knowledge base of evaluation

*2.0    Systematic inquiry*

2.1    Understands the knowledge base of evaluation (terms, concepts, theories, assumptions)

2.2    Is knowledgeable about quantitative methods

2.3    Is knowledgeable about qualitative methods

2.4    Is knowledgeable about mixed methods

2.5    Conducts literature reviews

2.6    Specifies program theory

2.7    Frames evaluation questions

2.8    Develops evaluation designs

2.9    Identifies data sources

2.10    Collects data

2.11    Assesses validity of data

2.12    Assesses reliability of data

2.13    Analyzes data

2.14    Interprets data

2.15    Makes judgments

2.16    Develops recommendations

2.17    Provides rationales for decisions throughout the evaluation

2.18    Reports evaluation procedures and results

2.19    Notes strengths and limitations of the evaluation

2.20    Conducts meta-evaluations

*3.0    Situational analysis*

3.1    Describes the program

3.2    Determines program evaluability

3.3    Identifies the interests of relevant stakeholders

3.4    Serves the information needs of intended users

3.5    Addresses conflicts

3.6    Examines the organizational context of the evaluation

3.7    Analyzes the political considerations relevant to the evaluation

3.8    Attends to issues of evaluation use

3.9    Attends to issues of organizational change

3.10   Respects the uniqueness of the evaluation site and client

3.11   Remains open to input from others

3.12   Modifies the study as needed

*4.0*    *Project management*

4.1    Responds to requests for proposals

4.2    Negotiates with clients before the evaluation begins

4.3    Writes formal agreements

4.4    Communicates with clients throughout the evaluation process

4.5    Budgets an evaluation

4.6    Justifies cost given information needs

4.7    Identifies needed resources for evaluation, such as information, expertise, personnel, and instruments

4.8    Uses appropriate technology

4.9    Supervises others involved in conducting the evaluation

4.10   Trains others involved in conducting the evaluation

4.11   Conducts the evaluation in a nondisruptive manner

4.12   Presents work in a timely manner

*5.0*    *Reflective practice*

5.0    Aware of self as an evaluator (knowledge, skills, dispositions)

5.2    Reflects on personal evaluation practice (competencies and areas for growth)

5.3    Pursues professional development in evaluation

5.4    Pursues professional development in relevant content areas

5.5    Builds professional relationships to enhance evaluation practice

*6.0*    *Interpersonal competence*

6.1    Uses written communication skills

6.2    Uses verbal/listening communication skills

6.3    Uses negotiation skills

6.4    Uses conflict resolution skills

6.5    Facilitates constructive interpersonal interaction (teamwork, group facilitation, processing)

6.6    Demonstrates cross-cultural competence

*Source:* Stevahn and others 2005.

different levels, and were adopted in 2008—may also be helpful (the link to UNEG's Web site is given at the end of this chapter).

Some believe that the evaluation field will never agree on a set of competencies for evaluators, that, instead, each organization or other entity will develop competencies for evaluators specific to their business, culture, and traditions. We predict that a set of global core competencies will be developed for development evaluation. Organizations will likely have additional competencies for evaluators, specific to their business, and will customize, but they will expect the core competencies to be attained.

Another argument is that one would have to be superhuman to attain all the competencies needed for all evaluations in all situations. Certainly, there will be extra requirements for those seeking evaluation specialties, such as expertise in social and environmental evaluation or the like. However, just as a brain surgeon is trained in general medicine but physicians are not trained in brain surgery, the core is central.

### *Certifying Development Evaluators*

Should there be a process whereby development evaluators can acquire certification of skills that is recognized worldwide? Such certification has certainly been useful for auditors, among whom designation as a certified public accountant is recognized and respected internationally. A recent survey by IDEAS of its membership indicated strong support for increased professionalization through competencies and, ultimately, certification (Morra Imas 2009).

Certifying evaluators would provide a mechanism for protecting consumers from substandard work and practitioners who deceptively embellish their credentials. It is also a mechanism for distinguishing evaluation and those who conduct it from audit reviews and auditors. Concerns center on fears that creating a mechanism might create a barrier to entry, especially in an environment in which demand outstrips supply and in a field in which on-the-job learning has been a traditional entry method.

Where evaluation quality and evaluator competence are of concern, especially because of the high external demand, a strong push for core competencies is likely. Our view is that if core competencies are set for development evaluators, discussion of certification will not be far behind.

In the end, the greatest challenges for development evaluation may be learning to set realistic expectations for interventions, building public demand for evaluation in countries without democratic traditions, reconciling results-based evaluation with participatory evaluation, and promoting evaluative thinking within all organizations. We look forward to meeting these challenges.

## Application Exercise 15.1: Building Evaluation Capacity

You (or your group) have been asked by the government to create a strategic plan for increasing evaluation capacity in your home country. Use the questions below to guide your thinking in preparing a one- to two-page strategic plan.

1. What are the two or three most difficult development issues to be tackled in the next several years?
2. To the best of your knowledge, what evaluation capacity already exists (availability of evaluators, skills, resources, infrastructure)?
3. Given current and future development needs and issues and your assessment of current evaluation capacity, list the six most important enhancements that would improve evaluation capacity in your country.
4. What is driving the need for M&E systems in your country?
5. Where in your government does accountability for the effective (and efficient) delivery of programs lie?
6. Is there a codified (through statute or mandate) strategy or organization in the government for tracking development goals?
7. Where does capacity with the requisite skills for designing and using M&E systems lie in your country? How has this capacity (or lack thereof) contributed to the use of M&E in your country?
8. Prioritize the needs for your country by identifying them as critical, very important, or important.

# References and Further Reading

AEA (American Evaluation Association). 2008. "Professional Designation for Evaluators in Canada: Where Are We Now?" Session at the annual conference of the American Evaluation Association, Denver, CO, November 5–8.

Beywl, W., and K. Harich. 2008. "University-Based Continuing Education in Evaluation: The Baseline in Europe." *Evaluation* 13 (1): 121–34.

Boyle, Richard. 1999. "Professionalizing the Evaluation Function: Human Resource Development and the Building of Evaluation Capacity." In *Building Effective Evaluation Capacity: Lessons from Practice,* eds. Richard Boyle and Donald Lemaire, 135-51. New Brunswick, NJ: Transaction Publishers.

Boyle, Richard, and Donald Lemaire, eds. 1999. *Building Effective Evaluation Capacity: Lessons from Practice.* New Brunswick, NJ: Transaction Publishers.

Dewey, J. D., B. E. Montrosse, D. C. Schroter, C. D. Sullins, and J. R. Mattox II. 2008. "Evaluator Competencies: What's Taught versus What's Sought." *American Journal of Evaluation* 29 (3): 268–87.

Ghere, G., J. A. King, L. Stevahn, and J. Minnema. 2006. "A Professional Development Unit for Reflecting on Program Evaluator Competencies." *American Journal of Evaluation,* 27 (1): 108–23.

Kusek, Jody Zall, and Ray C. Rist. 2004. *Ten Steps to a Results-Based Monitoring and Evaluation System.* World Bank, Washington, DC. http://www.oecd.org/dataoecd/23/27/35281194.pdf.

Mackay, Keith. 2007. *How to Build M&E Systems to Support Better Government.* World Bank, Independent Evaluation Group, Washington, DC. http://www.worldbank.org/ieg/ecd/docs/How_to_build_ME_gov.pdf.

McDonald, K. E., and S. E. Myrick. 2008. "Principles, Promises, and a Personal Plea: What Is an Evaluator to Do?" *American Journal of Evaluation* 29 (3): 343–51.

Morra Imas, Linda. 2009. "The Competencies and Credentials Debate in Evaluation: What Is It all About?" Presentation to the International Development Evaluation Association's Global Assembly, Johannesburg, March.

Porteous, Nancy L., Barbara J. Sheldrick, and Paula J. Stewart. 1999. "Enhancing Managers' Evaluation Capacity: A Case Study for Ontario Public Heath." *Canadian Journal of Program Evaluation* (Special Issue): 137–54.

Rist, Ray C., and Nicoletta Stame, eds. 2006. From Studies to Streams: *Managing Evaluative Systems.* Piscataway, NJ: Transaction Publishers.

Schaumberg-Müller, Henrik. 1996. *Evaluation Capacity Building: Donor Support and Experiences.* Copenhagen: Organisation for Economic Co-operation and Development. http://www.oecd.org/dataoecd/20/52/16546669.pdf.

Sonnichsen, Richard C. 1999. "Building Evaluation Capacity within Organizations." In *Building Effective Evaluation Capacity: Lessons from Practice,* eds. Richard Boyle and Donald Lemaire, 53–73. New Brunswick, NJ: Transaction Publishers.

Stevahn, Laurie, Jean A. King, Gail Ghere, and Jane Minnema. 2005. "Establishing Essential Competencies for Program Evaluators." *American Journal of Evaluation* 26 (1): 43–59.

Toulemonde, Jacques. 1999. "Incentives, Constraints, and Culture-Building as Instruments for Development of Evaluation Demand." In *Building Effective Evaluation Capacity: Lessons from Practice,* eds. Richard Boyle and Donald Lemaire, 153–68. New Brunswick, NJ: Transaction Publishers.

Treasury of Board of Canada Secretariat. 2005. *Improving the Professionalism of Evaluation*. Final report. http://www.tbs-sct.gc.ca/eval/dev/Professionalism/profession_e.asp.

World Bank. 1999. *Evaluation Capacity Development: A Diagnostic Guide and Action Framework*. ECD Working Paper 6, Operations Evaluation Department, Washington, DC.

———. 2006. *Diagnostic Guides*. Washington, DC. http://www.worldbank.org/ieg/ecd/diagnostic_guides.html.

## Web Sites

Campbell, Patricia B., and Beatriz Chu Clewell. 2008. *Building Evaluation Capacity: Designing a Cross-Project Evaluation. Guide I*. Urban Institute, Washington, DC. http://www.uquebec.ca/observgo/fichiers/43799_GRA-1a.pdf.

———. 2008. *Building Evaluation Capacity: Collecting and Using Data in Cross-Project Evaluations. Guide II*. Urban Institute, Washington, DC. http://www.uquebec.ca/observgo/fichiers/42773_GRA-1b.pdf.

Canadian Evaluation Society. www.evaluationcanada.ca.

———. *Professional Designation Project*. http://www.evaluationcanada.ca/site.cgi?s=5&ss=6&_lang=EN.

UNEG (United Nations Evaluation Group).2004a. *Evaluation Capacity Development: A Strategy Paper*. http://cfapp1-docs-public.undp.org/eo/evaldocs1/uneg_2006/eo_doc_350011048.doc.

———. 2004b. *Evaluation Capacity Development Task Force: Highlights*. http://cfapp1-docs-public.undp.org/eo/evaldocs1/uneg_2006/eo_doc_562044935.doc.

Weiss, Carol. *Evaluating Capacity Development: Experiences from Research and Development Organizations around the World*. http://www.agricta.org/pubs/isnar2/ECDbood(H-ch7).pdf.

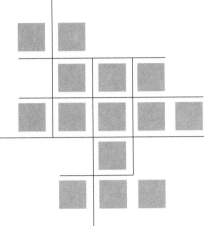

# APPENDIXES

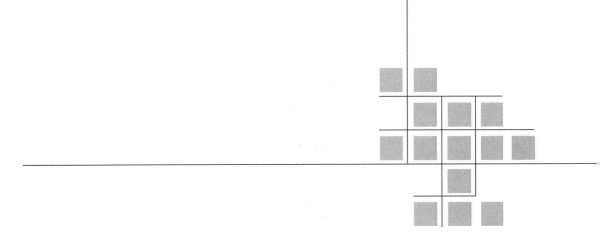

# OECD DAC Network on Development Evaluation Evaluating Development Cooperation: Summary of Key Norms and Standards

## Table of Contents

## Introduction

The DAC Network on Development Evaluation is a unique international forum that brings together evaluation managers and specialists from development co-operation agencies in OECD member countries and multilateral development institutions. Its goal is to increase the effectiveness of international development programmes by supporting robust, informed and independent evaluation. The Network is a subsidiary body of the OECD Development Assistance Committee (DAC).

A key component of the Network's mission is to develop internationally agreed norms and standards for development evaluation. These inform evaluation policy and practice and contribute to harmonised approaches in line with the commitments of the Paris Declaration on Aid Effectiveness. The body of norms and standards is based on experience, and evolves over time to fit the changing aid environment. The norms and standards serve as an international reference point, guiding efforts to improve development results through high quality evaluation.

The norms and standards summarised here should be applied discerningly and adapted carefully to fit the purpose, object and context of each evaluation. As this summary document is not an exhaustive evaluation manual readers are encouraged to refer to the complete texts available on the DAC Network on Development Evaluation's website:

**www.oecd.org/dac/evaluationnetwork.**

This and other key definitions are covered in the *Glossary of Key Terms in Evaluation and Results Based Management*. The glossary is a useful capacity development tool that helps build shared understandings of fundamental evaluation concepts. The DAC glossary is available in Arabic, Chinese, Dutch, English, French, Italian, Japanese, Kiswahili, Portuguese, Russian, Spanish, Swedish and Turkish.

## Development of Norms and Standards for Evaluation

A set of core **principles for evaluation of development assistance** (summarised in Part I) were adopted by the OECD DAC in 1991 and are at the heart of the Evaluation Network's approach to evaluation. The principles focus on the management and institutional arrangements of the evaluation system within development agencies.

During a **review of the evaluation principles** in 1998, most DAC members reported having made progress in implementing the core principles and found them useful and relevant. These fundamental evaluation principles not only remain a key benchmark for development evaluation but also serve as the basis for DAC Peer Reviews—the only internationally agreed mechanism to assess the performance of OECD DAC members' development co-operation programmes. However, the review also highlighted areas requiring adjustment or more specific guidance, setting the stage for further developments.

The **DAC criteria for evaluating development assistance** (detailed in Part II) are based on the evaluation principles and serve as a general guide of measures that can be applied, and are useful for assessing development work.

A thorough analysis of members' evaluation policies and practices undertaken in 2006, based on a review of peer reviews conducted over a period of eight years, led to the development of **Evaluation Systems and Use: A Working Tool for Peer Reviews and Assessments** (Part III). This document provides the key elements of a strong evaluation function in development agencies and is used to advance implementation of the principles.

The most recent step in the development of a normative framework is the definition of **evaluation quality standards** (presented in draft form in Part IV). These standards provide guidance on evaluation process and product. They will be finalised in 2009-2010 following a test phase of three years.

In addition to these general norms and standards, OECD DAC members recognise the need for specific guidance in certain areas of development evaluation. Building on evaluation experiences and the texts described above, guidance has been developed in a number of areas. The most significant of these **guidance documents** are presented in Part V.

## Part I: DAC Principles for Evaluation of Development Assistance

Adopted at the OECD DAC High Level Meeting in 1991, the evaluation principles were published in 1992 as part of the *DAC Principles for Effective Aid*. An overview of key elements of the original document is provided below.

### I. Central Messages

The principles provide general guidance on the role of aid evaluation in the aid management process, with the following central messages:

- Aid agencies should have an evaluation policy with clearly established guidelines and methods and with a clear definition of its role and responsibilities and its place in institutional aid structure.
- The evaluation process should be impartial and independent from the process concerned with policy-making, and the delivery and management of development assistance.
- The evaluation process must be as open as possible with the results made widely available.
- For evaluations to be useful, they must be used. Feedback to both policy makers and operational staff is essential.

- Partnership with recipients and donor co-operation in aid evaluation are both essential; they are an important aspect of recipient institution-building and of aid co-ordination and may reduce administrative burdens on recipients.
- Aid evaluation and its requirements must be an integral part of aid planning from the start. Clear identification of the objectives which an aid activity is to achieve is an essential prerequisite for objective evaluation. (Para. 4)

## II. Purpose of Evaluation

The main purposes of evaluation are:

- to improve future aid policy, programmes and projects through feedback of lessons learned;
- to provide a basis for accountability, including the provision of information to the public.

Through the evaluation of failures as well as successes, valuable information is generated which, if properly fed back, can improve future aid programmes and projects. (Para. 6)

## III. Impartiality and Independence

The evaluation process should be impartial and independent from the process concerned with policy making, and the delivery and management of development assistance. (Para. 11)

Impartiality contributes to the credibility of evaluation and the avoidance of bias in findings, analyses and conclusions. Independence provides legitimacy to evaluation and reduces the potential for conflict of interest which could arise if policy makers and managers were solely responsible for evaluating their own activities. (Para. 12)

Impartiality and independence will best be achieved by separating the evaluation function from the line management responsible for planning and managing development assistance. This could be accomplished by having a central unit responsible for evaluation reporting directly to the minister or the agency head responsible for development assistance, or to a board of directors or governors of the institution. To the extent that some evaluation functions are attached to line management they should report to a central unit or to a sufficiently high level of the management structure or to a management committee responsible for programme decisions. In this case, every effort should be made to avoid compromising the evaluation process

and its results. Whatever approach is chosen, the organisational arrangements and procedures should facilitate the linking of evaluation findings to
programming and policy making. (Para. 16)

## IV. Credibility

The credibility of evaluation depends on the expertise and independence
of the evaluators and the degree of transparency of the evaluation process.
Credibility requires that evaluation should report successes as well as failures. Recipient countries should, as a rule, fully participate in evaluation in
order to promote credibility and commitment. (Para. 18)

Transparency of the evaluation process is crucial to its credibility and
legitimacy . . . (Para. 20)

## V. Usefulness

To have an impact on decision-making, evaluation findings must be perceived as relevant and useful and be presented in a clear and concise way.
They should fully reflect the different interests and needs of the many parties involved in development co-operation. Easy accessibility is also crucial
for usefulness . . . (Para. 21)

Evaluations must be timely in the sense that they should be available at
a time which is appropriate for the decision-making process. This suggests
that evaluation has an important role to play at various stages during the
execution of a project or programme and should not be conducted only as
an ex post exercise. Monitoring of activities in progress is the responsibility of operational staff. Provisions for evaluation by independent evaluation
staffs in the plan of operation constitute an important complement to regular monitoring. (Para. 22)

## VI. Participation of Donors and Recipients

. . . whenever possible, both donors and recipients should be involved
in the evaluation process. Since evaluation findings are relevant to both
parties, evaluation terms of reference should address issues of concern
to each partner, and the evaluation should reflect their views of the
effectiveness and impact of the activities concerned. The principle of
impartiality and independence during evaluation should apply equally to
recipients and donors. Participation and impartiality enhance the quality
of evaluation, which in turn has significant implications for long-term

sustainability since recipients are solely responsible after the donor has left. (Para. 23)

Whenever appropriate, the views and expertise of groups affected should form an integral part of the evaluation. (Para. 24)

Involving all parties concerned gives an opportunity for learning by doing and will strengthen skills and capacities in the recipient countries, an important objective which should also be promoted through training and other support for institutional and management development. (Para. 25)

## VII. Donor Co-operation

Collaboration between donors is essential in order to learn from each other and to avoid duplication of effort. Donor collaboration should be encouraged in order to develop evaluation methods, share reports and information, and improve access to evaluation findings. Joint donor evaluations should be promoted in order to improve understanding of each others' procedures and approaches and to reduce the administrative burden on the recipient. In order to facilitate the planning of joint evaluations, donors should exchange evaluation plans systematically and well ahead of actual implementation. (Para. 26)

## VIII. Evaluation Programming

An overall plan must be developed by the agency for the evaluation of development assistance activities. In elaborating such a plan, the various activities to be evaluated should be organised into appropriate categories. Priorities should then be set for the evaluation of the categories and a timetable drawn up. (Para. 27)

Aid agencies which have not already done so should elaborate guidelines and/or standards for the evaluation process. These should give guidance and define the minimum requirements for the conduct of evaluations and for reporting. (Para. 31)

## IX. Design and Implementation of Evaluations

Each evaluation must be planned and terms of reference drawn up in order to:

- define the purpose and scope of the evaluation, including an identification of the recipients of the findings;
- describe the methods to be used during the evaluation;

- identify the standards against which project/programme performance are to be assessed;
- determine the resources and time required to complete the evaluation. (Para. 32)

It is essential to define the questions which will be addressed in the evaluation—these are often referred to as the "issues" of the evaluation. The issues will provide a manageable framework for the evaluation process and the basis for a clear set of conclusions and recommendations . . . (Para. 35)

## X. Reporting Dissemination and Feedback

Evaluation reporting should be clear, as free as possible of technical language and include the following elements: an executive summary; a profile of the activity evaluated; a description of the evaluation methods used; the main findings; lessons learned; conclusions and recommendations (which may be separate from the report itself). (Para. 39)

Feed back is an essential part of the evaluation process as it provides the link between past and future activities. To ensure that the results of evaluations are utilised in future policy and programme development it is necessary to establish feedback mechanisms involving all parties concerned. These would include such measures as evaluation committees, seminars and workshops, automated systems, reporting and follow-up procedures. Informal means such as networking and internal communications would also allow for the dissemination of ideas and information. In order to be effective, the feedback process requires staff and budget resources as well as support by senior management and the other actors involved. (Para. 42)

# Review of the DAC Principles for Evaluation of Development Assistance

In 1998, members of the Working Party on Aid Evaluation (now the DAC Network on Development Evaluation) completed a review of their experience with the application of the *DAC Principles for Evaluation of Development Assistance*. The objective was to examine the implementation and use of the principles, in order to assess their impact, usefulness and relevance and to make recommendations. The extract provided below demonstrates the ongoing efforts to implement the principles and point the way towards some of the later work presented in Parts II–V of this document. The full text includes detailed findings and further recommendations from evaluators and users.

The review demonstrated that evaluation in development co-operation is evolving and changing focus. Most members of the Network have re-organised their central evaluation offices to provide them with a new role with a strong focus on aid effectiveness. Moreover, central evaluation offices have moved away from traditional project evaluation to programme, sector, thematic and country assistance evaluations. In OECD countries, domestic interest in the results of development assistance has grown. Greater interest in decentralised evaluations has also been reported and there is evidence to suggest that evaluation in developing countries is beginning to take root.

Most members reported that they have reached a good degree of compliance with the essential *DAC Principles for Evaluation of Development Assistance*. They also claim to have found them useful and relevant in guiding their work and, in some cases, in re-organising their evaluation offices. Based on these results, it was concluded that the principles are still valid and sound.

Nevertheless, it was recognised that the principles needed to be complemented and reinforced with guidance (e.g. good or best practices) in key areas. These include ways to: effectively handle the trade-off between independence and involvement required to gain partnership; improve feedback and communication practices; promote an evaluation culture; implement country programme and joint evaluations; promote partnerships; and evaluate humanitarian aid.

## Part II: Evaluation Criteria

When evaluating development co-operation programmes and projects it is useful to consider the following criteria, laid out in the *DAC Principles for Evaluation of Development Assistance*.

### Relevance

The extent to which the aid activity is suited to the priorities and policies of the target group, recipient and donor.

In evaluating the relevance of a programme or a project, it is useful to consider the following questions:

- To what extent are the objectives of the programme still valid?
- Are the activities and outputs of the programme consistent with the overall goal and the attainment of its objectives?
- Are the activities and outputs of the programme consistent with the intended impacts and effects?

## Effectiveness

A measure of the extent to which an aid activity attains its objectives.

In evaluating the effectiveness of a programme or a project, it is useful to consider the following questions:

- To what extent were the objectives achieved/are likely to be achieved?
- What were the major factors influencing the achievement or non-achievement of the objectives?

## Efficiency

Efficiency measures the outputs—qualitative and quantitative—in relation to the inputs. It is an economic term which is used to assess the extent to which aid uses the least costly resources possible in order to achieve the desired results. This generally requires comparing alternative approaches to achieving the same outputs, to see whether the most efficient process has been adopted.

When evaluating the efficiency of a programme or a project, it is useful to consider the following questions:

- Were activities cost-efficient?
- Were objectives achieved on time?
- Was the programme or project implemented in the most efficient way compared to alternatives?

## Impact

The positive and negative changes produced by a development intervention, directly or indirectly, intended or unintended. This involves the main impacts and effects resulting from the activity on the local social, economic, environmental and other development indicators. The examination should be concerned with both intended and unintended results and must also include the positive and negative impact of external factors, such as changes in terms of trade and financial conditions.

When evaluating the impact of a programme or a project, it is useful to consider the following questions:

- What has happened as a result of the programme or project?
- What real difference has the activity made to the beneficiaries?
- How many people have been affected?

## Sustainability

Sustainability is concerned with measuring whether the benefits of an activity are likely to continue after donor funding has been withdrawn. Projects need to be environmentally as well as financially sustainable.

When evaluating the sustainability of a programme or a project, it is useful to consider the following questions:

- To what extent did the benefits of a programme or project continue after donor funding ceased?
- What were the major factors which influenced the achievement or non-achievement of sustainability of the programme or project?

## Part III: Evaluation Systems and Use: A Working Tool for Peer Reviews and Assessments

This framework was developed in March 2006, on the basis of a thorough analysis of peer reviews conducted over a period of eight years. It was designed to strengthen the evaluation function and promote transparency and accountability in development agencies. It has been developed with peer reviews in mind and as a management device for improving evaluation practice in aid agencies. It is a "living" tool, meant to be updated in function of experience.

1. Evaluation policy: role, responsibility and objectives of the evaluation unit
   - Does the ministry/aid agency have an evaluation policy?
   - Does the policy describe the role, governance structure and position of the evaluation unit within the institutional aid structure?
   - Does the evaluation function provide a useful coverage of the whole development cooperation programme?
   - According to the policy, how does evaluation contribute to institutional learning and accountability?
   - How is the relationship between evaluation and audit conceptualised within the agency?
   - In countries with two or more aid agencies, how are the roles of the respective evaluation units defined and coordinated?
   - ➤ **Is the evaluation policy adequately known and implemented within the aid agency?**

2. Impartiality, transparency and independence
   - To what extent are the evaluation unit and the evaluation process independent from line management?
   - What are the formal and actual drivers ensuring/constraining the evaluation unit's independence?
   - What is the evaluation unit's experience in exposing success and failures of aid programmes and their implementation?
   - Is the evaluation process transparent enough to ensure its credibility and legitimacy? Are evaluation findings consistently made public?
   - How is the balance between independence and the need for interaction with line management dealt with by the system?
   - ➤ **Are the evaluation process and reports perceived as impartial by non-evaluation actors within and outside the agency?**
3. Resources and staff
   - Is evaluation supported by appropriate financial and staff resources?
   - Does the evaluation unit have a dedicated budget? Is it annual or multiyear? Does the budget cover activities aimed at promoting feedback and use of evaluation and management of evaluation knowledge?
   - Does staff have specific expertise in evaluation, and if not, are training programmes available?
   - Is there a policy on recruiting consultants, in terms of qualification, impartiality and deontology?
4. Evaluation partnerships and capacity building
   - To what extent are beneficiaries involved in the evaluation process?
   - To what extent does the agency rely on local evaluators or, when not possible, on third party evaluators from partner countries?
   - Does the agency engage in partner-led evaluations?
   - Does the unit support training and capacity building programmes in partner countries?
   - ➤ **How do partners/beneficiaries/local NGOs perceive the evaluation processes and products promoted by the agency/country examined in terms of quality, independence, objectivity, usefulness and partnership orientation?**
5. Quality
   - How does the evaluation unit ensure the quality of evaluation (including reports and process)?
   - Does the agency have guidelines for the conduct of evaluation, and are these used by relevant stakeholders?
   - Has the agency developed/adopted standards/benchmarks to assess and improve the quality of its evaluation reports?

➤ **How is the quality of evaluation products/processes perceived throughout the agency?**

6. Planning, coordination and harmonisation
   - Does the agency have a multi-year evaluation plan, describing future evaluations according to a defined timetable?
   - How is the evaluation plan developed? Who, within the aid agency, identifies the priorities and how?
   - In DAC members where ODA responsibility is shared among two or more agencies, how is the evaluation function organised?
   - Does the evaluation unit coordinate its evaluation activities with other donors?
   - How are field level evaluation activities coordinated? Is authority for evaluation centralised or decentralised?
   - Does the evaluation unit engage in joint/multi donor evaluations?
   - Does the evaluation unit/aid agency make use of evaluative information coming from other donor organisations?
   - In what way does the agency assess the effectiveness of its contributions to multilateral organisations? To what extent does it rely on the evaluation systems of multilateral agencies?
   - In what way does the agency assess the effectiveness of its contributions to multilateral organisations? To what extent does it rely on the evaluation systems of multilateral agencies?

7. Dissemination, feedback, knowledge management and learning
   - How are evaluation findings disseminated? In addition to reports, are other communication tools used? (Press releases, press conferences, abstracts, annual reports providing a synthesis of findings)?
   - What are the mechanisms in place to ensure feedback of evaluation results to policy makers, operational staff and the general public?
   - What mechanisms are in place to ensure that knowledge from evaluation is accessible to staff and relevant stakeholders?

   ➤ **Is evaluation considered a 'learning tool' by agency staff?**

8. Evaluation use
   - Who are the main users of evaluations within and outside the aid agency?
   - Does evaluation respond to the information needs expressed by parliament, audit office, government, and the public?
   - Are there systems in place to ensure the follow up and implementation of evaluation findings and recommendations?
   - How does the aid agency/ministry promote follow up on findings from relevant stakeholders (through e.g. steering groups, advisory panels, and sounding boards)?

- Are links with decision making processes ensured to promote the use of evaluation in policy formulation?
- Are there recent examples of major operation and policy changes sparked by evaluation findings and recommendations?
- Are there examples of how evaluation serves as an accountability mechanism?
- ➤ **What are the perceptions of non evaluation actors (operation and policy departments, field offices, etc) regarding the usefulness and influence of evaluation?**

## Part IV: DAC Evaluation Quality Standards

The DAC Evaluation Quality Standards were approved in 2006 for a test phase application of three years. Experience with the use of the standards by members and interested partners will inform the final agreement of the standards in 2009.

The standards support evaluations that adhere to the *DAC Principles for Evaluation of Development Assistance,* including impartiality and independence, credibility and usefulness, and should be read in conjunction with those principles. The principles focus on the management and institutional arrangements of the evaluation systems within development agencies; by contrast, the standards provide guidance on the conduct of evaluations and for reports. The standards identify the key pillars needed for a quality evaluation process and product. The standards constitute a guide to good practice and aim to improve the quality of development evaluation. While the standards are not binding on every evaluation, they should be applied as widely as possible and a brief explanation provided where this is not possible.

1. Rationale, purpose and objectives of an evaluation
   1.1 The rationale of the evaluation
   Describes why and for whom the evaluation is undertaken and why it is undertaken at a particular point in time.
   1.2 The purpose of the evaluation
   The evaluation purpose is in line with the learning and accountability function of evaluations. For example the evaluation's purpose may be to:
   - Contribute to improving an aid policy, procedure or technique
   - Consider a continuation or discontinuation of a project/programme
   - Account for aid expenditures to stakeholders and tax payers

1.3 The objectives of the evaluation

The objectives of the evaluation, specify what the evaluation aims to achieve.

For example:

- To ascertain results (output, outcome, impact) and assess the effectiveness, efficiency and relevance of a specific development intervention;
- To provide findings, conclusions and recommendations with respect to a specific policy, programme etc.

2. Evaluation scope

2.1 Scope of the evaluation

The scope of the evaluation is clearly defined by specifying the issues covered, funds actually spent, the time period, types of interventions, geographical coverage, target groups, as well as other elements of the development intervention addressed in the evaluation.

2.2 Intervention logic and findings

The evaluation report briefly describes and assesses the intervention logic and distinguishes between findings at the different levels: inputs, activities, outcomes and impacts.

2.3 Evaluation criteria

The evaluation report applies the five DAC criteria for evaluating development assistance: relevance, efficiency, effectiveness, impact and sustainability. The criteria applied for the given evaluation are defined in unambiguous terms. If a particular criterion is not applied this is explained in the evaluation report, as are any additional criteria applied.

2.4 Evaluation questions

The questions asked, as well as any revisions to the original questions, are documented in the report for readers to be able to assess whether the evaluation team has sufficiently assessed them.

3. Context

3.1 The development and policy context

The evaluation report provides a description of the policy context relevant to the development intervention, the development agency's and partners' policy documents, objectives and strategies. The development context may refer to: regional and national economy and levels of development. The policy context may refer to: poverty reduction strategies, gender equality, environmental protection and human rights.

3.2 The institutional context

The evaluation report provides a description of the institutional environment and stakeholder involvement relevant to the development intervention, so that their influence can be identified and assessed.

3.3 The socio-political context

The evaluation report describes the socio-political context within which the intervention takes place, and its influence on the outcome and impact of the development intervention.

3.4 Implementation arrangements

The evaluation report describes the organisational arrangements established for implementation of the development intervention, including the roles of donors and partners.

4. Evaluation methodology

4.1 Explanation of the methodology used

The evaluation report describes and explains the evaluation method and process and discusses validity and reliability. It acknowledges any constraints encountered and their impact on the evaluation, including their impact on the independence of the evaluation. It details the methods and techniques used for data and information collection and processing. The choices are justified and limitations and shortcomings are explained.

4.2 Assessment of results

Methods for assessment of results are specified. Attribution and con-tributing/confounding factors should be addressed. If indicators are used as a basis for results assessment these should be SMART (spe-cific, measurable, attainable, relevant and time bound).

4.3 Relevant stakeholders consulted

Relevant stakeholders are involved in the evaluation process to identify issues and provide input for the evaluation. Both donors and partners are consulted. The evaluation report indicates the stakeholders consulted, the criteria for their selection and describes stakeholders' participation. If less than the full range of stakeholders was consulted, the methods and reasons for selection of particular stakeholders are described.

4.4 Sampling

The evaluation report explains the selection of any sample. Limita-tions regarding the representativeness of the evaluation sample are identified.

4.5 Evaluation team

The composition of evaluation teams should possess a mix of evalua-tive skills and thematic knowledge, be gender balanced, and include professionals from the countries or regions concerned.

5. Information sources

   5.1 Transparency of information sources

      The evaluation report describes the sources of information used (documentation, respondents, literature etc.) in sufficient detail, so that the adequacy of the information can be assessed. Complete lists of interviewees and documents consulted are included, to the extent that this does not conflict with the privacy and confidentiality of participants.

   5.2 Reliability and accuracy of information sources

      The evaluation cross-validates and critically assesses the information sources used and the validity of the data using a variety of methods and sources of information.

6. Independence

   6.1 Independence of evaluators vis-à-vis stakeholders

      The evaluation report indicates the degree of independence of the evaluators from the policy, operations and management function of the commissioning agent, implementers and beneficiaries. Possible conflicts of interest are addressed openly and honestly.

   6.2 Free and open evaluation process

      The evaluation team is able to work freely and without interference. It is assured of cooperation and access to all relevant information. The evaluation report indicates any obstruction which may have impacted on the process of evaluation.

7. Evaluation ethics

   7.1 Evaluation conducted in a professional and ethical manner

      The evaluation process shows sensitivity to gender, beliefs, manners and customs of all stakeholders and is undertaken with integrity and honesty. The rights and welfare of participants in the evaluation are protected. Anonymity and confidentiality of individual informants should be protected when requested and/or as required by law.

   7.2 Acknowledgement of disagreements within the evaluation team

      Evaluation team members should have the opportunity to dissociate themselves from particular judgements and recommendations. Any unresolved differences of opinion within the team should be acknowledged in the report.

8. Quality assurance

   8.1 Incorporation of stakeholders' comments

      Stakeholders are given the opportunity to comment on findings, conclusions, recommendations and lessons learned. The evaluation report reflects these comments and acknowledges any substantive disagreements. In disputes about facts that can be verified, the evaluators should investigate and change the draft where necessary. In the case of opinion or interpretation, stakeholders' comments should be reproduced verbatim, such as in an annex, to the extent that this does not conflict with the rights and welfare of participants.

8.2 Quality control

Quality control is exercised throughout the evaluation process. Depending on the evaluation's scope and complexity, quality control is carried out either internally or through an external body, peer review, or reference group. Quality controls adhere to the principle of independence of the evaluator.

9. Relevance of the evaluation results

9.1 Formulation of evaluation findings

The evaluation findings are relevant to the object being evaluated and the purpose of the evaluation. The results should follow clearly from the evaluation questions and analysis of data, showing a clear line of evidence to support the conclusions. Any discrepancies between the planned and actual implementation of the object being evaluated are explained.

9.2 Evaluation implemented within the allotted time and budget

The evaluation is conducted and results are made available in a timely manner in relation to the purpose of the evaluation. Un-envisaged changes to timeframe and budget are explained in the report. Any discrepancies between the planned and actual implementation and products of the evaluation are explained.

9.3 Recommendations and lessons learned

Recommendations and lessons learned are relevant, targeted to the intended users and actionable within the responsibilities of the users. Recommendations are actionable proposals and lessons learned are generalizations of conclusions applicable for wider use.

9.4 Use of evaluation

Evaluation requires an explicit acknowledgement and response from management regarding intended follow-up to the evaluation results. Management will ensure the systematic dissemination, storage and management of the output from the evaluation to ensure easy accessibility and to maximise the benefits of the evaluation's findings.

10. Completeness

10.1 Evaluation questions answered by conclusions

The evaluation report answers all the questions and information needs detailed in the scope of the evaluation. Where this is not possible, reasons and explanations are provided.

10.2 Clarity of analysis

The analysis is structured with a logical flow. Data and information are presented, analysed and interpreted systematically. Findings and conclusions are clearly identified and flow logically from the analysis of the data and information. Underlying assumptions are made explicit and taken into account.

10.3 Distinction between conclusions, recommendations and lessons learned

Evaluation reports must distinguish clearly between findings, conclusions and recommendations. The evaluation presents conclusions, recommendations and lessons learned separately and with a clear logical distinction between them. Conclusions are substantiated by findings and analysis. Recommendations and lessons learned follow logically from the conclusions.

10.4 Clarity and representativeness of the summary

The evaluation report contains an executive summary. The summary provides an overview of the report, highlighting the main conclusions, recommendations and lessons learned.

# Part V: Guidance Documents

In response to the need for more specific guidance in certain areas of development evaluation, and building on evaluation experiences and the norms and standards described above, a number of documents have been developed to steer evaluation policy and practice. Some of these guidance documents are presented below.

## Guidance on Evaluating Conflict Prevention and Peacebuilding Activities: Working Draft for Application Period
*(OECD, 2008)*

This document features challenges and emerging best practices for evaluating conflict prevention and peacebuilding activities.

With growing shares of aid resources, time and energy being dedicated to conflict prevention and peacebuilding, there is increased interest to learn what works, as well as what does not work and why. This guidance seeks to help answer these questions by providing direction to those undertaking evaluations of conflict prevention and peacebuilding projects, programmes and policies. It should enable systematic learning, enhance accountability and ultimately improve the effectiveness of peacebuilding work.

Some of the emerging key messages of the guidance include:

- Donors should promote systematic, high quality evaluation of all conflict prevention and peacebuilding work—including work carried out by implementing partners such as NGOs.
- Evaluations should be facilitated through better programme design.
- Coherent and co-ordinated intervention and policy strategies are needed to make progress towards peace.
- Concepts and definitions of conflict prevention and peacebuilding require clarification.

### Guidance for Managing Joint Evaluations
### (OECD, 2006)

This publication provides practical guidance for managers of joint evaluations of development programmes aiming to increase the effectiveness of joint evaluation work. It draws on a major review of experiences presented in "Joint Evaluations: Recent Experiences, Lessons Learned and Options for the Future" and the earlier guidance *Effective Practices in Conducting a Joint Multi-Donor Evaluation* (2000).

The focus in this publication is not on participatory evaluation with its techniques for bringing stakeholder communities into the process, but on evaluations undertaken jointly by more than one development co-operation agency. Such collaborative approaches, be they between multiple donors, multiple partners or some combination of the two, are increasingly useful at a time when the international community is prioritising mutual responsibility for development outcomes and joint approaches to managing aid.

Joint evaluations have the potential to bring benefits to all partners, such as:

- mutual capacity development and learning between partners;
- building participation and ownership;
- sharing the burden of work;
- increasing the legitimacy of findings;
- reducing the overall number of evaluations and the total transaction costs for partner countries.

Nevertheless, joint work can also generate specific costs and challenges and these can put significant burdens on the donor agencies. For example, building consensus between the agencies and maintaining effective co-ordination processes can be costly and time-consuming; delays in the completion of complex joint evaluations can adversely affect timeliness and relevance.

## Evaluation Feedback for Effective Learning and Accountability
### (OECD, 2001)

This publication highlights different feedback systems, and outlines the areas identified as most relevant for improving evaluation feedback. It also outlines the main concerns and challenges facing evaluation feedback and the means to address these.

A major challenge lies in conveying evaluation results to multiple audiences both inside and outside development agencies. Thus, feedback and communication of evaluation results are integral parts of the evaluation cycle. Effective feedback contributes to improving development policies, programmes and practices by providing policy makers with the relevant information for making informed decisions. The differences between agencies in their background, structure and priorities means that this is not an area where a blueprint approach is appropriate. Moreover, there is a need to tailor feedback approaches to suit different target audiences. However, a number of areas for action can be identified at various levels.

Suggested actions to improve evaluation feedback include:

- take steps to understand how learning happens within and outside the organisation, and identify where blockages occur;
- assess how the relevance and timeliness of evaluation feedback can be improved, and take steps to ensure this happens;
- develop a more strategic view of how feedback approaches can be tailored to the needs of different audiences;
- put much more effort into finding better ways of involving partner country stakeholders in evaluation work, including the feedback of evaluation lessons;
- take steps to increase the space and incentives for learning within the organisation (both from evaluations and other sources).

## Guidance on Evaluating Humanitarian Assistance in Complex Emergencies
### (OECD, 1999)

This publication is aimed at those involved in the commissioning, design and management of evaluations of humanitarian assistance programmes.

Historically, humanitarian assistance has been subjected to less rigorous evaluation procedures than development aid. As the share of ODA allocated to humanitarian assistance has risen, and awareness of its complexity has increased, the need to develop appropriate methodologies for its evaluation became steadily more apparent. This guidance complements the *DAC Principles for Evaluation of Development Assistance* by highlighting aspects of evaluation which require special attention in the field of humanitarian assistance.

**OECD DAC Network on Development Evaluation**
# EVALUATING DEVELOPMENT CO-OPERATION
**Summary of Key Norms and Standards**

A key component of the DAC Network on Development Evaluation's mission is to develop internationally agreed norms and standards for development evaluation. These inform evaluation policy and practice and contribute to harmonised approaches in line with the commitments of the Paris Declaration on Aid Effectiveness. The body of norms and standards is based on experience, and evolves over time to fit the changing aid environment. The norms and standards serve as an international reference point, guiding efforts to improve development results through high quality evaluation.

The norms and standards summarised here should be applied discerningly and adapted carefully to fit the purpose, object and context of each evaluation. As this summary document is not an exhaustive evaluation manual readers are encouraged to refer to the complete texts available on the DAC Network on Development Evaluation's website:

**www.oecd.org/dac/evaluationnetwork.**

# Design Matrix For Outer Baldonia Secondary School Vocational Training Program

Design Matrix For Outer Baldonia Secondary School Vocational Training Program, page 1

**Main Evaluation Issue:** Should this program be reauthorized? **General Approach:** Quasi-Experimental Impact Evaluation

| Questions | Subquestions | Type of (sub) question | Measures or indicators | Target or standard (if normative) | Baseline data? |
|---|---|---|---|---|---|
| 1. What services did the program provide to whom? | 1.A.1. In what vocational skill areas were participants trained? | Descriptive | Vocational skill areas program offered to trainees for certification | NA | NA |
| | 1.A.2. Were there changes over time in participation by skill area? | Descriptive | Same as above by number of participants each year NA | NA | Yes |
| | 1.B.1. What support services were offered by the program? | Descriptive | Support services (e.g. literacy, counseling) offered by the program | NA | NA |
| | 1.B.2. What proportion of participants received support services? | Descriptive | Number and percent of trainees receiving each type of support | NA | NA |
| | 1.C. What were the most popular certification areas selected by trainees in the vocational training program? | Descriptive | Number of trainees by certificate areas | NA | NA |
| | 1.D. To what extent did the program provide certification in areas forecast as high demand for the next 5-10 years? | Descriptive | List of vocational areas forecast as high demand over the next 5-10 years | NA | NA |
| 2. To what extent was there gender equity in the services delivered? | 2.A.1. Did equal numbers of males and females participate in the program? | Normative | Number and proportion males/females receiving vocational training | Program authorizing documents indicate 50% participation goal for females | NA |
| | 2.A.2 Is receipt of support services related to gender? | Normative | Proportions by gender receiving each of the support services offered | Program authorizing documents indicate gender equality a goal | NA |

Design Matrix, page 1 continued

| Design | Data sources | Sample | Data collection instrument | Data analysis | Comments |
|---|---|---|---|---|---|
| **1.A.1.** One Shot | Program records (MIS)<br><br>Program Director | For each of past 5 years | Record Retrieval Document 1<br><br>Program Officials Interview Guide | Frequency count<br><br>Content analysis | Data sources should match; note any discrepancy and explain |
| **1.A.2.** Time Series | Same as above | Same as above | Same as above | Same as above by year | Graphic would be good here |
| **1.B.1.** One Shot | Program records (MIS) | Census over past 5 years | Record Retrieval Document 2 | List | Check for duplicates such as M. Smith and Mary Smith |
| **1.B.2.** Same as above | Same as above | Same as above | Same as above | Frequency count | Note that participants can receive more than one support service |
| **1.C.** One Shot | Program records (MIS) | Census over past 5 years | Record Retrieval Document 2 | Frequency count | Graphic |
| **1.D.** Time Series | Labor Ministry Annual Reports on Short-, Mid-, and Long-Term Labor projections | Reports for each of past 5 years | Record Retrieval Document 3 | Trend analysis and forecast for each certification area offered over the past 5 years | Note changes in trends and program's responsiveness to them<br><br>Note whether there were potential growth areas in which the program did not offer training |
| **2.A.1.** Time Series | Program records (MIS) | For each of past 5 years | Record Retrieval Document 1 | Frequency counts by gender; present as line chart so trend over 5 years is clear. Compare to standard | Show standard in heavy black line across the line chart so it is easy to see. |
| **2.A.2.** Same as above | Same as above | Same as above | Same as above | Same as above | Note if there were changes over time |

| Questions | Subquestions | Type of subquestion | Measures or indicators | Target or standard (if normative) | Baseline data? |
|---|---|---|---|---|---|
| 3. Was the program effective? | 3.A. To what extent were the annual job placement targets met or exceeded? | Normative | Job placement rates by year | Yes. 80% of those completing the program | NA |
| | 3.B. To what extent were the annual average placement wage rates met or exceeded? | Normative | Job placement wages for each year | Yes. $2 per hour years 1-3 and $3 an hour years 4&5 | NA |
| | 3.C. To what extent were participants placed in jobs that matched their certification areas? | Descriptive | Trainee certificate area and job placement area | Implicit standard only so treated as descriptive question | NA |
| | 3.D, What was the program's drop-out rate? | Normative | Number entering the program each year and number graduating each year | Program documents indicate should not be more than 10% | NA |
| 4. Was the program cost-efficient? | 4.A. Was the program cost per participant reasonable in relation to similar programs? | Descriptive | Cost per placed trainee compared to other similar training programs | Implicit standard only so treated as descriptive question | NA |
| 5. To what extent was instructor turnover a problem? | 5.A, What was the turnover rate of instructors? | Descriptive | Turnover rate annually and for instructors | None set. Implicit standard is that it should be low | NA |
| | 5.B. How long did instructor positions stay vacant? | Descriptive | Average length of vacancies and range | None set. Implicit standard is that it should be low | NA |
| | 5.C. Were equally qualified instructors found as replacements? | Descriptive | Years teaching experience Years working in area of certification | None set. Implicit standard is that they should be comparable | NA |

| Design | Data sources | Sample | Data collection instrument | Data analysis | Comments |
|---|---|---|---|---|---|
| **3.A.** Time Series | Trainee records by year for each of 5 years (MIS) | Census of those placed by year | Record Retrieval Form 4 | Comparison to standard each year and cumulatively across the 5 years. | Need to validate the information in the records by confirming placements and starting rates with employers for a sample of trainees. Recall will likely be a problem for past two years. |
| One Shot | Trainee records for the last year (MIS) Employers/ Employers' records | Random sample | Employer Interview Guide Employer Record Form 1 | Match of MIS info with employer information | |
| **3.B.** Time Series | Trainee records by year for each of 5 years | Census of those placed by year | Record Retrieval Form 4 | Comparison to standard each year and cumulatively across the 5 years. | Need to validate the information in the records by confirming placements and starting rates with employers for a sample of trainees. Recall will likely be a problem for past two years. |
| One Shot | Trainee records for the last two years (MIS) Employers/ Employers' records | Random sample | Employer Interview Guide Employer Record Form i | Match of MIS info with employer information | |
| **3.C.** One Shot | Trainee records for past 2 years showing certification area (MIS) | Census of those placed | Record Retrieval Form 4 | Frequency count of matches by year and cumulatively | |
| | Employers hiring trainees over past 2 years | Random sample | Employer Interview Guide Employer Record Form 1 | | |
| **3.D. Time Series** | Trainee records by year for each of 5 years (MIS) | Census | Record Retrieval Form 4 | Comparison to standard each year and cumulatively | |
| **4.** One Shot | Program Financial Officer Placement rates (see 3A) Program Financial Statements | Census- all 5 years of financial statements | Interviews | Cost per participant Cost per participant placed | Hope to be able to compare cost per placed trainee to that of other similar training programs. |
| | Existing evaluations of similar training programs | | Literature review | Content analysis | |
| **5.A.** Time Series | Program employment records | All 5 years | Record Retrieval Form 5 | Frequency counts by year, range and average | |
| **5.B.** Time Series | Program financial records | All 5 years | Record Retrieval Form 5 | Frequency counts, range and average | |
| **5.C.** Time Series | Program employment records- c.v.s | All 5 years | Record Retrieval Form 6 | Comparisons of staff c.v.s Across the 5 years | |

Design Matrix For Outer Baldonia Secondary School Vocational Training Program

| Questions | Subquestions | Type of (sub) question | Measures or indicators | Target or standard (if normative) | Baseline data? |
|---|---|---|---|---|---|
| 6. To what extent were trainee dropouts a concern? | **6.A.** What were the numbers and percentages of males and females dropping out of the program each year? | Descriptive Proportions by gender | Number and proportion males/females starting the program by year and dropout rates by year. | Background documents indicate 10% is acceptable; Implicit that it would be the same rate for each gender | NA |
| | **6.B.** What were the certification areas from which they dropped? | Descriptive | Above by certification area. | NA | NA |
| | **6.C.** What were the common reasons for dropping out of the program? | Descriptive | Most frequent reasons for dropping out. | NA | NA |
| | **6.D.** How concerned were program officials about drop-out rates? | Descriptive | Awareness of drop-out rates Opinion on whether problem Actions taken | None specified. | NA |
| 7. To what extent do those trainees placed in jobs earn more than they would have absent the training program? | **7.A.** What are the job retention, salary increase, promotion, and firing rates of placed participants compared with others similar in characteristics who dropped out of the training program? | Cause & Effect | Placed participant job retention, starting salary, salary increases, and promotion and firing rates over two years compared with (i) others hired by the firms for similar positions over a comparable period; (ii) pre-program earnings; (iii) earnings of program drop-outs. | None specified | Yes, on placement wages |
| | **7.B.** What are employers' views of the performance of placed employees compared with others hired with similar characteristics who did not receive the training program? | Cause & Effect | (i)Likelihood of hiring training participants absent the program and (ii) hiring more program grads; (iii) views on job performance compared with others. | None specified | Initial placement wages; pre-training wage, if any |

| Design | Data sources | Sample | Data collection instrument | Data analysis | Comments |
|---|---|---|---|---|---|
| **6.A.** Time series | Trainee records by year for each of 5 years | Census by year | Record Retrieval Form 4 | Frequency distribution of drop-outs by year; percent drop-out by year by gender, and totals | |
| **6.B.** Time series | Trainee records by year for each of 5 years | Census by year | Record Retrieval Form 4 | Cross tab of certification areas by frequency of program drop-out annually and cumulatively | Might run test of significance—Chi Square? |
| **6.C.** One Shot | Trainee records for past two years | Census of program drop-outs for the two year period | Former participant survey | Frequency distribution of reasons for dropping out of program from (i) participant perspectives, and (ii) training program officials' views | Triangulate |
| | Training program officials | Senior officials | Program Officials Interview Guide | | |
| **6.D.** One Shot | Trainee records for past two years | Census of program drop-outs for the two year | Program Officials Interview Guide | Content Analysis and frequency counts | |
| | Training program officials | | | | |
| **7.A.** Quasi-experimental Design- Non-equivalent Groups | Employers and Employer records | Census for prior two years | Employer Interview Guide | Content analysis/ frequencies | No comparison group formed at program initiation; proxies need to be used |
| | | | Employer Record Form 1 | | |
| | Program drop-outs | | Former Participant Survey | | |
| **7.B.** One Shot | Employers and Employer records | Census for prior two years | Employer Interview Guide Employer Record Form 1 | Content analyses/ frequencies | Note C&E design limitations; are confidential, no access |

*Source:* Authors.

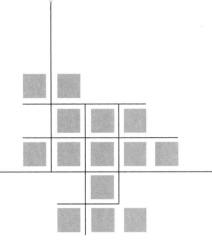

# Index

*Boxes, figures, and tables are denoted by b, f, and t, following the page numbers.*

ANOVA (analysis of variance), 400–401
ANSI (American National Standards Institute), 31
AnSWR (data analysis software), 382
anthropology, 26
anti-money laundering programs, 82–83
aptitude tests, 347
Asian Community of Practice, 62
Asian Development Bank (ADB), 10, 63, 66, 510
Asia–Pacific Finance Department Center, 63, 66
assertiveness in negotiation, 505–6
assessments
 beneficiary, 205, 210*t*
 environmental and social, 190–93, 202*b*, 208*t*, 346
 evaluability, 183–84, 207*t*
 rapid, 199–201, 209*t*
 readiness, 65, 113–15
 social, 189–90, 191*b*, 208*t*
 standard for complete and fair, 507
 of theory of change, 169–70
association, measures of, 398–99
Association of Southeast Asian Nations (ASEAN), 40*b*. *See also specific countries*
associations for professional evaluation, 28–29. *See also specific organizations*
assumptions, theory of change, 152, 154–55, 155*f*, 157–59, 159*f*
Atlas-ti (data analysis software), 382
attributional questions. *See* cause-and-effect questions
auditing, 23–26, 24*b*, 131, 275, 275*t*
Australasian Evaluation Society, 28, 508
Australia
 evaluation culture in, 51
 IPDET in, 63
 whole-of-government approach in, 52, 53–55
autonomy vs. conservatism, 507
axis titles and scales, 480
Azerbaijan, agricultural development program in, 191*b*

**B**

Bamberger, Michael, 257, 278
Bangladesh, evaluations in, 37*b*
banks, commercial, 90–91
BankTrack, 91
bar charts, 481*t*, 482, 484–85*f*
Barzelay, M., 275

baseline data collection
 propensity score matching and, 267
 results-based monitoring and evaluation, 119–21, 120*f*, 121*t*, 123*t*
before-and-after designs, 263–64, 273, 279*t*, 282*t*
behavioral independence, 32, 33–34*t*
Belgium and joint external evaluations, 425*b*
bell curve, 393, 393*f*
benchmarks, 224–25
beneficiary assessments, 205, 210*t*
BE Snapshots (IFC), 88
bias, 299. *See also* selection bias
bilateral donors, 72, 517
Bill & Melinda Gates Foundation, 79, 431
biological gradient, 270
Bosnia–Herzegovina, postconflict reconstruction in, 80
Botswana, IPDET in, 63
brainstorming, 345, 453, 454
Brazil, evaluation systems in, 64
Breier, Horst, 418, 419
Bribe Payers Index (Transparency International), 81
brochures, 470, 470*b*
Brossart, Daniel F., 258
budgets
 capacity-building and, 522
 enclave approach and, 67
 management of, 456–57
 performance budgeting, 21
 results-based evaluation reports and, 130
Business Environment Snapshots (IFC), 88

**C**

Cambodia, evaluations in, 40*b*
Campbell, D. T., 258
Canada
 evaluation culture in, 51
 evaluation in, 20, 21, 22, 26
 IPDET in, 63
 joint external evaluations and, 425*b*
Canadian Evaluation Society (CES), 508, 523
Canadian International Development Agency (CIDA), 26, 62, 196
capacity audits, 114, 275, 275*t*
capacity-building
 in developing countries, 74, 78–79
 for evaluations, 134, 519–22
 HIPC Initiative and, 78–79
 institutional, 61–62
 recommendations for, 517, 519–22, 520–21*b*

results-based evaluations and, 134
sustainability of M&E system and, 133
CAQDAS. *See* computer-assisted qualitative
data analysis software
Caracelli, V. J., 401
Caribbean, Minga initiative in, 9. *See also*
*specific countries*
Carleton University, 3, 62
Carney, R. N., 477
case study designs, 271–72, 272*b*, 377
categorical data, 482
CATI (computer-assisted telephone
interviewing), 319
causal list inference, 269
causal tracing strategies, 269–71
cause-and-effect questions
before-and-after designs, 263–64
case study designs, 271–72
causal tracing strategies, 269–71
control groups, 254–55
correlational designs, 266
cross-sectional designs, 267–68
defined, 227–29, 228–29*b*, 242
design process for, 252–72, 280
experimental designs, 252–61
flow charts and, 165
internal validity and, 257–61
interrupted time series comparison
designs, 265
longitudinal designs, 265
nonexperimental designs, 267–72
one-shot designs, 268
panel designs, 265
post-only nonequivalent comparison
designs, 264
pre- and post-nonequivalent comparison
designs, 264
propensity score matching, 266
quasi-experimental designs, 261–67,
262*b*, 276*b*
random assignment and, 255–57
simple cross-sectional designs, 267–68
theory of change and, 227
census, 356
Center for Evaluation of Science &
Technology, 65
Center for Global Development (CGD), 277
centralized management structures, 419
central tendency, measures of, 391–92, 393*t*
certification of evaluators, 526
CES. *See* Canadian Evaluation Society
CGD (Center for Global Development), 277
chain referral samples, 362–63

change frameworks. *See* theory of change
ChannahSorah, Vijaya Vinita, 57
chartjunk, 486–87, 487*b*, 488*f*
charts and graphs, 478–83
Chatterji, M., 257
Chelimsky, Eleanor, 12, 28, 201
chemical testing, 346
children
child scavenging assessment, 427–28, 427*b*
maturation effect and, 259
mortality reduction programs, 170*t*, 274*b*
poverty and, 85
Chile, evaluation systems in, 64
China
enclave approach in, 65–67
evaluation in, 19
IPDET in, 63
China International Engineering
Consulting Company, 65
chi-square test, 399–400
Christie, Christina, 204
chronological organization of data, 377
CIDA. *See* Canadian International
Development Agency
CIS (Commonwealth of Independent
States), 87–88. *See also specific*
*countries*
citizen groups, 130, 448
citizen report cards, 327–30, 330*t*, 331*t*
civil rights movement, 22
civil society, 130
classic experiments, 253
classic multipartner arrangements, 418
classification tables, 484–86, 486*t*
Clay, Daniel L., 258
cleaning data, 389–90
clientism fallacy, 497
clients. *See* main client
closed-ended questions, 320
closing phase, 457, 460*t*
cluster evaluations, 188–89, 208*t*, 517
cluster samples, 360–61, 361*b*
CODE (Committee on Development
Effectiveness), 474
*Code of Ethics and Auditing Standards*
(INTOSAI), 24*b*
coding data
qualitative, 377–78, 378*b*, 379, 383*b*
quantitative, 37*b*, 388–89
coherence, 270
Cohn, R., 497
collectivism vs. individualism, 507
commercial banks, 90–91

environmental and social assessments, 190–93, 202*b,* 208*t*
  data collection for, 346
  Equator Principles, 192
  evaluation synthesis used for, 202*b*
  ISO 14031, 192
  *Sustainable Development Strategies* (OECD), 192–93
environmental influences on results, 153, 153*f,* 223*f*
environmental sustainability, 90–91
  Equator Principles, 90, 192
equipment costs, 456
ESEA (Elementary and Secondary Education Act of 1965, U.S.), 22
*Ethical Guidelines* (UNEG), 508–9
ethical issues
  auditing, 24*b*
  evaluation purpose and, 11
  for evaluators, 496–99, 508–9
Ethnograph (data analysis software), 382
European Bank for Reconstruction and Development (EBRD), 26
Europe and European Union. *See also specific countries*
  capacity building for evaluation, 58–59
  child scavenging assessment, 427*b*
  contracting of evaluations in, 442
  evaluation culture in, 51
  evaluation in, 20, 21
European Evaluation Society, 28
European Social Fund, 59
evaluability assessments, 183–84, 207*t*
*Evaluating the World Bank's Approach to Global Programs* (World Bank), 92
evaluation approaches, 181–218, 207–10*t*
  beneficiary assessments, 205, 210*t*
  cluster evaluations, 188–89, 208*t*
  empowerment evaluations, 203–4, 210*t*
  environmental and social assessments, 190–93, 202*b,* 208*t*
  evaluability assessments, 183–84, 207*t*
  evaluation synthesis, 201–3, 202*b,* 209*t*
  goal-based evaluations, 185–86, 207*t*
  goal-free evaluations, 186–87, 207*t*
  horizontal evaluations, 206, 210*t*
  inclusive evaluations, 205, 210*t*
  multisite evaluations, 187–88, 208*t*
  outcome mapping, 196–99, 209*t*
  participatory evaluations, 193–96, 194*t,* 197*t,* 209*t*
  prospective evaluations, 182–83, 183*t,* 207*t*

rapid assessments, 199–201, 209*t*
  realist evaluations, 204–5, 210*t*
  social assessments, 189–90, 191*b,* 208*t*
  utilization-focused evaluations, 203, 210*t*
Evaluation Capacity Development Task Force (UNEG), 523–26
Evaluation Cooperation Group (MDB), 25, 32, 423, 519
evaluation corruptibility, 496–97
evaluation design matrix, 241–43, 442, 444
evaluation fallacies, 497
evaluation managers, 449–50
evaluations design matrix, 241–43, 243*f*
evaluation synthesis, 201–3, 202*b,* 209*t*
*Evaluation Toolkit* (Kellogg Foundation), 456–57
evaluators, 495–514
  activities of, 18–19
  certification of, 526
  conflicts of interest, 510
  core competencies, 523–26, 524–25*b*
  corruptibility of evaluation, 496–97
  DAC standards, 509–10
  data collection and, 376
  ethics and, 496–99, 508–9
  external, 18
  fallacies of evaluation, 497
  guiding principles, 508
  human weaknesses, 501–2
  internal, 18
  negotiation skills of, 503–6
  politics and, 499–506
  roles and responsibilities, 17–19, 450–51
  standards for, 506–8
  technical weaknesses, 500–501
  triangulation of, 300
ex ante evaluations, 11
executing phase, 457, 460*t*
executive summaries, 471–72
experimental designs, 249–50, 252–61, 279, 279*t,* 282*t*
expert judgment data collection method, 342–44, 344*t*
external audits, 23–24, 24*b*
external evaluations, 17, 18, 419, 420*t,* 518–19
extreme-case samples, 362

## F

face validity, 294
fair assessment evaluation standard, 507
fallacies of evaluation, 497
false negatives and positives, 254

incentives
  capacity-building, 522
  readiness assessment, 113–14
  sustainability of M&E system and, 133–34
inclusive evaluations, 205, 210*t*
independence, organizational, 32, 33*t*
Independent Evaluation Group (World
    Bank)
  country program evaluations and, 422*b*
  on Doing Business indicators, 89
  on global public goods, 92
  GRPPs and, 430–31
  independent evaluations and, 519
  IPDET and, 3, 62, 63
  recommendations by, 474
  sector program evaluations and, 424
independent evaluations, 32, 33–35*t*
independent variables, 398
India
  child scavenging assessment in, 427*b*
  IPDET in, 63
indicators
  CREAM characteristics of, 117
  in results-based M&E, 108*b*
  selection of, 116–18, 118*t*, 121*t*, 123*t*
  for social impact, 190
individualism vs. collectivism, 507
Indonesia, evaluation systems in, 64
inductive analysis, 386
inferential statistics, 391, 399–401
informal communications, 468
information infrastructure, 522
information strategies for sharing results,
    130–31. *See also* presentation of
    results
information technology. *See also* Internet
  computer-assisted content analysis, 380
  computer-assisted qualitative data
    analysis software (CAQDAS),
    382, 383*b*
  computer-assisted telephone
    interviewing (CATI), 319
  evaluators and, 450
initiating phase, 457, 458*t*
inputs, as component of theory of change,
    109–11, 109*t*, 110*f*, 111*f*, 223*f*
Institute of Internal Auditors, 24*b*
institutional capacity, 61–62
Institutional Integrity, Department of
    (World Bank), 499
instrumentation effect, 261
Integrated Framework for Trade, 430

integrated mixed-method approach, 402
integrated results-based management
    system (IRBM), 67–68
internal audits, 24–25, 24*b*
internal evaluations, 17, 18, 518–19
internal validity, 257–61
International Board of Standards for
    Training, Performance, and
    Instruction, 523
International Council on Security and
    Development, 343
International Development, Department
    for (DfID, UK), 26, 37*b*, 62, 202*b*
International Development Evaluation
    Association (IDEAS), 2, 29, 523, 526
International Development Research
    Centre (IDRC), 9, 62, 196
International Finance Corporation (IFC),
    88, 90, 474, 475*f*
*International Journal of Educational*
    *Research,* 156*b*
International Labour Organisation
    (ILO), 427
International Monetary Fund (IMF), 74
International Narcotics Control Board, 343
International Organisation for Cooperation
    in Evaluation (IOCE), 29
International Organization for Migration
    (IOM) Evaluation Guidelines, 423–24
International Organization for
    Standardization (ISO), 192
International Organization of Supreme
    Audit Institutions (INTOSAI), 24*b*
International Program for Development
    Evaluation Training (IPDET),
    3, 62–64
International Program on the Elimination
    of Child Labour, 427
Internet
  presentation of results via, 470*b*
  random number generation via, 357
  results-based evaluation reports and, 130
  sample size determination tools, 365, 366
interpersonal skills, 452–53
interpretation of qualitative data, 385–86,
    387*t. See also* data analysis
interrupted time series comparison
    designs, 265, 274, 283*t*
interval data, 392, 393*t*, 479
interviews, 295, 330–33, 332–33*b*, 333*t*
INTOSAI (International Organization of
    Supreme Audit Institutions), 24*b*

inverse relationships, 399
investment climate, 86–89
IOCE (International Organisation for
    Cooperation in Evaluation), 29
IOM (International Organization for
    Migration) Evaluation Guidelines,
    423–24
IPDET (International Program for
    Development Evaluation Training),
    3, 62–64
Iraq, ODA for, 87
IRBM (integrated results-based
    management system), 67–68
Ireland
    capacity building for evaluation in,
        58–59
    evaluation culture in, 51
    mixed evaluation approach in, 58
Irish–EU Community Support Framework
    (CSF), 58–59
ISO (International Organization for
    Standardization), 192
issue papers, 470, 470*b*
Italian Evaluation Association, 508
Italy, evaluation culture in, 51

**J**

Jackson, Gregg, 320, 325
Japan International Cooperation Agency
    (JICA), 40*b*
JEEAR (Joint Evaluation of Emergency
    Assistance to Rwanda), 39*b*
job training programs, 276*b*
Johnson, John, 266
Johnson, Lyndon B., 20–21
Joint Evaluation of Emergency Assistance
    to Rwanda (JEEAR), 39*b*
joint evaluations, 417–20, 420*t,* 425–26*b*
Jordan, enclave approach in, 58
Jospin, Lionel, 59
*Journal of Educational Research,* 156*b*
journals and diaries, 340–41, 341*t,* 342*t*
judgment samples, 362

**K**

Kellogg Foundation, 153–54, 160, 169,
    456–57, 507
Kenya, Delphi technique used in, 344
Key Evaluation Checklist (Scriven), 446
keyword frequencies, 379
knowledge fund, 150, 150*b*
Korea, Republic of, evaluation culture in, 51

Kosovo, evaluations in, 39*b*
Kripendorff, Klaus, 380
Kusek, Jody Zall, 66, 109, 121
Kyrgyz Republic
    enclave approach in, 58
    readiness assessment of, 65

**L**

Labor Market and Employment Act of 1969
    (Federal Republic of Germany), 21
land surveys, 303
land use mapping, 302
Lao PDR, evaluations in, 40*b*
Latin America, Minga initiative in, 9. *See
    also specific countries*
Lawrenz, Frances, 470*b*
legal framework
    ethics and, 496
    for joint evaluations, 419
Levin, J. R., 477
line drawing illustrations, 477, 477*f*
line graphs, 479, 480*f,* 481*t*
listening skills, 452, 453
literacy
    diary data collection and, 340–41
    survey response and, 319
Living Standards Measurement Survey
    (LSMS, World Bank), 320
lock-frame model, 168
Lofland, John, 315
logical framework, 168–69, 170*t*
logic models. *See* theory of change
longitudinal designs, 265, 266, 274, 283*t*
long-term maturation, 259
"look good–avoid blame" (LGAB)
    mindset, 501
LSMS (Living Standards Measurement
    Survey, World Bank), 320

**M**

Madagascar, capacity-building in, 79
main client
    communication strategy and, 468
    ethical issues and, 498
    evaluation uses by, 14–15
    identification of, 144
    management of, 446–47
Malawi, monitoring system in, 16
Malaysia
    auditing in, 24
    enclave approach in, 67–68
    professional evaluation associations, 28

management, 441–66
  of budgets, 456–57
  capacity audits, 275, 275*t*
  conflict resolution, 452, 452*b*
  contracting evaluations, 442–45, 445*b*
  of design matrix, 442
  evaluation manager, roles and
    responsibilities, 449–50
  evaluator, roles and responsibilities,
    450–51
  joint evaluations and, 418–19
  main client, roles and responsibilities,
    446–47
  of people, 451–54, 452–53*b*
  of projects, 457–60, 458–60*t*
  stakeholders, roles and responsibilities,
    447–48
  of tasks, 454–55
  teambuilding, 453–54, 453*b*
Management Action Tracking Record
    (MATR), 474, 475*f*
management information system (MIS),
    67–68. *See also* information
    technology
Management Sciences for Health, 147
managerial purpose, 11
M&E. *See* monitoring and evaluation
    systems
manual analysis of qualitative data,
    382–85, 385*f*
mapping
  concept mapping, 454
  at country level, 517
  data collection and, 302–3
  demographic, 302
  health mapping, 302
  historical mapping, 302
  land use mapping, 302
  NGO activities, 517
  outcome mapping, 196–99, 209*t*
  for reports, 476
  resource mapping, 302, 303
  social mapping, 303, 304*b*
  task maps, 454, 455*t*
  wealth mapping, 302
market-based curriculum, 229*b*
Markiewicz, Anne, 503–4, 505
mastery vs. harmony, 507
MATR (Management Action Tracking
    Record), 474, 475*f*
matrices, 484–86, 486*t*
maturation effect, 259

maximum variation samples, 362
MBS (Modified Budgeting System,
    Malaysia), 67
McCaston, M. Katherine, 306, 309
McDonaldization of society, 143
McNamara, Robert, 21
MDB (Multilateral Development Banks),
    25, 517
mean (measure of central tendency),
    391, 393*t*
measures of association, 398–99
measures of central tendency, 391–92, 393*t*
measures of dispersion, 392–95,
    393–94*f*, 395*b*
media, reporting of results through, 130
median (measure of central tendency),
    391, 393*t*
  samples, 362
Medicines for Malaria Venture, 430, 431
meta-evaluation, 202–3
"method in search of an application"
    technique, 248
methodologicalism fallacy, 497
methodological triangulation, 28
Mexico, enclave approach in, 58
midterm evaluations, 9–10
Miles, Mathew B., 401
Millennium Development Goals, 73–75, 74*b*
  country assistance evaluations and, 422*b*
  joint external evaluations and, 425*b*, 426*b*
  results-based M&E and, 50, 106, 276, 516
mini-IPDETs, 63
MIS (management information system),
    67–68. *See also* information
    technology
misconduct. *See* ethical issues
mixed evaluation approach, 58–60
Mnookin, Robert H., 505–6
mode, measure of central tendency, 391, 393*t*
moderators, focus group, 336–38, 339*t*
Modified Budgeting System (MBS,
    Malaysia), 67
modus operandi inference, 269
money laundering, 82–83
Mongolia, summative evaluations in, 10
monitoring. *See also* results-based
    monitoring and evaluation
  evaluation relationship with, 16–17, 17*t*
  results, 124–25*f*, 124–27
Monterrey Consensus, 76, 276
Morra, L. G., 201
Morris, M., 497

mortality effect, 260
motivational purpose, 11
Mozambique, evaluations in, 38*b*
Multilateral Development Banks (MDB),
    25, 517
multilateral donors, 72
multimedia coding, 382, 383*b*
multipartner arrangements, 418
multiple bar charts, 481*t*, 482, 485*f*
multisite evaluations, 187–88, 208*t*
multistage random samples, 361–62
multivariate analysis, 396–97
Murray, Vic V., 500–503
Myanmar, evaluations in, 40*b*

## N

Nambiar, Devaki, 363
National Audit Department (NAD,
    Malaysia), 24
National Poverty Reduction Strategy
    (Uganda), 70
National Strategy for Growth and
    Reduction of Poverty (NSGRP,
    Tanzania), 425*b*, 426*b*
negotiation skills, 503–6
Netherlands
    evaluation culture in, 51
    joint external evaluations and, 425*b*
    Policy and Operations Evaluation
      Department, 65
Network on Development Evaluations
    (DAC), 421, 509–10
Neuendorf, Kimberly A., 380
Newcomer, K. E., 186
New Zealand Evaluation Association, 523
NGOs. *See* nongovernmental organizations
Nigeria, ODA for, 87
nominal data, 392, 393*t*, 482
nonequivalent groups, 264
nonexperimental designs, 250–51, 267–72,
    279, 279*t*
nongovernmental organizations (NGOs)
    Equator Principles and, 91
    evaluation uses by, 14–15
    mapping activities of, 517
    participatory evaluations and, 448
    as research source, 155
nonnormal distributions, 393, 394*f*
nonrandom sampling strategy,
    362–63, 367
NORAD (Norwegian Agency for
    Development Cooperation), 62

normal distributions, 393, 393*f*, 394*f*
normative questions, 25, 224–27, 226*b*, 242,
    275–80
norm-referenced tests, 347, 348
Norwegian Agency for Development
    Cooperation (NORAD), 62
notation
    before-and-after designs, 264, 273
    case study designs, 272
    correlational designs, 266
    cross-sectional designs, 268
    design process, 251
    interrupted time series comparison
      designs, 265, 274
    longitudinal designs, 265, 274
    one-shot designs, 268
    panel designs, 265
    post-only nonequivalent comparison
      designs, 264
    pre- and post-nonequivalent comparison
      designs, 264
    quasi-experimental designs, 262
notes, importance of, 315, 376
NSGRP (National Strategy for Growth and
    Reduction of Poverty, Tanzania),
    425*b*, 426*b*
N6 (data analysis software), 382, 383*b*
null hypothesis, 401
NVivo 8 (data analysis software), 382

## O

objectives-based evaluations. *See* goal-
    based evaluations
objectives-referenced tests, 347
observation data collection method, 310–16
    for qualitative data, 295
    sample forms, 311*f*, 312–13*f*
    semistructured, 314, 314*t*
    structured, 310, 312–13*f*
    training for, 315–16
obtrusive methods, 298, 299*b*
ODA (official development assistance),
    86–87
OECD countries. *See also* Organisation for
    Economic Co-operation and
    Development
    evaluation in, 22
    M&E systems in, 50, 106
    performance audits in, 275
official development assistance (ODA), 86–87
one-shot designs, 268, 279*t*
open-ended questions, 320

stakeholders
  analysis of, 147–48, 148*b*
  communication strategy and, 468
  ethical issues and, 498
  evaluation manager and, 449
  evaluators and, 451
  GRPP evaluations and, 432
  horizontal evaluations and, 206
  identification of, 144–48
  management of, 447–48
  negotiation and, 503–6
  political games played by, 503
  realist evaluation and, 204
  roles of, 145–47, 146*t*
Stame, Nicoletta, 71–72
standard audits, 23
standard deviation, 393, 394*f,* 395*b*
standard flow chart, 165, 166*f*
standardized tests, 348
standard results chain, 166–68, 167*f*
Standards for Evaluation (UNEG), 509
*Standards for the Professional Practice of*
    *Internal Auditing* (Institute of
    Internal Auditors), 24*b*
Stata (software tool), 267
*Statement of Responsibilities of Internal*
    *Auditing* (Institute of Internal
    Auditors), 24*b*
statistical analysis, 390–401
  descriptive statistics, 391–99, 397*t*
    measures of association, 398–99
    measures of central tendency,
      391–92, 393*t*
    measures of dispersion, 392–95,
      393–94*f,* 395*b*
  inferential statistics, 399–401
    analysis of variance (ANOVA), 400–401
    chi-square test, 399–400
    *t*-test, 400
Stattrek (software tool), 357
Stewart, P. J., 382
story conference, 236
storytelling approach, 377
stratified random samples, 360
strength of association, 270
structured data collection, 291, 292*b*
structured observations, 310, 312–13*f*
structured surveys, 316–17, 317*t,* 318*t*
student achievement programs, 156*b,*
    161, 162*f*
"subjective interpretation of reality" (SIR)
    phenomenon, 501

summative evaluations, 9, 223*f*
supply costs, 456
surveys, 316–34, 319*t*
  administration modes, 318–19
  guidelines for, 328–29*b*
  questions in, 319, 320–27, 321*t,* 322*b*
  response rates, 334
  self-administered, 318
  semistructured, 317–18, 317*t,* 318*t*
  structured, 316–17, 317*t,* 318*t*
Susan Thompson Buffet Foundation, 79
sustainability
  environmental, 90–91
  as evaluation criteria, 30, 40*b,* 421, 433
  of M&E systems, 132–34
  social, 90–91
*Sustainable Development Strategies* (OECD
    & UNDP), 192–93
SWAps. *See* sectorwide approaches
Sweden, evaluation culture in, 19, 21, 22, 51
Swedish International Development
    Cooperation Agency (SIDA), 62
Swiss Agency for Development and
    Coordination (SDC), 62
Swiss Evaluation Society, 508
Switzerland, joint external evaluations
    and, 425*b*

## T

tables, informational, 484–86, 486*t*
Tanzania
  capacity-building in, 79
  child scavenging assessment, 427*b*
  data collection in, 341
  sector program evaluations, 424, 425–26*b*
targets
  normative questions and, 224–25
  performance, 121–23, 122*f,* 123*t*
  results-based M&E and, 108*b*
task forces, 342–43
task management, 454–55
task maps, 454, 455*t*
Taut, Sandy, 507–8
Tavistock Institute, 52
teambuilding, 453–54, 453*b*
technical design issues, 234
technical weaknesses in evaluators,
    500–501
*Teenage Pregnancy: 500,000 Births a*
    *Year but Few Tested Programs*
    (GAO), 10–11
telephone surveys, 318

## ECO-AUDIT
### Environmental Benefits Statement

The World Bank is committed to preserving endangered forests and natural resources. We have chosen to print *The Road to Results: Designing and Conducting Effective Development Evaluations* on 60-pound Finch Opaque, a recycled paper with 30% post-consumer waste. The Office of the Publisher has agreed to follow the recommended standards for paper usage set by the Green Press Initiative, a nonprofit program supporting publishers in using fiber that is not sourced from endangered forests. For more information, visit www.greenpressinitiative.org.

Saved:

- 71 trees
- 28 million BTUs of total energy
- 515 pounds of net greenhouse gases
- 32,500 gallons of waste water
- 1,099 pounds of solid waste